西安统计年鉴

XI'AN STATISTICAL YEARBOOK

2018

中英文对照 Chinese/English

中国统计出版社
China Statistics Press

西安市统计局
XI'AN MUNICIPAL BUREAU OF STATISTICS
国家统计局西安调查队
NBS SURVEY OFFICE IN XI'AN

图书在版编目（CIP）数据

西安统计年鉴. 2018 / 西安市统计局, 国家统计局西安调查队编. -- 北京 : 中国统计出版社, 2018.9
ISBN 978-7-5037-8598-6

Ⅰ. ①西… Ⅱ. ①西… ②国… Ⅲ. ①统计资料－西安－2018－年鉴 Ⅳ. ①C832.411-54

中国版本图书馆CIP数据核字(2018)第191381号

西安统计年鉴—2018

作　　者/ 西安市统计局 国家统计局西安调查队
责任编辑/ 陈越月
装帧设计/ 西安乐成品牌策划设计有限公司
出版发行/ 中国统计出版社
地　　址/ 北京市丰台区西三环南路甲6号 邮政编码/100073
电　　话/ 邮购（010）63376909 书店（010）68783171
网　　址/ http://csp.stats.gov.cn
印　　刷/ 西安一印制版有限责任公司
经　　销/ 新华书店
开　　本/ 890mm × 1240mm 1/16
字　　数/ 1566千字
印　　张/ 45
版　　别/ 2018年9月第1版
版　　次/ 2018年9月第1次印刷
定　　价/ 260元

如有印装差错，由本社发行部调换。

《西安统计年鉴—2018》编辑部

XI'AN STATISTICAL YEARBOOK-2018
EDITORLAL STAFF

编者说明

一、《西安统计年鉴—2018》系统收录了全市、区县及开发区2017年经济、社会各方面统计数据，以及重要历史年份主要统计数据，是一部全面记载西安市国民经济和社会发展情况的大型连续性统计文献资料和重要工具书。

二、本年鉴正文内容分为二十二个篇章：（一）综合；（二）基本单位；（三）国民经济核算；（四）人口、从业人员与职工工资；（五）固定资产投资；（六）财政；（七）物价指数；（八）人民生活；（九）城市公用事业；（十）环境保护；（十一）农业；（十二）工业；（十三）能源；（十四）建筑业；（十五）运输和邮电及信息化；（十六）国内贸易；（十七）对外经济贸易和旅游；（十八）服务业；（十九）金融业；（二十）教育和科技；（二十一）文化、体育、卫生、社会福利和其他；（二十二）企业调查。同时，为方便读者使用，各篇章前设有简要说明和主要统计指标，对本篇章的主要内容、资料来源、以及历史变动情况予以简要概述，篇末附有《主要统计指标解释》。

三、本年鉴统计资料的统计标准，按当时国家统计制度执行，有关指标的涵义、口径、范围、计算方法等，在不同时期可能有所不同，使用时请注意。如国民经济行业分类按GB/T4754—2011标准执行。

四、为便于国内外读者查阅，本年鉴全部内容均采用中英文对照编辑。

五、本年鉴中国民经济核算部分的2013年数据为全国第三次经济普查数据，2009-2012年数据为依据第三次经济普查修订数据；工业部分的2013年数据为第三次经济普查数据；国内贸易部分的2009—2013年为依据第三次经济普查调整后数据。

六、数据口径：本年鉴中2017年全市数据口径，基本单位、国民经济核算、农业(除个别指标)、工业、建筑业、国内贸易、服务业、能源、固定资产投资、常住人口、从业人员和职工工资、信息化、企业调查、城市公用事业（除城市公共交通部分等）、财政、教育、文化、卫生、社会福利和行政区划等指标数据包含西咸新区，并且在分全市及区县、开发区数据表中，西咸新区数据暂未单列；物价指数、人民生活、运输邮电、环境保护、对外贸易和旅游(除少部分指标)、金融、体育、户籍人口、土地面积、气象等指标数据为西安原口径数据或不包含西咸新区，具体情况见表下附注。

七、本年鉴中的部分指标合计数或相对数由于单位取舍不同产生的计算误差均未作机械调整。

八、本年鉴所使用的计量单位均依据2017年相关统计报表制度。

九、本年鉴使用的符号说明："空白"表示该项统计指标无数据或数据不详；"#"表示其中项；"*"表示另有注解。

感谢社会各界长期以来对《西安统计年鉴》的广泛关注和大力支持。为进一步做好工作，更好地为广大读者服务，希望社会各界提出宝贵意见。

PREFACE

I. Xi'an Statistical Yearbook 2018 is a periodical statistic yearbook which record economic and social development of Xi'an all-around in 2017 and some selected data series in historical important years. With its features of comprehensive and intensive information, this practically provides data covering the situation of social and economic developments in Xi' an. II. The book contains twenty-two parts, 1.General Survey; 2.Basic Unit; 3.National Economic Account; 4.Population, Employment and Wages; 5.Investment in Fixed Assets; 6.Government Finance; 7.Price Indices; 8.People's Livelihood; 9.Urban Public Utilities; 10.Environmental Protection; 11.Agriculture; 12.Industry; 13.Energy; 14.Construction; 15.Transportation, Post and Informatization; 16.Domestic Trade; 17.Foreign Trade; 18. Tertiary Industry; 19.Banking and Insurance; 20.Education, Science and Technology; 21.Culture, Sports, Public Health, Social Welfare and Other Social Activities; 22.Enterprises Investigation. Meanwhile, for the convenience of the reader, a brief explanation and major statistical indicators are provided before each chapter, the main contents, sources and historical changes of this chapter are briefly summarized. The final part is accompanied by the interpretation of major statistical indicators. III. The data of various years in conformity to the statistical standards prescribed by national statistical system of the time. The meaning, scope and calculating method of indicators may have some difference in different periods, which readers must pay attention to. For example, national industries classification is carried out according to standard GB/T4754 -2011. For the sake of comparison of the old and new industry standards, we edit the division' s data in some major indicators according to standard GB/T4754 -2011.

IV. For the convenience of being consulted by foreigners, the book is Chinese-English bilingual edition.

V. In this yearbook, data of 2013 at the part of National Economic Accounting and Industry is the results of Third National Economic Census, the data from 2009 to 2012 at the part of National Economic Account and data from 2009 to 2013 at the part of Domestic Trade have adjusted by Third National Economic Census.

VI. Statistical scope: in this yearbook, data of 2017 about the basic unit, the national economic accounting, agriculture, industry, construction industry, domestic trade, services, energy, investment in fixed assets, labor wages, informatization, enterprise survey, urban public utilities (except urban public transport,etv) , finance, education, culture, health and social welfare contains Xi Xian New Area; data of 2017 about price index, people's livelihood, transportation, post and telecommunications, environmental protection, foreign trade, finance, science and technology, sports, household population, land area, and meteorological information are original ones from Xi' an or excluding Xi Xian New Area.

VII .Statistical discrepancies due to rounding are not adjusted automatically in this yearbook.

VIII. Unit of measurement is used in this yearbook according to 2017 statistics system.

IX. Explanations on symbols used in this yearbook:

(Blank) indicates the data not available;

\# indicates the items of the total.

* indicates some other explanatory note.

Here we would like to express our sincere thanks to the people for their concerning and support to the Xi'an statistical yearbook. In order to do better and provide better service to readers, we hope that the whole society fields can propose constructive advices.

生产总值（亿元）

Gross Domestic Product (100 million yuan)

生产总值指数（以上年为100）

Indices of Gross Domestic Product (preceding year = 100)

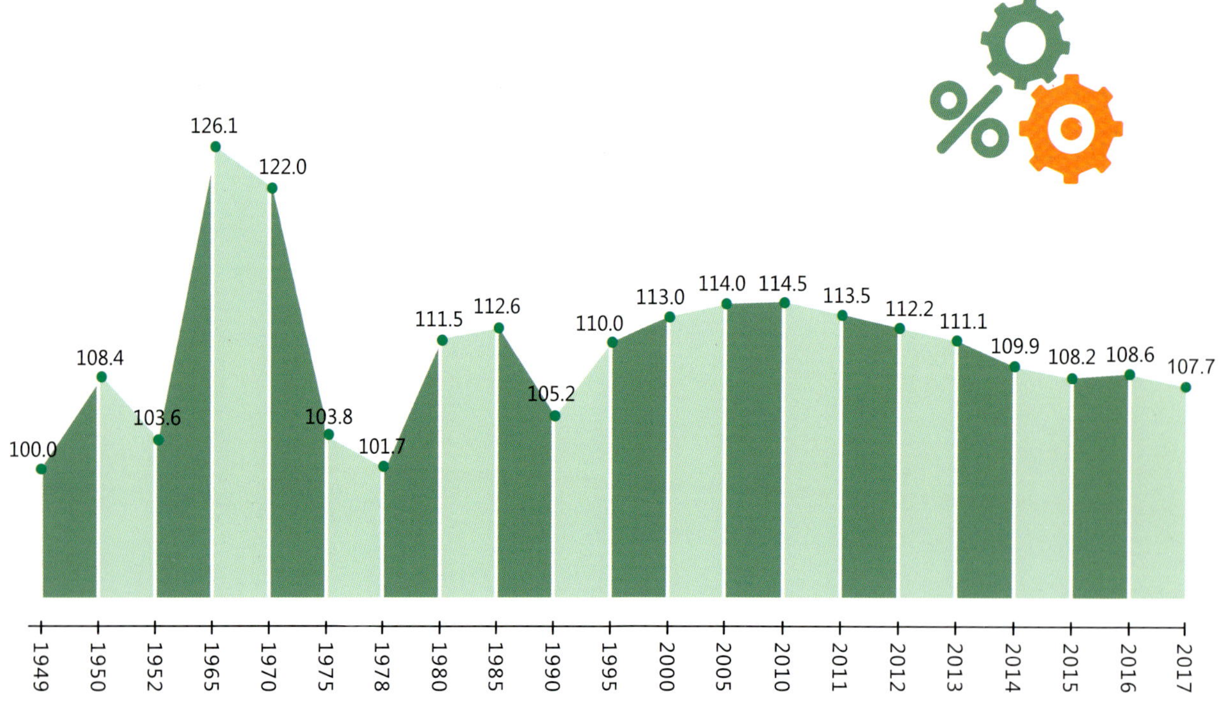

生产总值构成（%）

Composition of Gross Domestic Product (%)

 第一产业Primary Industry  第二产业 Secondary Industry  第三产业 Tertiary Industry

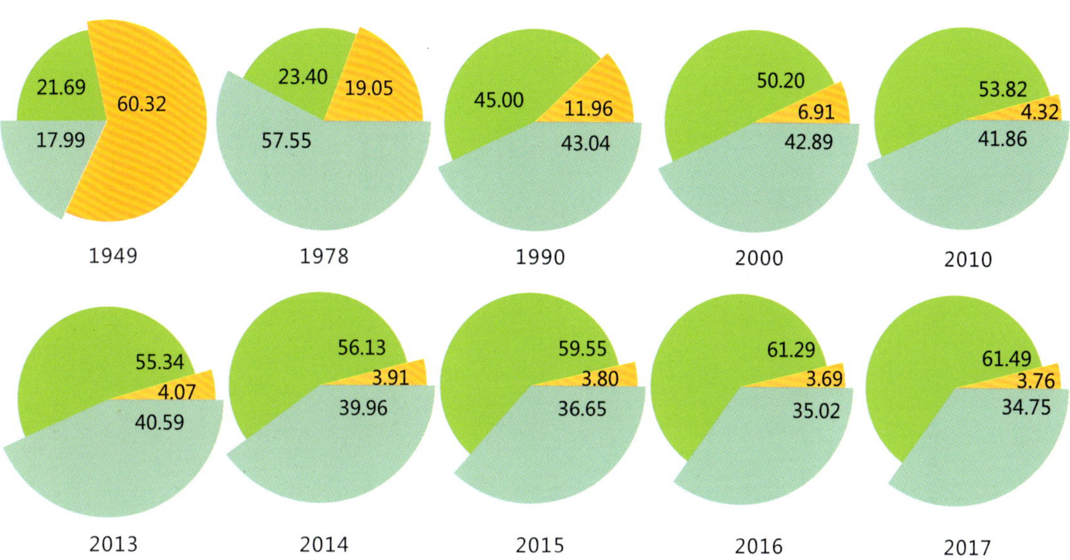

人均GDP（元/人）

Per Capita GDP(yuan/person)

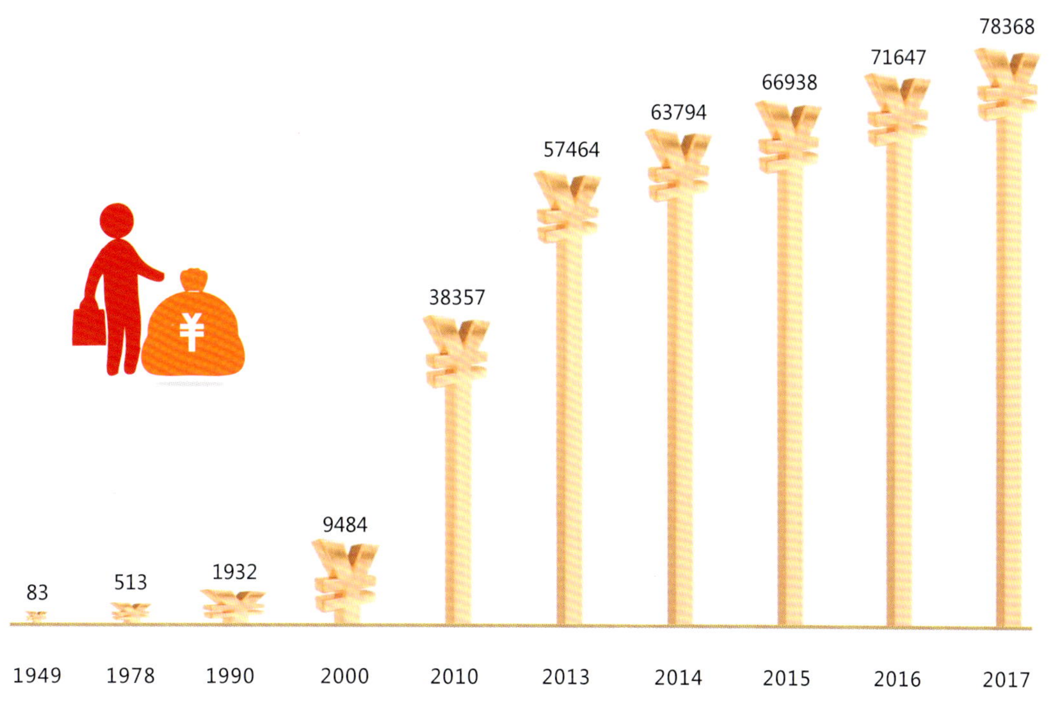

年末常住人口（万人）
Year-end Permanent Population(10000 persons)

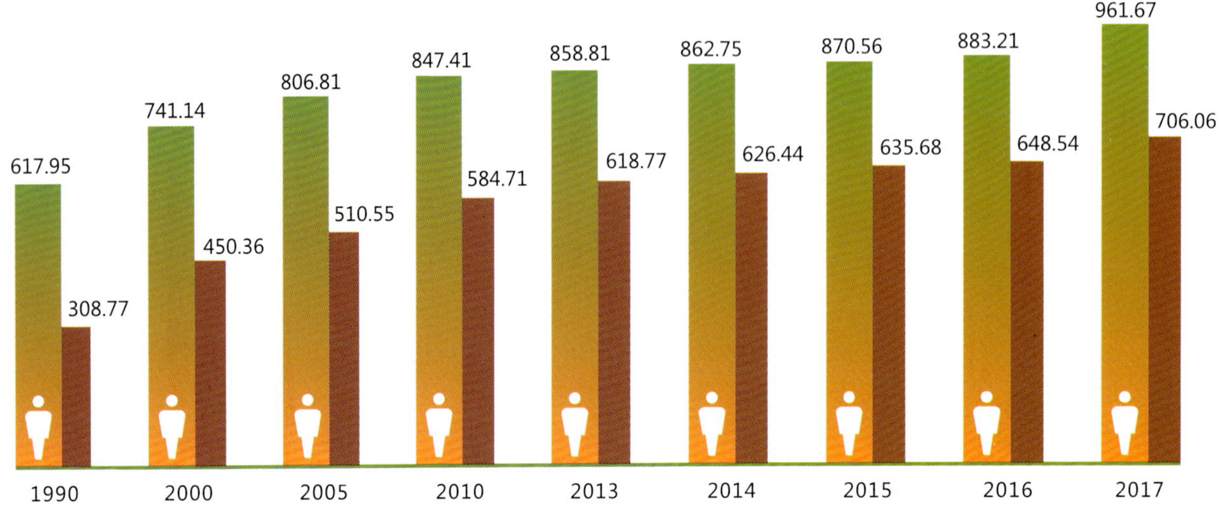

社会从业人数（万人）
Social Workers(10000 persons)

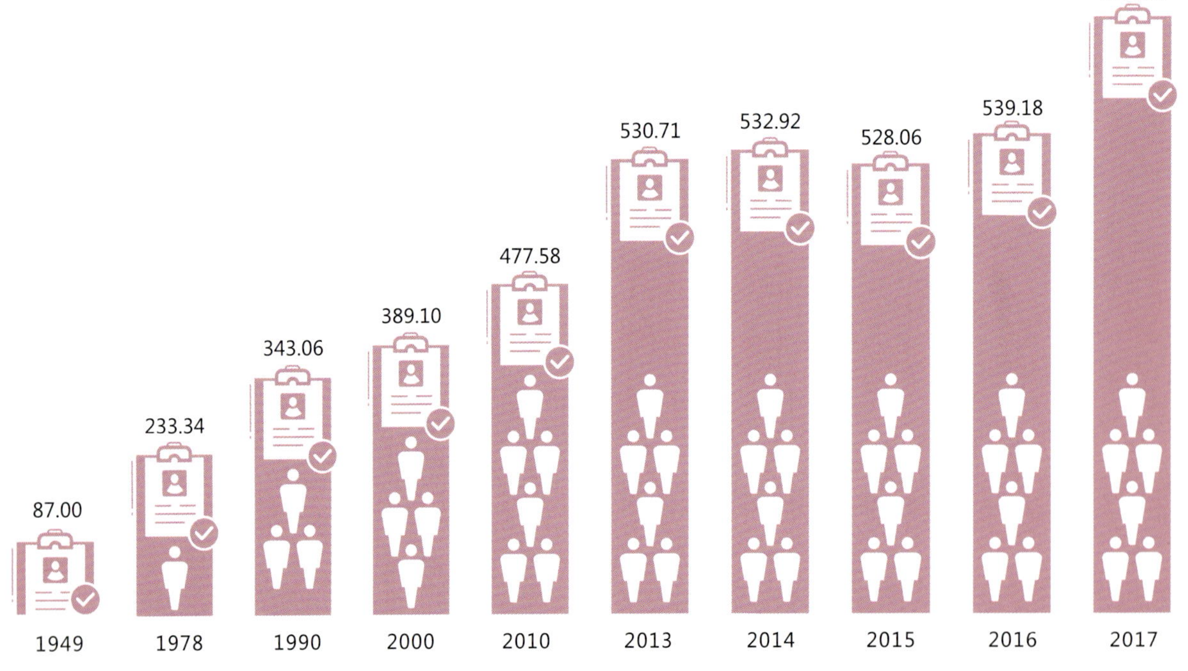

固定资产投资（亿元）

Investment in Fixed Assets(100 million yuan)

新增固定资产及住宅竣工面积

Newly Increased Fixed Assets and Residential Area of Completion

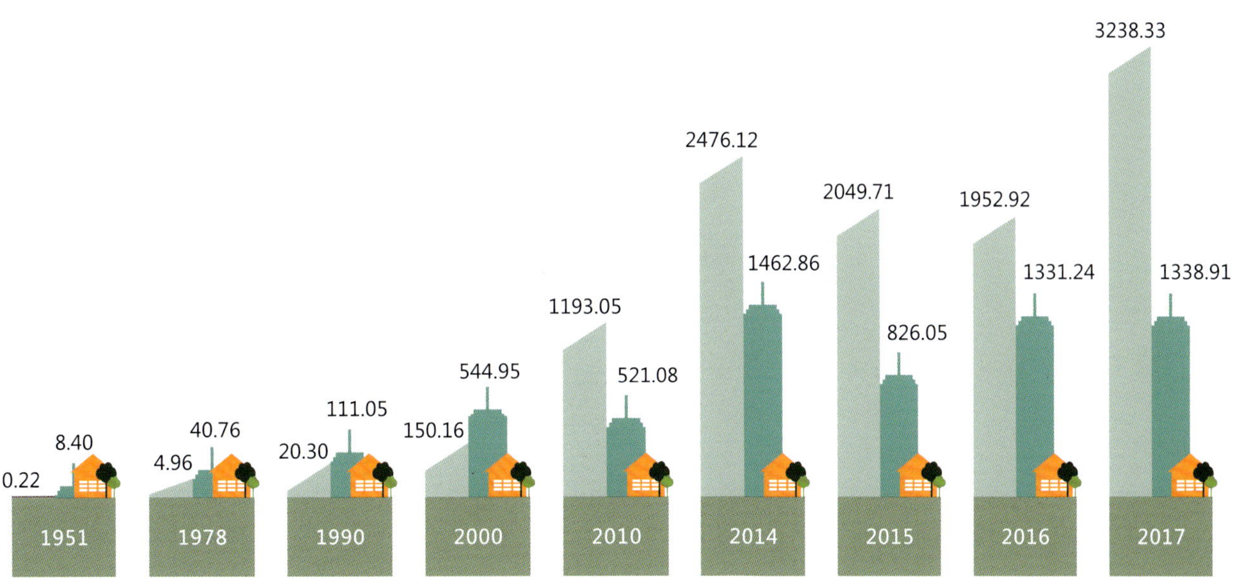

农林牧渔及服务业总产值（亿元）

Gross Output Value of Farming,Forestry, Animal Husbandry, Fishery and Service(100 million yuan)

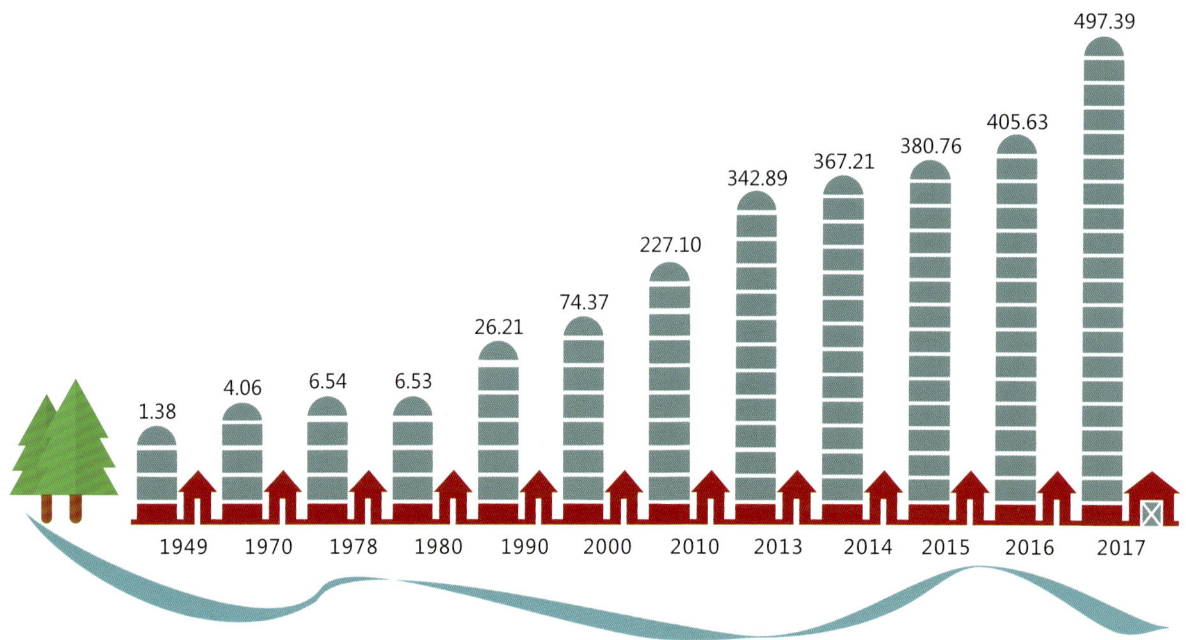

粮食产量（万吨）

Grain Product(10000 ton)

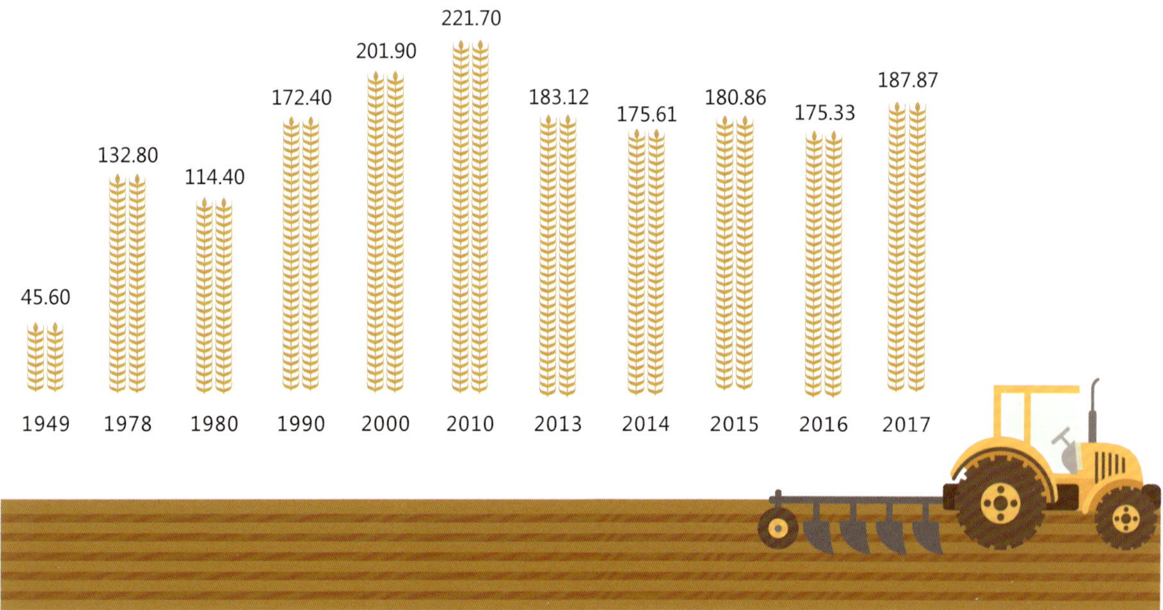

蔬菜产量（万吨）
Vegetables Product(10000 ton)

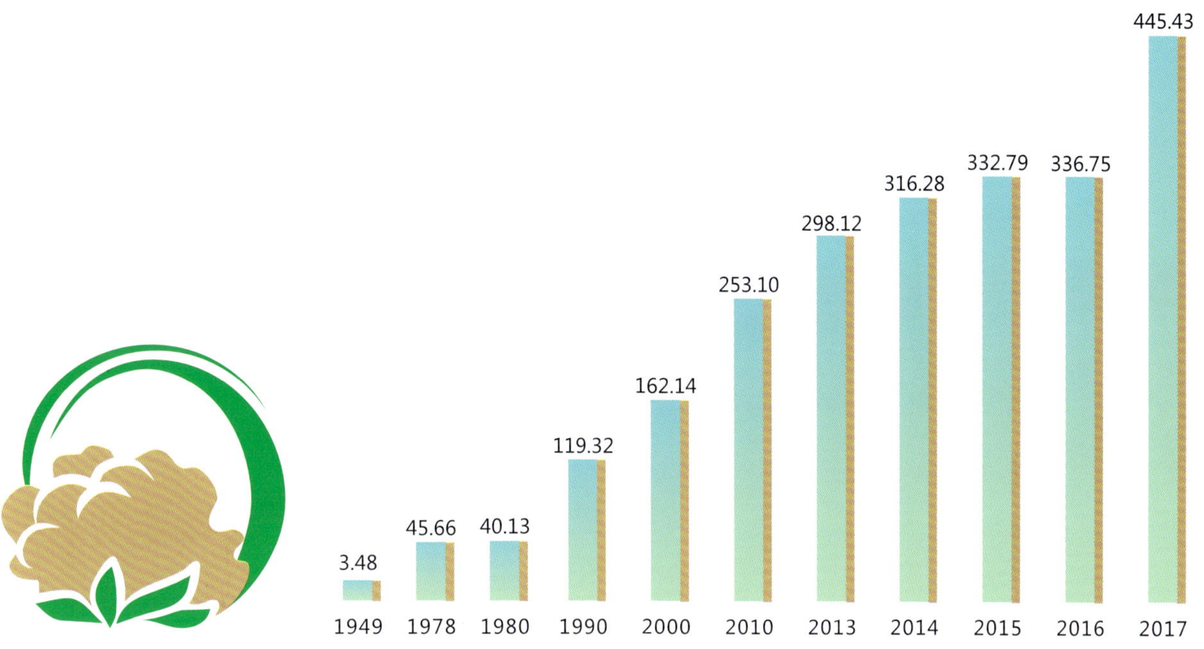

规模以上工业企业主要产品产量
Output of Major Industrial Products Of Enterprises Above Designated Size

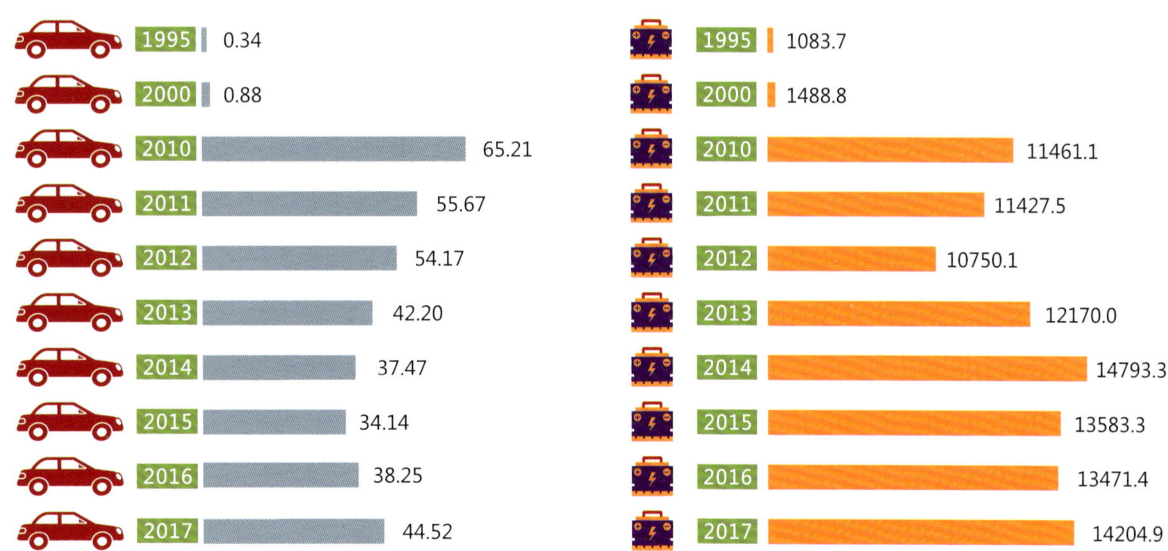

交通
Traffic

等级公路（公里）
Expressways and Class I to IV Highways(KM)

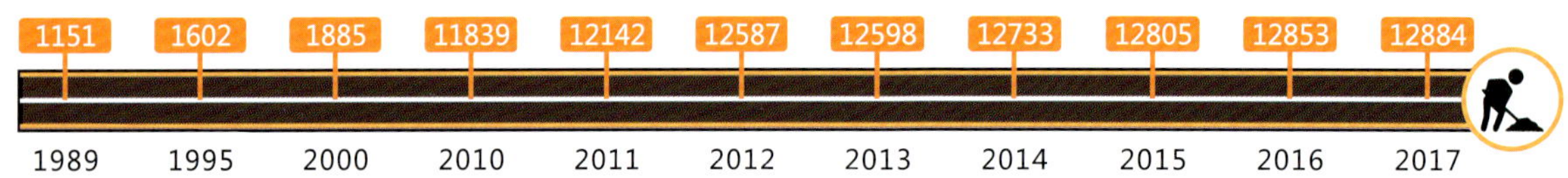

高速公路（公里）
Expressway(KM)

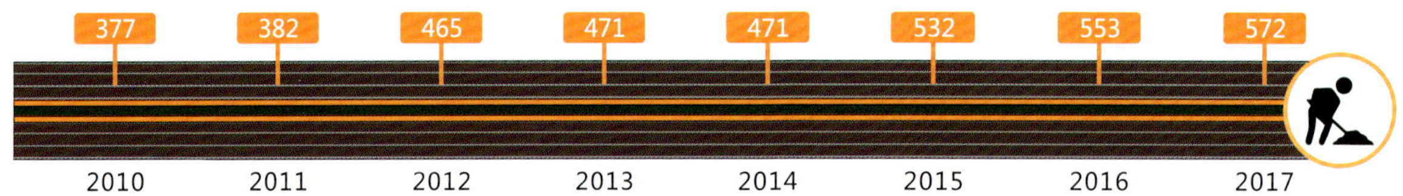

全社会车辆数（万辆）
Possession of Civil Vehicles(10000 unit)

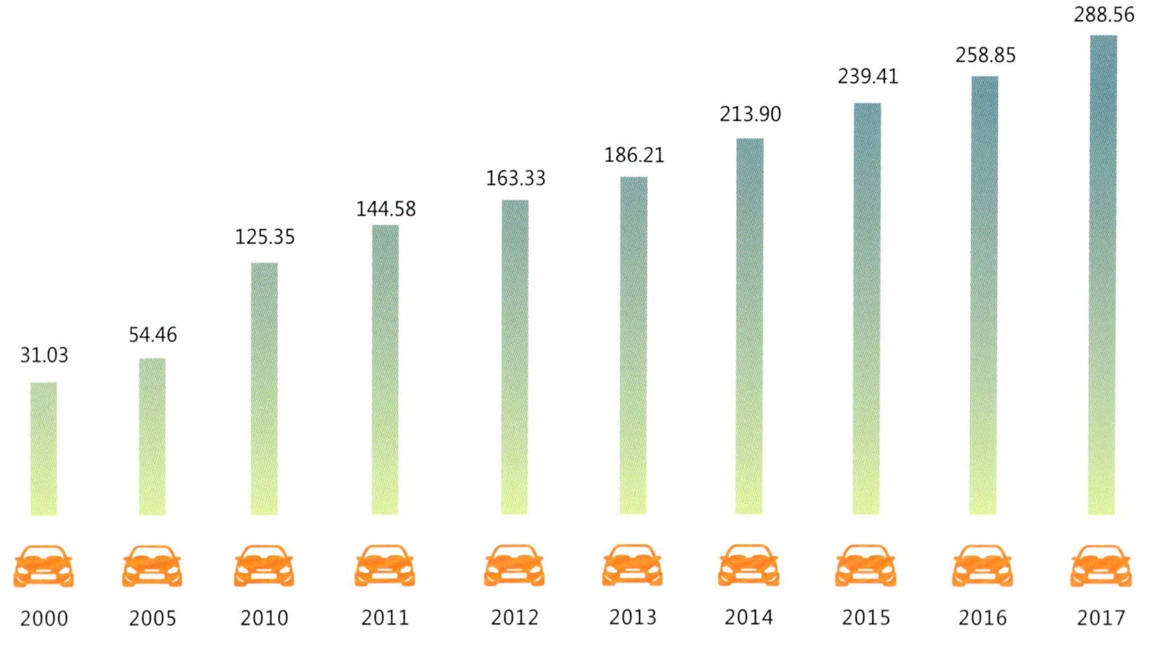

社会消费品零售总额（亿元）

Total Retail Sales of Consumer Goods(100 million yuan)

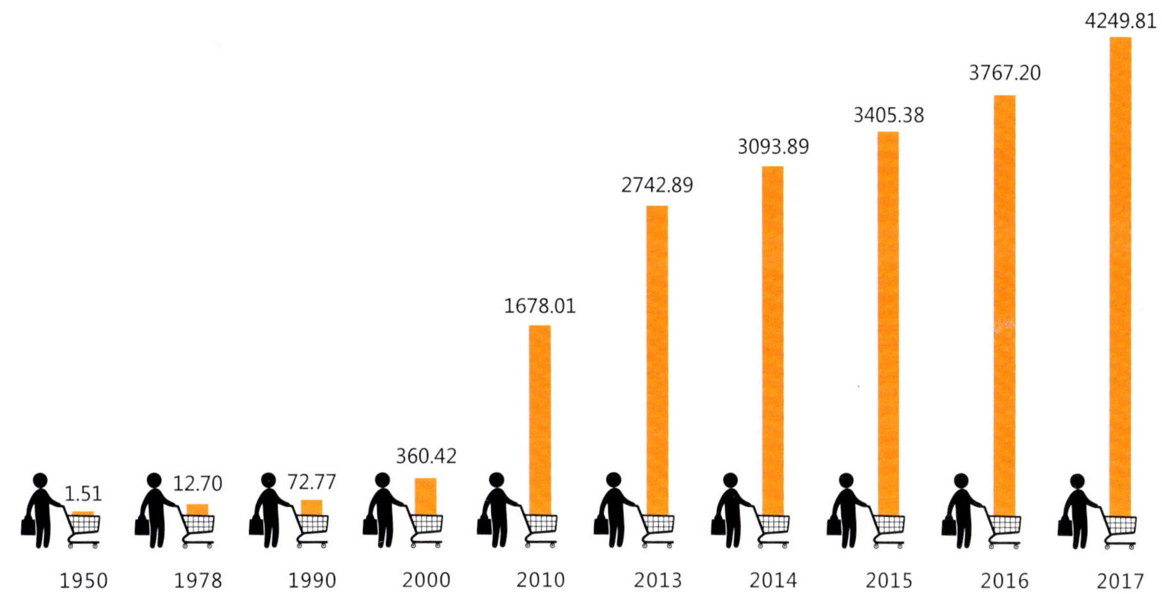

实际利用外商直接投资额（亿美元）

Foreign Direct Investment(USD 100 million)

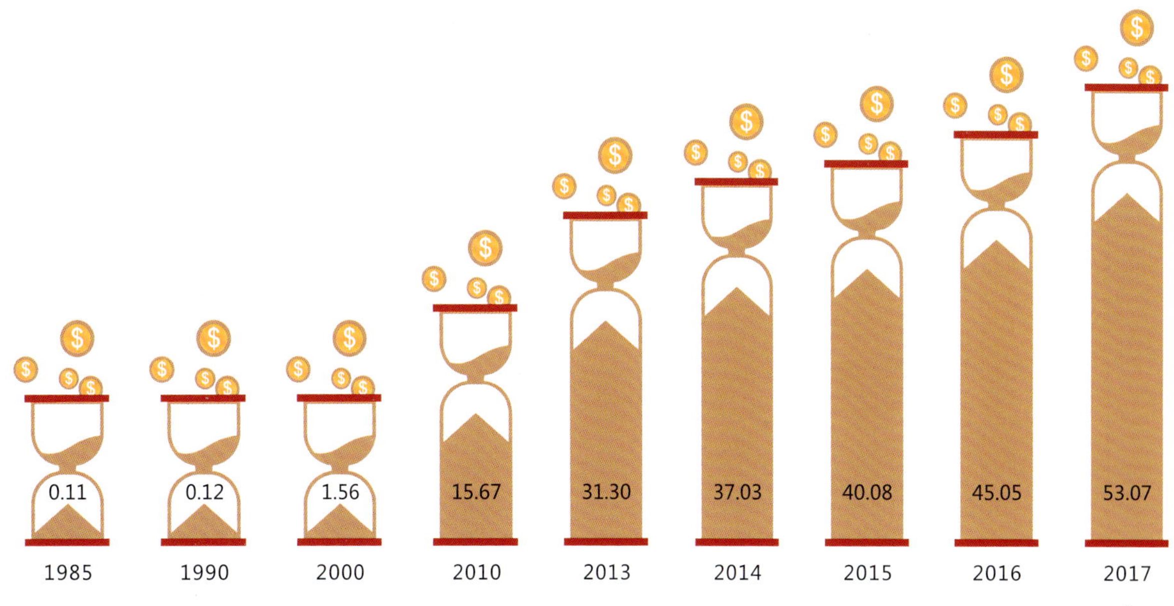

进出口总值（亿美元）

Total Value of Imports and Exports(USD 100 million)

	1987	1990	2000	2010	2011	2012	2013
进出口总值	1.36	3.82	17.37	103.92	126.02	130.14	179.85
出口总值	0.75	2.83	10.61	53.17	58.27	72.99	84.78
进口总值	0.61	0.99	6.76	50.75	67.75	57.16	95.07

	2014	2015	2016	2017
进出口总值	1532.15	1761.69	1829.95	2545.08
出口总值	734.68	819.88	947.31	1552.22
进口总值	797.47	941.81	882.64	992.86

注：2014年起单位为人民币（亿元）

旅游人数及收入

Number of Tourists and Tourism Income

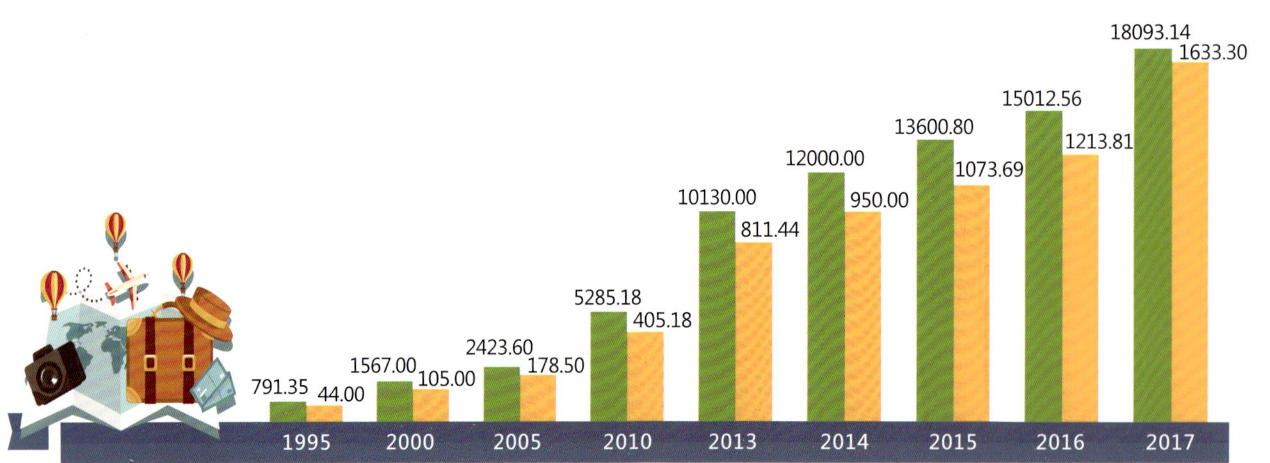

财政收支（亿元）
Government Revenue and Expenditure(100 million yuan)

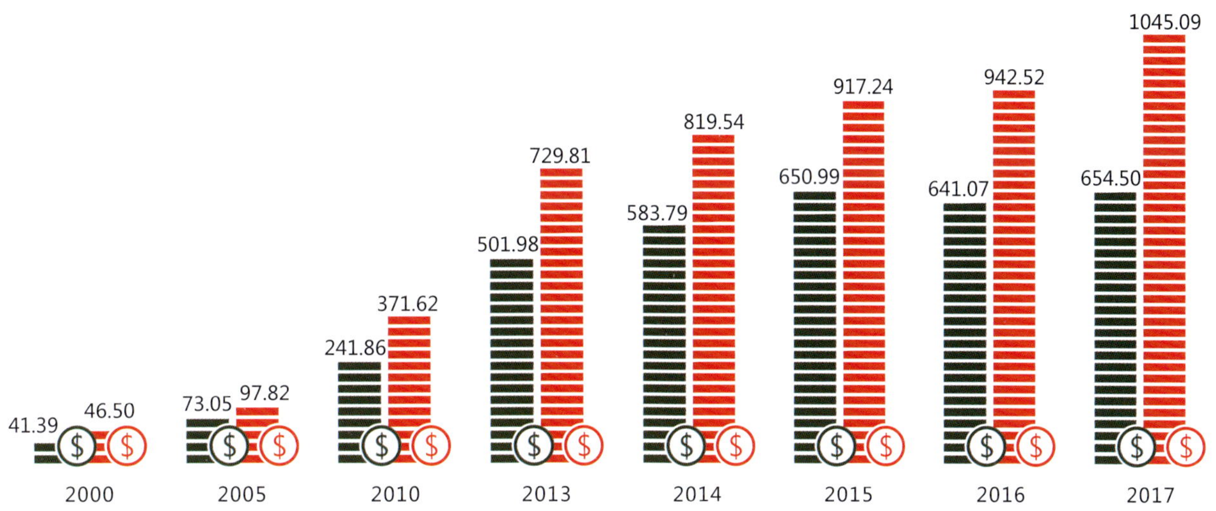

金融机构人民币存贷款年末余额（亿元）
Year-end Deposit and Loans in Financial Institutions (100 million yuan)

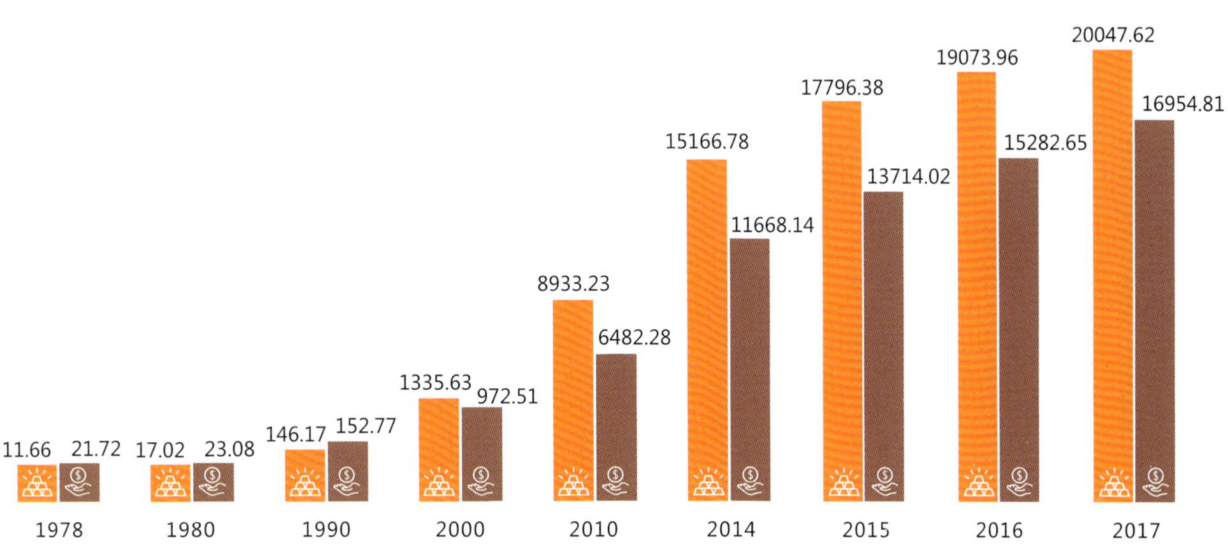

建成区面积（平方公里）
Area of Regions Built-up（sq.km）

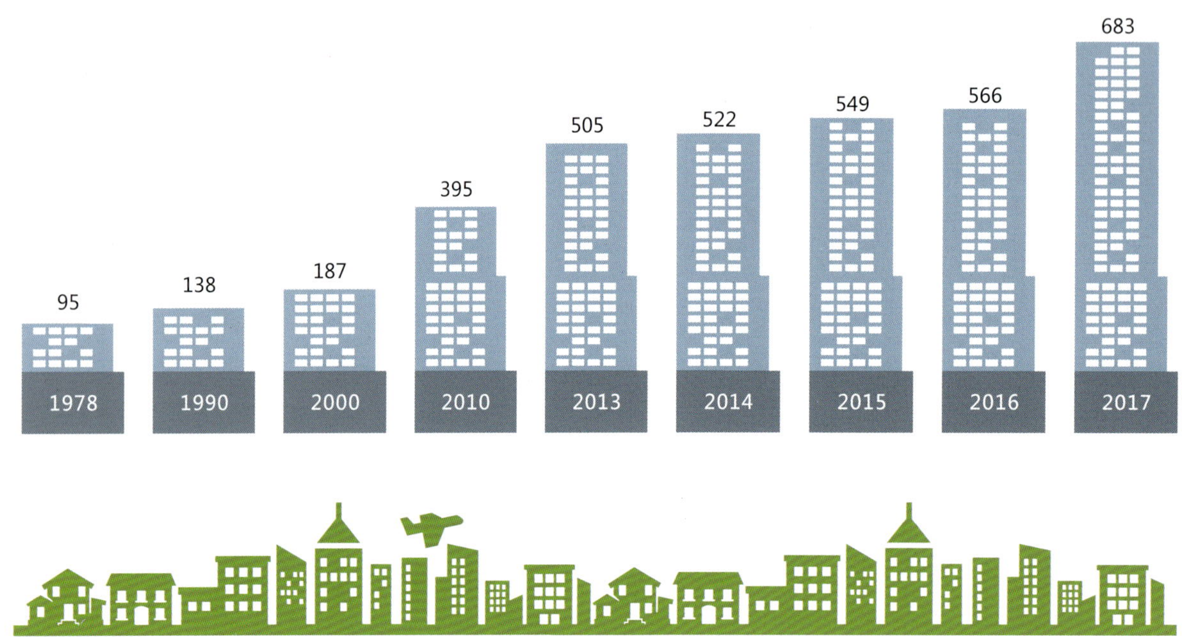

城市公共运营车辆（辆）
City Operating Vehicles(unit)

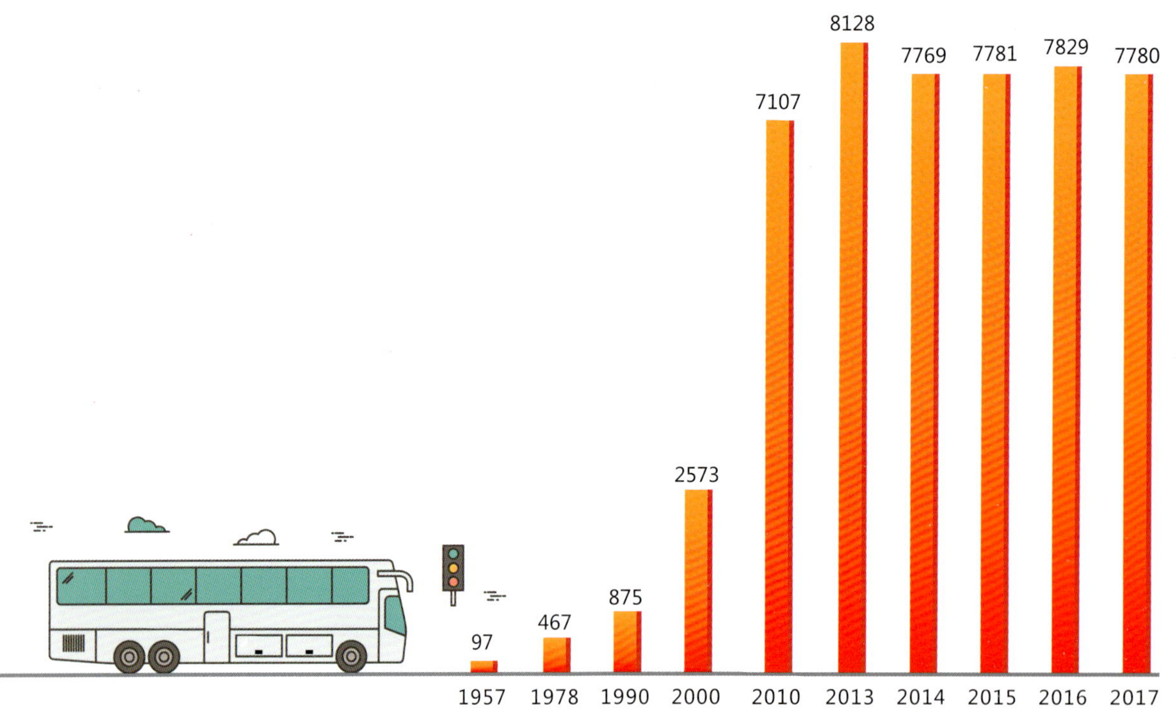

天然气供气总量（万立方米）

Total Natural Gas Supply(10000 cu.m)

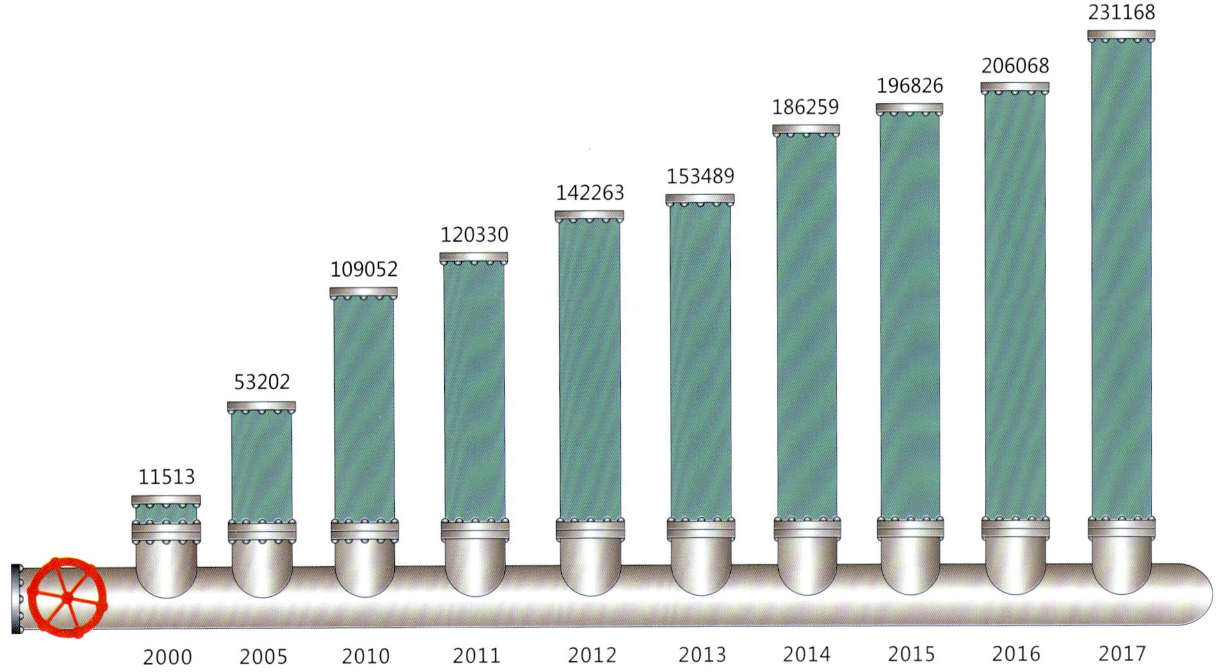

绿地面积（公顷）

Green Area（hectare）

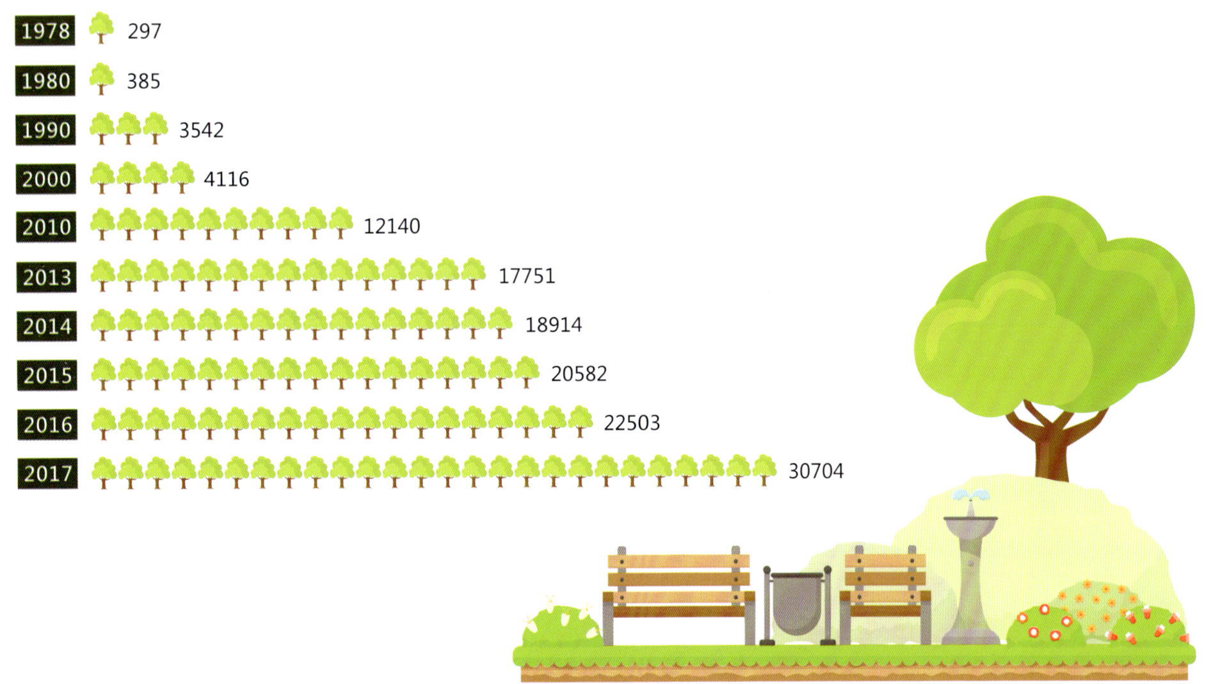

普通教育在校学生（万人）

Total Enrollment of Regular Education（10000 persons）

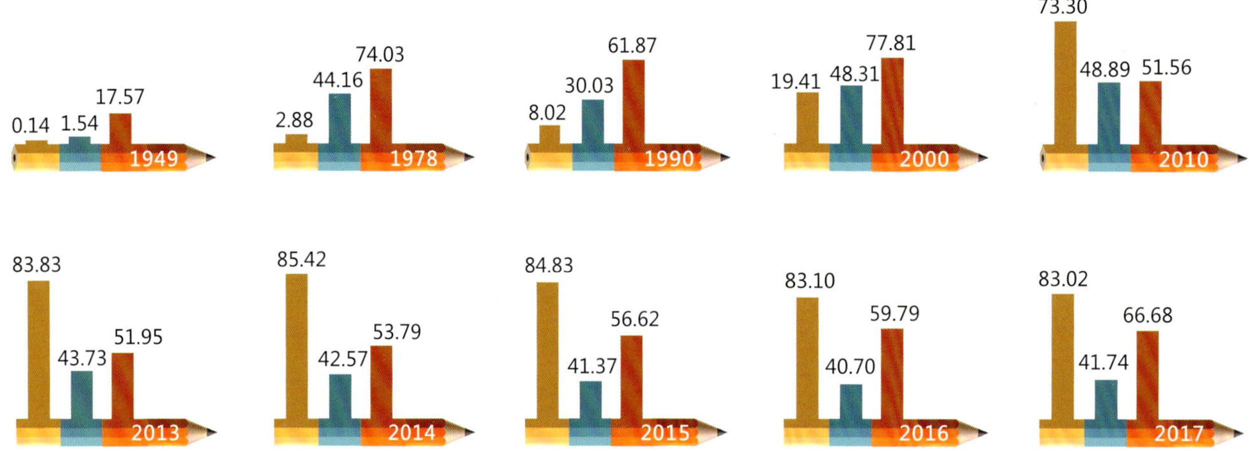

专任教师（万人）

Full-time Teachers (10000 persons)

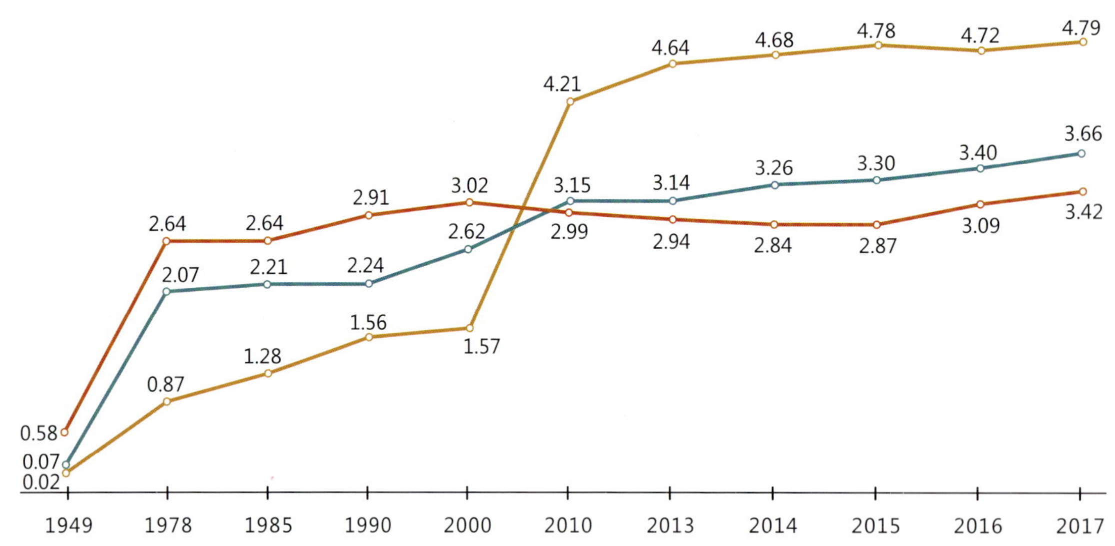

城乡居民收入（元）

The Income of Urban and Rural Residents(yuan)

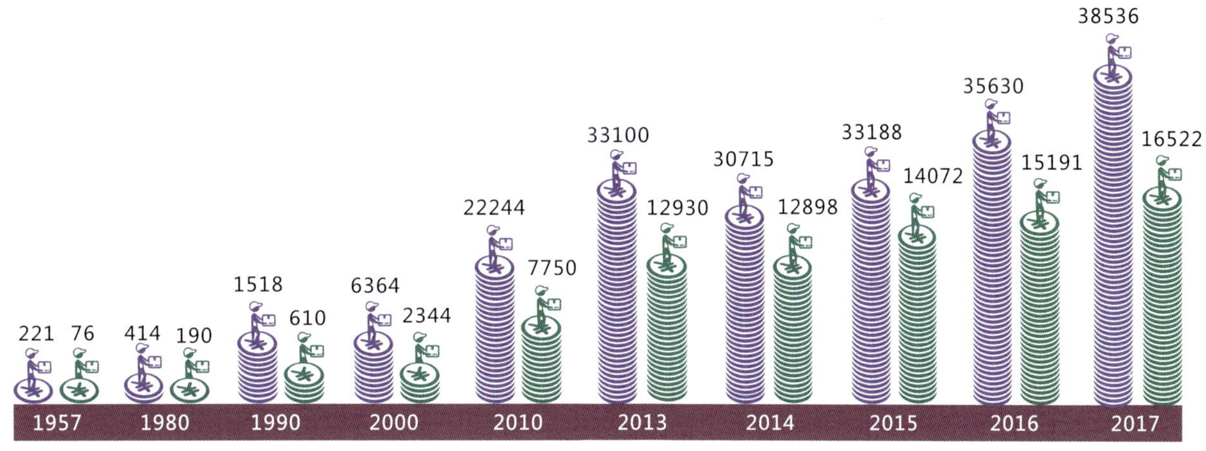

注：2014年起“农村居民人均纯收入”改为“农村居民人均可支配收入”

价格指数（以上年价格为100）

Price Indices(the price of preceding year=100)

● 居民消费价格指数 Consumer Price Index　　● 商品零售价格指数 Retail Price Index

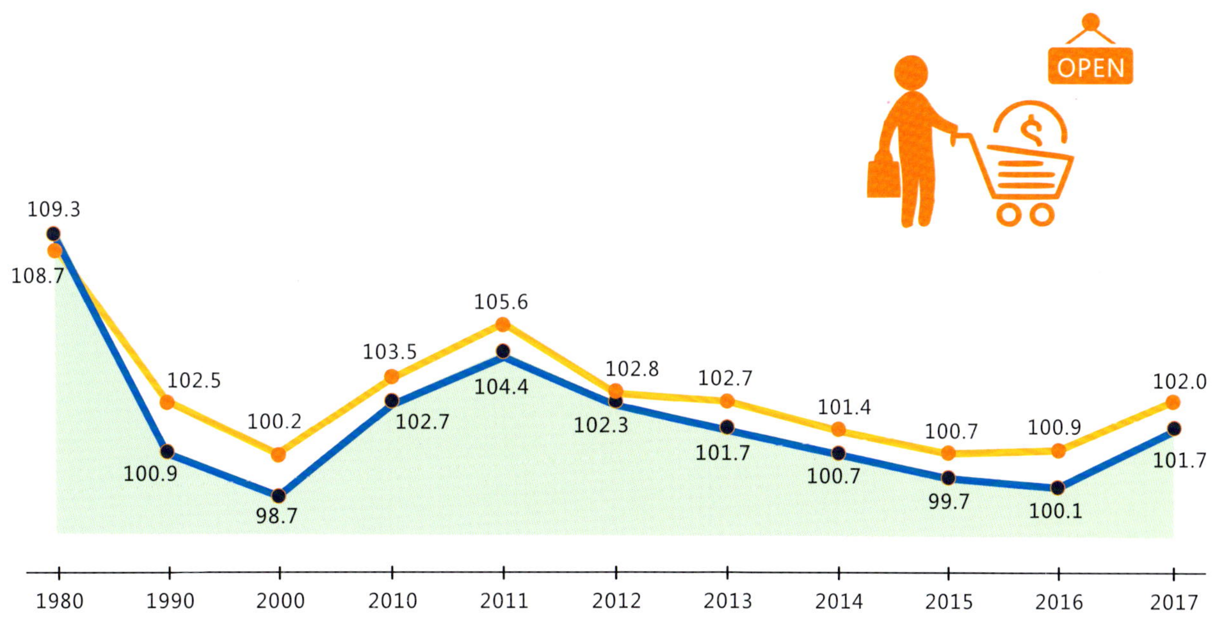

目　录

CONTENTS

西安市2017年国民经济和社会发展统计公报……1
Statistical Communique of Xi'an City on 2017 National Economic and Social Development ……7

一、综　合

GENERAL SURVEY

简要说明
Brief Introduction
1-1 行政区划（2017年）……17
Administrative Division（2017）
1-2 土地面积和常住人口密度（2017年）……18
Statistics on Land Area and Density of Permanent Population（2017）
1-3 自然状况和资源（2017年）……19
Nature Conditions and Resources（2017）
1-4 气象情况（2017年）……20
Climate Condition（2017）
1-5 市区及县各月平均气温（2017年）……20
Average Temperature of Xi'an and the Districts of Each Month（2017）
1-6 市区及县各月日照时数（2017年）……21
Sunshine Duration of Xi'an and the Districts of Each Month（2017）
1-7 市区及县各月降水天数（2017年）……21
Precipitation Days of Xi'an and the Districts of Each Month（2017）
1-8 市区及县各月降水量（2017年）……22
Amount of Precipitation of Xi'an and the Districts of Each Month（2017）
1-9 市区及区县各月平均风速（2017年）……22
Average Wind Velocity of Xi'an and the Districts of Each Month（2017）

1-10 主要年份国有土地使用权出让、划拨情况……23
The Transfer and Allocation of State-Owned Land Use Right in Representative Years
1-11 主要年份国民经济和社会发展总量与速度指标……24
Total and Speed Index of National Economy and Social Development in Representative Years
1-12 主要年份国民经济和社会发展结构指标……34
Structural Indicators of National Economic and Social Development in Representative Years
1-13 主要年份国民经济和社会发展比例和效益指标……42
Proportions of National Economic and Social Development and Benefit Index in Representative Years
1-14 主要年份平均每天主要社会经济活动……48
Major Social and Economic Activities Per Day in Representative Years
1-15 各区县国民经济和社会发展主要指标（2017年）……50
Major Indicators of National Economy and Social Development by Region（2017）
主要统计指标解释……52
Explanatory Notes on Main Statistical Indicators

二、基本单位

BASIC UNIT

简要说明
Brief Introduction
2-1 按登记注册类型分法人单位数（2017年）……57
Impersonal Entities by Status of Registion（2017）
2-2 按国民经济行业分法人单位数（2017年）……58
Impersonal Entities by Industry of the National Economy（2017）
2-3 按行政区划分法人单位数（2017年）……62
Impersonal Entities by Region（2017）
2-4 按登记注册类型分产业活动单位数（2017年）……63
Industrial Active Units by Status of Registion（2017）
2-5 按国民经济行业分产业活动单位数（2017年）……65
Industrial Active Units by Industry of the National Economy（2017）
2-6 按行政区划分产业活动单位数（2017年）……69
Industrial Active Units by Region（2017）
2-7 按统计机构分企业一套表调查单位数（2017年）……70
Number of Survey Units by Statistical Agencies of "One Sheet"（2017）
2-8 按行政区划分企业一套表调查单位数（2017年）……71

Number of Survey Units of "One Sheet" by Region (2017)

2-9 按行政区划和国民经济行业分法人单位数（2017年）……72

Impersonal Entities by Administravive Districts and Industry of the National Economy (2017)

2-10 按行政区划和机构类型分法人单位数（2017年）……76

Impersonal Entities by Agencies Types of Legal Entities Corporate Units and Administrative Districts (2017)

2-11 按行政区划和登记注册类型分企业法人单位数（2017年）……77

The Corporate Units by Types of Corporate Registration and Adminstration Districts (2017)

主要统计指标解释……78

Explanatory Notes on Main Statistical Indicators

三、国民经济核算

NATIONAL ECONOMIC ACCOUNTS

简要说明

Brief Introduction

3-1 主要年份生产总值……85

Gross Domestic Product in Representative Years

3-2 主要年份生产总值指数（上年＝100）……86

Indices of Gross Domestic Product in Representative Years (preceding year = 100)

3-3 主要年份生产总值指数（1952年=100）……87

Indices of Gross Domestic Product in Representative Years (1952= 100)

3-4 主要年份生产总值构成……88

Composition of Gross Domestic Product in Representative Years

3-5 主要年份分行业增加值……89

The Value added by Industry in Representative Years

3-6 主要年份分行业增加值指数（上年＝100）……91

Indices of the Value added by Industry in Representative Years (preceding year = 100)

3-7 主要年份三次产业贡献率……93

Three Industries Contribution Rate in Representative Years

3-8 主要年份三次产业拉动率……94

Three Industries Pulling Rate in Representative Years

3-9 分行业增加值……95

Value added by Industry

3-10 各区县生产总值（2017年）……96

Gross Domestic Product by Region (2017)

3-11 各区县生产总值指数（2017年）（上年=100）……97
Indices of Gross Domestic Product by Region（2017）（preceding year = 100）
3-12 主要年份非公有制经济增加值……98
The Added Value of Non-public-owned Economic in Representative Years
主要统计指标解释……99
Explanatory Notes on Main Statistical Indicators

四、人口、从业人员与职工工资

POPULATION, EMPLOYMENT AND WAGES

简要说明
Brief Introduction
4-1 主要年份人口数、人口密度和人口发展情况……105
Population, Population Density and Population Development in Representative Years
4-2 主要年份人口自然变动情况……106
Natural Population Movements in Representative Years
4-3 人口年龄构成和抚养比……107
Population Age Composition and Dependency Ratio
4-4 全市及各区县人口数和户数（2017年）……107
Population and Households by Region（2017）
4-5 全市及各区县常住人口数和人口变动情况（2017年）……108
Permanent Population and Population Changes by Region（2017）
4-6 主要年份常住人口数……108
Permanent Population in Representative Years
4-7 主要年份社会从业人数……109
Number of Social Laborers in Representative Years
4-8 按国民经济行业分从业人数（2017年）……110
Number of Employed Persons Grouped by Industry of the National Economy（2017）
4-9 全部单位从业人员情况（2017年）……112
Basic Facts on All Employees（2017）
4-10 国有单位从业人员情况（2017年）……114
Basic Facts on Employees in State-owned Units（2017）
4-11 城镇集体单位从业人员情况（2017年）……116
Basic Facts on Employees in Urban Collective-owned Units（2017）
4-12 其他经济类型单位从业人员情况（2017年）……118

Basic Facts on Employees in Other Units（2017）
4-13 城镇非私营单位分行业从业人员年平均工资……120
Average Wages of Urban Non-private Employees by Industry
4-14 主要年份单位从业人员数及工资总额……122
Number of Employees and Remuneration in Representative Years
4-15 全部单位从业人员工资总额（2017年）……123
Total Wages of All Employees of All Units（2017）
4-16 国有单位从业人员工资总额（2017年）……125
Total Wages of State-owned Units Employees（2017）
4-17 城镇集体单位从业人员工资总额（2017年）……127
Total Wages of Urban Collective-owned Units Employees（2017）
4-18 其他经济类型单位从业人员工资总额（2017年）……129
Total Wages of Other Units Employees（2017）
4-19 主要年份城镇登记失业人数及失业率……131
Registered Unemployed Persons and Unemployment Rate in Urban Area in Representative Years
主要统计指标解释……132
Explanatory Notes on Main Statistical Indicators

五、固定资产投资

INVESTMENT IN FIXED ASSETS

简要说明
Brief Introduction
5-1 主要年份按类别分全社会固定资产投资……137
Total Investment in Fixed Assets in the Whole Country by Classifications in Representative Years
5-2 主要年份按经济类型分全社会固定资产投资……138
Total Investment in Fixed Assets in the Whole Country by Economic Type in Representative Years
5-3 主要年份按产业分全市固定资产投资……139
Total Investment in Fixed Assets in the Whole City by Three Strata of Industry in Representative Years
5-4 主要年份按资金来源及建设性质分全市固定资产投资……140
Total Investment in Fixed Assets in the Whole City by Sources of Funds and Type of Construction in Representative Years
5-5 主要年份全市新增固定资产投资及房屋竣工面积……142
Newly Added Fixed Assets and Floor Spaces Completed of Municipal Units in Representative Years
5-6 全市固定资产投资（2017年）……143
Total Investment in Fixed Assets in the Whole City（2017）

5-7 按国民经济行业分全市固定资产投资（2017年）……146
Investment in Fixed Assets in the Whole City by Industry （2017）
5-8 按国民经济行业分民间投资（2017年）……148
Private Investment of Municipal Units by Industry （2017）
5-9 按国民经济行业分基础设施投资（2017年）……149
Investment for Basic Infrastructure of Municipal Units by Industry （2017）
5-10 全市固定资产投资资金来源（2017年）……149
Source of Funds for Total Fixed Assets Investment of Whole City（2017）
5-11 全市按行业分施工项目（2017年）……150
Construction Project Grouped by Industry in the Whole City（2017）
5-12 全市固定资产投资效果（2017年）……152
Achievements of Total Assets Investment of Whole City（2017）
5-13 固定资产投资新增生产能力或效益（2017年）……153
Newly Increased Production Capacity or Project Efficiency through Investment（2017）
5-14 全市按国民经济行业分房屋建筑面积（2017年）……154
Floors Space of Buildings Construction of Municipal Units by Industry （2017）
5-15 主要年份市属固定资产投资……156
Investment In Fixed Assets of Municipal Units in Representative Years
5-16 市属固定资产投资（2017年）……157
Investment in Fixed Assets of Municipal Units （2017）
5-17 按国民经济行业分市属固定资产投资（2017年）……159
Investment in Fixed Assets of Municipal Units by Industry （2017）
5-18 按资金来源及建设性质分市属固定资产投资（2017年）……161
Investment in Fixed Assets of Municipal Units by Sources of Funds and Type of Construction （2017）
5-19 分区县、开发区全社会固定资产投资额（2017年）……162
Total Investment in Fixed Assets by Region and Development Zone（2017）
5-20 分区县工业投资（2017年）……163
Industrial Investment by Region（2017）
5-21 分区县、开发区新增固定资产及房屋施工、竣工面积（2017年）……164
Newly Added Fixed Assets and Floor Space of Constructing and Completed Buildings by Region and Development Zone （2017）
5-22 主要年份房地产开发投资主要指标……166
Main Indicators of Investment in Real Estate Development in Representative Years
5-23 分区县、开发区房地产开发主要指标（2017年）……168
Main Indicators of Real Estate Development by Region and Development Zone （2017）
5-24 房地产开发投资主要指标（2017年）……170

Main Indicators of Investment in Real Estate Development（2017）
5-25 商品房销售情况（2017年）……171
Sales of Commercial Houses（2017）
5-26 房地产开发投资资金来源（2017年）……172
Source of Funds for Investment in Real Estate Development（2017）
5-27 房地产开发经营情况（2017年）……173
Running of Real Estate Development（2017）
主要统计指标解释……174
Explanatory Notes on Main Statistical Indicators

六、财 政

GOVERNMENT FINANCE

简要说明
Brief Introduction
6-1 主要年份地方财政一般预算收入及支出……183
General Public Budgetary Revenue and Expenditure of Local Finance in Representative Years
6-2 财政收入（2017年）……184
Government Revenue（2017）
6-3 财政支出（2017年）……185
Government Expenditures（2017）
6-4 各区县、开发区财政收入（2017年）……186
Government Revenue by Region and Development Zone（2017）
6-5 各区县、开发区财政支出（2017年）……190
Government Expenditure by Region and Development Zone（2017）
主要统计指标解释……195
Explanatory Notes on Main Statistical Indicators

七、物价指数

PRICE INDICES

简要说明
Brief Introduction
7-1 主要年份各种价格指数……203
Price Indices in Representative Years

7-2 居民消费价格指数（2017年）……204
Residents Consumer Price Indices（2017）
7-3 商品零售价格指数（2017年）……206
Retail Price Indices（2017）
7-4 主要年份工业生产者出厂价格指数……208
Producer Price Indices（PPI）for Industrial Producers in Representative Years
7-5 主要年份工业生产者购进价格指数……210
Industrial Purchasing Indices（IPI）for Industrial Producers in Representative Years
7-6 住宅销售价格指数（2017年）……211
Selling Price Indices of Residential Buildings（2017）
7-7 主要年份固定资产投资价格指数……211
Price Indices for Investment in Fixed Assets in Representative Years
主要统计指标解释……212
Explanatory Notes on Main Statistical Indicators

八、人民生活

PEOPLE'S LIVELIHOOD

简要说明
Brief Introduction
8-1 主要年份城乡居民人均收入及恩格尔系数……217
Per Capita Annual Income and Engel's Coefficient of Urban and Rural Households in Representative Years
8-2 主要年份城乡居民人民币储蓄存款……218
Savings Deposit of Urban and Rural Households in Representative Years
8-3 各区县城乡居民人均可支配收入……219
Per Capita Income of Urban and Rural Households by Region
8-4 全市居民家庭基本情况……220
Basic Conditions of All Households
8-5 全市居民人均可支配收入……221
Per Capita Annual Disposable Income of All Households
8-6 全市居民年人均消费支出……222
Per Capita Living Expenditure of All Households
8-7 全市居民家庭人均购买主要商品数量……223
Per Capita Annual Purchases of Major Commodities of All Households
8-8 全市居民家庭每百户年末耐用品拥有情况……224

Ownership of Major Durable Consumer Goods Every 100 Households

8-9 城镇常住居民家庭基本情况……225

Basic Conditions of Urban Households

8-10 城镇常住居民人均消费支出……226

Per Capita Living Expenditure of Urban Households

8-11 城镇常住居民家庭人均购买主要商品数量……227

Per Capita Annual Purchases of Major Commodities of Urban Households

8-12 城镇常住居民家庭每百户耐用品拥有情况……228

Ownership of Major Durable Consumer Goods Every 100 Urban Households

8-13 城镇常住居民家庭居住情况……229

Housing Conditions of Urban Households

8-14 农村常住居民家庭基本情况……230

Basic Conditions of Rural Households

8-15 农村常住居民人均消费支出……231

Per Capita Living Expenditure of Rural Households

8-16 农村常住居民家庭人均购买主要商品数量……232

Per Capita Annual Purchases of Major Commodities of Rural Households

8-17 农村常住居民家庭平均每百户耐用品拥有情况……233

Ownership of Major Durable Consumer Goods Every 100 Rural Households

8-18 农村常住居民家庭居住情况……234

Housing Conditions of Rural Households

主要统计指标解释……235

Explanatory Notes on Main Statistical Indicators

九、城市公用事业

URBAN PUBLIC UTILITIES

简要说明

Brief Introduction

9-1 城市（县城）供水……241

Urban (County) Water Supply

9-2 城市（县城）供燃气……241

Gas Supply in Urban Area (County)

9-3 城市（县城）供热……242

Heating in Urban Area (County)

9-4 城市公共交通……242
Urban Public Traffic
9-5 市政设施……243
Municipal Facilities
9-6 城市（县城）设施水平……243
Urban（County）Municipal Facilities
9-7 城市（县城）规模及用地情况……244
City（County）Scale and Land Use
9-8 城市（县城）园林绿化……244
Urban（County）Parks,Gardens and Green Areas in Cities
9-9 城市（县城）环境卫生……245
Urban（County）Environment Sanitation
9-10 市区及县供水（2017年）……245
Urban and County Water Supply（2017）
9-11 市区及县供燃气（2017年）……246
Urban and County Gas Supply（2017）
9-12 市区及县供热（2017年）……246
Urban and County Heating（2017）
9-13 市区及县市政设施（2017年）……247
Urban and County Municipal Facilities（2017）
9-14 市区及县市政设施水平（2017年）……247
Urban and County Municipal Facilities Level（2017）
主要统计指标解释……248
Explanatory Notes on Main Statistical Indicators

十、环境保护

ENVIRONMENT PROTECTION

简要说明
Brief Introduction
10-1 城市环境保护（2017年）……253
Urban Environmental Protection（2017）
10-2 主要年份工业“三废”排放及处理利用情况……254
Discharge and Treatrment of Waste Gas, Water & Solid Wastes in Repersentative Years
10-3 工业污染排放及处理利用情况（2017年）……256

Discharge and Treatment of Industrial Pollution（2017）
10-4 城市污水处理情况（2017年）……257
Urban Sewage Treatment（2017）
10-5 危险废物（医疗废物）集中处理情况（2017年）……258
Condition of Concentrated Disposal of Dangerous Wastes（Medical Wastes）（2017）
10-6 生活及其他污染情况（2017年）……258
Domestic Pollution and Other Conditions（2017）
10-7 工业污染治理项目建设情况（2017年）……259
Condition of Anti-Industrial-Pollution Projects（2017）
10-8 各区县、开发区环境保护基本情况（2017年）……260
Condition of Environment Protection by Regions（2017）
主要统计指标解释……262
Explanatory Notes on Main Statistical Indicators

十一、农　业
AGRICULTURE

简要说明
Brief Introduction
11-1 主要年份农村基层组织、乡村户数、人口及劳动力情况……269
Grassroots Organizations in Rural Areas, Rural Households, Population and Labor Force in Representative Years
11-2 各区县乡村从业人员数（2017年）……270
Number of Rural Employees by Region（2017）
11-3 主要年份耕地面积……271
Area of Cultivated Land in Representative Years
11-4 各区县耕地面积（2017年）……272
Area of Cultivated Land by Region（2017）
11-5 主要年份农业机械拥有量（年末数）……274
Possession of Agricultural Machinery in Representative Years（Number of year-end）
11-6 各区县农业机械拥有量（2017年）……276
Possession of Agricultural Machinery by Region（2017）
11-7 主要年份农业机械化、化肥、水利、水电情况……278
Agricultural Machinery,Chemical Fertilizers,Water Conservancy,Hydropower in Representative Years
11-8 各区县农业机械化、化肥、水利、水电情况（2017年）……280
Agricultural Machinery,Chemical Fertilizers,Water Conservancy, Hydropower by Region（2017）

11-9 主要年份农林牧渔及服务业总产值及指数……282
Gross Output Value of Farming,Forestry,Animal Husbandry,Fishery, Service and Related Indices in Representative Years
11-10 主要年份农林牧渔及服务业总产值指数……283
Related Indices of Gross Output Value of Farming,Forestry， Animal Husbandry,Fishery and Service in Representative Years
11-11 主要年份农林牧渔及服务业总产值构成……283
Gross Output Value and Its Composition of Farming, Forestry,Animal Husbandry,Fishery and Service at Current Price in Representative Years
11-12 各区县农林牧渔及服务业总产值（2017年）……284
Gross Output Value of Farming, Forestry, Animal Husbandry,Fishery and Service by Region（2017）
11-13 各区县农林牧渔及服务业总产值指数和构成（2017年）……285
Gross Output Value and Its Composition of Farming, Forestry, Animal Husbandry,Fishery and Service at Current Price by Region（2017）
11-14 主要年份农林牧渔及服务业增加值……286
Value-Added of Farming, Forestry, Animal Husbandry,Fishery and Service in Representative Years
11-15 主要年份农林牧渔及服务业增加值指数……287
Indices of Value-Added of Farming, Forestry, Animal Husbandry,Fishery and Service in Representative Years
11-16 各区县农林牧渔及服务业增加值（2017年）……287
Value-Added of Farming, Forestry, Animal Husbandry,Fishery and Service by Region（2017）
11-17 各区县农林牧渔及服务业增加值指数（2017年）……288
Indices of Value-Added of Farming, Forestry, Animal Husbandry， Fishery and Service by Region（2017）
11-18 主要年份农作物播种面积……289
Sown Areas of Farm Crops In Representative Years
11-19 各区县主要农作物播种面积（2017年）……290
Sown Areas of Major Farm Crops by Region（2017）
11-20 主要年份农作物产品产量……291
Yield of Major Farm Crops in Representative Years
11-21 各区县主要农作物产品产量（2017年）……292
Yield of Major Farm Crops by Region（2017）
11-22 主要年份农作物单位面积产量……293
Yield of Farm Crops Per Unit Area in Representative Years
11-23 各区县主要农作物单位面积产量（2017年）……294
The Output of Main Crops Per Unit Area by Region（2017）
11-24 设施农业生产情况（2017年）……295
Agricultural Production Facilities（2017）

11-25 主要年份林业生产情况……295
Statistics on Forestry in Representative Years
11-26 各区县林业生产情况（2017年）……296
Statistics On Forestry by Region（2017）
11-27 主要年份果业生产情况……296
Statistics on Fruits in Representative Years
11-28 各区县果业生产情况（2017年）……297
Area and Output of Fruits by Region（2017）
11-29 果品加工、销售及生产服务情况……298
The Situation of Fruit Processing, Sales and Production Service
11-30 主要年份畜牧业生产情况……300
Statistics on Livestock Husbandry in Representative Years
11-31 各区县畜牧业生产情况（2017年）……301
Statistics On Livestock, Animal Husbandry by Region（2017）
11-32 主要年份畜产品和水产品产量……302
Output of Livestock Products and Aquatic Products in Representative Years
11-33 各区县主要畜产品和水产品产量（2017年）……304
Output of Major Livestock Products and Aquatic Products by Region（2017）
11-34 农业科技、教育情况（2017年）……305
Agricultural Science and Technology Education（2017）
11-35 主要年份农产品人均占有量……305
Per Capita Output of Major Farm Products in Representative Years
11-36 主要年份农村经济效益指标……306
Main Indicators of Rural Economic Benefit in Representative Years
主要统计指标解释……307
Explanatory Notes on Main Statistical Indicators

十二、工　业

INDUSTRY

简要说明
Brief Introduction
12-1 主要年份全部工业总产值……313
Gross Output Value of Industry in Representative Years
12-2 主要年份各区县规模以上工业总产值……315

Gross Output Value of Industry above Designated Size in Representative Years
12-3 各区县规模以上工业企业工业总产值（2017年）……316
Gross Output Value of Industrial Enterprises above Designated Size by Region （2017）
12-4 主要年份规模以上工业企业主要经济指标……318
Major Economic Indicators of Industrial Enterprises above Designated Size in Representative Years
12-5 各区县规模以上工业企业主要经济指标（2017年）……320
Major Economic Indicators of Industrial Enterprises above Designated Size by Region（2017）
12-6 规模以上工业企业主要工业产品产量（2017年）……322
Major Output of Industrial Enterprises above Designated Size（2017）
12-7 主要年份规模以上工业企业经济效益指标……327
Indicators of Economic Performance of Industrial Enterprises above Designated Size in Representative Years
12-8 规模以上工业企业主要经济指标（2017年）……328
Major Economic Indicators of Industrial Enterprises above Designated Size （2017）
12-9 规模以上国有及国有控股工业企业主要经济指标（2017年）……346
Major Economic Indicators of State-owned and State-holding Share Industrial Enterprises above Designated Size（2017）
12-10 规模以上外商及港澳台商投资工业企业主要经济指标（2017年）……358
Major Economic Indicators of Foreign,Hong Kong,Macao and Taiwan Invested Industrial Enterprises above Designated Size （2017）
12-11 规模以上大中型工业企业主要经济指标（2017年）……370
Major Economic Indicators of Large and Medium-sized Industrial Enterprises above Designated Size（2017）
12-12 规模以上高技术产业工业企业主要经济指标（2017年）……388
Major Economic Indicators of High Technology Industry Industrial Enterprises above Designated Size （2017）
12-13 规模以上工业企业主要经济效益指标（2017年）……400
Major Indicators of Economic Performance of Industrial Enterprises above Designated Size （2017）
12-14 规模以上大中型工业企业主要经济效益指标（2017年）……404
Major Economic Indicators of Large and Medium-sized Industrial Enterprises above Designated Size（2017）
12-15 规模以上工业主要产品生产能力（2017年）……408
Production Capacity of Major Products of Industrial Enterprises above Designated Size（2017）
主要统计指标解释……409
Explanatory Notes on Main Statistical Indicators

十三、能　源

ENERGY

简要说明

Brief Introduction

13-1 全市及各区县单位GDP能耗……419

Energy Consumption per Unit of GDP by Region

13-2 主要年份全社会用电量……420

Electricity Consumption of the Whole Society in Representative Years

13-3 规模以上工业企业能源购进、消费及库存（2017年）……422

Energy Purchases，Consumption and Inventory of Industrial Enterprises above Designated Size（2017）

13-4 规模以上工业企业分行业主要能源品种消费量（2017年）……424

Major Energy Consumption above Designated Size by Industry（2017）

13-5 规模以上工业企业分行业综合能源消费量（2017年）……426

Comprehensive Energy Consumption by Sector above Designated Size（2017）

13-6 规模以上工业企业用水情况（2017年）……427

Statistics on Water Use of Industrial Enterprises above Designated Size（2017）

13-7 规模以上工业企业分行业用水情况（2017年）……428

Volume of Water Use of Industrial Enterprises above Designated Size by Industry（2017）

13-8 分区县规模以上工业企业综合能源消费量（2017年）……430

Comprehensive Energy Consumption above Designated Size by Region（2017）

主要统计指标解释……431

Explanatory Notes on Main Statistical Indicators

十四、建筑业

CONSTRUCTION

简要说明

Brief Introduction

14-1 主要年份建筑业总产值……437

Total Output Value of Construction in Representative Years

14-2 全市建筑施工总承包企业基本情况（2017年）……437

Basic Situation of Construction General Contracting Contractors in Whole City（2017）

14-3 施工总承包和专业承包建筑企业生产情况（2017年）……438

Main Indicators on General Constructing Contractors and Professional Contractors（2017）

14-4 施工总承包和专业承包建筑业企业主要指标（2017年）……442
Major Indicators of General Construction Contractors and Professional Contractors（2017）
14-5 施工总承包和专业承包建筑业企业财务状况（2017年）……444
Financial Status of General Constructing Contractors and Professional Contractors（2017）
14-6 劳务分包建筑业企业生产经营情况（2017年）……448
Production and Management Situation of Subcontractor Construction Enterprises（2017）
14-7 各区县建筑业主要经济指标（2017年）……452
Major Indicators of Construction Enterprises by Region（2017）
14-8 各区县建筑业房屋施工及竣工面积（2017年）……453
Floor Space of Buildings under Construction & Completed by Region（2017）
14-9 各区县建筑业企业主要经济效益指标（2017年）……454
Major Economic Performance Indicators on Construction Enterprises by Region（2017）
主要统计指标解释……455
Explanatory Notes on Main Statistical Indicators

十五、运输邮电和信息化

TRANSPORT，POSTAL TELECOMMUNICATION SERVICE AND INFORMATIZATION

简要说明
Brief Introduction
15-1 主要年份各种交通线路和桥梁……459
Transportation Routes and Bridges in Representative Years
15-2 各种交通线路里程和桥梁数（2017年）……461
Length of Transportation Routes and Number of Bridges（2017）
15-3 主要年份全社会车辆数……462
Possession of Civil Vehicles in Representative Years
15-4 全社会车辆数（2017年）……463
Possession of Civil Vehicles（2017）
15-5 主要年份交通运输量及周转量……464
Passenger Traffic and Kilometers and Freight Traffic and Ton-kilometers in Representative Years
15-6 交通运输量及运输周转量（2017年）……465
Passenger Traffic and Kilometers and Freight Traffic and Ton-kilometers（2017）
15-7 主要年份邮政电信情况……466
Basic Statistic on Postal and Telecommunication Service in Representative Years
15-8 邮政业务及服务网点……468

Postal Service and Branch Post Office
15-9 电信业务情况……469
Telecommunication Service
15-10 一套表单位信息化基本情况（2017年）……470
Basic Statistics on Informatization of “One Sheet” Units（2017）
15-11 一套表单位信息化设施及投入情况（2017年）……472
Information Technology Facilities and Investment of “One Sheet” Units （2017）
15-12 一套表单位信息化管理情况（2017年）……474
Information Management Situation of “One Sheet” Units （2017）
15-13 一套表单位电子商务交易情况（2017年）……476
E-commerce Transactions of “One Sheet” Units（2017）
主要统计指标解释……478
Explanatory Notes on Main Statistical Indicator

十六、国内贸易

DOMESTIC TRADE

简要说明
Brief Introduction
16-1 主要年份社会消费品零售额……485
Total Retail Sales of Consumer Goods in Representative Years
16-2 社会消费品零售总额……486
Total Retail Sales of Consumer Goods
16-3 各区县社会消费品零售总额……487
Total Retail Sales of Consumer Goods by Region
16-4 限额以上批发零售贸易企业财务状况（2017年）……488
Financial Status of Wholesale and Retail Enterprises above Designated Size （2017）
16-5 限额以上住宿和餐饮企业财务状况（2017年）……500
Finacial Status of Hotels and Catering Eenterprises above Designated Size（2017）
16-6 限额以上批发零售贸易业商品购进、销售、库存总额（2017年）……508
Total Purchases,Sales and Inventories of Wholesale and Retail Enterprises above Designated Size（2017）
16-7 限额以上住宿和餐饮业经营情况（2017年）……516
Statistic on Hotel Services and Catering Services above Designed Size（2017）
16-8 限额以上批发和零售业主要商品分类销售额（2017年）……520
Sale Values of Wholesale and Retail Enterprises above Designated Size by Category of Main Commodities（2017）

16-9 亿元以上商品交易市场成交情况（2017年）……521
Basic Statistics on Commodity Exchange Markets of Transaction Value over 100 Million Yuan（2017）
16-10 批发和零售业连锁经营情况（2017年）……522
Basic Statistics on Chain Business of Wholesale and Retail Trades（2017）
16-11 住宿和餐饮业连锁经营情况（2017年）……523
Basic Statistics on Chain Business of Hotels and Catering Services（2017）
16-12 限额以上住宿和餐饮业经营情况（2017年）……524
Statistic on Hotel Services and Catering Services above Designed Size（2017）
主要统计指标解释……528
Explanatory Notes on Main Statistical Indicators

十七、对外经济贸易和旅游

FOREIGN TRADE AND ECONOMIC COOPERATION TOURISM

简要说明
Brief Introduction
17-1 主要年份外资、外贸基本情况……535
Main Indicators on Foreign Investments and International Trading in Representative Years
17-2 主要年份利用外资情况……537
Utilization of Foreign Capital in Representative Years
17-3 外国和港澳台地区在西安投资情况（2017年）……538
Foreign, Hong Kong, Macao and Taiwan Investment Situation in Xi'an （2017）
17-4 各区县、开发区实际利用外资……540
Actual Utilized Investment by Foreign Entrepreneurs by Region and Development Zone
17-5 主要年份进出口总值……541
Total Imports and Exports in Representative Years
17-6 外贸商品进出口总值分国别和地区（2017年）……542
Total Value of Imports and Exports by Country and Region（2017）
17-7 主要商品分大类出口金额……543
Export Value of Major Merchandise by Type
17-8 主要商品分大类进口金额……546
Import Value of Major Merchandise by Type
17-9 按贸易方式分外贸出口总值……547
Total Value of Exports in Foreign Trade by Type of Trade
17-10 按贸易方式分外贸进口总值……548

Total Value of Imports in Foreign Trade by Type of Trade

17-11 主要年份旅游人数及收入……549

Number of Tourists and Tourism Earnings in Representative Years

17-12 主要年份旅行社及A级景点……549

Statistics of Travel Agencies and Level-A Scenic Spots in Representative Years

主要统计指标解释……550

Explanatory Notes on Main Statistical Indicators

十八、服务业

SERVICE INDUSTRY

简要说明

Brief Introduction

18-1 规模以上服务业按登记注册类型分主要经济指标（2017年）……555

Main Economic Indicators for Services above the Designated Size grouped by Registration Type（2017）

18-2 规模以上服务业按规模分主要经济指标（2017年）……560

Main Economic Indicators for Services above the Designated Size grouped by Size of Enterprises（2017）

18-3 规模以上服务业按行业分主要经济指标（2017年）……562

Main Economic Indicators for Services above the Designated Size grouped by Industry（2017）

18-4 规模以上服务业按隶属关系分主要经济指标（2017年）……566

Main Economic Indicators for Services above the Designated Size grouped by Affiliation（2017）

主要统计指标解释……568

Explanatory Notes on Main Statistical Indicators

十九、金融业

FINANCIAL INTERMEDIATION

简要说明

Brief Introduction

19-1 西安银行系统机构、人员数……575

Number of Institution and Employed Person in Finance System in Xi'an

19-2 金融机构（含外资）本外币存贷款年末余额（2017年）……576

Deposits and Loans of Local Currency and Foreign Currency in Financial Institution（Including Foreign-Funded Institution）at Year-end（2017）

19-3 金融机构（不含外资）本外币存贷款年末余额（2017年）……577
Deposits and Loans Domestic Funded Financial Institution of Local Currency and Foreign Currency at Year-end （2017）
19-4 主要年份金融机构（含外资）人民币存贷款年末余额……578
Deposits and Loans in Financial Institutions （Including Foreign-funded） in Representative Years
19-5 金融机构（含外资）人民币存贷款年末余额（2017年）……579
Loans in Financial Institutions（Including Foreign-funded） in Representative Years（2017）
19-6 金融机构（不含外资）人民币存贷款年末余额（2017年）……580
Year-end Balance of RMB Deposits and Loans in Financial Institutionst （Not Including Foreign-funded）(2017)
19-7 保险业务情况……581
Indicators of Insurance Business
19-8 西安地区证券期货系统机构、人员数……582
Number of Institution and Employed Person in Securities and Futures System in Xi'an
19-9 证券期货市场基本情况（2017年）……583
Basic Facts on Securities and Futures Markets（2017）
主要统计指标解释……584
Explanatory Notes on Main Statistical Indicators

二十、教育和科技

EDUCATION，SCIENCE AND TECHNOLOGY

简要说明
Brief Introduction
20-1 主要年份各类普通教育基本情况……589
Basic Statistics on Regular Eduction in Representative Years
20-2 各级各类学校、教职工情况（2017年）……590
Situation of All Kinds of Schools and Staff Members at All Levels （2017）
20-3 各级各类教育学生情况（2017年）……591
Basic Facts on Education Student by School Type （2017）
20-4 主要年份普通高等学校和科研机构研究生情况……592
Basic Statistics of Postgraduates on Regular Institutions of Higher Education and Scientific Research Institution in Representative Years
20-5 主要年份普通高等学校基本情况（本专科）……593
Basic Statistics on Regular Institution of Higher Education in Representative Years
20-6 主要年份普通中等专业学校基本情况……594
Basic Statistics on Regular Specialized Secondary Schools in Representative Years

20-7 主要年份普通中等教育基本情况……595
Basic Situation of General Secondary Education in Major Years
20-8 各区县普通中等教育基本情况（2017年）……596
Basic Situation of Ordinary Secondary Education in Various Districts and Counties（2017）
20-9 主要年份职业高中基本情况……597
Basic Statistics on Vocational Secondary Schools in Representative Years
20-10 各区县职业高中基本情况（2017年）……598
Basic Statistics on Vocational Secondary Schools by Region （2017）
20-11 主要年份普通初等教育基本情况……599
Basic Situation of General Primary Education in Major Years
20-12 各区县普通初等教育基本情况（2017年）……600
Basic Situation of General Primary Education in Various Districts and Counties （2017）
20-13 主要年份学前教育基本情况……601
Basic Conditions of Pre-school Education in Representative Years
20-14 主要年份特殊教育基本情况……602
Basic Statistics on Special Education in Representative Years
20-15 基础教育监测评价情况（2017年）……603
Monitoring and Evaluation of Basic Education（2017）
20-16 主要年份平均每万人口在校学生数及构成……604
The Average Number of Students in the School every 10000 Individuals in Representative Years
20-17 民办教育情况（2017年）……606
Private Education Situation （2017）
20-18 全市科技活动情况（2017年）……608
Scientific and Technological Activizies in the Whole City（2017）
20-19 规模以上重点行业企业研究与试验发展（R&D）情况（2017年）……608
R&D Project Status of Key Enterprises above Designated Size（2017）
20-20 规模以上工业企业研究与试验发展（R&D）基本情况（2017年）……609
R&D Project Status of Industrial Enterprises above Designated Size（2017）
20-21 规模以上工业企业研究与试验发展（R&D）人员和经费支出情况（2017年）……612
R&D Personnel and Expenditure Conditions of Industrial Enterprises above Designated Size（2017）
20-22 规模以上工业企业研究和试验发展（R&D）项目情况（2017年）……616
R&D Project Status of Industrial Enterprises above Designated Size（2017）
20-23 规模以上工业企业新产品开发、生产及销售情况（2017年）……620
New Product Development, Production and Sales of Above-scale Industrial Enterprises（2017）
20-24 规模以上非工业重点行业企业研究与试验发展（R&D）基本情况（2017）……624
R&D Project Status of Non-Industrial Key Enterprises above Designated Size（2017）

20-25 规模以上非工业重点行业企业研究与试验发展（R&D）人员和经费支出情况（2017年）………625
R&D Personnel and Expenditure of Non-Industrial Key Enterprises above Designated Size（2017）
20-26 规模以上非工业重点行业企业研究与试验发展（R&D）项目情况（2017年）………………………628
The Situation of Non-Industrial Key Enterprises above Designated Size Projects（2017）
20-27 主要年份知识产权情况………………………………………………………………………………629
Intellectual Property Rights in Major Years
20-28 主要年份民事知识产权维权情况……………………………………………………………………629
Protection of Civil Intellectual Property Rights in Major Years
20-29 规模以上工业企业自主知识产权情况（2017年）…………………………………………………630
The Independent Intellectual Property Rights of Industrial Enterprises above Designated Size（2017）
20-30 规模以上非工业重点行业企业知识产权（2017年）………………………………………………632
Intellectual Property Rights of Non–Industrial Key Enterprises above Designated Size（2017）
主要统计指标解释……………………………………………………………………………………633
Explanatory Notes on Main Statistical Indicators

二十一、文化、体育、卫生、社会福利和其他

CULTURE, SPORTS, PUBLIC HEALTH, SOCIAL WELFARE INSTITUTIONS AND OTHER SOCIAL ACTIVITIES

简要说明
Brief Introduction
21-1 电影基本情况（2017年）…………………………………………………………………………641
The Basic Situation of Film（2017）
21-2 图书馆基本情况（2017年）………………………………………………………………………642
The Basic Situation of Library（2017）
21-3 艺术表演基本情况（2017年）……………………………………………………………………642
The Basic Situation of Art Performance（2017）
21-4 主要年份群众艺术馆、文化馆（站）活动情况……………………………………………………643
Basic Statistics on Activities of Mass Art Centers and Cultural Centers in Representative Years
21-5 文物保护业基本情况（2017年）…………………………………………………………………643
Basic Statistics on Cultural Relics Protection（2017）
21-6 主要年份广播电台及节目制作情况…………………………………………………………………644
Basic Statistics of Broadcasting Stations and Program Production in Representative Years
21-7 主要年份电视台及节目制作情况……………………………………………………………………644
Basic Statistics of TV Stations and Production of TV Program in Representative Years

21-8 竞技体育情况（2017年）……645
The Situation of Competitive Sports（2017）
21-9 群众体育情况（2017年）……646
The Situation of Mass Sports（2017）
21-10 体育产业情况（2017年）……647
The Situation of Sport Industry（2017）
21-11 主要年份医疗卫生机构、床位、人员情况……647
Number of Health Care Institutions, Beds and Personnel in Health Care Institutions in Representative Years
21-12 医疗卫生机构、床位及人员情况（2017年）……648
Number of Health Care Institutions, Beds and Personnel in Health Care Institutions（2017）
21-13 各区县医疗卫生机构、床位及人员情况（2017年）……652
Number of Health Care Institutions, Beds and Employed Persons in Health Care Institutions By Region（2017）
21-14 各区县农村村级卫生组织情况（2017年）……653
Village Level Health Organization in the Rural Area by Region（2017）
21-15 各区县社区卫生服务中心（站）情况（2017年）……654
Situations of Community Health Service Center（Station）by Region（2017）
21-16 主要年份医疗卫生机构各类人员情况……655
Number of Personnel in Health Care Institutions in Representative Years
21-17 医疗卫生机构门诊、住院及病床使用情况（2017年）……656
Medical and Health Institutions Outpatient, Inpatient and Utilization of Beds（2017）
21-18 提供住宿的社会服务机构（2017年）……660
Social Welfare Insititutions Providing Accommodation （2017）
21-19 主要年份社会福利事业单位机构及人员情况……660
Number of Social Welfare Institutions and Personnel
21-20 社会保障基本情况（2017年）……661
Basic Situation of Social Security（2017）
21-21 全市及各区县新型农村合作医疗情况（2017年）……661
Situation of the New Rural Cooperative Medical Care of the Whole City and Area County（2017）
21-22 全市及各区县优抚对象人员情况（2017年）……662
Statistics on Persons Enjoying Favoured Treatment by Region（2017）
21-23 全市及各区县计划生育和婚姻登记情况（2017）……663
Conditions of Birth Control and Marriage Registration by Region（2017）
21-24 全市及各区县妇幼卫生保健情况（2017年）……664
Care Health Conditions of Women and Child by Region（2017）
21-25 主要年份律师、公证及调解情况……665
Basic Statistics on Lawyer, Notaries and Mediation in Representative Years

21-26 主要年份共青团组织情况……666
Basic Facts on Communist Youth League in Representative Years
21-27 妇联组织及工作情况（2017年）……666
The Basic Situation of Women's Federation （2017）
21-28 主要年份交通、火灾及安全生产情况……667
Transportation, Fire and Safety Production in Representative Years
21-29 主要年份刑事案件情况……668
Data on Criminal Cases in Representative Years
21-30 主要年份治安案件情况……668
Data on Public Order Cases in Representative Years
21-31 主要年份西安市人民检察院案件办理情况……669
Data on Acceptance of Cases of Xi'an People's Procuratorate
21-32 西安市中级人民法院案件基本情况（2017年）……669
Law Cases Basic Data of Xi'an Intermediate People's Court （2017）
主要统计指标解释……670
Explanatory Notes on Main Statistical Indicators

二十二、企业调查

ENTERPRISES INVESTIGATION

22-1 企业景气指数（2017年）……677
Business Climate Index（2017）
22-2 企业家信心指数（2017年）……677
Entrepreneur Expectation Indicator（2017）
主要统计指标解释……678
Explanatory Notes on Main Statistical Indicators

西安市2017年国民经济和社会发展统计公报[1]

西安市统计局　国家统计局西安调查队

2018年3月12日

2017年，全市上下认真学习贯彻党的十九大精神，以习近平新时代中国特色社会主义思想为指导，紧扣“五新战略”和“聚焦三六九、振兴大西安”奋斗目标，坚持稳中求进工作总基调，统筹推进稳增长、促改革、调结构、惠民生、防风险各项工作，实现了经济平稳健康发展与社会和谐稳定，开启了大西安建设新格局。

一、综合

初步核算，全年地区生产总值[2]（GDP）7469.85亿元，比上年增长7.7%。其中，第一产业增加值281.12亿元，增长4.6%；第二产业增加值2596.08亿元，增长5.5%；第三产业增加值4592.65亿元，增长9.2%。三次产业构成为3.8:34.7:61.5。按常住人口计算，全年人均生产总值78346元，比上年增长6.0%。

全年非公有制经济增加值3962.50亿元，占生产总值的比重为53.0%，比上年提高0.2个百分点。

全年居民消费价格比上年上涨2.0%，其中，食品烟酒价格上涨0.5%。商品零售价格上涨1.7%。工业生产者出厂价格上涨0.3%。工业生产者购进价格上涨4.7%。固定资产投资价格上涨5.4%。新建住宅销售价格上涨11.5%。

图1　2017年居民消费价格月度涨跌幅度（%）

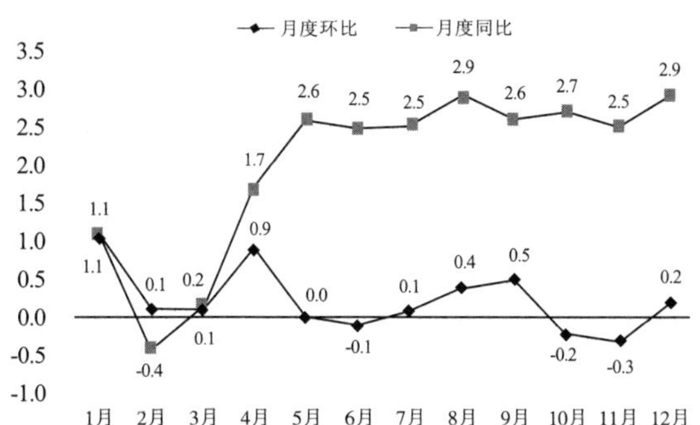

表1　2017年居民消费价格比上年涨跌幅度

指　标	涨跌幅度（%）
居民消费价格总指数	2.0
食品烟酒	0.5
衣着	0.7
居住	1.7
生活用品及服务	0.6
交通和通信	2.4
教育文化和娱乐	2.6
医疗保健	8.7
其他用品和服务	1.0

全年新增城镇就业14.09万人，城镇失业人员再就业6.16万人，农村劳动力转移就业78.89万人。年末城镇登记失业率为3.32%。引进产业发展与科技创新类人才14.59万人，培养实用型人才6.29万人。

全年新登记各类市场主体28.32万户，比上年增长99.7%；其中，新登记企业9.27万户，增长66.0%；新登记个体工商户18.92万户，增长1.2倍。

全年财政总收入1364.71亿元，比上年增长12.6%。全年地方财政一般公共预算收入654.50亿元，增长9.8%，其中税收收入448.99亿元，增长20.4%。全年地方财政一般公共预算支出1045.09亿元，比上年增长7.1%。

二、农业

全年粮食种植面积569.96万亩，比上年下降3.9%；蔬菜种植面积132.29万亩，增长5.2%；瓜果种植面积17.30万亩，增长2.9%；油料种植面积6.44万亩，下降14.8%；棉花种植面积0.25万亩，下降5.9%。

全年粮食产量187.87万吨，比上年下降4.3%，其中，夏粮98.58万吨，下降2.6%；秋粮89.29万吨，下降6.1%；蔬菜产量445.43万吨，增长5.0%；水果产量134.77万吨，增长3.9%。

表2　2017年主要农产品产量及其增长速度

产品名称	单位	产量	比上年增长（%）
粮食	万吨	187.87	-4.3
蔬菜	万吨	445.43	5.0
水果	万吨	134.77	3.9
肉类	万吨	18.31	3.5
#猪肉	万吨	13.09	2.6
奶类	万吨	55.84	-11.3
禽蛋	万吨	14.63	-10.5
猪年末存栏数	万头	96.91	-7.4
牛年末存栏数	万头	18.41	-2.6
羊年末存栏数	万只	31.02	-4.7
家禽年末存栏数	万只	1243.40	-7.5

三、工业和建筑业

全年全部工业增加值 1677.48亿元，比上年增长5.8%。规模以上工业增加值1361.77亿元，增长5.8%。在规模以上工业中，轻工业增加值270.89亿元，增长1.1%；重工业增加值1090.88亿元，增长7.0%。

图2　2017年规模以上工业增加值增长速度（%）

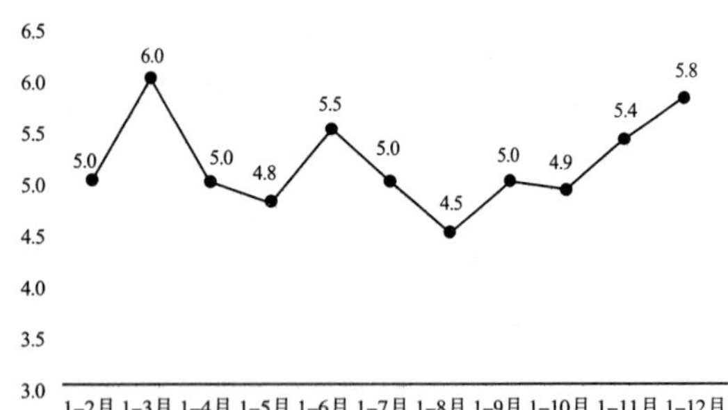

全年规模以上工业中，装备制造业[3]增加值增长14.8%，占规模以上工业增加值的比重为57.5%。其中，汽车制造业增长35.5%，铁路、船舶、航空航天和其他运输设备制造业增长30.8%，计算机、通信和其他电子设备制造业增长13.9%。六大高耗能行业[4]增加值下降10.2%，其中，非金属矿物制品业下降30.1%，有色金属冶炼和压延加工业下降19.5%，黑色金属冶炼和压延加工业下降70.3%，石油加工、炼焦和核燃料加工业下降8.4%，化学原料和化学制品制造业增长9.1%，电力、热力生产和供应业增长11.9%。

全年规模以上工业中，战略性新兴产业[5]实现总产值2226.45亿元，占规模以上工业比重为39.2%，同比增长14.1%，高于规模以上工业增速8.7个百分点。高技术制造业[6]实现总产值1410.37亿元，占规模以上工业比重为24.8%，同比增长14.9%，高于规模以上工业增速9.5个百分点，其中，电子及通信设备制造业实现工业总产值731.48亿元，占高技术制造业的比重为51.9%，同比增长15.4%，增速高于规模以上工业10.0个百分点，信息化学品制造业增长26.1%，航空、航天器及设备制造业增长22.1%，计算机及办公设备制造业增长20.9%。

工业新产品产量快速增长。单晶硅1629.53万千克，增长93.3%；新能源汽车8.15万辆，增长67.7%；光纤529.55万千米，增长61.4%；多晶硅639.86万千克，增长46.7%；锂离子电池2651.16万只，增长43.2%；智能手机3023.05万台，增长30.3%；集成电路圆片151.70万片，增长19.5%；光缆586.35万芯千米，增长16.8%。

表3　2017年主要工业产品产量及其增长速度

产品名称	单位	产量	比上年增长（%）
发电量	亿千瓦小时	176.74	-3.9
软饮料	万吨	191.11	-9.7
小麦粉	万吨	100.52	-26.3
机制纸	万吨	18.62	-8.0
配合饲料	万吨	17.25	56.1
乳制品	万吨	96.23	-1.8
中成药	万吨	0.68	4.2
钢材	万吨	54.91	-4.9
交流电动机	万千瓦	196.31	-38.3
变压器	万千伏安	14204.85	5.4
汽车	万辆	44.52	16.4
其中：载货汽车	万辆	18.92	63.0
轿车	万辆	18.14	-7.4
运动型多用途乘用车(SUV)	万辆	7.36	7.7
新能源汽车	万辆	8.15	67.7
单晶硅	万千克	1629.53	93.3
电力电缆	万千米	12.88	268.3
光纤	万千米	529.55	61.4
锂离子电池	万只	2651.16	43.2
智能手机	万台	3023.05	30.3
电子元件	亿只	4.44	-25.8
集成电路圆片	万片	151.70	19.5

规模以上工业企业主营业务收入5166.00亿元，增长7.3%。实现利润总额333.00亿元，增长9.1%。

全年全社会建筑业增加值938.30亿元，比上年增长5.3%。全市具有资质等级的总承包和专业承包建筑业企业实现建筑业总产值3304.54亿元，增长13.7%，其中，国有及国有控股企业2588.18亿元，增长13.1%。所有资质等级企业签订合同额9085.74亿元，增长18.0%。

图3　2013-2017年建筑业增加值及其增长速度

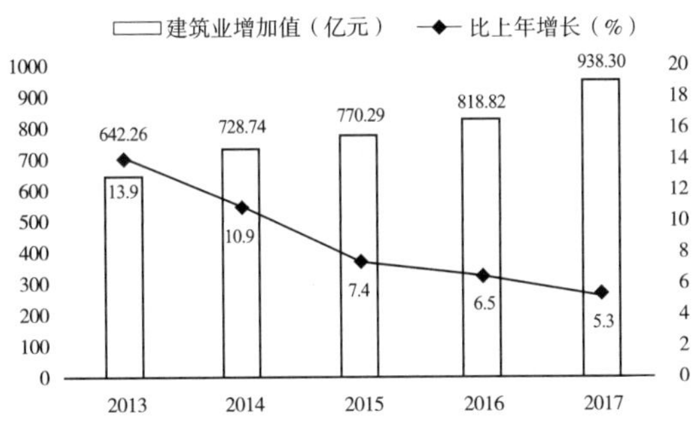

四、固定资产投资

全年全社会固定资产投资7556.47亿元，比上年增长12.9%。其中，固定资产投资（不含农户）7463.31亿元，增长13.0%。

图4　2017年固定资产投资（不含农户）增长速度（%）

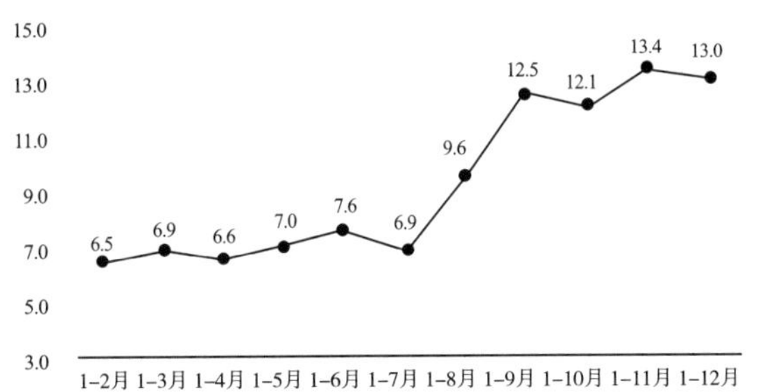

在固定资产投资（不含农户）中，第一产业投资123.20亿元，比上年增长2.3%；第二产业投资1086.93亿元，下降10.2%，其中，工业投资1072.06亿元，下降10.6%；第三产业投资6253.18亿元，增长18.6%。民间固定资产投资[7]3120.22亿元，比上年增长11.1%，占固定资产投资（不含农户）的比重为41.8%。全市PPP项目52个，PPP项目引资额达到1052.66亿元。

表4　2017年分行业固定资产投资（不含农户）及其增长速度

行业	投资额（亿元）	比上年增长（%）
农、林、牧、渔业	134.08	1.6
采矿业	7.04	906.6
制造业	853.37	-12.7
电力、热力、燃气及水的生产和供应业	211.64	-4.1
建筑业	20.55	15.0
批发和零售业	128.06	8.8
交通运输、仓储和邮政业	412.93	-3.2
住宿和餐饮业	51.60	36.5
信息传输、软件和信息技术服务业	131.48	2.2
金融业	8.36	3.5
房地产业	2837.71	5.2
租赁和商务服务业	133.47	18.6
科学研究和技术服务业	85.47	-17.2
水利、环境和公共设施管理业	1971.43	55.1
居民服务和其他服务业	20.86	126.5
教育	230.91	103.8
卫生和社会工作	80.76	4.7
文化、体育和娱乐业	109.75	39.8
公共管理和社会组织	33.83	-53.3

全年房地产开发投资[8]2333.34亿元，比上年增长15.0%。其中，住宅投资1566.37亿元，增长12.3%；办公楼投资221.21亿元，增长26.6%；商业营业用房投资319.73亿元，增长4.5%。房屋施工面积15843.92万平方米，增长5.4%；房屋竣工面积1634.63万平方米，增长4.0%。

表5　2017年房地产开发和销售主要指标及其增长速度

指　标	单位	绝对数	比上年增长（%）
房地产开发投资	亿元	2333.34	15.0
其中：住宅	亿元	1566.37	12.3
房屋施工面积	万平方米	15843.92	5.4
其中：住宅	万平方米	11134.28	4.6
房屋竣工面积	万平方米	1634.63	4.0
其中：住宅	万平方米	1281.70	1.3
商品房销售面积	万平方米	2509.78	20.8
其中：住宅	万平方米	2147.67	13.2

五、国内贸易

全年社会消费品零售总额4329.51亿元，比上年增长10.5%，扣除价格因素，实际增长8.7%。其中，限额以上企业（单位）消费品零售额2909.54亿元，增长9.6%。按经营地统计，城镇消费品零售额4177.70亿元，增长10.5%；乡村消费品零售额151.81亿元，增长9.5%。按消费形态统计，商品零售额3995.90亿元，增长10.6%；餐饮收入333.61亿元，增长9.6%。

图5　2017年社会消费品零售总额增长速度（%）

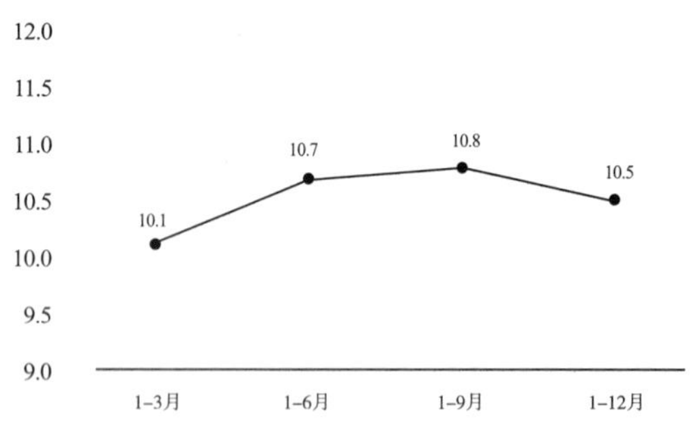

限额以上企业（单位）消费品零售额中，网上商品零售额[9] 240.30亿元，占限额以上消费品零售额的8.3%，较上年提高2.0个百分点；同比增长54.9%，高于限额以上消费品零售额45.3个百分点。

在限额以上企业（单位）商品零售额中，粮油、食品类零售额比上年增长20.6%，服装、鞋帽、针、纺织品类增长7.8%，化妆品类增长22.4%，金银珠宝类下降2.4%，日用品类增长17.2%，体育、娱乐用品类增长63.2%，电子出版物及音像制品类下降18.6%，家用电器和音像器材类增长24.9%，通讯器材类增长23.2%，家具类增长3.1%，石油及制品类增长10.4%，建筑及装潢材料类下降0.8%，汽车类增长7.3%。

六、对外经济

全年进出口总值2545.41亿元，比上年增长39.1%。其中，出口1552.38亿元，增长63.9%；进口993.03亿元，增长12.5%。

在进出口总值中，加工贸易进出口1712.78亿元，增长36.0%，占进出口总值的67.3%；一般贸易进出口533.57亿元，增长26.9%，占进出口总值的21.0%。

主要进口商品有，机电产品进口795.13亿元，增长14.5%；精炼铜进口22.91亿元，增长6.6%；矿砂进口54.80亿元，增长53.8%；医药品进口18.58亿元，增长15.3%。主要出口商品有，机电产品出口1401.80亿元，增长69.2%；单晶硅片出口27.93亿元，增长25.0%；农产品出口26.39亿元，增长22.9%；纺织服装出口14.92亿元，增长32.1%；矿产品出口19.33亿元，增长32.9%；有机化学品出口14.87亿元，增长27.0%。

全年吸收外商直接投资项目143个，批准合同外资44.50亿美元，比上年增长3.4倍；实际利用外商直接投资53.07亿美元，增长17.8%。

七、交通、邮电和旅游

全年货物运输总量2.55亿吨，比上年增长6.7%；货物运输周转量597.91亿吨公里，增长8.3%。旅客运输总量2.43亿人次，增长2.6%；旅客运输周转量326.72亿人公里，增长10.2%。国际航线条数57条，境外航班通航架次16231架。年末全市机动车保有量288.56万辆，比上年末增长11.5%。私人汽车保有量246.66万辆，增长11.0%。

表6　2017年各种运输方式完成货物运输量及其增长速度

指标	单位	绝对数	比上年增长（%）
货物运输总量	万吨	25496.62	6.7
公路	万吨	24477.00	6.4
铁路	万吨	993.63	16.4
民航（吞吐量）	万吨	25.99	11.2
货物运输周转量	亿吨公里	597.91	8.3
公路	亿吨公里	350.97	8.3
铁路	亿吨公里	245.92	8.3
民航	亿吨公里	1.02	1.9

表7　2017年各种运输方式完成旅客运输量及其增长速度

指　标	单位	绝对数	比上年增长（%）
旅客运输总量	万人次	24286.53	2.6
公路	万人次	15601.00	-1.1
铁路	万人次	4499.79	7.2
民航（吞吐量）	万人次	4185.74	13.1
旅客运输周转量	亿人公里	326.72	10.2
公路	亿人公里	90.03	-0.9
铁路	亿人公里	68.10	0.7
民航	亿人公里	168.59	22.2

全年邮政业务总收入54.46亿元,比上年增长23.8%。电信业务总收入147.55亿元，增长3.6%。年末全市固定电话用户269.21万户。移动电话用户1854.21万户。固定互联网宽带接入用户[10]348.30万

户。

全年接待国内外游客18093.14万人次，比上年增长20.5%；旅游业总收入1633.30亿元，增长34.6%。

八、金融

年末全市金融机构本外币存款余额20378.11亿元，比上年末增长4.6%；其中人民币存款余额20047.62亿元，增长5.1%，其中，住户存款余额7497.30亿元，增长6.6%。金融机构本外币贷款余额17155.11亿元，增长10.4%；其中人民币贷款余额16954.81亿元，增长10.9%。

全年证券市场各类证券交易总额46812.95亿元，比上年增长9.0%。年末全市拥有上市股份公司33家，上市总股本517.32亿股，总市值5154.10亿元。

年末全市共有保险公司59家，其中，财产险28家，人寿险31家。保险专业中介机构123家。全年保费收入420.73亿元，比上年增长21.7%，其中，财产险保费收入103.71亿元，增长11.1%；人身险保费收入317.02亿元，增长25.5%。全年支付各类赔款给付118.71亿元，比上年增长2.4%，其中，财产险业务48.94亿元，增长15.8%；人身险业务69.77亿元，下降5.3%。

九、教育、科技、文化和体育

全市普通高校63所，在校学生72.68万人，毕业生20.50万人，另有研究生培养单位43个，在学研究生10.41万人，毕业生2.55万人；普通中学448所，在校学生41.70万人，毕业生8.38万人；小学1125所，在校学生66.68万人，毕业生9.06万人。小学、初中学龄人口入学率分别为99.99%和99.98%。

全年实施市级科技计划项目243项。国家级高新技术企业数1839家，比上年增加333家。全年技术市场合同交易额809亿元。全年专利申请量81110件，其中，发明专利申请量40439件；专利授权量25042件，其中发明专利授权量7902件。全市众创空间422个，众创空间面积1389.50万平方米。

全市博物馆126座。各级别文物保护单位392处。公共图书馆13个，群众艺术馆2个，文化馆14个，文化站188个。地市广播电视台2座，县级广播电视台6座。全年举办各类会展活动199个，其中举办国际性会展活动46个；全年参展参会人数238万人次。

全年举办各类群众体育展示表演和竞赛活动共计260项次，体育社团举办和承办体育赛事306项次，其中，国际性和全国性赛事48项次。新建和更新社区全民健身路径150个。全市新增社会体育指导员1315名。已有晨晚练点1600个，健身气功站点310个，在册练功人数10517人。2017年，我市培养输送运动员参加国际、国内各项比赛获得金牌33枚、银牌27枚、铜牌1枚。

十、卫生和社会服务

年末全市共有各类卫生机构5879个。其中，医院313个，社区卫生服务中心（站）214个，卫生院100个。各类卫生技术人员9.11万人，其中，执业（含助理）医师3.03万人。各类卫生机构床位6.22万张。

全市提供住宿的法定社会服务机构152个，床位2.9万张，年末收养人数1.9万人。年末城市低保对象1.9万户、3.1万人，发放低保金2.6亿元；农村低保对象2.6万户、7.4万人，发放低保金3.0亿元。6075人享受农村特困人员救助供养，发放供养金4597万元。全年民政部门直接医疗救助3.2万人次。

十一、人口、人民生活和社会保障

年末全市户籍总人口905.68万人，其中西咸新区咸阳片区60.59万人。西安原口径户籍人口845.09万人，比上年净增加20.15万人，增长2.4%；其中，男性人口424.98万人，占50.3%，女性人口420.11万人，占49.7%，性别比为101.16（以女性为100，男性对女性的比例）。

全年全市居民人均可支配收入32597元，比上年增长8.5%。其中，城镇常住居民人均可支配收入38536元，比上年增长8.2%；农村常住居民人均可支配收入16522元，比上年增长8.8%。

年末全市城镇基本医疗保险参保人数467.33万人；城镇企业职工养老保险参保人数360.45万人；失业保险参保人数154.96万人；工伤保险参保人数172.04万人；职工生育保险参保人数151.16万人。年末农村新型合作医疗参保人数393.65万人，实际参合率99.72%。

十二、城市建设、环境和安全生产

全年完成市政公用设施投资677.31亿元，增长54.9%。新建人行天桥及地下通道4座，新建改造绿地广场62个。年末建成区面积595.26平方公里，市区人均公园绿地面积12.31平方米，建成区绿化覆盖率43.44%。年末城市污水处理厂日处理能力277.6万吨，比上年末增长6.3%。

全年城市环境空气质量达到二级以上的天数180天。二氧化硫年平均浓度为19微克/立方米，二氧化氮年平均浓度为59微克/立方米。颗粒物（PM10）年平均浓度为130微克/立方米，颗粒物（PM2.5）年平均浓度为73微克/立方米。全市集中式饮用水源地的水质达标率为98.1%。区域环境噪声等效声级均值为56.5分贝，道路交通噪声等效声级均值为70.6分贝。

全年发生各类生产安全事故492起，死亡177人；其中，生产经营性道路交通事故457起，死亡136人；工矿商贸事故33起，死亡41人。

注释：

[1]本公报中2017年数据为初步统计数，部分数据因四舍五入的原因，存在着分项与合计不等的情况。

[2]2017年西安生产总值统计口径发生变化，一是实施研发支出核算方法改革，将研发支出资本化数据计入地区生产总值；二是西咸新区数据纳入西安生产总值核算范围。生产总值、各产业增加值和人均生产总值绝对数按现价计算，增长速度按不变价格计算。

[3]装备制造业包括金属制品业，通用设备制造业，专用设备制造业，汽车制造业，铁路、船舶、航空航天和其他运输设备制造业，电气机械和器材制造业，计算机、通信和其他电子设备制造业，仪器仪表制造业。

[4]六大高耗能行业包括石油加工、炼焦和核燃料加工业，化学原料和化学制品制造业，非金属矿物制品业，黑色金属冶炼和压延加工业，有色金属冶炼和压延加工业，电力、热力生产和供应业。

[5]工业战略性新兴产业包括节能环保产业，新一代信息技术产业，生物产业，高端装备制造产业，新能源产业，新材料产业，新能源汽车产业等七大产业中的工业相关行业。

[6]高技术制造业包括医药制造业，航空、航天器及设备制造业，电子及通信设备制造业，计算机及办公设备制造业，医疗仪器设备及仪器仪表制造业，信息化学品制造业。

[7]民间固定资产投资是指具有集体、私营、个人性质的内资企事业单位以及由其控股（包括绝对控股和相对控股）的企业单位建造或购置固定资产的投资。

[8]房地产业投资除房地产开发投资外，还包括建设单位自建房屋以及物业管理、中介服务和其他房地产投资。

[9]网上商品零售额是指通过公共网络交易平台（主要从事实物商品交易的网上平台，包括自建网站和第三方平台）实现的商品零售额。

[10]固定互联网宽带接入用户是指报告期末在电信企业登记注册，通过xDSL、FTTx+LAN、FTTH/0以及其他宽带接入方式和普通专线接入公众互联网的用户。

数据口径：本公报中2017年物价、居民人均可支配收入、进出口、利用外资、交通运输、邮政电信、金融证券和保险、会展、体育、卫生、城市建设、环境监测等指标数据为西安原口径数据，就业与引进人才、市场主体、财政、PPP项目、旅游、教育、博物馆、文化、社会服务、低保、农村特困人员救助供养、户籍人口、安全生产、生产总值、农业、工业、建筑业、固定资产投资、国内贸易等指标数据为包含西咸新区数据。科技数据中，2017年科技计划项目、高新技术企业、技术市场合同交易额和专利数据为西安原口径数据，众创空间为包含西咸新区数据。社会保障数据中，2017年农村新型合作医疗和城镇企业职工养老保险参保人数为西安原口径数据，城镇基本医疗保险、失业保险、工伤保险和职工生育保险参保人数为包含西咸新区数据。

资料来源：本公报中物价、居民人均可支配收入数据来自国家统计局西安调查队；城镇新增就业、登记失业率、引进人才、社会保障数据来自西安市人力资源和社会保障局；市场主体数据来自市工商局；财政数据来自市财政局；PPP项目数据来自市发改委；进出口数据来自西安海关；利用外资数据来自市投资委；旅游数据来自市旅发委；铁路运输数据来自西安铁路局；公路运输数据来自市交通局；民航运输数据来自西安咸阳国际机场；机动车数据来自市车管所；邮政业务数据来自市邮政管理局；电信业务数据来自中国移动西安分公司、中国电信西安分公司、中国联通西安分公司；货币金融数据来自中国人民银行西安分行营业管理部；证券数据、保险业数据来自市金融办；教育数据来自市教育局；科技数据来自市科技局；博物馆数据来自市文物局；艺术表演团体、公共图书馆、文化馆、广播、电视数据来自市文化广电新闻出版局；会展数据来自市会展办；体育数据来自市体育局；卫生、新农合数据来自市卫计委；社会服务、低保、农村特困人员救助供养数据来自市民政局；户籍人口数据来自市公安局；城市建设数据来自市城乡建设委员会；环境监测数据来自市环境保护局；安全生产数据来自市安全生产监督管理局；其他数据均来自市统计局。

Statistical Communique of Xi'an City On 2017 National Economic and Social Development[1]

Xi'an Municipal Bureau of Statistics and NBS Survey Office in Xi'an

Mar. 12th, 2018

In 2017, the whole city earnestly studied and implemented the spirit of the 19th Party Congress, guided by Xi Jinping's new era of socialism with chinese characteristics, and closely focused on the "five new strategies" and the goal of "gathering 369 and revitalizing the great Xi'an." Adhere to the general tone of steady progress, strive to promote steady growth, promote reform, adjust structure, protect people's livelihood, prevent risks, achieve stable and healthy economic development and social harmony and stability, and open a new pattern of construction in Xi'an.

I. General Outlook

Based on the preliminary calculation, the gross domestic product[2] (GDP) preliminarily estimated was 746.985 billion yuan, up by 7.7% against the previous year. Analyzed by different industries, the value added of the primary industry was 28.112 billion yuan, up by 4.6%; the value added of the secondary industry was 259.608 billion yuan, a rise of 5.5%; and the value added of the tertiary industry was 459.265 billion yuan, up by 9.2%. The composition of the three industries is 3.8:34.7:61.5. According to the resident population calculation, the per capita GDP of the year was 78.346 thousand yuan, up by 6.0% against the previous year.

The value added of non-public sectors of the economy is 396.250 billion yuan, accounted for the proportion of GDP is 53.0%, an increase of 0.2percentage points over the previous year.

The general level of consumer prices in Xi'an was up by 2.0% against the previous year. The prices of food, tobacco and liquor went up by 0.5%. The retail prices of commodities went up by 1.7%. The producer prices of manufactured goods went up by 0.3%. The purchasing prices of manufactured goods went up by 4.7%. The fixed asset investment price went up 5.4% and the price of newly founded house increased by 11.5%.

Table 1 The Rate of Increase and Decrease of CPI in 2017 (%)

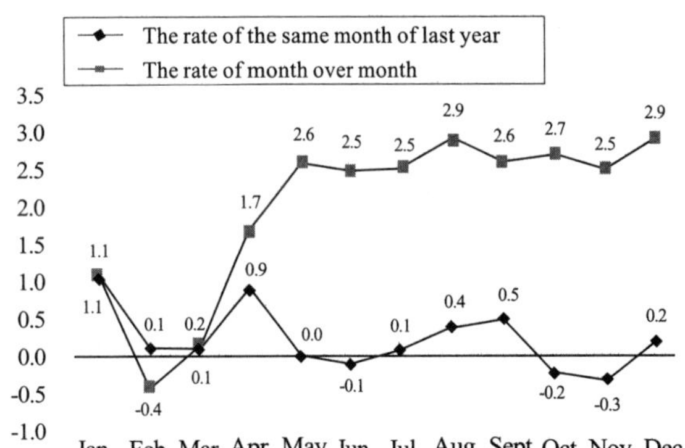

Sheet 1 Up and Fall Extent of Residents Consumer Price Indices against Previous Year (2017)

Item	2017(%)
Consumer Price Index	2.0
Food, Tobacco and Liquor	0.5
Clothing	0.7
Residence	1.7
Household Goods and Services	0.6
Transportation and Communication	2.4
Education, Culture and Entertainment	2.6
Health Care	8.7
Other Supplies and Services	1.0

In 2017, the number of newly increased employees in urban areas in Xi'an was 140.9 thousand, the number of reemployment of laid-off workers was 61.6 thousand, the number of transfer employment rural labors was 788.9 thousand, the urban unemployment rate through unemployment registration was 3.32% at the end of 2017. Introduced 145.9 thousand people in industrial development and scientific and technological innovation, trained practical talents 62.9 thousand.

In total ,The city registered new market entities of various types was 283.2 thousand, an increase of 99.7% compared with the previous year,the number of newly registered enterprises reached 92.7 thousand, an increase of 66.0%. The number of newly registered individual industrial and commercial households increased by 1.2 times to 189.2 thousand.

The financial revenue totaled 136.471 billion yuan, an increase of 12.6% compared with the previous year. In total, the General Budget Revenue of Regional Finance reached 65.450 billion yuan, up by 9.8%, tax revenue was 44.899 billion yuan, an increase of 20.4% compared with the previous year. the General Budget Expenditure of Regional Finance totaled 104.509 billion yuan, up by 7.1%.

II. Agriculture

In 2017, the sown area of grain was 5699.6 thousand mu, a decrease of 3.9% compared with the previous year; the sown area of vegetables was 1322.9 thousand mu, an increase of 5.2%; the planting area of melon and fruit was 173.0 thousand mu, an increase of 2.9%; the sown area of oil-bearing crops was 64.4 thousand mu, a decrease of 14.8%; the sown area of cotton was 2.5 thousand mu, a decrease of 5.9%.

The total output of grain in 2017 was 1.8787 million tons, a decrease of 4.3%, the output of summer crops was 0.9858 million tons, went down by 2.6% and that of the autumn grain was 0.8929 million tons, a decrease of 6.1%. Vegetable production was 4.4543 million tons, an increase of 5.0%. Fruit production was 1.3477 million tons, an increase of 3.9%.

Sheet 2 Mail Product of Agriculture Production in 2017

Name of Product	Units	Output	Increase over the last year (%)
Grain	10,000 tons	187.87	-4.3
Vegetable	10,000 tons	445.43	5.0
Fruit	10,000 tons	134.77	3.9
Meat	10,000 tons	18.31	3.5
#Pork	10,000 tons	13.09	2.6
Milk	10,000 tons	55.84	-11.3
Poultry eggs	10,000 tons	14.63	-10.5
Year-end Pig on hand	10,000 head	96.91	-7.4
Year-end Ox on hand	10,000 head	18.41	-2.6
Year-end Sheep on hand	10,000 head	31.02	-4.7
Year-end Fowl on hand	10,000 head	1243.40	-7.5

III. Industry and Construction

In 2017, the value added by the industrial sectors was 167.748 billion yuan, up by 5.8% over the previous year. In total, the value added of industrial enterprises above the designated size was 136.177 billion yuan, up by 5.8%, the value added of the light industry was 27.089 billion yuan, up by 1.1% and that of the heavy industry was 109.088 billion yuan, up by 7.0%.

Table 2 Growth of Above-Scale Industrial added Value in 2017 (%)

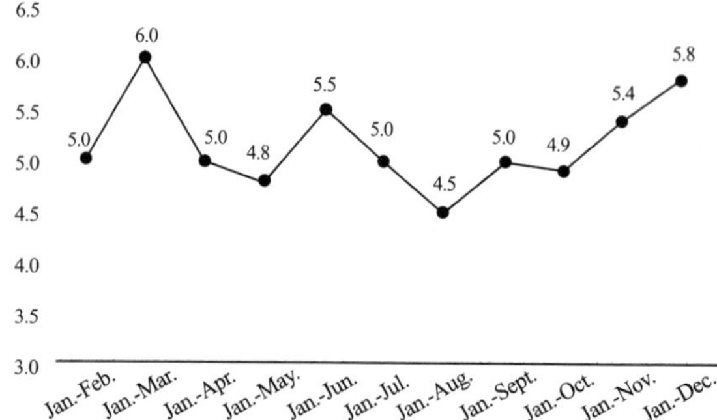

In 2017, of the industrial enterprises above designated size, the growth of value added of equipment manufacturing industry[3] was up by 14.8%, accounted for 57.5% of the added value of industrial enterprises above designated size. Manufacture of car increased by 35.5%, manufacturing of railways, ships, aerospace and other transportation equipment increased by 30.8%. The growth of value added for manufacture of computer, communication and other electrical devices were up by 13.9% over the previous year. The growth of the value added of the major six high energy consuming industries[4] was down by 10.2%. Manufacture of raw chemical materials and chemical products down by 30.1%, smelting and pressing of non-ferrous metals down by 19.5%, smelting and pressing of ferrous metals down by 70.3% and 8.4% decrease for processing of petroleum, coking, processing of nuclear fuel, manufacture of raw chemical materials and chemical products up by 9.1%, production and supply of electric power and heat power up by 11.9%.

In 2017, strategic emerging industries[5] achieved a total output value of 222.645 billion yuan, accounted for 39.2% of the value for industrial enterprises above designated size, soared by nearly 14.1% compared with last year, the growth rate was 8.7percentage points higher than that of industries above designated size. The gross output value of high technology industry industrial manufacturing enterprises above designated size[6] was 141.037 billion yuan, accounted for 24.8% of the value for industrial enterprises above designated size, soared by nearly 14.9% compared with last year, the growth rate was 9.5percentage points higher than that of industries above designated size. The gross output value of the electronic and communication equipment manufacturing was 73.148 billion yuan, accounted for 51.9% of the value for high technology industry, soared by 15.4% compared with last year.

The growth rate was 10.0percentage points higher than that of industries above designated size. The information chemicals manufacturing industry up by 26.1%, the aviation, spacecraft and equipment manufacturing industry up by 22.1%, and the computer and office equipment manufacturing industry up by 20.9%.

In 2017, the output of new industrial products increased rapidly. Single crystal silicon was 16.2953 million kilograms, an increase of 93.3%; the number of the new energy vehicle was 81.5 thousand, up by 67.7% over the previous year; the length of the optical fiber was 5.2955 million kilometers, up by 61.4% over the previous year; polysilicon was 639.86 million kilograms, an increase of 46.7%; the number of the lithium ion battery was 26.5116 million, up by 43.2% over the previous year; the number of smart phone was 30.2305 million, an increase of 30.3%; the number of the integrated circuit wafer sums up to 1.5170 million, an increase of 19.5%; the length of the optical cable was 5.8635 billion core kilometers, up by 16.8% over the previous year.

Sheet 3 Output of Major Industrial Products above Designated Size in Xi'an(2017)

Name of Product	Units	Output	Increase over the last year (%)
Electricity	100 million kilo watt-hour	176.74	-3.9
Soft Drink	10,000 tons	191.11	-9.7
Wheat Meal	10,000 tons	100.52	-26.3
Machine-made Paper	10,000 tons	18.62	-8.0
Mixed Feed	10,000 tons	17.25	56.1
Dairy	10,000 tons	96.23	-1.8
Chinese Patent Medicine	10,000 tons	0.68	4.2
Steel	10,000 tons	54.91	-4.9
AC Motors	10,000 kilowatt	196.31	-38.3
Transformer	10,000 kilovolt amperes	14204.85	5.4
Motor Vehicle	10,000 units	44.52	16.4
Truck	10,000 units	18.92	63.0
Car	10,000 units	18.14	-7.4
Sports Utility Vehicle	10,000 units	7.36	7.7
New Energy Vehicle	10,000 units	8.15	67.7
Mono-crystalline Silicon	10,000 kg	1629.53	93.3
Electric Cable	10,000 km	12.88	268.3
Optical Fiber	10,000 km	529.55	61.4
Lithium Battery	10,000 units	2651.16	43.2
Smart Phone	10,000 units	3023.05	30.3
Electronic Component	100 million units	4.44	-25.8
Integrated Circuit Chip	10,000 chips	151.70	19.5

The main business income of the industrial enterprises above designated size is 516.600 billion yuan, up by 7.3% over the previous year. The profit was 33.300 billion yuan, up by 9.1%.

In 2017, the added value of construction sector was 93.830 billion yuan, increased by 5.3% over the previous year. The total output value created of qualified contractors and professional building contractor companies was 330.454 billion yuan, increased by 13.7%. The output of state-owned and state holding corporations was 258.818 billion yuan, increased by 13.1%. Contracts signed by all qualified enterprises amounted to 908.574 billion yuan, increased by 18.0%.

Table 3 The Added Value of Construction and Growth Rate Between Year 2013–2017

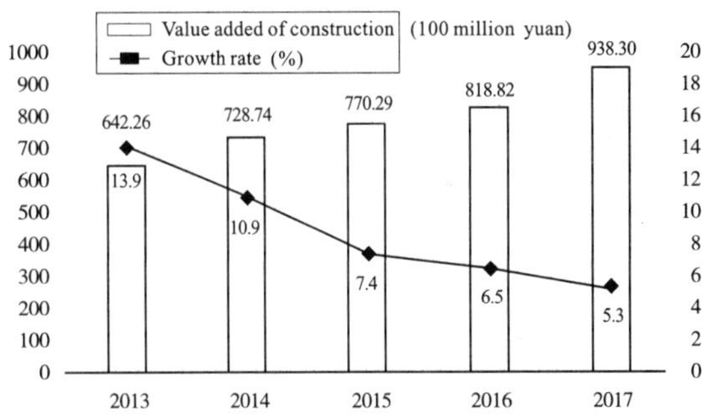

IV. Investment in Fixed Assets

The completed investment in fixed assets of the city in 2017 was 755.647 billion yuan, up by 12.9% over the previous year. Investment in fixed assets (excluding farmers) was 746.331 billion yuan, up by 13.0%.

Table 4 Growth Rate of Investment in Fixed Assets(excluding farmers) in 2017 (%)

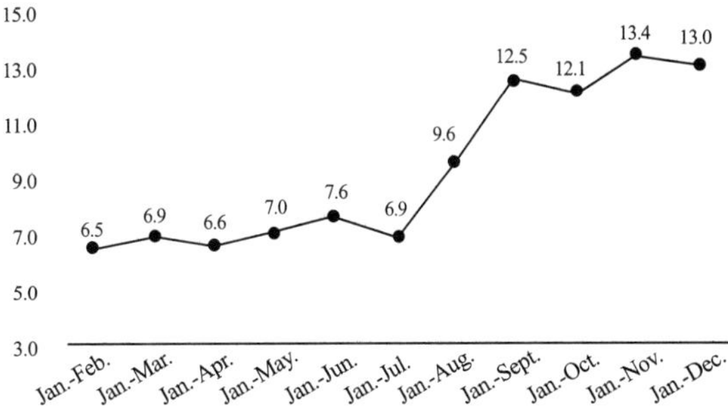

In whole investment(excluding farmers), the investment in the primary industry was 12.320 billion yuan, up by 2.3% against the previous year. In the secondary industry, it was 108.693 billion yuan, down by 10.2% in total, industrial investment was 107.206 billion yuan, down by 10.6%. In the tertiary industry, it was 625.318 billion yuan, up by 18.6%. Private investment in fixed assets[7] was 312.022 billion yuan, up by 11.1%, accounted for 41.8% of investment in fixed assets. There are 52 PPP projects in the city, and the investment amount of PPP projects reached 105.266 billion yuan.

Sheet 4 The Investment in Fixed Assets and Growth Rate in Main Industries in 2017

Industries	Investment (100 million Yuan)	Growth rate (%)
Agriculture, Forestry, Animal husbandry and fishery	134.08	1.6
Mining Industry	7.04	906.6
Manufacturing	853.37	-12.7
Electricity, Heat, Gas and Water Production and Supply Industry	211.64	-4.1
Construction Industry	20.55	15.0
Wholesale and Retail Trade	128.06	8.8
Transportation, Storage and Postal Services	412.93	-3.2
Hotels and Catering Services	51.60	36.5
Information Transmission, Computer Services and Software Industry	131.48	2.2
Finance	8.36	3.5
Real Estate Industry	2837.71	5.2
Leasing and Business Services	133.47	18.6
Scientific Research and Technical Service	85.47	-17.2
Water Conservancy, Environment and Public Facilities Administration Industry	1971.43	55.1
Residential Services and Other Services	20.86	126.5
Education	230.91	103.8
Sanitations and Social Work	80.76	4.7
Culture, Sports and Entertainment	109.75	39.8
Public Administration and Social Organizations	33.83	-53.3

In 2017, the investment in real estate development[8] was 233.334 billion yuan, up by 15.0%. Housing investment was 156.637 billion yuan, up by 12.3%. Office building investment was 22.121 billion yuan, up by 26.6%. Commercial and business building investment was 31.973 billion yuan, up by 4.5%. Housing construction area was 158.4392 million square meters, up by 5.4%. Floor space completed was 16.3463 million square meters, up by 4.0%.

Sheet 5 Mail Indicators of Real Estate Development and Sales in 2017

Item	Units	Absolute Number	Increase over the last year(%)
Investment in Real Estate Development	100 million yuan	2333.34	15.0
#Residential Building	100 million yuan	1566.37	12.3
Building construction area	10,000 sq.m	15843.92	5.4
# Residential Building	10,000 sq.m	11134.28	4.6
Floor Space of Buildings Completed	10,000 sq.m	1634.63	4.0
# Residential Building	10,000 sq.m	1281.70	1.3
Commercial housing sales area	10,000 sq.m	2509.78	20.8
# Residential Building	10,000 sq.m	2147.67	13.2

V. Domestic Trade

In 2017, the total retail sales of consumer goods reached 432.951 billion yuan, a growth of 10.5% over the previous year or a real growth of 8.7% after deducting price factors. The total retail sales by wholesale and retail enterprises above designated size was 290.954 billion yuan, up by 9.6%. Statistics on different areas showed that the retail sales of consumer goods in urban areas stood at 417.770 billion yuan, up by 10.5%, and that in rural areas reached 15.181 billion yuan, up by 9.5%. Grouped by consumption patterns, the income of retail sales of commodities was 399.590 billion yuan, up by 10.6%; that of catering industry was 33.361 billion yuan, up by 9.6%.

Table 5 The Total Retail Sales of Social Consumer Goods Growth Rate in 2017(%)

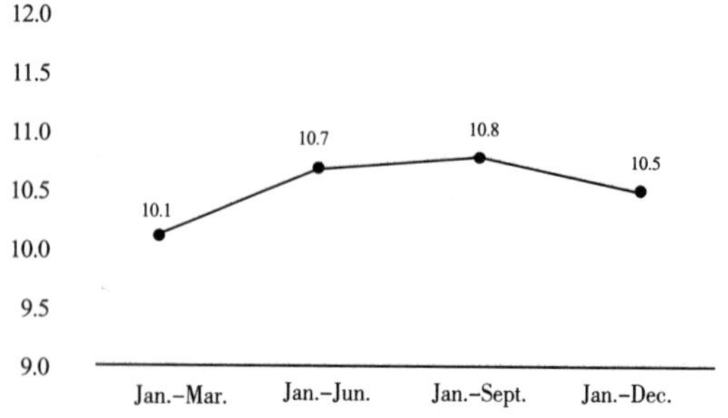

The online sales by wholesale and retail enterprises[9] above designated size was 24.030 billion yuan, accounted for 8.3% of retail sales of consumer goods above designated size, 2.0percentage points higher than the previous year, with year-on-year growth of 54.9%, 45.3percentage points higher than the retail sales of consumer goods above designated size.

Of the total retail sales by wholesale and retail enterprises above designated size, the sales of cereals, oils and food was up by 20.6%; clothing, shoes, hats and needle textiles up by 7.8%; cosmetics up by 22.4%; gold, silver and jewelry down by 2.4%; daily necessities up by 17.2%; sports-recreation up by 63.2%; electronic appliances and audio-video productions down by 18.6%, household appliances and audio-video equipment up by 24.9%; telecommunication equipment up by 23.2%; furniture increased by 3.1%; oil and oil products up by 10.4%; building decoration materials down by 0.8% and motor vehicles up by 7.3%.

VI. Foreign Economic Relations

In 2017, the total value of imports and exports reached 254.541 billion yuan, up by 39.1% over the previous year. The value of exports was 155.238 billion yuan, up by 63.9% and that of imports was 99.303 billion yuan, up by 12.5% respectively.

In total imports and exports, the value of processing trade was 171.278 billion yuan, up by 36.0%, accounted for 67.3% of import and export whole value of Xi'an region. The value of imports and exports of general trade was 53.357 billion yuan, increased by 26.9%, accounted for 21.0% of total import and export value of Xi'an region.

Among the main import commodities, the value of imports of electromechanical products was 79.513 billion yuan, up by 14.5%; the value of imports of refined copper was 2.291 billion yuan, up by 6.6%; the value of imports of ore sand was 5.480 billion yuan, up by 53.8%; the value of imports of medical products was 1.858 billion yuan, up by 15.3%. Among the main export commodities, the value of exports of electromechanical products was 140.180 billion yuan, up by 69.2%; the value of exports of monocrystalline silicon was 2.793 billion yuan, an increase of 25.0%; the value of exports of agricultural product was 2.639 billion yuan, an increase of 22.9%; textile and clothing exports totaled 1.492 billion yuan, up 32.1%; the value of exports of mineral products was 1.933 billion yuan, up by 32.9%; the organic chemicals was 1.487 billion yuan, up by 27.0%.

In 2017, there were 143 foreign direct investment projects approved and 4.450 billion US dollars were approved for contractual foreign investment, an increase of 3.4 times over the previous year; actual utilized foreign direct investment was 5.307 billion US dollars, up by 17.8%.

VII. Transportation, Post, Telecommunications and Tourism

In 2017, the total freight traffic reached 255 million ton, up by 6.7% over the previous year. The total goods transportation turnover reached 59.791 billion ton-kilometers, up by 8.3% over the previous year. The total passenger transport reached 243 million person-times, up by 2.6% over the previous year. The passenger transport turnover reached 32.672 billion people-kilometers person-times, up by 10.2% over the previous year. There are 57 international flights and 16,231 overseas flights. The total number of motor vehicles for civilian use reached 2885.6 thousand by the end of 2017, up by 11.5%, private-owned vehicles numbered 2466.6 thousand, up by 11.0%.

Sheet 6 The Total Freight Traffic and Growth Rate created by Kinds of Transport Mode in 2017

Index	Unit	Amount	Growth rate (%)
Total Freight Traffic	10,000 tons	25496.62	6.7
Highway	10,000 tons	24477.00	6.4
Railway	10,000 tons	993.63	16.4
Airway	10,000 tons	25.99	11.2
Goods Transportation Turnover	100 million ton-kilometers	597.91	8.3
Highway	100 million ton-kilometers	350.97	8.3
Railway	100 million ton-kilometers	245.92	8.3
Airway	100 million ton-kilometers	1.02	1.9

Sheet 7 The Total Passenger Traffic and Growth Rate created by Kinds of Transport Mode in 2017

Index	Unit	Amount	Growth rate (%)
Total Passenger	100 million people	24286.53	2.6
Highway	100 million people	15601.00	-1.1
Railway	100 million people	4499.79	7.2
Airway	100 million people	4185.74	13.1
Passenger Transport Turnover	100 million people -kilometers	326.72	10.2
Highway	100 million people -kilometers	90.03	-0.9
Railway	100 million people -kilometers	68.10	0.7
Airway	100 million people -kilometers	168.59	22.2

The revenue of post services totaled 5.446 billion yuan, an increase of 23.8% over the previous year. That of telecommunication services was 14.755 billion yuan, up by

3.6%. At the end of 2017, there were 2.6921 million fixed telephone users and 18.5421 million mobile phone users. The number of fixed internet broadband access users[10] was 3.4830 million.

The annual domestic and foreign tourists count was 180.9314 million person-times, up by 20.5%. The revenue from tourism totaled 163.330 billion yuan, up by 34.6%.

VIII. Finance

Savings deposit in RMB and foreign currencies in all items of financial institutions totaled 2037.811 billion yuan at the end of 2017, an increase of 4.6% compared with the end of the previous year. The savings deposit in RMB stood at 2004.762 billion yuan, an increase of 5.1%. The household deposit was 749.730 billion yuan, up by 6.6%. Loans in all items of financial institutions in RMB and foreign currencies reached 1715.511 billion yuan, an increase of 10.4% as compared with the end of the previous year. The loans in RMB stood at 1695.481 billion yuan, an increase of 10.9%.

The trading volume of stock exchange market was 4681.295 billion yuan in 2017, an increase of 9.0% compared with the previous year. There were 33 listed companies in Xi'an at the end of 2017 of which the total capital stock was 51.732 billion shares, and the total market value was 515.410 billion yuan.

By the end of 2017, there were 59 insurance institutions. The number of property insurance was 28 and that of life insurance was 31 respectively. There were 123 intermediary organs of insurance. The received by the insurance companies totaled 42.073 billion yuan in 2017, up by 21.7%. The revenue from property insurance was 10.371 billion yuan, up by 11.1% and that from life insurance was 31.702 billion yuan, up by 25.5% respectively. In total, insurance companies paid an indemnity worth of 11.871 billion yuan, up by 2.4% over the previous year. The property insurance was 4.894 billion yuan, up by 15.8% and the personal insurance business was 6.977 billion yuan, down by 5.3%.

IX. Education, Science & Technology, Culture and Sports

There were 63 general universities and colleges, with 726.8 thousand students in school, including 205.0 thousand graduates; there were 43 post-graduate training units, with 104.1 thousand students in school and 25.5 thousand graduates. There were 448 general middle schools and high schools, with 417.0 thousand students in school and 83.8 thousand graduates; there were 1125 primary schools, with 666.8 thousand students in school and 90.6 thousand graduates. The enrollment rates for school-age population of primary school and junior high school were 99.99% and 99.98% respectively.

243 science and technology projects were carried out in 2017. The number of state-level high-tech enterprises was 1839, an increase of 333 over the previous year. The turnover in technology market reached 80.9 billion yuan, and the number of annual patent applications was 81,110. Among them, the number of invention patent applications was 40,439; the number of patents granted was 25,042. 7,902 were invention patents. There are 422 space creations in the city, and the space area of the creation is 13.895 million square meters.

By the end of 2017, there were 126 museums, 392 cultural relics protection units at all levels, 13 public libraries, 2 mass art museums, 14 cultural centers, 188 culture stations. There were 2 city radio and television stations and 6 county radio and television stations. There were 199 various exhibitions held throughout the year, including 46 international exhibitions; the number of participants in the year was 2.38 million.

260 mass sports performances and competition activities were organized in 2017, and 306 sports competition were organized and hosted by sports associations, including 48 international and national sports competitions. In 2017, there were 150 public national fitness paths of community built. The number of social sports instructors newly increased 1,315. There were 1600 sites for morning and evening exercise and 310 sites for fitness Qigong, with 10,517 people taking part in fitness Qigong. In 2017, the delegation of Xi'an won 33 gold medals, 27 silver medals and 1 bronze medal in the National and international Games.

X. Health and Social Service

At the end of 2017, there were 5,879 health institutions in Xi'an, including 313 general hospitals, 214 community health centers, and 100 health centers. There were all 91.1 thousand health care workers, including 30.3 thousand practicing (assistant) doctors. General health centers in Xi'an possessed 62.2 thousand beds.

There were 152 social welfare adoption class units, with a total of 29 thousand beds, and 19 thousand people adopted at the end of 2017. There were 19 thousand of urban low-income households, with 31 thousand people, and 260 million yuan were distributed to them. There were 26 thousand of village low-income households, with 74 thousand people, and 300 million yuan were distributed to them. 6075 people were in the rural five guarantees and 45.97 million yuan were distributed. 32 thousand people gained medical relief directly from civil affairs departments in 2017.

XI. Population, Living Conditions and Social Security

At the end of the year, the total registered population of the city was 9.0568 million people, 605.9 thousand were in Xian Yang District of Xi'an New District. The number of registered population in Xi'an was 8.4509 million, a net increase of 201.5 thousand people over the previous year, an increase of 2.4%. Among them, the male population was 4.2498 million, accounting for 50.3%, the female population was 4.2011 million, accounting for 49.7%, and the sex ratio was 101.16 (take female as 100, male to female ratio).

In 2017, the annual per capita disposable income of all the city residents in Xi'an was 32,597 yuan, growth of 8.5% over the previous year. That of urban households was 38536 yuan, growth of 8.2% over the previous year. And that of rural households was 16,522 yuan, growth of 8.8% over the previous year.

By the end of 2017, 4.6733 million people participated in urban basic health insurance program; 3.6045 million people participated in basic pension program for staff and workers of enterprises; 1.5496 million people participated in unemployment insurance programs; 1.7204 million people participated in work accident insurance; 1.5116 million people participated in maternity insurance programs for staff and workers. The number of farmers taking part in the new cooperative medical care system in rural areas reached 3.9365 million, with a participation rate of 99.72% covered.

XII. Urban Construction, Environment and Work Safety

The total investment of municipal utilities was 67.731 billion yuan, up by 54.9%. 4 pedestrian bridges, and 62 underground passages were newly built. By the end of the year, the built-up area was 595.26 square kilometers, and the per capita green space of the city was 12.31 square meters, with a green coverage rate of 43.44% in the built-up area. At the end of the year, the municipal wastewater treatment plant has a daily capacity of 2.776 million tons, an increase of 6.3% over the previous year.

In 2017, there were 180 days with air quality better than standard Grade II. The average annual concentration of sulfur dioxide was 19 micrograms / m3. The average annual concentration of nitrogen dioxide was 59 micrograms / m3. The average annual concentration of PM10 was 130 micrograms / m3.The average annual concentration of PM12.5 was 73 micrograms / m3.The water quality compliance rate of centralized drinking water sources in the city was 98.1%. The average equivalent level of regional environmental noise is 56.5 decibels, and the average equivalent noise level of road traffic noise is 70.6 decibels.

In 2017, various kinds of work accidents amounted to 492, death of 177 people. There were 457 road traffic accidents in production and operation, 136 deaths, 33 industrial and mining accidents and 41 deaths.

Notes:

[1] All figures in this Communique are preliminary statistics, some data are not equal to the total due to rounding.

[2] The statistical caliber of Xi'an's GDP has changed in 2017. Firstly, the reform of accounting methods for Research and Development expenditure has been carried out, and the capitalization data of Research and Development expenditure has been included in the regional GDP. Secondly, the data of Xi'xian new district has been included in the accounting scope of Xi'an GDP. the absolute number of GDP, the added value of each industry and GDP per capita were calculated at current prices, and the growth rate was calculated at constant prices.

[3] Equipment manufacturing industry includes metal products industry, general equipment manufacturing industry, special equipment manufacturing industry, automobile manufacturing, railway, marine, aerospace and other transportation equipment manufacturing, electrical machinery and equipment manufacturing, computer, communications and other electronic equipment manufacturing, instrumentation manufacturing, metal products, machinery and equipment repair industry.

[4] Six highly energy-consuming industries are manufacture of raw chemical materials and chemical products, manufacture of non-metallic mineral products, smelting and pressing of ferrous metals, smelting and pressing of non-ferrous metals, oil processing, coking and nuclear fuel processing, and production and supply of electricity and heat.

[5] Industrial strategic emerging industries includes energy conservation, environmental protection industry, a new generation of information technology industry, biology industry, high-end equipment manufacturing industry, new energy industry, new material industry, new energy automotive industry and so on seven big industry in the industrial industry.

[6] High tech manufacturing industry includes pharmaceutical manufacturing, aviation, aerospace and equipment manufacturing industry, electronics and

communications equipment manufacturing, computer and office equipment manufacturing, medical equipment and instrument manufacturing and photographic equipment manufacturing.

[7] Private investment in fixed assets is the construction or purchase of fixed assets investment by collective, private and individual domestic enterprises or institutions and enterprise units by its holdings (including absolute holdings and relative holdings).

[8] The real estate investment, in addition to investment in real estate development, also includes the construction of self-built housing units, as well as property management, intermediary services and other real estate investment.

[9]Online retail sales of goods refers to the retail sales of goods through the public website trading platform (the online platform mainly engaged in physical goods trading, including the self-established website and the third-party platform).

[10] Fixed Internet broadband access users are people who have the registration of Telecom Enterprises at the end of the reporting period and access to the public Internet by xDSL、FTTx+LAN、FTTH/0 or other broadband access ways and common line access.

The Data Size:

In this communique, items in 2017 such as prices, the per capita disposable income, import and export, external use of foreign capital, transportation, postal telecommunications, finance, securities and insurance, exhibition, sports, health, urban construction, environmental monitoring index data for Xi'an is the original diameter. Items such as employment and the introduction of talent, market main body, finance, the PPP projects, tourism, education, museums, cultural, social services, and rural strands personnel assistance support, census register population, production safety, gross domestic product, agriculture, industry, construction industry, investment in fixed assets and domestic trade index data include Xi'xian new district. In data of science and technology, the volume of contract transaction and patent data of 2017 science and technology plan project, high-tech enterprise, technology market are the original data of Xi'an, and the crowd-creation space is the data include Xi'xian new district. In the data of Social security in 2017, the new rural cooperative medical care system and town enterprise worker endowment insurance number is of Xi'an original diameter, urban basic medical insurance, unemployment insurance, employment injury insurance and worker bears insurance number include Xi'xian new district.

Data Sources:

In this communique, data of price and the per capita disposable income are from NBS Survey Office in Xi'an; data of newly increased employed people, unemployment rate through unemployment registration ,the introduction of talent and social security are from the Xi'an Municipal Bureau of Human Resources and Social Security; The main market data comes from the Industrial and Commercial Bureau; financial data are from the Xi'an Municipal Bureau of Finance; PPP project data came from the Municipal Development and Reform Commission; data of imports and exports are from the Xi'an Customs; data on the utilization of foreign capital came from the Municipal Investment Commission; tourism data from the city Tourism Commission; data of railway transportation are from the Xi'an Municipal Bureau of Railways; data of highway transportation are from the Xi'an Municipal Bureau of Transport; data of air transport are from the Xi'an- Xian yang International Airport; data of motor vehicles for civilian use are from the Xi'an vehicle administration; data of post services are from the Xi'an Municipal Bureau of post; data of telecommunications are from Xi'an branch of China Mobile、China Unicom and China Telecom; data of monetary and financial are from business management department for Xi'an branch of the People's Bank of China; data of listed companies and insurance are from Xi'an Municipal Finance Office; data of education are from the Xi'an Municipal Bureau of Education; data of technology are from Xi'an Municipal Bureau of Technology; data of museum are from Xi'an Municipal Bureau of Heritage; data of art-performing groups, public libraries, culture centers, radio and television are from the Xi'an Municipal Bureau of Culture, Radio, Press and Publication; the exhibition data comes from the Municipal Exhibition Office; data of sports are from the Xi'an Municipal Bureau of Sport; data of health and new cooperative medical care system in rural areas are from the Xi'an Municipal Bureau of Health; data on social services, subsistence allowances for the poor and the rural poor came from the Civil Affairs Bureau; the household registration data came from the Municipal Public Security Bureau; data of urban construction are from Urban and Rural Construction Commission; data of sewage treatment in urban and environment monitoring from the Xi'an Municipal Bureau of Environmental Protection; data of work safety are from the State Administration of Work Safety; all the other data are from Xi'an Municipal Bureau of Statistics.

1 综　合

GENERAL SURVEY

资料整理：李　芬
Data management：Li Fen
数据审核：陈　英
Data audit：Chen Ying

第一部分　综合

一、简要说明

本章资料主要包括西安市行政区划、自然地理、自然资源、气象、国民经济和社会发展等综合资料，由西安市统计局综合处根据局内各专业处及有关部门统计资料进行整理和编辑。

二、主要指标

生产总值（亿元）	7471.89	比上年增长	7.7%
农林牧渔及服务业总产值（亿元）	497.39	比上年增长	4.8%
全部工业总产值（亿元）	6285.34	比上年增长	15.1%
全社会固定资产投资额（亿元）	7556.47	比上年增长	12.9%
社会消费品零售总额（亿元）	4249.81	比上年增长	8.5%
财政一般公共预算收入（亿元）	654.50	比上年增长	9.8%
财政一般公共预算支出（亿元）	1045.09	比上年增长	7.1%
进出口总值（亿元）	2545.08	比上年增长	39.1%
城镇居民人均可支配收入（元）	38536	比上年增长	8.2%
农村居民人均可支配收入（元）	16522	比上年增长	8.8%

1　GENERAL SURVEY

Ⅰ.Brief Introduction

This chapter consists of mainly unified data of administrative divisions, natural geography, natural resources, meteorology, national economy and social development of Xi'an city. It is compiled by Integration Division according to the reported data from other divisions of the Xi'an Bureau of Statistics and other departments of the municipal government.

Ⅱ. Major Indicators

		Increase over Preceding Year
Gross Domestic Product (100 mil. Yuan)	7471.89	7.7%
Gross Output Value of Farming, Forestry, Animal, Husbandry and Fishery (100 mil. Yuan)	497.39	4.8%
Gross Output Value of Industry (100 mil. Yuan)	6285.34	15.1%
Total Investment In Fixed Assets (100 mil. Yuan)	7556.47	12.9%
Total Retail Sales of Consumer Goods (100 mil. Yuan)	4249.81	8.5%
Government General Public Budgetary Revenue (100 mil. Yuan)	654.50	9.8%
Government General Public Budgetary Expenditures (100 mil. Yuan)	1045.09	7.1%
Total Value of Imports and Exports (RMB 100 mil.Yuan)	2545.08	39.1%
Per Capita Annual Disposable Income of Urban Households (Yuan)	38536	8.2%
Per Capita Annual Disposable Income of Rural Households (Yuan)	16522	8.8%

1-1 行政区划（2017年）

Administrative Division（2017）

单位：个　　(unit)

地　区	Region	乡镇及街道办 Township and Urban Subdistrict Office	镇数 Town	街道办事处 Urban Subdistrict Office	村民委员会 Villagers' Committee	社区居委会 Neighbourhood Committee
西安市	**Xi'an**	**187**	**57**	**130**	**2219**	**950**
#新城区	Xincheng	9		9		101
碑林区	Beilin	8		8		100
莲湖区	Lianhu	9		9		131
灞桥区	Baqiao	9		9	195	51
未央区	Weiyang	10		10	68	124
雁塔区	Yanta	10		10	64	153
阎良区	Yanliang	7	2	5	73	24
临潼区	Lintong	23		23	226	41
长安区	Chang'an	21		21	306	102
高陵区	Gaoling	7		7	86	17
鄠邑区	Huyi	13	12	1	245	20
蓝田县	Lantian	19	18	1	337	9
周至县	Zhouzhi	20	19	1	264	16

注：本表数据来源市民政局。

1-2 土地面积和常住人口密度（2017年）

Statistics on Land Area and Density of Permanent Population（2017）

地　区	Region	土地面积 Area 绝对数（平方公里）Absolute Value (sq.km)	比重（%）Proportion (%)	常住人口（万人）Total of Permanent Population (10 000 persons)	常住人口密度（人/平方公里）Density of Permanent Population (person/sq.km)
西安市	**Xi 'an**	**10096.81**	**100.0**	**961.67**	
市区	**Urban**	**5145.66**	**51.0**	**750.69**	
新城区	Xincheng	30.12	0.3	62.06	20604
碑林区	Beilin	23.37	0.2	65.18	27890
莲湖区	Lianhu	38.32	0.4	73.67	19225
灞桥区	Baqiao	324.50	3.2	64.06	1974
未央区	Weiyang	264.41	2.6	70.17	
雁塔区	Yanta	151.44	1.5	125.49	8286
阎良区	Yanliang	244.55	2.4	29.47	1205
临潼区	Lintong	915.97	9.1	68.99	753
长安区	Chang'an	1588.53	15.7	100.97	
高陵区	Gaoling	285.03	2.8	35.70	1252
鄠邑区	Huyi	1279.42	12.7	54.93	
二县	**Two Counties**	**4951.15**	**49.0**	**112.20**	**227**
蓝田县	Lantian	2005.95	19.9	53.26	266
周至县	Zhouzhi	2945.20	29.2	58.94	200

注：1.本表土地面积数据来源市国土资源局，为西安原口径数据。
2.全市常住人口数据包含西咸新区。
3.由于全市、市区及相关区县常住人口与土地面积口径不一致，暂不计算人口密度。

1-3 自然状况和资源（2017年）

Nature Conditions and Resources（2017）

指　标	Item	2017
一、自然状况	**Nature Conditions**	
土地总面积（平方公里）	Total Land Area (sq.km)	10096.81
#市区面积	Urban Area	5145.66
气候（市区）	Climate (Urban)	
年平均气温（℃）	Average Annual Temperature (℃)	15.6
年降水量（毫米）	Total Annual Precipitation (mm)	649.0
日照总时数（小时）	Total Sunshine Time (hour)	1965.7
平均风速（米/秒）	Average Wind-speed (m/sec.)	2.1
二、自然资源	**Natural Resources**	
年末实有耕地面积（千公顷）	Cultivated Area Year-end (1 000 hectare)	249.63
林业用地面积（千公顷）	Area of Forestry (1 000 hectare)	480.54
全市水面面积（千公顷）	Whole Water Area (1 000 hectare)	3.97
水资源总量（亿立方米）	Total Water Resource (0.1 billion cu.m)	24.45
#天然地表水资源总量	Total Savageness Surface Water Resource	20.31
地下水资源总量（亿立方米）	Total Underground Water Resource (0.1 billion cu.m)	9.27

注：1. 全市水面面积包括湖泊、水库、鱼塘、城市段河流面积等。
2. 本表数据来源市气象局、林业局、水务局等。
3. 本表年末实有耕地面积含西咸新区，其他指标数据均为西安原口径数据。

1-4 气象情况（2017年）

Climate Condition（2017）

地 区	Region	平均气温（℃）Average Temperature (℃)	日照时数（小时）Sunshine Time (hour)	降水天数（天）Raining days (day)	年降水量（毫米）Total Annual Precipitation (mm)	平均风速（米/秒）Average Wind-speed (m/second)
市 区	Urban	15.6	1965.7	107	649.0	2.1
临潼区	Lintong	15.1	2194.5	78	582.5	1.8
长安区	Chang'an	14.1	1808.1	97	939.7	1.3
高陵区	Gaoling	14.7	2161.1	91	591.5	1.9
鄠邑区	Huyi	14.8	2058.7	115	778.1	1.8
蓝田县	Lantian	13.8	1653.4	243	826.8	1.5
周至县	Zhouzhi	14.3	1898.1	110	792.8	1.6

注：本表数据来源市气象局，为西安原口径数据。

1-5 市区及县各月平均气温（2017年）

Average Temperature of Xi'an and the Districts of Each Month（2017）

单位：℃ (℃)

月 份	Month	市区 Urban	临潼区 Lintong	长安区 Chang'an	高陵区 Gaoling	鄠邑区 Huyi	蓝田县 Lantian	周至县 Zhouzhi
一月	January	2.7	2.3	1.2	1.3	1.7	0.8	1.7
二月	February	5.6	4.8	4.0	4.1	4.4	3.5	4.5
三月	March	9.8	9.3	8.3	8.8	8.8	7.6	8.6
四月	April	17.0	16.5	15.3	15.9	15.8	14.8	15.9
五月	May	22.2	21.9	20.1	21.1	21.1	19.8	20.7
六月	June	26.1	25.7	24.2	25.7	25.3	24.7	24.4
七月	July	30.5	30.1	29.3	30.2	30.3	29.3	29.3
八月	August	26.6	26.3	25.3	26.2	25.8	25.3	25.0
九月	September	21.3	20.7	20.0	20.9	20.4	20.3	20.0
十月	October	13.7	13.2	13.0	13.4	13.2	12.8	12.9
十一月	November	8.8	8.2	7.2	7.6	7.9	6.8	7.3
十二月	December	3.0	2.6	1.4	1.3	2.3	0.2	1.6

注：本表数据来源市气象局，为西安原口径数据。

1-6 市区及县各月日照时数(2017年)

Sunshine Duration of Xi'an and the Districts of Each Month(2017)

单位：小时 (hour)

月 份	Month	市区 Urban	临潼区 Lintong	长安区 Chang'an	高陵区 Gaoling	鄠邑区 Huyi	蓝田县 Lantian	周至县 Zhouzhi
一月	January	106.9	103.4	96.8	118.9	107.7	93.4	111.9
二月	February	162.7	160.9	147.3	169.8	152.0	142.0	155.1
三月	March	161.8	182.2	143.0	171.7	161.9	143.5	133.8
四月	April	195.9	223.3	179.2	208.0	186.6	171.9	183.9
五月	May	232.2	270.6	217.3	239.3	240.7	195.4	222.7
六月	June	216.1	243.3	218.7	249.3	230.8	190.4	197.7
七月	July	290.9	301.7	258.8	301.8	281.6	234.5	294.3
八月	August	180.1	202.0	126.9	190.6	185.0	165.2	159.5
九月	September	103.8	103.6	93.2	120.7	119.7	76.2	85.5
十月	October	34.3	59.4	37.7	52.4	56.3	31.0	39.2
十一月	November	121.8	144.9	117.4	147.5	140.0	80.2	108.2
十二月	December	158.8	199.2	171.8	191.1	196.4	129.7	206.3

注：本表数据来源市气象局，为西安原口径数据。

1-7 市区及县各月降水天数(2017年)

Precipitation Days of Xi'an and the Districts of Each Month(2017)

单位：天 (day)

月 份	Month	市区 Urban	临潼区 Lintong	长安区 Chang'an	高陵区 Gaoling	鄠邑区 Huyi	蓝田县 Lantian	周至县 Zhouzhi
一月	January	2	2	3	2	4	3	4
二月	February	2	3	3	4	6	8	5
三月	March	12	7	6	9	13	16	11
四月	April	9	8	9	9	12	25	11
五月	May	10	6	8	10	9	20	11
六月	June	8	7	13	8	10	21	8
七月	July	10	6	6	7	6	19	8
八月	August	14	12	13	14	13	43	11
九月	September	16	13	18	12	18	46	17
十月	October	18	10	16	13	19	34	19
十一月	November	6	4	2	3	5	8	5
十二月	December							

注：本表数据来源市气象局，为西安原口径数据。

1-8 市区及县各月降水量（2017年）

Amount of Precipitation of Xi'an and the Districts of Each Month（2017）

单位：毫米 (mm)

月 份	Month	市区 Urban	临潼区 Lintong	长安区 Chang'an	高陵区 Gaoling	鄠邑区 Huyi	蓝田县 Lantian	周至县 Zhouzhi
一月	January	3.6	3.8	3.0	4.7	2.6	2.5	4.7
二月	February	11.1	14.8	12.3	11.2	7.0	17.0	6.0
三月	March	50.6	48.7	54.4	49.6	59.1	45.5	58.3
四月	April	55.9	39.6	67.0	41.9	49.3	57.1	50.4
五月	May	63.6	66.2	87.1	57.5	54.9	75.5	44.3
六月	June	72.2	56.4	70.8	65.3	76.8	57.1	100.4
七月	July	82.5	47.4	60.9	30.5	40.9	82.9	68.9
八月	August	64.5	69.0	127.1	83.5	138.4	156.9	132.9
九月	September	98.6	118.6	204.8	89.4	185.7	186.7	143.3
十月	October	140.0	111.6	146.8	151.8	159.3	134.0	182.9
十一月	November	6.4	6.4	5.5	6.1	4.1	11.6	0.7
十二月	December							

注：本表数据来源市气象局，为西安原口径数据。

1-9 市区及区县各月平均风速（2017年）

Average Wind Velocity of Xi'an and the Districts of Each Month（2017）

单位：米/秒 (m/s)

月 份	Month	市区 Urban	临潼区 Lintong	长安区 Chang'an	高陵区 Gaoling	鄠邑区 Huyi	蓝田县 Lantian	周至县 Zhouzhi
一月	January	2.1	1.8	1.3	1.8	1.6	1.5	1.5
二月	February	2.2	1.7	1.4	1.8	1.6	1.7	1.6
三月	March	2.4	1.9	1.5	2.1	1.8	1.6	1.6
四月	April	2.3	2.0	1.3	2.0	1.7	1.5	1.6
五月	May	2.2	2.0	1.4	1.9	2.2	1.7	2.0
六月	June	2.3	1.9	1.2	2.2	2.0	1.6	1.7
七月	July	2.4	2.0	1.4	2.2	2.1	1.8	2.0
八月	August	2.3	1.9	1.3	1.8	2.0	1.5	1.7
九月	September	2.0	1.5	1.1	1.6	1.5	1.3	1.2
十月	October	2.1	1.7	1.1	1.8	1.5	1.4	1.3
十一月	November	2.0	1.7	1.2	1.7	1.5	1.4	1.4
十二月	December	1.8	1.7	1.4	1.4	1.5	1.2	1.4

注：本表数据来源市气象局，为西安原口径数据。

1-10 主要年份国有土地使用权出让、划拨情况

The Transfer and Allocation of State-Owned Land Use Right in Representative Years

项　　目	Item	2009	2010	2011	2012	2013	2014	2015	2016	2017
国有土地使用权出让	**Lease of the Use Right of State-owned Land**									
出让地块(宗)	Land leased (item)	297	386	474	581	550	506	416	457	397
协议	Agreement	100	173	133	80	90	109	72	82	69
招标	Invitation for Bid		3							
拍卖	Auction	1	11							25
挂牌交易	Listed Transaction	196	199	341	500	460	397	344	375	303
出让面积（公顷）	Area of Totally Leased Land (hectare)	1047	1364	1386	1853	2195	1789	1294	1599	1736
土地使用权出让总收入（万元）	**Total Revenue from Leasing of the Use Right(10 000 yuan)**	**284405**	**358098**	**334069**	**218817**	**292945**	**183901**	**109116**	**2832632**	**3988818**
国有土地使用权划拨	**Administrative Allocation of the Use Right of State-owned Land**									
划拨地块（宗）	Land Allocated (item)	79	108	253	154	234	152	141	132	130
划拨面积（公顷）	Area of Land Allocated(hectare)	1721	1027	1426	1617	1986	1739	1209	1135	1411

注：1、本表数据来自市国土资源局，2017年数据为西安原口径数据。
　　2、2016年起土地使用权出让总收入，包括协议出让和招拍挂出让收入。

1-11 主要年份国民经济和社会发展总量与速度指标

指 标	Item	总量指标 Total quantity index 1995	2000	2005	2010
人口与就业	**Population and Employment**				
人口	**Population**				
年底户籍总人口(万人)	Population at the Year-end (10 000 persons)	648.21	688.01	741.73	782.73
城镇人口	Urban Population	255.71	285.79	333.14	374.64
乡村人口	Rural Population	392.50	402.22	408.59	408.09
男性人口	Male Population	334.75	355.18	382.02	398.80
女性人口	Female Population	313.46	332.83	359.71	383.93
就业	**Employment**				
全社会从业人员数(万人)	Employment(10 000 persons)	372.60	389.10	415.83	477.58
#全部单位在岗职工人数	Number of Employed Staff and Workers	141.17	109.62	119.73	130.70
城镇登记失业人数	Registered Unemployed in Urban Areas	5.92	3.85	8.45	10.46
宏观经济	**Macroeconomic Indicator**				
国民经济核算(亿元)	**National Accounts(100 mil. yuan)**				
生产总值(亿元)	Gross Domestic Product(100 mil. yuan)	330.35	646.13	1313.93	3242.86
第一产业	Primary Industry	41.40	44.65	66.01	140.06
第二产业	Secondary Industry	135.33	277.13	540.50	1357.53
第三产业	Tertiary Industry	153.62	324.35	707.42	1745.27
工业	Industry	112.50	218.44	420.00	954.38
建筑业	Construction			120.50	403.15
在生产总值中：最终消费	Total Consumption	239.64	413.43	766.62	1598.51
资本形成总额	Total Investment	151.55	287.82	839.01	2835.42
固定资产投资	**Investment in Fixed Assets**				
全社会固定资产投资总额(亿元)	Total Investment in Fixed Assets(100 mil. yuan)	103.42	232.37	835.10	3250.56
按类别分：	By classification:				
固定资产投资（不含农户）	Investment in Fixed Assets (excluding farmers)	88.50	203.01	776.33	3104.92
#房地产开发投资	Real Estate Investment	21.65	51.85	225.23	842.34
农户投资	Farmer Investment	14.92	29.36	58.77	145.64
按经济成分划分:	By Economic Component				
国有单位	State-owned	69.08	159.60	373.70	1348.76
集体单位	Collective-Owned	9.78	14.65	59.23	326.44
个体经济	Self-employed Individual	11.13	24.40	79.04	54.73
其他经济	Other	13.43	33.72	323.13	1520.63
财政	**Public Finance**				
地方财政一般公共预算收入（亿元）	General Public Budgetary Revenue of Local Government (100 mil. yuan)	18.21	41.39	73.05	241.86
地方财政一般公共预算支出（亿元）	General Public Budgetary Expenditure of Local Government (100 mil. yuan)	18.42	46.50	97.82	371.62
物价指数(上年=100)	**Price Indices(preceding year=100)**				
商品零售价格指数	Retail Price Index	114.6	98.7	99.7	102.7
居民消费价格指数	Consumer Price Index	117.0	100.2	100.3	103.5
工业生产者出厂价格指数	Producer Price Indices (PPI) for Manufactured Goods	110.8	99.4	103.9	102.3
利用外资	**Utilization of Foreign Capital**				
利用外资签定协议额(万美元)	Amount of Foreign Capital for Utilization Through Signed Contracts or Agreements(USD 10 000)	28956	54123	121499	119689
外商实际直接投资额(万美元)	Amount of Foreign Capital Actually Utilized (USD 10 000)	18653	15633	57113	156653

注：1.国民经济核算2004—2008年为全国第二次经济普查修订数据。2009—2012年为三经普修订数据，2013年为全国第三次经济普查数据。2014—2015年为年报最终核实数。
2.2009年及以前年份财政收支为一般预算收支与基金预算收支之和。部分历史年份数据有所修订。
3.由于2010年固定资产投资起报点的变化，指数和平均增长速度为可比口径计算。
4.2015年，市公安局提供户籍人口分类为“城镇人口”和“乡村人口”，2015年之前，分类为“非农业人口”和“农业人口”。
5.2015年，国家取消了城乡投资分组，“农户投资”2014年之前为原来的“农村投资”。
6.由于2017年部分指标包含有西咸新区数据,速度指标为同口径计算数据。
7.本表数据2017年数据口径情况详见总说明和相关章节表下注释。

Total and Speed Index of National Economy and Social Development in Representative Years

					速度指标 （%） Indices and Growth Rates（%）						
2013	2014	2015	2016	2017	指数（2017比以下各年） (2017 as percentage of the following years)				平均增长速度 Average Annual Growth Rate		
					2005	2010	2015	2016	2006-2010	2011-2015	2016-2017
806.93	815.29	815.66	824.93	845.09	113.9	107.8	103.5	102.4	1.1	0.8	1.7
409.82	418.16	545.95	552.21	567.26	170.2	151.3	103.8	102.7	2.4	7.8	1.9
397.11	397.13	269.71	272.72	277.83	68.0	68.1	103.0	101.9	－0.02	-7.9	1.5
408.78	412.46	412.23	416.54	424.98	111.2	106.5	103.0	102.0	0.9	0.7	1.5
398.15	402.83	403.43	408.39	420.11	116.8	109.5	104.1	102.9	1.3	1.0	2.0
530.71	532.92	528.06	539.18	596.21	132.8	115.6	104.6	102.4	2.8	2.0	2.3
183.60	183.22	181.86	184.93	188.42	155.1	142.1	102.1	100.4	1.8	6.8	1.0
10.13	10.84	10.74	11.29	11.51	136.1	110.0	107.1	101.9	4.4	0.5	3.5
4924.97	5492.64	5801.20	6282.65	7471.89	395.5	196.8	117.0	107.7	15.0	11.0	8.2
200.45	214.55	220.20	232.01	281.12	194.1	141.9	108.6	104.6	6.5	5.5	4.2
1998.82	2194.78	2126.29	2200.36	2596.52	375.5	188.7	114.3	105.3	14.8	10.6	6.9
2725.70	3083.31	3454.71	3850.28	4594.25	431.8	207.4	119.2	109.4	15.8	11.7	9.2
1376.74	1488.02	1376.72	1397.25	1684.02	357.4	190.1	115.5	105.8	13.4	10.5	7.5
642.26	728.74	770.29	818.82	928.30	441.8	185.5	111.0	104.2	19.0	10.8	5.4
5134.56	5903.98	5165.98	5191.36	7556.47	899.5	231.1	115.2	112.9	31.2	14.9	7.3
4982.25	5682.42	5086.93	5097.00	7463.31	979.1	244.8	116.8	113.0	31.9	15.9	8.1
1595.64	1761.88	1831.67	1955.82	2333.34	998.9	267.1	122.8	115.0	30.2	16.8	10.8
152.31	221.56	79.05	78.65	93.16	141.3	57.0	105.0	105.5	19.9	-11.5	2.5
1770.84	1916.31	1826.62	2332.08	4127.66	853.9	236.7	138.4	119.4	29.3	11.3	17.6
219.88	203.35	158.14	152.05	153.36	250.6	45.5	74.3	90.1	40.7	-9.4	-13.8
84.43	83.28	80.47	81.68	93.94	150.0	216.7	116.7	115.0	-7.1	13.2	8.0
3059.41	3701.04	3100.75	2625.55	3181.51	1205.4	256.2	99.8	107.0	36.6	20.7	-0.1
501.98	583.79	650.99	641.07	654.50	1143.6	342.5	122.0	109.8	27.3	22.9	10.5
729.81	819.54	917.24	942.52	1045.09	1041.9	274.0	110.1	107.1	30.6	20.0	4.9
101.7	100.7	99.7	100.1	101.7					2.5	1.7	0.9
102.7	101.4	100.7	100.9	102.0					3.1	2.6	1.4
99.5	99.5	98.5	97.8	100.3					2.2	0.1	-1.0
251874	255321	193684	102103	464954	382.5	388.5	240.0	455.4	-0.3	10.1	54.9
312994	370310	400833	450466	530680	929.2	338.8	132.4	117.8	22.4	20.7	15.1

1-11 续表1

指 标	Item	总量指标 Total quantity index			
		1995	2000	2005	2010
产 业	**Industry**				
农业	**Agriculture**				
耕地面积(万亩)	Cultivated Areas(10 000 hectares)	463.97	443.37	400.17	383.32
农林牧渔及服务业总产值 (亿元)	Gross Output Value of Farming Forestry, Animal Husbandry and Fishery(100 mil yuan)	75.46	74.37	106.54	227.10
主要农产品产量(万吨)	Output of Major Farm Products(10 000 tons)				
粮 食	Grain	175.30	201.90	205.50	221.70
奶 类	Milk	13.29	24.59	42.22	63.37
油 料	Oil-bearing Crops	2.17	1.34	1.16	1.20
蔬 菜	Vegetables	133.60	162.14	195.70	253.10
水 果	Fruits	24.10	34.36	51.29	84.78
肉 类	Meat	12.78	14.76	18.20	13.65
水产品	Aquatic Products	0.85	1.14	0.94	1.19
工业	**Industry**				
全部工业总产值（亿元）	Gross Industrial Output Value(100 mil. yuan)	405.90	639.48	1308.56	3562.88
规模以上工业企业主要经济指标（亿元）	Main Economic Indicators of Industrial Enterprises above Designated Size				
资产总计	Total Assets		958.05	1503.85	3592.13
主营业务收入	Revenue from Principal Business		420.42	980.97	3011.19
利润总额	Profits		16.11	28.72	245.37
从业人员年平均人数（万人）	Annual Average Employees(10 000 persons)		43.25	37.92	47.11
主要工业产品产量	Output of Major Industrial Products				
布(亿米)	Cloth(100 mil.m)	3.03	2.48	2.70	2.38
机制纸及纸板(万吨)	Machine-Made Paper(10 000ton)	36.44	5.47	22.19	49.60
发电量(亿千瓦时)	Electricity(100 million kwh)	22.00	19.00	48.00	96.94
钢材(万吨)	Steel Products(10 000ton)	31.44	10.00	24.02	110.77
汽车(万辆)	Motor Vehicle (10 000 units)	0.30	0.90	4.10	65.21
建筑业	**Construction**				
建筑业企业从业人数(人)	Number of Employed Persons(person)		136718	158311	539000
建筑业总产值(亿元)	Gross Output Value(100 mil. yuan)	42.55	105.93	326.65	1334.00
房屋建筑施工面积 (万平方米)	Floor Space of Buildings under Construction (10 000 sq.m)	601.70	793.30	1801.20	4592.57
房屋建筑竣工面积 (万平方米)	Floor Space of Buildings Completed (10 000 sq.m)	177.15	336.80	569.01	1391.91

注：规模以上工业2013年为全国第三次经济普查数据。以前年份未做修订。
由于2010年规模以上工业起报点的变化，指数和平均增长速度为可比口径计算。

continued 1

					速度指标 （%）				Indices and Growth Rates（%）		
2013	2014	2015	2016	2017	指数（2017比以下各年） (2017 as percentage of the following years)				平均增长速度 Average Annual Growth Rate		
					2005	2010	2015	2016	2006-2010	2011-2015	2016-2017
366.23	360.73	356.89	346.80	374.45	84.8	88.5	95.1	97.8	-9.0	-1.4	-2.5
342.89	367.21	380.76	405.63	497.39	199.6	142.9	109.2	104.8	6.8	5.5	4.5
183.12	175.61	180.86	175.33	187.87	81.6	75.7	92.7	95.7	1.5	-4.0	-3.7
65.77	65.80	63.73	56.20	55.84	118.1	78.7	78.2	88.7	8.5	0.1	-11.6
1.00	0.98	0.95	0.86	0.93	64.8	62.7	79.2	87.5	0.0	-4.6	-11.0
298.12	316.28	332.79	336.75	445.43	180.7	139.8	106.3	105.0	5.3	5.6	3.1
95.19	99.66	105.20	107.74	134.77	218.2	132.1	106.4	103.9	10.6	4.4	3.2
15.74	16.19	16.13	15.68	18.31	89.1	118.8	100.6	103.5	-5.6	3.4	0.3
1.42	1.42	1.42	1.34	1.38	146.8	115.9	97.2	103.0	5.7	3.6	-1.4
5042.64	5660.63	5159.91	5462.43	6285.34	461.7	176.8	121.9	115.1	21.2	7.7	10.4
5127.69	6048.34	6740.26	7473.07	7862.59	533.4	223.2	119.0	107.3	19.0	13.4	9.1
4171.21	4566.20	4374.11	5028.28	5710.70	550.2	179.3	123.4	107.3	25.1	7.8	11.1
211.26	226.17	206.88	290.96	367.77	1104.9	129.3	153.4	109.1	53.6	-3.4	23.9
44.27	49.53	50.59	49.55	51.11	123.8	99.6	92.8	94.8	4.4	1.4	-3.7
1.40	1.12	1.04	1.22	1.27	46.9	53.2	121.8	103.8	-2.5	-15.3	10.4
16.00	11.24	12.22	13.44	18.62	55.8	24.9	101.2	92.0	17.5	-24.4	0.6
184.50	179.58	158.68	161.00	176.74	322.5	159.7	97.5	96.1	15.1	10.4	-1.3
54.30	42.87	37.03	43.92	54.91	173.9	37.7	112.8	95.1	35.8	-19.7	6.2
42.20	37.47	34.14	38.25	44.52	1085.5	68.3	130.4	116.4	73.9	-12.1	14.2
577944	394070	596245	588418	703169	438.6	128.9	116.5	118.0	27.8	2.0	7.9
2228.41	2586.33	2650.41	2897.55	3304.54	1008.4	247.0	124.3	113.7	41.0	14.7	11.5
9753.45	11182.18	11979.16	11945.73	13491.49	736.0	288.6	110.7	111.0	20.6	21.1	5.2
2229.97	2536.71	2712.01	2233.20	2553.10	420.8	172.0	88.3	107.3	19.6	14.3	-6.0

1–11 续表2

指 标	Item	总量指标 Total quantity index			
		1995	2000	2005	2010
交通运输	**Transportation**				
货运量(万吨)	Freight Traffic(10 000 tons)	9590	6999	12051	34323
铁 路	Railways	3317	3101	540	706
公 路	Highways	6268	3890	11505	33610
民用航空	Civil Aviation	5	8	6	7
客运量(万人次)	Passenger Traffic(10 000 persons-times)	9069	8068	10479	30294
铁 路	Railways	2678	2130	1796	2781
公 路	Highways	6128	5578	8294	26536
民用航空	Civil Aviation	263	360	389	977
邮电通信业	**Post and Telecommunication Services**				
邮电业务总量(亿元)	Total Business Revenue(100 mil. yuan)	7.65	46.16	132.04	323.11
函 件(万件)	Number of Letters Delivered(10 000 pieces)	14647	8230	9526	8176
本地电话局用交换机容量 (万门)	Capacity of Local Office Telephone Exchanges (10 000 line)	58.30	204.80	457.30	449.00
本地电话年末用户(万户)	Local fixed telephone end users (million)	29.95	124.26	321.48	261.77
城市电话用户	Urban Telephone Subscribers	29.11	107.24	271.40	228.26
乡村电话用户	Rural Telephone Subscribers	0.84	17.02	50.08	33.50
移动电话用户(万户)	Number of Mobile Telephone Subscribers (10 000 subscribers)		73.10	419.96	1423.08
互联网年末宽带用户(万户)	Number of Subscribers of Intemet Services (10 000 subscribers)			33.93	146.18
国内贸易	**Domestic Trade**				
社会消费品零售总额 (亿元)	Total Retail Sales of Consumer Goods (100 mil. yuan)	186.60	360.42	670.56	1678.01
对外经济贸易	**Foreign Trade**				
进出口总值(万美元)	Total Value of Exports and Imports(USD 10 000)	137510	173696	390146	1039273
出口总值	Exports	110163	106062	263441	531729
进口总值	Imports	27347	67634	126705	507544
旅游	**Tourism**				
旅游者人数(万人次)	Number of Tourists(10 000 persons)	791.35	1567.00	2423.60	5285.18
旅游总收入(亿元)	Earnings from Tourism (10 000yuan)	44.00	105.00	178.50	405.18
金融业	**Financial Intermediation**				
金融机构（不含外资）人民币存款余额(亿元)	Balance of Deposits in Domestic Funded Financial Institutions (100 mil. yuan)	359.51	1335.63	3599.70	8863.36
金融机构（不含外资）人民币贷款余额 (亿元)	Balance of Loans in Domestic Funded Financial Institutions (100 mil. yuan)	334.50	972.52	2158.10	6420.72
保险公司保费收入(亿元)	Insurance premium income (100 million Yuan)	4.70	13.58	44.94	129.38
保险公司赔款及付给金额(亿元)	Indemnity Insurance and Amount Paid(100 million yuan)	1.70	1.39	9.50	26.39

注：1.2006年铁路数据按新口径统计；
2.2006年国际互联网络用户改为互联网宽带用户。
3.2009—2013年社会消费品零售总额为全国第三次经济普查修订数据。
4.2014年起，海关不发布美元口径数据，为了数据可持续性，使用年均汇率折算为美元口径。
5.2016年社会消费品零售总额数据依据第三次农业普查和相关制定进行了修订。

continued 2

					速度指标 （%）				Indices and Growth Rates（%）		
					指数（2017比以下各年） (2017 as percentage of the following years)				平均增长速度 Average Annual Growth Rate		
2013	2014	2015	2016	2017	2005	2010	2015	2016	2006-2010	2011-2015	2016-2017
50119	42039	46270	23888	25497				106.7	23.3		
858	900	848	854	994				116.4	5.5		
49243	41120	45401	23011	24477				106.4	23.9		
18	19	21	23	26				113.0	3.1		
38289	25719	26904	23671	24287				102.6	23.7		
3071	3511	3982	4199	4500				107.2	9.1		
32614	19282	19625	15773	15601				98.9	26.2		
2604	2926	3297	3699	4186				113.2	20.2		
247.94	292.20	331.53	383.11	439.85	333.3	136.2	132.7	114.8	19.6	0.5	15.2
2856	2112	1707	1367	1360	14.2	16.6	79.7	99.5	-3.0	-26.9	-10.7
378.00	230.00	145.10	75.92						-0.4	-20.2	
319.11	306.66	292.08	284.33	273.22	85.0	104.4	93.5	96.1	-4.0	2.2	-3.3
286.05	269.38	261.44	252.88	243.81	89.7	106.7	93.2	96.4	-3.4	2.8	-3.5
33.06	37.28	30.63	31.45	29.41	58.8	87.8	96.0	93.5	-7.7	-1.8	-2.0
2160.67	2025.32	1767.00	1739.50	1854.21	441.4	130.3	104.9	106.6	27.6	4.4	2.4
267.05	277.95	289.97	335.83	346.79	1022.3	237.3	119.6	103.3	33.9	14.7	9.4
2742.89	3093.89	3405.38	3767.20	4249.81	603.8	241.3	118.9	108.5	19.5	15.2	9.0
1798534	2494223	2828479	2754991	3769490	966.1	362.7	133.2	136.8	21.6	39.6	15.4
847819	1196005	1316350	1426175	2298972	872.4	432.3	174.6	161.2	15.1	35.3	32.1
950715	1298218	1512129	1328816	1470518	1161.2	289.9	97.3	110.7	32.0	43.9	-1.4
10130.00	12000.00	13600.80	15012.56	18093.14	746.6	342.3	133.0	120.5	21.6	37.0	15.3
811.44	950.00	1073.69	1213.81	1633.30	915.7	403.4	152.2	134.6	15.1	38.4	23.4
13665.89	15064.10	17682.94	18957.55	19943.41	554.0	225.0	112.8	105.2	19.7	14.8	6.2
9930.04	11576.30	13604.89	15159.40	16831.48	779.6	262.1	123.7	111.0	24.4	16.2	11.2
202.41	219.49	263.02	345.85	421.10	937.5	325.6	160.2	121.8	23.6	15.2	26.6
66.49	80.77	87.62	115.91	118.71	1249.5	449.7	135.5	102.4	24.8	27.1	16.4

1-11 续表3

指 标	Item	总量指标 Total quantity index 1995	2000	2005	2010
教育、科技、文化	**Education, Science and Technology and Culture**				
教育	**Education**				
专任教师数(人)	Full-time Teachers(person)				
#普通高等学校	Institutions of Higher Education	15914	15679	29498	42098
普通中等专业学校	Regular Specialized Secondary Schools	2533	3172	2130	1845
普通中学	Regular Middle Schools	21984	26230	31094	31506
小 学	Primary Schools	30270	30215	29647	29944
在校学生数(万人)	Students Enrollment(10 000 person)				
#普通高等学校	Institutions of Higher Education	11.67	19.41	53.06	73.3
普通中等专业学校	Regular Specialized Secondary Schools	3.74	6.02	6.16	6.75
普通中学	Regular Schools	32.32	48.31	55.74	48.89
小 学	Primary Schools	79.36	77.81	60.47	51.56
科技	**Science and Technology**				
高新技术企业(个)	Hi-tech Enterprises (unit)				827
企事业单位累计授权专利数（件）	Accumulated patents awarded(unit)	3164	6139	11670	31999
文化	**Cultural**				
图书馆总藏量(千册件)	Total Collections in Library (1000 Volume-time)	2830	3214	3671	4465
文化馆、站（个）	Cultural Centers or Stations (unit)	201	251	192	197
电视节目制作时间(小时)	Time for TV Programs Production(hour)	5738	11871	27377	29626
家庭、生活、环境	**Family, People's Livelihood and Environment**				
家庭	**Family**				
家庭总户数(户籍人口)(万户)	Total Number of Households(10 000 household)	171.25	187.08	203.04	226.71
城镇常住居民平均每户家庭人口(人)	Average Household Size in Urban Areas(person)	3.88	2.99	2.93	2.81
农村常住居民平均每户家庭人口(人)	Average Household Size in Rural Areas(person)	4.60	4.30	4.22	3.94
婚姻	**Marriages and Divorces**				
结婚(对)	Number of Marriages(couple)	47236	46415	49962	83645
离婚(对)	Number of Divorces(couple)	4296	5161	12747	19060
居住	**Housing**				
城镇居民人均现住房建筑面积(平方米)	Per Capita Building Area of Urban Residents (sq.m)	13.05	14.82	16.38	28.7
农村居民人均现住房建筑面积(平方米)	Per Capita Building Area of Rural Residents(sq.m)	21.77	28.31	36.73	66.73

注：1.2008年及以前图书馆总藏量为图书馆藏书量。
2.2005年以前城镇居民人均现住房总建筑面积为城镇人均住房使用面积。
3.2014年城乡居民人均住房面积为城乡住户调查一体化改革后新口径数据，与往年不可比。

continued 3

2013	2014	2015	2016	2017	速度指标（%） Indices and Growth Rates（%）						
					指数（2017比以下各年） (2017 as percentage of the following years)				平均增长速度 Average Annual Growth Rate		
					2005	2010	2015	2016	2006-2010	2011-2015	2016-2017
46436	46766	47768	47158	47917	162.4	113.8	100.3	101.6	7.4	2.6	0.1
1474	1346	1228	1210	998	46.9	54.1	81.3	82.5	-2.8	-7.8	-9.8
31419	32615	33014	33962	36565	110.6	109.1	104.1	101.2	0.3	0.9	2.0
29421	28395	28748	30941	34163	106.3	105.2	110.9	103.1	0.2	-1.1	5.3
83.83	85.42	84.83	83.10	83.02	156.5	113.3	97.9	99.9	6.7	3.0	-1.1
4.66	4.07	3.47	3.11	2.74	44.4	40.6	78.9	88.1	1.9	-12.5	-11.2
43.73	42.57	41.37	40.7	41.74	72.1	82.2	97.2	98.8	-2.6	-3.3	-1.4
51.95	53.79	56.62	59.79	66.68	104.3	122.4	111.5	105.6	-3.1	1.9	5.6
1026	1253	1316	1506	1839		222.2	139.7	122.1		9.7	18.2
69368	86639	103910	150021	175063	1500.4	547.2	168.5	116.7	22.4	26.6	29.8
6647	6285	6522	6957	7340	200.0	164.5	112.6	105.5	4.0	7.9	6.1
198	199	199	190	202	94.7	92.4	91.5	95.8	0.6	0.2	-4.3
46614	35182	43563	54200	49001	178.9	165.3	112.5	90.4	1.6	8.0	6.1
245.53	250.26	253.13	256.65	267.68	131.8	118.2	105.8	104.3	2.2	2.2	2.9
2.73	2.7	2.8	2.8	2.8	95.6	99.6	100.0	100.0	-0.8	-0.1	
4.09	3.5	3.6	3.6	3.6	85.3	91.4	100.0	100.0	-1.6	-1.8	
89136	91123	80790	77371	70954	142.0	84.8	87.8	91.7	10.9	-0.7	-6.3
20304	21887	22748	25448	28811	226.1	151.1	126.7	113.2	8.4	3.6	12.6
33.43	32.06	32.1	33.4	33.7					11.9		
81.00	48.83	50.7	51.7	52.4					12.7		

1-11 续表4

指 标	Item	总量指标 Total quantity index			
		1995	2000	2005	2010
生活	**People's Livelihood**				
城镇居民人均可支配收入(元)	Per Capita Annual Disposable Income of Urban Households (yuan)	4153	6364	9628	22244
农村居民人均纯收入(元)	Per Capita Net Income of Rural Residents(yuan)	1353	2344	3460	7750
住户存款	Household deposits	291.46	675.83	1716.76	3641.09
工资	**Wages**				
在岗职工工资总额(亿元)	The Gross Salary of Workers (100 mil. yuan)	67.23	101.68	211.14	501.76
城镇非私营单位从业人员年平均工资(元)	Aunual Average Wage of Stuff and Workers in Urban Non-privite Enterprises(yuan)	4763	9179	17728	37870
卫生	**Health Care**				
医院、卫生院(个)	Number of Hospitals(unit)	368	426	479	412
执业（助理）医师（人）	Licensed (Assistant) Doctors (person)	18846	18750	17730	18763
医院、卫生院床位数(张)	Number of Hospital Beds(unit)	28265	28697	30087	36796
市政建设	**City Construction**				
自来水供应量(万立方米)	Volume of Tap Water Supply(10 000 cu.m)	35885	30273	35776	41089
自来水供水管道长度(公里)	Length of Water Supply Pipelines(km)	1066	2237	2315	2416
城市天然气供气总量 (万立方米)	Volume of Natural Gas Supply in Urban Areas (10 000 cu.m)	8419	11513	53202	109052
城市公共运营车辆(辆)	Total Number of Public Buses and Trolley Buses(unit)	977	2573	4762	7107
道路长度(公里)	Length of Paved Roads(km)	835	975	1382	2662
绿地面积(公顷)	Areas of Green Land(hectare)	5603	4116	4867	12140
环境、灾害	**Environment and Disaster**				
工业废水排放量(万吨)	Volume of Waste Water up to the Standard for Discharge(10 000 tons)	12479	9145	16969	13840
火灾发生数(起)	Number of Fire Disasters(case)	426	1040	2664	1825
火灾事故损失额（万元）	Fire Loss(10 000 yuan)	742.1	472.4	1565.5	2224.2
交通事故发生数（起）	Number of Traffic Accidents(case)	3065	4099	4903	2323
交通事故损失额（万元）	Loss of Traffic Accidents(10 000 yuan)	1103.2	1116.1	2024.4	736.6

注：1、城镇非私营单位从业人员年平均工资2012年前为城镇非私营单位在岗职工年平均工资。
2、2014年及以后城乡居民人均收入为新口径数据，“农村居民人均纯收入”改为“农村居民人均可支配收入”
3、部门对住户存款部分历史年代数据进行了修订。
4、市政建设大部分指标2017年包含西咸新区，故不计算相关速度指标。

continued 4

					速度指标（%） Indices and Growth Rates（%）						
					指数（2017比以下各年） (2017 as percentage of the following years)				平均增长速度 Average Annual Growth Rate		
2013	2014	2015	2016	2017	2005	2010	2015	2016	2006-2010	2011-2015	2016-2017
33100	30715	33188	35630	38536	470.8	203.8	116.2	108.2	18.2	15.1	7.8
12930	12898	14072	15191	16522	535.8	239.3	117.5	108.8	17.5	15.3	8.4
5357.05	5698.15	6571.18	7035.81	7497.30	437.1	206.1	114.2	106.6	13.3	12.5	6.9
987.8	1094.02	1202.01	1309.69	1488.71	681.3	286.8	119.7	109.8	18.9	19.1	9.4
49350	54573	60557	67205	75262	426.6	199.7	124.9	112.5	16.4	9.8	11.8
381	381	395	392	448	83.9	97.6	101.8	102.6	-3.0	-0.8	0.9
23885	24820	26626	27864	30820	167.8	158.5	111.7	106.8	1.1	7.3	5.7
44190	47075	51345	53008	60513	192.2	157.1	112.6	109.1	4.1	6.9	6.1
51372	53799	56055	59953	89216					2.8	6.4	
3385	3500	4371	4522	4900					0.9	12.6	
153489	186259	196826	206068	231168					15.4	12.5	
8128	7769	7781	7829	7780	163.4	109.5	100.0	99.4	8.3	1.8	
3387	3461	3571	3683	4399					14.0	6.1	
17751	18914	20582	22503	30704					20.1	11.1	
8973	6340	5204	4030	4448	26.3	32.1	85.4	110.4	-4.0	-17.8	-7.6
4062	3199	2590	3434	2353	88.3	128.9	90.8	68.5	-7.3	7.3	-4.7
3011.9	4381.1	2401.5	1901.1	1659.1	106.1	74.6	69.1	87.3	7.3	1.5	-16.9
2252	1970	2392	2943	2858	58.3	123.0	119.4	97.1	-13.9	0.6	9.3
1143.9	1264	1470.2	1653.7	1777.3	87.8	241.4	120.9	107.5	-18.3	14.8	10.0

1-12 主要年份国民经济和社会发展结构指标

单位: %

指　　标	Item	1995	2000	2005
人口与就业	Population and Employment			
人　口	Population			
城乡结构	Structure			
城镇人口	Urban Population	39.45	41.54	44.91
乡村人口	Rural Population	60.55	58.46	55.09
性别结构	Sexual Structure			
男	Male	51.64	51.62	51.50
女	Female	48.36	48.38	48.50
就　业	Employment			
全社会从业人员产业结构	Industrial Structure of the Whole Society			
第一产业	Primary Industry	41.17	37.78	32.78
第二产业	Secondary Industry	29.43	27.57	27.46
第三产业	Tertiary Industry	29.40	34.65	39.76
宏观经济	Macro Economy			
国民经济核算	National Accounting			
生产总值产业结构	Industrial Structure			
第一产业	Primary Industry	12.53	6.91	5.02
第二产业	Secondary Industry	40.97	42.89	41.14
第三产业	Tertiary Industry	46.50	50.20	53.84
生产总值支出结构	Structure of Gross Domestic by Expenditures			
最终消费	Total Consumption	72.54	63.99	58.35
资本形成总额	Total Investment	45.88	44.55	63.85
货物和服务净出口	Net Export of Goods and Services	-18.42	-8.54	-22.20
投　资	Investment			
全社会固定资产投资结构	Structure of Total Investment in Fixed Assets			
报表种类结构	By classification			
固定资产投资（不含农户）	Investment in Fixed Assets (excluding farmers)	85.57	87.36	92.96
#房地产开发投资	Real Estate Investment	20.93	22.31	27.00
农户投资	Farmer Investment	14.43	12.64	7.04
经济成分结构	Registion Status Composition			
国有经济	State-owned Enterprises Investment	66.79	68.68	44.75
集体经济	Collective-owned Enterprises Investment	9.46	6.30	7.09
个体经济	Self-employed Individual	10.76	10.50	9.46
其他经济	Other	12.99	14.51	38.69

注：2015年，市公安局提供户籍人口分类为“城镇人口”和“乡村人口”，2015年之前，分类为“非农业人口”和“农业人口”。

Structural Indicators of National Economic and Social Development in Representative Years

(%)

	2009	2010	2011	2012	2013	2014	2015	2016	2017
	47.42	47.86	49.42	50.05	50.79	51.29	66.93	66.94	67.12
	52.58	52.14	50.58	49.95	49.21	48.71	33.07	33.06	32.88
	51.08	50.95	50.83	50.75	50.66	50.59	50.54	50.49	50.29
	48.92	49.05	49.17	49.25	49.34	49.41	49.46	49.51	49.71
	26.40	25.65	24.41	22.33	20.81	19.71	20.39	19.50	18.98
	28.45	29.65	30.51	31.55	28.55	28.49	24.53	23.72	22.73
	45.15	44.70	45.08	46.12	50.64	51.80	55.08	56.78	58.29
	4.05	4.32	4.47	4.45	4.07	3.91	3.80	3.69	3.76
	42.01	41.86	40.91	40.53	40.59	39.96	36.65	35.02	34.75
	53.94	53.82	54.62	55.02	55.34	56.13	59.55	61.29	61.49
	51.51	49.31	48.07	47.93					
	83.77	87.47	84.52	86.65					
	-35.28	-36.78	-32.60	-34.58					
	94.70	95.52	95.87	96.80	97.03	96.25	98.47	98.18	98.77
	27.85	25.91	29.79	30.21	31.08	29.84	35.46	37.67	30.88
	5.30	4.48	4.13	3.20	2.97	3.75	1.53	1.52	1.23
	37.31	41.49	36.00	39.15	34.49	32.46	35.36	44.92	54.62
	11.60	10.04	7.71	4.59	4.28	3.44	3.06	2.93	2.03
	3.91	1.68	2.23	1.95	1.64	1.41	1.56	1.57	1.24
	47.18	46.78	54.05	54.31	59.58	62.69	60.02	50.58	42.10

1-12 续表1

单位: %

指　标	Item	1995	2000	2005
财 政	**Government Finance**			
财政收入结构	Structure of Government Revenue			
中　央	Central Government		31.94	58.30
地　方	Local Governments		68.06	41.70
产　业	**Industry**			
农　业	**Agriculture**			
农林牧渔及服务业总产值结构	Structure of Gross Output Value of Farming,Forestry,Animal Husbandry, Fishery and Service			
农　业	Farming	68.03	69.23	61.69
林　业	Forestry	0.96	1.14	1.23
牧　业	Animal Husbandry	30.29	28.58	30.96
渔　业	Fishery	0.72	1.05	0.69
农林牧渔服务业	Farming,Forestry,Animal Husbandry, Fishery and Service			5.43
工 业	**Industry**			
工业总产值经济类型结构	Structure of Gross Output Value of Industry by Registion Status			
国有经济	State-owned Enterprises	51.04	43.00	45.21
集体经济	Collective-owned Enterprises	40.98	32.76	5.16
其他经济类型	Others	7.98	24.24	49.63
工业总产值轻重结构	Structure of Gross Output Value of Industry by Light Industry and Heavy Industry			
轻工业	Light Industry	40.31	48.81	31.17
重工业	Heavy Industry	59.69	51.19	68.83
工业总产值规模结构	Structure of Gross Output Value of Industry by Size of Enterprises			
大型企业	Large Enterprises	38.80	36.29	35.46
中型企业	Medium-sized Enterprises	9.14	5.14	24.67
小型企业	Small Enterprises	52.06	58.57	39.87

注：本表2008年以后财政收入结构中地方指地方财政一般公共预算收入。

continued 1

(%)

2009	2010	2011	2012	2013	2014	2015	2016	2017
39.68	37.28	35.78	32.37	30.80	29.61	28.94	31.68	35.63
45.32	47.36	49.02	52.71	55.60	57.25	58.39	56.45	47.96
59.42	63.36	63.42	62.69	63.38	64.37	64.19	63.79	65.31
1.27	1.18	1.27	2.02	2.34	2.37	2.57	2.52	2.73
30.56	27.72	27.68	26.61	25.19	23.95	23.30	23.20	21.03
0.66	0.56	0.55	0.65	0.66	0.65	0.51	0.48	0.46
8.09	7.18	7.09	8.04	8.42	8.66	9.43	10.01	10.48
51.07	51.52	50.46	52.20	50.29	48.32	48.47	44.85	45.74
1.38	1.22	0.92	0.81	0.64	0.59	0.31	0.25	0.32
47.55	47.26	48.62	46.99	49.07	51.09	51.22	54.90	53.94
23.47	22.01	21.97	21.95	18.44	18.32	19.55	17.89	17.48
76.53	77.99	78.03	78.05	81.56	81.68	80.45	82.11	82.52
43.54	42.11	41.15	48.46	34.49	43.95	51.33	52.36	54.82
21.88	23.96	15.17	13.41	14.42	15.47	16.34	14.78	15.99
34.58	33.93	43.68	38.13	51.09	40.58	32.33	32.86	29.19

1-12 续表2

单位: %

指　　标	Item	1995	2000	2005
建筑业	**Construction**			
建筑业总产值结构	Structure of Gross Output Value of Construction Industry			
房屋建筑业	Building Construction	12.84	9.28	34.05
土木工程建筑业	Civil Engineering Construction	86.27	88.50	56.59
建筑安装业	Installation of Construction			
建筑装饰和其他建筑业	Decoration and others	0.89	2.22	9.36
交通运输业	**Transportation**			
客运量结构	Structure of Passenger Traffic			
铁　路	Railways	29.53	26.40	17.14
公　路	Highways	67.57	69.14	79.15
民　航	Civil Aviation	2.90	4.46	3.71
货运量结构	Structure of Freight Traffic			
铁　路	Railways	34.59	44.30	26.92
公　路	Highways	65.36	55.58	73.04
民　航	Civil Aviation	0.05	0.12	0.04
国内贸易	**Domestic Trade**			
社会消费品零售总额结构	Composition of Retail Sales of Consumer Goods			
城　镇	Urban Area	88.95	87.99	90.17
农　村	Rural Area	11.05	12.01	9.83
国际旅游	**International Tourism**			
国际旅游人数结构	Structure of Tourists			
外国人	Foreigners	89.76	84.03	84.91
华侨及港澳台同胞	Overseas Chinese and Compatriots form Hong Kong, Macao and Taiwan	10.24	15.97	15.09
教育文化、卫生、人民生活	**Education and Culture，Health Care，People's Livelihood**			
教　育	**Education**			
在校学生结构	Structure of Student Enrollment			
#普通高等学校	Institutions of Higher Education	8.81	12.44	28.48
普通中等专业学校	Regular Specialized Secondary Schools	2.84	3.84	3.33
普通中学	Regular Schools	24.55	30.93	29.89
小　学	Primary Schools	59.91	49.89	32.45

continued 2

(%)

2009	2010	2011	2012	2013	2014	2015	2016	2017
25.50	24.63	36.81	43.03	43.03	41.58	38.41	36.69	36.64
67.14	68.61	53.75	47.57	47.86	49.43	51.84	53.63	54.13
	4.39	6.70	6.49	5.86	5.32	5.91	6.61	6.30
7.36	2.37	2.74	2.91	3.25	3.67	3.84	3.07	2.93
9.01	9.18	8.57	8.07	8.02	13.65	14.80	17.74	18.53
88.07	87.59	87.96	85.45	85.18	74.97	72.95	66.63	64.24
2.92	3.23	3.46	6.48	6.80	11.38	12.25	15.63	17.24
2.01	2.06	2.10	1.84	1.71	2.14	1.83	3.58	3.90
97.97	97.92	97.88	98.13	98.25	97.81	98.12	96.32	96.00
0.02	0.02	0.02	0.04	0.04	0.05	0.05	0.10	0.10
95.57	96.00	96.53	96.92	96.89	96.85	96.69	96.46	96.43
4.43	4.00	3.47	3.08	3.11	3.15	3.31	3.54	3.57
87.81	86.97	88.43	87.91	88.26				
12.19	13.03	11.58	12.08	11.74				
31.54	32.60	29.74	31.00	33.09	33.16	32.78	31.38	29.13
3.32	3.02	2.37	2.08	1.84	1.58	1.34	1.17	0.96
22.70	21.74	18.32	17.40	17.26	16.53	16.00	15.37	14.65
23.56	22.95	19.95	19.52	20.51	20.88	21.88	22.58	23.40

1-12 续表3

单位: %

指　　标	Item	1995	2000	2005
专任教师结构	Structure of Full-time Teachers			
#普通高等学校	Institutions of Higher Education	21.25	19.89	29.93
普通中等专业学校	Regular Specialized Secondary Schools	3.38	4.02	2.16
普通中学	Regular Middle Schools	29.37	33.21	31.55
小 学	Primary Schools	40.41	38.34	30.08
人民生活	**People's Livelihood**			
城镇居民消费结构	Consumption Structure of Urban Residents			
食品烟酒	Food,Tobacco and Alcohol	44.68	36.46	37.04
衣 着	Clothing	12.67	8.13	9.03
居 住	Residence	6.49	11.23	9.10
生活用品及服务	Living Articles and Services	13.75	11.33	4.73
交通和通信	Transport and Communication Services	5.58	6.93	9.67
教育文化娱乐	Recreation, Education and Culture Services	9.05	13.74	17.18
医疗保健	Medical and Health Care Services	3.27	7.23	9.45
其他用品和服务	Other Commodities and Services	4.51	4.95	3.80
农村居民消费结构	Consumption Structure of Rural Residents			
食品烟酒	Food,Tobacco and Alcohol	50.31	36.63	36.34
衣 着	Clothing	8.39	6.65	6.11
居 住	Residence	5.92	21.41	17.76
生活用品及服务	Living Articles and Services	5.17	5.47	5.11
交通和通信	Transport and Communication Services	8.09	4.21	8.19
教育文化娱乐	Recreation, Education and Culture Services	18.53	14.49	16.15
医疗保健	Medical and Health Care Services	1.78	6.93	8.19
其他用品和服务	Other Commodities and Services	1.81	4.21	2.15
卫 生	**Health Care**			
卫生技术人员结构	Medical Technical Personnel by Types			
执业（助理）医师	Licensed（Assistant） Doctors	45.42	44.82	41.96
注册护士	Registered Nurses	32.68	34.29	33.14
药 师	Junior Paramedics	8.78	8.31	7.30
技 师	Technicians	5.21	5.21	5.33
其 他	Others	7.91	7.37	12.27

注：2014年及以后为城乡住户调查一体化改革后数据，居民消费结构与2014年之前不可比。

continued 3

(%)

2009	2010	2011	2012	2013	2014	2015	2016	2017
31.90	32.47	31.97	32.96	33.91	33.87	34.52	32.63	30.90
1.35	1.42	1.29	1.18	1.08	0.97	0.89	0.84	0.64
24.68	24.30	23.70	23.36	22.95	23.62	23.86	23.50	23.58
23.83	23.10	22.37	21.97	21.49	20.57	20.52	21.41	22.03
32.43	31.29	31.29	32.48	32.44	29.21	29.59	29.26	29.44
10.98	11.11	12.27	12.17	12.02	9.09	8.78	8.22	8.12
8.86	9.33	8.26	8.47	7.82	17.89	17.78	17.87	17.84
7.28	7.56	8.11	7.87	7.80	7.21	7.42	7.59	7.57
11.33	12.06	12.81	14.26	14.01	14.16	13.31	13.67	13.00
14.34	14.66	14.27	14.33	14.17	12.60	12.48	12.29	12.61
9.65	9.50	9.00	8.52	7.99	7.32	7.92	8.14	8.28
5.13	4.49	4.00	1.91	3.76	2.53	2.72	2.96	3.15
35.81	32.54	31.89	33.83	32.96	29.93	28.18	26.86	27.27
6.40	6.55	7.20	7.42	7.87	7.44	7.12	6.65	6.50
19.47	24.41	23.92	21.91	19.82	21.99	23.28	23.38	23.54
6.97	6.53	7.10	7.46	7.76	6.97	6.60	7.59	7.85
9.83	8.45	9.01	10.19	9.86	10.66	10.70	10.76	10.69
11.13	11.20	10.43	10.20	10.56	10.26	11.68	11.86	11.90
8.50	8.54	8.65	8.85	8.41	11.07	10.68	11.17	10.47
1.89	1.78	1.80	0.14	2.77	1.68	1.76	1.73	1.79
37.34	33.16	35.17	34.46	33.58	32.66	32.69	32.30	32.71
39.05	40.01	40.87	41.61	42.13	42.28	42.74	43.50	44.15
5.45	5.36	5.10	5.05	4.99	4.88	4.86	4.72	4.54
6.49	8.11	5.91	5.91	5.75	5.63	5.76	5.86	5.94
11.67	13.36	12.95	12.97	13.55	14.56	13.97	13.62	12.66

1-13 主要年份国民经济和社会发展比例和效益指标

指　　标	Item	1995
人口与就业	**Population and Employment**	
人口	**Population**	
出生率(‰)	Birth Rate (‰)	11.95
死亡率(‰)	Death Rate(‰)	4.98
自然增长率(‰)	Natural Growth Rate(‰)	6.79
就业	**Employment**	
就业者负担人口	Dependency Ratio	1.7
三次产业就业者比例	Employment Ratio by Type of Industry	
(以第一产业为100)	(Employment in primary industry=100)	
第一产业	Primary Industry	100
第二产业	Secondary Industry	71.5
第三产业	Tertiary Industry	71.4
城镇登记失业率(%)	Unemployment Rate in Urban Areas(%)	3.1
宏观经济	**Macro Economy**	
国民经济核算	**National Accounting**	
三次产业增加值比例	Ratio of Value-added by Type of Industry	
(以第一产业为100)	(Employment in primary industry=100)	
第一产业	Primary Industry	100
第二产业	Secondary Industry	326.9
第三产业	Tertiary Industry	371.1
全社会劳动生产率(元／人)	Overall Labor Productivity(yuan/person)	8963
第一产业	Primary Industry	2698
第二产业	Secondary Industry	12404
第三产业	Tertiary Industry	14488
人均生产总值(元)	Per Capita GDP(yuan)	5131
固定资产投资	**Investment in Fixed Assets**	
全社会固定资产投资相当于生产总值比例(%)	Proportion of Investment in fixed Assets to GDP(%)	31.3
房屋建筑面积竣工率(%)	Rate of Floor Space of Buildings Completed in Construction(%)	33.4
固定资产交付使用率(%)	Rate of Fixed Assets Completed in Capital Construction and Put into Use(%)	70.7
建设项目建成投产率(%)	Rate of Projects Completed in Capital Construction and Put into Use(%)	43.7
财政	**Finance**	
财政总收入相当于生产总值比例(%)	Proportion of Government Revenue to GDP(%)	5.5
一般公共预算支出相当于生产总值比例(%)	Proportion of Government General Public Budgeary Expenditures to GDP(%)	5.6
利用外资	**Utilization of Foreign Capital**	
外商实际直接投资额相当于利用外资协议金额比例(%)	Proportion of Foreign Capital Actually Used to Total Amount of Foreign Capital for Utilization by Signed Contracts or Agreements (%)	64.4

注：本表财政收入数据2009年及以前为一般预算财政收入和基金收入之和。依据部门历史年份修订结果对财政相关数据进行了重新计算。

Proportions of National Economic and Social Development and Benefit Index in Representative Years

2000	2005	2009	2010	2011	2012	2013	2014	2015	2016	2017
13.07	9.58	10.08	9.73	9.71	10.13	9.57	10.11	10.15	11.54	12.62
5.96	5.16	5.63	5.34	5.38	5.57	5.37	5.47	5.51	5.40	5.42
7.11	4.42	4.45	4.39	4.33	4.56	4.20	4.64	4.64	6.14	7.20
1.8	1.8	1.9	1.8	1.7	1.7	1.6	1.6	1.6	1.6	1.6
100	100	100	100	100	100	100	100	100	100	100
73.0	83.8	107.7	124.0	125.0	141.3	137.2	144.6	120.3	121.7	119.7
91.7	121.3	171.0	183.3	184.7	206.5	243.3	262.9	270.1	291.3	307.1
3.4	4.3	4.3	4.2	3.9	3.5	3.4	3.4	3.4	3.3	3.3
100	100	100	100	100	100	100	100	100	100	100
620.7	818.8	1037.1	969.3	914.4	910.6	997.2	1023.0	965.6	948.4	923.6
726.4	1071.7	1331.5	1246.1	1220.7	1236.2	1359.8	1437.1	1568.9	1659.5	1634.3
16367	31837	59850	68990	79498	86971	94233	103281	109356	117736	131617
2960	4747	8830	11701	14530	16578	17789	19915	20705	21805	25755
25443	47853	87452	98027	106710	113561	127374	144703	151144	170975	197154
24024	44024	73714	82377	96392	104914	107722	113188	121876	128977	140561
9484	16406	32420	38357	45561	51499	57464	63794	66938	71647	78368
36.0	65.8	91.8	100.2	86.5	96.6	104.3	107.5	89.1	82.6	101.1
42.0	28.1	16.0	6.9	10.0	8.7	13.2	11.4	6.8	9.9	11.2
74.0	52.8	42.8	38.4	40.4	42.4	37.1	42.5	40.3	38.3	43.4
44.2	54.2	72.5	53.9	54.9	56.1	56.1	62.5	61.0	64.6	62.4
9.5	12.5	14.7	15.7	16.8	17.1	18.3	18.6	19.2	18.1	18.3
7.2	7.4	10.2	11.5	12.8	13.6	14.8	14.9	15.8	15.0	14.0
28.9	47.0	203.0	130.9	167.0	68.8	124.3	145.0	207.0	441.2	114.1

1-13 续表1

指　　标	Item	1995
能　　源	**Energy**	
单位生产总值能耗降低率(%)	Decreasing Rate of Energy Consumption per Unit GDP(%)	
规模以上工业单位工业增加值能耗降低率(%)	Decreasing Rate of Energy Consumption per Unit Industrial value-added of Industry Above Designated Size(%)	
单位生产总值电耗降低率(%)	Decreasing Rate of Electricity Consumption per Unit GDP(%)	
产　　业	**Industries**	
农业	**Agriculture**	
农业从业者人均耕地面积(公顷)	Cultivated Land per Agricultural Laborer(hectare)	0.20
每公顷耕地农业机械总动力(千瓦)	Total Power of Agricultural Machinery per Hectare of Cultivated Land(kw)	5.23
每公顷耕地化肥施用量(公斤)	Chemical Fertilizer Consumption per Hectare of Cultivated Land(kg)	536
每公顷耕地生产的农业总产值(元)	Agricultural Output Value per Hectare of Cultivated Land(yuan)	24396
每个农林牧渔及服务业劳动力农产品生产量(公斤)	Output of Farm Products per Farming,Forestry,Animal Husbandry,Fishery and Service Husbandry and Fishery Laborer (kg)	
粮食	Grain	1150
蔬菜	Vegetables	877
禽蛋	Poultry Eggs	93
肉类	Meat	84
水产品	Aquatic Products	6
每公顷播种面积农产品产量(公斤)	Output of Farm Crops per Hectare of Sown Area(kg)	
粮食	Grain	3806
油料	Oil-bearing Crops	1753
蔬菜	Vegetables	34800
工业	**Industrial**	
规模以上工业企业经济效益	**Economic Benefit of Industrial Enterprises above Designated Size**	
总资产贡献率(%)	Ratio of Total Assets to Industrial Output Value (%)	
资产负债率(%)	Assets-Liability Ratio (%)	
流动资产周转次数（次/年）	Rate of Annual Turnover Working Capitals(times/year)	
成本费用利润率(%)	Ratio of Profits to Cost (%)	
产品销售率(%)	Proportion of Industrial Products Sold(%)	
全员劳动生产率（元/人）	Overall Labor Productivity (yuan/person)	
建筑业	**Construction**	
机械装备率(元／人)	Value of Machinery per Laborer(yuan/person)	5990
产值利润率(%)	Ratio of Per-tax Profits to Gross Output Value (%)	3.5
全员劳动生产率(元／人)(按总产值计算)	Overall Labor Productivity(yuan/person) (in terms of gross output value per employee)	37689
邮电通信业	**Post and Communication Services**	
电话普及率(含移动电话）(部/百人)	Access to Telephones, National(include mobilphone) (set/100 persons)	7.9
移动电话普及率(部/百人)	Access to Mobilphones (set/100 persons)	0.48

continued 1

2000	2005	2009	2010	2011	2012	2013	2014	2015	2016	2017
		5.56	2.06	3.56	3.51	3.57	5.89	3.20	3.83	4.61
		10.48	12.18	15.44	10.56	17.69	15.21	19.48		
		5.33	1.00	4.43	2.92	2.26				
0.20	0.22	0.21	0.22	0.22	0.22	0.23	0.22	0.23	0.22	0.22
6.78	8.39	10.12	10.48	11.50	12.10	12.73	13.32	13.68	11.31	10.19
664	794	891	922	953	987	982	1045	1035	1050	1023
25161	39937	69106	88869	108457	125041	140441	152695	160033	175446	199248
1382	1493	1792	1901	1567	1700	1688	1592	1721	1668	1660
1110	1421	1990	2171	2253	2452	2748	2867	3166	3203	3936
95	86	96	106	108	115	125	123	133	134	129
101	132	104	117	124	134	145	147	153	149	162
8	7	11	10	10	12	13	13	14	13	12
4342	4796	5206	5349	4764	5045	4837	4777	5045	4983	4944
1526	1821	1956	2004	1988	1987	1956	2097	2086	2087	2166
37797	35231	38344	39667	40475	42607	44767	46713	48235	49037	50506
	8.4	11.3	12.2	8.6	7.7	8.5	7.4	5.7	6.4	7.2
65.0	65.0	61.1	57.6	57.7	59.4	59.5	59.7	57.3	55.7	53.0
1.0	1.3	1.7	1.7	1.5	1.5	1.5	1.4	1.3	1.3	1.4
4.2	3.1	8.1	8.8	5.2	4.5	5.2	5.2	4.8	6.0	6.6
97.1	97.5	97.6	97.1	97.4	96.7	95.7	94.9	94.5	96.0	97.3
29496	82815	161289	188483	194105	230032	264324	275288	268182	277240	294393
6805	13332	11928	9461	28669	12216	10339		12712	14193	10051
3.4	4.8	6.3	4.4	4.4	2.8	2.6	2.3	2.3	3.1	2.8
74347	206337	285854	321340	334172	479232	354419	347000	406962	422421	411690
31.2	100.0	167.1	199.0	221.3	247.2	288.7	270.3	236.5	229.1	221.2
10.62	56.62	132.79	168.00	189.58	210.87	251.59	234.75	203.0	197.0	192.8

1-13 续表2

指　　标	Item	1995
国内贸易	**Domestic Trade**	
人均批发零售和住宿餐饮业消费品零售额(元)	Per Capita Retail Sales of Wholesale,Retail Trade and Accommodation Catering Trade (yuan)	1979
对外经济贸易	**Foreign Trade**	
进出口总值相当于地区生产总值比例(%)	Proportion of Total Imports & Exports to GDP(%)	34.76
旅游	**International Tourism**	
每一游客花费(元)	Expenditure per Tourist (yuan)	556
金融业	**Finance and Insurance**	
金融机构存款相当于生产总值比例(%)	Bank Deposits as Percentage of GDP(%)	108.83
金融机构贷款相当于生产总值比例(%)	Bank Loans as Percentage of GDP(%)	101.26
教育、科技、文化	**Education, Science and Technology and Culture**	
教育	**Education**	
毕业率(%)	Graduation Rate(%)	
小学	Primary Schools	
初中	Junior Schools	
学校教师负担系数	Student-teacher Ratio(in percentage)	
高等学校	Colleges and Universities	6.83
中等学校	Secondary Schools	14.42
小学	Primary Schools	26.22
文化	**Culture (unit)**	
每百万人有艺术表演团体	Number of Troupes per Million Persons	3.39
每百万人有公共图书馆	Number of Public Libraries per Million Persons	2.31
家庭、生活、环境	**Family, People's Livelihood and Environment**	
家庭	**Family**	
城市居民家庭	Urban Households	
平均每户就业面(%)	Percentage of Employees Per Household (%)	55.9
平均每一劳动力负担人口（人）	Persons supported by Each Laborer (person)	1.8
农村居民家庭	Rural Households	
平均每一劳动力负担人口（人）	Persons supported by Each Laborer (person)	1.6
卫生	**Health Care**	
每万人医院数（个）	Number of Hospitals per 10 000 Persons(unit)	0.60
每万人医生数(人)	Number of Doctors per 10 000 Persons(person)	29.10
每万人医院床位数(张)	Number of Hospital Beds per 10 000 Persons(unit)	43.60
市政建设	**City Construction**	
城市自来水普及率(%)	Percentage of Households with Access to Tap Water(%)	
城市用气普及率(%)	Percentage of Households with Access to Tap Gas (%)	
人均公园绿地面积(平方米)	Public Green Areas per 10 000 Persons(hectare)	3.80

continued 2

2000	2005	2009	2010	2011	2012	2013	2014	2015	2016	2017
4027	8795	16638	19848	24007	28132	32004	35943	39293	42545	46071
22.25	24.79	18.16	21.22	20.52	18.61	22.27	27.89	30.37	29.13	34.06
645	737	757	767	797	820	801	792	789	809	903
206.71	283.41	273.69	273.32	267.47	274.09	277.48	274.26	304.82	301.74	266.91
150.51	169.91	162.81	198.00	193.71	194.77	201.63	210.76	234.52	241.29	225.26
			100.4	100.2	100.2	99.8	99.6	99.6	99.8	99.8
			99.7	100.6	98.7	99.3	99.9	98.3	98.7	98.3
12.38	17.99	17.32	17.41	17.92	18.15	18.05	18.27	17.76	17.62	17.33
17.84	18.47	18.27	17.78	16.91	16.43	15.07	14.01	13.88	13.05	12.78
25.75	20.38	17.32	17.22	18.06	17.15	17.66	18.94	19.94	11.98	11.42
3.20	2.56	2.13	1.53	3.52	2.22	2.10	2.09	2.07	2.04	1.87
2.18	2.02	1.78	1.77	1.76	1.75	1.75	1.74	1.49	1.47	1.35
45.7	47.4	53.2	53.7	54.8	54.0	54.6	54.5	50.4	48.7	46.4
2.2	2.1	1.9	1.9	1.8	1.9	1.8	1.3	1.3	1.3	1.3
1.6	1.6	1.5	1.5	1.5	1.5	1.5	1.4	1.4	1.4	1.4
0.57	0.59	0.49	0.49	0.43	0.44	0.44	0.44	0.45	0.44	0.47
25.30	21.98	22.86	22.14	25.31	26.95	27.81	28.77	30.58	31.55	32.05
38.72	37.29	41.38	43.42	43.77	47.45	51.45	54.56	58.98	60.02	62.92
98.95	99.00	100.00	98.77	99.95	100	100	100	100	100	99.25
81.51	91.30	98.15	97.02	97.46	98.19	98.68	98.71	98.79	98.89	96.07
5.12	5.63	7.90	9.11	9.89	10.22	10.70	11.22	11.47	11.61	12.04

1-14 主要年份平均每天主要社会经济活动

指 标	Item	1995	2000
一、每天创造的财富	**Daily Production**		
生产总值(万元)	Gross Domestic Product(10 000 yuan)	9050.7	17702.2
第一产业	Primary Industry	1134.3	1223.3
第二产业	Secondary Industry	3707.7	7592.6
第三产业	Tertiary Industry	4208.8	8886.3
工业	Industry	3082.2	5984.7
建筑业	Construction	625.5	1608.0
批发和零售业	Wholesale and Retail Trade	909.6	1804.7
交通运输、仓储和邮政业	Transport, Storage, Post & Telecommunication Services	674.0	1178.4
住宿和餐饮业	Hotels and Catering Services		505.8
财政总收入(万元)	Total Government Revenue(10 000 yuan)	498.8	1686.8
财政一般公共预算支出(万元)	Government General Public Budgetary Expenditures(10 000 yuan)	504.7	1274.0
粮食(吨)	Grain(ton)	4801	5532
奶类(吨)	Milk(ton)	364	674
蔬菜(吨)	Vegetables(ton)	3660	4442
肉类(吨)	Meat(ton)	350	404
水产品(吨)	Aquatic Products(ton)	23	31
布(万米)	Cloth(10 000 m)	83.0	77.0
发电量(万千瓦小时)	Electricity(10 000 kwh)	610	534
钢材(吨)	Steel(ton)	861	274
汽车(辆)	Motor Vehicle(unit)	8	25
二、每天消费量	**Daily National Consumption**		
最终消费(万元)	Final Consumption Expenditure(10 000 yuan)	6565.5	11326.9
社会消费品零售总额(万元)	Total Retail Sales of Consumer Goods (10 000 yuan)	5112.3	9874.5
三、每天其他经济活动	**Other Daily Economic Activities**		
资本形成总额(万元)	Gross Capital Formation(10 000 yuan)	4152.1	7885.5
固定资本形成	Fixed Capital Formation		
存货增加	Changes in Stock		
竣工住宅面积(平方米)	Floor Space of Buildings Completed (sq.m)	6927	14930
货运量(万吨)	Freight Traffic(10 000 tons)	26.3	19.2
客运量(万人次)	Passenger Traffic(10 000 person-times)	24.8	22.1
邮电业务总量(万元)	Business Volume of Postal and Telecommunications Services(10 000 yuan)	209.6	1264.7
进出口总值(万美元)	Total Value of Imports and Exports (USD 10 000)	110.2	475.9
出口值	Exports	82.5	290.6
进口值	Imports	27.7	185.3
外商实际直接投资额(万美元)	Foreign Capital Actually Used(USD 10 000)	51.1	42.8
旅游者人数（人次）	Number of Tourists (person-time)	21681	42932
四、每天人口变动和婚姻	**Daily Population Changes and Marriages**		
出 生(人)	Births(person)	211	247
死 亡(人)	Deaths(person)	88	113
结 婚(对)	Marriages(couple)	129	129
离 婚(对)	Divorces(couple)	12	14

注：本表财政收入数据2009年及以前为一般预算财政收入和基金收入之和。依据部门历史年份修订结果对财政相关数据进行了重新计算。

Major Social and Economic Activities Per Day in Representative Years

2005	2009	2010	2011	2012	2013	2014	2015	2016	2017
35998.1	74654.2	88845.5	106023.0	120396.4	134930.7	150483.3	158937.0	172127.4	204709.3
1808.5	3024.1	3837.3	4743.6	5358.6	5491.8	5878.1	6032.9	6356.4	7701.9
14808.2	31363.0	37192.6	43375.6	48797.0	54762.2	60131.0	58254.5	60283.8	71137.5
19381.4	40267.1	47815.6	57903.8	66240.8	74676.7	84474.2	94649.6	105487.1	125869.9
11506.9	22381.6	26147.7	30095.9	33644.9	37718.9	40767.7	37718.4	38280.8	46137.5
3301.4	8981.6	11045.2	13279.5	15151.8	17596.2	19965.5	21103.8	22433.4	25432.9
4032.9	8172.3	9654.0	12047.9	14053.7	15773.2	17360.3	18301.1	19241.1	21124.4
1816.4	3069.0	3717.8	4525.5	5272.9	5893.4	6454.2	7132.3	8178.6	9151.2
1381.9	2570.4	2816.4	3233.4	3550.1	3714.5	3949.3	4360.0	4675.9	5155.6
4489.6	10946.0	13991.5	17805.0	20632.1	24733.3	27936.7	30547.4	31114.5	37389.3
2680.0	7584.9	10181.4	13550.0	16369.6	19994.8	22453.2	25129.9	25822.5	28632.6
5631	5978	6074	4987	5275	5017	4811	4955	4804	5147
1157	1694	1736	1775	1826	1802	1803	1746	1540	1530
5362	6641	6934	7169	7611	8168	8665	9118	9226	12204
499	346	374	396	416	431	444	442	430	502
26	36	33	32	38	39	39	39	37	38
74.0	60.8	65.2	44.8	39.1	38.0	33.0	28.5	33.4	34.8
1316	2280	2656	2603	2726	5055	4920	4347	4411	4842
658	3028	3035	506	857	1488	1175	1015	1203	1504
112	1389	1787	1525	1484	1156	1027	935	1048	1220
21003.3	38441.1	43794.8	50874.2	57341.6					
18371.5	37838.9	44850.4	53862.5	62023.6	75147.7	84764.1	93298.1	102211.0	116433.0
22986.6	62518.1	77682.7	89447.4	103646.6					
20918.4	58878.9	72237.8	83395.6	97509.0					
2068.2	3639.2	5444.9	6051.8	6137.5					
16400	22537	12287	23601	24762	23014	40078	22632	36472	36683
33.0	83.9	94.0	107.5	123.1	137.3	115.2	126.8	65.4	69.9
28.7	78.6	83.0	91.4	99.1	104.9	70.5	73.7	64.9	66.5
3617.7	8189.6	8852.3	5494.8	5923.6	6793.0	8016.4	9083.1	10496.2	12050.7
1068.9	1985.3	2847.3	3452.5	3565.6	4927.5	6833.5	7749.3	7547.9	10327.4
721.8	912.6	1456.8	1596.3	1999.7	2322.8	3276.7	3606.4	3907.3	6298.6
347.1	1072.6	1390.5	1856.2	1565.9	2604.7	3556.8	4142.8	3640.6	4028.8
156.5	333.9	429.2	549.4	678.9	857.5	1014.5	1098.2	1234.2	1453.9
66400	107652	144799	182280	218585	277534	328767	372625	411303	495702
210	232	225	226	237	225	238	241	277	330
63	130	124	125	130	126	129	131	130	142
137	241	229	259	246	244	250	221	212	194
35	43	52	53	51	56	60	62	70	79

1-15 各区县国民经济和社会发展主要指标（2017年）

指 标	Item	新城区 Xincheng	碑林区 Beilin
一、年底总人口（常住人口）（万人）	Population at the Year-end Permanent population(10 000 persons)	62.06	65.18
二、生产总值（亿元）	Gross Domestic Product(100 mil. yuan)	616.10	873.49
第一产业	Primary Industry		
第二产业	Secondary Industry	216.83	179.21
第三产业	Tertiary Industry	399.27	694.28
三、全社会固定资产投资总额（亿元）	Total Investment in Fixed Assets(100 mil. yuan)	248.95	223.93
固定资产投资（不含农户）	Investment in Fixed Assets (excluding farmers)	248.95	223.93
#房地产开发投资	Real Estate	123.39	77.24
四、财政一般公共预算收入（亿元）	General Public Budgetary Revenue(100 mil. yuan)	27.02	40.93
财政一般公共预算支出（亿元）	General Public Budgetary Expenditure(100 mil. yuan)	28.30	35.65
五、农林牧渔及服务业总产值（万元）	Gross Output Value of Farming Forestry Animal Husbandry and Fishery(10 000 yuan)		
主要农产品产量（万吨）	Output of Major Farm Products(10 000 tons)		
粮食	Grain		
蔬菜	Vegetables		
瓜果	Melon and Fruit		
肉类(吨)	Meat (Ton)		
奶类(吨)	Milk (Ton)		
六、规模以上工业总产值（亿元）	Gross industrial Output Value(100 mil. yuan)	394.86	31.15
七、建筑业	Construction		
房屋建筑施工面积（万平方米）	Floor Space of Buildings under Construction (10 000 sq.m)	1290.28	4222.08
房屋建筑竣工面积（万平方米）	Floor Space of Buildings Completed(100 mil. yuan)	288.03	812.57
八、社会消费品零售总额（亿元）	Total Retail Sales of Consumer Goods (100 mil. yuan)	667.03	625.92
九、城镇居民人均可支配收入（元）	Per Capita Annual Disposable Income of Urban Households (yuan)	40292	40636
农村居民人均可支配收入（元）	Per Capita Disposable Income of Rural Households (yuan)		
十、医疗机构数（个）	Number of Health Care Institutions(unit)	248	400
卫生技术人员（人）	Number of Medical Technical Personnel (person)	11862	13332
床位数（张）	Number of Beds(unit)	7424	8781

注：本表城镇居民人均可支配收入和农村居民人均可支配收入为西安原口径数据，其他指标均不包含西咸新区。

Major Indicators of National Economy and Social Development by Region（2017）

莲湖区 Lianhu	灞桥区 Baqiao	未央区 Weiyang	雁塔区 Yanta	阎良区 Yanliang	临潼区 Lintong	长安区 Chang'an	高陵区 Gaoling	鄠邑区 Huyi	蓝田县 Lantian	周至县 Zhouzhi
73.67	64.06	70.17	125.49	29.47	68.99	100.97	35.70	54.93	53.26	58.94
749.47	428.35	844.53	1521.15	240.21	221.01	791.03	377.10	197.41	143.49	134.26
	21.82	0.66		24.24	31.45	33.95	32.62	27.74	30.15	33.91
239.80	140.22	405.79	331.31	117.58	66.76	401.86	250.13	82.72	39.10	29.15
509.67	266.31	438.08	1189.84	98.39	122.80	355.22	94.35	86.95	74.24	71.20
240.30	678.30	914.44	1061.91	180.27	171.53	554.48	523.32	183.55	311.77	155.19
240.30	672.13	912.26	1061.91	176.53	158.81	540.79	519.63	172.97	299.08	141.97
164.13	227.72	466.75	650.13	34.99	36.02	198.66	62.21	26.53	3.88	7.61
45.69	44.92	19.18	33.61	11.89	12.79	23.98	11.73	8.48	2.85	2.50
44.34	36.10	29.37	33.10	23.95	40.67	53.08	25.31	40.70	35.76	39.89
	364717	13836		412635	588206	556509	607588	496405	539025	591455
	4.96	0.01		8.48	30.48	26.53	17.92	26.90	25.38	20.66
	30.94	0.19		83.88	50.44	56.78	54.03	28.31	19.17	21.94
	1.14	0.01		24.86	7.62	7.37	3.73	3.66	0.49	4.55
	7820	2510		7734	46275	15072	9512	17300	21899	25818
	30815	270		103187	211056	24731	55070	14035	43297	13676
471.67	137.52	1014.93	721.42	316.66	181.43	1001.19	939.03	359.94	74.43	65.64
1820.99	142.67	3078.31	2077.88	54.31	66.74	175.16	119.00	104.77	114.55	74.42
410.44	50.83	239.07	353.21	17.36	19.91	39.85	70.98	67.99	87.90	27.69
503.68	232.31	558.35	782.59	45.59	96.47	231.40	51.78	77.75	70.42	57.08
40575	39794	40034	40660	39914	33261	37437	31974	30224	28596	29039
	22280			22034	17859	18239	17934	15918	13151	13348
326	466	347	503	172	528	726	218	567	619	534
11454	4258	9229	16108	2208	3043	7429	2848	4143	2391	2735
7860	2852	5674	9582	1463	2756	6021	1999	3080	1528	2185

主要统计指标解释

行政区划 指国家对行政区域的划分。根据有关法规规定，我国的行政区域划分如下：（1）全国分为省、自治区、直辖市；（2）省、自治区分为自治州、县、自治县、市；（3）自治州分为县、自治县、市；（4）县、自治县分为乡、民族乡、镇；（5）直辖市和较大的市分为区、县；（6）国家在必要时设立的特别行政区。

气候 指地球与大气之间长期能量交换与质量交换所形成的一种自然环境状态，它是多种因素综合作用的结果。气候既是人类生活和生产的环境要素之一，又是供给人类生活和生产的重要资源。气温、降水、湿度等气象要素的多年平均值是用来描述一个地区气候状况的主要参数，而各种气象要素某年、某月的平均值（或总量）则可以反映出该时期天气气候状况的重要特征。

自然资源 指人类可以直接从自然界获得，并用于生产和生活的物质资源。自然资源一般可以分成可再生资源和非再生资源两大类。可再生资源指在较短时间内可以再生、可以循环利用的资源，包括土地资源、水资源、气候资源、生物资源和海洋资源等。非再生资源指在使用后不能再生的资源，包括矿产资源和地热能源。

土地资源 土地指陆地的表层部分，它主要由岩石、岩石的风化物和土壤构成。土地资源按利用类型可以分为农用地、建筑用地和未利用地。农用地包括耕地、园地、林地、牧草地和水面。建筑用地包括居民点及工矿用地、交通用地和水利设施用地。未利用地指农用地和建筑用地以外的土地，包括滩涂、荒漠、戈壁、冰川和石山等。

耕地面积 指经过开垦用以种植农作物并经常进行耕耘的土地面积。包括种有作物的土地面积、休闲地、新开荒地和抛荒未满三年的土地面积。

森林面积 指由乔木树种构成，郁闭度0.2以上（含0.2）的林地或冠幅宽度10米以上的林带的面积，即有林地面积。森林面积包括天然起源和人工起源的针叶林面积、阔叶林面积、针阔混交林面积和竹林面积，不包括灌木林地面积和疏林地面积。

林业用地面积 指生长乔木、竹类、灌木、沿海红树林等林木的土地面积，包括有林地、灌木林、疏林地、未成林造林地、迹地、苗圃等。

水资源总量 指评价区内降水形成的地表和地下产水总量，即地表产流量与降水入渗补给地下水量之和，不包括过境水量。

地表水资源量 指评价区内河流、湖泊、冰川等地表水体中可以逐年更新的动态水量，即当地天然河川径流量。

地下水资源量 指评价区内降水和地表水对饱水岩土层的补给量，包括降水入渗补给量和河道、湖库、渠系、渠灌田间等地表水体的入渗补给量。

气温 指空气的温度，我国一般以摄氏度（℃）为单位表示。气象观测的温度表是放在离地面约1.5米处通风良好的百叶箱里测量的，因此，通常说的气温指的是离地面1.5米处百叶箱中的温度。其统计计算方法为：

月平均气温是将全月各日的平均气温相加，除以该月的天数而得。

年平均气温是将12个月的月平均气温累加后除以12而得。

降水量 指从天空降落到地面的液态或固态（经融化后）水，未经蒸发、渗透、流失而在地面上积聚的深度。其统计计算方法为：

月降水量是将全月各日的降水量累加而得。

年降水量是将12个月的月降水量累加而得。

日照时数 指太阳实际照射地面的时间。其统计方法与降水量相同。

平均增长速度 平均增长速度表明社会经济现象在一个较长的时期内逐期平均增长变化的程度，它不能根据各个环比增长速度直接求得，但与平均发展速度之间存在着一定的数量关系：平均增长速度 = 平均发展速度 - 1。

平均发展速度 是一种根据环比发展速度计算的序时平均数,由于各时期对比的基础不同，所以计算平均发展速度不能采用一般的序时平均数的计算方法，计算方法分为水平法和累计法。水平法，又称几何平均法，即将环比发展速度按连乘法用几何平均数公式计算。累计法，也称方程法，根据一段时期内各年发展水平总和与基期水平的关系，列出方程式计算平均发展速度。水平法着重考虑最后一年所达到的发展水平；累计法着重考虑整个时期累计发展水平的总量。

本《年鉴》内所列的平均增长速度，均用“水平法”计算。从某年到某年平均增长速度的年份，均不包括基期年在内。如建国六十年以来的平均增长速度是以1949年为基期计算的，则写为1950-2009年平均增长速度，其余类推。

Explanatory Notes on Main Statistical Indicators

Divisions of Administrative Areas refers to the division of administrative areas by the State. The relative laws stipulate that (1)the whole country is divided into provinces, autonomous regions and municipalities directly under the Central Government;(2)provinces and autonomous regions are further divided into autonomous prefectures, counties, autonomous counties and cities; (3)autonomous prefectures are further divided into counties, autonomous counties and cities; (4)counties and autonomous counties are further divided into townships, ethnic townships and towns; (5)municipalities directly under the Central Government and large cities are divided into districts and counties, (6)the State shall, when necessary, establish special administrative regions.

Climate refers to the natural environmental status formed by the long-term exchange of energy and mass between the earth and the atmosphere, and is the result of interaction of many factors. Climate is both one of the environment factors and also the important resources for living and production activities of the human being. The average values across several years of meteorological factors such as temperature, rainfall and humidity are used as important parameters to describe the climate of a region, while the average values (or total values)of a given year or month of meteorological factors reflect the key characteristics of climate for that period of time.

Natural Resources refer to material resources that could be obtained from the nature by human being and used for production and living. Natural resources in general can be classified as renewable resources and non-renewable resources. Renewable resources refer to resources that could be renewed and recycled during a relatively short period of time, including land resource, water resource, climate resource, biology resource and marine resource. Non-renewable resources include resources that could not be renewed, such as minerals and geothermal resource.

Land Resource Land refers to the surface of the earth, consisting of mainly rocks and its whethering and earth. Land resource can be classified, by its utilization, as land for agriculture, land for construction and unused land. Land for agriculture includes cultivated land, plantation land, forestland, grassland and waters. Land for construction includes land for residential purpose, for manufacturing and mining, for transportation and for water-conservancy projects. Unused land refers to land other than land for agriculture and.construction, including beaches, deserts, Gobi, glaciers and rock mountains.

Area of Cultivated Land refers to area of land reclaimed for the regular cultivation of various farm crops, including crop-cover land, fallow, newly reclaimed land and land laid idle for less than 3 years.

Forest Area refers to the area of trees and bamboo grow with canopy density above 0.2, the area of shrubby tree according to regulations of the government, the area of forest land inside farm land and the area of trees planted by the side of villages, farm houses and along roads and rivers.

Area of Afforested Land refers to area for land for trees bamboo, bushes and mangrove, including forest-covered land, bush-covered land, sparse forest land, land planned for afforestation and nurseries of young trees.

Total Water Resources refers to total volume of water resources measured as run-off for surface water from rainfall and recharge for groundwater in a given area, excluding transit water.

Surface Water Resources refers to total renewable resources which exist in rivers, lakes, glaciers and other collectors from rainfall and are measured as run-off of rivers.

Groundwater Resources refers to replenishment of aquifers with rainfall and surface water.

Temperature refers to the air temperature. China uses centigrade as the unit. The thermometry used for weather observation is put in a breezy shutter, which is 1.5 meters high from the ground. Therefore, the commonly used temperature refers to the temperature in the breezy shutter 1.5 meters away from the ground. The calculation method is as follows:

Monthly average temperature is the summation of average daily temperature of one month divided by the actual days of that particular month.

Annual average temperature is the summation of monthly average of a year divided by 12 months.

Volume of Precipitation refers to the deepness of liquid state or solid state (thawed)water falling from the sky to the ground that has not been evaporated, infiltrated or run off. The calculation method is as follows:

Monthly precipitation is the summation of daily precipitation of a month.

Annual precipitation is the summation of 12 months precipitation of a year.

Sunshine Hours refer to the actual hours of sun irradiating the earth. The calculation method is the same as that of the precipitation.

Average Annual Growth Rate shows the average growth rate of social and economic development during a longer period. It can not be directly calculated by chain based growth rate. The relation is:

Average Annual Growth Rate=Average Speed of Development 1

Average speed of development is the time series average of speed which calculated by chain based.Because the reference bases during the different periods are not same, average speed of development can not be calculated by the general method. Level approach and accumulative approach for calculating average speed of development rate are applied. The "level approach" , or the method of calculating the geometric average, is derived by the formula of geometric average of the chain-based speeds of development, or comparing the level of the last year of the interval with that of the beginning year; the other is called the "accumulative approach" or the "algebraic average" , "equation" method, which is derived by the summation of the actual figure of each year in the interval divided by the figure in the base year. The level approach focuses on the level of the last year, while the accumulative approach emphasizes the aggregate development in the duration.

The average annual growth rates listed in the Yearbook are calculated by the level approach except for the growth rate of investment in fixed assets. The base year is not listed in the duration for which average annual growth rates are computed. For instance, the average annual growth rate of the 60 years since 1949 is shown as the average annual growth rate of 1950-2009 without showing the base year 1949.

2 基本单位

BASIC UNIT

资料整理：张　奇　张　斌
Data management：Zhang Qi　Zhang Bin
数据审核：张利民
Data audit：Zhang Limin

第二部分　基本单位

一、简要说明

本章资料主要包括法人单位、产业活动单位和企业一套表调查单位数等资料，由西安市统计局普查中心提供。本年统计年鉴一套表单位数为年报数，使用时请注意。

二、主要指标

法人单位数（个）	153875	比上年增长	13.0%
产业活动单位数（个）	166731	比上年增长	17.1%
规模以上工业企业数（个）	1366	比上年增长	15.2%
限额以上批发零售住宿餐饮业企业数（个）	1932	比上年增长	22.1%
资质内建筑业企业数（个）	1055	比上年增长	18.1%
房地产开发经营企业数（个）	1044	比上年增长	13.1%
规模以上服务业企业数（个）	1547	比上年增长	25.9%

2　BASIC UNIT

Ⅰ.Brief Introduction

This chapter consists of unified data of enterprises and industrial active unites and investigation unit in “Enterprises Data in One sheet”, provided by census center of Xi’an Municipal Bureau of statistics . Data of “Enterprises Data in One Sheet ” in this Yearbook is the number of annual reports, please note that when used.

Ⅱ.Major Indicators

		Increase over Preceding Year
Number of Enterprises (unit)	153875	13.0%
Number of Industrial Active Units (unit)	166731	17.1%
Number of Industrial Enterprises above Designed Size (unit)	1366	15.2%
Number of Enterprises about Wholesale、Retail、Accommodation and Catering above Designed Size (unit)	1932	22.1%
Number of Qualified Construction Enterprises (unit)	1055	18.1%
Number of Real Estate Development Enterprises (unit)	1044	13.1%
Number of service Enterprises above Designed Size (unit)	1547	25.9%

2-1 按登记注册类型分法人单位数（2017年）

Impersonal Entities by Status of Registion（2017）

单位：个 (unit)

分 组	Classify	法人单位数 Number of Enterprises	企业 Enterprises
总 计	**Total**	**153875**	**133465**
#非公有制企业法人	Non-public corporate	127370	127370
按登记注册类型分	**Grouped by Status of Registion**		
（一）内资	Domestic Funded Enterprises	152817	132411
国有	State-owned Enterprises	7487	1590
集体	Collective-owned Enterprises	2711	1542
股份合作	Cooperative Enterprises	324	307
联营	Joint Ownership Enterprises	217	177
国有联营	State Joint Ownership Enterprises	24	17
集体联营	Collective Joint Ownership Enterprises	124	115
国有与集体联营	Joint State-collective Ownership Enterprises	13	7
其他联营	Other Joint Ownership Enterprises	56	38
有限责任公司	Limited Liability Corporations	44243	44119
国有独资公司	State Sole Funded Corporations	393	393
其他有限责任公司	Other Limited Liability Corporations	43850	43726
股份有限公司	Share-holding Corporations Limited	1201	1194
私营	Private Enterprises	79770	79471
私营独资企业	Private-funded Enterprises	13874	13673
私营合伙	Private Partnership Enterprises	1731	1688
私营有限责任公司	Private Limited Liability Corporations	62862	62809
私营股份有限公司	Private Share-holding Corporations Ltd.	1303	1301
其他	Other Domestic Funded Enterprises	16864	4011
（二）港、澳、台商投资企业	Enterprises with Funds from Hong Kong, Macao and Taiwan	368	367
与港、澳、台商合资经营	Joint-venture with Funds from Hong Kong,Macao and Taiwan	133	133
与港、澳、台商合作经营	Cooperative Enterprises with Funds from Hong Kong Macau and Taiwan	10	9
港澳台商独资经营	Enterprises with Sole Investment from Hong Kong Macau and Taiwan	179	179
港澳台商投资股份有限公司	Share-holding Corporations Ltd. with funds from Hong Kong, Macao & Taiwan	18	18
其他港澳台商投资	Other Enterprises with Funds from Hong Kong, Macao and Taiwan	28	28
（三）外商投资	Foreign Funded Enterprises	690	687
中外合资经营	Sino-foreign Joint Ventures	234	233
中外合作经营	Sino-Foreign Cooperation Enterprises	14	14
外资企业	Foreign Owned Enterprises	377	376
外商投资股份有限公司	Limited Company Funded by Foreign Investment	35	35
其他外商投资	Other Foreign Funded Enterprises	30	29

2-2 按国民经济行业分法人单位数（2017年）

Impersonal Entities by Industry of the National Economy（2017）

单位：个 (unit)

分 组	Classify	法人单位数 Number of Enterprises	企业 Enterprises
总 计	**Total**	**153875**	**133465**
（一）农、林、牧、渔业	Agriculture,Forestry,Animal Husbandry and Fishery	6294	3149
农业	Farming	3034	1212
林业	Forestry	844	516
畜牧业	Animal Husbandry	1852	1114
渔业	Fishery	97	59
农、林、牧、渔服务业	Services in Support of Agriculture	467	248
（二）采矿业	Mining	258	258
煤炭开采和洗选业	Mining and Washing of Coal	9	9
石油和天然气开采业	Extraction of Petroleum and Natural Gas	21	21
黑色金属矿采选业	Mining of Ferrous Metal Ores	13	13
有色金属矿采选业	Mining of Non-ferrous Metal Ores	21	21
非金属矿采选业	Mining and Processing of Nonmetal Ores	77	77
开采辅助活动	Ancillary activitives for mining	97	97
其他采矿业	Mining of Other Ores	20	20
（三）制造业	Manufacturing	16931	16896
农副食品加工业	Processing of Food from Agricultural Products	567	552
食品制造业	Manufacture of Foods	571	569
酒、饮料和精制茶制造业	Manufacture of Beverages	228	225
烟草制品业	Manufacture of Tobacco	3	3
纺织业	Manufacture of Textile	179	177
纺织服装、服饰业	Manufacture of Textile Wearing Apparel	161	160
皮革、毛皮、羽毛及其制品和制鞋业	Manufacture of Leather, Fur, Feather and Related Products and Footware	39	36
木材加工和木、竹、藤、棕、草制品业	Timber Processing,Bamboo,Cane, Palm Fiber and Straw Products	273	273
家具制造业	Manufacture of Furniture	506	506
造纸及纸制品业	Manufacture of Paper and Paper Products	389	388
印刷和记录媒介复制业	Printing,Reproduction of Recording Media	634	634
文教、工美、体育和娱乐用品制造业	Manufacture of Articles For Culture, Education and Sport Activities	271	270

2-2 续表1 continued 1

单位：个 (unit)

分 组	Classify	法人单位数 Number of Enterprises	企业 Enterprises
石油加工、炼焦和核燃料加工业	Processing of Petroleum, Coking, Processing of Nuclear Fuel	67	67
化学原料和化学制品制造业	Manufacture of Raw Chemical Materials and Chemical Products	861	860
医药制造业	Manufacture of Medicines	371	371
化学纤维制造业	Manufacture of Chemical Fibers	19	19
橡胶和塑料制品业	Manufacture of Rubber and Manufacture of Plastics	584	584
非金属矿物制品业	Manufacture of Non-metallic Mineral Products	1728	1727
黑色金属冶炼和压延加工业	Smelting and Pressing of Ferrous Metals	244	244
有色金属冶炼和压延加工业	Smelting and Pressing of Non-ferrous Metals	212	212
金属制品业	Manufacture of Metal Products	1206	1206
通用设备制造业	Manufacture of General Purpose Machinery	2188	2188
专用设备制造业	Manufacture of Special Equipment	1610	1608
汽车制造业	Manufacture of Motor Vehicle	217	217
铁路、船舶、航空航天和其他运输设备制造业	Railways,Shipbuilding,Aerospace and Other Transportation Equipment Manufacturing Industry	373	373
电气机械和器材制造业	Manufacture of Electric Equipment and Machinery	1543	1543
计算机、通信和其他电子设备制造业	Manufacture of Communication Equipment, Computers and other Electronic Equipment	892	892
仪器仪表制造业	Manufacture of Measuring Instruments and Machinery	592	592
其他制造业	Other Manufacturing	125	125
废弃资源综合利用	Recycling and Disposal of Waste	61	60
金属制品、机械和设备修理业	Metal Products,Machinery and Equipment Repair Industry	217	215
（四）电力、热力、燃气及水的生产供应业	Production and Distribution of Electricity,Heat,Gas and Water	458	452
电力、热力生产和供应业	Production and Supply of Electric Power and Heat Power	288	287
燃气生产和供应业	Gas mining and supplying industry	53	52
水的生产和供应业	Production and Supply of Water	117	113
（五）建筑业	Construction	12861	12861
房屋建筑业	Construction of Building	2639	2639
土木工程建筑业	Civil Engineering	2613	2613
建筑安装业	Architectural Installation	2101	2101
建筑装饰和其他建筑业	Architectural Decoration and Other Construction	5508	5508
（六）批发和零售业	Wholesale and Retail Trades	49313	48695

2-2 续表2 continued 2

单位：个

分 组	Classify	法人单位数 Number of Enterprises	企业 Enterprises
批发业	Wholesale Trade	27023	26528
零售业	Retail Trade	22290	22167
（七）交通运输、仓储和邮政业	Traffic, Transport, Storage and Post	2981	2896
铁路运输业	Transport Via Railway	31	30
道路运输业	Transport Via Road	1798	1762
水上运输业	Water Transport	4	4
航空运输业	Air Transport	79	78
管道运输业	Transport Via Pipeline	2	2
装卸搬运和运输代理服务业	Loading, Unloading, Portage and Other Transport Services	578	576
仓储业	Storage	360	315
邮政业	Post	129	129
（八）住宿和餐饮业	Hotels and Catering Services	4057	4039
住宿业	Hotels	1490	1484
餐饮业	Catering Services	2567	2555
（九）信息传输、软件和信息技术服务业	Information Transmission, Computer Services and Software	7285	7263
电信、广播电视和卫星传输服务	Telecom & Other Information Transmission Services	311	305
互联网和相关服务	Internet and Relevant Services	901	899
软件和信息技术服务	Software Industry	6073	6059
（十）金融业	Financial Intermediation	847	831
货币金融服务	Monetary and Financial Services	266	259
资本市场服务	Capital Market Services	307	305
保险业	Insurance	170	166
其他金融业	Other Financial Intermediation	104	101
（十一）房地产业	Real Estate	8016	8000
房地产业	Real Estate	8016	8000
（十二） 租赁和商务服务业	Leasing and Business Services	15161	14857
租赁业	Leasing	1263	1258
商务服务业	Business Services	13898	13599
（十三）科学研究和技术服务业	Scientific Research, Technical Sevice	6319	5626
研究与试验发展	Research and Experimental Development	707	624
专业技术服务业	Professional Technical Services	3923	3623

2-2 续表3 continued 3

单位：个 (unit)

分 组	Classify	法人单位数 Number of Enterprises	企业 Enterprises
科技推广和应用服务业	Services of Science and Technology Exchanges and Promotion	1689	1379
（十四）水利、环境和公共设施管理业	Management of Water Conservancy, Environment and Public Facilities	1308	1097
水利管理业	Management of Water Conservancy	172	79
生态保护和环境治理业	Environmental Management	140	121
公共设施管理业	Management of Public Facilities	996	897
（十五）居民服务、修理和其他服务业	Services to Households and Other Services	3134	3068
居民服务业	Services to Households	1122	1067
机动车、电子产品和日用产品修理业	The Repair Service Industry for Motor Vehicle、Electronic	1435	1431
其他服务业	Other Services	577	570
（十六）教育	Education	4172	585
教育	Education	4172	585
（十七）卫生和社会工作	Health, Social Security	3627	378
卫生	Health	3374	336
社会工作	Social	253	42
（十八）文化、体育和娱乐业	Culture, Sports and Entertainment	2856	2511
新闻和出版业	Journalism and Publishing Activities	164	119
广播、电视、电影和影视录音制作业	Broadcasting, Movies, Television and Audiovisual Activities	512	499
文化艺术业	Cultural and Art Activities	886	640
体育	Sports Activities	238	207
娱乐业	Entertainment	1056	1046
（十九）公共管理、社会保障和社会组织	Public Management and Social Organizaion	7997	3
中国共产党机关	Organs of Communist Party of China	176	
国家机构	Government Agencies	2278	
人民政协、民主党派	People's Political Consultative	29	
	Conference and Democratic Parties	73	3
社会保障	Social Security		
群众团体、社会团体和其他成员组织	Mass organizations、Social Groups and other members of the organization	1399	
基层群众自治组织	Grass-roots Mass Self-Government Organizations	4042	
（二十）国际组织	International Organizations		
国际组织	International Organizations		

2-3 按行政区划分法人单位数（2017年）

Impersonal Entities by Region（2017）

单位：个 (unit)

区 县	Region	法人单位数 Number of Enterprises	企业 Enterprises
总 计	**Total**	**153875**	**133465**
新城区	Xincheng	9194	8299
碑林区	Beilin	13314	12350
莲湖区	Lianhu	13817	12885
灞桥区	Baqiao	6808	5768
未央区	Weiyang	25940	24927
雁塔区	Yanta	38183	37126
阎良区	Yanliang	3293	2580
临潼区	Lintong	5064	3072
长安区	Chang'an	12552	10155
高陵区	Gaoling	4080	2972
鄠邑区	Huyi	5820	3593
蓝田县	Lantian	5378	3177
周至县	Zhouzhi	4591	2193

2-4 按登记注册类型分产业活动单位数（2017年）

Industrial Active Units by Status of Registion（2017）

单位：个 (unit)

分 组	Classify	产业活动单位数 Number of Industrial Active Units	企业 Enterprises
总计	**Total**	**166731**	**143390**
按登记注册类型分	Grouped by Status of Registion		
（一）内资	Domestic Funded Enterprises	164772	141435
国有	State-owned Enterprises	10933	2809
集体	Collective-owned Enterprises	3417	1927
股份合作	Cooperative Enterprises	570	553
联营	Joint Ownership Enterprises	291	245
国有联营	State Joint Ownership Enterprises	43	36
集体联营	Collective Joint Ownership Enterprises	149	136
国有与集体联营	Joint State-collective Ownership Enterprises	20	12
其他联营	Other Joint Ownership Enterprises	79	61
有限责任公司	Limited Liability Corporations	47408	47280
国有独资公司	State Sole Funded Corporations	421	421
其他有限责任公司	Other Limited Liability Corporations	46987	46859
股份有限公司	Share-holding Corporations Limited	2399	2392
私营	Private Enterprises	82313	82001
私营独资企业	Private-funded Enterprises	14295	14087
私营合伙	Private Partnership Enterprises	1816	1770
私营有限责任公司	Private Limited Liability Corporations	64798	64742
私营股份有限公司	Private Share-holding Corporations Ltd.	1404	1402
其他	Other Enterprises	17441	4228

2-4 续表 continued

单位：个 (unit)

分 组	Classify	产业活动单位数 Number of Industrial Active Units	企业 Enterprises
（二）港、澳、台商投资企业	Enterprises with Funds from Hong Kong,Macao and Taiwan	596	595
与港、澳、台商合资经营	Joint-venture with Funds from Hong Kong,Macao and Taiwan	160	160
与港、澳、台商合作经营	Cooperative Enterprises with Funds from Hong Kong Macau and Taiwan	21	20
港澳台商独资经营	Enterprises with Sole Investment from Hong Kong Macau and Taiwan	348	348
港澳台商投资股份有限公司	Share-holding Corporations Ltd. with funds from Hong Kong, Macao & Taiwan	26	26
其他港澳台商投资	Other Enterprises with Funds from Hong Kong,Macao and Taiwan	41	41
（三）外商投资	Foreign Funded Enterprises	1363	1360
中外合资经营	Sino-foreign Joint Ventures	351	350
中外合作经营	Sino-Foreign Cooperation Enterprises	24	24
外资企业	Foreign Owned Enterprises	780	779
外商投资股份有限公司	Limited Company Funded by Foreign Investment	130	130
其他外商投资	Other Foreign Funded Enterprises	78	77

2-5 按国民经济行业分产业活动单位数（2017年）

Industrial Active Units by Industry of the National Economy（2017）

单位：个 (unit)

分组	Classify	产业活动单位数 Number of Industrial Active Units	企业 Enterprises
总计	**Total**	**166731**	**143390**
（一）农、林、牧、渔业	Agriculture,Forestry,Animal Husbandry and Fishery	6318	3162
农业	Farming	3041	1218
林业	Forestry	849	517
畜牧业	Animal Husbandry	1857	1119
渔业	Fishery	97	59
农、林、牧、渔服务业	Services in Support of Agriculture	474	249
（二）采矿业	Mining	271	271
煤炭开采和洗选业	Mining and Washing of Coal	10	10
石油和天然气开采业	Extraction of Petroleum and Natural Gas	24	24
黑色金属矿采选业	Mining of Ferrous Metal Ores	13	13
有色金属矿采选业	Mining of Non-ferrous Metal Ores	21	21
非金属矿采选业	Mining and Processing of Nonmetal Ores	77	77
开采辅助活动	Ancillary activitives for mining	106	106
其他采矿业	Mining of Other Ores	20	20
（三）制造业	Manufacturing	17290	17255
农副食品加工业	Processing of Food from Agricultural Products	582	567
食品制造业	Manufacture of Foods	585	583
酒、饮料和精制茶制造业	Manufacture of Beverages	237	234
烟草制品业	Manufacture of Tobacco	3	3
纺织业	Manufacture of Textile	181	179
纺织服装、服饰业	Manufacture of Textile Wearing Apparel	164	163
皮革、毛皮、羽毛及其制品和制鞋业	Manufacture of Leather, Fur, Feather and Related Products and Footware	39	36
木材加工和木、竹、藤、棕、草制品业	Timber Processing,Bamboo,Cane, Palm Fiber and Straw Products	279	279
家具制造业	Manufacture of Furniture	513	513
造纸及纸制品业	Manufacture of Paper and Paper Products	392	391
印刷和记录媒介复制业	Printing,Reproduction of Recording Media	650	650
文教、工美、体育和娱乐用品制造业	Manufacture of Articles For Culture, Education and Sport Activities	275	274

2-5 续表1 continued 1

单位：个 (unit)

分　组	Classify	产业活动单位数 Number of Industrial Active Units	企业 Enterprises
石油加工、炼焦和核燃料加工业	Processing of Petroleum, Coking, Processing of Nuclear Fuel	67	67
化学原料和化学制品制造业	Manufacture of Raw Chemical Materials and Chemical Products	874	873
医药制造业	Manufacture of Medicines	379	379
化学纤维制造业	Manufacture of Chemical Fibers	19	19
橡胶和塑料制品业	Manufacture of Rubber and Manufacture of Plastics	592	592
非金属矿物制品业	Manufacture of Non-metallic Mineral Products	1761	1760
黑色金属冶炼和压延加工业	Smelting and Pressing of Ferrous Metals	247	247
有色金属冶炼和压延加工业	Smelting and Pressing of Non-ferrous Metals	215	215
金属制品业	Manufacture of Metal Products	1236	1236
通用设备制造业	Manufacture of General Purpose Machinery	2229	2229
专用设备制造业	Manufacture of Special Equipment	1642	1640
汽车制造业	Manufacture of Motor Vehicle	231	231
铁路、船舶、航空航天和其他运输设备制造业	Railways,Shipbuilding,Aerospace and Other Transportation Equipment Manufacturing Industry	380	380
电气机械和器材制造业	Manufacture of Electric Equipment and Machinery	1576	1576
计算机、通信和其他电子设备制造业	Manufacture of Communication Equipment, Computers and other Electronic Equipment	914	914
仪器仪表制造业	Manufacture of Measuring Instruments and Machinery	612	612
其他制造业	Other Manufacturing	130	130
废弃资源综合利用	Recycling and Disposal of Waste	63	62
金属制品、机械和设备修理业	Metal Products,Machinery and Equipment Repair Industry	223	221
（四）电力、热力、燃气及水的生产供应业	Production and Distribution of Electricity,Heat,Gas and Water	560	549
电力、热力生产和供应业	Production and Supply of Electric Power and Heat Power	377	371
燃气生产和供应业	Gas mining and supplying industry	59	58
水的生产和供应业	Production and Supply of Water	124	120
（五）建筑业	Construction	13476	13476
房屋建筑业	Construction of Building	2957	2957
土木工程建筑业	Civil Engineering	2704	2704
建筑安装业	Architectural Installation	2174	2174
建筑装饰和其他建筑业	Architectural Decoration and Other Construction	5641	5641
（六）批发和零售业	Wholesale and Retail Trades	53019	52401

2-5 续表2 continued 2

单位：个 (unit)

分组	Classify	产业活动单位数 Number of Industrial Active Units	企业 Enterprises
批发业	Wholesale Trade	27684	27189
零售业	Retail Trade	25335	25212
（七）交通运输、仓储和邮政业	Traffic, Transport, Storage and Post	3571	3454
铁路运输业	Transport Via Railway	57	56
道路运输业	Transport Via Road	1969	1913
水上运输业	Water Transport	5	5
航空运输业	Air Transport	86	85
管道运输业	Transport Via Pipeline	6	6
装卸搬运和运输代理服务业	Loading, Unloading, Portage and Other Transport Services	655	652
仓储业	Storage	380	335
邮政业	Post	413	402
（八）住宿和餐饮业	Hotels and Catering Services	4796	4775
住宿业	Hotels	1661	1653
餐饮业	Catering Services	3135	3122
（九）信息传输、软件和信息技术服务业	Information Transmission, Computer Services and Software	7761	7725
电信、广播电视和卫星传输服务	Telecom & Other Information Transmission Services	540	523
互联网和相关服务	Internet and Relevant Services	941	938
软件和信息技术服务	Software Industry	6280	6264
（十）金融业	Financial Intermediation	2443	2418
货币金融服务	Monetary and Financial Services	1456	1443
资本市场服务	Capital Market Services	362	360
保险业	Insurance	511	505
其他金融业	Other Financial Intermediation	114	110
（十一）房地产业	Real Estate	8402	8381
房地产业	Real Estate	8402	8381
（十二） 租赁和商务服务业	Leasing and Business Services	15914	15541
租赁业	Leasing	1311	1306
商务服务业	Business Services	14603	14235
（十三）科学研究和技术服务业	Scientific Research, Technical Sevice	6636	5871
研究与试验发展	Research and Experimental Development	732	647
专业技术服务业	Professional Technical Services	4134	3812

2-5　续表3 continued 3

单位：个　　(unit)

分　组	Classify	产业活动单位数 Number of Industrial Active Units	企业 Enterprises
科技推广和应用服务业	Services of Science and Technology Exchanges and Promotion	1770	1412
（十四）水利、环境和公共设施管理业	Management of Water Conservancy, Environment and Public Facilities	1408	1133
水利管理业	Management of Water Conservancy	215	82
生态保护和环境治理业	Environmental Management	144	122
公共设施管理业	Management of Public Facilities	1049	929
（十五）居民服务、修理和其他服务业	Services to Households and Other Services	3414	3330
居民服务业	Services to Households	1305	1239
机动车、电子产品和日用产品修理业	The repair service industry for motor vehicle、electronic	1511	1507
其他服务业	Other Services	598	584
（十六）教育	Education	4770	661
教育	Education	4770	661
（十七）卫生和社会工作	Health, Social Security	3987	405
卫生	Health	3722	362
社会工作	Social	265	43
（十八）文化、体育和娱乐业	Culture, Sports and Entertainment	3009	2578
新闻和出版业	Journalism and Publishing Activities	178	127
广播、电视、电影和影视录音制作业	Broadcasting, Movies, Television and Audiovisual Activities	528	513
文化艺术业	Cultural and Art Activities	971	649
体育	Sports Activities	257	225
娱乐业	Entertainment	1075	1064
（十九）公共管理、社会保障和社会组织	Public Management and Social Organizaion	9686	4
中国共产党机关	Organs of Communist Party of China	193	
国家机构	Government Agencies	3788	
人民政协、民主党派	People's Political Consultative Conference and Democratic Parties	39	
社会保障	Social Security	102	4
群众团体、社会团体和其他成员组织	Mass organizations、Social Groups and other members of the organization	1515	
基层群众自治组织	Grass-roots Mass Self-Government Organizations	4049	
（二十）国际组织	International Organizations		
国际组织	International Organizations		

2-6 按行政区划分产业活动单位数（2017年）

Industrial Active Units by Region（2017）

单位：个 (unit)

区 县	Region	产业活动单位数 Number of Industrial Active Units	企业 Enterprises
总 计	**Total**	**166731**	**143390**
新城区	Xincheng	10415	9392
碑林区	Beilin	15242	14150
莲湖区	Lianhu	15190	14111
灞桥区	Baqiao	7573	6254
未央区	Weiyang	27079	25942
雁塔区	Yanta	39815	38620
阎良区	Yanliang	3618	2819
临潼区	Lintong	5987	3549
长安区	Chang'an	13301	10793
高陵区	Gaoling	4352	3202
鄠邑区	Huyi	6434	3998
蓝田县	Lantian	6209	3483
周至县	Zhouzhi	5182	2404

2-7 按统计机构分企业一套表调查单位数（2017年）

Number of Survey Units by Statistical Agencies of "One Sheet"（2017）

单位：个 (unit)

区县、开发区	Region	合计 Total	规模以上工业 Industrial Enterprises above Designed Size	限额以上批发零售住宿餐饮业 Above wholesale and Retail Accommodation and Catering Industry	资质内建筑业 Qualified Construction Enterprises	房地产开发经营企业 Real Estate Development Enterprises	规模以上服务业 Service Enterprises above Designed Size
全　市	**Total**	**6944**	**1366**	**1932**	**1055**	**1044**	**1547**
新城区	Xincheng	335	7	153	57	33	85
碑林区	Beilin	727	12	286	150	91	188
莲湖区	Lianhu	493	24	159	77	88	145
灞桥区	Baqiao	184	56	32	25	45	26
未央区	Weiyang	292	29	85	61	55	62
雁塔区	Yanta	571	44	144	165	70	148
阎良区	Yanliang	189	68	49	26	26	20
临潼区	Lintong	180	72	38	30	16	24
长安区	Chang'an	244	37	97	32	45	33
高陵区	Gaoling	198	79	44	13	39	23
鄠邑区	Huyi	178	63	52	9	39	15
蓝田县	Lantian	103	42	23	11	14	13
周至县	Zhouzhi	153	51	53	14	18	17
高新区	GaoXin	1000	288	180	191	78	263
经开区	JingKai	855	235	217	121	81	201
曲江新区	Qujiang	254		38	12	83	121
航空基地	Aviation Industry Base	61	37	6		10	8
航天基地	Aerospace Base	120	32	19	5	46	18
浐灞生态区	Chanba Eco-District	181	5	54	14	71	37
国际港务区	International Trade &Logistic Park	104	18	27	3	15	41

注：由于统计口径不同，一套表调查单位数与各专业有差异。

2-8 按行政区划分企业一套表调查单位数（2017年）

Number of Survey Units of "One Sheet" by Region (2017)

单位：个 (unit)

区县	Region	合计 Total	规模以上工业 Industrial Enterprises above Designed Size	限额以上批发零售住宿餐饮业 Above wholesale and Retail Accommodation and Catering Industry	资质内建筑业 Qualified Construction Enterprises	房地产开发经营企业 Real Estate Development Enterprises	规模以上服务业 Service Enterprises above Designed Size
全　市	**Total**	**6944**	**1366**	**1932**	**1055**	**1044**	**1547**
新城区	Xincheng	337	8	153	59	33	84
碑林区	Beilin	719	14	286	142	88	189
莲湖区	Lianhu	501	26	159	77	92	147
灞桥区	Baqiao	426	83	103	43	103	94
未央区	Weiyang	1250	214	352	197	201	286
雁塔区	Yanta	1627	210	339	358	212	508
阎良区	Yanliang	249	104	55	26	36	28
临潼区	Lintong	187	72	39	30	20	26
长安区	Chang'an	514	151	140	51	103	69
高陵区	Gaoling	290	156	50	13	42	29
鄠邑区	Huyi	223	106	54	9	39	15
蓝田县	Lantian	103	42	23	11	14	13
周至县	Zhouzhi	155	52	53	14	18	18

2-9 按行政区划和国民经济行业分法人单位数（2017年）

单位：个

区 县	Region	合计 Total	农、林、牧、渔业 Agriculture Forestry Animal Husbandry and Fishery	采矿业 Mining	制造业 Manufacturing	电力、燃气及水的生产和供应业 Production and Distribution of Electricity Gas and Water
全 市	**Total**	**153875**	**6294**	**258**	**16931**	**458**
新城区	Xincheng	9194	5		303	2
碑林区	Beilin	13314		6	219	6
莲湖区	Lianhu	13817	8	3	369	6
灞桥区	Baqiao	6808	170		1130	23
未央区	Weiyang	25940	93	45	2874	53
雁塔区	Yanta	38183	140	90	3252	97
阎良区	Yanliang	3293	284		777	20
临潼区	Lintong	5064	867		685	26
长安区	Chang'an	12552	739	25	2553	40
高陵区	Gaoling	4080	500	12	802	25
鄠邑区	Huyi	5820	743	26	1787	26
蓝田县	Lantian	5378	1155	24	656	70
周至县	Zhouzhi	4591	858	24	324	31

Impersonal Entities by Administrative Districts and Industry of the National Economy (2017)

(unit)

建筑业 Construction	批发和零售业 Wholesale and Retail Trades	交通运输、仓储和邮政业 Traffic Transport Storage and Post	住宿和餐饮业 Hotels and Catering Services	信息传输、软件和信息技术服务业 Information Transmission Software and Information Technology Services	金融业 Financial Intermediation
12861	**49313**	**2981**	**4057**	**7285**	**847**
458	4243	261	463	186	36
985	5566	114	629	538	71
1093	6496	310	541	394	107
532	1954	374	133	181	37
2537	12201	688	467	619	90
4039	11285	280	786	4366	306
201	729	103	83	53	17
461	748	113	101	67	10
1107	2211	147	369	663	65
300	746	126	87	38	11
197	542	95	67	41	16
432	669	59	114	45	17
164	980	129	67	34	7

2-9 续表

单位：个

区 县	Region	房地产业 Real Estate	租赁和商务服务业 Leasing and Business Services	科学研究和技术服务业 Scientific Research Technical Services	水利、环境和公共设施管理业 Management of Water Conservancy, Environment and Public Facilities
全 市	**Total**	**8016**	**15161**	**6319**	**1308**
新城区	Xincheng	976	685	268	47
碑林区	Beilin	845	1964	779	90
莲湖区	Lianhu	777	1628	491	121
灞桥区	Baqiao	381	485	248	76
未央区	Weiyang	1283	2108	1026	183
雁塔区	Yanta	2257	5917	2350	233
阎良区	Yanliang	114	209	67	36
临潼区	Lintong	104	307	182	60
长安区	Chang'an	553	935	450	146
高陵区	Gaoling	203	212	70	43
鄠邑区	Huyi	138	162	137	80
蓝田县	Lantian	89	199	49	49
周至县	Zhouzhi	100	79	104	76

continude

(unit)

居民服务、修理和其他服务业 Services to Households Repairs and Other Services	教育 Education	卫生和社会工作 Health and Social Work	文化、体育和娱乐业 Culture Sports and Entertainment	公共管理、社会保障和社会组织 Public Administration Social Security and Social Organizations	国际组织 International Orgnizations
3134	**4172**	**3627**	**2856**	**7997**	
237	204	73	161	586	
318	319	118	302	445	
341	285	130	243	474	
151	282	67	108	476	
491	301	102	209	570	
774	489	164	896	462	
62	101	105	66	266	
72	258	359	125	519	
258	509	472	248	1062	
95	201	208	82	319	
69	277	528	90	799	
68	240	566	103	774	
44	385	468	88	629	

2-10 按行政区划和机构类型分法人单位数（2017年）

Impersonal Entities by Agencies Types of Legal Entities Corporate Units and Administrative Districts（2017）

单位：个 (unit)

区 县	Region	法人单位数 Number of Enterprises	企业法人 Business Entity	事业法人 Institution Entity	机关法人 Government Entity	社会团体 Social Organization	其他 Other
全 市	**Total**	**153875**	**133465**	**4995**	**1314**	**1251**	**12850**
新城区	Xincheng	9194	8299	279	157	220	239
碑林区	Beilin	13314	12350	317	88	199	360
莲湖区	Lianhu	13817	12885	325	93	139	375
灞桥区	Baqiao	6808	5768	240	73	78	649
未央区	Weiyang	25940	24927	309	147	58	499
雁塔区	Yanta	38183	37126	331	93	70	563
阎良区	Yanliang	3293	2580	146	62	46	459
临潼区	Lintong	5064	3072	575	77	62	1278
长安区	Chang'an	12552	10155	725	77	46	1549
高陵区	Gaoling	4080	2972	311	78	25	694
鄠邑区	Huyi	5820	3593	385	71	82	1689
蓝田县	Lantian	5378	3177	223	105	73	1800
周至县	Zhouzhi	4591	2193	384	70	103	1841

2-11 按行政区划和登记注册类型分企业法人单位数（2017年）

The Corporate Units by Types of Corporate Registration and Adminstration Districts（2017）

单位：个 (unit)

区 县	Region	企业单位数 Number of Enterprises	内资企业 Domestic Investment Enterprises	国有企业 State-owned Enterprises	集体企业 Collective-owned Enterprises	股份合作企业 Share-holding Corperative Enterprises	联营企业 Joint Ownership Enterprises
全 市	**Total**	**133465**	**132411**	**1590**	**1542**	**307**	**177**
新城区	Xincheng	8299	8270	272	291	44	20
碑林区	Beilin	12350	12281	227	117	34	25
莲湖区	Lianhu	12885	12830	244	222	18	25
灞桥区	Baqiao	5768	5708	79	120	15	6
未央区	Weiyang	24927	24744	115	156	38	24
雁塔区	Yanta	37126	36714	159	82	41	17
阎良区	Yanliang	2580	2562	38	48	16	4
临潼区	Lintong	3072	3060	65	83	8	2
长安区	Chang'an	10155	10042	84	104	42	15
高陵区	Gaoling	2972	2949	53	32	16	7
鄠邑区	Huyi	3593	3566	87	111	14	7
蓝田县	Lantian	3177	3158	47	94	10	16
周至县	Zhouzhi	2193	2192	52	29	4	3

2-11 续表 continued

区 县	Region	有限责任公司 Limited Liability Corporations	股份有限公司 Share-holding Corperation Ltd.	私营企业 Private Enterprises	港、澳、台商投资企业 Enterprises with Funds from Hong Kong, Macao and Taiwan	外商投资企业 Enterprises with Foreign Investment
全 市	**Total**	**44119**	**1194**	**79471**	**367**	**687**
新城区	Xincheng	4226	103	3239	11	18
碑林区	Beilin	5868	126	5683	30	39
莲湖区	Lianhu	1265	93	10071	27	28
灞桥区	Baqiao	2378	34	2951	31	29
未央区	Weiyang	9148	157	14988	84	99
雁塔区	Yanta	14992	311	21001	108	304
阎良区	Yanliang	833	37	1179	8	10
临潼区	Lintong	206	9	2672	5	7
长安区	Chang'an	2380	138	6457	24	89
高陵区	Gaoling	999	53	1696	5	18
鄠邑区	Huyi	399	47	2717	12	15
蓝田县	Lantian	359	26	2232	7	12
周至县	Zhouzhi	182	29	1446		1

主要统计指标解释

企业（单位）登记注册类型 是以在工商行政管理机关登记注册的各类企业为划分对象，以工商行政管理部门对企业登记注册的类型为依据，将企业登记注册类型分为内资企业、港澳台商投资企业和外商投资企业三大类。内资企业包括国有企业、集体企业、股份合作企业、联营企业、有限责任公司、股份有限公司、私营公司和其他企业；港澳台商投资企业和外商投资企业分别包括合资经营企业、合作经营企业、独资经营企业和股份有限公司。对不在工商行政管理部门进行登记注册的行政机关、事业单位和社会团体，主要按其经费来源和管理方式进行划分。

国有企业 指企业全部资产归国家所有，并按《中华人民共和国企业法人登记管理条例》规定登记注册的非公司制的经济组织。不包括有限责任公司中的国有独资公司。

集体企业 指企业资产归集体所有，并按《中华人民共和国企业法人登记管理条例》规定登记注册的经济组织。

股份合作企业 指以合作制为基础，由企业职工共同出资入股，吸收一定比例的社会资产投资组建，实行自主经营，自负盈亏，共同劳动，民主管理，按劳分配与按股分红相结合的一种集体经济组织。

联营企业 指两个及两个以上相同或不同所有制性质的企业法人或事业单位法人，按自愿、平等、互利的原则，共同投资组成的经济组织。联营企业包括国有联营企业、集体联营企业、国有与集体联营企业和其他联营企业。

有限责任公司 指根据《中华人民共和国公司登记管理条例》规定登记注册，由两个以上、五十个以下的股东共同出资，每个股东以其所认缴的出资额对公司承担有限责任，公司以其全部资产对其债务承担责任的经济组织。有限责任公司包括国有独资公司以及其他有限责任公司。

股份有限公司 指根据《中华人民共和国公司登记管理条例》规定登记注册，其全部注册资本由等额股份构成并通过发行股票筹集资本，股东以其认购的股份对公司承担有限责任，公司以其全部资产对其债务承担责任的经济组织。

私营企业 指由自然人投资设立或由自然人控股，以雇佣劳动为基础的营利性经济组织。包括按照《公司法》、《合伙企业法》、《私营企业暂行条例》规定登记注册的私营有限责任公司、私营股份有限公司、私营合伙企业和私营独资企业。

其他企业 指上述企业之外的其他内资经济组织。

与港澳台商合资经营企业 指港澳台地区投资者与内地企业依照《中华人民共和国中外合资经营企业法》及有关法律的规定，按合同规定的比例投资设立、分享利润和分担风险的企业。

与港澳台商合作经营企业 指港澳台地区投资者与内地企业依照《中华人民共和国中外合作经营企业法》及有关法律的规定，依照合作合同的约定进行投资或提供条件设立、分配利润和分担风险的企业。

港澳台商独资经营企业 指依照《中华人民共和国外资企业法》及有关法律的规定，在内地由港澳台地区投资者全额投资设立的企业。

港澳台商投资股份有限公司 指根据国家有关规定，经原外经贸部依法批准设立，其中港、澳、台商的股本占公司注册资本的比例达25%以上的股份有限公司。凡其中港、澳、台商的股本占公司注册资本的比例小于25%的，属于内资企业中的股份有限公司。

中外合资经营企业 指外国企业或外国人与中国内地企业依照《中华人民共和国中外合资经营企业法》及有关法律的规定，按合同规定的比例投资设立、分享利润和分担风险的企业。

中外合作经营企业 指外国企业或外国人与中国内地企业依照《中华人民共和国中外合作经营企业法》及有关法律的规定，依照合作合同的约定进行投资或提供条件设立、分配利润和分担风险的企业。

外资企业 指依照《中华人民共和国外资企业法》及有关法律的规定，在中国内地由外国投资者全额投资设立的企业。

外商投资股份有限公司 指根据国家有关规定，经原外经贸部依法批准设立，其中外资的股本占公司注册资本的比例达25%以上的股份有限公司。凡其中外资股本占公司注册资本的比例小于25%的，属于内资企业中的股份有限公司。

行政机关、事业单位和社会团体 参照企业登记注册类型，主要按其经费来源和管理方式划分。具体规定如下：

（1）行政机关：包括国家机关和政党机关，原则上均列为“国有”。但有特殊规定的，如供销社等，则列为“集体”。

（2）事业单位：包括经国家机构编制部门和有关业务主管部门批准成立的各类事业单位，不包括实行企业化管理的事业单位。事业单位的划分办法如下：

①由国家财政预算拨款或列入财政预算外资金管理以及经费主要来源于国有主管部门或国有上级单位的事业单位，列为“国有”。

②经费主要来源于集体单位的事业单位，列为“集体”。

③公民个人（或个人合伙）开办的事业单位，列为“私营”。

④上述以外的其他事业单位，如果其经费来源不明确，按管理方式进行归类。

（3）社会团体：包括经民政部门批准成立以及未纳入社会团体管理条例范围的工会、妇联等各类社会团体。社会团体的划分办法如下：

①未纳入民政部社会团体管理条例范围的工会、妇联、共青团、青联、工商联、科协、侨联等社会团体，国家拨款设立的基金会或基金管理组织以及经费主要来源于国有业务主管部门或国有上级单位的社会团体，列为“国有”。

②经费主要来源于集体单位的社会团体，列为“集体”。

③公民个人（或个人合伙）开办的社会团体，划为“私营”。

④上述以外的其他社会团体，如果其经费来源不明确，改按管理方式进行归类。

Explanatory Notes on Main Statistical Indicators

Registration Status of Enterprises Enterprises are classified into 3 categories, namely domestic-funded enterprises, enterprises with investment from Hong Kong, Macau and Taiwan, and enterprises with foreign investment, according to the registration status of an enterprise in industrial and commercial administration agencies. Domestic-funded enterprises include State- owned enterprises, collective-owned enterprises, cooperative enterprises, joint ownership enterprises, limited liability corporations, share-holding corporations Ltd., private enterprises and other enterprises. Included in the enterprises with investment from Hong Kong, Macau and Taiwan and enterprises with foreign investment are joint-venture enterprises, cooperative enterprises, sole investment enterprises and share-holding corporations Ltd. For government agencies, institutions and social organizations which are not registered in industrial and commercial administration agencies, they are classified mainly by their sources of funding and manner of management.

State–owned Enterprises refer to non-corporation economic units where the entire assets are owned by the State and which have been registered in accordance with the Regulation of the People's Republic of China on the Management of Registration of Corporate Enterprises. Not included from this category are solely State-funded corporations in the limited liability corporations.

Collective–owned Enterprises refer to economic units where the assets are owned collectively and which have been registered in accordance with the Regulation of the People's Republic of China on the Management of Registration of Corporate Enterprises.

Cooperative Enterprises refer to a form of collective economic units (enterprises)where capitals come mainly from employees as their shares, with certain proportion of capital from the outside, where production is organized on the basis of independent operation, independent accounting for profits and losses, joint work, democratic management, and a distribution system that integrates remuneration according to work with dividend according to capital share.

Joint Ownership Enterprises refer to economic units established by two or more corporate enterprises or corporate institutions of the same or different ownership, through joint investment on the basis of voluntary participation, equality, and mutual benefits. They include State joint ownership enterprises; collective joint ownership enterprises; joint State-collective enterprises; and other joint ownership enterprises.

Limited Liability Corporations refer to economic units established with investment from 2-50 investors and registered in accordance with the Regulation of the People's Republic of China on the Management of Registration of Corporations, each investor bearing limited liability to the corporation depending on its share of investment, and the corporation bearing liability to its debt to the maximum of its total assets. Limited liability corporations include solely State-funded limited liability corporations and other limited liability corporations.

Share–holding Corporations Ltd. refer to economic units registered in accordance with the Regulation of the People's Republic of China on the Management of Registration of Corporations, with total registered capital divided into equal shares and raised through issuing stocks. Each investor bears limited liability to the corporation depending on the holding of shares, and the corporation bears liability to its debt to the maximum of its total assets.

Private Enterprises refer to profit-making economic units invested and established by natural persons, or controlled by natural persons using employed labour~ Included in this category are private limited liability corporations, private share-holding corporations Ltd., private partnership enterprises and private-funded enterprises registered in accordance with the Company Law, the Law on Partnership Business and Interim Regulations on Private Enterprises.

Other Domestic–funded Enterprises refer to domestic-funded economic units other than those mentioned above.

Joint Venture Enterprises with Funds from Hong Kong, Macau and Taiwan are enterprises established by investors from Hong Kong, Macau and Taiwan with enterprises in the mainland of China in accordance with the Law of the People's Republic of China on Sino-foreign Equity Joint Ventures and other relevant laws, where the establishment of the investment and the sharing of profits and risks are stipulated under joint venture contracts.

Cooperative Enterprises with Funds from Hong Kong, Macan and Taiwan established by investors from Hong Kong, Macau and Taiwan with enterprises in the mainland of China in accordance with the Law of the People's Republic of China on Sino-foreign Contractual Joint Venture and other relevant laws, where the investment or provision of facilities and the sharing of profits and risks are stipulated under cooperative contracts.

Enterprises with Sole (exclusive)Investment from

Hong Kong, Macau and Taiwan refer to enterprises established in the mainland of China with exclusive investment from investors from Hong Kong, Macau and Taiwan in accordance with the Law of the People's Republic of China on Wholly Foreign-owned Enterprises and other relevant laws.

Share-holding Corporations Ltd. with Investment from Hong Kong, Macau and Taiwan refer to share- holding corporations Ltd. established with the approval from the former Ministry of Foreign Trade and Economic Relations in line with relevant State regulations, where the share of investment from Hong Kong, Macau or Taiwan businessmen exceeds 25% of the total registered capital of the corporation. In case the share of investmentfrom Hong Kong, Macau or Taiwan is less than 25% of thetotal registered capital, the enterprise is to be classified as domestic-funded share-holding corporation Ltd.

Joint Venture Enterprises with Foreign Investment refer to enterprises jointly established byforeign enterprises or foreigners with enterprises in themainland of China in accordance with the Law of thePeople's Republic of China on Sino-foreign Equity JointVentures and other relevant laws, where the sharing ofinvestment, profits and risks is stipulated under contract.

Cooperative Enterprises with Foreign Investment refer to enterprises jointly established by foreign enterprises or foreigners with enterprises in the mainland of China in accordance with the Law of the People's Republic of China on Sino-foreign Contractual Joint Venture and other relevant laws, where the investment or provision of facilities and the sharing of profits and risks are stipulated under cooperative contracts.

Enterprises with Sole (exclusive)Foreign Investment refer to enterprises established in the mainland of China with exclusive investment from foreign investors in accordance with the Law of the People's Republic of China on Wholly Foreign-owned Enterprises and other relevant laws.

Share-holding Corporations Ltd. with Foreign Investment refer to share-holding corporations Ltd. established with the approval from the former Ministry of Foreign Trade and Economic Relations in line with relevant State regulations, where the share of investment from foreign investors exceeds 25% of the total registered capital of the corporation. In case the share of foreign investment is less than 25% ofthe total registered capital, the enterprise is to be classified as domestic-funded share-holding corporation Ltd.

Government Agencies, Institutions and Social Organizations are classified into the following categories by source of funds and manner of management taking reference of thc registration status of enterprises:

(1)Government agencies: include State and party agencies, classified in principle as State-owned. There are exceptions, such as supply and marketing cooperatives which are classified as collective-owned.

(2)Institutions: include institutions of various types established with the approval by organization and staffing departments of the government, but exclude institutions where enterprise management system is introduced. Institutions are further classified as follows:

(a)Institutions for which their main budgets are from government budget appropriations or extra-budget funds, or allocated from the budget of their competent government agencies. Such institutions are classified as state-owned.

(b)Institutions for which their budget mainly come from collective units. Such institutions are classified as collective-owned.

(c)Social institutions established by individual or a group of citizens, which are classified as private.

(d)Institutions other than those mentioned above for which their sources of budget are not clear. Such institutions are classified by the manner of management.

(3)Social organizations: include social organizations established with the approval from the Ministry of Civil Affairs, and organizations that are not covered by social organization management regulations such as trade unions, women's federations etc.. Social organizations are further classified as follows:

(a)Social organizations that are not covered by social organization management regulations of the Ministry of Civil Affairs such as trade unions, women federations, communist youth leagues, youth associations, industrial and commerce associations, scientist associations, overseas Chinese associations, etc., foundations and fund management organizations established with funds from the state, and social organizations whose funds mainly come from the budget of their competent government agencies. Such institutions are classified as State-owned.

(b)Social organizations for which their budget mainly come from collective units. Such institutions are classified as collective-owned.

(c)Social organizations established by individual or a group of citizens, which are classified as private.

(d)Social organizations other than those mentioned above for which their sources of budget are not clear. Such organizations are classified by the manner of management.

3 国民经济核算

NATIONAL ECONOMIC ACCOUNTS

资料整理：刘晓敏　段　斐　张　洁
Data management：Li xiaomin　Duan Fei　Zhang Jie
数据审核：连　鹏
Data audit：Lian Peng

第三部分　国民经济核算

一、简要说明

本章资料包括西安市生产总值、构成和指数，分区县生产总值和指数，非公有制经济增加值及占比等。根据国家统计局的统一要求，2009年—2012年数据为第三次经济普查修订结果，2013年数据为第三次经济普查结果，2014年、2015年、2016年、2017年数据为年报最终核实数据；区县2017年数据为初步核算数；2013年（含）之后三次产业分类依据国家统计局2012年制定的新《三次产业划分规定》；2004年（含）之前人均GDP按户籍人口计算，2005年（含）之后按常住人口计算。资料由西安市统计局国民经济核算处提供。

二、主要指标

生产总值（亿元）	7471.89	比上年增长	7.7%
第一产业	281.12	比上年增长	4.6%
第二产业	2596.52	比上年增长	5.3%
第三产业	4594.25	比上年增长	9.4%
人均生产总值（元/人）	78368	比上年增长	6.0%

3　NATIONAL ECONOMIC ACCOUNTS

Ⅰ.Brief Introduction

The data in this chapter consists of Xi'an GDP, composition, index, and sub-county gross production, index the added value of non-public-owned economics According to the uniform requirements of National Bureau of Statistics date between 2009 to 2012 were amended by the Third Economic Census, of 2013 data was revised by the Third Economic Census, data of 2014 and 2015 and 2016and 2017 was the Annual Report final verification data. The data of the districts and counties in Xi'an in 2017 are preliminary accounting data.Three industrial classification after 2013（included） based on the new "three industrial division rule" for mulated according to National Bureau of Statistics in 2012.per capita GDP was calculated on permanent population after 2005（included）, had been calculated on register population before 2005.Data in this chapter is provided by National Economics Accounting Division of the Xi'an Bureau of Statistics.

Ⅱ.Major Indicators

		Increase over Preceding Year
Gross Domestic Product(100 mil. yuan)	7471.89	7.7%
Primary Industry	281.12	4.6%
Secondary Industry	2596.52	5.3%
Tertiary Industry	4594.25	9.4%
Per Capita Gross Domestic Product (yuan/person)	78368	6.0%

3-1 主要年份生产总值

Gross Domestic Product in Representative Years

(本表按当年价格计算)　　(Data in the table are calculated at current prices)
单位：亿元　　(100 million yuan)

年份 Year	生产总值 Gross Domestic Product	第一产业 Primary Industry	第二产业 Secondary Industry	第三产业 Tertiary Industry	人均生产总值（元/人）Per Capita GDP (yuan/person)
1952	3.37	1.59	0.88	0.90	135
1965	12.76	2.62	7.22	2.92	323
1970	17.76	3.13	10.96	3.67	412
1975	21.33	4.14	12.63	4.56	448
1978	25.35	4.83	14.59	5.93	513
1980	31.66	4.73	18.69	8.24	623
1983	35.89	5.22	20.14	10.53	674
1984	44.14	7.45	24.17	12.52	817
1985	57.58	8.76	30.83	17.99	1049
1986	65.78	9.59	33.86	22.33	1178
1987	80.16	10.73	37.69	31.74	1409
1988	99.22	11.47	46.58	41.17	1711
1989	109.38	12.78	48.91	47.69	1861
1990	116.51	13.94	50.15	52.42	1932
1991	136.14	17.17	57.06	61.91	2224
1992	164.85	18.78	69.22	76.85	2662
1993	229.56	22.58	110.88	96.10	3661
1994	289.82	31.68	128.27	129.87	4563
1995	330.35	41.40	135.33	153.62	5131
1996	406.95	46.94	161.63	198.38	6246
1997	488.82	51.33	197.97	239.52	7424
1998	525.85	51.91	216.32	257.62	7906
1999	577.29	45.53	243.35	288.41	8599
2000	646.13	44.65	277.13	324.35	9484
2001	734.86	45.87	312.90	376.09	10628
2002	826.68	47.77	353.58	425.33	11831
2003	946.66	50.72	407.38	488.56	13341
2004	1102.39	60.21	476.92	565.26	15294
2005	1313.93	66.01	540.50	707.42	16406
2006	1538.94	70.44	645.65	822.85	18890
2007	1856.63	82.51	781.94	992.18	22463
2008	2318.14	103.45	981.58	1233.11	27794
2009	2724.88	110.38	1144.75	1469.75	32420
2010	3242.86	140.06	1357.53	1745.27	38357
2011	3869.84	173.14	1583.21	2113.49	45561
2012	4394.47	195.59	1781.09	2417.79	51499
2013	4924.97	200.45	1998.82	2725.70	57464
2014	5492.64	214.55	2194.78	3083.31	63794
2015	5801.20	220.20	2126.29	3454.71	66938
2016	6282.65	232.01	2200.36	3850.28	71647
2017	7471.89	281.12	2596.52	4594.25	78368

注：1.2004年（含）之前人均GDP按户籍人口计算，2005年（含）之后按常住人口计算。
2.全市2009年—2012年数据为第三次经济普查修订结果，2013年数据为第三次经济普查结果。
3.2013年（含）之后三次产业分类依据国家统计局2012年制定的新《三次产业划分规定》。
4.2017年数据包含研发支出核算改革、西咸新区由西安代管统计范围变化两部分新增GDP，之前年份则不含（下同）。

3-2 主要年份生产总值指数（上年＝100）

Indices of Gross Domestic Product in Representative Years(preceding year = 100)

(本表按可比价格计算)

(Data in the table are calculated at constant prices)

年 份	Year	生产总值 Gross Domestic Product	第一产业 Primary Industry	第二产业 Secondary Industry	第三产业 Tertiary Industry	人均生产总值 Per Capita GDP
1952		103.6	92.2	137.5	123.7	
1965		126.1	134.1	133.0	106.7	
1970		122.0	109.4	140.0	100.1	
1975		103.8	92.6	107.1	107.5	
1978		101.7	101.6	99.4	108.2	
1980		111.5	83.3	119.7	116.5	
1985		112.6	107.5	111.8	116.9	
1986		111.4	107.7	108.4	118.8	
1987		113.6	100.8	109.1	126.6	
1988		111.4	81.2	115.5	114.7	
1989		106.7	103.0	104.5	110.8	
1990		105.2	103.0	102.5	109.6	
1991		109.8	118.6	108.6	108.6	108.2
1992		115.6	109.4	118.1	115.0	114.3
1993		123.9	112.5	142.7	108.4	122.3
1994		110.3	98.4	110.6	113.2	108.8
1995		110.0	104.5	112.1	108.6	108.5
1996		114.9	106.8	118.8	111.7	113.5
1997		114.4	109.1	116.7	112.4	113.2
1998		113.3	106.5	117.5	108.8	112.1
1999		112.2	97.4	115.7	110.1	111.2
2000		113.0	103.5	115.1	111.5	111.4
2001		113.1	102.5	115.3	112.6	111.4
2002		113.3	103.1	115.0	113.0	112.1
2003		113.5	101.8	117.5	111.2	111.7
2004		113.5	106.7	115.9	112.0	111.7
2005		114.0	107.5	112.3	116.3	112.2
2006		114.0	107.1	113.7	114.9	112.9
2007		115.6	104.5	115.7	116.4	113.9
2008		116.3	107.6	116.4	116.9	115.3
2009		114.5	106.3	112.8	116.3	113.7
2010		114.5	106.9	115.2	114.5	113.8
2011		113.5	106.7	112.5	114.9	113.0
2012		112.2	106.0	112.0	112.9	111.7
2013		111.1	104.7	113.6	109.7	110.6
2014		109.9	105.1	109.3	110.7	109.4
2015		108.2	105.0	105.6	110.4	107.5
2016		108.6	103.8	108.5	109.0	107.4
2017		107.7	104.6	105.3	109.4	106.0
平均每年增长	**Yearly Average Growth Rates**					
“一五”时期	**The First Five-Year Plan Period**	**15.8**	**5.9**	**37.7**	**16.9**	
“二五”时期	**The Second Five-Year Plan Period**	**2.0**	**-3.7**	**2.5**	**8.4**	
1963--1965年	**Readjust Period**	**14.2**	**16.1**	**23.4**	**0.3**	
“三五”时期	**The Third Five-Year Plan Period**	**7.1**	**0.1**	**11.7**	**5.4**	
“四五”时期	**The Fourth Five-Year Plan Period**	**5.0**	**4.0**	**5.3**	**5.0**	
“五五”时期	**The Fifth Five-Year Plan Period**	**6.0**	**-0.7**	**6.5**	**10.1**	
“六五”时期	**The Sixth Five-Year Plan Period**	**10.7**	**7.9**	**10.4**	**12.9**	
“七五”时期	**The Seventh Five-Year Plan Period**	**9.6**	**-1.3**	**7.9**	**15.9**	
“八五”时期	**The Eighth Five-Year Plan Period**	**13.8**	**8.5**	**17.8**	**10.7**	**12.3**
“九五”时期	**The Ninth Five-Year Plan Period**	**13.6**	**4.6**	**16.8**	**10.9**	**12.3**
“十五”时期	**The Tenth Five-Year Plan Period**	**13.5**	**4.3**	**15.2**	**13.0**	**11.8**
“十一五”时期	**The Eleventh Five-Year Plan Period**	**15.0**	**6.5**	**14.8**	**15.8**	**13.9**
“十二五”时期	**The Twelve Five-Year Plan Period**	**11.0**	**5.5**	**10.6**	**11.7**	**10.4**

3–3 主要年份生产总值指数（1952年=100）

Indices of Gross Domestic Product in Representative Years(1952= 100)

(本表按可比价格计算) (Data in the table are calculated at constant prices)

年份 Year	生产总值 Gross Domestic Product	第一产业 Primary Industry	第二产业 Secondary Industry	第三产业 Tertiary Industry
1952	100.0	100.0	100.0	100.0
1965	341.6	173.3	1048.3	329.2
1970	481.6	174.3	1821.0	428.6
1975	614.2	211.9	2362.5	547.9
1978	678.7	231.3	2560.8	643.8
1980	821.4	204.2	3237.2	885.2
1983	988.4	222.5	3846.2	1154.4
1984	1213.6	278.2	4748.8	1388.7
1985	1366.8	299.1	5310.6	1632.4
1986	1523.1	322.3	5756.7	1928.9
1987	1730.0	324.9	6280.6	2441.6
1988	1926.3	263.7	7256.6	2801.2
1989	2054.8	271.6	7583.1	3104.6
1990	2162.5	279.7	7772.7	3403.6
1991	2374.4	331.7	8441.2	3696.3
1992	2744.8	362.9	9969.1	4250.7
1993	3400.8	408.2	14225.9	4607.8
1994	3751.1	401.8	15733.8	5216.0
1995	4126.2	419.9	17637.6	5664.6
1996	4741.0	448.5	20953.5	6327.4
1997	5423.7	489.3	24452.7	7112.0
1998	6145.1	521.1	28731.9	7737.9
1999	6894.8	507.6	33242.8	8519.4
2000	7791.1	525.4	38262.5	9499.1
2001	8811.7	538.5	44116.7	10696.0
2002	9983.7	555.2	50734.2	12086.5
2003	11331.5	565.2	59612.7	13440.2
2004	12861.3	603.1	69091.1	15053.0
2005	14661.9	648.3	77589.3	17506.6
2006	16714.6	694.3	88219.0	20115.1
2007	19322.1	725.5	102069.4	23414.0
2008	22471.6	780.6	118808.8	27371.0
2009	25730.0	829.8	134016.3	31832.5
2010	29460.8	887.0	154386.8	36448.2
2011	33438.0	946.5	173685.2	41879.0
2012	37517.5	1003.3	194527.4	47281.3
2013	41681.9	1050.4	220983.1	51867.6
2014	45808.4	1104.0	241534.5	57417.5
2015	49580.4	1158.8	255076.2	63393.7
2016	53863.1	1202.3	276727.1	69125.3
2017	57999.0	1257.7	291436.6	75632.5

3-4 主要年份生产总值构成

Composition of Gross Domestic Product in Representative Years

(本表按当年价格计算)　　　　(Data in the table are calculated at current prices)

单位:%　　　　(%)

年份	Year	生产总值 Gross Domestic Product	第一产业 Primary Industry	第二产业 Secondary Industry	第三产业 Tertiary Industry
1952		100	47.18	26.11	26.71
1965		100	20.53	56.58	22.89
1970		100	17.62	61.71	20.67
1975		100	19.41	59.21	21.38
1978		100	19.05	57.55	23.40
1980		100	14.94	59.03	26.03
1985		100	15.21	53.54	31.25
1986		100	14.58	51.47	33.95
1987		100	13.39	47.02	39.59
1988		100	11.56	46.95	41.49
1989		100	11.68	44.72	43.60
1990		100	11.96	43.04	45.00
1991		100	12.61	41.91	45.48
1992		100	11.39	41.99	46.62
1993		100	9.84	48.30	41.86
1994		100	10.93	44.26	44.81
1995		100	12.53	40.97	46.50
1996		100	11.53	39.72	48.75
1997		100	10.50	40.50	49.00
1998		100	9.87	41.14	48.99
1999		100	7.89	42.15	49.96
2000		100	6.91	42.89	50.20
2001		100	6.24	42.58	51.18
2002		100	5.78	42.77	51.45
2003		100	5.36	43.03	51.61
2004		100	5.46	43.26	51.28
2005		100	5.02	41.14	53.84
2006		100	4.58	41.95	53.47
2007		100	4.44	42.12	53.44
2008		100	4.46	42.34	53.20
2009		100	4.05	42.01	53.94
2010		100	4.32	41.86	53.82
2011		100	4.47	40.91	54.62
2012		100	4.45	40.53	55.02
2013		100	4.07	40.59	55.34
2014		100	3.91	39.96	56.13
2015		100	3.80	36.65	59.55
2016		100	3.69	35.02	61.29
2017		100	3.76	34.75	61.49
"一五"时期	**The First Five-Year Plan Period**	**100**	**32.88**	**43.92**	**23.20**
"二五"时期	**The Second Five-Year Period**	**100**	**18.08**	**58.63**	**23.29**
1963--1965年	**Readjust Period**	**100**	**19.36**	**55.38**	**25.26**
"三五"时期	**The Third Five-Year Plan Period**	**100**	**18.60**	**57.33**	**24.07**
"四五"时期	**The Fourth Five-Year Plan Period**	**100**	**20.46**	**59.59**	**19.95**
"五五"时期	**The Fifth Five-Year Plan Period**	**100**	**18.41**	**57.69**	**23.90**
"六五"时期	**The Sixth Five-Year Plan Period**	**100**	**16.03**	**55.01**	**28.96**
"七五"时期	**The Seventh Five-Year Plan Period**	**100**	**12.42**	**46.11**	**41.47**
"八五"时期	**The Eighth Five-Year Plan Period**	**100**	**11.44**	**43.52**	**45.04**
"九五"时期	**The Ninth Five-Year Plan Period**	**100**	**9.09**	**41.45**	**49.46**
"十五"时期	**The Tenth Five-Year Plan Period**	**100**	**5.49**	**42.47**	**52.04**
"十一五"时期	**The Eleventh Five-Year Plan Period**	**100**	**4.34**	**42.04**	**53.62**
"十二五"时期	**The Twelve Five-Year Plan Period**	**100**	**4.10**	**39.55**	**56.35**

3-5 主要年份分行业增加值

The Value added by Industry in Representative Years

单位：亿元 （100 million yuan）

年份 Year	地区生产总值 Gross Domestic Product	农、林、牧、渔业 Farming Forestry Animal Husbandry Fishery	工业 Industry	建筑业 Construction	批发和零售业 Wholesale and Retail Trades
1992	164.85	18.78	61.33	7.89	18.16
1993	229.56	22.58	98.88	12.00	22.63
1994	289.82	31.68	110.52	17.75	27.83
1995	330.35	41.40	112.50	22.83	33.20
1996	406.95	46.94	132.52	29.11	44.51
1997	488.82	51.33	161.97	36.00	59.31
1998	525.85	51.91	175.00	41.32	64.93
1999	577.29	45.53	194.00	49.35	70.27
2000	646.13	44.65	218.44	58.69	65.87
2001	734.86	45.87	246.90	66.00	78.38
2002	826.68	47.77	280.20	73.38	91.57
2003	946.66	50.72	324.88	82.50	106.82
2004	1102.39	60.21	383.46	93.46	125.12
2005	1313.93	66.01	420.00	120.50	147.20
2006	1538.94	70.44	494.22	151.43	166.72
2007	1856.63	82.51	594.95	186.99	195.51
2008	2318.14	103.45	721.40	260.18	242.91
2009	2724.88	110.38	816.92	327.83	298.29
2010	3242.86	140.06	954.38	403.15	352.37
2011	3869.84	173.14	1098.51	484.70	439.75
2012	4394.47	195.59	1228.05	553.04	512.96
2013	4924.97	217.76	1376.74	642.26	575.72
2014	5492.64	233.61	1488.02	728.74	633.65
2015	5801.20	241.69	1376.72	770.29	667.99
2016	6282.65	256.38	1397.25	818.82	702.30
2017	7471.89	312.46	1684.02	928.30	771.04

注：1999年（含）之前，批发和零售业与住宿和餐饮业无法分类，故1999年（含）之前批发和零售业数据为批发和零售业与住宿和餐饮业合计数。

3-5 续表 continued

单位：亿元 (100 million yuan)

年 份 Year	交通运输、仓储和邮政业 Transport, Storage and Post	住宿和餐饮业 Accommodation and Catering Trade	金融业 Financial Intermediation	房地产业 Real Estate	其他服务业 Others Services
1992	15.21		16.28	1.58	25.62
1993	18.01		20.59	1.97	32.90
1994	22.02		31.19	3.76	45.07
1995	24.60		35.20	4.90	55.72
1996	32.73		40.15	7.42	73.57
1997	43.02		37.50	8.74	90.95
1998	48.64		32.95	11.95	99.15
1999	55.35		30.37	14.42	118.00
2000	43.01	18.46	33.00	16.96	147.05
2001	45.50	21.97	36.21	21.38	172.65
2002	48.25	25.27	43.48	26.90	189.86
2003	51.37	29.41	50.76	32.42	217.78
2004	55.10	35.89	61.49	39.05	248.61
2005	66.30	50.44	75.00	52.48	316.00
2006	74.08	52.23	96.50	62.32	371.00
2007	84.21	70.09	128.50	75.26	438.61
2008	99.16	85.65	160.84	92.97	551.58
2009	112.02	93.82	197.87	128.18	639.57
2010	135.70	102.80	236.36	186.42	731.62
2011	165.18	118.02	294.44	235.20	860.90
2012	192.46	129.58	359.63	260.53	962.63
2013	215.11	135.58	429.51	292.41	1039.88
2014	235.58	144.15	534.00	326.10	1168.79
2015	260.33	159.14	658.90	398.34	1267.80
2016	298.52	170.67	724.35	459.20	1455.16
2017	334.02	188.18	800.94	550.35	1902.58

3-6 主要年份分行业增加值指数（上年＝100）

Indices of the Value added by Industry in Representative Years（preceding year＝100）

(本表按可比价格计算) (Data in the table are calculated at constant prices)

年 份 Year	地区生产总值 Gross Domestic Product	农、林、牧、渔业 Farming Forestry Animal Husbandry Fishery	工业 Industry	建筑业 Construction	批发和零售业 Wholesale and Retail Trades
1992	115.6	109.4	118.1	118.2	130.7
1993	123.9	112.5	143.7	135.6	108.0
1994	110.3	98.4	106.8	141.3	103.1
1995	110.0	104.5	108.1	136.6	109.6
1996	114.9	106.8	117.1	126.8	116.0
1997	114.4	109.1	116.4	117.8	124.0
1998	113.3	106.5	116.1	123.4	110.7
1999	112.2	97.4	114.0	122.8	106.4
2000	113.0	103.5	113.8	120.1	111.4
2001	113.1	102.5	116.3	111.8	110.5
2002	113.3	103.1	116.4	109.3	115.3
2003	113.5	101.8	115.7	125.0	110.8
2004	113.5	106.7	115.5	117.3	109.1
2005	114.0	107.5	110.3	120.0	112.7
2006	114.0	107.1	112.3	118.7	112.5
2007	115.6	104.5	114.9	118.4	112.9
2008	116.3	107.6	115.7	118.9	115.0
2009	114.5	106.3	110.1	121.2	121.8
2010	114.5	106.9	114.3	117.6	115.0
2011	113.5	106.7	112.8	111.7	119.5
2012	112.2	106.0	112.7	110.3	114.0
2013	111.1	104.8	114.0	113.9	110.4
2014	109.9	105.1	108.4	110.9	109.3
2015	108.2	105.1	104.8	107.4	105.6
2016	108.6	104.0	109.2	106.5	104.8
2017	107.7	104.7	105.8	104.2	105.6

注：1999年（含）之前，批发和零售业与住宿和餐饮业无法分类，故1999年（含）之前批发和零售业数据为批发和零售业与住宿和餐饮业合计数。

3-6 续表 continued

(本表按可比价格计算) (Data in the table are calculated at constant prices)

年 份 Year	交通运输、仓储和邮政业 Transport, Storage and Post	住宿和餐饮业 Accommodation and Catering Trade	金融业 Financial Intermediation	房地产业 Real Estate	其他服务业 Others Services
1992	111.3		107.6	119.5	112.2
1993	102.7		109.7	107.4	111.4
1994	102.5		126.9	160.7	114.8
1995	102.6		103.7	119.7	113.6
1996	115.1		98.7	130.8	114.2
1997	122.4		87.0	109.6	115.1
1998	114.4		88.8	138.3	110.3
1999	111.9		90.6	118.6	117.0
2000	111.7	111.7	107.7	116.6	111.7
2001	111.6	114.2	103.6	123.5	114.2
2002	106.1	116.5	104.6	106.0	116.5
2003	113.6	111.6	107.4	108.8	111.6
2004	115.6	112.9	107.1	110.3	112.9
2005	113.2	136.1	109.3	112.9	117.7
2006	112.3	116.6	107.3	117.5	117.7
2007	110.3	117.3	126.7	119.7	116.3
2008	108.4	111.6	113.6	107.6	122.5
2009	111.0	106.6	123.7	130.8	112.5
2010	119.4	106.6	116.1	128.1	111.9
2011	115.7	108.5	117.9	113.5	112.9
2012	112.6	105.4	124.8	108.8	110.4
2013	108.2	100.7	119.0	111.9	106.1
2014	106.2	102.0	121.1	107.7	110.2
2015	111.3	109.2	119.3	107.9	109.7
2016	109.5	105.7	109.3	113.1	110.7
2017	107.4	105.4	105.7	109.6	113.8

3-7 主要年份三次产业贡献率

Three Industries Contribution Rate in Representative Years

(本表按可比价格计算) (Data in the table are calculated at constant prices)

年 份 Year	生产总值 Gross Domestic Product	第一产业 Primary Industry	第二产业 Secondary Industry	第三产业 Tertiary Industry
2000	100	1.8	66.9	31.3
2001	100	1.3	50.4	48.3
2002	100	1.5	49.4	49.1
2003	100	0.8	57.7	41.5
2004	100	2.5	54.1	43.4
2005	100	2.6	41.3	56.1
2006	100	2.5	40.2	57.3
2007	100	1.4	41.4	57.2
2008	100	2.0	41.4	56.6
2009	100	1.7	36.5	61.8
2010	100	1.7	42.5	55.8
2011	100	2.1	38.5	59.4
2012	100	2.0	40.7	57.3
2013	100	1.5	50.3	48.2
2014	100	1.7	39.3	59.0
2015	100	1.9	28.4	69.7
2016	100	1.7	36.0	62.3
2017	100	2.4	26.1	71.5

3-8 主要年份三次产业拉动率

Three Industries Pulling Rate in Representative Years

(本表按可比价格计算) (Data in the table are calculated at constant prices)

年 份 Year	生产总值 Gross Domestic Product	第一产业 Primary Industry	第二产业 Secondary Industry	第三产业 Tertiary Industry
2000	13.0	0.2	8.7	4.1
2001	13.1	0.2	6.6	6.3
2002	13.3	0.2	6.6	6.5
2003	13.5	0.1	7.8	5.6
2004	13.5	0.3	7.3	5.9
2005	14.0	0.4	5.8	7.8
2006	14.0	0.4	5.7	7.9
2007	15.6	0.2	6.4	9.0
2008	16.3	0.3	6.8	9.2
2009	14.5	0.2	5.3	9.0
2010	14.5	0.3	6.2	8.0
2011	13.5	0.3	5.2	8.0
2012	12.2	0.2	5.0	7.0
2013	11.1	0.2	5.6	5.3
2014	9.9	0.2	3.9	5.8
2015	8.2	0.2	2.3	5.7
2016	8.6	0.1	3.1	5.4
2017	7.7	0.2	2.0	5.5

3-9 分行业增加值

Value added by Industry

单位：亿元 (100 million yuan)

指　标	Item	增加值 Value Added		指数（上年=100） Index	
		2016	2017	2016	2017
地区生产总值	**Gross Domestic Product**	**6282.65**	**7471.89**	**108.6**	**107.7**
农、林、牧、渔业	Farming Forestry Animal Husbandry Fishery	**256.38**	**312.46**	**104.0**	**104.7**
工业	Industry	1397.25	1684.02	109.2	105.8
建筑业	Construction	818.82	928.30	106.5	104.2
批发和零售业	Wholesale and Retail Trades	702.30	771.04	104.8	105.6
交通运输、仓储和邮政业	Transport, Storage and Post	298.52	334.02	109.5	107.4
住宿和餐饮业	Accommodation and Catering Trade	170.67	188.18	105.7	105.4
金融业	Financial Intermediation	724.35	800.94	109.3	105.7
房地产业	Real Estate	459.20	550.35	113.1	109.6
其他服务业	Others Services	1455.16	1902.58	110.7	113.8
第一产业	Primary Industry	232.01	281.12	103.8	104.6
第二产业	Secondary Industry	2200.36	2596.52	108.5	105.3
第三产业	Tertiary Industry	3850.28	4594.25	109.0	109.4

3-10 各区县生产总值（2017年）

Gross Domestic Product by Region（2017）

单位：亿元　　　　（100 million yuan）

指　标	Item	生产总值 Gross Domestic Product	第一产业 Primary Industry	第二产业 Secondary Industry	第三产业 Tertiary Industry	人均生产总值（元）Per Capita GDP（yuan）
全　市	**Total**	**7471.89**	**281.12**	**2596.52**	**4594.25**	**78368**
新城区	Xincheng	616.10		216.83	399.27	100203
碑林区	Beilin	873.49		179.21	694.28	135372
莲湖区	Lianhu	749.47		239.80	509.67	102737
灞桥区	Baqiao	428.35	21.82	140.22	266.31	67568
未央区	Weiyang	844.53	0.66	405.79	438.08	122104
雁塔区	Yanta	1521.15		331.31	1189.84	122377
阎良区	Yanliang	240.21	24.24	117.58	98.39	82053
临潼区	Lintong	221.01	31.45	66.76	122.80	32224
长安区	Chang'an	791.03	33.95	401.86	355.22	79095
高陵区	Gaoling	377.10	32.62	250.13	94.35	106510
鄠邑区	Huyi	197.41	27.74	82.72	86.95	36139
蓝田县	Lantian	143.49	30.15	39.10	74.24	27043
周至县	Zhouzhi	134.26	33.91	29.15	71.20	22864

注：本表区县数据为初步核算数。

3-11 各区县生产总值指数（2017年）（上年＝100）

Indices of Gross Domestic Product by Region（2017）（preceding year = 100）

(本表按可比价格计算) (Data in the table are calculated at constant prices)

指 标	Item	生产总值 Gross Domestic Product	第一产业 Primary Industry	第二产业 Secondary Industry	第三产业 Tertiary Industry	人均生产总值 Per Capita GDP
全 市	**Total**	**107.7**	**104.6**	**105.3**	**109.4**	**106.0**
新城区	Xincheng	108.2		112.5	106.0	106.7
碑林区	Beilin	108.4		110.7	107.8	106.5
莲湖区	Lianhu	109.1		112.3	107.7	107.3
灞桥区	Baqiao	113.8	104.3	114.3	114.3	111.4
未央区	Weiyang	109.2	85.7	110.6	107.9	106.5
雁塔区	Yanta	108.5		100.6	111.5	106.5
阎良区	Yanliang	107.0	105.1	106.0	108.7	105.8
临潼区	Lintong	109.6	104.7	107.5	112.7	108.5
长安区	Chang'an	111.7	104.3	117.4	106.8	109.6
高陵区	Gaoling	115.6	104.2	115.4	120.7	114.1
鄠邑区	Huyi	110.1	105.1	114.9	107.9	109.1
蓝田县	Lantian	108.5	105.9	109.1	109.3	107.8
周至县	Zhouzhi	107.9	104.4	109.1	109.2	107.1

注：本表区县数据为初步核算数。

3-12 主要年份非公有制经济增加值

The Added Value of Non-public-owned Economic in Representative Years

年 份 Year	非公有制经济增加值（亿元） the Added Value of Non-public-owned Economic (100 million yuan)	第一产业 Primary Industry	第二产业 Secondary Industry	第三产业 Tertiary Industry
2005	568.45	20.86	232.66	314.93
2006	684.66	26.27	279.06	379.33
2007	854.26	25.25	365.24	463.77
2008	1103.96	36.42	468.58	598.96
2009	1327.87	36.32	535.02	756.53
2010	1611.71	42.66	636.73	932.32
2011	1956.41	52.93	761.31	1142.17
2012	2258.95	59.79	831.93	1367.23
2013	2569.20	53.72	970.24	1545.24
2014	2892.90	57.40	1079.59	1755.91
2015	3060.38	58.09	1060.92	1941.37
2016	3314.20	61.42	1071.54	2181.24
2017	3962.95	67.89	1322.16	2572.90

3-12 续表 continued

年 份 Year	非公有制经济增加值占GDP比重(%) the Added Value of Non-public-owned Economic Percentage to GDP(%)	第一产业 Primary Industry	第二产业 Secondary Industry	第三产业 Tertiary Industry
2005	43.3	31.6	43.1	44.5
2006	44.5	37.3	43.2	46.0
2007	46.0	30.6	46.7	46.7
2008	47.6	35.2	47.7	48.6
2009	48.7	32.9	46.7	51.5
2010	49.7	30.5	46.9	53.4
2011	50.6	30.6	48.1	54.0
2012	51.4	30.6	46.7	56.6
2013	52.2	26.8	48.5	56.7
2014	52.7	26.8	49.2	56.9
2015	52.8	26.4	49.9	56.2
2016	52.8	26.5	48.7	56.7
2017	53.0	24.1	50.9	56.0

注：1、2009年—2012年数据根据第三次经济普查GDP修订结果相应进行了调整。
2、2013年—2017年数据为年报最终核实数据。

主要统计指标解释

生产总值（GDP） 是按市场价格计算的一个地区（或国家）所有常住单位在一定时期内生产活动的最终成果。生产总值有三种表现形态，即价值形态、收入形态和产品形态。从价值形态看，它是所有常住单位在一定时期内生产的全部货物和服务价值超过同期中间投入的全部非固定资产货物和服务价值的差额，即所有常住单位的增加值之和；从收入形态看，它是所有常住单位在一定时期内创造并分配给常住单位和非常住单位的初次收入分配之和；从产品形态看，它是所有常住单位在一定时期内最终使用的货物和服务价值与货物和服务净出口价值之和。在实际核算中，生产总值有三种计算方法，即生产法、收入法和支出法。三种方法分别从不同的方面反映生产总值及其构成。

人均生产总值 即"人均GDP"，常作为发展经济学中衡量经济发展状况的指标，是最重要的宏观经济指标之一，它是人们了解和把握一个国家或地区的宏观经济运行状况的有效工具。将一个国家核算期内（通常是一年）实现的国内生产总值与这个国家的常住人口（或户籍人口）相比进行计算，得到人均生产总值。

三次产业 指根据社会生产活动历史发展的顺序对产业结构的划分。目前我国的三次产业划分是：

第一产业是指农、林、牧、渔业（不含农、林、牧、渔服务业）。

第二产业是指采矿业（不含开采辅助活动），制造业（不含金属制品、机械和设备修理业），电力、热力、燃气及水生产和供应业，建筑业。

第三产业即服务业，是指除第一产业、第二产业以外的其他行业。

劳动者报酬 指劳动者因从事生产活动所获得的全部报酬。包括劳动者获得的各种形式的工资、奖金和津贴，既包括货币形式的，也包括实物形式的，还包括劳动者所享受的公费医疗和医药卫生费、上下班交通补贴、单位支付的社会保险费、住房公积金等。

生产税净额 指生产税减生产补贴后的余额。生产税指政府对生产单位从事生产、销售和经营活动以及因从事生产活动使用某些生产要素（如固定资产、土地、劳动力）所征收的各种税、附加费和规费。生产补贴与生产税相反，指政府对生产单位的单方面转移支出，因此视为负生产税，包括政策亏损补贴、价格补贴等。

固定资产折旧 指一定时期内为弥补固定资产损耗按照规定的固定资产折旧率提取的固定资产折旧，或按国民经济核算统一规定的折旧率虚拟计算的固定资产折旧。它反映了固定资产年当期生产中的转移价值。各类企业和企业化管理的事业单位的固定资产折旧是指实际计提的折旧费；不计提折旧的政府机关、非企业化管理的事业单位和居民住房的固定资产折旧是按照统一规定的折旧率和固定资产原值计算的虚拟折旧。原则上，固定资产折旧应按固定资产当期的重置价值计算，但是目前我国尚不具备对全社会固定资产进行重估价的基础，所以暂时只能采用上述办法。

营业盈余 指常住单位创造的增加值扣除劳动者报酬、生产税净额和固定资产折旧后的余额。它相当于企业的营业利润加上生产补贴，但要扣除从利润中开支的工资和福利等。

三次产业贡献率 各产业不变价增加值增量与不变价GDP增量之比。

三次产业拉动率 GDP增长速度与各产业贡献率之乘积。

非公有制经济 非公有制经济是指国民经济中除国有经济和集体经济以外的部分，对其中的混合制经济要依据实收资本之间的比例，按经济成分对各主要经济总量进行划分。

Explanatory Notes on Main Statistical Indicators

Gross Domestic Product (GDP) refers to the final products at market prices produced by all resident units in a country (or a region) during a certain period of time. Gross domestic product is expressed in three different perspectives, namely value, income, and products respectively. GDP in its value perspective refers to the total value of all goods and services produced by all resident units during a certain period of time, minus the total value of input of goods and services of the nature of non-fixed assets; in other words, it is the sum of the value-added of all resident units. GDP from the perspective of income includes the primary income created by all resident units and distributed to resident and non-resident units. GDP from the perspective of products refers to the value of all goods and services for final demand by all resident units plus the net exports of goods and services during a given period of time. In the practice of national accounting, gross domestic product is calculated from three approaches, namely production approach, income approach and expenditure approach, which reflect gross domestic product and its composition from different angles.For a region, it is called as Gross Regional Product (GRP) or regional GDP.

Per capita gross domestic product: "per capita GDP", often used as a measure of economic development in development economics, it is one of the most important macroeconomic indicators, and people's understanding and grasp of a country or a region effective tool of macroeconomic performance. The gross domestic product (GDP) of a country's accounting period (usually one year) is divided by the country's resident population (or household population), resulting in per capita GDP.

Three Strata of Industry Classification of economic activities into three strata of industry is a common practice in the world, although the grouping varies to some extent from country to country. In China economic activities are categorized into the following three strata of industry:

Primary industry refers to agriculture, forestry, animal husbandry and fishery and services in support of these industries.

Secondary industry refers to mining and quarrying, manufacturing, production and supply of electricity, water and gas, and construction.

Tertiary industry refers to all other economic activities not included in the primary or secondary industries.

Compensation of Employees refers to the total payment of various forms to employees for the productive activities they are engaged in. It includes wages, bonuses and allowances, which the employees earn in cash or in kind. It also includes the free medical services provided to the employees and the medicine expenses, transport subsidies and social insurance, and housing fund paid by the employers.

Net Taxes on Production refers to taxes on production less subsidies on production. The taxes on production refers to the various taxes, extra charges and fees levied on the production units on their production, sale and business activities as well as on the use of some factors of production, such as fixed assets, land and labour in the production activities they are engaged in. In contrast to taxes on production, subsidies on production refer to the unilateral government transfer to the production units and are therefore regarded as negative taxes on production. They include subsidies on the loss due to implementation of government policies, price subsidies, etc.

Depreciation of Fixed Assets refers to the depreciation of fixed assets in a given period, drawn in accordance with the stipulated depreciation rate for the purpose of compensating the wear-and-tear loss of the fixed assets or the depreciation of fixed assets imputed in accordance with the stipulated unified depreciation rate in the national economic accounting system. It reflects the value of transfer of the fixed assets in the production of the current period. The depreciation of fixed assets in various enterprises and institutions managed as enterprises refers to the depreciation expenses actually drawn. In government agencies and institutions not managed as enterprises which do not draw the depreciation expenses, as well as for the houses of residents, the depreciation of fixed assets is the imputed depreciation, which is calculated in accordance with the stipulated unified depreciation rate. In principle, the depreciation of fixed assets should be calculated on the basis of the re-purchased value of the fixed assets. However, currently the conditions in China do not facilitate the revaluation of all the fixed assets. Therefore, only the above-mentioned methods can be adopted at present.

Operating Surplus refers to the balance of the value added created by the resident units after deducting the labourers remuneration, net taxes on production and the depreciation of fixed assets. It is equivalent to the business profit of the enterprises plus subsidies to production, but the wages and welfare expenses paid from the profits should be deducted.

Three Industry Contribution Rate The ratio of all industries incremental value added to GDP increment at constant prices.

Three Industries Pulling Rate The product of GDP growth rate and the contribution rate of each industry.

Non-public Economy It refers to the part of in addition to state-owned economy and collective economy in the national economy,On which the mixed-economy should be divided according to the major economic components of total economic output based on the proportion in paid-in capital.

4 人口、从业人员与职工工资

POPULATION,EMPLOYMENT AND WAGES

资料整理：王义龙　安海军　张　叶
Data management：Wang Yilong An Haijun Zhang ye
数据审核：冯军魁
Data audit：Feng Junkui

第四部分　人口、从业人员与职工工资

一、简要说明

本章资料包括主要年份人口、分区县户籍和常住人口及变动、从业人员及劳动报酬等。户籍人口数为公安年报数，1991年以前年份市区数未包括临潼、长安。主要数据由西安市统计局人口就业处提供。

二、主要指标

年末户籍人口（万人）	845.09	比上年增长	2.4%
人口自然增长率（‰）	7.20	比上年上升	1.06个千分点
常住人口（万人）	961.67	比上年增长	1.7%
男女性别比（以女性为100）	105.40	比上年下降	0.1个百分点
户籍人口密度（人／平方公里）	837	比上年增加	20人/平方公里
城镇非私营单位在岗职工年平均工资（元）	77774	比上年增长	11.7%

4　POPULATION,EMPLOYMENT AND WAGES

Ⅰ.Brief Introduction

This chapter consists of the data about registered population and permanent resident population in representative years population of all the districts and counties and the correspondent changes, the employed and their wages. The registered population data are from the annual report of the Xi'an Bureau of Public Security, with Lintong, Chang'an not included before 1991. The population data is provided primarily by Population & Employment Office of the Xi'an Bureau of Statistics.

Ⅱ.Major Indicators

		Increase over Preceding Year
Total registered Population of Year-end(10 000 persons)	845.09	2.4%
Natural Growth Rate(‰)	7.20	1.06per thousand
Permanent Population(10 000 persons)	961.67	1.7%
Sex Ratio (Female=100)	105.40	-0.1percentage points
Density of Population (person/sq.km)	837	20 person/sq.km
Annual Average Wage of Staff and Workers in Urban Non-privite Enterprises(yuan)	77774	11.7%

4-1 主要年份人口数、人口密度和人口发展情况

Population, Population Density and Population Development in Representative Years

单位：万人 (10 000 persons)

年份 Year	总人口 Total Population	市区 Urban Area	女性人口 Number of Female	城填人口 Urban Population	人口密度（人/平方公里） Density of Population (person/sq.km)	总人口指数（上年为100） Total Population Index (100 for preceding year) 全市 Whole City	市区 Urban Area
1952	252.92	92.42	118.81	57.61	254	102.6	103.1
1965	400.05	179.88	190.72	136.39	401	102.5	103.4
1970	435.12	188.12	210.47	139.12	436	101.9	101.4
1978	498.10	210.15	241.82	159.98	499	101.7	102.7
1980	511.91	221.19	249.26	172.85	513	101.4	102.6
1985	553.11	245.76	268.40	201.90	554	101.6	102.2
1986	563.97	251.80	273.30	205.92	565	102.0	102.5
1987	574.46	257.69	278.12	210.25	575	101.9	102.3
1988	585.85	264.94	283.68	216.99	587	102.0	102.8
1989	597.36	270.80	289.44	222.54	598	102.0	102.2
1990	608.89	275.69	295.29	226.98	610	101.9	101.8
1991	615.48	419.29	298.13	230.85	617	101.1	152.1
1992	623.20	429.54	301.92	236.45	624	101.3	102.4
1993	630.91	435.41	305.30	240.85	632	101.2	101.4
1994	639.45	442.30	309.17	248.35	641	101.4	101.6
1995	648.21	448.65	313.46	255.71	645	101.4	101.4
1996	654.87	454.68	316.60	261.28	653	101.0	101.3
1997	662.06	461.17	320.18	267.52	663	101.1	101.4
1998	668.22	466.31	323.20	271.75	669	100.9	101.1
1999	674.50	463.56	326.12	276.14	676	100.9	99.4
2000	688.01	483.10	332.83	285.79	689	102.0	104.2
2001	694.84	489.88	336.04	292.62	696	101.0	101.4
2002	702.59	497.38	339.51	300.05	704	101.1	101.5
2003	716.58	510.26	346.26	312.88	718	102.0	102.6
2004	725.01	516.30	350.85	318.50	717	101.2	101.2
2005	741.73	533.21	359.71	333.14	734	102.3	103.3
2006	753.11	540.97	365.74	343.78	745	101.5	101.5
2007	764.25	549.19	371.84	353.85	756	101.5	101.5
2008	772.30	554.73	376.76	363.87	764	101.1	101.0
2009	781.67	561.58	382.39	370.66	773	101.2	101.2
2010	782.73	562.65	383.93	374.64	774	100.1	100.2
2011	791.83	568.77	389.31	391.31	783	101.2	101.1
2012	795.98	572.76	392.04	398.40	788	100.5	100.7
2013	806.93	580.60	398.15	409.82	799	101.4	101.4
2014	815.29	587.16	402.83	418.16	807	101.0	101.1
2015	815.66	588.43	403.43	545.95	808	100.0	100.2
2016	824.93	629.24	408.39	552.21	817	101.1	106.9
2017	845.09	649.08	420.11	567.26	837	102.4	103.2

注：本表为公安年报数据,系户籍人口。2016年起公安年报调整至11月30日，市区数1991年增加临潼、长安，2016年增加高陵，行政区划面积自2012年发生变更，调整了2012年和2013年户籍人口密度。2015年公安局户籍改革，按统计上城乡划分标准统计城镇与乡村人口。2017年公安年报数为原西安口径数据。

4-2 主要年份人口自然变动情况

Natural Population Movements in Representative Years

单位：万人 (10 000 persons)

年份 Year	出生 Birth 人数 Population	出生率（‰） Birth Rate (‰)	死亡 Death 人数 Population	死亡率（‰） Death Rate (‰)	自然增长率（‰） Natural Growth Rate (‰)	迁入人口 Immigrant Population	迁出人口 Emigrant Population
1985	8.95	16.30	3.01	5.48	10.82	11.60	8.74
1986	10.14	18.15	2.78	4.97	13.18	11.79	8.39
1987	9.76	17.14	2.83	4.97	12.17	12.58	9.26
1988	9.42	16.24	2.89	4.98	11.26	13.54	8.97
1989	11.78	19.92	3.04	5.13	14.79	12.73	10.15
1990	12.40	20.55	3.45	5.72	14.83	11.82	9.86
1991	8.73	14.25	3.26	5.33	8.92	8.98	6.09
1992	8.98	14.49	3.39	5.48	9.01	13.94	9.54
1993	9.25	14.75	3.37	5.38	9.37	11.50	8.33
1994	8.08	12.71	3.16	4.97	7.74	13.40	8.59
1995	7.69	11.95	3.21	4.98	6.97	14.41	8.85
1996	7.26	11.15	3.41	5.24	5.91	11.94	8.88
1997	6.84	10.38	3.12	4.75	5.63	12.58	8.62
1998	6.40	9.62	3.10	4.66	4.96	10.89	8.36
1999	6.19	9.22	3.88	5.78	3.44	12.58	9.23
2000	8.90	13.07	4.06	5.96	7.11	17.12	9.23
2001	5.11	7.39	2.89	4.19	3.20	15.16	10.83
2002	5.34	7.64	3.08	4.41	3.23	13.90	9.41
2003	6.02	8.48	3.32	4.68	3.80	20.60	9.15
2004	6.63	9.19	4.23	5.87	3.32	15.56	10.19
2005	7.67	9.58	4.13	5.16	4.42	22.61	9.46
2006	8.13	9.98	4.45	5.46	4.52	17.23	11.75
2007	8.27	10.00	4.53	5.48	4.52	19.90	14.01
2008	8.47	10.15	4.65	5.57	4.58	18.49	15.04
2009	8.47	10.08	4.73	5.63	4.45	16.84	13.14
2010	8.23	9.73	4.51	5.34	4.39	14.09	13.50
2011	8.25	9.71	4.57	5.38	4.33	14.21	11.74
2012	8.64	10.13	4.75	5.57	4.56	12.55	13.10
2013	8.20	9.57	4.60	5.37	4.20	10.83	8.60
2014	8.70	10.11	4.71	5.47	4.64	9.10	7.61
2015	8.80	10.15	4.78	5.51	4.64	8.08	11.61
2016	10.12	11.54	4.74	5.40	6.14	6.21	4.68
2017	12.03	12.62	5.17	5.42	7.20	25.22	4.94

注：2004年以前为公安年报数据。迁入人口和迁出人口为公安年报数据。2010年出生、死亡、自然增长率根据第六次人口普查数据推算得出。2005-2009、2011-2017年出生、死亡、自然增长率为人口变动抽样调查推算数据。2017年公安年报数为原西安口径数据。

4-3 人口年龄构成和抚养比

Population Age Composition and Dependency Ratio

单位：%　　(%)

年　份 Year	各年龄段人口比重 Proportion of Population of All Ages 0-14岁 0-14 year old	15-64岁 15-64 year old	65岁及以上 65 year old and above	总抚养比 Total Dependency Ratio	少年儿童 Children	老年人口 Elderly Population
1990	25.71	69.08	5.21	44.76	37.21	7.55
2000	22.27	71.26	6.47	40.33	31.25	9.08
2010	12.89	78.65	8.46	27.15	16.39	10.76
2011	12.57	78.33	9.10	27.66	16.04	11.62
2012	12.54	78.02	9.44	28.17	16.07	12.10
2013	12.46	77.88	9.66	28.40	16.00	12.40
2014	12.52	77.46	10.02	29.10	16.16	12.94
2015	12.56	76.94	10.50	29.98	16.33	13.65
2016	12.76	76.35	10.89	30.97	16.71	14.26
2017	13.63	75.20	11.17	32.97	18.12	14.85

注：1990、2000、2010年数据根据人口普查数据加工整理，2011-2017年数据根据人口变动抽样调查数据推算，2017年为纳入西咸新区咸阳片区后的结构。抚养比指0-14岁、65岁及以上人口占15-64岁人口的比重。

4-4 全市及各区县人口数和户数（2017年）

Population and Households by Region（2017）

单位：万人　　(10 000 persons)

区县	Region	总户数（万户） Number of Households (10 000 households)	总人口 Total Population	城镇人口 Urban Population	按性别划分Grouped by Sex 男 Male	女 Female	迁入人口(人) Immigrant Population (person)	迁出人口(人) Emigrant Population (person)
全　市	**Total**	**267.68**	**845.09**	**567.26**	**424.98**	**420.11**	**252163**	**49412**
新城区	Xincheng	17.46	49.69	49.69	24.97	24.72	11765	2360
碑林区	Beilin	21.92	67.96	67.96	34.07	33.89	21336	9438
莲湖区	Lianhu	24.31	66.97	66.97	33.35	33.62	24508	2733
灞桥区	Baqiao	18.68	56.40	54.23	27.65	28.75	15917	1330
未央区	Weiyang	23.50	68.58	68.58	33.91	34.67	55042	3552
雁塔区	Yanta	32.46	95.03	95.03	46.99	48.04	70990	10319
阎良区	Yanliang	8.16	26.63	12.31	13.34	13.29	1920	753
临潼区	Lintong	21.20	71.72	24.08	36.24	35.48	4232	1686
长安区	Chang'an	34.30	112.18	48.78	55.74	56.44	30422	3328
高陵区	Gaoling	10.59	33.92	22.24	16.82	17.10	6277	694
鄠邑区	Huyi	18.06	61.28	22.14	31.48	29.80	4371	4234
蓝田县	Lantian	19.17	65.60	18.51	34.02	31.58	2660	4333
周至县	Zhouzhi	17.87	69.13	16.74	36.40	32.73	2723	4652

注：本表均为公安年报数据。总户数未机械配平。2017年公安年报数为原西安口径数据。

4-5 全市及各区县常住人口数和人口变动情况(2017年)

Permanent Population and Population Changes by Region (2017)

区 县	Region	常住人口(万人) Permanent Population (10 000 persons)	城镇 Urban	出生率(‰) Birth Rate (‰)	死亡率(‰) Death Rate (‰)	自然增长率(‰) Natural Growth Rate (‰)
全 市	**Total**	**961.67**	**706.06**	**12.62**	**5.42**	**7.20**
新城区	Xincheng	62.06	62.06	10.02	3.41	6.61
碑林区	Beilin	65.18	65.18	11.71	4.03	7.68
莲湖区	Lianhu	73.67	73.67	11.03	3.76	7.27
灞桥区	Baqiao	64.06	60.82	12.90	5.49	7.41
未央区	Weiyang	70.17	68.18	12.72	5.40	7.32
雁塔区	Yanta	125.49	125.49	11.81	4.52	7.29
阎良区	Yanliang	29.47	16.89	11.86	5.55	6.31
临潼区	Lintong	68.99	24.11	12.49	5.68	6.81
长安区	Chang'an	100.97	61.18	14.11	7.00	7.11
高陵区	Gaoling	35.70	23.02	13.48	5.87	7.61
鄠邑区	Huyi	54.93	23.14	13.65	6.19	7.46
蓝田县	Lantian	53.26	17.69	14.49	7.15	7.34
周至县	Zhouzhi	58.94	19.93	14.48	7.28	7.20

注：本表数据均为人口变动抽样调查推算数据。2017年常住口径数据为大西安范围，含西咸新区。

4-6 主要年份常住人口数

Permanent Population in Representative Years

单位：万人 (10 000 persons)

年 份 Year	年末常住人口 Permanent Population (year-end)	城镇 Urban	乡村 Rural
2000	741.14	450.36	290.78
2005	806.81	510.55	296.26
2006	822.52	530.94	291.58
2007	830.54	548.99	281.55
2008	837.52	565.16	272.36
2009	843.46	581.4	262.06
2010	847.41	584.71	262.7
2011	851.34	596.79	254.55
2012	855.29	611.62	243.67
2013	858.81	618.77	240.04
2014	862.75	626.44	236.31
2015	870.56	635.68	234.88
2016	883.21	648.54	234.67
2017	961.67	706.06	255.61

注：2000年常住人口为普查数据。2010年常住人口为年末常住人口数，根据第六次人口普查数据推算得出。2005-2009、2011-2017年常住人口为人口变动抽样调查推算数据。2017年常住口径数据为大西安范围，含西咸新区。

4-7 主要年份社会从业人数

Number of Social Laborers in Representative Years

单位：万人 (10 000 persons)

年 份 Year	合计 Total	一、按城乡分 Grouped by Urban area and Rural area					二、按三次产业分 Grouped by Industry		
		1.城镇 Urban	国有经济 State-owned Enterprises	集体经济 Collective Enterprises	其他经济 Others	2.乡村 Village	第一产业 Primary Industry	第二产业 Secondary Industry	第三产业 Tertiary Industry
1985	**296.80**	129.07	96.80	29.07	3.20	167.73	135.89	98.61	62.30
1986	**299.45**	132.82	101.28	28.43	3.11	166.63	127.46	100.61	71.38
1987	**312.16**	138.56	104.58	30.72	3.26	173.60	130.36	107.75	74.05
1988	**327.76**	142.24	106.46	30.73	5.05	185.52	138.87	108.12	80.77
1989	**332.65**	145.65	108.80	30.44	6.41	187.00	142.21	106.40	84.04
1990	**343.06**	147.93	110.95	29.78	7.20	195.13	149.64	106.74	86.68
1991	**347.65**	149.48	111.87	29.80	7.81	198.17	152.24	108.19	87.22
1992	**357.51**	151.67	113.19	29.97	8.51	205.84	154.75	110.22	92.54
1993	**363.70**	155.72	112.98	29.77	12.97	207.98	154.02	114.02	95.66
1994	**364.56**	154.88	113.39	27.97	13.52	209.68	153.51	108.53	102.52
1995	**372.60**	158.80	113.79	25.58	19.43	213.80	153.39	109.67	109.54
1996	**379.29**	164.54	113.29	24.82	26.43	214.75	153.43	109.17	116.69
1997	**385.14**	169.52	112.44	23.52	33.56	215.62	153.23	109.46	122.45
1998	**393.95**	177.20	106.06	21.50	49.64	216.75	153.00	110.45	130.50
1999	**400.43**	180.27	105.08	20.50	54.69	220.16	154.64	110.58	135.21
2000	**389.10**	176.45	103.46	18.40	54.59	212.65	147.03	107.26	134.81
2001	**389.30**	177.94	100.47	17.10	60.37	211.36	145.09	108.96	135.25
2002	**397.16**	181.85	100.54	16.90	64.41	215.31	143.04	111.62	142.50
2003	**404.92**	183.23	94.51	16.78	71.94	221.69	146.67	109.09	149.16
2004	**409.57**	187.53	93.43	15.41	78.69	222.04	141.81	111.70	156.06
2005	**415.83**	192.53	93.27	14.47	84.79	223.30	136.31	114.20	165.32
2006	**422.15**	196.16	84.46	14.41	97.29	225.99	135.10	116.09	170.96
2007	**436.36**	214.27	90.58	11.88	111.81	222.09	133.33	125.06	177.97
2008	**448.05**	224.20	90.17	10.60	123.43	223.85	127.87	130.23	189.95
2009	**462.52**	239.39	90.83	7.63	140.93	223.13	122.13	131.57	208.82
2010	**477.58**	252.54	94.01	5.48	153.05	225.04	117.27	145.40	214.91
2011	**495.99**	265.43	91.62	5.33	168.48	230.56	121.05	151.33	223.61
2012	**514.57**	287.65	95.33	5.10	187.22	226.92	114.92	162.35	237.30
2013	**530.71**	308.04	86.06	7.29	214.69	222.67	110.45	151.50	268.76
2014	**532.92**	316.59	84.83	6.67	225.09	216.33	105.02	151.85	276.05
2015	**528.06**	327.68	84.52	5.29	237.87	200.38	107.68	129.51	290.87
2016	**539.18**	335.07	87.15	4.85	243.07	204.11	105.12	127.88	306.18
2017	**596.21**	370.33	86.06	4.46	279.81	225.88	113.17	135.52	347.52

注：第一产业从业人员中包括城镇农林牧渔及服务业企业人员。

4-8 按国民经济行业分从业人数（2017年）

单位：万人

行　业	Sector	合计 Total
总计	**Total**	**596.21**
（一）农、林、牧、渔业	Agriculture ,Forestry,Animal Husbandry and Fishery	113.17
（二）采矿业	Mining	0.94
（三）制造业	Manufacturing	74.61
（四）电力、燃气及水的生产供应业	Production and Distribution of Electricity,Gas and Water	4.53
（五）建筑业	Construction	55.60
（六）批发和零售业	Wholesale and Retail Trades	93.70
（七）交通运输、仓储和邮政业	Traffic,Transport,Storage and Post	34.10
（八）住宿和餐饮业	Hotels and Catering Services	44.45
（九）信息传输、软件和信息技术服务业	Information Transmission,Software and Information Technology Services	19.29
（十）金融业	Financial Intermediation	11.46
（十一）房地产业	Real Estate	12.31
（十二）租赁和商务服务业	Leasing and Business Services	23.11
（十三）科学研究和技术服务业	Scientific Research and Technical Services	17.94
（十四）水利、环境和公共设施管理业	Management of Water Conservancy, Environment and Public Facilities	3.29
（十五）居民服务、修理和其他服务业	Services to Households, Repairs and Other Services	26.71
（十六）教育	Education	24.06
（十七）卫生和社会工作	Health and Social Work	18.46
（十八）文化、体育和娱乐业	Culture, Sports and Entertainment	4.15
（十九）公共管理、社会保障和社会组织	Public Administration, Social Security and Social Organizations	14.33
（二十）国际组织	International Organizations	

Number of Employed Persons Grouped by Industry of the National Economy (2017)

(10 000 persons)

国有经济 State-owned Enterprises	集体经济 Collective Enterprises	城镇其他经济 Urban Other Enterprises	城镇私营经济及个体劳动者 Urban Private Enterprises and Individual Labors	乡村从业人员 Rural Employed Persons
86.06	**4.46**	**111.77**	**168.04**	**225.88**
0.19		0.01	2.60	110.37
0.19		0.51	0.24	
17.81	0.56	30.07	9.29	16.88
2.61	0.06	1.70	0.16	
2.29	2.46	17.21	15.62	18.02
1.07	0.16	12.22	60.04	20.21
11.21	0.01	5.20	6.13	11.55
0.44	0.02	5.24	28.33	10.42
0.09		9.07	9.08	1.05
1.76	0.20	8.25	0.27	0.98
0.67	0.04	6.83	4.77	0.00
0.61	0.65	4.66	9.32	7.87
9.67	0.04	4.41	2.97	0.85
1.34	0.01	1.33	0.61	
0.40	0.05	0.51	14.33	11.42
14.41	0.03	1.85	0.65	7.12
7.34	0.17	1.14	1.92	7.89
0.93		1.51	1.71	
13.03		0.05		1.25

4-9 全部单位从业人员情况（2017年）

单位：人

分　组	Classify	单位从业人员 Employed Persons	女性 Female
总计	**Total**	**2022926**	**772257**
一、按机构类型分组	**Grouped by Organization Type**		
#企业	Enterprises	1621349	578876
事业	Public Institutions	274934	148694
机关	Government Units	117212	38832
二、按国民经济行业分组	**Grouped by Economic Sector**		
（一）农业	Agriculture ,Forestry,Animal Husbandry and Fishery	1973	591
（二）采矿业	Mining	5064	1375
（三）制造业	Manufacturing	484423	158739
（四）电力、燃气及水的生产供应业	Production and Distribution of Electricity,Gas and Water	44127	13217
（五）建筑业	Construction	219593	35262
（六）批发和零售业	Wholesale and Retail Trades	134430	70039
（七）交通运输、仓储和邮政业	Traffic,Transport,Storage and Post	164794	45772
（八）住宿和餐饮业	Hotels and Catering Services	56953	34007
（九）信息传输、软件和信息技术服务业	Information Transmission,Software and Information Technology Services	91660	35978
（十）金融业	Financial Intermediation	102074	57301
（十一）房地产业	Real Estate	75465	30980
（十二） 租赁和商务服务业	Leasing and Business Services	59186	21635
（十三）科学研究和技术服务业	Scientific Research and Technical Services	141423	46128
（十四）水利、环境和公共设施管理业	Management of Water Conservancy, Environment and Public Facilities	27304	11019
（十五）居民服务、修理和其他服务业	Services to Households, Repairs and Other Services	9546	3960
（十六）教育	Education	162982	90523
（十七）卫生和社会工作	Health and Social Work	86649	60321
（十八）文化、体育和娱乐业	Culture, Sports and Entertainment	24477	11618
（十九）公共管理、社会保障和社会组织	Public Administration, Social Security and Social Organizations	130803	43792
（二十）国际组织	International Organizations		

注：采矿业因企业行业代码发生变化，故从业人员与上年同比变化较大。

Basic Facts on All Employees（2017）

(person)

在岗职工合计 Total Fully Employed Staff and Workers	其他从业人员 Other Employed Persons	单位从业人员 平均人数 Average Employment	在岗职工合计 Staff and Workers	其他从业人员 Other Employed Persons
1884195	**138731**	**2049319**	**1914136**	**135183**
1509419	111930	1642545	1533388	109157
261077	13857	281467	268047	13420
104641	12571	116221	103985	12236
1797	176	1970	1797	173
4433	631	5036	4412	624
475310	9113	502295	493548	8747
42757	1370	49479	48153	1326
190957	28636	211677	183972	27705
130815	3615	132559	128522	4037
158751	6043	170679	164357	6322
51926	5027	55573	51385	4188
90582	1078	92383	91275	1108
70982	31092	102393	69443	32950
73071	2394	75447	73105	2342
44687	14499	55779	45269	10510
136412	5011	147569	142081	5488
25549	1755	26941	25200	1741
9265	281	9891	9618	273
153331	9651	167968	158330	9638
83428	3221	87532	84284	3248
23215	1262	24689	23458	1231
116927	13876	129459	115927	13532

4-10 国有单位从业人员情况（2017年）

单位：人

分 组	Classify	单位从业人员 Employed Persons	女性 Female
总计	**Total**	**860643**	**341157**
一、按机构类型分组	**Grouped by Organization Type**		
#企业	Enterprises	471815	155692
事业	Public Institutions	270504	146089
机关	Government Units	117162	38817
二、按国民经济行业分组	**Grouped by Economic Sector**		
（一）农业	Agriculture ,Forestry,Animal Husbandry and Fishery	1906	566
（二）采矿业	Mining		
（三）制造业	Manufacturing	178183	61771
（四）电力、燃气及水的生产供应业	Production and Distribution of Electricity,Gas and Water	26465	8030
（五）建筑业	Construction	22873	3757
（六）批发和零售业	Wholesale and Retail Trades	10680	5527
（七）交通运输、仓储和邮政业	Traffic,Transport,Storage and Post	112719	28969
（八）住宿和餐饮业	Hotels and Catering Services	4443	2385
（九）信息传输、软件和信息技术服务业	Information Transmission,Software and Information Technology Services	917	277
（十）金融业	Financial Intermediation	17606	8542
（十一）房地产业	Real Estate	6714	2532
（十二）租赁和商务服务业	Leasing and Business Services	6083	2472
（十三）科学研究和技术服务业	Scientific Research and Technical Services	96942	32576
（十四）水利、环境和公共设施管理业	Management of Water Conservancy, Environment and Public Facilities	13846	5490
（十五）居民服务、修理和其他服务业	Services to Households, Repairs and Other Services	3956	932
（十六）教育	Education	144102	78690
（十七）卫生和社会工作	Health and Social Work	73567	50809
（十八）文化、体育和娱乐业	Culture, Sports and Entertainment	9321	4235
（十九）公共管理、社会保障和社会组织	Public Administration, Social Security and Social Organizations	130320	43597
（二十）国际组织	International Organizations		

Basic Facts on Employees in State-owned Units (2017)

(person)

在岗职工合计 Total Fully Employed Staff and Workers	其他从业人员 Other Employed Persons	单位从业人员 平均人数 Average Employment	在岗职工合计 Staff and Workers	其他从业人员 Other Employed Persons
820842	**39801**	**899898**	**861363**	**38535**
458334	13481	505548	492549	12999
256763	13741	277047	263755	13292
104591	12571	116171	103935	12236
1730	176	1903	1730	173
175057	3126	198582	195977	2605
26457	8	31919	31887	32
21025	1848	19165	17812	1353
10245	435	10695	10255	440
109242	3477	119764	116008	3756
4087	356	4397	4022	375
906	11	912	899	13
17390	216	16329	16142	187
6164	550	6960	6417	543
5756	327	6097	5770	327
94213	2729	102870	99943	2927
12492	1354	13858	12511	1347
3885	71	4196	4131	65
136145	7957	149216	141307	7909
70610	2957	74769	72137	2632
8994	327	9303	8984	319
116444	13876	128963	115431	13532

4-11 城镇集体单位从业人员情况（2017年）

单位：人

分组	Classify	单位从业人员 Employed Persons	女性 Female
总计	**Total**	**44572**	**9872**
一、按机构类型分组	**Grouped by Organization Type**		
#企业	Enterprises	43313	9119
事业	Public Institutions	1195	715
机关	Government Units		
二、按国民经济行业分组	**Grouped by Economic Sector**		
（一）农业	Agriculture ,Forestry,Animal Husbandry and Fishery		
（二）采矿业	Mining		
（三）制造业	Manufacturing	5648	2333
（四）电力、燃气及水的生产供应业	Production and Distribution of Electricity,Gas and Water	632	57
（五）建筑业	Construction	24611	3271
（六）批发和零售业	Wholesale and Retail Trades	1582	572
（七）交通运输、仓储和邮政业	Traffic,Transport,Storage and Post	72	36
（八）住宿和餐饮业	Hotels and Catering Services	151	73
（九）信息传输、软件和信息技术服务业	Information Transmission,Software and Information Technology Services	24	7
（十）金融业	Financial Intermediation	1962	925
（十一）房地产业	Real Estate	422	155
（十二）租赁和商务服务业	Leasing and Business Services	6465	850
（十三）科学研究和技术服务业	Scientific Research and Technical Services	370	144
（十四）水利、环境和公共设施管理业	Management of Water Conservancy, Environment and Public Facilities	133	57
（十五）居民服务、修理和其他服务业	Services to Households, Repairs and Other Services	523	206
（十六）教育	Education	293	145
（十七）卫生和社会工作	Health and Social Work	1661	1028
（十八）文化、体育和娱乐业	Culture, Sports and Entertainment	23	13
（十九）公共管理、社会保障和社会组织	Public Administration, Social Security and Social Organizations		
（二十）国际组织	International Organizations		

Basic Facts on Employees in Urban Collective-owned Units（2017）

(person)

		单位从业人员		
在岗职工合计 Total Fully Employed Staff and Workers	其他从业人员 Other Employed Persons	平均人数 Average Employment	在岗职工合计 Staff and Workers	其他从业人员 Other Employed Persons
43169	**1403**	**44474**	**42806**	**1668**
41916	1397	43216	41566	1650
1189	6	1192	1174	18
5539	109	5593	5486	107
632		586	551	35
23847	764	24601	23624	977
1361	221	1594	1369	225
68	4	76	72	4
151		142	142	
24		26	26	
1842	120	2024	1894	130
382	40	412	377	35
6418	47	6486	6439	47
344	26	366	342	24
133		132	132	
457	66	519	453	66
291	2	290	288	2
1657	4	1604	1588	16
23		23	23	

4-12 其他经济类型单位从业人员情况（2017年）

单位：人

分 组	Classify	单位从业人员 Employed Persons	女性 Female
总计	**Total**	**1117711**	**421228**
一、按机构类型分组	**Grouped by Organization Type**		
#企业	Enterprises	1106221	414065
事业	Public Institutions	3235	1890
机关	Government Units	50	15
二、按国民经济行业分组	**Grouped by Economic Sector**		
（一）农业	Agriculture ,Forestry,Animal Husbandry and Fishery	67	25
（二）采矿业	Mining	5064	1375
（三）制造业	Manufacturing	300592	94635
（四）电力、燃气及水的生产供应业	Production and Distribution of Electricity,Gas and Water	17030	5130
（五）建筑业	Construction	172109	28234
（六）批发和零售业	Wholesale and Retail Trades	122168	63940
（七）交通运输、仓储和邮政业	Traffic,Transport,Storage and Post	52003	16767
（八）住宿和餐饮业	Hotels and Catering Services	52359	31549
（九）信息传输、软件和信息技术服务业	Information Transmission,Software and Information Technology Services	90719	35694
（十）金融业	Financial Intermediation	82506	47834
（十一）房地产业	Real Estate	68329	28293
（十二）租赁和商务服务业	Leasing and Business Services	46638	18313
（十三）科学研究和技术服务业	Scientific Research and Technical Services	44111	13408
（十四）水利、环境和公共设施管理业	Management of Water Conservancy, Environment and Public Facilities	13325	5472
（十五）居民服务、修理和其他服务业	Services to Households, Repairs and Other Services	5067	2822
（十六）教育	Education	18587	11688
（十七）卫生和社会工作	Health and Social Work	11421	8484
（十八）文化、体育和娱乐业	Culture, Sports and Entertainment	15133	7370
（十九）公共管理、社会保障和社会组织	Public Administration, Social Security and Social Organizations	483	195
（二十）国际组织	International Organizations		

Basic Facts on Employees in Other Units（2017）

(person)

在岗职工合计 Total Fully Employed Staff and Workers	其他从业人员 Other Employed Persons	单位从业人员 平均人数 Average Employment	在岗职工合计 Staff and Workers	其他从业人员 Other Employed Persons
1020184	**97527**	**1104947**	**1009967**	**94980**
1009169	97052	1093781	999273	94508
3125	110	3228	3118	110
50		50	50	
67		67	67	
4433	631	5036	4412	624
294714	5878	298120	292085	6035
15668	1362	16974	15715	1259
146085	26024	167911	142536	25375
119209	2959	120270	116898	3372
49441	2562	50839	48277	2562
47688	4671	51034	47221	3813
89652	1067	91445	90350	1095
51750	30756	84040	51407	32633
66525	1804	68075	66311	1764
32513	14125	43196	33060	10136
41855	2256	44333	41796	2537
12924	401	12951	12557	394
4923	144	5176	5034	142
16895	1692	18462	16735	1727
11161	260	11159	10559	600
14198	935	15363	14451	912
483		496	496	

4-13 城镇非私营单位分行业从业人员年平均工资

单位：元

分 组	Classify	2010
总计	**Grouped by Economic Sector**	**37870**
（一）农业	Agriculture ,Forestry,Animal Husbandry and Fishery	21436
（二）采矿业	Mining	32154
（三）制造业	Manufacturing	26663
（四）电力、燃气及水的生产供应业	Production and Distribution of Electricity,Gas and Water	39508
（五）建筑业	Construction	26875
（六）批发和零售业	Wholesale and Retail Trades	25103
（七）交通运输、仓储和邮政业	Traffic,Transport,Storage and Post	41737
（八）住宿和餐饮业	Hotels and Catering Services	19647
（九）信息传输、软件和信息技术服务业	Information Transmission,Software and Information Technology Services	45904
（十）金融业	Financial Intermediation	63952
（十一）房地产业	Real Estate	45273
（十二）租赁和商务服务业	Leasing and Business Services	30267
（十三）科学研究和技术服务业	Scientific Research and Technical Services	55456
（十四）水利、环境和公共设施管理业	Management of Water Conservancy, Environment and Public Facilities	25322
（十五）居民服务、修理和其他服务业	Services to Households, Repairs and Other Services	26443
（十六）教育	Education	53084
（十七）卫生和社会工作	Health and Social Work	44035
（十八）文化、体育和娱乐业	Culture, Sports and Entertainment	31925
（十九）公共管理、社会保障和社会组织	Public Administration, Social Security and Social Organizations	39964
（二十）国际组织	International Organizations	

Average Wages of Urban Non-private Employees by Industry

(yuan)

2011	2012	2013	2014	2015	2016	2017
41679	**44533**	**49350**	**54573**	**60557**	**67205**	**75262**
23567	31846	36658	42881	43426	48626	52020
38551	33489	40605	42116	46645	108827	118026
34698	38957	44321	49482	56686	61434	66067
47705	55409	59955	61252	65887	69092	77674
29773	35828	39507	48275	52783	60475	68025
27996	34382	37362	40915	46203	48210	55793
48231	48760	54147	59189	62816	63583	69469
22925	26637	29497	30914	33746	37507	41147
51135	63328	67495	100550	109448	137210	142407
72195	75652	97140	104433	106807	108569	114884
34626	37567	44832	48120	52423	56979	57970
31549	34291	42109	46828	52637	54395	53474
64448	68274	69951	69958	72731	79539	86199
26009	29938	38429	43033	45356	44062	48277
23993	25103	32066	32478	37019	35721	35979
54442	54581	59143	58451	63761	71635	86672
48836	56764	61602	59892	61623	74797	86521
34717	40833	50201	57239	61561	65974	70202
42163	47691	49893	47000	51681	59437	77660

4-14 主要年份单位从业人员数及工资总额

Number of Employees and Remuneration in Representative Years

年 份 year	单位从业人员（万人） Number of Employed Persons (10 000 persons)	从业人员工资总额（亿元） Remuneration of Employed Persons (100mil. yuan)	城镇非私营单位从业人员年平均工资（元） Annual Average Wage of Employees in Urban Non-private Units(yuan)	国有单位从业人员年平均工资（元） Annual Average Wage of Employees in State-owned Units(yuan)	城镇集体单位从业人员年平均工资（元） Annual Average Wage of Employees in Urban Collective Units(yuan)	其他经济类型单位从业人员年平均工资（元） Annual Average Wage of Employees in Other Units (yuan)
1978	67.19	4.71	713	705	609	
1980	91.76	7.31	859	849	699	
1985	127.04	14.17	1148	1215	923	1409
1986	132.78	16.87	1311	1388	1048	1659
1987	135.48	19.13	1446	1544	1107	1583
1988	137.56	22.81	1702	1842	1216	2065
1989	139.86	25.64	1873	2010	1385	2188
1990	141.55	29.48	2133	2290	1545	2044
1991	142.86	26.88	2276	2435	1657	2966
1992	144.51	30.80	2545	2758	1709	3504
1993	146.03	43.25	2999	3274	1910	3551
1994	142.37	58.87	4172	4588	2337	5243
1995	141.17	67.23	4763	5168	2837	5863
1996	140.60	75.64	5407	5858	3216	6225
1997	138.89	80.83	5785	6204	3437	7487
1998	138.78	82.85	6900	7445	3964	6942
1999	115.88	90.13	7764	8238	4374	8217
2000	112.45	103.80	9179	9742	5178	9451
2001	113.93	123.12	10786	11570	5431	10781
2002	115.77	138.88	12138	12877	6230	12543
2003	116.68	155.95	13504	14217	6892	14215
2004	118.15	184.63	15473	15994	7428	17030
2005	123.66	215.67	17728	18420	7612	19066
2006	125.10	250.87	20475	21392	8494	21859
2007	129.40	319.23	25012	25696	9768	27400
2008	130.85	379.29	29749	30246	10834	33344
2009	135.64	450.48	34032	34611	11940	37307
2010	140.38	520.88	37870	38122	12505	40721
2011	154.33	658.73	41679	45217	23241	37643
2012	165.59	770.86	44533	47493	29988	41218
2013	198.42	1031.46	49350	52782	34591	47462
2014	199.41	1151.53	54573	54138	41006	55766
2015	198.46	1255.75	60557	60301	43291	61590
2016	199.19	1358.95	67205	66295	48098	68847
2017	202.29	1542.35	75262	76682	54755	74999

4-15 全部单位从业人员工资总额（2017年）

Total Wages of All Employees of All Units (2017)

单位：万元 (10 000yuan)

分 组	Classify	单位从业人员工资总额 Total Wages of Employment	在岗职工工资总额 Total Wages of Employed Staff and Workers
总计	**Total**	**15423493**	**14887058**
一、按机构类型分组	**Grouped by Organization Type**		
#企业	Enterprises	12061900	11604453
事业	Public Institutions	2412042	2365921
机关	Government Units	901442	869417
二、按国民经济行业分组	**Grouped by Economic Sector**		
（一）农业	Agriculture ,Forestry,Animal Husbandry and Fishery	10248	10095
（二）采矿业	Mining	59438	51227
（三）制造业	Manufacturing	3318530	3270063
（四）电力、燃气及水的生产供应业	Production and Distribution of Electricity, Gas and Water	384320	380602
（五）建筑业	Construction	1439940	1294432
（六）批发和零售业	Wholesale and Retail Trades	739582	719947
（七）交通运输、仓储和邮政业	Traffic,Transport,Storage and Post	1185690	1157947
（八）住宿和餐饮业	Hotels and Catering Services	228669	217740
（九）信息传输、软件和信息技术服务业	Information Transmission,Software and Information Technology Services	1315594	1308237
（十）金融业	Financial Intermediation	1176327	1082466
（十一）房地产业	Real Estate	437367	429714
（十二）租赁和商务服务业	Leasing and Business Services	298271	255950
（十三）科学研究和技术服务业	Scientific Research and Technical Services	1272029	1245787
（十四）水利、环境和公共设施管理业	Management of Water Conservancy, Environment and Public Facilities	130064	124608
（十五）居民服务、修理和其他服务业	Services to Households, Repairs and Other Services	35587	34787
（十六）教育	Education	1455807	1421046
（十七）卫生和社会工作	Health and Social Work	757337	744267
（十八）文化、体育和娱乐业	Culture, Sports and Entertainment	173321	168421
（十九）公共管理、社会保障和社会组织	Public Administration, Social Security and Social Organizations	1005372	969722
（二十）国际组织	International Organizations		

注：采矿业因企业行业代码发生变化，故从业人员与上年同比变化较大。

4-15 续表 continued

单位：万元　　　　　　　　　　　　　　　　　　　　　　　　　　　　　(10 000 yuan)

分　组	Classify	其他从业人员工资总额 Remuneration of Other Employed Persons	城镇非私营单位从业人员平均工资（元） Annual Average Wage of Employees in UrbanNon-private Units(yuan)
总计	**Total**	**536435**	**75262**
一、按机构类型分组	**Grouped by Organization Type**		
#企业	Enterprises	457447	73434
事业	Public Institutions	46121	85695
机关	Government Units	32025	77563
二、按国民经济行业分组	**Grouped by Economic Sector**		
（一）农业	Agriculture ,Forestry,Animal Husbandry and Fishery	153	52020
（二）采矿业	Mining	8211	118026
（三）制造业	Manufacturing	48467	66067
（四）电力、燃气及水的生产供应业	Production and Distribution of Electricity, Gas and Water	3718	77674
（五）建筑业	Construction	145509	68025
（六）批发和零售业	Wholesale and Retail Trades	19635	55793
（七）交通运输、仓储和邮政业	Traffic,Transport,Storage and Post	27743	69469
（八）住宿和餐饮业	Hotels and Catering Services	10929	41147
（九）信息传输、软件和信息技术服务业	Information Transmission,Software and Information Technology Services	7357	142407
（十）金融业	Financial Intermediation	93861	114884
（十一）房地产业	Real Estate	7652	57970
（十二）租赁和商务服务业	Leasing and Business Services	42321	53474
（十三）科学研究和技术服务业	Scientific Research and Technical Services	26242	86199
（十四）水利、环境和公共设施管理业	Management of Water Conservancy, Environment and Public Facilities	5457	48277
（十五）居民服务、修理和其他服务业	Services to Households, Repairs and Other Services	800	35979
（十六）教育	Education	34761	86672
（十七）卫生和社会工作	Health and Social Work	13070	86521
（十八）文化、体育和娱乐业	Culture, Sports and Entertainment	4900	70202
（十九）公共管理、社会保障和社会组织	Public Administration, Social Security and Social Organizations	35650	77660
（二十）国际组织	International Organizations		

4-16 国有单位从业人员工资总额（2017年）

Total Wages of State-owned Units Employees （2017）

单位：万元 （10 000yuan）

分 组	Classify	单 位 从业人员 工资总额 Total Wages of Employment	在岗职工 工资总额 Total Wages of Employed Staff and Workers
总计	**Total**	**6892934**	**6762604**
一、按机构类型分组	**Grouped by Organization Type**		
#企业	Enterprises	3603956	3550848
事业	Public Institutions	2378267	2333096
机关	Government Units	901247	869222
二、按国民经济行业分组	**Grouped by Economic Sector**		
（一）农业	Agriculture ,Forestry,Animal Husbandry and Fishery	9994	9841
（二）采矿业	Mining		
（三）制造业	Manufacturing	1270895	1260973
（四）电力、燃气及水的生产供应业	Production and Distribution of Electricity, Gas and Water	234946	234694
（五）建筑业	Construction	107531	102085
（六）批发和零售业	Wholesale and Retail Trades	61505	60377
（七）交通运输、仓储和邮政业	Traffic,Transport,Storage and Post	859120	841557
（八）住宿和餐饮业	Hotels and Catering Services	18160	16342
（九）信息传输、软件和信息技术服务业	Information Transmission,Software and Information Technology Services	5256	5070
（十）金融业	Financial Intermediation	280810	279900
（十一）房地产业	Real Estate	33071	32095
（十二）租赁和商务服务业	Leasing and Business Services	39053	38286
（十三）科学研究和技术服务业	Scientific Research and Technical Services	787950	777344
（十四）水利、环境和公共设施管理业	Management of Water Conservancy, Environment and Public Facilities	67802	64257
（十五）居民服务、修理和其他服务业	Services to Households, Repairs and Other Services	15360	15074
（十六）教育	Education	1350178	1322370
（十七）卫生和社会工作	Health and Social Work	678256	666709
（十八）文化、体育和娱乐业	Culture, Sports and Entertainment	71566	69799
（十九）公共管理、社会保障和社会组织	Public Administration, Social Security and Social Organizations	1001481	965831
（二十）国际组织	International Organizations		

4-16 续表 continued

单位：万元 （10 000yuan）

分 组	Classify	其他从业人员工资总额 Remuneration of Other Employed Persons	城镇非私营单位从业人员平均工资（元） Annual Average Wage of Employees in UrbanNon-private Units(yuan)
总计	**Total**	**130330**	**76682**
一、按机构类型分组	**Grouped by Organization Type**		
#企业	Enterprises	53108	71429
事业	Public Institutions	45171	85843
机关	Government Units	32025	77579
二、按国民经济行业分组	**Grouped by Economic Sector**		
（一）农业	Agriculture ,Forestry,Animal Husbandry and Fishery	153	52517
（二）采矿业	Mining		
（三）制造业	Manufacturing	9922	63999
（四）电力、燃气及水的生产供应业	Production and Distribution of Electricity, Gas and Water	252	73607
（五）建筑业	Construction	5446	56108
（六）批发和零售业	Wholesale and Retail Trades	1128	57509
（七）交通运输、仓储和邮政业	Traffic,Transport,Storage and Post	17563	72339
（八）住宿和餐饮业	Hotels and Catering Services	1818	41300
（九）信息传输、软件和信息技术服务业	Information Transmission,Software and Information Technology Services	186	57638
（十）金融业	Financial Intermediation	910	171970
（十一）房地产业	Real Estate	976	47515
（十二）租赁和商务服务业	Leasing and Business Services	767	64052
（十三）科学研究和技术服务业	Scientific Research and Technical Services	10606	76597
（十四）水利、环境和公共设施管理业	Management of Water Conservancy, Environment and Public Facilities	3545	48926
（十五）居民服务、修理和其他服务业	Services to Households, Repairs and Other Services	286	36606
（十六）教育	Education	27808	90485
（十七）卫生和社会工作	Health and Social Work	11547	90714
（十八）文化、体育和娱乐业	Culture, Sports and Entertainment	1767	76928
（十九）公共管理、社会保障和社会组织	Public Administration, Social Security and Social Organizations	35650	77656
（二十）国际组织	International Organizations		

4-17 城镇集体单位从业人员工资总额（2017年）

Total Wages of Urban Collective-owned Units Employees（2017）

单位：万元 （10 000yuan）

分组	Classify	单位从业人员工资总额 Total Wages of Employment	在岗职工工资总额 Total Wages of Employed Staff and Workers
总计	**Total**	**243517**	**235597**
一、按机构类型分组	**Grouped by Organization Type**		
#企业	Enterprises	236456	228618
事业	Public Institutions	6872	6789
机关	Government Units		
二、按国民经济行业分组	**Grouped by Economic Sector**		
（一）农、林、牧、渔业	Agriculture ,Forestry,Animal Husbandry and Fishery		
（二）采矿业	Mining		
（三）制造业	Manufacturing	29900	29621
（四）电力、燃气及水的生产供应业	Production and Distribution of Electricity, Gas and Water	5791	5467
（五）建筑业	Construction	137192	132010
（六）批发和零售业	Wholesale and Retail Trades	5190	4538
（七）交通运输、仓储和邮政业	Traffic,Transport,Storage and Post	278	270
（八）住宿和餐饮业	Hotels and Catering Services	585	585
（九）信息传输、软件和信息技术服务业	Information Transmission,Software and Information Technology Services	72	72
（十）金融业	Financial Intermediation	23358	22572
（十一）房地产业	Real Estate	1681	1605
（十二）租赁和商务服务业	Leasing and Business Services	23659	23465
（十三）科学研究和技术服务业	Scientific Research and Technical Services	3435	3246
（十四）水利、环境和公共设施管理业	Management of Water Conservancy, Environment and Public Facilities	471	471
（十五）居民服务、修理和其他服务业	Services to Households, Repairs and Other Services	2308	2161
（十六）教育	Education	2127	2115
（十七）卫生和社会工作	Health and Social Work	7371	7300
（十八）文化、体育和娱乐业	Culture, Sports and Entertainment	99	99
（十九）公共管理、社会保障和社会组织	Public Administration, Social Security and Social Organizations		
（二十）国际组织	International Organizations		

4-17 续表 continued

单位：万元　　　　　　　　　　　　　　　　　　　　　　　　　　　　　(10 000 yuan)

分　组	Classify	其他从业人员工资总额 Remuneration of Other Employed Persons	城镇非私营单位从业人员平均工资（元） Annual Average Wage of Employees in UrbanNon-private Units(yuan)
总计	**Total**	**7920**	**54755**
一、按机构类型分组	**Grouped by Organization Type**		
#企业	Enterprises	7838	54715
事业	Public Institutions	83	57650
机关	Government Units		
二、按国民经济行业分组	**Grouped by Economic Sector**		
（一）农、林、牧、渔业	Agriculture ,Forestry,Animal Husbandry and Fishery		
（二）采矿业	Mining		
（三）制造业	Manufacturing	279	53460
（四）电力、燃气及水的生产供应业	Production and Distribution of Electricity, Gas and Water	324	98833
（五）建筑业	Construction	5182	55767
（六）批发和零售业	Wholesale and Retail Trades	652	32561
（七）交通运输、仓储和邮政业	Traffic,Transport,Storage and Post	8	36605
（八）住宿和餐饮业	Hotels and Catering Services		41211
（九）信息传输、软件和信息技术服务业	Information Transmission,Software and Information Technology Services		27577
（十）金融业	Financial Intermediation	786	115406
（十一）房地产业	Real Estate	76	40794
（十二）租赁和商务服务业	Leasing and Business Services	194	36478
（十三）科学研究和技术服务业	Scientific Research and Technical Services	189	93858
（十四）水利、环境和公共设施管理业	Management of Water Conservancy, Environment and Public Facilities		35659
（十五）居民服务、修理和其他服务业	Services to Households, Repairs and Other Services	147	44461
（十六）教育	Education	12	73331
（十七）卫生和社会工作	Health and Social Work	71	45955
（十八）文化、体育和娱乐业	Culture, Sports and Entertainment		43043
（十九）公共管理、社会保障和社会组织	Public Administration, Social Security and Social Organizations		
（二十）国际组织	International Organizations		

4-18 其他经济类型单位从业人员工资总额（2017年）

Total Wages of Other Units Employees（2017）

单位：万元 （10 000yuan）

分 组	Classify	单位从业人员工资总额 Total Wages of Employment	在岗职工工资总额 Total Wages of Employed Staff and Workers
总计	**Total**	**8287044**	**7888859**
一、按机构类型分组	**Grouped by Organization Type**		
#企业	Enterprises	8221487	7824987
事业	Public Institutions	26903	26035
机关	Government Units	195	195
二、按国民经济行业分组	**Grouped by Economic Sector**		
（一）农、林、牧、渔业	Agriculture ,Forestry,Animal Husbandry and Fishery	254	254
（二）采矿业	Mining	59438	51227
（三）制造业	Manufacturing	2017735	1979470
（四）电力、燃气及水的生产供应业	Production and Distribution of Electricity, Gas and Water	143582	140441
（五）建筑业	Construction	1195218	1060337
（六）批发和零售业	Wholesale and Retail Trades	672885	655031
（七）交通运输、仓储和邮政业	Traffic,Transport,Storage and Post	326292	316119
（八）住宿和餐饮业	Hotels and Catering Services	209924	200813
（九）信息传输、软件和信息技术服务业	Information Transmission,Software and Information Technology Services	1310266	1303095
（十）金融业	Financial Intermediation	872159	779994
（十一）房地产业	Real Estate	402616	396015
（十二）租赁和商务服务业	Leasing and Business Services	235559	194199
（十三）科学研究和技术服务业	Scientific Research and Technical Services	480644	465197
（十四）水利、环境和公共设施管理业	Management of Water Conservancy, Environment and Public Facilities	61792	59880
（十五）居民服务、修理和其他服务业	Services to Households, Repairs and Other Services	17919	17552
（十六）教育	Education	103503	96562
（十七）卫生和社会工作	Health and Social Work	71710	70258
（十八）文化、体育和娱乐业	Culture, Sports and Entertainment	101656	98523
（十九）公共管理、社会保障和社会组织	Public Administration, Social Security and Social Organizations	3892	3892
（二十）国际组织	International Organizations		

4-18 续表 continued

单位：万元 (10 000 yuan)

分组	Classify	其他从业人员工资总额 Remuneration of Other Employed Persons	城镇非私营单位从业人员平均工资（元） Annual Average Wage of Employees in UrbanNon-private Units(yuan)
总计	**Total**	**398185**	**74999**
一、按机构类型分组	**Grouped by Organization Type**		
#企业	Enterprises	396500	75166
事业	Public Institutions	868	83342
机关	Government Units		39080
二、按国民经济行业分组	**Grouped by Economic Sector**		
（一）农、林、牧、渔业	Agriculture ,Forestry,Animal Husbandry and Fishery		37896
（二）采矿业	Mining	8211	118026
（三）制造业	Manufacturing	38265	67682
（四）电力、燃气及水的生产供应业	Production and Distribution of Electricity, Gas and Water	3141	84590
（五）建筑业	Construction	134881	71182
（六）批发和零售业	Wholesale and Retail Trades	17854	55948
（七）交通运输、仓储和邮政业	Traffic,Transport,Storage and Post	10173	64181
（八）住宿和餐饮业	Hotels and Catering Services	9111	41134
（九）信息传输、软件和信息技术服务业	Information Transmission,Software and Information Technology Services	7171	143285
（十）金融业	Financial Intermediation	92165	103779
（十一）房地产业	Real Estate	6601	59143
（十二）租赁和商务服务业	Leasing and Business Services	41360	54533
（十三）科学研究和技术服务业	Scientific Research and Technical Services	15447	108417
（十四）水利、环境和公共设施管理业	Management of Water Conservancy, Environment and Public Facilities	1912	47712
（十五）居民服务、修理和其他服务业	Services to Households, Repairs and Other Services	367	34619
（十六）教育	Education	6941	56063
（十七）卫生和社会工作	Health and Social Work	1452	64262
（十八）文化、体育和娱乐业	Culture, Sports and Entertainment	3133	66169
（十九）公共管理、社会保障和社会组织	Public Administration, Social Security and Social Organizations		78458
（二十）国际组织	International Organizations		

4-19　主要年份城镇登记失业人数及失业率

Registered Unemployed Persons and Unemployment Rate in Urban Area in Representative Years

年 份 year	城镇登记失业人员数（万人） Real Number of Registered Unemployed Persons (10 000 persons)	城镇登记失业率（%） Registered Unemployment in Urban Area (%)
2002		3.7
2003		4.5
2004	8.29	4.3
2005	8.45	4.3
2006	8.74	4.3
2007	8.77	4.3
2008	9.40	4.2
2009	10.02	4.3
2010	10.46	4.2
2011	10.37	3.9
2012	9.60	3.5
2013	10.13	3.4
2014	10.84	3.4
2015	10.74	3.4
2016	11.29	3.3
2017	11.51	3.3

主要统计指标解释

人口数 指一定时点、一定地区范围内的有生命的个人的总和。年度统计的年末人口数，指每年12月31日24时的人口数。

常住人口 指实际经常居住在某地区一定时间（半年以上，含半年）的人口。常住人口包括户口在本辖区人也在本辖区居住的人，户口在本辖区之外但在户口登记地半年以上的人，户口待定（无户口和口袋户口）的人，户口在本辖区但离开本辖区半年以下的人。

城镇人口和乡村人口 城镇人口是指居住在城镇范围内的全部常住人口；乡村人口是除上述人口以外的全部人口。

出生率（又称粗出生率） 指在一定时期内（通常为一年）平均每千人所出生的人数的比率，一般用千分率表示。其计算公式为：

出生率＝年出生人数／年平均人数×1000‰

式中：出生人数指活产婴儿，即胎儿脱离母体时（不管怀孕月数），有过呼吸或其他生命现象。年平均人数指年初、年底人口数的平均数，也可用年中人口数代替。

死亡率（又称粗死亡率） 指在一定时期内（通常为一年）一定地区的死亡人数与同期内平均人数（或期中人数）之比，一般用千分率表示。本资料中的死亡率指年死亡率，其计算公式为：

死亡率＝年死亡人数／年平均人数×1000‰

人口自然增长率 指在一定时期内（通常为一年）人口自然增加数（出生人数减死亡人数）与该时期内平均人数（或期中人数）之比，一般用千分率表示。计算公式为：

人口自然增长率＝（本年出生人数—本年死亡人数）／年平均人数×1000‰。

从业人员 指在16周岁及以上，从事一定社会劳动并取得劳动报酬或经营收入的人员。这一指标反映了一定时期内全部劳动力资源的实际利用情况，是研究我国基本国情国力的重要指标。

单位从业人员 指在各级国家机关、政党机关、社会团体及企业、事业单位中工作，取得工资或其他形式的劳动报酬的全部人员。包括在岗职工、再就业的离退休人员、民办教师以及在各单位中工作的外方人员和港澳台方人员、兼职人员、借用的外单位人员和第二职业者。不包括离开本单位仍保留劳动关系的职工。各单位的就业人员反映了各单位实际参加生产或工作的全部劳动力。

城镇私营和个体就业人员 城镇私营就业人员指在工商管理部门注册登记，其经营地址设在县城关镇（含城关镇）以上的私营企业就业人员；包括私营企业投资者和雇工。城镇个体就业人员指在工商管理部门注册登记，并持有城镇户口或在城镇长期居住，经批准从事个体工商经营的就业人员；包括个体经营者和在个体工商户劳动的家庭帮工和雇工。

国有单位 指资产归国家所有的经济组织。包括按《中华人民共和国企业法人登记管理条例》规定登记注册的非公司制的经济组织，以及中央、地方各级国家机关、事业单位和社会团体。

集体单位 指生产资料归集体所有，并按《中华人民共和国企业法人登记管理条例》规定登记注册的经济组织。

其他单位 包括股份合作单位、联营单位、有限责任公司、股份有限公司、港澳台商投资单位以及外商投资单位等其他登记注册类型单位。

在岗职工 指在本单位工作并由单位支付工资的人员，以及有工作岗位，但由于学习、病伤产假等原因暂未工作，仍由单位支付工资的人员。

职工工资总额 指各单位在一定时期内直接支付给本单位全部职工的劳动报酬总额。工资总额的计算原则应以直接支付给职工的全部劳动报酬为根据。各单位支付给职工的劳动报酬以及其他根据有关规定支付的工资，不论是计入成本的还是不计入成本的，不论是按国家规定列入计征奖金税项目的，还是未列入计征奖金税项目的，不论是以货币形式支付的还是以实物形式支付的，均包括在工资总额内。

职工平均工资 指企业、事业、机关单位的职工在一定时期内平均每人所得的货币工资额。它表明一定时期职工工资收入的高低程度，是反映职工工资水平的主要指标。计算公式为：

职工平均工资＝报告期实际支付的全部职工工资总额/报告期全部职工平均人数

城镇登记失业人员 指有非农业户口，在一定的劳动年龄内，有劳动能力，无业而要求就业，并在当地就业服务机构进行求职登记的人员。

城镇登记失业率 指城镇登记失业人数同城镇从业人数与城镇从业人数与城镇登记失业人数之和的比。计算公式为：

$$\text{城镇登记失业率}=\frac{\text{城镇登记失业人数}}{\text{（城镇单位就业人员-使用的农村劳动力-聘用的离退休人员-聘用的港澳台及外方人员）+不在岗职工+城镇私营业主+城镇个体户主+城镇私营企业及个体就业人员+城镇登记失业人数}}\times 100\%$$

Explanatory Notes on Main Statistical Indicators

The annual statistics on total population is taken at midnight, the 31st of December, not including residents in Taiwan province, Hong Kong SAR and Macao SAR and Chinese national residing abroad.

Permanent population refers to the population of actual habitual residence in a certain area six months or over six months. Permanent popul ation include the accounts in this area which are also living in this area, accounts outside this area but with more than half a year of household registration, accounts to be determined including people without accounts or pockets of accounts, and accounts in the area but leaving this area less than six months.

Urban Population and Rural Population Urban population refers to all people residing in cities and towns, while rural population refers to population other than urban population.

Birth Rate (or Crude Birth Rate) refers to the ratio of the number of births to the average population (or mid-period population) during a certain period of time (usually one year), expressed in ‰. Birth rate in the chapter refers to annual birth rate. The following formula is used:

$$\text{Birth Rate}=\frac{\text{Number of Births}}{\text{Annual Average Population}}\times 1000‰$$

Number of births in the formula refers to live births, i.e. when a baby has breathed or showed any vital phenomena regardless of the length of pregnancy.

Annual average population is the average of the number of population at the beginning of the year and that at the end of the year. Sometimes it is substituted by the mid-year population.

Death Rate (or Crude Death Rate) refers to the ratio of the number of deaths to the average population (or mid-period population) during a certain period of time (usually one year), expressed in ‰. Death rate in the chapter refers to annual death rate. The following formula is used:

$$\text{DeathRate}=\frac{\text{Number of Deaths}}{\text{Annual Average Population}}\times 1000‰$$

Natural Growth Rate of Population refers to the ratio of natural increase in population (number of births minus number of deaths) in a certain period of time (usually one year) to the average population (or mid-period population) of the same period, expressed in ‰. The following formula is applied:

Natural Growth Rate of Population =(Number of Births-Number of Deaths)/Annual Average Population× 1000‰

Employed Persons refer to the ones aged 16 and over who are engaged in gainful employment and thus receive remuneration payment or earn business income. This indicator reflects the actual utilization of total labour force during a certain period of time and is often used for the research on China's economic situation and national power.

Persons Employed in Various Units refer to all the persons working in government agencies of various levels, political and party organizations, social organizations, enterprises and institutions, and receiving wages or other forms of payment. They include fully-employed staff and workers, re-employed retirees, teachers in the schools run by the local people, foreigners and Chinese compatriots from Hong Kong, Macao, and Taiwan working in various units, part-time employees, employees of other units working temporarily at current posts, and employees holding the second job, but do not include persons who have left their working units while keeping their labour contract (employment relation) unchanged. This indicator reflects the total number of laborers actually engaged in production or other operations in various units.

Persons Employed in Private Enterprises and Self- Employed Individuals in Urban Areas Persons employed in private enterprises refer to the persons employed in the private enterprises which have been registered at the departments of industrial and commercial administration for which the business operation are situated at a county town (i.e. a town where the county government is located), or at urban areas with administrative hierarchy higher than a county town. The self-employed individuals in urban areas refer to persons who hold the certificates of residence in urban areas or have resided in the urban areas for a long time and have been registered at the departments of industrial and commercial administration and approved to be engaged in individual industrial or commercial business, including self-employed persons as well as helpers and hired labourers who work in individual households.

State-owned Units refer to economic units whose assets are owned by the state, including non-corporation units registered according to Regulation of the People's Republic of China on the Registration of Enterprises and

Corporations, state organs, institutions and social organizations at the central-level and local levels.

Collective-owned Units refer to economic units registered according to Regulation of the People's Republic of China on the Registration of Enterprises and Corporations where the means of production are collectively owned.

Units of Other Types of Ownership refer to units registered with other types of ownership, including cooperative units, joint ownership units, limited liability corporations, share holding corporations, units funded by entrepreneurs from Hong Kong, Macao, and Taiwan, and foreign- funded units.

Employed Staff and Workers refer to persons who work in, and receive wages from their working units, including persons who have their work posts but are temporarily absent from work for reasons of study or on sick, injury or maternal leave and still receive wages from their working units.

Total Wage Bill refers to the total remuneration payment to employed persons in various units during a certain period of time. The calculation of total wage bill is based on the total remuneration payment to employed persons . Therefore, all the wages and salaries and other payments to employed persons are included in the total wage bill regardless of sources, reckoning the cost of production or not, category, listing as items of premium taxation or not, and forms, paying in cash or in kind.

Average Wage refers to the average wage in money terms per person during a certain period of time for employed persons in enterprises, institutions, and government agencies, which reflects the general level of wage income during a certain period of time and is calculated as follows:

$$\text{AverageWage}=\frac{\text{TotalWage Billof Employed Personsat Reference Time}}{\text{Average Number of Persons Employedat Reference Time}}$$

Registered Unemployed Persons in Urban Areas refer to the persons with non-agricultural household registration at certain working ages (16 years old to retirement age), who are capable of working, unemployed and willing to work, and have been registered at the local employment service agencies to apply for a job.

Registered Unemployment Rate in Urban Areas refers to the ratio of the number of the registered unemployed persons to the sum of the number of persons employed in various units (minus the employed rural labour force, re-employed retirees, and Hong Kong, Macao, Taiwan or foreign employees), laid-off staff and workers in urban units, owners of private enterprises in urban areas, owners of self-employed individuals in urban areas, employees of private enterprises in urban areas, employee of self-employed individuals in urban areas, and the registered unemployed persons in urban areas. The formula is as follows:

$$\text{Registered Unemployment rate in urban areas}=\frac{\text{numberof registered urban unemployed persons}}{\text{number of persons employed in urbanunits-employed rurallabour force re-employed retirees - HongKong, Macao,Taiwan or foreign employees + laid-off staff and workers+owners of urban private Enterprises+ owners of urbanself-employed Individuals + employees ofurbanprivate Enterprises+employees of urbanself- employed Individuals+ registered unemployed persons in urbanareas}}\times 100\%$$

5 固定资产投资

INVESTMENT IN FIXED ASSETS

资料整理：康　敏　王　峰
Data management: Kang Min Wang Feng
数据审核：席锋旭
Data audit: Xi Fengxu

第五部分　固定资产投资

一、简要说明

本章资料主要包括全社会固定资产投资、项目投资、房地产开发投资和农户投资以及分区县情况，由西安市统计局固定资产投资处提供。

二、主要指标

全社会固定资产投资（亿元）	7556.47	比上年增长	12.9%
#国有经济单位	4127.66	比上年增长	19.4%
集体经济单位	153.36	比上年下降	9.9%
#固定资产投资	7463.31	比上年增长	13.0%
#房地产开发	2333.34	比上年增长	15.0%
全市新增固定资产（亿元）	3238.33	比上年增长	24.6%
全市竣工住宅面积（万平方米）	1338.91	比上年增长	5.8%

5　INVESTMENT IN FIXED ASSETS

Ⅰ.Brief Introduction

This chapter consists of primarily the data on fixed asset investment, Project investment real estate development investment, and farmer Investment provided by Fixed Asset Investment Division of the Xi'an Bureau of Statistics.

Ⅱ.Major Indicators

		Increase over Preceding Year
Total Investment In Fixed Assets(100 mil. yuan)	7556.47	12.9%
State-owned Enterprises	4127.66	19.4%
Collective-owned Enterprises	153.36	-9.9%
Project Investment	7463.31	13.0%
Real Estate Development	2333.34	15.0%
Investment Newly Increased Fixed Assets(100 mil. yuan)	3238.33	24.6%
Total Floor Space of Building Completed(10 000 sq.m)	1338.91	5.8%

5-1 主要年份按类别分全社会固定资产投资

Total Investment in Fixed Assets in the Whole Country by Classifications in Representative Years

单位：亿元 (100 million yuan)

年 份 Year	全社会固定资产投资合计 Total Investment in Fixed Assets in the Whole Country	固定资产投资 Fixed Assets Investment	房地产开发投资 Real Estate Investment	农户投资 Farmer Investment
1979	4.08	3.01		1.07
1980	6.12	4.48		1.64
1981	5.59	4.56		1.03
1982	9.49	8.02		1.47
1983	10.46	9.17		1.29
1984	12.89	10.69		2.20
1985	18.44	14.44		4.00
1986	22.15	18.54		3.61
1987	27.05	23.15		3.90
1988	29.14	24.43		4.71
1989	28.30	23.85		4.45
1990	26.39	23.10	0.91	3.29
1991	30.76	25.55	2.01	5.21
1992	38.48	32.85	3.32	5.63
1993	75.06	66.65	7.39	8.41
1994	85.57	73.47	12.02	12.10
1995	103.42	88.50	21.65	14.92
1996	114.38	96.98	24.66	17.40
1997	116.90	95.17	24.68	21.73
1998	154.80	138.68	38.21	16.12
1999	197.31	172.64	44.30	24.67
2000	232.37	203.01	51.85	29.36
2001	287.72	256.95	67.42	30.77
2002	338.15	307.24	79.37	30.91
2003	478.10	445.74	124.82	32.36
2004	646.69	612.03	169.67	34.66
2005	835.10	776.33	225.23	58.77
2006	1066.62	971.84	285.76	94.78
2007	1435.33	1340.59	387.33	94.74
2008	1906.36	1786.60	540.26	119.76
2009	2500.13	2367.58	696.34	132.55
2010	3250.56	3104.92	842.34	145.64
2011	3346.26	3207.97	996.81	138.29
2012	4243.43	4107.54	1281.90	135.89
2013	5134.56	4982.25	1595.64	152.31
2014	5903.98	5682.42	1761.88	221.56
2015	5165.98	5086.93	1831.67	79.05
2016	5191.36	5097.00	1955.82	78.65
2017	7556.47	7463.31	2333.34	93.16

注：2015年国家取消了城乡投资分组，表中“农户投资”2014年以前为原先的农村投资。
2016年全社会固定资产投资不含跨省项目，固定资产投资不含跨省和跨市项目。

5-2 主要年份按经济类型分全社会固定资产投资

Total Investment in Fixed Assets in the Whole Country by Economic Type in Representative Years

单位：亿元 (100 million yuan)

年 份 Year	合计 Total	国有经济 State-owned	集体经济 Collective-owned	个体经济 Self-employed Individual	其他经济 Others
1985	18.44	13.96	1.36	3.12	
1986	22.15	18.05	0.97	3.13	
1987	27.05	22.18	1.50	3.37	
1988	29.14	23.72	1.86	3.56	
1989	28.30	23.22	1.46	3.62	
1990	26.39	22.21	1.44	2.74	
1991	30.76	24.42	2.26	4.08	
1992	38.48	32.04	1.45	4.99	
1993	75.06	59.66	3.03	6.55	5.82
1994	85.57	64.71	4.14	10.09	6.63
1995	103.42	69.08	9.78	11.13	13.43
1996	114.38	80.66	8.73	12.50	12.49
1997	116.90	77.46	10.21	15.11	14.12
1998	154.80	113.07	7.89	10.59	23.25
1999	197.31	136.50	13.62	16.22	30.97
2000	232.37	159.60	14.65	24.40	33.72
2001	287.72	175.58	14.67	38.57	58.90
2002	338.15	200.06	13.70	44.68	79.71
2003	478.10	264.83	22.33	73.43	117.51
2004	646.69	329.14	40.06	48.95	228.54
2005	835.10	373.70	59.23	79.04	323.13
2006	1066.62	401.14	110.68	107.33	447.47
2007	1435.33	476.78	207.08	183.09	568.38
2008	1906.36	694.89	246.89	50.43	914.15
2009	2500.13	932.91	289.91	97.86	1179.45
2010	3250.56	1348.76	326.44	54.73	1520.63
2011	3346.26	1204.80	258.15	74.64	1808.67
2012	4243.43	1661.22	194.71	82.72	2304.78
2013	5134.56	1770.84	219.88	84.43	3059.41
2014	5903.98	1916.31	203.35	83.28	3701.04
2015	5165.98	1826.62	158.14	80.47	3100.75
2016	5191.36	2332.08	152.05	81.68	2625.55
2017	7556.47	4127.66	153.36	93.94	3181.51

注：集体经济：包括城镇集体和农村集体。
个体经济：包括私营个体投资及城镇工矿区私人建房和农村私人建房。

5-3 主要年份按产业分全市固定资产投资

Total Investment in Fixed Assets in the Whole City by Three Strata of Industry in Representative Years

单位：亿元 (100 million yuan)

年 份 Year	全市固定资产投资合计 Total Investment in Fixed Assets in The Whole City	第一产业 Primary Industry	第二产业 Secondary Industry	工业 Industry	第三产业 Tertisry Industry
1979	3.01	0.06	1.24	1.20	1.71
1980	4.48	0.06	2.09	1.99	2.33
1981	4.56	0.11	2.10	1.83	2.35
1982	8.02	0.04	4.07	3.63	3.91
1983	9.17	0.11	4.97	4.41	4.09
1984	10.69	0.19	4.56	3.99	5.94
1985	14.44	0.18	7.22	6.45	7.04
1986	18.54	0.16	8.98	8.37	9.40
1987	23.15	0.19	11.81	11.26	11.15
1988	24.43	0.15	11.95	11.20	12.33
1989	23.85	0.13	11.94	11.50	11.78
1990	23.10	0.25	11.03	10.59	11.82
1991	25.55	0.27	12.48	11.95	12.80
1992	32.85	0.10	15.60	14.73	17.15
1993	66.65	0.07	24.50	22.44	42.08
1994	73.47	0.03	27.04	25.85	46.40
1995	88.50	0.14	28.80	27.71	59.56
1996	96.98	0.13	25.96	24.24	70.89
1997	95.17	0.24	23.65	21.66	71.28
1998	138.68	0.48	35.33	29.86	102.87
1999	172.64	0.94	39.88	36.40	131.82
2000	203.01	0.76	57.21	54.37	145.04
2001	256.95	0.86	63.31	61.28	192.78
2002	307.24	4.29	74.34	68.45	228.61
2003	445.74	3.34	83.25	78.41	359.15
2004	612.03	3.38	97.69	95.67	510.96
2005	776.33	5.26	144.25	140.44	626.82
2006	971.84	10.04	213.43	206.48	748.37
2007	1340.59	10.20	297.53	286.61	1032.86
2008	1786.60	23.75	369.74	356.12	1393.11
2009	2367.58	24.46	458.44	442.70	1884.68
2010	3104.92	39.83	556.10	498.62	2508.99
2011	3207.97	43.10	474.73	390.30	2690.14
2012	4165.99	99.34	671.92	578.17	3394.73
2013	5055.23	73.15	983.09	868.57	3998.99
2014	5824.53	75.15	1261.70	1205.53	4487.68
2015	5086.93	99.78	1158.30	1135.87	3828.85
2016	5097.00	89.70	963.80	949.27	4043.50
2017	7463.31	123.20	1086.93	1072.06	6253.18

5-4 主要年份按资金来源及建设性质分全市固定资产投资

单位：万元

指标	Item	1995	2000	2001	2002	2003	2004
一. 投资总额(万元)	**Total Investment (10 000 yuan)**	**884994**	**2030122**	**2569496**	**3072442**	**4457381**	**6120324**
（一）按资金来源分	Grouped by Funds Source						
1. 国家预算内投资	State Budgetary Funds	69185	160982	256403	355960	365263	436496
2. 国内贷款	Domestic Loans	216565	432282	672379	666146	1219234	1565246
3. 债券	Bonds	873	32460	6753	766	3278	
4. 利用外资	Utilization of Foreign Funds	80792	31622	54907	15192	47509	47401
5. 自筹资金	Self-raising Funds	385047	875352	1121502	1392915	1733132	2629720
6. 其他资金	Others	132532	497424	457552	641463	1088965	1441461
（二）按构成分	Grouped by Composition of Funds						
1. 建筑安装工程	Construction and Installation Projects	527220	1404184	1698777	2119151	3067309	4127677
2. 设备、工器具购置	Purchasing of Equipment and Instruments	233730	382495	452602	552251	577240	708988
3. 其它费用	Others	124044	243443	418117	401040	812832	1283659
（三）按建设性质分	Grouped by Type of Construction						
#新建	New Construction	210926	533058	723957	874392	1294032	1874116
扩建	Expansion	180210	542510	581138	868603	1102914	1169537
改建	Reconstruction	157457	263657	344879	343184	447944	670229
二. 房屋施工面积（万平方米）	**Floor Space Under Construction (10 000sq.m)**	**1070.58**	**1702.58**	**1767.13**	**2396.89**	**2716.18**	**3177.36**

Total Investment in Fixed Assets in the Whole City by Sources of Funds and Type of Construction in Representative Years

(10 000 yuan)

2005	2006	2007	2008	2009	2010	2011	2012	2013	2014	2015	2016	2017
7763283	**9718418**	**13405920**	**17865977**	**23675759**	**31049184**	**32079666**	**41659924**	**50552171**	**58245332**	**50869319**	**50970036**	**74633058**
728885	677145	670592	1555809	2562756	1649563	1480412	1851860	1439721	1622413	2250911	2528528	2959768
1257175	1631689	1619218	2162957	3301919	4288663	3546561	4023452	4146647	5592450	4510474	5018722	7782466
								11356				1985
40583	165390	183422	261325	144124	126802	89047	135147	182153	789982	2067810	957646	235730
4001700	5538393	8565573	12771844	15776565	18279153	19400468	28680236	36446760	41430249	33936574	30562975	43941535
1734940	1705801	2367115	1114042	1890395	6705003	7563178	6969229	8325534	8810238	8103551	11902165	19711574
5086664	6486233	9165668	12864657	16337466	21690205	25553161	34268466	41672647	44701184	41024301	39843259	56988374
1021079	1409589	1858720	2024631	2619783	3094336	1911180	3311375	4861642	8847403	4990590	5682434	6908078
1655540	1822596	2381532	2976689	4718510	6264643	4615325	4080083	4017882	4696745	4854428	5444343	10736606
2907551	3511432	5123975	6356716	8567540	14292899	16077747	21651399	26063028	29798357	26685245	26057561	43898511
1208430	1101740	994841	2118013	3054929	2649749	1956527	1685922	1232264	1102377	1017226	1714627	2278259
782953	1099304	1548130	1921664	2738799	2620997	2155112	2810903	3183300	2605272	1439734	1622434	2978772
4030.38	**4589.39**	**5759.28**	**6570.94**	**9571.25**	**11166.19**	**12353.11**	**14093.91**	**14749.84**	**16249.30**	**16325.63**	**18977.88**	**17676.88**

5-5 主要年份全市新增固定资产投资及房屋竣工面积

Newly Added Fixed Assets and Floor Spaces Completed of Municipal Units in Representative Years

年 份 Year	新增固定资产（亿元） Newly Increased Fixed Assets (10 000 mil.yuan)	房屋竣工面积（万平方米） Floor Space of Buildings Completed (10 000sq.m)	住宅 Residential Buildings
1978	4.96	99.10	40.76
1980	4.64	164.87	100.15
1985	8.62	222.42	129.07
1986	13.40	272.95	155.91
1987	16.72	241.48	119.21
1988	16.82	211.83	102.43
1989	16.58	178.45	87.77
1990	20.30	211.88	111.05
1991	17.86	185.34	95.84
1992	22.33	204.75	112.66
1993	41.70	257.90	144.88
1994	55.37	282.91	184.49
1995	62.58	357.67	252.84
1996	60.04	332.18	249.52
1997	62.88	374.46	286.54
1998	80.23	382.80	275.63
1999	118.92	681.04	550.83
2000	150.16	714.83	544.95
2001	167.77	692.56	502.26
2002	198.97	773.28	486.13
2003	279.44	917.96	578.06
2005	261.95	776.59	498.33
2004	409.72	1131.41	598.61
2006	453.01	1199.45	583.10
2007	667.97	1672.16	929.50
2008	725.17	1113.31	693.42
2009	1013.44	1529.13	822.62
2010	1193.05	775.16	521.08
2011	1297.35	1231.91	861.44
2012	1765.05	1626.25	1189.04
2013	1875.00	1118.69	840.02
2014	2476.12	1856.70	1462.86
2015	2049.71	1109.00	826.05
2016	1952.92	1884.05	1331.24
2017	3238.33	1987.95	1338.91

5-6 全市固定资产投资（2017年）

Total Investment in Fixed Assets in the Whole City（2017）

单位：万元 (10 000 yuan)

指　标	Item	合计 Total	房地产开发投资 Real Estate Investment
一、本年完成投资（万元）	**Investment Completed This Year(10 000 yuan)**	**74633058**	**23333373**
#住宅	Residential Buildings	16213609	15663673
（一）按登记注册类型分	**Grouped by Registion Status**		
内资	Domestic Funded Enterprises	71503454	22615441
国有	State-owned Enterprises	26059748	487218
集体	Collective-owned Enterprises	648610	9284
股份合作	Cooperative Enterprises	32717	
联营	Joint Ownership Enterprises	18539	
国有联营	State Joint Ownership Enterprises		
集体联营	Collective Joint Ownership Enterprises	18539	
国有与集体联营	Joint State-collective Ownership Enterprises		
其他联营	Other Joint Ownership Enterprises		
有限责任公司	Limited Liability Corporations	31656145	15941938
国有独资公司	State-funded Corporations	5600024	1352779
其他有限责任公司	Other Limited Liability Corporations	26056121	14589159
股份有限公司	Stock Limited Corporation	1313818	385993
私营	Private Enterprises	10932769	5725355
私营独资	Private -funded Enterprises	889718	67874
私营合伙	Private Limited Liability Corporations	16126	
私营有限责任公司	Private Limited Liability Corporations	9690252	5509071
私营股份有限公司	Private Share Holding Corporations	336673	148410
其他	Others	841108	65653
港澳台商投资	Enterprises Funded by Hong Kong, Macao and Taiwan	1288593	410797
与港澳台合资经营	Joint-venture Enterprises	581017	40716
与港澳台合作经营	Cooperative Enterprises	53090	53090
港澳台独资	Wholly Funded from Hong Kong,Macao and Taiwan	616353	278858
港澳台投资股份有限公司	Share-holding Corporations Ltd.		
其他港澳台投资	Investment From Hongkong,Macao,Taiwan	38133	38133

5-6 续表1 continued 1

单位：万元 (10 000 yuan)

指 标	Item	合计 Total	房地产开发投资 Real Estate Investment
外商投资	Foreign Owned Enterprises	1833050	307135
中外合资经营	Joint-venture Enterprises	689618	130756
中外合作经营	Cooperation Enterprises		
外资企业	Foreign Funded Enterprises	1118616	151563
外商投资股份有限公司	Share-holding Corporations Ltd. With Foreign Funds	24816	24816
其他外商投资	Foreign Investment		
（二）按隶属关系分	**Grouped by Jurisdiction of Management**		
中央	Central	3336373	488741
省属	Provincial	8091583	643960
市属	Municipal	63205102	22200672
（三）按建设性质分	**Grouped by Type of Construction**		
#新建	New Construction	43898511	
扩建	Expansion	2278259	
改建和技术改造	Reconstruction	2978772	
（四）按构成分	**Grouped by Composition**		
1. 建筑工程	Construction Projects	50791624	15282995
2. 安装工程	Installment Projects	6196750	2912289
3. 设备、工器具购置	Purchasing of Equipment and Instruments	6908078	529814
4. 其他费用	Others	10736606	4608275

5-6 续表2 continued 2

单位：万元 (10 000 yuan)

指　标	Item	合计 Total	房地产开发投资 Real Estate Investment
二、构成(%)	**Proportion (%)**		
（一）按登记注册类型分组	**Grouped by Regisition Status**		
#国有经济	State-owned	21.1	10.2
集体经济	Collective-owned	-35.9	-97.0
（二）按隶属关系分组	**Grouped by Jurisdiction of Management**		
中央	Central	4.4	-11.1
省属	Provincial	2.3	-5.1
市属	Municipal	15.1	16.4
（三）按建设性质分	**Grouped by Type of Construction**		
#新建	New Construction	13.1	
扩建	Expansion	-20.1	
改建和技术改造	Reconstruction	60.0	
（四）按构成分	**Grouped by Composition of Funds**		
1. 建筑工程	Construction Projects	4.5	3.9
2. 安装工程	Installation Projects	29.2	11.0
3. 设备、工器具购置	Purchasing of the Equipment and Instruments	10.8	90.1
4. 其他	Others	67.7	71.9
三、本年新增固定资产（万元）	**Newly Increase in Fixed Assets This Year(10 000 yuan)**	**32383343**	**8072589**
四、房屋面积（万平方米）	**Floor Space (10 000 sq.m)**		
房屋施工面积	Floor Space of Buildings Under Construction	17677	15844
#住宅	Residential Buildings	11518	11134
房屋竣工面积	Floor Space of Buildings Completed	1988	1635
#住宅	Residential Buildings	1339	1282
五、本年房屋竣工价值（万元）	**Value of the Building Completed This Year (10 000 yuan)**	**5719558**	**5719558**
#住宅	Residential Buildings	4480159	4480159

5-7 按国民经济行业分全市固定资产投资（2017年）

Investment in Fixed Assets in the Whole City by Industry（2017）

单位：万元 (10 000 yuan)

行业	Sector	固定资产投资 Grouped by Sector	工业改建和技术改造 Industrial Reconstruction and Technical Transformation
本年完成固定资产投资（万元）	**Grouped by Sector (10 000 yuan)**	**74633058**	**2388201**
（一）农、林、牧、渔业	Agriculture,Forestry,Animal Husbandry and Fishery	1340782	
（二）采矿业	Mining	70402	24343
（三）制造业	Manufacturing	8533746	2056417
农副食品加工业	Processing of Food from Agricultural Products	74731	3345
食品制造业	Manufacture of Foods	270117	55930
酒、饮料和精制茶制造业	Wine, Soft Drinks and Refined Tea Industry	84815	22984
烟草制品业	Tobacco Processing	9265	1065
纺织业	Textile Industry	24231	2458
纺织服装、服饰业	Textile, Apparel Industry	27260	3100
皮革、毛皮、羽毛及其制品和制鞋业	Leather, Fur, Feather (eiderdown) and Their Products Industry	164	
木材加工和木、竹、藤、棕、草制品业	Timber Processing,Bamboo,Cane, Palm Fiber and Straw Products	82401	600
家具制造业	Furniture Manufacturing	201533	66718
造纸及纸制品业	Papermaking and Paper products	66599	18926
印刷和记录媒介复制业	Printing,Record Medium Reproduction	52130	14913
文教、工美、体育和娱乐用品制造业	Culture, Education, Craft Art, Sports and Entertainment Goods Manufacturing Industry	50506	26772
石油加工、炼焦和核燃料加工业	Petroleum Refining, Ccoke Making and Nuclear Fuel Processing Industry	10572	3000
化学原料和化学制品制造业	Raw Chemical Materials and Chemical Products	259252	65273
医药制造业	Medical and Pharmaceutical Products	389062	109609
化学纤维制造业	Chemical Fiber		
橡胶和塑料制品业	Rubber and Plastic Products Industry	190674	15916
非金属矿物制品业	Nonmetal Mineral Products	352152	69576
黑色金属冶炼和压延加工业	Smelting and Pressing of Ferrous Metals	28058	2350
有色金属冶炼和压延加工业	Smelting and Pressing of Nonferrou Metals	412628	59964
金属制品业	Metal Products	256909	38130

5-7 续表 continued

单位：万元 (10 000 yuan)

行 业	Sector	固定资产投资 Grouped by Sector	工业改建和技术改造 Industrial Reconstruction and Technical Transformation
通用设备制造业	General Equipment Manufacturing Industry	479043	144581
专用设备制造业	Special Purpose Equipment	1023740	236523
汽车制造业	Automotive Manufacturing	664823	83457
铁路、船舶、航空航天和其他运输设备制造业	Railroad, Marine, Aerospace and other Transportation Equipment Manufacturing	803777	256324
电气机械和器材制造业	Electric Equipment and Machinery	997081	251907
计算机、通信和其他电子设备制造业	Communication Equipment, Computer and Other Electronic Equipment Manufacturing Industry	1186379	422664
仪器仪表制造业	Instrument Manufacturing Industry	250051	67438
其他制造业	Other Manufacturing	214557	4374
废弃资源综合利用	Comprehensive Utilization of waste Resources	25936	6800
金属制品、机械和设备修理业	Metal Products, Machinery and Equipment Repair Industry	45300	1720
（四）电力、燃气及水的生产供应业	Production & Supply of Electricity,Gas & Water	2116431	307441
（五）建筑业	Construction	205531	
（六）批发和零售业	Wholesale and Retail Trades	1280618	
（七）交通运输、仓储和邮政业	Transport, Storage and Post	4129303	
（八）住宿和餐饮业	Hotels and Catering Services	516004	
（九）信息传输、软件和信息技术服务业	Information Transmission,Computer Service and Software	1314806	
（十）金融业	Financial Intermediation	83579	
（十一）房地产业	Real Estate	28377081	
（十二） 租赁和商务服务业	Leasing and Business Services	1334697	
（十三）科学研究和技术服务业	Scientific Research,Technical Service and Geologic Prospecting	854738	
（十四）水利、环境和公共设施管理业	Management of Water Conservancy, Environment and Public Facilities	19714266	
（十五）居民服务、修理和其他服务业	Services to Households, Repairs and Other Services	208566	
（十六）教育	Education	2309133	
（十七）卫生和社会工作	Health and Social Work	807587	
（十八）文化、体育和娱乐业	Culture, Sports and Entertainment	1097510	
（十九）公共管理、社会保障和社会组织	Public Administration, Social Security and Social Organizations	338278	
（二十）国际组织	International Organizations		

5-8 按国民经济行业分民间投资（2017年）

Private Investment of Municipal Units by Industry（2017）

行 业	Sector	投资额（万元）Investment (10000 yuan)	占民间投资比重（%）Rate(%)
民间投资总计	**Total**	**31202195**	**100.0**
（一）农、林、牧、渔业	Agriculture, Forestry, Animal Husbandry and Fishery	921245	3.0
（二）采矿业	Mining	31843	0.1
（三）制造业	Manufacturing	5399227	17.3
（四）电力、燃气及水的生产供应业	Generation and Supply of Electricity, Production and Supply of Gas and Water	297921	1.0
（五）建筑业	Construction	45948	0.1
（六）批发和零售业	Wholesale and Retail Trades	806579	2.6
（七）交通运输、仓储和邮政业	Transportation, Storage and Post	810053	2.6
（八）住宿和餐饮业	Hotels and Catering Services	317644	1.0
（九）信息传输、软件和信息技术服务业	Information Transmission, Computer Service and Software	157713	0.5
（十）金融业	Financial Intermediation	14787	
（十一）房地产业	Real Estate	17665992	56.5
（十二） 租赁和商务服务业	Leasing and Business Services	771884	2.5
（十三）科学研究和技术服务业	Scientific Research and Technical Service	265774	0.9
（十四）水利、环境和公共设施管理业	Management of Water Conservancy, Environment and Public Facilities	2294991	7.4
（十五）居民服务、修理和其他服务业	Services to Households, Repairs and Other Services	44890	0.1
（十六）教育	Education	246753	0.8
（十七）卫生和社会工作	Health and Social Work	453078	1.5
（十八）文化、体育和娱乐业	Culture, Sports and Entertainment	625361	2.0
（十九）公共管理、社会保障和社会组织	Public Administration, Social Security and Social Organizations	30512	0.1
（二十）国际组织	International Organizations		

5-9 按国民经济行业分基础设施投资（2017年）

Investment for Basic Infrastructure of Municipal Units by Industry（2017）

指 标	Item	投资额（万元）Investment (10000 yuan)	占基础设施投资比重（%）Rate(%)
基础设施投资总计	**Total Investment of Infrastructure**	**25475595**	**100.0**
一、交通运输、仓储和邮政业	**Traffic, Transport, Storage and Post**	**4129303**	**16.2**
铁路运输业	Railway Transport Industry	525592	2.1
道路运输业	The Road Transport Industry	2156366	8.5
水上运输业	Water Transportation		
航空运输业	The Air Transport Industry	209533	0.8
管道运输业	Pipeline Transportation	4396	
装卸搬运和运输代理服务业	Handling and Transport Industry	27465	0.1
仓储业	Warehousing Industry	1107414	4.3
邮政业	The Postal Service	98537	0.4
二、信息传输、软件和信息技术服务业	**Information Transmission,Software and Information Technology Services**	**1314806**	**5.2**
三、水利、环境和公共设施管理业	**Management of Water Conservancy, Environment and Public Facilities**	**19714266**	**77.4**
水利管理业	Water Resources Management Industry	890047	3.5
生态保护和环境治理业	Ecological Protection and Environmental Control Industries	441270	1.7
公共设施管理业	Public Facilities Management Industry	18382949	72.2

5-10 全市固定资产投资资金来源（2017年）

Source of Funds for Total Fixed Assets Investment of Whole City（2017）

单位：万元 (10 000 yuan)

指 标	Item	固定资产投资 Fixed Assets Investment	房地产开发 Real Estate
一、本年资金来源合计	**Total of Sources of Funds This Year**	**123987978**	**73725178**
1. 上年末结余资金	Balance of Last Year	18737288	16940172
2. 本年实际到位资金	Fully Funded Capital this Year	105250690	56785006
(1) 国家预算资金	State Budgetary Funds	4173990	
(2) 国内贷款	Domestic Loans	10975162	6964189
(3) 债券	Bonds	2800	
(4) 利用外资	Utilization of Foreign Funds	332436	2184
(5) 自筹资金	Self-raising Funds	61968208	23188023
(6) 其他资金来源	Others	27798094	26630610
二、各项应付款合计	**Total Sums of Money to be Paid This Year**	**15156179**	**10687846**

5-11 全市按行业分施工项目（2017年）

Construction Project Grouped by Industry in the Whole City（2017）

行 业	Sector	本年新增固定资产（万元）Increased Fixed Assets This Year (10 000 yuan)	施工项目个数（个）Number of Constructing Projects (unit)
总计	**Total**	**32383343**	**5434**
（一）农、林、牧、渔业	Agriculture, Forestry, Animal Husbandry and Fishery	790179	387
（二）采矿业	Mining	76015	6
（三）制造业	Manufacturing	4635742	943
（四）电力、燃气及水的生产供应业	Generation and Supply of Electricity,Production and Supply of Gas and Water	890033	240
（五）建筑业	Construction	95462	12
（六）批发和零售业	Wholesale and Retail Trades	751984	199
（七）交通运输、仓储和邮政业	Transportation, Storage and Post	1426965	244
（八）住宿和餐饮业	Hotels and Catering Services	261429	121
（九）信息传输、软件和信息技术服务业	Information Transmission, Computer Service and Software	721278	116
（十）金融业	Financial Intermediation	25728	11
（十一）房地产业	Real Estate	10096311	244
（十二） 租赁和商务服务业	Leasing and Business Services	769626	72
（十三）科学研究和技术服务业	Scientific Research and Technical Service	425949	81
（十四）水利、环境和公共设施管理业	Management of Water Conservancy, Environment and Public Facilities	8618144	2177
（十五）居民服务、修理和其他服务业	Services to Households, Repairs and Other Services	112180	45
（十六）教育	Education	1381746	275
（十七）卫生和社会工作	Health and Social Work	446225	91
（十八）文化、体育和娱乐业	Culture, Sports and Entertainment	635904	112
（十九）公共管理、社会保障和社会组织	Public Administration, Social Security and Social Organizations	222443	58
（二十）国际组织	International Organizations		

5-11 续表 continued

行 业	Sector	本年新开工 Newly Started This Year	本年投产项目个数（个） Projects put into Use (unit)
总计	**Total**	**3884**	**3393**
（一）农、林、牧、渔业	Agriculture, Forestry, Animal Husbandry and Fishery	330	256
（二）采矿业	Mining	4	3
（三）制造业	Manufacturing	583	636
（四）电力、燃气及水的生产供应业	Generation and Supply of Electricity,Production and Supply of Gas and Water	156	113
（五）建筑业	Construction	9	29
（六）批发和零售业	Wholesale and Retail Trades	150	131
（七）交通运输、仓储和邮政业	Transportation, Storage and Post	144	133
（八）住宿和餐饮业	Hotels and Catering Services	100	96
（九）信息传输、软件和信息技术服务业	Information Transmission, Computer Service and Software	99	81
（十）金融业	Financial Intermediation	9	9
（十一）房地产业	Real Estate	128	89
（十二） 租赁和商务服务业	Leasing and Business Services	47	65
（十三）科学研究和技术服务业	Scientific Research and Technical Service	36	59
（十四）水利、环境和公共设施管理业	Management of Water Conservancy, Environment and Public Facilities	1684	1272
（十五）居民服务、修理和其他服务业	Services to Households, Repairs and Other Services	40	43
（十六）教育	Education	188	177
（十七）卫生和社会工作	Health and Social Work	63	85
（十八）文化、体育和娱乐业	Culture, Sports and Entertainment	75	66
（十九）公共管理、社会保障和社会组织	Public Administration, Social Security and Social Organizations	39	50
（二十）国际组织	International Organizations		

5-12 全市固定资产投资效果（2017年）

Achievements of Total Assets Investment of Whole City（2017）

指　标	Item	固定资产投资 Fixed Assets Investment	房地产开发投资 Real Estate Investment
一、建设项目投产率（%）	**Rate of Projects Put Into Use(%)**	**62.4**	
施工项目个数（个）	Number of Constructing Projects (unit)	5434	
本年投产项目个数（个）	Number of Projects Put into Use (unit)	3393	
二、固定资产交付使用率（%）	**Rate of Fixed Assets Put into Use(%)**	**43.4**	**34.6**
本年新增固定资产（亿元）	Newly Increased Fixed Assets This Year(100 million yuan)	3238.33	807.26
本年完成投资（亿元）	Investment Completed This Year (100 million yuan)	7463.31	2333.34
三、建设周期（年）	**Construction Period (year)**	**4.2**	**6.4**
计划总投资（亿元）	Total Planned Investment(100 million yuan)	31380.03	14879.57
本年完成投资（亿元）	Investment Completed This Year (100 million yuan)	7463.31	2333.34
四、房屋建筑面积竣工率（%）	**Completion Rate of Buildings (%)**	**11.2**	**10.3**
本年房屋施工面积（万平方米）	Floor Space of the Constructing Buildings This Year (10 000 sq.m)	17676.90	15843.90
本年房屋竣工面积（万平方米）	Floor Space of the Buildings Completed This Year (10 000 sq.m)	1987.90	1634.60

5-13 固定资产投资新增生产能力或效益（2017年）

Newly Increased Production Capacity or Project Efficiency through Investment（2017）

能源名称	Name	累计新增生产能力或效益 Cumulative Newly Increased Production Capacity or Project Efficiency
太阳能发电（万千瓦）	Solar Energy (10 000 kw)	1865.9
其他发电（万千瓦）	Others (10 000 kw)	1.1
输电线路长度（11万伏及以上）（公里）	Length of Transmission Lines (above 110 000 VA) (km)	15.0
水泥（万吨/年）	Cement (10 000 tons/year)	
平板玻璃（万重量箱/年）	Plate Glass (10 000 Weight-boxs/year)	
氮肥（吨/年）	Nitrogen Fertilizers (ton/year)	
磷肥（吨/年）	Phosphate Fertilizer (ton/year)	
钾肥（吨/年）	Potash Fertilizer (ton/year)	
塑料树脂及共聚物（吨/年）	Plastic Resin and Copolymer (ton/year)	70
合成橡胶（吨/年）	Synthetic Rubber (ton/year)	
轿车制造（辆/年）	Car Manufacturing (car/year)	1450
化学纤维（吨/年）	Chemical Fiber (ton/year)	30000
棉纺锭（锭）	Cotton Spirit（Spindle）	
啤酒（万吨/年）	Beer (10 000 tons/year)	
白酒（万吨/年）	White Spirit (10 000 tons/year)	2.0
其他酒（万吨/年）	Other Alcohols (10 000 tons/year)	
新建公路（公里）	Newly Highways (km)	123.5
#高速公路（公里）	Expressway (km)	
一级公路（公里）	First Class (km)	17.3
二级公路（公里）	Second Class (km)	36.0
改建公路（公里）	Reconstructed Highways (km)	41.0
新建独立公路桥梁（延长米）	New-built Separate Highway Bridge (extended meters)	457
新建独立公路隧道（延长米）	New-built Separate Highway Tunnel (extended meters)	1
新（扩）建客、货运站（个）	New (expanded) Passenger and Freight Stations（unit）	1
新（扩）建客、货运站（平方米）	New (expanded) Passenger and Freight Stations（sq.m）	10000
城市自来水供水能力（万吨/日）	Tap Water Supply Capacity in City(10 000 tons/day)	5.7
城市污水处理能力（万吨/日）	Waste Water Treated Capacity in City(10 000 tons/day)	17.6

5-14 全市按国民经济行业分房屋建筑面积（2017年）

单位：平方米

行 业	Sector	本年施工房屋面积 Floor Space of Buildings Under Construction This Year	住宅 Residential Residence
总 计	**Total**	**176768812**	**115175542**
（一）农、林、牧、渔业	Agriculture, Forestry, Animal Husbandry and Fishery	80155	1285
（二）采矿业	Mining	99152	
（三）制造业	Manufacturing	2549434	14024
（四）电力、燃气及水的生产供应业	Generation and Supply of Electricity, Production and Supply of Gas and Water	132894	4629
（五）建筑业	Construction	19800	
（六）批发和零售业	Wholesale and Retail Trades	821692	85300
（七）交通运输、仓储和邮政业	Transportation, Storage and Post	556775	
（八）住宿和餐饮业	Hotels and Catering Services	527686	56760
（九）信息传输、软件和信息技术服务业	Information Transmission, Computer Service and Software	155656	16600
（十）金融业	Financial Intermediation	4100	
（十一）房地产业	Real Estate	165128232	114271835
（十二） 租赁和商务服务业	Leasing and Business Services	421719	
（十三）科学研究和技术服务业	Scientific Research and Technical Service	445857	7098
（十四）水利、环境和公共设施管理业	Management of Water Conservancy, Environment and Public Facilities	308299	90620
（十五）居民服务、修理和其他服务业	Services to Households, Repairs and Other Services	67899	810
（十六）教育	Education	2529073	564019
（十七）卫生和社会工作	Health and Social Work	2243240	25392
（十八）文化、体育和娱乐业	Culture, Sports and Entertainment	335366	37170
（十九）公共管理、社会保障和社会组织	Public Administration, Social Security and Social Organizations	341783	
（二十）国际组织	International Organizations		

Floors Space of Buildings Construction of Municipal Units by Industry（2017）

(sq.m)

本年竣工房屋面积 Floor Space of Buildings Completed This Year	住宅 Residential Residence	本年竣工房屋价值（万元） Value of Buildings Completed this Year (10 000 yuan)	住宅 Residential Residence
19879485	**13389117**	**5719558**	**4480159**
60685	285		
604238	12674		
117800	2100		
2100			
288785	300		
20851			
164343			
23000	5000		
2300			
17468946	13249209	5719558	4480159
25500			
48185	800		
114674	37720		
44089	120		
562931	55517		
278782	25392		
26207			
26069			

5-15 主要年份市属固定资产投资

Investment In Fixed Assets of Municipal Units in Representative Years

单位：万元 (10 000 yuan)

指 标	Item	1995	2000	2002	2003	2004	2005	2006	2007	2008
一、投资总额	**Total Investment**	**432451**	**1263023**	**1848833**	**2978747**	**4355271**	**5788693**	**7835681**	**10555849**	**14648360**
#房地产开发	Real Estate	171291	473787	702233	1114809	1492693	2062940	2641871	3515719	4938202
按经济类型分	Grouped by Economic Type									
国有经济	State-owned Enterprises	258545	890546	1006245	1586057	1884624	2198836	2591184	2972840	4480627
集体经济	Collective-owned Enterprises	5720	52893	63877	142849	257226	258327	363909	1366567	1646111
其他经济	Others	168186	319584	778711	1249841	2213421	3331530	4880588	6216442	8521622
二、本年新增固定资产	**Newly Increased Fixed Assets this Year**	**273324**	**953173**	**1295389**	**1812099**	**1962795**	**3011104**	**3495179**	**5279938**	**6488364**
三、本年房屋竣工面积（万平方米）	**Floor Space of the Building this Year Completed(10 000sq.m)**	**202.52**	**509.48**	**537.44**	**631.89**	**606.23**	**767.7**	**914.8**	**1343.88**	**987.05**
#住宅	Residential Buildings	143.30	373.51	331.45	387.82	388.79	436.43	432.43	734.05	602.69

5-15 续表1 continued 1

单位：万元 (10 000 yuan)

指 标	Item	2009	2010	2011	2012	2013	2014	2015	2016	2017
一、投资总额	**Total Investment**	**19063075**	**25474854**	**26820029**	**35875223**	**44187825**	**50533650**	**45066446**	**44832319**	**63205102**
#房地产开发	Real Estate	6575526	8020893	9001953	11655613	14410956	16107323	17238478	18472701	22200672
按经济类型分	Grouped by Economic Type									
国有经济	State-owned Enterprises	6527566	9306901	8750285	12264895	12847731	12835067	13496036	17842932	31080614
集体经济	Collective-owned Enterprises	1614290	2253851	1897980	1932578	2148977	1927394	1493122	1318545	1370650
其他经济	Others	10921219	13914102	16171764	21677750	29191117	35771189	30077288	25670842	30753838
二、本年新增固定资产	**Newly Increased Fixed Assets this Year**	**8380033**	**10423906**	**10663882**	**15376910**	**16019776**	**21603094**	**17837619**	**17090770**	**27720621**
三、本年房屋竣工面积（万平方米）	**Floor Space of the Building this Year Completed(10 000sq.m)**	**1359.46**	**668.49**	**1002.82**	**1450.29**	**975.03**	**1591.28**	**902.22**	**1725.49**	**1823.00**
#住宅	Residential Buildings	727.41	448.46	531.38	1069.61	760.87	1262.20	640.60	1245.54	1203.36

5-16 市属固定资产投资（2017年）

Investment in Fixed Assets of Municipal Units（2017）

单位：万元　　　　(10 000 yuan)

指　标	Item	固定资产投资 Fixed Assets Investment	房地产开发 Real Estate
一、本年完成投资	**Investment Completed This Year**	**63205102**	**22200672**
#住宅	Residential Buildings	15261264	14905313
（一）按登记注册类型分	**Grouped by Registion Status**		
内资	Domestic Funded Enterprises	60208437	21482740
国有	State-owned Enterprises	19009022	463099
集体	Collective-owned Enterprises	632682	9284
股份合作	Cooperative Enterprises	29049	
联营	Joint Ownership Enterprises	4905	
国有联营	State Joint Ownership Enterprises		
集体联营	Collective Joint Ownership Enterprises	4905	
国有与集体联营	Joint State-collective Ownership Enterprises		
其他联营	Other Joint Ownership Enterprises		
有限责任公司	Limited Liability Corporations	27922975	14833356
国有独资公司	State-funded Corporations	4468243	946050
其他有限责任公司	Other Limited Liability Corporations	23454732	13887306
股份有限公司	Stock Limited Corporation	924596	385993
私营	Private Enterprises	10932769	5725355
私营独资	Private -funded Enterprises	889718	67874
私营合伙	Private Limited Liability Corporations	16126	
私营有限责任公司	Private Limited Liability Corporations	9690252	5509071
私营股份有限公司	Private Share Holding Corporations	336673	148410
其他	Others	752439	65653
港澳台商投资	Enterprises Funded by Hong Kong, Macao and Taiwan	1238324	410797
与港澳台合资经营	Joint-venture Enterprises	581017	40716
与港澳台合作经营	Cooperative Enterprises	53090	53090
港澳台独资	Wholly Funded from Hong Kong,Macao and Taiwan	566084	278858
港澳台投资股份有限公司	Share-holding Corporations Ltd.		
其他港澳台投资	Investment From Hongkong,Macao,Taiwan	38133	38133
外商投资	Foreign Owned Enterprises	1750380	307135
中外合资经营	Joint-venture Enterprises	628278	130756
中外合作经营	Cooperation Enterprises		
外资企业	Foreign Funded Enterprises	1097286	151563

5-16 续表 continued

单位：万元 (10 000 yuan)

指　标	Item	固定资产投资 Fixed Assets Investment	房地产开发 Real Estate
外商投资股份有限公司	Share-holding Corporations Ltd. With Foreign Funds	24816	24816
其他外商投资	Foreign Investment		
（二）按建设性质分	**Grouped by Type of Construction**		
#新建	New Construction	35671980	
扩建	Expansion	1713410	
改建和技术改造	Reconstruction	2073211	
（三）按构成分	**Grouped by Composition**		
建筑工程	Construction Projects	43625616	14461298
安装工程	Installment Projects	5002517	2727544
设备、工器具购置	Purchasing of Equipment and Instruments	5282298	527069
其他费用	Others	9294671	4484761
二、本年完成投资额构成(%)	**the Constitution of Compeleted Investment this Year (%)**		
（一）按登记注册类型分组	**Grouped by Status**		
# 国有经济	State-owned	26.7	4.4
集体经济	Collective-owned	-36.3	-96.7
（二）按建设性质分	**Grouped by Type of Construction**		
# 新建	New Construction	13.4	
扩建	Expansion	4.3	
改建和技术改造	Reconstruction	120.5	
（三）按构成分	**Grouped by Composition of Funds**		
建筑工程	Construction Projects	7.1	5.0
安装工程	Installation Projects	19.6	11.1
设备、工器具购置	Purchasing of the Equipment and Instruments	8.5	90.2
其他	Others	80.7	74.9
三、本年新增固定资产	**Newly Increase in Fixed Assets this Year**	**27720621**	**7803981**
四、房屋面积（万平方米）	**Floor Space (10 000 sq.m)**		
本年房屋施工面积	Floor Space of Buildings Under Construction This Year	16299.96	14942.86
#住宅	Residential Buildings	10649.57	10475.74
本年房屋竣工面积	Floor Space of Buildings Completed this Year	1823.00	1512.87
#住宅	Residential Buildings	1203.36	1167.1
五、本年竣工房屋价值	**Value of the Building Completed this Year**	5480446	5480446
#住宅	Residential Buildings	4260847	4260847

5-17 按国民经济行业分市属固定资产投资（2017年）

Investment in Fixed Assets of Municipal Units by Industry（2017）

单位：万元 (10 000 yuan)

行 业	Sector	2017
本年完成固定资产投资	**Grouped by Sector**	63205102
（一）农、林、牧、渔业	Agriculture,Forestry,Animal Husbandry and Fishery	1288071
（二）采矿业	Mining	54993
（三）制造业	Manufacturing	7262474
农副食品加工业	Processing of Food from Agricultural Products	74731
食品制造业	Manufacture of Foods	270117
酒、饮料和精制茶制造业	Wine, Soft Drinks and Refined Tea Industry	48978
烟草制品业	Tobacco Processing	
纺织业	Textile Industry	24231
纺织服装、服饰业	Textile, Apparel Industry	27260
皮革、毛皮、羽毛及其制品和制鞋业	Leather, Fur, Feather (eiderdown) and Their Products Industry	
木材加工和木、竹、藤、棕、草制品业	Timber Processing,Bamboo,Cane,Palm Fiber and Straw Products	82401
家具制造业	Furniture Manufacturing	201533
造纸及纸制品业	Papermaking and Paper products	66599
印刷和记录媒介复制业	Printing,Record Medium Reproduction	49518
文教、工美、体育和娱乐用品制造业	Culture, Education, Craft Art, Sports and Entertainment Goods Manufacturing Industry	47466
石油加工、炼焦和核燃料加工业	Petroleum Refining, Ccoke Making and Nuclear Fuel Processing Industry	10572
化学原料和化学制品制造业	Raw Chemical Materials and Chemical Products	235819
医药制造业	Medical and Pharmaceutical Products	340372
化学纤维制造业	Chemical Fiber	
橡胶和塑料制品业	Rubber and Plastic Products Industry	190674
非金属矿物制品业	Nonmetal Mineral Products	326652
黑色金属冶炼和压延加工业	Smelting and Pressing of Ferrous Metals	27700
有色金属冶炼和压延加工业	Smelting and Pressing of Nonferrou Metals	410412
金属制品业	Metal Products	244144

5-17 续表 continued

单位：万元 (10 000 yuan)

行 业	Sector	2017
通用设备制造业	General Equipment Manufacturing Industry	387706
专用设备制造业	Special Purpose Equipment	863038
汽车制造业	Automotive Manufacturing	588140
铁路、船舶、航空航天和其他运输设备制造业	Railroad, Marine, Aerospace and Other Transportation Equipment Manufacturing	620838
电气机械和器材制造业	Electric Equipment and Machinery	833539
计算机、通信和其他电子设备制造业	Communication Equipment, Computer and Other Electronic Equipment Manufacturing Industry	969136
仪器仪表制造业	Instrument Manufacturing Industry	200076
其他制造业	Other Manufacturing	64356
废弃资源综合利用	Comprehensive Utilization of Waste Resources	19136
金属制品、机械和设备修理业	Metal Products, Machinery and Equipment Repair Industry	37330
（四）电力、燃气及水的生产供应业	Production & Supply of Electricity,Gas & Water	1516207
（五）建筑业	Construction	122691
（六）批发和零售业	Wholesale and Retail Trades	1178707
（七）交通运输、仓储和邮政业	Transport, Storage and Post	3257458
（八）住宿和餐饮业	Hotels and Catering Services	463204
（九）信息传输、软件和信息技术服务业	Information Transmission,Computer Service and Software	287699
（十）金融业	Financial Intermediation	44931
（十一）房地产业	Real Estate	26381035
（十二） 租赁和商务服务业	Leasing and Business Services	1239495
（十三）科学研究和技术服务业	Scientific Research,Technical Service and Geologic Prospecting	543123
（十四）水利、环境和公共设施管理业	Management of Water Conservancy, Environment and Public Facilities	15580882
（十五）居民服务、修理和其他服务业	Services to Households, Repairs and Other Services	177974
（十六）教育	Education	1976628
（十七）卫生和社会工作	Health and Social Work	738000
（十八）文化、体育和娱乐业	Culture, Sports and Entertainment	845302
（十九）公共管理、社会保障和社会组织	Public Administration, Social Security and Social Organizations	246228
（二十）国际组织	International Organizations	

5-18 按资金来源及建设性质分市属固定资产投资（2017年）

Investment in Fixed Assets of Municipal Units by Sources of Funds and Type of Construction (2017)

单位：万元 (10 000 yuan)

指　标	Item	2017
投资总额	**Total Investment**	**63205102**
一、按资金来源分	**Grouped by Funds Sources**	
1. 国家预算内资金	State Budgetary Funds	3578519
2. 国内贷款	Domestic Loans	10164060
3. 债券	Bonds	2800
4. 利用外资	Utilization of Foreign Funds	322286
5. 自筹资金	Self-raising Funds	53713115
6. 其他资金	Others	26080010
二、按建设性质分	**Grouped by Type of Construction**	
#新建	New Construction	35671980
扩建	Expansion	1713410
改建	Reconstruction	2073211
三、按构成分	**Grouped by Composition of Funds**	
1. 建筑工程	Construction Project	43625616
2. 安装工程	Installation Projects	5002517
3. 设备、工器具购置	Purchasing of Equipment and Instruments	5282298
4. 其他费用	Others	9294671
四、房屋施工面积（万平方米）	**Floor Space of Buildings Under Construction (10 000 sq.m)**	**16299.96**

5-19 分区县、开发区全社会固定资产投资额（2017年）

Total Investment in Fixed Assets by Region and Development Zone（2017）

单位：亿元 （100 million yuan）

区县、开发区	Region	全社会固定资产投资 Fixed Assets Investment	固定资产投资 Urban Area	房地产 Real Estate	农户投资 Farmer Investment
区县	**Region**	**5447.94**	**5369.26**	**2079.26**	**78.68**
新城区	Xincheng	248.95	248.95	123.39	
碑林区	Beilin	223.93	223.93	77.24	
莲湖区	Lianhu	240.30	240.30	164.13	
灞桥区	Baqiao	678.30	672.13	227.72	6.17
未央区	Weiyang	914.44	912.26	466.75	2.18
雁塔区	Yanta	1061.91	1061.91	650.13	
阎良区	Yanliang	180.27	176.53	34.99	3.74
临潼区	Lintong	171.53	158.81	36.02	12.72
长安区	Chang'an	554.48	540.79	198.66	13.69
高陵区	Gaoling	523.32	519.63	62.21	3.69
鄠邑区	Huyi	183.55	172.97	26.53	10.58
蓝田县	Lantian	311.77	299.08	3.88	12.69
周至县	Zhouzhi	155.19	141.97	7.61	13.22
#开发区	**Development Zones**	**3091.42**	**3091.42**	**1236.90**	
高新区	GaoXin	842.71	842.71	322.43	
经开区	JingKai	775.84	775.84	270.87	
曲江新区	Qujiang	422.59	422.59	267.24	
浐灞生态区	Chanba Eco-District	539.64	539.64	230.17	
航空基地	Aviation Industry Base	129.66	129.66	21.99	
航天基地	Aerospace Base	169.22	169.22	96.01	
国际港务区	International Trade&Logistic Park	211.76	211.76	28.19	

5-20 分区县工业投资（2017年）

Industrial Investment by Region（2017）

单位：万元　　　　(10 000 yuan)

区县	Region	投资额 Investment	工业企业技术改造 Technological Transformation of Industrial Enterprises
全　市	**Total**	**10720579**	**2388201**
新城区	Xincheng	138708	63107
碑林区	Beilin	164226	15102
莲湖区	Lianhu	117388	14883
灞桥区	Baqiao	165330	50838
未央区	Weiyang	1317652	150324
雁塔区	Yanta	806694	463022
阎良区	Yanliang	707871	240748
临潼区	Lintong	287034	42471
长安区	Chang'an	1661624	716130
高陵区	Gaoling	1966580	169003
鄠邑区	Huyi	603877	123787
蓝田县	Lantian	385533	138697
周至县	Zhouzhi	244268	107349

5-21 分区县、开发区新增固定资产及房屋施工、竣工面积（2017年）

区县、开发区	Region	本年新增固定资产（亿元）Increased Fixed Assets this Year (100 million yuan)	房屋施工面积（万平方米）Floor Space of Buildings Under Construction (10 000sq.m)	住宅 Residential Buildings
区县	**Region**	**2283.30**	**16368.72**	**10672.61**
新城区	Xincheng	87.68	827.05	583.04
碑林区	Beilin	208.85	1073.30	679.97
莲湖区	Lianhu	87.73	1559.15	1243.83
灞桥区	Baqiao	263.52	1695.84	1247.25
未央区	Weiyang	374.72	3762.31	2364.27
雁塔区	Yanta	357.67	3883.04	2307.72
阎良区	Yanliang	60.55	213.51	135.36
临潼区	Lintong	57.62	290.10	176.51
长安区	Chang'an	190.42	1911.45	1229.85
高陵区	Gaoling	274.51	572.43	392.47
鄠邑区	Huyi	47.05	354.20	151.88
蓝田县	Lantian	220.87	108.53	90.17
周至县	Zhouzhi	52.11	117.81	70.29
开发区	**Development Zones**	**955.12**	**7458.41**	**4424.24**
高新区	GaoXin	223.46	1356.40	502.19
经开区	JingKai	285.54	1591.26	864.42
曲江新区	Qujiang	118.35	1628.27	1064.25
浐灞生态区	Chanba Eco-District	143.71	1661.04	1266.54
航空基地	Aviation Industry Base	27.01	80.32	42.25
航天基地	Aerospace Base	58.75	979.10	615.94
国际港务区	International Trade&Logistic Park	98.30	162.02	68.65

Newly Added Fixed Assets and Floor Space of Constructing and Completed Buildings by Region and Development Zone（2017）

本年房屋竣工面积（万平方米）Floor Space of Buildings this Year Completed(10 000 sq.m)	住宅 Residential Buildings	本年房屋竣工价值（亿元）Value of Buildings Completed this Year (100 million yuan)	住宅 Residential Buildings	本年商品房销售面积（万平方米）Floor Space of Houses Sales this year (sq.m) Houses(10 000sq.m)	本年商品房销售额（亿元）Sales Income of Commercial Houses this year(100 million yuan)
1828.45	**1257.06**	**543.41**	**423.98**	**2399.71**	**2041.22**
118.45	79.92	38.77	19.80	65.09	51.17
344.93	211.65	72.55	58.58	107.41	86.28
106.13	85.71	29.72	26.96	128.40	106.66
110.37	82.43	32.94	25.56	275.97	203.98
443.30	312.12	161.00	114.02	601.49	490.33
375.91	308.77	156.87	137.46	676.36	729.99
29.45	21.27	8.70	6.88	29.31	14.31
56.17	24.80	1.59	1.54	44.70	30.11
92.60	55.87	21.71	17.06	287.85	244.27
73.24	50.73	14.77	12.09	107.69	49.64
31.14	10.98	2.33	2.11	49.31	25.29
21.88	10.46	1.63	1.46	14.91	5.41
24.88	2.35	0.83	0.46	11.22	3.78
430.35	**333.98**	**181.26**	**145.87**	**1343.60**	**1272.69**
62.35	49.04	23.21	19.52	217.75	272.91
131.71	95.76	41.42	29.41	283.81	205.14
49.84	44.85	52.05	43.58	387.73	402.36
104.40	85.27	43.46	35.76	303.11	276.87
2.50	2.50	1.10	1.10	6.36	4.30
78.67	56.56	20.02	16.50	104.35	86.69
0.88				40.49	24.42

5-22 主要年份房地产开发投资主要指标

单位：万平方米

指 标	Item	1997	1998	1999	2000	2001	2002
本年完成投资额（亿元）	Investment Completed This Year(100 million yuan)	24.68	38.21	44.30	51.85	67.42	79.37
本年房屋施工面积	Floor Space of Buildings Under Construction This Year	451.47	678.87	793.46	763.18	743.78	1172.58
#住宅	Residential Buildings	331.16	552.37	649.53	619.85	580.43	964.68
本年房屋竣工面积	Floor Space of Buildings Completed This Year	135.62	156.17	377.79	321.10	316.24	329.71
#住宅	Residential Buildings	120.33	133.33	352.28	295.55	269.61	290.30
本年房屋竣工价值（亿元）	Value of Floor Space of Buildings Completed this Year(100million yuan)	11.96	14.36	38.22	26.94	37.20	36.93
#住宅	Residential Buildings	9.63	11.00	33.02	22.97	28.62	30.46
本年商品房销售面积	Floor Space of Commercialized Buildings Sold	78.45	117.11	296.97	212.92	225.35	252.90
#住宅	Residential Buildings	72.69	108.61	284.95	200.77	192.20	237.04
本年商品房销售额（亿元）	Total Sales of Commercialized Buildings(100 million yuan)	12.81	17.74	35.19	32.52	47.22	51.35
#住宅	Residential Buildings	11.39	15.46	32.35	29.46	35.53	45.46
本年批准预售面积	Approved Pre-sale Area of This Year	26.35	252.02	30.25	253.03	67.44	61.02
#住宅	Residential Buildings	23.27	246.77	27.34	253.03	65.20	55.73
待售面积	Area for Sale	58.71	32.52	62.38	36.41	50.82	57.14
#住宅	Residential Buildings	50.26	22.81	52.32	24.02	34.18	44.70
房屋出租面积	Rental Housing Area	25.69	1.04	1.88	1.17	9.19	15.75
#住宅	Residential Buildings	22.87	0.01	0.15	0.02	0.10	1.13
本年新增固定资产（亿元）	Newly Increased Fixed Assets This Year(100 million yuan)	14.36	19.93	43.10	38.38	50.77	48.43

Main Indicators of Investment in Real Estate Development in Representative Years

(10 000 sq.m)

2003	2004	2005	2006	2007	2008	2009	2010	2011	2012	2013	2014	2015	2016	2017
124.82	169.67	225.23	285.76	387.33	540.26	696.34	842.34	996.81	1281.90	1595.64	1761.88	1831.67	1955.82	2333.34
1343.12	1633.68	2174.29	2383.56	2915.95	3632.87	5708.63	6697.39	8247.69	9947.89	10454.27	12422.10	13392.94	14727.10	15843.92
943.61	1204.01	1783.36	1890.27	2376.82	3079.13	4901.59	5777.71	7108.27	8294.92	8461.71	9727.60	9777.23	10468.80	11134.28
339.67	380.84	361.62	399.64	483.30	443.96	542.81	463.65	631.03	1063.70	795.35	1533.70	976.64	1560.18	1634.63
289.56	308.06	316.52	342.15	422.47	412.46	453.49	412.44	564.59	903.82	663.20	1307.64	766.58	1259.24	1281.71
54.73	73.75	80.58	82.02	101.13	106.50	168.08	145.62	213.29	310.57	279.63	442.74	301.86	456.48	571.96
44.01	55.58	68.11	65.80	77.13	96.02	137.42	128.69	185.31	260.04	222.64	368.25	236.66	351.46	448.02
252.74	305.47	497.34	621.50	833.92	760.72	1256.02	1587.81	1778.02	1538.91	1662.75	1707.71	1763.68	2047.67	2509.78
230.28	279.90	476.39	584.06	782.91	715.76	1202.12	1523.24	1674.85	1383.84	1522.50	1525.95	1584.08	1877.78	2147.67
54.29	81.35	171.29	206.15	281.79	296.44	488.55	707.00	1091.31	1017.74	1112.87	1100.71	1146.79	1347.08	2123.34
44.25	71.27	158.03	179.47	251.74	268.92	450.71	661.27	973.71	858.53	976.19	928.74	985.35	1194.41	1743.43
52.35	176.40	300.07	428.20	491.07	569.22	1125.44	1510.20	3105.76	2627.73	1787.89	842.98	751.15	717.54	634.50
49.12	159.10	287.13	408.11	457.54	541.20	1095.17	1452.20	2826.79	2340.69	1597.82	727.31	583.55	508.17	515.34
63.85	108.52	123.59	112.49	45.42	55.40	40.68	34.32	59.76	102.58	74.59	187.13	296.50	378.24	379.66
52.34	72.76	99.17	85.89	38.62	35.40	28.73	26.23	45.41	83.78	61.24	143.21	185.96	215.40	176.90
10.56	11.18	17.32	8.53	10.84	34.94	38.23	28.60	8.01	15.16	15.57	7.15	19.64	48.67	57.12
5.43	5.78	4.09	3.74	5.36	4.53	6.55	0.70	3.25	4.03	0.73	0.07	1.47	1.47	
62.13	83.36	92.78	100.22	143.17	124.02	195.71	168.20	25.53	358.03	334.41	531.44	335.91	574.54	807.26

5-23 分区县、开发区房地产开发主要指标（2017年）

单位：万元

区县、开发区	Region	企业（单位）个数（个）Number of Enterprises (unit)	本年完成投资 Investment Completed This Year	本年新增固定资产 Increased Fixed Assets This Year
区县	**Region**	**963**	**20792586**	**7776262**
新城区	Xincheng	35	1233913	423919
碑林区	Beilin	92	772404	1267611
莲湖区	Lianhu	90	1641345	673893
灞桥区	Baqiao	104	2277164	427104
未央区	Weiyang	170	4667528	2055021
雁塔区	Yanta	208	6501260	2282889
阎良区	Yanliang	36	349895	88788
临潼区	Lintong	20	360165	21246
长安区	Chang'an	94	1986633	293090
高陵区	Gaoling	41	622072	174200
鄠邑区	Huyi	40	265281	24341
蓝田县	Lantian	15	38833	16274
周至县	Zhouzhi	18	76093	27886
#开发区	**Development Zones**	**386**	**12368799**	**2289188**
高新区	GaoXin	78	3224263	248695
经开区	JingKai	81	2708669	564733
曲江新区	Qujiang	84	2672267	709348
浐灞生态区	Chanba Eco-District	72	2301719	435175
航空基地	Aviation Industry Base	10	219863	12000
航天基地	Aerospace Base	46	960068	245205
国际港务区	International Trade&Logistic Park	15	281950	74032

Main Indicators of Real Estate Development by Region and Development Zone（2017）

(10 000 yuan)

房屋施工面积（平方米）Floor Space of Buildings Under Constmction(sq.m)	住宅 Residential Buildings	本年房屋竣工面积（平方米）Floor Space of Buildings Completed this Year(sq.m)	住宅 Residential Buildings	本年房屋竣工价值 Value of Buildings Completed this Year	住宅 Residential Buildings
148508538	**104120607**	**15479428**	**12212769**	**5433902**	**4240124**
7300463	5473115	1175773	792352	387661	198024
8405535	6171905	2553335	2074371	725458	585847
15116693	12187924	843143	775538	297152	269625
16474977	12419948	1007363	771706	329376	255635
36417731	23596766	4327785	3113741	1609994	1140237
36298679	23032193	3620672	3087656	1568713	1374646
2024054	1353562	252039	212696	86997	68816
1984017	1692093	188301	177301	15926	15375
16397522	11810204	671721	522173	217144	170637
4806501	3895756	588494	478442	147681	120939
1499713	966753	120037	109799	23255	21059
841308	817835	81940	73799	16274	14645
941345	702553	48825	23195	8271	4639
68545097	**43764808**	**4086805**	**3326829**	**1812470**	**1458750**
12159912	5021924	571994	490398	232094	195243
15526436	8644227	1307214	957603	414183	294057
14202088	10642450	498377	448544	520483	435803
15899321	12626851	1008193	852662	434552	357632
803177	422466	25000	25000	11000	11000
8362768	5720367	676027	552622	200158	165015
1591395	686523				

5-24 房地产开发投资主要指标（2017年）

Main Indicators of Investment in Real Estate Development（2017）

单位：万元 (10 000 yuan)

指标	Item	全市合计 Total	国有 State-owned	市区 Urban	市属 Municipal
一、企业（单位）个数（个）	**Number of Enterprises(unit)**	**1044**	**58**	**929**	**979**
二、本年完成投资	**Investment Completed This Year**	**23333373**	**1839997**	**22078264**	**22200672**
按工程用途分	Grouped by Function				
住宅	Residential Buildings	15663673	1447112	14918652	14905313
#别墅、高档公寓	Villas and Top-Grade Apartments	588850		423975	588650
办公楼	Office Buildings	2212039	153116	2112745	2092318
商业营业用房	Houses for Business Use	3197315	103149	2832756	3057410
其他	Others	2260346	136620	2214111	2145631
三、本年新增固定资产	**Increased Fixed Assets This Year**	**8072589**	**343621**	**7819656**	**7803981**
四、房屋施工面积（平方米）	**Floor Space of Buildings Under Construction (sq.m)**	**158439241**	**12024938**	**151433319**	**149428611**
#住宅	Residential Buildings	111342753	8857047	106393699	104757410
五、本年房屋竣工面积（平方米）	**Floor Space of Buildings this Year Completed (sq.m)**	**16346323**	**1053857**	**15715333**	**15128670**
#住宅	Residential Buildings	12817071	961640	12277932	11671005
六、本年房屋竣工价值	**Value of Buildings Completed this Year**	**5719558**	**339681**	**5497100**	**5480446**
#住宅	Residential Buildings	4480159	316672	4278553	4260847
七、本年商品房屋销售面积（平方米）	**Floor Space of Commercialized Buildings Sold this Year(sq.m)**	**25097758**	**1064832**	**24028608**	**23596677**
本年商品房销售额	Sales Income of Commercialized Buildings	21233383	920537	20667867	20035664

5-25 商品房销售情况（2017年）

Sales of Commercial Houses（2017）

指 标	Item	全市合计 Total	国有 State-owned	市区 Urban	市属 Municipal
本年商品房销售面积（平方米）	**Floor Space of Commercialized Buildings Sold(sq.m)**	**25097758**	**1064832**	**24028608**	**23596677**
现房销售面积（平方米）	**Floor Space of Completed Apartment Sales (sq.m)**	**3609109**	**175899**	**3228160**	**3377877**
期房销售面积（平方米）	**Floor Space of Forward Delivery Housing Sales (sq.m)**	**21488649**	**888933**	**20800448**	**20218800**
住宅	Residential Buildings	21476743	995717	20492595	20183819
#别墅、高档公寓	Villas and High-grade Apartments	604239	149755	549114	552119
办公楼	Office Buildings	1451883	38714	1449683	1388937
商业营业用房	Houses for Business Use	1375392	26686	1293090	1279631
其他	Others	793740	3715	793240	744290
本年商品房销售额（万元）	**Real estate sales this year(10 000Yuan)**	**21233383**	**920537**	**20667867**	**20035664**
现房销售额（万元）	**Floor Space of Completed Apartment Sales**	**2504284**	**92894**	**2315921**	**2362763**
期房销售额（万元）	**Floor Space of Forward Delivery Housing Sales**	**18729099**	**827643**	**18351946**	**17672901**
住宅	Residential Buildings	17434263	800549	16927707	16470106
#别墅高档公寓	Villas and High-grade Apartments	795555	134724	713137	749238
办公楼	Office Buildings	1562763	78013	1561443	1456396
商业营业用房	Houses for Business Use	1773789	39830	1716292	1668136
其他	Others	462568	2145	462425	441026
待售面积（平方米）	**Area for Sale (sq.m)**	**3796551**	**93950**	**3443348**	**3502674**
#待售一年以上（一到三年）	Being Idle for One Year	1098794	49669	867722	959646
待售三年以上（含三年）	Being Idle for Three Years	54334	924	45473	53410
住宅	Residence	1768953	56763	1533937	1618899
#别墅高档公寓	Villas and High-grade Apartments	25040		5838	25040
办公楼	Office Buildings	212702		212702	212702
商业营业用房	Houses for Business Use	1202165	32769	1097726	1147834
其他	Others	612731	4418	598983	523239
房屋出租面积（平方米）	**Rental area (sq.m)**	**571221**	**2524**	**569121**	**571221**
住宅	Residential Buildings				
办公楼	Office Buildings	39865		39865	39865
商业营业用房	Houses for Business Use	524795	2524	522695	524795
其他	Others	6561		6561	6561

5-26 房地产开发投资资金来源（2017年）

Source of Funds for Investment in Real Estate Development（2017）

单位：万元 (10 000 yuan)

指 标	Item	全市合计 Total	国有 State-owned	市区 Urban	市属 Municipal
一. 本年资金来源合计	**Total**	**39135119**	**2790385**	**37459368**	**37406620**
1. 上年末结余资金	Balance of Last Year	8824106	558413	8571935	8429318
2. 本年实际到位资金	Fully Funded Capital this Year	30311013	2231972	28887433	28977302
(1) 国内贷款	Domestic Loans	3278891	296370	2987173	3180111
#银行贷款	Bank Loan	2490691	196170	2264308	2425891
非银行金融机构贷款	Loans from financial Institutions except Bank	788200	100200	722865	754220
(2) 自筹资金	Self-raising Funds	12315243	1513975	11739738	12026638
#定金及预收款	Earnest Money and Advance payment	8293213	187149	7994091	7824995
个人按揭贷款	Personal Mortgage Loan	4323182	108189	4151739	4071983
(3) 其他资金	Others	14714695	421627	14160288	13770319
二. 本年各项应付款合计	**Total Sums of Money to be Paid This Year**	**6658439**	**559226**	**6253134**	**6032161**
#工程款	Project Fund	3458509	175603	3250377	3245423

5-27 房地产开发经营情况（2017年）

Running of Real Estate Development（2017）

单位：万元 (10 000 yuan)

指 标	Item	全市合计 Total	国有 State-owned	市区 Urban	市属 Municipal
一、资产负债情况	**Assets and Liabilities**				
1. 资产总计	Total Assets	92085175	7432077	88975217	85189932
2. 负债合计	Total Liabilities	79543436	5717177	76715260	73380088
3. 所有者权益合计	Total Creditor's Equity	12541739	1714900	12259957	11809844
#实收资本	Held Capital	9089704	897293	8780245	8502431
二、损益及分配情况	**Profit or Loss and the Distribution**				
1. 主营业务收入	Revenue from Principal Business	15001437	888187	14649707	13660695
土地转让收入	Revenue of Land Transferred	1875		860	1875
商品房屋销售收入	Revenue of Commercial Houses Sold	14533051	762649	14191772	13210477
自持物业收入	Self-owned Property Income	232089	24410	231228	225195
#房屋出租收入	Revenue of Houses Leased	83578	12013	82987	80644
其他收入	Other Revenue	234422	101128	225847	223148
2. 主营业务成本	Cost of Principal Business	11526741	721524	11248880	10431551
3. 主营业务税金及附加	Taxes and Other Charges on Principal Business	579832	29871	573168	524458
4. 其他业务利润	Other Business Profit	7240	1578	7205	6774
5. 销售费用	Sales Expenditures	533594	22514	515186	496572
6. 管理费用	Management Cost	486067	47270	468649	444140
7. 财务费用	Fiscal Expenditure	220305	14336	213754	218629
#利息支出	Interest Exchange	171726	39866	167933	147456
8. 营业利润	Operating Profit	1560235	92167	1533258	1443558
投资收益	Investment Revenue	52366	36390	51752	31108
营业外收入	Non-business Revenue	40521	19502	32675	38834
营业外支出	Non-business Expenditures	62724	1601	46940	56348
9. 利润总额	Total Profit	1538031	110068	1518994	1426044
10. 应付职工薪酬	Salary Payable	448164	50890	426076	409460
11. 应交增值税	Value-added Tax Payable	320153	24853	315803	295240
三、全部从业人员年平均人数	**Average Number of Employed Persons**	**75447**	**6960**	**71674**	**13580**
四、本年应付工资总额	**Total Wages This Year**	**437366**	**33070**	**415497**	**78725**

主 要 统 计 指 标 解 释

全社会固定资产投资 是以货币形式表现的在一定时期内全社会建造和购置固定资产的工作量以及与此有关的费用的总称。该指标是反映固定资产投资规模、结构和发展速度的综合性指标，又是观察工程进度和考核投资效果的重要依据。全社会固定资产投资按登记注册类型可分为国有、集体、联营、股份制、私营和个体、港澳台商、外商、其他等。

固定资产投资(不含农户) 指城镇和农村各种登记注册类型的企业、事业、行政单位及城镇个体户进行的计划总投资500万元及500万元以上的建设项目投资和房地产开发投资，包含原口径城镇固定资产投资加上农村企事业组织项目投资，该口径自2011年起开始使用。

房地产开发投资 指各种登记注册类型的房地产开发公司、商品房建设公司及其他房地产开发法人单位和附属于其他法人单位实际从事房地产开发或经营活动的单位统一开发的包括统代建、拆迁还建的住宅、厂房、仓库、饭店、宾馆、度假村、写字楼、办公楼等房屋建筑物和配套的服务设施，土地开发工程（如道路、给水、排水、供电、供热、通讯、平整场地等基础设施工程)的投资；不包括单纯的土地交易活动。

农户投资 是指以农户为单位进行的房屋建设(主要指住宅建设)投资、农村对农、林、牧、渔及服务行业进行的投资(如农户近年广泛进行的设施农业投资)、以及农户购买生产性固定资产的投资。

固定资产投资的资金来源 根据固定资产投资的资金来源不同，分为国家预算资金、国内贷款、利用外资、自筹资金和其他资金。

（1）国家预算资金：包括一般预算、政府性基金预算、国有资本经营预算和社保基金预算等资金。

（2）国内贷款：指报告期固定资产投资单位向银行及非银行金融机构借入的用于固定资产投资的各种国内借款，包括银行利用自有资金及吸收的存款发放的贷款、上级主管部门拨入的国内贷款、国家专项贷款、地方财政专项资金安排的贷款、国内储备贷款、周转贷款等。

（3）利用外资：指报告期收到的用于固定资产建造和购置的境外资金（包括设备、材料、技术在内）。包括对外借款（外国政府、国际金融组织贷款、出口信贷、外国银行商业贷款、对外发行债券和股票）、外商直接投资及外商其他投资。不包括我国自有外汇资金（国家外汇、地方外汇、留成外汇、调剂外汇和中国银行自有资金发行的外汇贷款等）。计算利用外资时，需要折算成人民币，折算中所使用的外汇汇率按现汇计算，即按使用外汇时的汇率计算。

（4）自筹资金：指固定资产投资单位报告期收到的，由各地区、各部门及企、事业单位筹集用于固定资产投资的预算外资金，包括中央各部门、各级地方和企、事业单位的自筹资金。

（5）其他资金：指在报告期收到的除以上各种资金之外其他用于固定资产投资的资金，包括企业或金融机构通过发行各种债券筹集到的资金、社会集资、个人资金、无偿捐赠的资金及其他单位拨人的资金等。

固定资产投资按国民经济行业分 根据现有企业、事业、行政单位和建设项目建成投产后的主要产品种类或主要用途及社会经济活动性质来确定国民经济行业。一般情况下，一个建设项目或一个企业、事业单位只能属于一种国民经济行业。

固定资产投资按隶属关系分 是按建设单位或企业、事业、行政单位的主管上级机关确定的。

（1）中央：是指中共中央、人大常委会和国务院各部、委、局、总公司以及直属机构直接领导的建设项目和企业、事业、行政单位。这些单位的固定资产投资计划由国务院各部门直接编制和下达，建设中所需物资、主要设备以及建设中的问题都由中央有关部门安排和解决。

（2）地方：是由省（自治区、直辖市）、地区（州、盟、省辖市）、县（旗、县级市）三级政府及业务主管部门直接领导和管理的建设项目、企业、事业、行政单位。地方项目还包括不隶属以上各级政府及主管部门的建设项目和企业、事业单位，如外商投资企业和无主管部门的企业等。

固定资产投资按建设性质分 根据整个建设项目情况来确定。建设项目的性质一般分为新建、扩建、改建和技术改造、单纯建造生活设施、迁建、恢复、单纯购置。房地产开发单位、农户投资不划分建设性质。

（1）新建：一般指从无到有开始建设的企业、事业和行政单位或建设项目。有的单位原有基础很小，经过建设后新增的固定资产价值超过该企、事业、行政单位原有固定资产价值（原值）三倍以上的也应作为新建。

（2）扩建：指在厂内或其他地点，为扩大原有产品的生产能力（或效益）或增加新的产品生产能力，而增建主要的生产车间（或主要工程）、分厂、独立的生产线。行政、事业单位在原单位增建业务用房（如学校增建教学用房、医院增建门诊部、病房等）也作为扩建。

现有企、事业单位为扩大原有主要产品生产能力或增加新的产品生产能力，增建一个或几个主要生产车间（或主要工程）、分厂，同时进行一些更新改造工程的，也应作为扩建。

（3）改建和技术改造：指现有企业、事业单位，对原有设施进行技术改造或更新（包括相应配套的辅助性生产、生活福利设施）的建设项目。现有企业、事业单位为适应市场变化的需要，而改变企业的主要产品种类（如军工企业转产民用品等）的建设项目，应作为改建。原有产品生产作业线由于各工序（车间）之间能力不平衡，为填平补齐充分发挥原有生产能力而增建不增加本企业主要产品设计能力的车间，也应作为改建。技术改造是指企业、事业单位在现有基础上，用先进的技术代替落后的技术，用先进的工艺和装备代替落后的工艺和装备，以改变企业落后的技术经济面貌，实现以内涵为主的扩大再生产，达到提高产品质量、促进产品更新换代、节约能源、降低消耗、扩大生产规模、全面提高社会经济效益的目的。技术改造具体包括以下内容：机器设备和工具的更新改造；生产工艺改革、节约能源和原材料的改造；厂房建筑和公共设施的改造；劳动条件和生产环境的改造等。

固定资产投资按构成分 固定资产投资活动按其工作内容和实现方式分为建筑安装工程，设备工具器具购置和其他费用三个部分。

（1）建筑安装工程（建筑安装工作量）：指各种房屋、建筑物的建造工程和各种设备、装置的安装工程。包括各种房屋建造工程；各种用途设备基础和各种工业窑炉的砌筑工程及金属结构工程；为施工而进行的各种准备工作和临时工程以及完工后的清理工作等；铁路、道路的铺设，矿井的开凿及石油管道的架设等；水利工程；防空地下建筑等特殊工程；列入房屋工程预算内的暖气、卫生、通风、照明、煤气等设备的价值及装设油饰工程；列入建筑工程预算内的各种管道（蒸汽、压缩空气、石油、给排水等管道）、电力、电讯电缆导线等的敷设工程；以及各种机械设备的安装下程；为测定安装工程质量，对设备进行的试运工作；房地产开发单位进行的商品房屋开发建设工程、土地开发工程。

在建筑安装工程中，不包括被安装设备本身的价值。

（2）设备工具器具购置：指建设单位或企、事业单位购置或自制的，达到固定资产标准的设备、工具、器具的价值。新建单位及扩建单位的新建车间，按照设计或计划要求购置或自制的全部设备、工具、器具，不论是否达到固定资产标准均计入“设备工具器具购置”中。

（3）其他费用：指在固定资产建造和购置过程中发生的，除上述几项内容以外的各种应分摊计入固定资产的费用。

施工项目 指报告期内所有施工的建设项目个数，包括本年新开工的项目和以前年度开工在本年继续施工的建设项目。凡是报告期内施过工的建设项目，不论施工时间长短，均作为施工项目统计。施工项目个数可以反映一定时期固定资产投资的实际规模，与同期全部建成投产项目个数相比，可以从建设速度的角度反映固定资产投资的效果。

全部建成投产项目 指报告期内按设计文件规定的全部生产能力（或效益）建成投产，经验收合格交付使用的建设项目。

新增生产能力（或工程效益） 指通过固定资产投资活动而增加的设计能力（或工程效益）。主要指标包括建设规模、本年施工规模、自开始建设累计新增生产能力（或工程效益）、本年新增生产能力（或工程效益）等。

建设规模 指建设项目或工程设计文件中规定的全部设计能力（或工程效益）。包括已经建成投产和尚未建成投产的工程的生产能力（或工程效益）。

本年施工规模 指报告期内施工的单项工程的设计能力（或工程效益），即全部建设规模中在本年正式施工的部分。

自开始建设累计新增生产能力（或工程效益） 指自开始建设至本年底止建成投产的全部单项工程累计的新增生产能力（或工程效益）。

本年新增生产能力（或工程效益） 指在本年度内按照新增生产能力（或工程效益）的计算条件和标准，实际建成投入生产或交付使用的生产能力（或工程效益）。

施工房屋面积 指报告期内施工的全部房屋（包括地下室、半地下室以及配套房屋）建筑面积。包括本期新开工的面积和上期开工跨入本期继续施工的房屋面积，以及上期已停建在本期恢复施工的房屋面积。本期竣工和本期施工后又停缓建的房屋，其建筑面积仍计入本期房屋施工面积中。

竣工房屋面积 指在报告期内房屋建筑按照设计要求已经全部完工，达到住人和使用条件，经验收鉴定合格（或达到竣工验收标准），可正式移交使用单位的各栋房屋建筑面积的总和。

新增固定资产 指报告期内交付使用的固定资产价值。包括本年内建成投入生产或交付使用的工程投资和达到固定资产标准的设备、工具、器具的投资及有关应摊入的费用。该指标是表示固定资产投资成果的价值指标，也是反映建设进度，计算固定资产投资效果的重要指标。

项目建成投产率 指一定时期内全部建成投产项目个数与同期施工项目个数的比率。该指标是从建设单位建设速度的角度反映投资效果的指标。

固定资产交付使用率 指一定时期新增固定资产与同期完成投资额的比率。该指标是反映固定资产动用速度，衡量建设过程中宏观投资效果的综合指标。由于新增固定资产是较长时期内形成的结果，而投资额则是当年完成的，因此，该指标一般适宜于反映较长时期内固定资产的动用情况。

商品房销售面积 指报告期内出售商品房屋的合同总面积（即双方签署的正式买卖合同中所确定的建筑面积）。由现房销售建筑面积和期房销售建筑面积两部分组成。

商品房销售额 指报告期内出售商品房屋的合同总价款（即双方签署的正式买卖合同中所确定的合同总价）。该指标与商品房销售面积同口径，由现房销售额和期房销售额两部分组成。

经济适用房 指根据经济适用房计划安排建设的政策性住宅。经济是指房屋建筑造价和销售价格低于一般商品住宅；适用是指适合中低收入家庭购买使用。经济适用房主要是由地方政府统一下达投资计划，房地产公司开发，对外销售；用地一般采用行政划拨或招标投标方式，免收土地出让金；对各种经批准的收费减半征收，开发利润不超过3%；销售价格实行政府指导价。该指标可以分析房地产投资结构，反映中低收入家庭商品住宅的供求平衡情况。

Explanatory Notes on Main Statistical Indicators

Total Investment in Fixed Assets in the Whole Country refers to the volume of activities in construction and purchases of fixed assets of the whole country and related fees, expressed in monetary terms during the reference period. It is a comprehensive indicator which shows the size, structure and growth of the investment in fixed assets, providing a basis for observing the progress of construction projects and evaluating results of investment. Total investment in fixed assets in the whole country includes, by type of ownership, the investment by State-owned units, collective-owned units, joint ownership units, share-holding units, private units individuals as well as investments by entrepreneurs from Hong Kong, Macao and Taiwan, foreign investors and others.

Investment in Fixed Assets (Excluding Rural Households) refers to the investment in construction projects with a total planned investment of 5 million yuan and above by enterprises of various ownerships, public institutions, administrative units and urban self-employed individuals, and the investment in real estate development in both urban and rural areas. Since 2011, it covers the urban investment in fixed assets of original statistical ranges and project investments by rural enterprises and public institutions.

Investment in Real Estate Development refers to investment by real estate development companies, commercialized buildings construction companies and other real estate development units of various types of ownership in the construction of buildings, such as residential buildings, factory buildings, warehouses, hotels, guesthouses, holiday villages, office buildings, and the complementary service facilities and land development projects, such as roads, water supply, water drainage,power supply,heating sup ply, telecommunications, land leveling and other infrastructural projects. It does not include activities in pure land transactions.

Investmentof Rural Households refers to the Housing construction investment (mainly residential construction) taken by the Rural Households as one unit, rural investment in agriculture, forestry, animal husbandry, fishery and service industries (such as the extensive facility agriculture investment of farmers in recent years) and investment in productive fixed assets purchased by farmers.

Sources of Funds for Investment in Fixed Assets are categorized as funds from the State budget, domestic loans, foreign investment, self-raised funds, and others, depending on the sources of investment.

(1) Fund from the State budget consists of budgetary appropriation and loans from the State budget. More specifically, it includes, from the budget of the central government, capital construction fund (operation fund and non-operational fund), special expenses, loans from repayment, discount fund, expenses on innovation and trial production of new products, expenses on urban construction, expenses on temporary construction from business departments, development fund for less developed areas, as well as local budgetary fund transferred from the central budget.

(2) Domestic loans refer to loans of various forms borrowed by investing units from banks and non-bank financial institutions during the reference period for the purpose of investment in fixed assets, including loans issued by banks from their self-owned funds and deposit, loans appropriated by higher authorities, special loans by government, loans arranged by local government from special funds, domestic reserve loan, and working loan.

(3) Foreign investment refers to overseas funds received during the reference period for the construction and purchase of investment in fixed assets (covering equipment, materials and technology), including foreign borrowings (loans from foreign governments and international financial institutions, export credit, commercial loans from foreign banks, issue of bonds and stocks overseas), foreign direct investment and other foreign investments. Excluded from this category is capital in foreign exchanges owned by China (foreign exchanges owned by the central and local governments, foreign exchanges retained by enterprises, foreign exchanges by enterprises through the regulating mechanism, loans in foreign exchanges issued by the Bank of China with its own fund, etc). In calculating the utilization of foreign capital, foreign currencies are converted into Chinese Renminbi applying the current exchange rate when the foreign capitals are actually used.

(4) Self-raised funds refer to extra-budgetary funds for investment in fixed assets received during the reference period by investing units from central government ministries, local governments, enterprises and institutions, including their self-raised funds.

(5) Others refer to funds for investment in fixed assets received from sources other than those listed above, including capital raised through issuing bonds by

enterprises or financial institutions, funds raised from individuals and through donations, and funds transferred from other units.

Investment in Fixed Assets by Sector The classification of construction projects by sector is determined by enterprises, institutions, administrative units and the major products or the purpose of the projects of existing enterprises, institutional and administrative units when they are put into production or use, and by the nature of their social economic activities. In general, one project or one enterprise or institution can only be classified into one sector.

Investment in Fixed Assets by Jurisdiction of Management refers to the classification of investment by the competent authorities under which investment is made by construction units, enterprises, institutions or administrative units.

(1) Central investment refers to the investment in projects or by enterprises, institutions or administrative units which are under the direct leadership and management of the State Council and of the national commissions, ministries, agencies and State-owned large corporations. Various ministries and departments of the State Council prepare and implement plans for investment in fixed assets by those departments, and arrange and ensure the supply of materials and key equipment required for the projects.

(2) Local investment refers to the investment in projects or by enterprises, institutions or administrative units which are under the direct leadership and management of departments under the provincial, prefecture and county governments. Also included are projects by foreign-invested enterprises and enterprises without competent managing authorities.

Investment in Fixed Assets by Type of Construction Construction projects in general can be classified, by the type of construction, into new construction, expansion, reconstruction and technical transformation, purely construction of living facilities, moving, restoration and purely purchasing. However, investment by type of construction is not applied to investment by real-estate development units and investment by rural households.

(1) New construction in general refers to construction projects, which start from scratch, of enterprises, institutions, administrative agencies. In case the size of the existing unit is quite small, and the value of newly added fixed assets is more than three times of the original value, the expansion will be considered as new construction.

(2) Expansion refers to construction of new major production workshop, branch factory or independent production line within a factory or in other locations, for the purpose of increasing the production capacity (or improving efficiency) or adding new production capacity. Newly constructed accommodation for the operation of institutions and administrative organizations (such as newly constructed buildings for teaching in schools, buildings for clinics or wards in hospitals, etc.) are also classified as expansion.

Also included in expansion are investments by existing enterprises or institutions in building major production line(s) or branch factory(ies) along with some work on innovation, for the purpose of expanding the production capacity of original products or producing new products.

(3) Reconstruction and technical transformation refers to construction projects by existing enterprises or institutions in innovation or technical transformation of the old facilities (including auxiliary production equipment and welfare facilities). Also considered as reconstruction is the construction of new workshops by the existing enterprises or institutions to change the variety of products to meet the market demand (such as the production of civil products by defence industries), or to bring the designed production capacity into full play through a more balanced production process on production lines. Technical transformation refers to replacement of old technology or equipment by new technology or equipment, in order to expand the reproduction through improvement of technology contents in production, to improve product quality, to promote new products to save energy,to reduce consumption, to expand the production scale and to improve overall social-economic efficiency. Contents of technical transformation include: updating of machinery, equipment and tools; reforming production process by using energy or materials saving technology; construction of factory workshops and transformation of public facilities; improvement of working conditions and environment, etc.

Investment in Fixed Assets by Structure By their

contents and the mode of implementation, investment activities are classified into 3 categories, i.e. construction and installation, purchase of equipment and instrument, and other expenses.

(1) Construction and installation (work volume of construction and installation) refers to the construction of houses and buildings and the installation of various kinds of equipment and instruments. They include construction of houses; equipment foundations, industrial kilns and stoves, and metal structure work; preparation works and temporary works for project construction, and clearing up works post project construction; pavement of railways and roads, drilling of mines and putting up of oil pipes; construction of water conservancy; construction of underground air-raid shelters and construction of other special projects; value of equipment for heating, sanitation, ventilation, lighting, gas, painting, etc. that are covered by the budget of housing projects; laying out of various pipelines (for steam, compressed air, petroleum, tap water and sewage) and wiring and cabling for electric power and for communications; installation of various machinery and equipment; testing operation for pre- testing the quality of installation projects, and land and other development work conducted by real estate developers for commercialized housing.

The value of equipment installed is itself not included in the value of construction and installation projects.

(2) Purchase of equipment and instruments refers to the total value of equipment, tools, and instruments purchased or self-produced which come up to the cut-off point for fixed assets by the construction units or investing enterprises or institutions. Equipment, tools and instruments purchased or self-produced for new workshops by newly established or expanded units are categorized as "purchase of equipment and instruments" no matter whether they come up to the cut-off point for fixed assets.

(3) Other expenses refer to expenses arising during the construction or purchase of fixed assets other than those mentioned above.

Projects under Construction refer to number of all projects with construction activities newly started in current year or left-over from the previous year in the reference period. All projects that have construction activities undertaken during the reference period are reported as projects under construction irrespective of the length of construction work. The number of projects under construction can reflect the actual size of investment in fixed assets during a given period, and when compared with the number of projects completed and put into use during the same period, it demonstrates the results of investment in fixed assets from the angle of the speed of the construction.

Projects Completed and Put into Use refer to projects have been completed in accordance with the design documents, resulting in forming production capacity (efficiency) and have been checked and accepted after relevant tests, and have been formally delivered for use.

Newly Increased Production Capacity (or Project Efficiency) refers to the increase in design capacity (or project efficiency) through investment in fixed assets. The main indicators include: construction scale, scale of projects under construction in current year, the accumulated newly increased production capacity (project efficiency) since the start of the projects and the newly increased production capacity (project efficiency) of current year.

Construction Scale refers to the total designed production capacity (project efficiency) of the construction projects in accordance with the design document, including those have been put into operation and those that have not been completed.

Scale of Projects under Construction in Current Year refers to the designed production capacity (project efficiency) of a single project under construction in the reference period, i.e. the part of the total scale of project which is officially under construction in current year.

The Accumulated Newly Increased Production Capacity (project efficiency) since the Start of the Projects refers to the accumulated newly increased production capacity of all the single projects which have been put into use from the beginning of the projects till the end of current year.

The Newly Increased Production Capacity (project efficiency) of Current Year refers to the production capacity (project efficiency) that has been completed and put into operation in current year according to the calculation conditions and standards on newly increased production capacity (project efficiency).

Floor Space of Buildings under Construction refers to the total floor space of all the buildings (including basement, semi-basement and auxiliary buildings), including the effective area and the area occupied by the structure. This indicator is one of the important indicators in physical terms to reflect the scale and accomplishment of the construction industry and also an important basis for monitoring the progress, Calculating the cost, analyzing the efficiency and studying the supply of building materials in relation to the construction projects.

Floor Space Completed refers to the floor space of all buildings completed in the reference period, which have been appraised and accepted (or come up to the designed standards) and have been transferred to owner units.

Newly Increased Fixed Assets refer to the value of fixed that has been put into use, including investment in projects that have been completed and put into operation in current year and the investment in equipment, tools and appliance that meet the standard of fixed assets and fees that should be apportioned. This is an indicator that demonstrates the results of investment in fixed assets in monetary terms, and an important indicator to reflect the speed of construction and to calculate the efficiency of investment.

Rate of Construction Projects Completed and Put into Use refers to the ratio of the number of construction projects completed and put into use in a certain period of time to the number of projects under construction in the same period. This reflects the investment efficiency from the perspective of the speed of projects construction.

Rate of Projects of Fixed Assets Completed and Put into Operation refers to the ratio of the newly increased fixed assets to the total investment made in the same period. This is a comprehensive indicator reflecting the speed of the employment of fixed assets and the investment efficiency at the macro-level. As the newly increase fixed assets is the result of a long period while the investment is completed in the current year, this indicator is expected to be used to reflect the employment of fixed assets over a long period of time.

6 财 政

GOVERNMENT FINANCE

资料整理：罗延庆
Data management:Luo yanqing
数据审核：陈　英
Data audit:Chen Ying

第六部分　财政

一、简要说明

本章资料主要包括地方财政收入、支出总额构成及分区县情况，由西安市统计局综合处根据西安市财政局提供资料整理。

二、主要指标

财政总收入（亿元）	1364.71	比上年增长	12.6%
一般公共预算收入（亿元）	654.50	比上年增长	9.8%
一般公共预算支出（亿元）	1045.09	比上年增长	7.1%

6　GOVERNMENT FINANCE

Ⅰ.Brief Introduction

This chapter consists of primarily data on regional revenue, expenditure of the municipal government, regional revenue and expenditure of the districts and the counties. The data are provided by the Xi'an Bureau of Finance and are compiled by Integration division of the Xi'an Bureau of Statistics.

Ⅱ.Major Indicators

		Increase over Preceding Year
Total Government Revenue(100 mil. yuan)	1364.71	12.6%
General Pubilc Budgetary Revenue(100 mil. yuan)	654.50	9.8%
General Pubilc Budgetary Expenditures(100 mil. yuan)	1045.09	7.1%

6-1 主要年份地方财政一般预算收入及支出

General Public Budgetary Revenue and Expenditure of Local Finance in Representative Years

单位：亿元 （100 million yuan）

年 份 Year	财政总收入 Fiscal Revenue	一般公共预算收入 General Public Budgetary Revenue	一般公共预算支出 General Public Budgetary Expenditure	收支差额 Balance of Payments	财政总收入比上年增长（%） Fiscal Revenue Increased over the Previous Year（%）	一般公共预算收入比上年增长（%） General Public Budget Revenue Growth over the Previous Year（%）	一般公共预算支出比上年增长（%） General Public Budget Expenditures Growth over the Previous Yea r（%）
2000	61.57	41.39	46.50	-5.11		14.4	
2001	75.79	51.45	54.21	-2.76	23.1	9.9	10.2
2002	99.84	54.49	63.80	-9.31	31.7	16.9	11.3
2003	120.64	64.80	72.37	-7.57	20.8	21.6	22.6
2004	133.52	75.31	84.20	-8.89	10.7	20.0	16.3
2005	163.87	73.05	97.82	-24.77	22.7	18.2	16.2
2006	195.96	85.89	119.22	-33.33	19.6	18.6	21.9
2007	260.70	112.92	161.25	-48.33	33.0	31.5	35.3
2008	324.49	145.61	226.99	-81.38	24.5	28.9	40.8
2009	399.53	181.40	276.85	-95.45	23.4	24.6	22.0
2010	510.69	241.86	371.62	-129.76	27.6	33.3	34.2
2011	649.88	318.55	494.58	-176.03	27.3	31.7	33.1
2012	753.08	396.96	597.49	-200.53	15.9	24.6	20.8
2013	902.76	501.98	729.81	-227.83	19.9	26.5	22.1
2014	1019.69	583.79	819.54	-235.75	13.0	16.3	12.3
2015	1114.98	650.99	917.24	-266.25	9.3	16.3	12.9
2016	1135.68	641.07	942.52	-301.45	8.5	11.1	2.8
2017	1364.71	654.50	1045.09	-390.59	12.6	9.8	7.1

注：本表数据来源于市财政局，对部分历史年份数据进行了修订。

6-2 财政收入（2017年）

Government Revenue（2017）

单位：万元 （10 000 yuan）

指　　标	Item	2017
财政总收入	**Total Government Revenue**	**13647091**
#一般公共预算收入	**General Public Budgetary Revenue**	**6544997**
一、税收收入	**Total Tax Revenue**	**4489896**
1. 国内增值税	Value-added Tax	789230
2. 改征增值税	Levying VAT	885126
3. 营业税	Business Tax	21926
4. 企业所得税	Corporate Income Tax	494491
5. 个人所得税	Individual Income Tax	262652
6. 城建税	City Maintenance and Construction Tax	382082
7. 房产税	House Property Tax	207007
8. 城镇土地使用税	Urban Land Use Tax	114348
9. 印花税	Stamp Tax	137343
10. 车船税	Tax on the Use of Vehicles and Ships	89819
11. 土地增值税	Land Appreciation Tax	369350
12. 资源税	Resource Tax	438
13. 耕地占用税	Farm Land Occupatian Tax	226075
14. 契税	Deed Tax	510009
二、非税收入	**Total Non-tax Revenue**	**2055101**
1. 行政性收费收入	Charge of Adminnistrative and Institutional Units	169029
2. 罚没收入	Penalty Receipts	548623
3. 专项收入	Special Program Receipts	322456
4. 国有资本经营收入	State-owned Assets Profit	298396
5. 国有资源（资产）有偿使用收入	Revenue for the Use of State-owned Assets (Resources)	600802
6. 捐赠收入	Donation Income	138
7. 政府住房基金收入	Governmental Housing Fund Income	68215
8. 其他收入	Other Revenue	47442
政府性基金预算收入	**Governmental Fund Budgetary Revenue**	**5505601**

注：本表数据来源于市财政局。

6-3 财政支出（2017年）

Government Expenditures (2017)

单位：万元 （10 000 yuan）

指　标	Item	2017
一、政府性基金支出	**Governmental Fund Budgetary Expenditure**	**4769664**
二、一般公共预算支出	**General Public Budgetary Expenditure**	**10450925**
1. 一般公共服务支出	Expenditure for General Public Services	836763
2. 国防支出	Expenditure for National Defense	16090
3. 公共安全支出	Expenditure for Public Security	639700
4. 教育支出	Expenditure for Education	1338949
5. 科学技术支出	Expenditure for Science and Technology	452846
6. 文化体育与传媒支出	Expenditure for Cultural, Sports and Media	255316
7. 社会保障和就业支出	Expenditure for Social Safety Net and Employment Effort	1256617
8. 医疗卫生与计划生育支出	Expenditure for Medical 、 Health Care and Brith Control Planning	881128
9. 节能环保支出	Expenditure for Energy Saving	432002
10. 城乡社区事务支出	Expenditure for Urban and Rural Community Affairs	2334825
11. 农林水事务支出	Expenditure for Agriculture, Forestry and Water Conservancy	593690
12. 交通运输支出	Expenditure for Transportation	143711
13. 资源勘探电力信息等事务支出	Expenditure for Exploration of the Power of Information	346587
14. 商业服务业等事务支出	Expenditure for Business Services	196353
15. 金融支出	Expenditure for Finance	32017
16. 国土海洋气象等支出	Expenditure for Land and Marine Meteorology	37381
17. 住房保障支出	Expenditure for Housing Security	441302
18. 粮油物资储备支出	Expenditure for Grain and Oil Stockpiles	17125
19. 债务付息支出	Debt Service Expenditure	169757
20. 其它支出	Other Expenditure	26355
21. 债务发行费用支出	Debt Issuance Expenditure	2411

注：本表数据来源于市财政局。

6-4 各区县、开发区财政收入（2017年）

单位：万元

区县、开发区	Region	一般公共预算收入 General Public Budgetary Revenue	税收收入 Tax Revenue	增值税 Value Added Tax	营业税 Business Revenue	企业所得税 Corporate Income Tax
合计	**Total**	**6544997**	**4489896**	**1674356**	**21926**	**494491**
市本级合计	**Sum of City Level**	**1109970**	**335462**	**66291**	**284**	**61341**
区、县合计	**Region**	**2855988**	**2188975**	**884759**	**10364**	**231609**
新城区	Xincheng	270221	181139	68608	-966	39063
碑林区	Beilin	409296	335724	155290	1709	56499
莲湖区	Lianhu	456934	320421	147334	222	33302
雁塔区	Yanta	449244	389913	159967	712	36292
灞桥区	Baqiao	191780	144956	49213	1499	10470
未央区	Weiyang	336148	259083	103887	3048	24581
阎良区	Yanliang	118939	84230	19166	107	3754
临潼区	Lintong	127946	104135	26485	497	4143
长安区	Chang'an	239837	184487	73487	2071	15445
高陵区	Gaoling	117293	94857	37452	1069	3773
鄠邑区	Huyi	84800	56616	29570	386	2886
蓝田县	Lantian	28507	17989	7722	10	1001
周至县	Zhouzhi	25043	15425	6578		400
开发区合计	**Sum of Development Zones**	**2123298**	**1571380**	**534129**	**9611**	**167659**
高新区	GaoXin	1024571	738843	273070	4591	97460
经开区	JingKai	411539	297205	134798	3194	26617
曲江新区	Qujiang	395018	297605	61359	712	21616
浐灞生态区	Chanba Eco-District	157985	119291	26769	152	8582
航天基地	Aerospace Base	55043	46115	12839	800	6307
航空基地	Aviation Industry Base	11918	9831	3668	69	1099
国际港务区	International Trade&Logistic Park	67224	62490	21626	93	5978

注：本表数据来源于市财政局。

Government Revenue by Region and Development Zone (2017)

(10 000 yuan)

一般公共预算收入 General Public Budgetary Revenue					
税收收入 Tax Revenue					
个人所得税 Individual Income Tax	资源税 Resource Tax	城市维护建设税 City Maintenance and Construction Tax	耕地占用税 Farm Land Occupation Tax	契税 Deed Tax	其他各项税收收入 Other Tax Revenue
262652	**438**	**382082**	**226075**	**510009**	**917867**
49056		**54797**			**103693**
115563	**432**	**173735**	**176785**	**226666**	**369062**
10119		15926		17439	30950
30227		29644		21812	40543
17281	1	29772		38943	53566
25762		31657	15613	54203	65707
3241		10535	20075	18055	31868
10018		22660	2182	32262	60445
4895		3193	41122	2640	9353
2548	4	5224	48563	4619	12052
6568	21	10962	23017	20302	32614
2604		8111	14785	9207	17856
1202	360	3941	4517	5011	8743
499	43	1220	3397	1141	2956
599	3	890	3514	1032	2409
87975	**2**	**125992**	**37531**	**233677**	**374804**
66259		69368	31200	51908	144987
10846	1	29174		36648	55927
5633	1	13060		90211	105013
1897		6013		35603	40275
1900		2850		7901	13518
372		1132		779	2712
1068		4395	6331	10627	12372

6-4 续表1

单位：万元

区县、开发区	Region	一般公共预算收入 General Public Budgetary Revenue 非税收入 Non-tax Revenue	专项收入 Special Program Receipts	行政事业性收费收入 Charge of Adiministrative and Institutional Units
合计	**Total**	**2055101**	**548623**	**322456**
市本级合计	**Sum of City Level**	**774508**	**216580**	**179415**
区、县合计	**Region**	**667013**	**162281**	**101924**
新城区	Xincheng	89082	8962	11312
碑林区	Beilin	73572	16809	8549
莲湖区	Lianhu	136513	17716	9681
雁塔区	Yanta	59331	16870	18145
灞桥区	Baqiao	46824	15626	5094
未央区	Weiyang	77065	12869	12032
阎良区	Yanliang	34709	26672	4589
临潼区	Lintong	23811	5311	2645
长安区	Chang'an	55350	24651	15042
高陵区	Gaoling	22436	6013	2720
鄠邑区	Huyi	28184	6223	8235
蓝田县	Lantian	10518	2021	1313
周至县	Zhouzhi	9618	2538	2567
开发区合计	**Sum of Development Zones**	**551918**	**131620**	**26847**
高新区	GaoXin	285728	39794	17789
经开区	JingKai	114334	17363	2873
曲江新区	Qujiang	97413	39489	4919
浐灞生态区	Chanba Eco-District	38694	27013	874
航天基地	Aerospace Base	8928	2782	25
航空基地	Aviation Industry Base	2087	1563	367
国际港务区	International Trade&Logistic Park	4734	3616	

continued 1

（10 000 yuan）

罚没收入 Penalty Receipts	国有资本经营收入 State-owned Assets Profit	国有资源(资产)有偿使用收入 The Revenues of the Compensation for the Use of State-owned Resoures(Assants)	其他收入 Other Income	政府性基金预算收入 Governmental Funds Budgetary Revenue
169029	**298396**	**600802**	**115795**	**5505601**
104283		**199371**	**74859**	**1489638**
55319	**2562**	**323394**	**21533**	**729951**
5119		63689		487
3075		44119	1020	
2964	2311	103841		137100
3718		20548	50	
2008		23980	116	162547
2967		29656	19541	13016
1884	171	1190	203	9879
11291	80	4484		77687
9184		6469	4	191573
2203		11436	64	45876
5608		7637	481	52528
2517		4633	34	6201
2781		1712	20	33057
6721	**295834**	**73460**	**17436**	**2303727**
2314	164977	54100	6754	293732
1927	91997	174		183985
1634	37810	13168	393	1153474
599		5817	4391	407231
186		37	5898	150574
52		105		21755
9	1050	59		92976

6-5 各区县、开发区财政支出（2017年）

单位：万元

区县、开发区	Region	一般公共预算支出 General Public Budgetary Expenditures	一般公共服务支出 General Public Services Expenditure	国防支出 Expenditure for National Defense	公共安全支出 Expenditure for Public Safety
合计	**Total**	**10450925**	**836763**	**16090**	**639700**
市本级合计	**Sum of City Level**	**3031973**	**213051**	**12912**	**300199**
区、县合计	**Region**	**4662268**	**348917**	**2071**	**294224**
新城区	Xincheng	283048	21627	141	29276
碑林区	Beilin	356500	30756		27601
莲湖区	Lianhu	443387	33013	294	31820
雁塔区	Yanta	361024	24971	160	41021
灞桥区	Baqiao	293695	23546	438	22215
未央区	Weiyang	330966	23993	191	28085
阎良区	Yanliang	239536	16612		13507
临潼区	Lintong	406723	24763		17215
长安区	Chang'an	530795	48735	236	27235
高陵区	Gaoling	253141	29372	116	12685
鄠邑区	Huyi	407011	25126	140	14377
蓝田县	Lantian	357590	21224	200	15533
周至县	Zhouzhi	398852	25179	155	13654
开发区合计	**Sum of Development Zones**	**2206967**	**195679**	**673**	**28696**
高新区	GaoXin	980236	42472	673	10542
经开区	JingKai	335000	26033		8616
曲江新区	Qujiang	329168	47658		1815
浐灞生态区	Chanba Eco-District	224181	39327		5927
航天基地	Aerospace Base	68836	6416		1056
航空基地	Aviation Industry Base	19906	1968		
国际港务区	International Trade&Logistic Park	249640	31805		740

注：本表数据来源于市财政局。

Government Expenditure by Region and Development Zone （2017）

（10 000 yuan）

教育支出 Expenditure for Education	科学技术支出 Expenditure for Science and Technology	文化体育与传媒支出 Expenditure for Culture,Sport and Media	社会保障和就业支出 Expenditure for Social Safety Net and Employment Effort	医疗卫生与计划生育支出 Medical 、 Health and Family Planning Expenditure	节能环保支出 Expenditure for Energy Saving and Environment Protection
1338949	**452846**	**255316**	**1256617**	**881128**	**432002**
141125	**107340**	**68731**	**425463**	**333244**	**128761**
999636	**23705**	**46761**	**752544**	**504745**	**54975**
51955	1496	753	69102	18352	4
59478	4092	1812	70121	20783	1525
86419	6087	948	78066	26878	1166
82816	1194	3797	67472	30807	1047
54021	766	5007	37607	27372	11238
79798	2399	2376	52480	22884	3724
37148	1310	1485	34873	24420	1819
87022	891	4789	65552	52972	5686
122686	778	7631	73467	84173	2751
46642	294	3199	36588	35657	2995
84987	2776	4291	53691	56619	10504
98373	557	4815	52471	50569	3787
108291	1065	5858	61054	53259	8729
125698	**317839**	**137894**	**9915**	**11749**	**210608**
29561	284668	5187	1769	1583	180101
14047	22069	110	915		17924
28268	600	90706	203	35	1401
10884		110			4250
15270	9342		527		4103
2500	1130				400
25168	30	41781	6501	10131	2429

6-5 续表1

单位：万元

区县、开发区	Region	一般公共预算支出 General Public Budgetary Expenditures			
		城乡社区支出 Expenditure for Urban and Rural Community Affairs	农林水支出 Expenditure for Agriculture, Foresty and Water Conservancy	交通运输支出 Expenditure for Transportation	资源勘探电力信息等支出 Expenditure for Exploration of the Power of Information
合计	**Total**	**2334825**	**593690**	**143711**	**346587**
市本级合计	**Sum of City Level**	**548247**	**90598**	**84235**	**138978**
区、县合计	**Region**	**910657**	**462538**	**50819**	**25667**
新城区	Xincheng	75012	1062	1484	945
碑林区	Beilin	136809	129	505	393
莲湖区	Lianhu	162668	1562	633	3123
雁塔区	Yanta	94504	4929	1483	2077
灞桥区	Baqiao	71315	20199	2409	1297
未央区	Weiyang	92532	7272	1641	821
阎良区	Yanliang	64161	29187	1791	6189
临潼区	Lintong	71171	55187	2229	1850
长安区	Chang'an	64418	57864	9046	752
高陵区	Gaoling	23154	32699	5875	1487
鄠邑区	Huyi	19172	101776	10277	4349
蓝田县	Lantian	18097	73326	4562	811
周至县	Zhouzhi	17644	77346	8884	1573
开发区合计	**Sum of Development Zones**	**787745**	**9630**	**6817**	**172460**
高新区	GaoXin	222529	434		155169
经开区	JingKai	232849	154		7343
曲江新区	Qujiang	142908	4526		1327
浐灞生态区	Chanba Eco-District	143170	1006		171
航天基地	Aerospace Base	21537		500	5977
航空基地	Aviation Industry Base	8627	210	500	2110
国际港务区	International Trade&Logistic Park	16125	3300	5817	363

continued 1

(10 000 yuan)

商业服务业等支出 Expenditure for Business Services	金融支出 Expenditure for Finance	国土海洋气象等支出 Land and Marine Meteorological and Other Expenses	住房保障支出 Expenditure for Housing Support	粮油物资储备支出 Expenditure for Grain and Oil Stockpiles
196353	**32017**	**37381**	**441302**	**17125**
87285	**3707**	**7087**	**225842**	**12676**
19545	**6941**	**24299**	**109120**	**3970**
2533	798	776	6669	3
350		828	492	
812	202	768	7777	
2088	24	2180		
507		1473	10913	279
1238		2107	5101	
888	208	1006	2098	383
2024	26	1624	11228	229
2615		3149	23331	1210
503	33	2283	18351	478
1480	71	3030	12366	688
2553	23	2669	5951	325
1954	5556	2406	4843	375
87752	**1078**	**3389**	**63943**	
2441	566	1536	11192	
1210	100	58	900	
1628	291	900	6143	
15143	4	489	3610	
126		360	3262	
14	117		941	
67190		46	37895	

6-5 续表2 continued 2

单位：万元 （10 000 yuan）

区县、开发区	Region	一般公共预算支出 General Public Budgetary Expenditures			政府性基金预算支出 Governmental Fund Budgetary Expenditure
		债务付息支出 Debt Service Expenditure	其他支出 Other Expenditure	债务发行费用支出 Debt Issuance Expenditure	
合计	**Total**	**169757**	**26355**	**2411**	**4769664**
市本级合计	**Sum of City Level**	**93168**	**7246**	**2078**	**932389**
区、县合计	**Region**	**19283**	**1851**		**767354**
新城区	Xincheng	1060			23632
碑林区	Beilin	826			40404
莲湖区	Lianhu	1151			118399
雁塔区	Yanta	454			58768
灞桥区	Baqiao	2975	118		117104
未央区	Weiyang	4319	5		19914
阎良区	Yanliang	2217	234		14495
临潼区	Lintong	2054	211		63127
长安区	Chang'an	548	170		179335
高陵区	Gaoling	400	330		35790
鄠邑区	Huyi	1051	240		51795
蓝田县	Lantian	1298	446		7631
周至县	Zhouzhi	930	97		36960
开发区合计	**Sum of Development Zones**	**29969**	**5433**		**2110666**
高新区	GaoXin	27128	2685		274570
经开区	JingKai	1085	1587		177652
曲江新区	Qujiang	598	161		1084422
浐灞生态区	Chanba Eco-District	60	30		386691
航天基地	Aerospace Base	60	300		135936
航空基地	Aviation Industry Base	739	650		22106
国际港务区	International Trade&Logistic Park	299	20		29289

主要统计指标解释

财政收入 指国家财政参与社会产品分配所取得的收入，是实现国家职能的财力保证。主要包括：

（1）税收收入：包括增值税、消费税、营业税、企业所得税、企业所得税退税、个人所得税、资源税、城市维护建设税、房产税、印花税、城镇土地使用税、土地增值税、车船税、船舶吨税、车辆购置税、关税、耕地占用税、契税、烟叶税等。

（2）非税收入：包括专项收入、行政事业性收费、罚没收入、国有资本经营收入、国有资源（资产）有偿使用收入和其他收入。

财政支出 指国家财政将筹集起来的资金进行分配使用，以满足经济建设和各项事业的需要。主要包括：

（1）一般公共服务支出：指政府提供基本公共管理与服务的支出，包括人大事务、政协事务、政府办公厅（室）及相关机构事务、发展与改革事务、统计信息事务、财政事务、税收事务、审计事务、海关事务、人力资源事务、纪检监察事务、商贸事务、知识产权事务、工商行政管理事务、质量技术监督与检验检疫事务、民族事务、宗教事务、港澳台侨事务、档案事务、民主党派及工商联事务、群众团体事务、共产党事务等。

（2）外交支出：指政府外交事务支出，包括外交管理事务、驻外机构、对外援助、国际组织、对外合作与交流、对外宣传、边界勘界联检等方面的支出。

（3）国防支出：指政府用于国防方面的支出，包括用于现役部队、国防科研事业、专项工程、国防动员等方面的支出。

（4）公共安全支出：指政府维护社会公共安全方面的支出，包括武装警察、公安、国家安全、检察、法院、司法、监狱、劳教、国家保密、缉私警察等。

（5）教育支出：指政府教育事务支出，包括教育管理、学前教育、普通教育、职业教育、成人教育、广播电视教育、留学教育、特殊教育、进修及培训、教育费附加安排的支出等。

（6）科学技术支出：指用于科学技术方面的支出，包括科学技术管理事务、基础研究、应用研究、技术研究与开发、科技条件与服务、社会科学、科学技术普及、科技交流与合作、科技重大专项等。

（7）文化体育与传媒支出：指政府在文化、文物、体育、广播影视、新闻出版等方面的支出。

（8）社会保障和就业支出：指政府在社会保障与就业方面的支出，包括人力资源和社会保障管理事务、民政管理事务、财政对社会保险基金的补助、补充全国社会保障基金、行政事业单位离退休、企业改革补助、就业补助、抚恤、退役安置、社会福利、残疾人事业、城市居民最低生活保障、其他城市生活救助、自然灾害生活救助、红十字事业、农村最低生活保障、其他农村生活救助、补充道路交通事故社会救助基金等。

（9）医疗卫生和计划生育支出：指政府医疗卫生方面的支出，包括医疗卫生管理事务、公立医院、基层医疗卫生机构、公共卫生、医疗保障、中医药、食品和药品监督管理、人口与计划生育事务等。

（10）节能环保支出：指政府节能环保支出，包括环境保护管理事务、环境监测与监察、污染治理、自然生态保护、天然林保护工程、退耕还林、风沙荒漠治理、退牧还草、已垦草原退耕、能源节约利用、污染减排、可再生能源和资源综合利用等支出。

（11）城乡社区支出：指政府城乡社区事务支出，包括城乡社区管理事务、城乡社区规划与管理、城乡社区公共设施、城乡社区环境卫生、建设市场管理与监督等。

（12）农林水支出：指政府用于农林水事务支出，包括农业、林业、水利、南水北调、扶贫、农业综合开发、农业综合改革、促进金融支农等。

（13）交通运输支出：指政府交通运输和邮政业方面的支出，包括公路水路运输、铁路运输、民用航空运输、石油价格改革对交通运输的补贴、邮政业、车辆购置税等。

（14）资源勘探电力信息支出：指政府用于资源勘探、制造业、建筑业、电力信息等方面的支出，包括资源勘探开发、制造业、建筑业、电力监管、工业和信息产业监管、安全生产监管、国有资产监管、支持中小企业发展和管理等。

（15）商业服务业支出：指政府用于商业服务业方面的支出，包括商业流通事务、旅游业管理与服务、涉外发展服务等。

（16）金融支出：指政府用于金融方面的支出，包括金融部门行政、金融部门监管、金融发展、金融调控等。

（17）援助其他地区支出：指用于援助方政府安排并管理的对其他地区各类援助、捐赠等资金支出。

（18）国土海洋气象支出：指政府用于国土资源、海洋、测绘、地震、气象等公益服务事业方面的支出。

（19）住房保障支出：指政府用于住房方面的支出，包括保障性安居工程、住房改革、城乡社区住宅等。

（20）粮油物资储备支出：指政府用于粮油物资储备方面的支出，包括粮油事务、物资事务、能源储备、粮油储备、重要商品储备等。

（21）国债还本付息支出：指国债还本、付息、发行等方面的支出。

（22）其他支出：指不能划分到上述功能科目的其它政府支出。

中央财政收入和地方财政收入 指按现行分税制财政体制划分的中央本级收入和地方本级收入。属于中央财政的收入包括关税，进口货物增值税和消费税，出口货物退增值税和消费税，消费税，铁道部门、各银行总行、各保险公司总公司等集中交纳的营业税和城市维护建设税，增值税75%部分，纳入共享范围的企业所得税60%部分，未纳入共享范围的中央企业所得税、中央企业上交的利润，个人所得税60%部分，车辆购置税，船舶吨税，证券交易印花税97%部分，海洋石油资源税，中央非税收入等。属于地方财政的收入包括营业税（不含铁道部门、各银行总行、各保险公司总公司集中交纳的营业税），地方企业上交利润，城市维护建设税（不含铁道部门、各银行总行、各保险公司总公司集中交纳的部分），房产税，城镇土地使用税，土地增值税，车船税，耕地占用税，契税，烟叶税，印花税，增值税25%部分，纳入共享范围的企业所得税40%部分，个人所得税40%部分，证券交易印花税3%部分，海洋石油资源税以外的其他资源税，地方非税收入等。

中央财政支出和地方财政支出 指根据政府在经济和社会活动中的不同职责，划分中央和地方政府的责权，按照政府的责权划分确定的支出。中央财政支出包括一般公共服务，外交支出，国防支出，公共安全支出，以及中央政府调整国民经济结构、协调地区发展、实施宏观调控的支出等。地方财政支出包括一般公共服务，公共安全支出，地方统筹的各项社会事业支出等。

Explanatory Notes on Main Statistical Indicators

Government Revenue refers to income for the government finance through participating in the distribution of social products. It is the financial guarantee to ensure government functioning. The contents of government revenue include the following main items:

(1)Tax revenue, including business tax, corporate income tax, corporate income tax refund ,individual income tax, resource tax, city maintenance and construct tax, house property tax, stamp tax, urban land use tax, land appreciation tax, tax on vehicles and boat operation, ship tonnage tax, vehicle purchase tax, tariffs, farm land occupation tax, deed tax, and tobacco leaf tax, etc.

(2) Non-tax revenue, including special program receipts, charge of administrative and institutional units, penalty receipts ,state-owned capital operating income,State-owned resources (assets) compensation for the use of incomeand others non-tax receipts.

Government Expenditure refers to the distribution and use of the funds which the government finance has raised, so as to meet the needs of economic construction and various causes. It includes the following main items:

(1) Expenditure for general public services: It refers to the spending on the basic public management and services which provided by governments, including the expense on affairs of People' s Congress, affairs of People' s Political Consultative Conference, affairs of government general office and relative institutions, affairs of development and reform, affairs of statistics, affairs of finance, affairs of taxation, affairs of audit, affairs of customs, affairs of human resources and social security, affairs of discipline inspection and supervision, affairs of population and family planning, affairs of commerce and trade, affairs of intellectual property, affairs of administration for industry and commerce, affairs of land and resources, affairs of oceanic administration, affairs of surveying and mapping, affairs of earthquake, ethnic affairs, religious affairs, affairs of Hong Kong, Macao, Taiwan, and Overseas Chinese, affairs of archives administration, affairs of Chinese Communist Party, affairs of democratic parties and federation of industry and commerce, affairs of mass organization, and affairs of lottery, etc.

(2) Expenditure for foreign affairs: It refers to the spending of government on foreign affairs, including the expense on administration of foreign affairs, missions overseas, external assistance, international organizations, foreign cooperation and communication, surveying and joint inspection on borderline, etc.

(3) Expenditure for national defense: It refers to the spending of government on national defense, including the expense on active force, scientific research on national defense, special projects, mobilization of national defense, etc.

(4) Expenditure for public security: It refers to the spending of government on maintaining social and public security, including the expense on armed police force, public security, state security, prosecution, courts, justice, prison, labor education and rehabilitation, protection of state secrecy, anti-smuggling police, etc.

(5) Expenditure for education: It refers to the spending of government on education, including the expense on the administration of education, pre-primary education, regular vocational school education, adult education,radio and television education, student abroad education, special education, education and training,education surtax arrangementsspending, etc.

(6) Expenditure for science and technology: It refers to the spending of government on science and technology (S&T), including the expense on the administration of S&T, basic research, applied research, research and development, conditions and services of S&T, popularization of social science, science and technology, exchanges and cooperation of S&T, etc.

(7) Expenditure for culture, sport and media: It refers to the spending of government on culture, cultural heritage, sports, radio, film, television, press and publication, etc.

(8) Expenditure for social safety net and employment effort: It refers to the spending of government on social safety net and employment, including the expense on administration of social safety net and employment, civil affairs, budgetary subsidy on the social insurance funds, subsidy on National Social Security Fund, retirees of administrative units and institutions, subsidy on enterprise reform, subsidy on

employment effort, pension, placement of ex-serviceman, social welfare, the handicapped undertakings, the system of cost of living allowances for urban residents, other urban social relief, rural social relief, living relief of natural disasters, affairs of Red Cross Society, etc.

(9) Expenditure for medical health care and birth control planning : It refers to gov ernment spending on health care, including health management services, public hospitals, primary health care institutions, public health, health care, the pharmaceutical, food and drug supervision and manangement, population and family planning affairs.

(10) Expenditure for energy saving: It refers to the government energy-saving and environmental protection expenditures, including environmental management services, environmental monitoring and surveillance, pollution control, ecological protection, natural forest protection project, forest, desert sand control, pasture, grassland of cultivated farmland, energy conservation and utilization expenditure pollution reduction, renewable energy and comprehensive utilization of resources, etc.

(11) Expenditure for urban and rural community affairs: It refers to the spending of government on urban and rural community affairs, including the expense on administration of urban and rural community, planning and management of urban and rural community, public facilities of urban and rural community, housing of urban and rural community, sanitation of urban and rural community, management and supervision on the construction market, etc.

(12) Expenditure for agriculture, forestry and water conservancy: It refers to the spending of government on agriculture, forestry and water conservancy, including the expense on agriculture, forestry, water conservancy, South-to-North Water Diversion Project, poverty alleviation, agricultural comprehensive development, comprehensive agricultural reform, promoting financial support for agriculture, etc.

(13) Expenditure for transportation: It refers to the spending of government on transportation and postal services, including the expense on road transport, sea transport, rail transport, civil aviation transportation, oil price reform subsidies for transportation, postal services, vehicle purchase tax, etc.

(14) Expenditure for exploration of the power of information: It refers to the spending on exploration, manufacturing, construction, electricity and other aspects of information, including resource exploration and development, manufacturing, construction, electricity regulation, industry and information industry regulation, safety supervision, the state-owned assets supervision and support of small and medium enterprise development and management, etc.

(15) Expenditure for business services: It refers to government spending on commercial aspects of services, including commercial distribution business, tourism management and services, foreign development services, etc.

(16) Expenditure for financial: It refers to government spending on financial aspects, including administrative of financial sector, financial sector supervision, financial development, financial control, etc.

(17) Expenditure for assistance to other parts: It refers to the various types of assistance to other regions, financial donations, donors, government expenditure and management arrangements, etc.

(18) Expenditure for Land and Marine Meteorology : It refers to government spending on land resources, marine, mapping, seismic, weather and other aspects of public service undertakings, etc.

(19) Expenditure for housing security: It refers to government spending on housing, including affordable housing projects, housing reform, urban and rural communities housing, etc.

(20) Expenditure for Grain and Oil stockpiles: It refers to government spending on supplies of grain and oil reserves, including grain and oil services, supplies services, energy reserves, grain and oil reserves, reserves of other important commodities, etc.

(21) Expenditure for Treasury debt service: It refers to the national debt principal, interest expenses, and other aspects of the issue, etc.

(22) Other expenditure:It refers to other government spending cannot be divided into the above functions subjects.

Revenue of the Central Government and Revenue of the Local Governments refers to the revenue collected by the Central Government and that by the local governments as defined by the decentralized taxation system. In accordance with this system, the revenue of the Central Government includes tariff, VAT and consumption tax from imports, VAT and consumption tax rebate for exports, consumption tax, business tax and city maintenance and construct tax from the Ministry of Railways, head offices of banks, head offices of insurance company, which are handed over to the government in a centralized way, 75% of the value added tax, 60% the share part of the corporate income tax, unshared part of corporate income tax of the central enterprises, profit handed in by the central enterprises, 60% of individual income tax, vehicle purchase tax, ship tonnage tax, 97% of stamp tax on securities transactions, resource tax on the offshore petroleum resources. The revenue of the local governments includes business tax (excluding the part of the Ministry of Railways, head offices of banks, head offices of insurance company, which are handed over to the government in a centralized way), profit handed in by the local enterprises, city maintenance and construct tax (excluding the part of the Ministry of Railways, head offices of banks, head offices of insurance company, which are handed over to the government in a centralized way), house property tax, urban land use tax, land appreciation tax, tax on vehicles and boat operation, farm land occupation tax, deed tax, and tobacco leaf tax, stamp tax, 25% of the value added tax, 40% the share part of the corporate income tax, 40% of individual income tax, 3% of stamp tax on securities transactions, resource tax other than the tax on offshore petroleum resources, local non-tax revenue, etc.

Expenditure of the Central Government and Expenditure of the Local Governments according to the different functions of the Central Government and local governments in economic and social activities, the rights of affairs administration are demarcated between those of the Central Government and those of local governments; and the classification of the expenditure between the Central Government and local governments are made on the basis of the classification of the rights of affairs administration between them. The expenditure of the Central Government includes the expenditure for general public services, expenditure for foreign affairs, expenditure for public security, and the expenditure of the Central Government for adjusting the national economic structure; coordinating the development among different regions; and exercising macroeconomic regulation. The expenditure of the local governments includes mainly the expenditure for general public services, expenditure for public security, and expenditures for social development which are planned by local governments, etc.

7 物价指数

PRICE INDICES

资料整理：周　文　王　晶　王　茹
Data management:Zhou Wen Wang Jing Wang Ru
数据审核：刘　青　李　欣　党　军　雷麦鸽
Data audit：Liu Qing Li xin Dang Jun Lei Maige

第七部分　物价指数

一、简要说明

本章资料主要包括居民消费、商品零售、工业生产者出厂、工业生产者购进、房地产销售以及固定资产投资等价格指数，由国家统计局西安调查队提供。本部分2017年数据为西安原口径数据。

二、主要指标

商品零售价格总指数（上年=100）	101.7	比上年上升	1.6个百分点
居民消费价格总指数（上年=100）	102.0	比上年上升	1.1个百分点

7　PRICE INDICES

Ⅰ.Brief Introduction

This chapter consists of primarily data on consumer price indices, retail price indices, producer price indices for industrial products,purchasing price indices for industrial products,real estate selling, fixed asset investment,provided by Fixed Asset NBS Survey Office in Xi'an.

Ⅱ.Major Indicators

		Increase over Preceding Year
Retail Price Index(the price of preceding year=100)	101.7	1.6 percentage points
Consumer Price Index(the price of preceding year=100)	102.0	1.1 percentage points

7-1 主要年份各种价格指数

Price Indices in Representative Years

(以上年价格为100) (the price of preceding year= 100)

年 份 Year	居民消费价格指数 Consumer Price Index	商品零售价格指数 Retail Price Index	工业生产者出厂价格指数 Producer Price Indices (PPI) for Industrial Producers	工业生产者购进价格指数 Industrial Purchasing Indices （IPI） for Industrial Producers	固定资产投资价格指数 Price Index for Investment in Fixed Assets
1980	108.7	109.3			
1981	102.4	102.7			
1982	100.9	101.0			
1983	102.6	102.0			
1984	104.7	104.8			
1985	109.7	109.3			
1986	108.5	107.4			
1987	110.6	111.4			
1988	122.8	123.2			
1989	118.3	117.8			
1990	102.5	100.9			
1991	109.4	108.3			
1992	112.2	112.4			
1993	117.2	112.8	102.5	104.3	
1994	128.5	126.2	132.2	115.0	
1995	117.0	114.6	110.8	113.1	
1996	110.9	107.9	100.7	103.8	
1997	106.0	101.5	98.6	102.5	
1998	97.9	95.5	94.4	97.5	
1999	96.8	97.4	97.5	96.9	100.8
2000	100.2	98.7	99.4	102.4	102.1
2001	99.9	98.9	99.3	101.0	101.3
2002	98.6	98.5	98.2	98.4	101.2
2003	100.5	100.0	101.5	105.3	102.4
2004	102.3	101.9	102.7	110.4	103.3
2005	100.3	99.7	103.9	109.6	102.4
2006	101.6	101.5	103.2	106.1	102.0
2007	104.7	103.7	101.9	106.2	103.5
2008	106.0	105.4	103.7	108.5	110.5
2009	99.7	99.5	99.9	100.7	97.9
2010	103.5	102.7	102.3	106.3	103.8
2011	105.6	104.4	102.5	108.8	105.4
2012	102.8	102.3	100.5	97.2	101.9
2013	102.7	101.7	99.5	97.2	100.8
2014	101.4	100.7	99.5	99.5	100.8
2015	100.7	99.7	98.5	94.5	97.9
2016	100.9	100.1	97.8	97.6	100.0
2017	102.0	101.7	100.3	104.7	105.4

注：本表数据来源国家统计局西安调查队。
本表2017年数据为西安原口径数据。下同。

7-2 居民消费价格指数（2017年）

Residents Consumer Price Indices（2017）

(以上年价格为100) (the price of preceding year=100)

指　标	Item	2017
居民价格消费指数	**Consumer Price Index**	**102.0**
非食品烟酒价格指数	Non-Food，Tobaccol and Liquor Price Index	102.6
服务价格指数	Price Index of Service	103.6
工业品价格指数	Industrial Price Index	101.5
鲜活食品价格指数	Price Index of Fresh Food	97.3
消费品价格指数	Price Index of Consumer Goods	101.1
能源价格指数	Energy Price Index	102.0
非食品价格指数	Non-foodstuff Price Index	102.5
扣除食品和能源价格指数	Price Index with Food And Energy Excluded	102.5
扣除鲜菜鲜果价格指数	Price Index with Fresh Vegetables Fruits Excluded	102.2
扣除自有住房价格指数	Price Index with Self-owned Housing Excluded	101.9
居住（扣自有住房）价格指数	Housing (Self-owned Housing Excluded) Price Index	100.9
一、食品和烟酒	**Food，To bacco and Liquor**	**100.5**
1. 食品	Food	99.8
（1）粮食	Grain	101.1
（2）薯类	Potato	95.2
（3）豆类	Beans	101.0
（4）食用油	Cooking Oil	103.7
（5）菜	Vegetables	90.9
（6）畜肉类	Livestock Meat	95.1
（7）禽肉类	Poultry Meat	103.1
（8）水产品	Aquatic Products	107.5
（9）蛋类	Eggs	95.1
（10）奶类	Milk	102.0
（11）干鲜瓜果类	Dried Fresh Melons and Fruits	107.3
（12）糖果糕点类	Sweets and Cakes	103.6
（13）调味品	Flavouring	102.8
（14）其他食品类	Other Food	103.1
2. 茶及饮料	Tea and Drinks	100.1
3. 烟酒	Tobacco and Liquor	100.2
（1）烟草	Tobacco	99.3
（2）酒类	Liquor	101.8
4. 在外用餐	Dining Out	102.3
二、衣着	**Clothing**	**100.7**
1. 服装	Garments	100.7
2. 服装材料	Clothing Material	100.0
3. 其他衣着及配件	Other Clothing And Accessories	95.1
4. 衣着加工服务费	Clothing Manufacturing Services	104.6
5. 鞋类	Footwear	100.9
三、居住	**Residence**	**101.7**
1. 租赁房房租	Rental Housing	101.3
2. 住房保养维修及管理	Housing Maintenance And Management	101.3
3. 水电燃料	Water,Electricity, Fuels	100.5
4. 自有住房	Private Housing	102.9

注：本表数据来源国家统计局西安调查队。

7-2 续表 continued

(以上年价格为100) (the price of preceding year= 100)

指 标	Item	2017
四、生活用品及服务	**Daily Necessities and Services**	**100.6**
1. 家具及室内装饰品	Furniture and Interior Decorations	100.3
2. 家用器具	Household Appliances	98.2
3. 家用纺织品	Home Textiles	96.7
4. 家庭日用杂品	Daily Use Household Articles	101.2
5. 个人护理用品	Personal Care Articles	103.4
6. 家庭服务	Home Services	103.7
五、交通和通信	**Transportation And Communication**	**102.4**
1. 交通	Transportation	102.8
（1）交通工具	Transportation Facility	102.8
（2）交通工具用燃料	Fuels For Vehicles	108.0
（3）交通工具使用和维修	Vehicles Use And Maintenance	100.5
（4）交通费	Traffic Fare	101.2
2. 通信	Communications	101.4
（1）通信工具	Telecommunication facility	104.8
（2）通信服务	Telecommunication Service	100.0
（3）邮递服务	Postal Service	99.9
六、教育文化和娱乐	**Education, Culture And Recreation**	**102.6**
1. 教育	Education	105.1
（1）教育用品	Educational Articles	104.9
（2）教育服务	Education Service	105.1
2. 文化娱乐	Culture And Recreation	100.2
（1）文娱耐用消费品	Durable Consumer Goods for Cultural and Recreational Use and Service	102.8
（2）其他文娱用品	Other Recreational Articles	102.6
（3）文化娱乐服务	Cultural And Recreational Services	100.6
（4）旅游	Touring	98.2
七、医疗保健	**Health Care**	**108.7**
1. 药品及医疗器具	Medical Instrument Articles	101.2
（1）中药	Traditional Chinese Medicine	105.0
（2）西药	Western Medicine	96.8
（3）滋补保健品	Health Care Articles	113.1
（4）医疗卫生器具	Medical Apparatus	100.0
（5）保健器具	Health Care Appliances	100.0
2. 医疗服务	Medical Service	115.0
八、其他用品和服务	**Other Supplies And Services**	**101.0**
1. 其他用品类	Other Supplies	101.1
（1）首饰手表	Jewelry and Watches	102.0
（2）其他杂项用品	Other Miscellaneous Articles	99.8
2. 其他服务类	Other Service	100.8

7-3 商品零售价格指数（2017年）

Retail Price Indices（2017）

(以上年价格为100) (the price of preceding year= 100)

指 标	Item	2017
商品零售价格指数	**Retail Price Indices**	**101.7**
一、食品	**Food**	**100.3**
1. 粮食	Grain	101.1
2. 薯类	Potato	95.2
3. 豆类	Beans	101.0
4. 食用油	Cooking Oil	103.7
5. 菜	Vegetables	90.9
6. 畜肉类	Livestock Meat	94.0
7. 禽肉类	Poultry Meat	103.1
8. 水产品	Aquatic Products	108.4
9. 蛋类	Eggs	95.1
10. 奶类	Milk	102.0
11. 干鲜瓜果类	Dried Fresh Melons and Fruits	107.3
12. 糖果糕点类	Sweets and Cakes	103.6
13. 调味品	Flavouring	102.8
14. 其他食品类	Other Food	103.1
15. 在外餐饮	Dining Out	102.3
二、饮料、烟酒	**Drinks, Tobacco and Liquor**	**100.4**
1. 茶及饮料	Tea and Drinks	100.1
2. 烟草	Tobacco	99.3
3. 酒类	Liquor	101.8
三、服装、鞋帽	**Garments, Shoes And Hats**	**100.6**
1. 服装	Garments	100.7
2. 鞋帽袜	Footwear and Hats	100.0
3. 其他衣着配件	Other Clothing Accessories	105.2
四、纺织品	**Textiles**	**97.2**
1. 服装材料	Cotton Cloth	100.0
2. 床上用品	Blend Cloth	96.9
五、家用电器及音像器材	**Household Appliances，Music and Video Equipment**	**101.2**
1. 家庭设备	Household Facility	98.3
2. 文娱用耐用消费品	Durable Consumer Goods for Cultural and Recreational Use	106.6
3. 专业音响器材	Music and Video Equipment	96.5

注：本表数据来源国家统计局西安调查队。

7-3 续表 continued

(以上年价格为100) (the price of preceding year= 100)

指 标	Item	2017
六、文化办公用品	**Cultural and Office Appliances**	**100.5**
七、日用品	**Articles for Daily Use**	**101.8**
1. 日用百货	General Merchandise for Daily Use	101.0
2. 厨具餐具茶具	Kitchenware, Tableware, Tea Set	101.5
3. 清洗用品	Daily Use Articles For Washing	104.8
4. 其他日用品	Other Daily Articles	99.1
八、体育娱乐用品	**Sports And Recreation Articles**	**101.5**
1. 体育户外用品	Sports Outdoor Articles	100.7
2. 娱乐用品	Recreation Articles	102.1
九、交通、通信用品	**Transportation And Communication Goods**	**104.4**
1. 交通运输机械	Transportation Machinery	104.1
2. 通信器材	Communication Equipment	106.0
十、家具	**Furniture**	**100.8**
十一、化妆品	**Cosmetics**	**103.2**
十二、金银饰品	**Gold , Silver and Jewelry**	**102.4**
十三、中西药品及医疗保健用品	**Traditional Chinese And Western Medicines And Health Care Articles**	**100.3**
1. 医疗卫生器具	Medical Apparatus	100.0
2. 中药	Traditional Chinese Medicine	105.0
3. 西药	Western Medicine	96.8
4. 保健器具及用品	Health Care Apparatus and Article	107.2
十四、书报杂志及电子出版物	**Books, Newspapers,Magazines And Electronic Publications**	**103.3**
1. 教材及参考书	Teaching Materials and Reference Books	104.9
2. 书报杂志	Books, Newspapers,Magazines	102.1
3. 计算机办公软件	Computer Office Software	100.5
十五、燃料	**Fuel**	**105.7**
1. 煤炭及制品	Coal and Its Products	108.5
2. 石油及制品	Oil and Its Products	105.0
十六、建筑材料及五金电料	**Building Materials And Hardware**	**101.9**
1. 建筑装潢材料	Building Decoration Materials	102.4
2. 五金水暖	Hardware Plumbing	99.6

7-4 主要年份工业生产者出厂价格指数

(上年价格=100)

类　别	Classify	1997	1998	1999	2000	2001	2002
工业生产者出厂价格指数	**Producer Price Index**	**98.6**	**94.4**	**97.5**	**99.4**	**99.3**	**98.2**
按轻重工业分	Grouped by Light Industry and Heavy Industry						
轻工业	Light Industry	98.2	91.1	95.9	97.8	99.6	98.4
以农产品为原料	Using Farm Products as Raw Materials	99.2	89.5	95.2	99.2	99.0	98.4
以非农产品为原料	Using Non-farm Products as Raw Materials	96.8	93.4	97.0	95.5	100.6	98.6
重工业	Heavy Industry	99.0	97.3	98.9	100.8	99.2	98.2
采掘	Mining & Quarrying		104.1	101.5	97.5	94.8	101.3
原料	Raw Materials	101.0	100.7	102.3	107.7	101.1	101.3
加工	Processing	97.9	95.6	98.0	98.4	98.5	97.7
按生产生活资料分	by means of production and livelihood						
生产资料	Means of Production	99.6	96.6	98.3	100.5	99.1	98.0
采掘	Mining & Quarrying		104.1	101.5	97.5	94.8	101.3
原料	Raw Materials	100.9	100.6	100.2	106.4	101.1	101.0
加工	Processing	98.9	94.7	97.6	98.7	98.5	97.4
生活资料	Consumer Goods	97.0	91.4	96.5	97.3	99.9	99.1
（1）食品	Food	108.2	97.8	95.8	94.4	99.6	101.2
（2）衣着	Clothing	93.0	83.9	95.2	101.6	99.4	100.8
（3）一般日用品	Articles for Daily Use	91.6	95.1	97.6	96.9	101.9	97.9
（4）耐用消费品	Durable Consumer Goods	99.7	95.4	98.0	95.9	97.0	98.1
按工业部门分	Grouped by Industrial Sector						
1. 冶金工业	Metallurgical Industry	99.2	97.5	91.2	98.2	97.2	98.7
2. 电力工业	Power Industry	111.3	111.2	109.3	109.6	102.4	100.0
3. 煤炭及炼焦工业	Coal and Coking Industry	98.9	98.5	96.3	100.5	110.3	106.7
4. 石油工业	Petroleum Industry			107.1	134.2	96.6	100.7
5. 化学工业	Chemical Industry	91.8	92.9	96.6	96.7	100.5	99.2
6. 机械工业	Machine Manufacturing Industry	98.8	94.6	98.1	98.0	98.3	97.6
7. 建筑材料工业	Building Materials Industry	98.2	99.3	96.7	98.5	100.6	99.6
8. 森林工业	Timber Industry	107.6	104.5	97.9	98.9	98.1	98.9
9. 食品工业	Food Industry	106.8	95.3	95.5	94.3	99.8	101.1
10. 纺织工业	Textiles Industry	94.3	82.6	93.7	103.4	97.5	94.9
11. 缝纫工业	Tailoring Industry	100.1	97.3	99.1	103.5	100.0	101.1
12. 皮革工业	Leather Industry	91.2	96.8	98.0	99.2	101.0	101.8
13. 造纸工业	Paper Industry			95.3	96.7	102.3	95.0
14. 文教艺术用品工业	Cultural,Educational & Handicrafts Articles			96.7	96.4	101.1	103.4
15. 其它工业	Other Industry	109.5	109.2	98.9	104.8	107.1	99.4

注：本表数据来源国家统计局西安调查队。

Producer Price Indices (PPI) for Industrial Producers in Representative Years

(the price of preceding year= 100)

2003	2004	2005	2006	2007	2008	2009	2010	2011	2012	2013	2014	2015	2016	2017
101.5	**102.7**	**103.9**	**103.2**	**101.9**	**103.7**	**99.9**	**102.3**	**102.5**	**100.5**	**99.5**	**99.5**	**98.5**	97.8	100.3
101.3	103.4	99.9	100.2	101.8	103.7	100.6	102.5	107.0	100.4	100.7	100.9	100.3	98.5	100.5
104.5	108.7	97.3	100.1	103.3	106.0	98.9	104.0	109.3	100.3	101.0	100.8	99.1	97.8	100.9
99.9	100.8	101.2	100.2	100.8	102.1	101.8	101.4	100.9	100.5	99.9	101.3	103.3	100.1	99.7
101.6	101.9	107.9	105.5	101.9	103.8	99.3	102.2	101.6	100.5	99.2	99.2	98.2	97.6	100.3
103.4	140.5	107.9	100.6	111.6	122.3	90.0	150.2	102.6	101.8	100.6	100.6	99.8	99.8	106.0
111.2	109.0	114.2	111.8	104.9	110.8	99.5	108.9	111.2	108.6	95.1	97.6	90.4	91.4	103.4
100.1	100.6	106.7	104.2	101.2	101.9	99.4	100.8	100.1	99.2	99.9	99.5	99.3	98.3	99.8
101.8	102.7	105.3	104.2	101.3	103.4	99.3	102.2	101.9	100.3	99.2	99.5	98.3	97.4	100.7
103.4	140.5	107.9	100.6	111.6	122.3	90.0	150.2	102.6	101.8	100.6	100.6	99.8	99.8	106.0
108.1	106.6	111.3	111.6	104.8	110.2	99.7	109.0	111.3	108.7	95.2	97.7	90.5	91.2	102.7
100.9	102.0	104.3	103.0	100.6	102.0	99.3	101.0	100.3	98.9	99.9	99.7	99.6	98.3	100.3
100.5	102.5	100.4	100.4	103.5	104.7	101.4	102.5	104.5	100.8	100.4	99.7	99.4	98.6	99.7
101.0	103.6	100.3	100.4	105.3	106.6	100.3	103.3	109.5	101.6	100.9	101.2	100.1	97.7	100.3
99.4	102.7	102.0	103.3	104.6	105.1	102.7	101.2	111.9	99.4	100.4	99.1	96.0	100.2	101.3
101.2	101.2	101.3	100.8	100.1	102.7	102.6	101.2	101.5	101.5	99.1	101.3	102.1	98.9	99.6
97.2	98.3	99.1	99.4	100.7	100.7	103.9	101.9	99.5	99.0	100.9	95.9	95.6	99.5	98.5
103.8	107.1	103.9	106.5	103.2	104.8	92.0	105.8	116.3	100.7	97.5	97.5	96.5	95.2	104.9
103.2	104.1	110.6	107.9	105.5	110.0	109.0	101.2	104.7	111.2	100.6	99.4	98.9	92.3	99.4
136.8	131.4	97.1	95.4	106.8	104.8	101.7	110.6	109.3	101.5	100.0	100.0	100.0		
118.6	110.5	121.7	117.6	104.8	115.6	96.7	114.2	108.4	108.2	89.7	97.2	81.0	95.4	102.5
100.2	100.8	103.2	100.8	101.1	104.1	102.6	100.8	104.2	100.3	99.6	100.9	100.6	96.8	100.6
99.8	100.6	104.9	103.4	101.0	101.7	99.9	100.9	99.5	99.0	100.0	99.4	99.5	98.6	99.5
99.7	100.0	98.6	98.9	98.9	101.8	101.9	99.9	100.6	99.6	99.3	99.1	99.5	98.0	106.1
100.1	100.2	101.6	101.6	101.1	101.1	101.1	101.7	105.2	103.2	103.4	101.6	91.7	99.9	100.0
102.8	107.5	98.3	99.0	106.1	109.3	98.3	104.3	110.1	101.7	101.0	101.3	99.8	97.0	99.9
117.3	119.1	89.9	102.4	98.4	99.7	97.5	108.9	107.2	88.7	103.9	99.3	96.0	93.7	103.5
100.2	103.6	100.8	103.5	104.6	105.1	102.6	101.3	113.4	99.4	100.4	99.0	93.4	100.5	102.7
98.7	99.6	101.2	100.0	99.0	99.6	99.7	99.6	98.0	99.9	99.9	100.0	118.9	99.8	99.6
96.9	100.2	101.2	100.0	100.1	104.5	98.4	100.4	103.4	99.2	98.4	98.1	98.1	100.9	109.7
97.5	96.5	98.1	100.1	99.1	99.2	102.2	99.9	100.7	106.0	97.5	100.0	102.6	98.0	99.0
103.3	105.0	103.4	105.7	111.4	104.3	99.7	100.5	104.3	101.2	99.6	100.0	100.0	99.7	96.2

7-5 主要年份工业生产者购进价格指数

Industrial Purchasing Indices (IPI) for Industrial Producers in Representative Years

(上年价格=100) (the price of preceding year= 100)

指 标	Item	2000	2001	2002	2003	2004	2005	2006	2007	2008
工业生产者购进价格指数	**Industrial Producer Price Index**	**102.4**	**101.0**	**98.4**	**105.3**	**110.4**	**109.6**	**106.1**	**106.2**	**108.5**
(一)燃料、动力类	Fuel and Power	105.0	101.8	100.9	105.7	109.4	123.5	112.6	107.0	109.8
(二)黑色金属材料类	Ferrous Metals	102.7	102.1	98.5	107.4	117.4	107.6	99.2	104.8	111.3
#钢材	Steel	103.4	102.4	97.9	106.0	114.8	107.5	98.5	104.9	111.7
(三)有色金属材料和电线类	Non-ferrous Metals and Electric Wires	105.2	95.5	96.8	105.8	114.1	107.8	116.5	110.7	99.1
(四)化工原料类	Raw Chemical Materials	104.6	102.5	97.9	102.4	106.3	106.1	101.6	105.6	111.4
(五)木材及纸浆类	Timber and Paper Pulp	101.2	102.8	99.4	101.2	100.3	108.2	111.7	105.9	106.5
(六)建筑材料及非金属矿类	Building Materials and Non-metal ores	100.3	99.7	98.6	99.6	110.4	99.3	100.7	104.0	104.8
(七)其它工业原材料及半成品类	Other Industrial Raw Materials and Semi-Products	98.8	100.8	98.9	102.5	111.2	106.1	104.3	108.8	110.6
(八)农副产品类	Agricultural Products	100.4	102.8	98.2	113.7	112.7	100.9	107.2	107.2	108.9
(九)纺织原料类	Textile Materials	98.0	96.8	90.6	103.4	103.9	97.6	101.5	100.5	99.8

注：本表数据来源国家统计局西安调查队。

7-5 续表 continued

(上年价格=100) (the price of preceding year= 100)

指 标	Item	2009	2010	2011	2012	2013	2014	2015	2016	2017
工业生产者购进价格指数	**Industrial Producer Price Index**	**100.7**	**106.3**	**108.8**	**97.2**	**97.2**	**99.5**	**94.5**	**97.6**	**104.7**
(一)燃料、动力类	Fuel and Power	105.1	108.6	113.5	102.3	96.8	98.2	95.3	98.3	101.6
(二)黑色金属材料类	Ferrous Metals	99.2	103.1	102.9	93.4	98.0	97.9	91.6	96.0	109.0
#钢材	Steel	98.7	103.5	102.9	93.3	98.0	97.9	91.5	96.0	109.0
(三)有色金属材料和电线类	Non-ferrous Metals and Electric Wires	93.9	113.6	118.9	93.0	94.5	96.6	96.3	99.3	117.7
(四)化工原料类	Raw Chemical Materials	95.0	103.9	108.1	87.7	90.8	104.6	91.3	94.1	104.2
(五)木材及纸浆类	Timber and Paper Pulp	102.6	101.1	105.4	100.9	99.2	100.7	101.0	98.7	107.3
(六)建筑材料及非金属矿类	Building Materials and Non-metal ores	106.8	102.1	102.9	97.4	102.2	101.1	98.1	97.1	101.0
(七)其它工业原材料及半成品类	Other Industrial Raw Materials and Semi-Products	101.4	108.1	109.4	100.3	98.9	100.9	99.1	98.9	100.8
(八)农副产品类	Agricultural Products	99.6	106.5	107.4	103.4	100.5	98.8	92.8	100.4	101.0
(九)纺织原料类	Textile Materials	97.6	104.6	107.0	89.1	97.6	99.3	89.7	94.1	102.7

7-6　住宅销售价格指数（2017年）

Selling Price Indices of Residential Buildings（2017）

(上年价格=100)　　(the price of preceding year= 100)

指　标	Item	2017
新建住宅	**Newly built residential buildings**	**111.5**
一、保障性住房	guaranteed house	
二、新建商品住宅	New commodity residential house	112.5
（一）90平方米及以下	90 square meters and less	112.7
（二）90-144平方米	90-144 square meters	112.9
（三）144平方米以上	144 square meters and more	111.6
二手住宅	**used/second hand residential buildings**	**104.8**
一、90平方米及以下	90 square meters and the following	105.3
二、90-144平方米	90-144 square meters	105.6
三、144平方米以上	144 square meters and more	102.1

注：本表数据来源国家统计局西安调查队。

7-7　主要年份固定资产投资价格指数

Price Indices for Investment in Fixed Assets in Representative Years

(上年价格=100)　　(the price of preceding year= 100)

指　标	Item	2000	2006	2007	2008	2009	2010	2011	2012	2013	2014	2015	2016	2017
固定资产投资价格指数	**Price Indices for Investment in Fixed Assets**	**102.1**	**102.0**	**103.5**	**110.5**	**97.9**	**103.8**	**105.4**	**101.9**	**100.8**	**100.8**	**97.9**	**100.0**	**105.4**
一、建筑安装工程	**Construction and Installation Engineering**	**103.9**	**102.6**	**104.9**	**114.9**	**97.1**	**105.5**	**107.2**	**102.6**	**101.0**	**100.8**	**97.0**	**100.5**	**107.8**
1. 材料费	Material Costs	104.4	101.1	104.3	117.6	94.1	105.2	106.3	99.0	97.5	98.1	93.3	99.8	111.9
钢材	Steel	109.0	97.0	104.5	127.2	86.7	106.4	107.9	94.7	92.9	93.7	84.6	100.0	120.3
木材	Wood	103.6	101.9	102.5	106.9	101.8	105.0	104.5	104.9	104.5	105.2	107.6	101.4	102.0
水泥	Cement	101.5	101.1	102.7	107.8	109.4	103.8	100.9	100.3	101.4	100.4	97.3	98.1	104.4
地方材料	Local Materials	101.6	102.6	103.5	108.5	103.8	104.7	105.8	102.0	102.4	102.0	100.4	100.0	105.3
化工材料	Chemical Materials	107.1	113.6	113.0	110.0	95.5	104.5	105.4	104.2	102.5	100.9	95.6	95.3	102.7
电料	Electrical Materials and Sppliances	100.6	107.5	110.4	110.1	102.6	104.1	104.1	101.5	100.9	99.9	97.8	99.1	104.2
其他材料	Other Materials	103.4	103.2	107.4	108.5	101.6	102.7	104.5	102.7	101.6	100.7	100.4	100.7	101.4
2. 人工费	Labor Costs	103.6	108.3	109.1	114.5	110.6	111.9	114.0	112.9	109.7	108.8	105.7	102.9	103.2
3. 机械使用费	Mechanical Service Costs	103.9	104.5	104.5	106.5	99.3	103.3	106.7	104.8	104.0	102.2	100.8	100.7	100.8
二、设备、工器具购置	**Purchase of Equipment and Instruments**	**97.9**	**100.8**	**100.7**	**101.0**	**98.6**	**100.0**	**100.6**	**99.1**	**99.5**	**99.9**	**99.1**	**99.1**	**99.7**
三、其他费用	**Others**	**100.0**	**100.5**	**100.6**	**101.9**	**100.9**	**100.8**	**102.8**	**102.7**	**101.9**	**101.8**	**100.4**	**99.0**	**100.9**

注：本表数据来源国家统计局西安调查队。

主 要 统 计 指 标 解 释

居民消费价格指数 是反映一定时期内城乡居民所购买的生活消费品和服务项目价格变动趋势和程度的相对数，是对城市居民消费价格指数和农村居民消费价格指数进行综合汇总计算的结果。通过该指数可以观察和分析消费品的零售价格和服务项目价格变动对城乡居民实际生活费支出的影响程度。

商品零售价格指数 是反映一定时期内城乡商品零售价格变动趋势和程度的相对数。商品零售价格的变动与国家的财政收入、市场供需的平衡、消费与积累的比例关系有关。因此，该指数可以从一个侧面对上述经济活动进行观察和分析。

工业生产者价格指数 是反映工业产品价格变化趋势和变动幅度的统计指标，是工业企业的产品价格在不同的时间和空间条件下平均变动的相对数。工业生产者价格包括工业品第一次出售时的出厂价格和企业作为中间投入的原材料、燃料、动力购进价格，简称工业生产者出厂价格和工业生产者购进价格。工业生产者价格指数是进行国民经济核算和经济管理的主要依据。

固定资产投资价格指数 是反映一定时期内固定资产投资品和取费项目价格的变动趋势和变动幅度的相对数。固定资产投资额是由建筑安装工程投资完成额、设备工器具购置投资完成额和其他费用投资完成额三部分组成的。编制固定资产投资价格指数应首先分别编制上述三部分投资的价格指数，然后采用加权算术平均法求出固定资产投资价格总指数。

该指数可以准确地反映固定资产投资中涉及的各类投资品和取费项目价格变动趋势和变动幅度，消除按现价计算的固定资产投资指标中的价格变动因素，真实地反映固定资产投资的规模、速度、结构和效益，为国家科学地制定、检查固定资产投资计划和进行国民经济核算提供科学的、可靠的依据。

Explanatory Notes on Main Statistical Indicators

Consumer Price Indices reflect the trend and degree of changes in prices of consumer goods and services purchased by urban and rural households during a given period. They are obtained by combining Consumer Price Indices of Urban Household and Consumer Price Indices of Rural Household. The Indices enable the observation and analysis of the degree of impact of the changes in the prices of retailed goods and services on the actual living expenses of urban and rural residents.

Retail Price Indices reflect the trend and degree of change in retail prices of commodities during a given period. The change in retail prices of commodities is related to government revenue, the equilibrium of market supply and demand, and the ratio of consumption to accumulation. Therefore, the retail price indices are useful from an oblique perspective for observing and analyzing the changes of the above economic activities.

Industrial Producer Price Index refelct the trend and degree of changes of industrial product price, which is the relative number of average change prices of industrial enterprises products under different condition of time and space. Including the first time of sale prices of industrial products and the price of raw materials, fuel and power as intermediate inputs, be called for short of PPI and IPI.

Industrial producer price Index is an important basis for national accounts and economic manegement.

Price Indices for Investment in Fixed Assets reflect the trend and degree of changes in prices of investment goods and projects in fixed assets during a given period. The investment in fixed assets consists of three components, namely the investment in construction and installation, the investment in purchases of equipment and instrument, and the investment in other items. Price indices for investment in fixed assets are calculated as the weighted arithmetic mean of the price indices for the three components of investment in fixed assets.

Removing the factor of price change in the aggregates of investment at current prices, this indicator shows the changes in the prices of commodities and fees involved in the investment of fixed assets, and can be used to observe the actual size, growth, structure, and efficiency of investment in fixed assets and provides reliable and scientific data for government planning and further improving the current national accounting .

8 人民生活

PEOPLE´S LIVELIHOOD

资料整理：王红梅
Data management：Wang Hongmei
数据审核：高小琴
Data audit：Gao Xiaoqin

第八部分　人民生活

一、简要说明

本章资料反映我市城乡常住居民生活现状及变化情况，2014年以后数据为实施城乡住户调查一体化改革后的全市居民生活主要数据，由国家统计局西安调查队住户专项处提供。本部分2017年数据为西安原口径数据。因样本调整，暂不编发按收入五等分分组的城镇和农村居民人均可支配收入表。

二、主要指标

全体居民人均可支配收入（元）	32597	比上年增长	8.5%
城镇常住居民人均可支配收入（元）	38536	比上年增长	8.2%
城镇常住居民人均消费支出（元）	25374	比上年增长	6.6%
农村常住居民人均可支配收入（元）	16522	比上年增长	8.8%
农村常住居民人均消费支出（元）	10966	比上年增长	7.5%

8 PEOPLE'S LIVELIHOOD

Ⅰ.Brief Introduction

The data in this chapter reflected the city's urban and rural residents living situation and changes in circumstances,Data reflected the implementation of the city's residents in 2014 integrated household survey reformed life.The data is provided by Resident Special Investigation offices of the Survey Office of National of Statistics Xi'an .

Ⅱ.Major Indicators

		Increase over Preceding Year
Per capita disposable income of all residents(yuan)	32597	8.5%
Per capita disposable income of Urban residents (yuan)	38536	8.2%
Per capita consumption expenditure of Urban residents (yuan)	25374	6.6%
Per capita disposable income of Rural residents (yuan)	16522	8.8%
Per capita consumption expenditure of Rural residents(yuan)	10966	7.5%

8-1 主要年份城乡居民人均收入及恩格尔系数

Per Capita Annual Income and Engel's Coefficient of Urban and Rural Households in Representative Years

年 份 Year	城镇居民人均可支配收入 Per Capita Annual Disposable Income of Urban		农村居民人均纯收入（可支配收入） Per Capita Annual Net Income of Rural （Disposable Income）		城镇居民家庭恩格尔系数（%） Engel's Coefficient of Urban Households（%）	农村居民家庭恩格尔系数（%） Engel's Coefficient of Rural Households（%）
	绝对数(元) Absolute number (yuan)	指数 1980年=100 Index year of 1980=100	绝对数(元) Absolute number (yuan)	指数 1978年=100 Index year of 1978=100		
1978			140	100.0		
1979						
1980	414	100.0	190	135.7	53.3	53.3
1981	446	107.7	207	147.9	52.9	53.7
1982	479	115.6	254	181.4	55.1	56.7
1983	509	122.9	245	175.0	55.1	58.4
1984	540	130.3	299	213.6	54.9	51.7
1985	719	173.5	351	250.7	49.5	48.5
1986	911	219.8	390	278.6	49.9	47.9
1987	1034	249.7	434	310.0	50.6	50.3
1988	1142	275.6	482	344.3	44.9	47.5
1989	1344	324.3	530	378.6	51.7	48.2
1990	1518	366.5	610	435.7	53.1	49.5
1991	1619	390.9	707	505.0	51.6	46.7
1992	1992	481.0	783	559.3	52.5	50.9
1993	2661	642.5	870	621.4	46.4	46.0
1994	3517	849.1	1078	770.0	45.2	50.1
1995	4153	1002.5	1353	966.4	44.7	50.3
1996	5023	1212.6	1586	1132.9	42.6	49.9
1997	5344	1290.1	1846	1318.6	40.7	49.2
1998	5670	1368.7	2052	1465.7	39.8	42.4
1999	5999	1448.3	2203	1573.6	36.3	39.1
2000	6364	1536.5	2344	1674.3	36.5	36.6
2001	6705	1618.8	2490	1778.6	34.8	33.9
2002	7184	1734.3	2641	1886.4	34.4	31.1
2003	7748	1870.7	2838	2027.1	34.8	37.6
2004	8544	2062.8	3143	2245.0	36.1	35.7
2005	9628	2324.5	3460	2471.4	37.0	36.3
2006	10905	2632.9	3808	2720.0	34.4	36.8
2007	12662	3057.0	4399	3142.1	36.6	38.2
2008	15207	3671.4	5212	3722.9	36.4	37.0
2009	18963	4578.2	6275	4482.3	32.4	35.8
2010	22244	5370.4	7750	5535.7	31.3	32.5
2011	25981	6272.6	9788	6991.4	31.3	31.9
2012	29982	7238.5	11442	8172.9	32.5	33.8
2013	33100	7991.3	12930	9235.7	32.5	33.0
2014	30715	8718.5	12898	10334.7	32.3	34.2
2015	33188	9422.0	14072	11270.0	32.7	32.2
2016	35630	10119.2	15191	12171.6	29.3	26.9
2017	38536	10948.9	16522	13267.0	29.1	27.3

注：2014年实施城乡住户一体化调查后，统计口径发生变化，新老口径存在差异。本表2014年开始为新口径数据，“农村居民人均纯收入”改为“农村居民人均可支配收入”。2014-2015年黑格尔系数按新口径进行了修订。

本表2017年数据为西安原口径数据。下同。

8-2 主要年份城乡居民人民币储蓄存款

Savings Deposit of Urban and Rural Households in Representative Years

单位：亿元 (100 million yuan)

年 份 Year	年末余额 Balance at Year-end	指数（上年＝100） Index(preceding year=100)
1978	2.57	
1979	3.30	128.4
1980	4.22	127.8
1981	4.90	116.0
1982	5.97	121.9
1983	7.35	123.1
1984	10.73	146.0
1985	14.26	132.9
1986	19.45	136.4
1987	33.95	174.6
1988	40.77	120.1
1989	56.65	138.9
1990	77.09	136.1
1991	97.42	126.4
1992	120.27	123.5
1993	158.28	131.6
1994	218.74	138.2
1995	291.46	133.2
1996	394.02	135.2
1997	433.56	110.0
1998	499.68	115.3
1999	586.40	117.4
2000	675.83	115.3
2001	800.86	118.5
2002	988.04	123.4
2003	1210.56	122.5
2004	1432.86	118.4
2005	1716.76	119.8
2006	1950.53	113.6
2007	2002.38	102.7
2008	2513.70	125.5
2009	3084.20	122.7
2010	3641.09	118.1
2011	4155.65	114.1
2012	4787.03	115.2
2013	5357.05	111.9
2014	5698.15	106.4
2015	6571.18	115.3
2016	7035.81	107.1
2017	7497.30	106.6

注：1.本表数据来源于人民银行西安营管部,对部分历史年份数据进行了修订。
2.2015年以后“储蓄存款”为“住户存款”。

8-3 各区县城乡居民人均可支配收入

Per Capita Income of Urban and Rural Households by Region

区 县	Region	城镇居民人均可支配收入 Per Capita Disposable Income of Urban Households			农村居民人均可支配收入 Per Capita Disposable Income of Rural Households		
		绝对数（元） Absolute number(yuan)		2017年比2016年增长% Growth of 2017 than 2016 (%)	绝对数（元） Absolute number(yuan)		2017年比2016年增长% Growth of 2017 than 2016 (%)
		2016	2017		2016	2017	
全 市	**Total**	**35630**	**38536**	**8.2**	**15191**	**16522**	**8.8**
新城区	Xincheng	37212	40292	8.3			
碑林区	Beilin	37539	40636	8.3			
莲湖区	Lianhu	37425	40575	8.4			
灞桥区	Baqiao	36784	39794	8.2	20431	22280	9.0
未央区	Weiyang	37085	40034	8.0	21294		
雁塔区	Yanta	37631	40660	8.0			
阎良区	Yanliang	36931	39914	8.1	20262	22034	8.7
临潼区	Lintong	30753	33261	8.2	16389	17859	9.0
长安区	Chang'an	34627	37437	8.1	16741	18239	8.9
高陵区	Gaoling	29464	31974	8.5	16431	17934	9.1
鄠邑区	Huyi	27970	30224	8.1	14638	15918	8.7
蓝田县	Lantian	26321	28596	8.6	12082	13151	8.8
周至县	Zhouzhi	26899	29039	8.0	12207	13348	9.3

8-4 全市居民家庭基本情况

Basic Conditions of All Households

指标名称	Item	2016	2017
调查户数（户）	**Number of Households Surveyed (household)**	**2369**	**2385**
调查户人口（人）	**Residents Surveyed(person)**		
平均每户常住人口	Average Household Size	3.0	3.0
平均每户劳动力人数	Average Number of Employed Persons	2.2	2.3
平均每劳动力负担人口	Average Number of Persons Supported by a Laborer	1.4	1.3
人均可支配收入（元）	**Annual Per Capita Disposable Income(yuan）**	**30032.5**	**32597.4**
工资性收入	Wages Income	18588.9	20402.5
经营净收入	Net Income from Business	2787.4	2880.7
财产净收入	Net Income from Property	2304.0	2387.5
转移净收入	Net Income from Transfer	6352.3	6926.9
人均消费支出（元）	**Annual Per Capita Consumption Expenditure (yuan)**	**20074.2**	**21487.5**
食品烟酒	Food,Tobacco and Alcohol	5806.5	6261.4
衣着	Clothing	1605.7	1696.7
居住	Residence	3740.9	4001.5
生活用品及服务	Living Articles and Services	1523.5	1634.1
交通通信	Transport and Communication Services	2663.4	2725.1
教育文化娱乐	Recreation, Education and Culture Services	2455.7	2688.7
医疗保健	Medical and Health Care Services	1718.8	1843.0
其他用品和服务	Other Commodities and Services	559.6	637.1

8-5 全市居民人均可支配收入

Per Capita Annual Disposable Income of All Households

单位：元 (yuan)

指标名称	Item	2016	2017
可支配收入	**Disposable income**	**30032.5**	**32597.4**
一、工资性收入	**Wage income**	**18588.9**	**20402.5**
（一）工资	Wage	17051.4	19140.9
（二）实物福利	Benefits in kind	77.2	81.8
（三）其他	Others	1460.3	1179.8
二、经营净收入	**Net Income from Business**	**2787.4**	**2880.7**
（一）第一产业经营净收入	Net Income from Primary Industry Business	494.9	667.6
（二）第二产业经营净收入	Net Income from Secondary Industry Business	119.0	176.2
（三）第三产业经营净收入	Net Income from Tertiary Industry Business	2173.4	2036.8
三、财产净收入	**Net Income from Properties**	**2304.0**	**2387.5**
#利息净收入	Net interest	32.4	129.8
红利收入	Bonus	154.0	240.7
转让承包土地经营权租金净收入	Net Rental from Transfer of Contracted Land Management Rights	64.5	25.4
出租房屋财产性收入	The Property Income by Renting House	1125.1	1040.0
出租机械、专利、版权等资产的收入	The Income by Renting Assets like Mechanical, Patents, Copyright ect.	82.7	32.3
四、转移净收入	**Net Income from Transfer**	**6352.3**	**6926.9**
（一）转移性收入	Net Income from Transfer	7837.8	8021.4
（二）转移性支出	Transfer Expenditure	1485.6	1094.5

8-6 全市居民年人均消费支出

Per Capita Living Expenditure of All Households

单位：元 (yuan)

指标名称	Item	2016	2017
消费支出	**Total Living Expenditure**	**20074.2**	**21487.5**
一、食品烟酒	**Food,Tobacco and Alcohol**	**5806.5**	**6261.4**
1.食品	food	3413.5	3821.5
2.烟酒	Alcohol and tobacco	639.9	595.4
3.饮料	Drink	158.7	186.7
4.饮食服务	Catering Services	1594.4	1657.8
二、衣着	**Clothing**	**1605.7**	**1696.7**
衣类	Garments	1220.2	1278.8
鞋类	Footwear	385.5	417.9
三、居住	**Residence**	**3740.9**	**4001.5**
#租赁房房租	Rental Housing Rent	303.1	374.7
住房维修及管理	Housing Repair and Management	652.2	596.2
水电燃料及其他	Water,Electric Power Fuel and Others	912.2	974.9
四、生活用品及服务	**Living Articles and Services**	**1523.5**	**1634.1**
家具及室内装饰品	Furniture and Interior Decorations	272.0	272.9
家用器具	Household Appliances	405.0	453.8
家用纺织品	Household textile	127.1	123.7
家庭日用杂品	Household Articles of Daily Use	352.8	382.3
个人用品	Personal Items	326.3	345.9
家庭服务	Household Services	40.2	55.5
五、交通通信	**Transportation and Communications**	**2663.4**	**2725.1**
交通	Transportation	1812.4	1651.9
通信	Communications	851.0	1073.2
六、教育文化娱乐	**Recreation, Education and Culture Services**	**2455.7**	**2688.7**
教育	Education	1187.1	1380.6
文化娱乐	Recreation	1268.5	1308.1
七、医疗保健	**Medicine and Medical Services**	**1718.8**	**1843.0**
医疗器具及药品	Medical Instruments and Medicines	739.9	743.2
医疗服务	Medical Services	978.9	1099.8
八、其他用品和服务	**Others**	**559.7**	**637.1**

8-7 全市居民家庭人均购买主要商品数量

Per Capita Annual Purchases of Major Commodities of All Households

单位：千克 (kg)

指标名称	Item	2016	2017
面粉	Flour	22.2	20.1
大米	Rice	18.0	17.0
薯类	Potato	13.1	13.6
豆类	Beans	9.8	10.5
食用植物油	Edible vegetable oil	11.2	11.4
鲜菜	Fresh vegetables	89.2	93.8
猪肉	Pork	10.0	10.0
牛肉	Beef	1.4	1.6
羊肉	Lamb	0.8	0.6
鸡	Chicken	2.7	2.5
鱼类	Fish	3.2	3.5
虾类	Shrimp	0.7	0.7
鲜蛋	Eggs	9.4	10.1
鲜奶	Milk	14.0	13.7
酸奶	Yogurt	5.5	6.5
奶粉	Milk	0.6	0.7
鲜瓜果	Fresh fruit	54.4	60.3
糕点	Cake	4.7	5.2
茶叶	Tea	0.4	0.8
卷烟（盒）	Cigarettes (box)	31.7	28.4
啤酒	Beer	4.4	4.3
白酒	Liquor	1.0	1.1
果酒	Wine	0.6	0.4
鞋(双)	Footwear (pair)	3.1	3.1
水（吨）	Water (tons)	24.5	26.0
电（度）	Electricity （kwh）	746.0	761.6
煤炭	Coal	50.8	29.7
管道天燃气（立方米）	Gas pipeline (cu.m)	55.4	59.3
罐装液化石油气	Bottled liquefied petroleum gas	3.7	5.0

8-8　全市居民家庭每百户年末耐用品拥有情况

Ownership of Major Durable Consumer Goods Every 100 Households

指标名称	Item	2016	2017
家用汽车（辆）	Automobile (unit)	31.0	32.3
摩托车（辆）	Motorcycles (unit)	17.5	16.7
助力车（台）	Strength-aid Cycle (unit)	44.6	44.2
洗衣机（台）	washing machine (unit)	99.3	100.3
电冰箱（柜）	Refrigerator (unit)	94.6	95.7
微波炉（台）	Microwave Oven (unit)	45.4	45.6
彩色电视机（台）	Color TV Set (unit)	115.6	115.7
#接入有线电视（台）	Cable TV Set(unit)	66.3	61.4
空调（台）	Air conditioning(unit)	129.2	136.8
热水器（台）	Water heaters(unit)	83.8	85.2
#太阳能热水器（台）	Solar water heaters (unit)	41.0	41.9
洗碗机（台）	Dishwasher (unit)	1.3	1.4
排油烟机（台）	Exhauster (unit)	66.9	63.7
固定电话（线）	Ordinary Telephone (unit)	39.2	34.3
移动电话（部）	Mobile phones (unit)	242.2	245.5
#接入互联网（部）	Access to the Internet(unit)	115.2	130.0
计算机（台）	Computer (a)	66.4	67.5
#接入互联网（台）	Access to the Internet(unit)	54.2	52.8
照相机（台）	Camera (unit)	33.8	34.6
中高档乐器（架）	High-end Instruments (unit)	3.5	4.9
健身器材（台）	Setting-up Apparatus (unit)	4.2	4.0

8-9 城镇常住居民家庭基本情况

Basic Conditions of Urban Households

指标名称	Item	2016	2017
调查户数（户）	**Number of Households Surveyed (household)**	**1670**	**1678**
调查户人口（人）	**Residents Surveyed(person)**		
平均每户常住人口	Average Household Size	2.8	2.8
平均每户劳动力人数	Average Number of Employed Persons	2.1	2.1
平均每劳动力负担人口	Average Number of Persons Supported by a Laborer	1.3	1.3
人均可支配收入（元）	**Annual Per Capita Disposable Income(yuan)**	**35630.1**	**38536.0**
工资性收入	Wages Income	22607.6	24740.4
经营净收入	Household Business Income	2329.0	2353.0
财产净收入	Property Income	3011.8	3101.6
转移净收入	Transfer Income	7681.7	8341.0
人均消费支出（元）	**Annual Per Capita Consumption Expenditure (yuan)**	**23798.9**	**25374.2**
食品烟酒	Food,Tobacco and Alcohol	6963.3	7469.8
衣着	Clothing	1955.6	2059.9
居住	Residence	4252.3	4526.2
生活用品及服务	Living Articles and Services	1806.5	1919.8
交通通信	Transport and Communication Services	3254.3	3298.9
教育文化娱乐	Recreation, Education and Culture Services	2925.6	3200.0
医疗保健	Medical and Health Care Services	1937.4	2099.7
其他用品和服务	Other Commodities and Services	703.9	799.9

8-10 城镇常住居民人均消费支出

Per Capita Living Expenditure of Urban Households

单位：元 (yuan)

指标名称	Item	2016	2017
消费支出	**Total Living Expenditure**	**23798.9**	**25374.2**
一、食品烟酒	**Food,Tobacco and Alcohol**	**6963.3**	**7469.8**
1.食品	food	3960.4	4470.6
2.烟酒	Alcohol and tobacco	772.3	698.1
3.饮料	Drink	196.1	227.8
4.饮食服务	Catering Services	2034.5	2073.3
二、衣着	**Clothing**	**1955.6**	**2059.9**
衣类	Garments	1487.6	1552.7
鞋类	Footwear	467.9	507.2
三、居住	**Residence**	**4252.3**	**4526.2**
#租赁房房租	Rental Housing Rent	402.1	495.8
住房维修及管理	Housing Repair and Management	819.4	731.4
水电燃料及其他	Water,Electric Power Fuel and Others	1066.6	1219.3
四、生活用品及服务	**Living Articles and Services**	**1806.5**	**1919.8**
家具及室内装饰品	Furniture and Interior Decorations	333.7	309.0
家用器具	Household Appliances	460.7	519.1
家用纺织品	Household textile	147.9	145.8
家庭日用杂品	Household Articles of Daily Use	406.8	449.5
个人用品	Personal Items	412.7	426.3
家庭服务	Household Services	44.7	70.1
五、交通通信	**Transportation and Communications**	**3254.3**	**3298.9**
交通	Transportation	2241.0	1979.2
通信	Communications	1013.4	1319.6
六、教育文化娱乐	**Recreation, Education and Culture Services**	**2925.6**	**3200.0**
教育	Education	1283.0	1552.4
文化娱乐	Recreation	1642.6	1647.6
#健身器材	Fitness Equipment	20.3	2.5
体育及户外用品	Sports and outdoor products	26.6	22.8
体育健身活动	Sports fitness activity	26.8	41.2
七、医疗保健	**Medicine and Medical Services**	**1937.4**	**2099.7**
医疗器具及药品	Medical Instruments and Medicines	889.5	906.8
医疗服务	Medical Services	1047.9	1192.9
八、其他用品和服务	**Others**	**703.9**	**799.9**

8-11 城镇常住居民家庭人均购买主要商品数量

Per Capita Annual Purchases of Major Commodities of Urban Households

单位：千克 (kg)

指标名称	Item	2016	2017
面粉	Flour	21.6	19.4
大米	Rice	20.5	19.0
薯类	Potato	14.5	14.9
豆类	Beans	10.8	11.4
食用植物油	Edible vegetable oil	11.5	11.7
鲜菜	Fresh vegetables	100.2	105.4
猪肉	Pork	11.2	11.0
牛肉	Beef	1.8	1.9
羊肉	Lamb	0.9	0.7
鸡	Chicken	3.3	3.1
鱼类	Fish	4.2	4.5
虾类	Shrimp	0.9	1.0
鲜蛋	Eggs	10.7	11.3
鲜奶	Milk	16.7	16.2
酸奶	Yogurt	6.6	7.5
奶粉	Milk	0.6	0.8
鲜瓜果	Fresh fruit	60.9	67.4
糕点	Cake	5.4	6.0
茶叶	Tea	0.5	0.9
卷烟（盒）	Cigarettes (box)	33.9	28.5
啤酒	Beer	4.7	4.9
白酒	Liquor	1.2	1.3
果酒	Wine	0.7	0.5
鞋(双)	Footwear (pair)	3.3	3.2
水（吨）	Water (tons)	29.6	30.8
电（度）	Electricity （kwh）	846.8	831.8
煤炭	Coal	48.1	26.1
管道天燃气（立方米）	Gas pipeline (cu.m)	70.5	73.4
罐装液化石油气	Bottled liquefied petroleum gas	3.6	5.1

8–12 城镇常住居民家庭每百户耐用品拥有情况

Ownership of Major Durable Consumer Goods Every 100 Urban Households

指标名称	Item	2016	2017
家用汽车（辆）	Automobile (unit)	32.5	33.2
摩托车（辆）	Motorcycles (unit)	7.3	7.4
助力车（台）	Strength-aid Cycle (unit)	32.7	35.6
洗衣机（台）	washing machine (unit)	98.6	99.7
电冰箱（柜）	Refrigerator (unit)	95.7	96.3
微波炉（台）	Microwave Oven (unit)	56.6	53.9
彩色电视机（台）	Color TV Set (unit)	111.2	111.5
空调（台）	Air conditioning(unit)	145.0	151.6
热水器（台）	Water heaters(unit)	88.0	88.6
#太阳能热水器（台）	Solar water heaters (unit)	33.6	33.7
洗碗机（台）	Dishwasher (unit)	1.4	1.4
排油烟机（台）	Exhauster (unit)	80.6	71.7
固定电话（线）	Ordinary Telephone (unit)	44.7	38.7
移动电话（部）	Mobile phones (unit)	226.7	225.8
计算机（台）	Computer (a)	78.1	79.8
照相机（台）	Camera (unit)	43.4	44.6
中高档乐器（架）	High-end Instruments (unit)	4.5	6.2
健身器材（台）	Setting-up Apparatus (unit)	5.2	4.6

8-13 城镇常住居民家庭居住情况

Housing Conditions of Urban Households

指标名称	Item	2016	2017
调查户数（户）	**Number of Households Surveyed (household)**	**1670**	**1678**
平均每户居住人口（人）	**Average Number of Resident Population (person)**	**2.8**	**2.8**
人均现住房建筑面积（平方米/人）	**The Average Floor Area Per Person (sq.m / person)**	**33.4**	**33.7**
一、按居住空间样式分（%）	**by Living space style（%）**	**100.0**	**100.0**
单栋楼房	Single building Room	6.1	6.4
单栋平房	Single-storey House	2.2	2.1
单元房	Apartment	84.9	84.2
筒子楼或连片平房	Tube-shaped Apartment or Lace Single-storey Houses	6.7	7.2
其他	Other	0.1	0.1
二、按主要建筑材料分（%）	**by main construction materials（%）**	**100.0**	**100.0**
钢筋混凝土	Reinforced concrete soil	29.9	30.5
砖混材料	Brick and concrete material	69.8	69.3
砖瓦砖土	Tile and brick earth	0.1	0.1
其他	Others	0.2	0.1
三、按房屋来源分（%）	**by Source of Housing（%）**	**100.0**	**100.0**
租赁住房	Rental housing	10.8	10.1
自建住房	Self-establish Housing	8.3	8.9
购买商品房	Commercial Residential Housing	35.0	34.2
购买房改住房	Private Housing through Housing Reform	35.2	35.5
购买保障性住房	Indemnificatory Housing	3.8	4.1
拆迁安置房	Resettlement Housing	3.8	4.2
继承或获赠住房	Inheriting and Donation Housing	0.9	0.8
其他	Others	2.2	2.2
四、住房外道路为硬化路面的户比重（%）	**proportion of households which outer road is Hardened road（%）**	**99.5**	**99.5**
五、按住宅有管道供水情况分（%）	**By Piped Water Supply Condition （%）**	**100.0**	**100.0**
管道供水入户	Pipe water into People's Homes	99.0	98.9
管道供水至公共取水点	Pipe water to Public Watering Points	0.9	1.0
没有管道设施	No Pipeline Facilities	0.1	0.1
六、按住户主要饮水来源情况分（%）	**By Source of main Drinking Water （%）**	**100.0**	**100.0**
经过净化处理的自来水	Purified Tap Water	91.2	91.0
受保护的井水和泉水	Protected Wells and Springs	6.7	7.6
不受保护的井水和泉水	Unprotected Wells and Springs	0.6	0.1
江河湖泊水	Rivers and Lakes Water	0.2	0.2
其他饮用水来源	Others	1.3	1.1
七、按住宅内厕所类型分（%）	**By Household Lavatory Type (%)**	**100.0**	**100.0**
水冲式卫生厕所	Sanitary Water Closet	96.1	96.1
水冲式非卫生厕所	Insanitary Water Closet	1.1	1.1
卫生旱厕	Sanitary Latrine	1.1	1.2
普通旱厕	Latrine	1.6	1.5
无厕所	No Lavatory	0.1	0.1
八、按主要炊用能源状况分（%）	**By Cooking Fuel Condition （%）**	**100.0**	**100.0**
天然气、煤气、液化石油气	Pipeline Natural Gas，Pipeline Gas，Pipeline Liquified Petroleum Gas	73.5	73.4
煤炭	Coal	0.6	0.2
电	Electricity	25.1	25.8
沼气	Methane		
其他	Others	0.8	0.6

8-14 农村常住居民家庭基本情况

Basic Conditions of Rural Households

指标名称	Item	2016	2017
调查户数（户）	**Number of Households Surveyed (household)**	**699**	**706**
调查户人口（人）	**Residents Surveyed(person)**		
平均每户常住人口	Average Household Size	3.6	3.6
平均每户劳动力人数	Average Number of Employed Persons	2.6	2.6
平均每劳动力负担人口	Average Number of Persons Supported by a Laborer	1.4	1.4
人均可支配收入（元）	**Annual Per Capita Disposable Income(yuan）**	**15191.2**	**16522.3**
工资性收入	Wages Income	7933.9	8660.2
经营净收入	Household Business Income	4002.5	4308.9
财产净收入	Property Income	427.3	454.3
转移净收入	Transfer Income	2827.6	3099.0
人均消费支出（元）	**Annual Per Capita Consumption Expenditure (yuan)**	**10198.7**	**10966.4**
食品烟酒	Food,Tobacco and Alcohol	2739.3	2990.3
衣着	Clothing	678.2	713.4
居住	Residence	2384.8	2581.2
生活用品及服务	Living Articles and Services	773.4	860.6
交通通信	Transport and Communication Services	1096.7	1171.9
教育文化娱乐	Recreation, Education and Culture Services	1209.9	1304.9
医疗保健	Medical and Health Care Services	1139.4	1148.1
其他用品和服务	Other Commodities and Services	177.0	196.1

8-15 农村常住居民人均消费支出

Per Capita Living Expenditure of Rural Households

单位：元 (yuan)

指标名称	Item	2016	2017
消费支出	**Total Living Expenditure**	**10198.7**	**10966.4**
一、食品烟酒	**Food,Tobacco and Alcohol**	**2739.3**	**2990.3**
1.食品	food	1963.6	2064.4
2.烟酒	Alcohol and tobacco	288.9	317.2
3.饮料	Drink	59.3	75.5
4.饮食服务	Catering Services	427.5	533.3
二、衣着	**Clothing**	**678.2**	**713.4**
衣类	Garments	511.2	537.4
鞋类	Footwear	167.1	176.0
三、居住	**Residence**	**2384.8**	**2581.2**
#租赁房房租	Rental Housing Rent	40.7	46.8
住房维修及管理	Housing Repair and Management	208.8	230.4
水电燃料及其他	Water,Electric Power Fuel and Others	502.9	313.4
四、生活用品及服务	**Living Articles and Services**	**773.4**	**860.6**
家具及室内装饰品	Furniture and External Decorations	108.7	175.1
家用器具	Household Appliances	257.3	276.9
家用纺织品	Household textile	72.1	63.9
家庭日用杂品	Household Articles of Daily Use	209.8	200.6
个人用品	Personal Items	97.3	128.0
家庭服务	Household Services	28.2	16.0
五、交通通信	**Transportation and Communications**	**1096.7**	**1171.9**
交通	Transportation	676.3	765.9
通信	Communications	420.4	406.0
六、教育文化娱乐	**Recreation, Education and Culture Services**	**1209.9**	**1304.9**
教育	Education	933.0	915.6
文化娱乐	Recreation	276.8	389.3
七、医疗保健	**Medicine and Medical Services**	**1139.4**	**1148.1**
医疗器具及药品	Medical Instruments and Medicines	343.3	300.5
医疗服务	Medical Services	796.0	847.5
八、其他用品和服务	**Others**	**177.0**	**196.1**

8-16 农村常住居民家庭人均购买主要商品数量

Per Capita Annual Purchases of Major Commodities of Rural Households

单位：千克 (kg)

指标名称	Item	2016	2017
面粉	Flour	23.8	21.9
大米	Rice	11.4	11.7
薯类	Potato	9.4	10.3
豆类	Beans	7.0	7.9
食用植物油	Edible vegetable oil	10.4	10.6
鲜菜	Fresh vegetables	60.2	62.7
猪肉	Pork	7.0	7.2
牛肉	Beef	0.3	0.6
羊肉	Lamb	0.4	0.3
鸡	Chicken	1.0	1.0
鱼类	Fish	0.8	0.9
虾类	Shrimp	0.1	0.2
鲜蛋	Eggs	5.8	7.1
鲜奶	Milk	7.1	6.8
酸奶	Yogurt	2.8	3.8
奶粉	Milk	0.8	0.6
鲜瓜果	Fresh fruit	37.1	41.2
糕点	Cake	2.7	3.0
茶叶	Tea	0.2	0.3
卷烟（盒）	Cigarettes (box)	25.7	28.2
啤酒	Beer	3.7	2.6
白酒	Liquor	0.5	0.7
果酒	Wine	0.3	0.3
鞋(双)	Footwear (pair)	2.5	2.7
水（吨）	Water (tons)	10.9	13.1
电（度）	Electricity （kwh）	478.9	571.5
煤炭	Coal	57.7	39.6
管道天燃气（立方米）	Gas pipeline (cu.m)	15.3	21.0
罐装液化石油气	Bottled liquefied petroleum gas	3.9	4.6

8-17 农村常住居民家庭平均每百户耐用品拥有情况

Ownership of Major Durable Consumer Goods Every 100 Rural Households

指标名称	Item	2016	2017
家用汽车（辆）	Automobile (unit)	27.3	30.2
摩托车（辆）	Motorcycles (unit)	41.8	38.8
助力车（台）	Strength-aid Cycle (unit)	73.2	73.9
洗衣机（台）	washing machine (unit)	100.9	101.6
电冰箱（柜）	Refrigerator (unit)	92.0	94.2
微波炉（台）	Microwave Oven (unit)	18.6	17.1
彩色电视机（台）	Color TV Set (unit)	126.0	125.9
空调（台）	Air conditioning(unit)	91.3	101.8
热水器（台）	Water heaters(unit)	73.7	76.9
#太阳能热水器（台）	Solar water heaters (unit)	58.7	61.3
洗碗机（台）	Dishwasher (unit)	0.9	1.5
排油烟机（台）	Exhauster (unit)	34.2	36.2
固定电话（线）	Ordinary Telephone (unit)	26.2	23.9
移动电话（部）	Mobile phones (unit)	279.1	292.2
计算机（台）	Computer (a)	38.4	38.4
#接入互联网（台）	Access to the Internet(unit)	31.2	30.7
照相机（台）	Camera (unit)	10.7	10.9
中高档乐器（架）	High-end Instruments (unit)	1.1	2.0
健身器材（台）	Setting-up Apparatus (unit)	1.9	1.9

8-18 农村常住居民家庭居住情况

Housing Conditions of Rural Households

指标名称	Item	2016	2017
调查户数（户）	**Number of Households Surveyed (household)**	**699**	**706**
平均每户居住人口（人）	**Average Number of Resident Population (person)**	**3.6**	**3.6**
人均现住房建筑面积（平方米/人）	**The Average Floor Area Per Person (sq.m / person)**	**51.7**	**52.4**
一、按居住空间样式分（%）	**by Living space style（%）**	**100.0**	**100.0**
单栋楼房	Single building Room	45.2	46.2
单栋平房	Single-storey House	38.7	38.3
单元房	Apartment	12.4	12.0
筒子楼或连片平房	Tube-shaped Apartment or Lace Single-storey Houses	2.4	2.3
其他	Other	1.3	1.3
二、按主要建筑材料分（%）	**by main construction materials（%）**	**100.0**	**100.0**
钢筋混凝土	Reinforced concrete soil	20.4	20.0
砖混材料	Brick and concrete material	74.9	75.5
砖瓦砖土	Tile and brick earth	4.0	3.8
竹草土坯	Bamboo grass mud	0.6	0.6
其他	Others	0.1	0.1
三、按房屋来源分（%）	**by Source of Housing（%）**	**100.0**	**100.0**
租赁住房	Rental housing	1.6	1.6
自建住房	Self-establish Housing	85.3	85.6
购买商品房	Commercial Residential Housing	4.1	4.0
购买房改住房	Private Housing through Housing Reform	1.4	1.3
购买保障性住房	Indemnificatory Housing	1.3	1.3
拆迁安置房	Resettlement Housing	6.0	6.1
继承或获赠住房	Inheriting and Donation Housing	0.1	0.1
其他	Others	0.1	0.1
四、住房外道路为硬化路面的户比重（%）	**proportion of households which outer road is Hardened road（%）**	**97.6**	**97.5**
五、按住宅有管道供水情况分（%）	**By Piped Water Supply Condition （%）**	**100.0**	**100.0**
管道供水入户	Pipe water into People's Homes	94.4	95.6
管道供水至公共取水点	Pipe water to Public Watering Points	1.0	0.7
没有管道设施	No Pipeline Facilities	4.6	3.7
六、按住户主要饮水来源情况分（%）	**By Source of main Drinking Water （%）**	**100.0**	**100.0**
经过净化处理的自来水	Purified Tap Water	66.1	69.7
受保护的井水和泉水	Protected Wells and Springs	29.0	26.2
不受保护的井水和泉水	Unprotected Wells and Springs	4.6	4.0
江河湖泊水	Rivers and Lakes Water	0.1	
其他饮用水来源	Others	0.1	0.1
七、按住宅内厕所类型分（%）	**By Household Lavatory Type (%)**	**100.0**	**100.0**
水冲式卫生厕所	Sanitary Water Closet	44.3	43.3
水冲式非卫生厕所	Insanitary Water Closet	7.3	7.8
卫生旱厕	Sanitary Latrine	18.3	18.7
普通旱厕	Latrine	29.2	29.5
无厕所	No Lavatory	1.0	0.7
八、按主要炊用能源状况分（%）	**By Cooking Fuel Condition （%）**	**100.0**	**100.0**
天然气、煤气、液化石油气	Pipeline Natural Gas，Pipeline Gas，Pipeline Liquified Petroleum Gas	32.6	29.9
煤炭	Coal	7.4	5.0
电	Electricity	37.2	42.8
沼气	Methane	0.3	0.1
其他	Others	22.5	22.2

主 要 统 计 指 标 解 释

住户 指居住在一个住宅内，共同分享生活开支或收入的一群人。居住在同一房间内、不共同分享生活开支的人群，每个人都视为一个住户。住家保姆、住家家庭帮工视为单独的住户。

常住居民 指住户成员中，经常在家居住、或者调查期内居住时间超过一半的人员，以及本住户供养的学生。常住居民是住户收支的调查对象。

整、半劳动力 整劳动力是指男子18周岁到50周岁，女子18周岁到45周岁；半劳动力是指男子16周岁到17周岁，51周岁到60周岁；女子16周岁到17周岁，46周岁到55周岁，同时具有劳动能力的人。虽然在劳动年龄之内，但已丧失劳动能力的人，不应算为劳动力；超过劳动年龄，但能经常参加劳动，计入半劳动力数内。常住人口中的职工，若这些职工为劳动力，就包括在本户的整半劳动力中。

居民人均可支配收入 指调查期内居民家庭成员人均获得的、可用于最终消费支出和储蓄的总和，即居民可以用来自由支配的收入，既包括现金收入，也包括实物收入。全体居民可支配收入可以体现各地区城乡一体的居民收入及生活水平变化情况。按照收入的来源，可支配收入包含四项，分别为：工资性收入、经营净收入、财产净收入、转移净收入。

工资性收入 指就业人员通过各种途径得到的全部劳动报酬和各种福利，包括受雇于单位或个人、从事各种自由职业、兼职和零星劳动得到的全部劳动报酬和福利。

经营净收入 指住户或住户成员从事生产经营活动所获得的净收入，是全部经营收入中扣除经营费用、生产性固定资产折旧和生产税净额（生产税减去生产补贴）之后得到的净收入。计算公式为：

经营净收入 = 经营收入 – 经营费用 – 生产性固定资产折旧 – 生产税净额（生产税–生产补贴）

财产净收入 指住户或住户成员将其所拥有的金融资产和自然资源交由其他机构单位、住户或个人支配而获得的回报并扣除相关的费用之后得到的净收入。计算公式为：

财产净收入 = 财产性收入 – 财产性支出

转移净收入 指国家、单位、社会团体对住户的各种经常性转移支付和住户之间的经常性收入转移。包括政府、非行政事业单位、社会团体对居民转移的养老金或退休金、社会救济和补助、政策性生活补贴、救灾款、经常性捐赠和赔偿以及报销医疗费等；住户之间的赡养收入、经常性捐赠和赔偿以及农村地区（村委会）在外（含国外）工作的本住户非常住成员寄回带回的收入等。计算公式为：

转移净收入=转移性收入–转移性支出

居民收入五等份分组 指将所有调查户按人均收入水平从低到高顺序排列，平均分为五个等份，处于最高20%的收入群体为高收入组，依此类推依次为中高收入组、中等收入组、中低收入组、低收入组。

居民人均生活消费支出 指住户用于满足家庭日常生活消费需要的全部支出，包括用于消费品的支出和用于服务性消费的支出。根据用途不同，消费支出可划分为食品烟酒、衣着、居住、生活用品及服务、交通通信、教育文化娱乐、医疗保健、其他用品及服务八大类。

居民人均可支配收入 指家庭总收入扣除交纳的个人所得税和个人交纳的各项社会保障支出之后，按照居民家庭人口平均的收入水平。其中家庭总收入是指该家庭中生活在一起的所有家庭人员从各种渠道得到的所有收入之和。计算公式为：

可支配收入= 家庭总收入– 交纳个人所得税–个人交纳的社会保障支出–记账补贴

农村居民人均纯收入（老口径） 指农村住户当年从各个来源得到的家庭总收入扣除有关费用性支出后，最终归农村居民所有的收入总和，按照农村住户人口平均的纯收入水平。计算公式为：

纯收入 = 总收入–家庭经营费用支出–税费支出–生产性固定资产折旧–赠送农村内部亲友

Explanatory Notes on Main Statistical Indicators

Households refer to persons living and sharing economically together in one house. When people don't share living expenses, every single person are deemed to be one household. Live-in Nanny and family helpers are deemed to be one household.

Usual Resident Population refers to persons staying at home regularly or for over half of time in survey period and students provided by the household. Usual resident population is the respondent of household living expenses.

Full/Semi Labour Force Full labour force refers to persons capable of work, aged 18-50 for males and 18-45 for females. Semi labour force refers to persons capable of work, aged 16-17 and 51-60 for males and 16-17 and 46-55 for females. Persons at their working ages but not capable of work are not to be included as labour force. Persons not at working ages but participating regularly in work are included in semi labour force. For staff and workers who are usual residents, are included as full or semi labour force of the household if they are in the labour force.

Disposable Income of Residents refers to the actual income at the disposal of members of the households which can be used for final consumption and savings in survey period, residents can use that at their disposal. It includes cash income and physical income. This income demonstrates the situation about incomes of both rural and urban residents and living standard in various regions. According to the source of income, disposable income include wage income, net business income, net property income and net transferability income.

Wages Income refers to the work reward and all benefits received in various ways by the members of rural households,include the work reward and all benefits received from employed by other units or individuals,liberal professions, part-time job and sporadic labor.

Net Business Income refers to the net income received by households engaged in manufacturing & managing activities.This equals to total business income minus operating costs, depreciation for productive plant assets and net product tax(production taxes minus production subsidies).The following formula is used:

Net business income=business income-operating costs-depreciation for productive plant assets- net product tax(production taxes-production subsidies)

Net Property Income refers to the income received as returns by owners of financial assets or nature sources by providing nature sources to other institutional units,households and individuals. The following formula is used:

Net property income = property income - property expenditure

Net Transferability Income refers to various current transfers of nation, units and social organizations pay to households and recurring revenue transfer between households. This income includes pension transferred from government, the non administrative institutions and social organizations to households, social assistance, policy living allowance, disaster relief funds, regular donation and compensation, recoverable medical cost; alimony income, regular donation and compensation, income from the ones who are not resident in rural areas between the households.The following formula is used:

Net transferability income = transfer income - transfer expenditure

Five Equal Groups of Resident Income According to income per head, all investigative households are arranged from low to high. Divided five groups equally, the maximum 20% of the income groups is high-income groups, and so on, there are middle and upper-income groups, middle-income groups, medium-low-income groups and low-income groups.

Consumption Expenditure of Households refers to total expenditure of households for consumption in daily life, including expenditure on the eight categories of food; clothing; housing; household appliances and services; health care and medical services; transport and communications; recreation, education and cultural services; and miscellaneous goods and services.

The per capita disposable income This equals to total income minus income tax , personal contribution to social security and subsidy for keeping diaries in being a sample household. The following formula is used:

Disposable income = total household income - income tax - personal contribution to social security - subsidy for keeping diaries for a sampled household

The Average Per Capita Net Income of Rural Residents(the old range) refers to the total income of rural households from all sources minus all corresponding expenses. The formula for calculation is as follows:

Net income = total income - household operation expenses - taxes and fees paid - taxes and fees depreciation of fixed assets for production - gifts to non-rural relatives.

9 城市公用事业

URBAN PUBLIC UTILITIES

资料整理：郝　静
Data management：Hao Jing
数据审核：王金桂
Data audit：Wang Jingui

第九部分　城市公用事业

一、简要说明

本章资料主要包括城市供水、供燃气、供热、公共交通、市政设施、市政设施水平、城市规模及用地状况、园林绿地、环境卫生等情况，由西安市统计局服务业和社会科技处根据西安市建委、市交通局、市地铁办及市水务局提供的数据整理。

二、主要指标

人均公园绿地面积（平方米）	12.04	比上年增加	0.43
人均城市道路面积（平方米）	19.73	比上年增加	1.58
用水普及率（%）	99.25	比上年降低	0.75个百分点
燃气普及率（%）	96.07	比上年降低	2.82个百分点

9　URBAN PUBLIC UTILITIES

Ⅰ.Brief Introduction

Data in this chapter reflects basic condition of urban public utilities of Xi'an City. Data on public utilities primarily consists of urban water supply, gas sales, urban heating, public transportation, municipal facilities, level of municipal construction, scale of the city, condition of land utilization, parks, greenbelt and environmental sanitation. Data in this chapter is compiled by Tertiary Industry and Social Science & Technology Division of Xi'an Bureau of Statistics according to the data provided by Committee of Urban Construction of Xi'an, Xi'an Burean of Transportation and Xi'an Metro Office.

Ⅱ.Major Indicators

		Increase over Preceding Year
Per Capita Public Green Areas (sq.m)	12.04	0.43
Per Captia Area of Roads (sq.m)	19.73	1.58
Water–Consuming Popularization (%)	99.25	–0.75 percenage points
Gas–Consuming Popularization (%)	96.07	–2.82 percenage points

9-1 城市（县城）供水

Urban (County) Water Supply

指　标	Item	2010	2013	2014	2015	2016	2017
年末水厂个数（个）	Number of Water Factory at Year-end (units)	9	15	16	22	22	24
供水综合生产能力（万立方米/日）	Total Volume of Water Supply (10 000 cu.m/day)	197.40	195.52	196.50	211.50	219.38	206.47
# 地下水	Undergronnd Water	55.80	51.35	51.33	62.86	64.61	65.11
年末供水管道总长度（公里）	Length of Water Supply Pipelines at Year-end (kms)	2416.00	3385.33	3499.97	4371.05	4522.46	4899.56
全年供水总量（万立方米）	Total Annual Volume of Water Supply (10 000 cu.m)	41089.00	51372.07	53798.99	56055.25	59953.03	89215.62
#生产运营用水	For Productive Use	6267.00	6272.62	15680.53	16146.29	16567.21	43095.31
居民家庭用水	For Residential Use	20944.00	26138.73	28497.40	30742.79	32182.87	34896.60
用水人口（万人）	Population with Access to Tap Water (10 000 persons)	410.90	444.35	452.57	463.05	475.00	506.26

注：本表数据来源于市建委和市水务局。
本表2017年数据含西咸新区。

9-2 城市（县城）供燃气

Gas Supply in Urban Area（County）

指　标	Item	2010	2013	2014	2015	2016	2017
一、天然气	**Natural Gas**						
管道长度（公里）	Total Length of Gas Pipelines (km)	4488	6163.39	6892.25	7465.73	8199.80	9174.87
供气总量（万立方米）	Total Gas Supply(10 000 cu.m)	109052	153488.90	186259.15	196826.38	206068.05	231168.38
#销售气量	Volume of Gas Sales	104055	147592.97	179536.78	189066.21	201078.36	224419.93
#家庭用量	Residential Households	20989	36671.17	59057.38	65952.81	67024.75	105249.81
用气人口（万人）	Population with Access to Gas (10 000 persons)	333	410.56	425.72	437.96	452.11	477.01
二、液化石油气	**Liquefied Petroleum Gas**						
供气总量（吨）	Total Gas Supply (tons)	11469	6047.90	5299.70	5030.30	4955.50	7607.20
#销售气量	Volume of Gas Sales	11441	5986.20	5244.00	4950.00	4875.20	7478.90
#家庭用量	Residential Households	7376	4945.00	4281.00	4064.00	4056.00	6081.47
用气人口（万人）	Population with Access to Gas (10 000 persons)	31.20	27.92	21.00	19.50	17.60	13.02

注：本表数据来源于市建委。
本表2017年数据含西咸新区。

9–3 城市（县城）供热

Heating in Urban Area（County）

指　标	Item	2010	2013	2014	2015	2016	2017
供热能力	Heating Capacity						
蒸气（吨/小时）	Steam (tons/hour)	2235	4283	2893	3013	3013	6200
热水（兆瓦）	Hot Water (megawatts)	3531	12691.10	13967.00	17191.90	17765.90	14477.00
供热总量(万吉焦)	Volume Supplied (10 000 gigajoules)						
蒸气	Steam	1674	1667.88	1743.87	1671.14	1789.13	2813.00
热水	Hot Water	2570	2990.38	3726.89	4241.30	5032.84	6338.00
集中供热管道长度（公里）	Length of Centralized Heating Pipelines(km)	541	812.45	894.24	1054.41	1141.24	1842.00
供热面积（万平方米）	Heated Area (10 000sq.m)	6094	10980.27	13492.55	16690.65	19566.81	29118.90
#住宅	Residential Buildings	5009	9874.54	11828.59	14730.49	17282.39	17541.10

注：本表数据来源于市建委。
　　本表2017年数据含西咸新区。

9–4 城市公共交通

Urban Public Traffic

指　标	Item	2010	2013	2014	2015	2016	2017
运营车辆（辆）	Operating Vehicles (units)	7107	8128	7769	7781	7829	7780
标准运营车辆（标台）	Standard Vehicles (units)	8139	9371	9050	9061	9140	9243
公交客运总量（万人次）	Total of Bus Passenger(10 000 person-times)	162400	174051	170960	161032	147089	133465
公交客运收入（万元）	Bus Passenger Transport Income (10 000 yuan)	129397	146417	140914	137492	129132	165072
出租汽车数（辆）	Number of Taxis (units)	12786	14139	14159	14459	14459	14509
地铁运营线路长度（公里）	Length of Subway Lines in Operation(km)		44.68	50.94	50.94	88.97	88.97
地铁客运量（万人次）	Total of Subway Passenger(10 000 person-times)		12189.61	29953.07	34209.35	40815.75	60534.01

注：本表数据来源于市交通局和地铁办。
　　本表数据为西安原口径。

9-5 市政设施

Municipal Facilities

指　标	Item	2010	2013	2014	2015	2016	2017
一、道路长度（公里）	**Length of Roads (km)**	**2662**	**3387.43**	**3461.18**	**3570.58**	**3683.14**	**4398.83**
二、道路面积（万平方米）	**Area of Roads (10 000 sq.m)**	**5965**	**7931.80**	**8144.22**	**8457.14**	**8618.93**	**10063.55**
三、人行道面积（万平方米）	**Area of Sidewalks (10 000 sq.m)**	**1834**	**2259.29**	**2310.46**	**2381.20**	**2423.70**	**2814.31**
四、桥梁数（座）	**Number of Bridges (units)**	**347**	**432**	**437**	**448**	**449**	**491**
#立交桥	Overpasses	71	97	105	106	107	127
五、路灯盏数（盏）	**Number of Street Lights (units)**	**291754**	**333393**	**337991**	**343465**	**349808**	**382979**
六、排水管道长度（公里）	**Length of Drainage Pipelines (km)**	**3765**	**4629.70**	**4839.49**	**4984.94**	**5161.83**	**5802.36**
七、污水年排放量（万立方米）	**Annual Discharge Volume of Sewage (10 000 cu.m)**	**34706**	**46186**	**51673**	**62092**	**56578**	**58303**
八、污水处理厂处理能力（万立方米/日）	**Daily Disposal Capacity of Sewage (10 000 cu.m/day)**	**106.5**	**153.1**	**153.1**	**200.6**	**212.1**	**147.6**
九、污水年处理量（万立方米）	**Yearly Disposal Capacity of Sewage Disposal Plant (10 000 cu.m)**	**25088**	**41898**	**47907**	**57034**	**52011**	**54279**

注：本表数据来源于市建委。
本表2017年数据含西咸新区。

9-6 城市（县城）设施水平

Urban（County）Municipal Facilities

指　标	Item	2010	2013	2014	2015	2016	2017
一、人均日生活用水量（升）	**Per Capita Daily Consumption of Tap Water For Residential Use (liters)**	**186.20**	**225.78**	**178.45**	**187.79**	**191.35**	**199.09**
二、用水普及率(%)	**Water-Consuming Popularization (%)**	**98.8**	**100**	**100**	**100**	**100**	**99.25**
三、每万人拥有公共交通车辆（标台）	**Number of Public Transport Vehicles Per 10 000 Population (units)**	**13.9**	**15.1**	**14.4**	**14.3**	**13.9**	**14.4**
四、燃气普及率(%)	**Gas-Consuming Popularization (%)**	97.0	98.68	98.71	98.79	98.89	96.07
五、人均城市道路面积（平方米）	**Per Captia Area of Roads (sq.m)**	15.4	17.85	18.00	18.26	18.15	19.73
六、建成区排水管道密度（公里/平方公里）	**Density of Drainage Pipelines in Developed Areas (km/sq.km)**	9.5	9.17	9.27	9.09	9.12	1.46
七、污水处理率(%)	**Rate of Sewerage Disposal (%)**	84.0	90.72	92.71	91.85	91.93	93.10
八、园林绿化	**Afforestation and Parks and Gardens**						
人均公园绿地面积（平方米）	Per Capita Public Green Areas (sq.m)	9.1	10.70	11.22	11.47	11.61	12.04
建城区绿地率（%）	Rate of Green Areas in Developed Areas (%)	29.2	32.32	32.60	34.03	34.95	36.78
九、生活垃圾无害化处理率(%)	**Rate of No Harm Disposal of Garbage (%)**	93.9	93.95	93.48	98.09	96.70	98.11

注：本表数据来源于市建委。
每万人拥有公共交通车辆计算数据口径调整，故与2009年前数据不可比。
本表2017年数据含西咸新区。其中，“每万人拥有公共交通车辆”指标数据为西安原口径。

9-7 城市（县城）规模及用地情况

City（County） Scale and Land Use

单位：平方公里 (sq.km)

指 标	Item	2010	2013	2014	2015	2016	2017
建成区面积	Area of the Constructed Regions	395	504.68	521.91	548.60	565.75	683.09
城市建设用地	Land use for Construction	336	489.03	507.66	536.10	553.29	646.54

注：本表数据来源于市建委。
本表2017年数据含西咸新区。

9-8 城市（县城）园林绿化

Urban（County） Parks,Gardens and Green Areas in Cities

指 标	Item	2010	2013	2014	2015	2016	2017
一、公园个数（个）	**Number of Parks (units)**	**68**	**81**	**85**	**91**	**95**	**103**
二、公园面积（公顷）	**Area of Parks (hectares)**	**1335**	**2406.00**	**2483.83**	**2599.83**	**2647.40**	**3259.70**
三、绿地面积（公顷）	**Total Area of Parks,Gardens and Green Areas (hectares)**	**12140**	**17751.00**	**18914.05**	**20582.44**	**22502.87**	**30703.66**
#公园绿地面积	Public Green Areas	3526	4756.00	5075.85	5310.58	5517.08	6142.98
四、年末绿化覆盖面积（公顷）	**Coverage Space of Green Areas at year-end (hectares)**	**15646**	**21865.00**	**23216.65**	**25639.88**	**27617.83**	**35936.49**
五、建成区绿化覆盖率（%）	**Coverage of Green Areas in Developed Areas (%)**	**37.50**	**40.29**	**40.76**	**42.04**	**42.57**	**40.79**

注：本表数据来源于市建委。
本表2017年数据含西咸新区。

9-9 城市（县城）环境卫生

Urban（County）Environment Sanitation

指 标	Item	2010	2013	2014	2015	2016	2017
清扫面积（万平方米）	Area Under Cleaning Program (10 000 sq.m)	6290	8725	10110	9842	9137	12241
生活垃圾清运量（万吨）	Volume of Residential Garbage Disposal (10 000 tons)	237	290.76	359.37	359.16	371.51	189.93
公共厕所（座）	Number of Public Lavatories (units)	1257	1770	2151	2239	2314	3274
市容环卫专用车辆设备总数（辆）	Special Vehicles of Environmental Sanitation (units)	1042	1639	1990	2050	2000	2571

注：本表数据来源于市建委。
本表2017年数据含西咸新区。
2017年生活垃圾清运量统计口径与2016年及以前不同。

9-10 市区及县供水（2017年）

Urban and County Water Supply (2017)

指 标	Item	西安 Xi'an	市区 City	蓝田 Lantian	周至 ZhouZhi
年末水厂个数（个）	Number of Water Factory at Year-end (units)	24	22	1	1
供水综合生产能力（万立方米/日）	Total Volume of Water Supply (10 000 cu.m/day)	206.47	201.43	2.54	2.50
#地下水	Groundwater	65.11	61.57	1.74	1.80
年末供水管道总长度（公里）	Length of Water Supply Pipelines at Year-end (km)	4899.56	4702.04	124.92	72.60
全年供水总量（万立方米）	Total Annual Volume of Water Supply (10 000 cu.m)	89215.62	87740.72	617.03	857.87
#生产运营用水	For Productive Use	43095.31	42500.74	266.57	328.00
居民家庭用水	For Residential Use	34896.60	34272.88	267.72	356.00
用水人口（万人）	Population with Access to Tap Water (10 000 persons)	506.26	490.84	8.13	7.29

注：本表数据来源于市建委及市水务局。
本表数据含西咸新区。

9-11 市区及县供燃气（2017年）

Urban and County Gas Supply (2017)

指 标	Item	西安 Xi'an	市区 Urban	蓝田 Lantian	周至 ZhouZhi
一、天然气	**Natural Gas**				
管道长度（公里）	Total Length of Gas Pipelines (km)	9174.87	9046.37	83.00	45.50
供气总量（万立方米）	Total Gas Supply(10 000 cu.m)	231168.38	228044.18	1702.00	1422.20
#销售气量	Volume of Gas Sales	224419.93	221301.93	1698.00	1420.00
#家庭用量	Residential Households	105249.81	103650.81	939.00	660.00
用气人口（万人）	Population with Access to Gas (10 000 persons)	477.01	463.80	7.01	6.20
二、液化石油气	**Liquefied Petroleum Gas**				
供气总量（吨）	Total Gas Supply (tons)	7607.20	4964.00	1478.00	1165.20
#销售气量	Volume of Gas Sales	7478.90	4868.40	1445.50	1165.00
#家庭用量	Residential Households	6081.47	3470.97	1445.50	1165.00
用气人口（万人）	Population with Access to Gas (10 000 persons)	13.02	10.70	1.12	1.20

注：本表数据来源于市建委。
本表数据含西咸新区。

9-12 市区及县供热（2017年）

Urban and County Heating (2017)

指 标	Item	西安 Xi'an	市区 Urban	蓝田 Lantian	周至 ZhouZhi
供热能力	Heating Capacity				
蒸气（吨/小时）	Steam (tons/hour)	6200	6200		
热水（兆瓦）	Hot Water (megawatts)	14477	14473		4
供热总量(万吉焦)	Volume Supplied(10 000 gigajoules)				
蒸气	Steam	2813	2813		
热水	Hot Water	6338	5938		400
集中供热管道长度（公里）	Length of Centralized Heating Pipelines(km)	1842	1840		2
供热面积（万平方米）	Heated Area (10 000sq.m)	29118.9	28417.1		701.8
#住宅	Residential Buildings	17541.1	17538.1		3.0

注：本表数据来源于市建委。
本表数据含西咸新区。

9-13 市区及县市政设施（2017年）

Urban and County Municipal Facilities (2017)

指 标	Item	西安 Xi'an	市区 Urban	蓝田 Lantian	周至 ZhouZhi
一、道路长度（公里）	**Length of Roads (km)**	**4398.83**	**4276.67**	**75.60**	**46.56**
二、道路面积（万平方米）	**Area of Roads (10 000 sq.m)**	**10063.55**	**9829.39**	**136.18**	**97.98**
三、人行道面积（万平方米）	**Area of Sidewalks (10 000 sq.m)**	**2814.31**	**2720.51**	**58.96**	**34.84**
四、桥梁数（座）	**Number of Bridges (units)**	**491**	**475**	**11**	**5**
#立交桥	Crossroads	127	127		
五、路灯盏数（盏）	**Number of Street Lights (units)**	**382979**	**375561**	**2232**	**5186**
六、排水管道长度（公里）	**Length of Drainage Pipelines (km)**	**5802.36**	**5652.51**	**89.45**	**60.40**
七、污水年排放量（万立方米）	**Annual Discharge Volume of Sewage (10 000 cu.m)**	**58303**	**57355**	**533**	**415**
八、污水处理厂处理能力（万立方米/日）	**Daily Disposal Capacity of Sewage (10 000 cu.m/day)**	**147.6**	**145.0**	**1.5**	**1.1**
九、污水年处理量（万立方米）	**Yearly Disposal Capacity of Sewage Disposal Plant (10 000 cu.m)**	**54279**	**53509**	**433**	**337**

注：本表数据来源于市建委。
本表数据含西咸新区。

9-14 市区及县市政设施水平（2017年）

Urban and County Municipal Facilities Level(2017)

指 标	Item	西安 Xi'an	市区 City	蓝田 Lantian	周至 ZhouZhi
一、人均日生活用水量（升）	**Per Capita Daily Consumption of Tap Water For Residential Use (liters)**	**199.09**	**200.95**	**107.59**	**175.51**
二、用水普及率(%)	**Water-Consuming Popularization (%)**	**99.25**	**99.39**	**98.78**	**91.13**
三、每万人拥有公共交通车辆（标台）	**Number of Public Transport Vehicles Per 10 000 Population (units)**	**14.4**			
四、燃气普及率（%）	**Gas-Consuming Popularization (%)**	**96.07**	**96.08**	**98.78**	**92.5**
五、人均城市道路面积（平方米）	**Per Captia Area of Roads (sq.m)**	**19.73**	**19.9**	**16.55**	**12.25**
六、建成区排水管道密度（公里/平方公里）	**Density of Drainage Pipelines (km/sq.km)**	**1.46**	**1.38**	**4.19**	**3.63**
七、污水处理率(%)	**Rate of Sewerage Disposal (%)**	**93.10**	**93.29**	**81.24**	**81.20**
八、园林绿化	**Afforestation and Parks and Gardens**				
人均公园绿地面积（平方米）	Per Capita Public Green Areas (sq.m)	12.04	12.05	8.86	14.75
建城区绿地率（%）	Rate of Green Areas in Developed Areas(%)	36.78	37.11	31.09	21.40
九、生活垃圾无害化处理率(%)	**Rate of No Harm Disposal of Garbage (%)**	**98.11**	**99.98**		**94.6**

注：本表数据来源于市建委。
本表数据含西咸新区。其中“每万人拥有公共交通车辆”指标数据为西安原口径。

主要统计指标解释

建成区面积 城市行政区内实际已成片开发建设、市政公用设施和公共设施基本具备的区域。对核心城市，它包括集中连片的部分以及分散的若干个已经成片建设起来，市政公用设施和公共设施基本具备的地区；对一城多镇来说，它包括由几个连片开发建设起来的，市政公用设施和公共设施基本具备的地区组成。因此建成区范围，一般是指建成区外轮廓线所能包括的地区，也就是这个城市实际建设用地所达到的范围。

供水综合生产能力 指按供水设施取水、净化、送水、出厂输水干管等环节设计能力计算的综合生产能力。包括在原设计能力的基础上，经挖、革、改增加的生产能力。计算时，以四个环节中最薄弱的环节为主确定能力。

供水管道长度 指从送水泵至用户水表之间所有管道的长度。不包括新安装尚未使用、水厂内以及用户建筑物内的管道。在同一条街道埋设两条或两条以上管道时，应按每条管道的长度计算。

供水总量 指报告期供水企业（单位）供出的全部水量。包括有效供水量和漏损水量。

用水普及率 指报告期末城区内用水人口与总人口的比率。计算公式:

$$用水普及率=\frac{用水人口（含暂住人口）}{人口+暂住人口}\times 100\%$$

供气管道长度 指报告期末从气源厂压缩机的出口或门站出口至各类用户引入管之间的全部已经通气投入使用的管道长度。不包括煤气生产厂、输配站、液化气储存站、灌瓶站、储配站、气化站、混气站、供应站等厂（站）内的管道。

供气总量 指报告期燃气企业（单位）向用户供应的燃气数量。包括销售量和损失量。

燃气普及率 指报告期末城区内使用燃气的人口与总人口的比率。计算公式：

$$燃气普及率=\frac{用气人口（含暂住人口）}{人口+暂住人口}\times 100\%$$

供热能力 指供热企业（单位）向城市热用户输送热能的设计能力。不是热电厂的生产能力。

供热总量 指在报告期供热企业（单位）向城市热用户输送全部蒸汽和热水的总热量。

供热管道长度 指从各类热源到热用户建筑物接入口之间的全部蒸汽和热水的管道长度。不包括各类热源厂内部的管道长度。

供热面积 指供热企业（单位）向城市各类房屋建筑物、构筑物及其附属设施供热的全部建筑面积。

道路长度 指道路长度和与道路相通的桥梁、隧道的长度，按车行道中心线计算。

道路面积 指道路实际铺装面积和与道路相通的广场、桥梁、隧道的铺装面积（统计时，将人行道面积单独统计）。

人行道面积按道路两侧面积相加计算，包括步行街和广场，不含人车混行的道路。

排水管道长度 指所有排水总管、干管、支管、检查井及连接井进出口等长度之和。计算时按单管计算，即在同一条街道上如有两条或两条以上并排的排水管道时，应按每条排水管道的长度相加计算。

绿化覆盖面积 指城市中的乔木、灌木、草坪等所有植被的垂直投影面积。包括公园绿地、防护绿地、生产绿地、附属绿地、其他绿地的绿化种植覆盖面积、屋顶绿化覆盖面积以及零散树木的覆盖面积，不含各类绿地中的水域面积以及没有被植被覆盖的面积（硬化道路、无屋顶绿化的建筑物等）。乔木树冠下重迭的灌木和草本植物不重复计算。

人均城市道路面积 指报告期末城区内平均每人拥有的城市道路面积。计算公式：

$$人均城市道路面积=\frac{城区道路面积}{城区人口+城区暂住人口}$$

建成区排水管道密度 指报告期末建成区排水管道分布的疏密程度，计算公式：

$$排水管道密度=\frac{排水管道长度}{建成区面积}$$

污水处理率 指报告期内污水处理总量与污水排放总量的比率。计算公式：

$$污水处理率=\frac{污水处理总量}{污水排放总量}\times 100\%$$

人均公园绿地面积 指报告期末城区内平均每人拥有的公园绿地面积。计算公式：

$$人均公园绿地面积=\frac{城区公园绿地面积}{城区人口+城区暂住人口}$$

建成区绿地率 指报告期末建成区内绿地面积与建成区面积的比率。计算公式：

$$建成区绿地率\frac{建成区绿地面积}{建成区面积}\times 100\%$$

Explanatory Notes on Main Statistical Indicators

Area of the Constructed Regions refers to developed and built city administrative area where basic municipal utilities and public facilities complete constructed. To core city, it includes part of contiguous centralized and a number of decentralized part where basic municipal utilities and public facilities complete constructed. To a multi-city town, it consists of several contiguous developed and build area where municipal utilities and public facilities with basic composition. Therefore, the range of built-up area, generally refers to the built-up areas in the contour line, which is the actual construction site of the city achieved range.

Production Capacity of Water Supply refers to the designed overall production capacity of water facilities, covering the four segments of water collection, purification, conveyance, and out flow through trunk pipelines. Increased capacity through transformation and innovation projects is included as well. The capacity is determined mainly on the weakest of the above-mentioned four segments.

Length of Water Supply Pipelines at Year-end refers to the total length of all the pipelines between the water pumps and the user water meters, excluding pipelines newly installed but not used yet, pipeline in the water factory, and pipeline in the user's buildings.

Volume of Water Supply refers to the total volume of water supplied by water-works(units) during the reference period, including both the effective water supply and loss during the water supply.

Coverage Rate of Urban Population with Access to Tap Water refers to the ratio of the urban population with access to tap water to the total urban population . The formula is :

$$\text{Coverage of urban population with access to tap water} = \frac{\text{population with access to tap water}}{\text{population}} \times 100\%$$

Length of Gas Pipeline refers to the total length of pipelines in use between the outlet of the compressor of gas-work of outlet gas stations and the leading pipe of users , excluding pipelines within gasworks , delivery stations ,LPG storage stations ,refilling stations, gas-mixing stations and supply stations.

Volume of Gas Supply refers to the total volume of gas provided to users by gas-producing enterprises (units) in a year ,including the volume sold and the volume lost .

Coverage Rate of Urban Population with Access to Gas refers to the ratio of the urban population with access to gas to the total urban population at the end of the reference period. The formula is :

$$\text{Coverage rate of urban population with access to gas} = \frac{\text{population with access to gas}}{\text{population}} \times 100\%$$

City Heating capacity in Urban Areas refers to the designed capacity of heating enterprises (units) in supplying heating energy to urban users during the reference period .

City Quantity of Heat Supplied in Urban Areas refers to the total quantity of heat from steam and hot water urban users by heating enterprises (units) during the reference period .

City Length of Urban Heating Pipelines refers to the total length of steam or hot water pipelines for sources of heat to the leading pipelines of the building of the users ,excluding internal pipelines in heat generating enterprises

Heated Area refers to the total structure area of heat supplied to urban constructions, structures and ancillary facilities by heating enterprises (units) during the reference period .

Length of Paved Roads refers to the length of roads with paved surface including bridges and tunnels connected with roads. Length of the roads is measured by the central lines .

Area of Paved Roads refers to the actual pavement area of roads and the actual pavement area of squares, bridges and tunnels connecting to the roads (the area of sidewalk pavements is calculated separately).

The area of sidewalk pavements is the sum of area of roads on sides of road, including pedestrian streets and squares, excluding roads for both pedestrians and vehicles .

Length of exhaust pipelines refers to the total length of all main drain piles ,trunk pipes ,branch pipes

,access manholes ,and connector well entrances and exits ,and so on . The whole length is calculated as of single pipes. Namely ,if there are two or more drain pipes parallel on a street ,the length of every pipe shall be summed .

Total area of green land refers to vertical projection area of all vegetation including trees, shrubs, lawns. Including parks, protective green space, production green space, green subsidiaries, green plants covering area, covering an area other green spaces, green roofs and covering area of scattered trees, excluding kinds of water area in kinds of green area and the area not covered by vegetation(hardened road, building of no green roof). shrubs and herbaceous plants overlap under the canopy of trees do not double counting.

Per Capita Area of Paved Roads refers to the area of urban roads per capita at the end of the reporting period. The formula is :

$$\text{Per capita area of paved roads} = \frac{\text{Area of urban roads}}{\text{Urban population+temporary resident population}}$$

Density of Drainage Pipelines refers to density of drainage pipelines in developed areas at the end of the reporting period .The formula is :

$$\text{Density of drainage pipelines} = \frac{\text{Length of drainage pipelines}}{\text{Ares of developed areas}}$$

Rate of Sewerage Disposal refers to the ratio of waste water disposed with the total discharge of waste water in the reporting period .The formula is:

$$\text{Rate of Sewerage Disposal} = \frac{\text{Waste Water Disposed}}{\text{Total Discharge of Waste Water}} \times 100\%$$

Per Capita Area of Public Green refers to the area of public green areas per capita at end of the reporting period .The formula is :

$$\text{Per capita area of public green} = \frac{\text{Area of public green areas}}{\text{Urban population+temporary resident population}}$$

Coverage of Green Areas in Developed Areas refers to the ratio of green areas in built-up areas with the area of developed areas at the end of reporting period . The formula is:

$$\text{Coverage of green land in developed areas} = \frac{\text{Area of green land in developed aresa}}{\text{Area of developed areas}} \times 100\%$$

10 环境保护

ENVIRONMENT PROTECTION

资料整理：张　育
Data management：Zhang Yu
数据审核：马建华
Data audit：Ma Jianhua

第十部分　环境保护

一、简要说明

本章资料反映环境保护、工业污染排放及处理利用情况、危险废物集中处置情况、生活及其他污染情况和工业污染治理项目建设情况，由西安市统计局能源与环境处根据西安市环保局提供的数据资料整理。本部分2017年数据不包含西咸新区。

二、主要指标

全年环境空气质量达标天数（天）	180	比上年减少	12天
工业固体废物综合利用率（%）	83.97	比上年下降	1.34个百分点

10 ENVIRONMENT PROTECTION

Ⅰ.Brief Introduction

This chapter contains information that reflect environment protection, discharge and treatment of industrial pollutant, centralized treatment of dangerous wastes, domestic pollution and other pollution, construction of projects of industrial pollution treatment. Data in this chapter is compiled by General Division of the Xi'an Bureau of Statistics according to the reported data from Xi'an Environment Protection Bureau.

Ⅱ.Major Indicators

		Increase over Preceding Year
Days of Air Quality up to the Standards（days）	180	−12days
Percentage of InduStrial Solid Waste Utilized(%)	83.97	−1.34percentage points

10-1 城市环境保护（2017年）

Urban Environmental Protection（2017）

指　标	Item	2017
一、饮用水环境	**Potable Water Environment**	
全市饮用水水质达标率(%)	Compliance Rate of the City's Potable Water Quality (%)	98.1
二、大气环境	**Atmospheric Environment**	
颗粒物（PM10）年平均浓度（微克/立方米）	Particulate matter (PM10) Annual average concentration (μg / m^3)	130
颗粒物（PM2.5）年平均浓度（微克/立方米）	Particulate matter (PM2.5) Annual average concentration (μg / m^3)	73
二氧化硫浓度年平均值（微克/立方米）	Annual Average Concentration of Sulphur Dioxide (μg / m^3)	19
二氧化氮浓度年平均值（微克/立方米）	Annual Average Concentration of Nitrogen Dioxide (μg / m^3)	59
一氧化碳第95百分位数（微克/立方米）	The 95th percentile of carbon monoxide (μg / m^3)	2.8
臭氧八小时第90百分位数（微克/立方米）	Ozone eight hours 90th percentile (μg / m^3)	185
全年环境空气质量达标天数(天)	Days of Air Quality up to the Standards(days)	180
全年环境空气质量达标率(%)	Annual compliance rate of Ambient Air Quality(%)	49.32
三、声环境	**Voice**	
1、功能区噪声平均值(dB(A))	Average Noise Value of Functional Districts(dB(A))	
0类区	Class 0	53
1类区	Class 1	61
2类区	Class 2	58
3类区	Class 3	59
4类区	Class 4	71
2、道路交通噪声平均值(dB(A))	Average Noise Value of Road Traffic(dB(A))	70.6
3、区域噪声平均值(dB(A))	Average Noise Value of Region(dB(A))	56.5
四、环境污染治理	**Environmental pollution treatment**	
当年完成环保验收项目环境保护投资（亿元）	Year Completed Investment in Environmental Protection Projects of Environmental acceptance(100 million yuan)	22.9

注：本表数据来源于市环保局。
2017年数据为不含西咸新区口径。下同。

10-2 主要年份工业“三废”排放及处理利用情况

指　标	Item	2000	2010
一、工业废水排放量（万吨）	**Volume of Waste Water Discharge (10 000 tons)**	**9145**	**13840**
工业废水处理量（万吨）	Volume of Industrial Wastewater Disposal (10 000 tons)		10673.52
废水治理设施数（套）	Number of Facilities for Treatment of Waste Water (sets)		267
二、工业废气排放量（亿立方米）	**Total Volume of Industrial Waste Gas Emission (100 million cu.m)**	**275.97**	**791.56**
废气治理设施数（套）	Number of Facilities for Treatment of Waste Gas(sets)		816
三、工业固体废物产生量（万吨）	**Volume of Industrial Solid Wastes Produced (10 000 tons)**	**107**	**267.29**
工业固体废物处置量（万吨）	Volume of Industrial Solid Wastes Treated (10 000 tons)	20	3.56
工业固体废物综合利用量（万吨）	Volume of Industrial Solid Waste Utilized (10 000 tons) in a Comprehensive Way	63	262
工业固体废物综合利用率（%）	Percentage of Volume of Industrial Solid Waste Utilized in a Comprehensive Way(%)	58.88	98.05
四、工业锅炉（台/蒸吨）	**Industrial Boilers (units/tons)**		

注：1.本表数据来源于市环保局。
2.2010年全国统一进行了污染源普查动态更新调查工作，“十二五”的环境统计体系与污染源普查体系相衔接，与“十一五”环境统计口径不同。
3.工业固体废物综合利用率依据环境统计口径计算。

Discharge and Treatrment of Waste Gas, Water & Solid Wastes in Repersentative Years

2011	2012	2013	2014	2015	2016	2017
13148	**10223.73**	**8972.97**	**6339.85**	**5203.56**	**4029.83**	**4247.60**
12632.38	9089.04	6798.71	5818.27	4783.60	4264.99	4448.08
314	312	295	305	315	266	275
1018.46	**1043.31**	**844.11**	**901.23**	**1108.48**	**1034.46**	**1444.60**
745	649	661	740	801	834	1048
279	**259.14**	**255.78**	**252.66**	**238.53**	**195.99**	**190.30**
6	9.24	9.68	17.54	20.95	28.66	28.00
271	248.58	244.08	233.52	216.64	167.20	159.80
97.30	95.92	95.43	92.43	90.82	85.31	83.97
	503/8785	**576/13466**	**520/14177**	**501/18278**	**480/12791.8**	**457/14682.3**

10-3 工业污染排放及处理利用情况（2017年）

Discharge and Treatment of Industrial Pollution (2017)

指 标	Item	2017
一、被调查企业基本情况	**Basic condition of Enterprises investigated**	
1. 企业数（个）	Number of Enterprises (units)	496
2. 工业总产值（亿元）	Gross Industry Output Value (100 millian yuan)	3067.6
3. 工业锅炉数（台/蒸吨）	Industrial Boilers (units/tons)	457/14682.3
4. 工业炉窑数（座）	Number of Industrial Grates (items)	149.0
二、工业废水	**Industrial Waste Water**	
1. 工业取水量（万吨）	Industrial water intake (10000 tons)	9197.10
#新鲜水量	Volume of Fresh Water	
重复用水量	Volume of Water Recycled	
2. 工业用水重复利用率（%）	Percentage of Industrial Water Recycled (%)	
3. 废水治理设施数（套）	Number of Facilities for Treatment of Waste Water (sets)	275
4. 废水治理设施处理能力（万吨/日）	Disposal Capacity of Facilities for Treatment of Waste Water (10 000 tons/day)	29.6
5. 废水治理设施运行费用（万元）	Operating Expense of Facilities for Treatment of Waste Water (10 000 yuan)	27056.9
6. 工业废水排放量（万吨）	Volume of Industrial Waste Water Discharged (10 000 tons)	4247.6
三、工业废气	**Industrial Waste Gas**	
1. 煤炭消费量（万吨）	Total Coal Consumption (10 000 tons)	673.7
2. 燃料油消费量（不含车船用）（万吨）	Fuel Oil Consumption (10 000 tons)	0.19
3. 天然气消费量（亿立方米）	Natural Gas Consumption (100 millian cu.m)	14.5
4. 工业废气排放总量（亿立方米）	Total Volume of Industrial Waste Gas Emission (100 millian cu.m)	1444.6
5. 废气治理设施数（套）	Number of Facilities for Treatment of Waste Gas (sets)	1048
6. 废气治理设施处理能力（万立方米/时）	Disposal Capacity of Facilities for Treatment of Waste Gas (10 000 cu.m./h)	5580.8
7. 废气治理设施设备运行费用（万元）	Operating Expense of Facilities for Treatment of Waste gas(10 000 yuan)	58786.0
8. 二氧化硫产生量（吨）	Sulfur dioxide production (tons)	79711.2
9. 二氧化硫排放量（吨）	Volume of Sulphur Dioxide Emission (tons)	3904.2
10. 氮氧化物产生量（吨）	Production of nitrogen oxides(tons)	30816.0
11. 氮氧化物排放量（吨）	Nitrogen oxide emissions(tons)	7402.6
12. 烟（粉）尘产生量（吨）	Tobacco (powder) dust production(tons)	1128552.3
13. 烟（粉）尘排放量（吨）	The smoke (powder) dust emissions(tons)	2757.5
四、工业固体废物	**Industrial Solid Waste**	
1. 工业固体废物产生量（万吨）	Volume of Industrial Solid Waste Produced (10 000tons)	190.3
2. 工业固体废物综合利用量（万吨）	Volume of Industrial Solid Waste Utilized (10 000tons)	159.8
3. 工业固体废物综合利用率（%）	Percentage of Industrial Solid Waste Utilized (%)	
4. 工业固体废物贮存量（万吨）	Volume of Industrial Solid Waste Accumulated (10 000tons)	2.5
5. 工业固体废物处置量（万吨）	Volume of Industrial Solid Waste Treated (10 000tons)	28.0
6. 工业固体废物倾倒丢弃量（吨）	Volume of Industrial Solid Waste Discharged (tons)	

注：本表数据来源于市环保局。

10-4 城市污水处理情况（2017年）

Urban Sewage Treatment（2017）

指 标	Item	2017
一、污水处理厂数（座）	**Number of Sewage Treatment Works(units)**	**37**
污水处理厂处理能力（万吨/日）	Daily Disposal Capacity of Sewage(10 000 tons/day)	242.8
二、污水处理	**Sewgae Disposal**	
污水实际处理量（万吨）	Volume of Sewgae Disposal(10 000 tons)	76087.1
生活污水处理量	Volume of Domestic Sewgae Disposal	70983.6
工业污水处理量	Volume of Industrial Sewage Disposal	5103.5
三、再生水（万吨）	**Recycled water (10 000 tons)**	
生产量	Production	4939.4
利用量	Utilization	3493
四、化学需氧量去除量（吨）	**Volume of COD Removed (tons)**	**342009.8**
五、氨氮去除量（吨）	**Volume of Ammonia and Nitrogen Removed(tons)**	**25277.5**
六、总磷去除量（吨）	**Volume of Total Phosphorus Removed(tons)**	**3519**
七、污泥产生量（吨）	**Volume of Sludge Produced(tons)**	**188233**
八、污泥处置量（吨）	**Volume of Sludge Disposal(tons)**	**187933**
九、污泥倾倒丢弃量（吨）	**Dumping sludge discards (tons)**	**300**
十、本年运行费用（万元）	**Operating Expense(10 000 yuan)**	**72396.9**

注：本表数据来源于市环保局。

10-5 危险废物（医疗废物）集中处理情况（2017年）

Condition of Concentrated Disposal of Dangerous Wastes（Medical Wastes）（2017）

指 标	Item	2017
一、危险废物集中处理（置）厂数（个）	**Number of Colleted Dangerous Wastes Treated Plants(items)**	**2**
二、医疗废物集中处理（置）厂数（个）	**The number of Manufacturing Plants of Medical waste treatment (units)**	**1**
三、危险废物设计处置能力（吨/日）	**Design hazardous waste disposal capacity (tons / day)**	**352.0**
四、实际处置危险废物量（吨）	**The actual amount of hazardous waste disposal (tons)**	**17686.2**
五、危险废物综合利用量（吨）	**Volume of Dangerous Wastes Utilized in a Comprehensive Way (tons)**	
六、焚烧残渣流向（千克）	**Flow Direction of Residuum after Burning (kg)**	
1. 焚烧残渣量	Volume of Residuum after Burning	696811.4
2. 焚烧残渣安全填埋处置量	Secure landfill disposal incineration residues	696301.4
3. 焚烧飞灰产生量	Fly ash production	77366.8
4. 焚烧飞灰安全填埋处置量	Fly ash landfill disposal safety	77366.8
七、当年运行费用（万元）	**Operating Expenses in Current year(10 000 yuan)**	**4443.0**

注：本表数据来源于市环保局。

10-6 生活及其他污染情况（2017年）

Domestic Pollution and Other Conditions（2017）

指 标	Item	2017
一、基本情况	**Basic Condition**	
1. 生活天然气消费量（万立方米）	Volume of Living natural gas consumption (10 000 cu.m)	104990
2. 生活用水总量（万吨）	Volume of Living water (10 000 tons)	88840
二、污染排放情况	**Discharge of Pollutant**	
1. 城镇生活污水排放量（万吨）	Volume of Urban Domestic Sewage Discharged(10 000 tons)	72021
2. 生活污水处理量（万吨）	Volume of Domestic Sewgae Disposal(10 000 tons)	70984
3. 生活CDD产生量（吨）	Volume of Life CDD production (tons)	340610
4. 生活CDD排放量（吨）	Volume of Life CDD emissions (tons)	23684
5. 生活氨氮产生量（吨）	Volume of Ammonia and Nitrogen in Urban Domestic Sewage Produced (tons)	22941
6. 生活氨氮排放量（吨）	Volume of Ammonia and Nitrogen in Urban Domestic Sewage Discharged (tons)	2557
7. 二氧化硫排放量（吨）	Volume of Domestic and Other Sulphur Dioxide Emission (tons)	38352
8. 氨氮化物排放量（吨）	Volume of Ammonia and Nitrogen in Urban Domestic Sewage Discharged (tons)	6480
9. 烟尘排放量（吨）	Volume of Soot Emission (tons)	25380

注：本表数据来源于市环保局。

10-7　工业污染治理项目建设情况（2017年）

Condition of Anti-Industrial-Pollution Projects（2017）

指　标	Item	2017
一、工业企业数（个）	**Number of Industrial Enterprises (units)**	**17**
二、老工业污染源项目治理本年施工总数（个）	**The total number of construction projects of Old industrial pollution sources control this year(units)**	**15**
#工业废水治理项目	Treatment of Waste Water	2
工业废气治理项目	Treatment of Waste Gas	11
工业固体废物治理项目	Treatmen of Solid Wastes	
三、老工业污染源项目治理本年竣工总数（个）	**The Total Number of Old Industrial Pollution Control Projects Completed this year(units)**	**14**
#工业废水治理项目	Treatment of Waste Water	2
工业废气治理项目	Treatment of Waste Gas	10
工业固体废物治理项目	Treatmen of Solid Wastes	
四、老工业污染源治理项目本年完成投资（万元）	**Investment completed in Old industrial pollution control projects this Year(10 000 yuan)**	**25962**
#废水治理项目	Treatment of Waste Water	2057
废气治理项目	Treatment of Waste Gas	21219
固体废物治理项目	Treatmen of Solid Wastes	
五、老工业污染源治理项目本年投资来源（万元）	**Source of Investment in Old industrial pollution control projects this Year(10 000 yuan)**	**25962**
#排污费补助	Pollution Charges Subsidies	
政府其他补助	Other Government Subsidies	1268
企业自筹	Self-raising Funds	24694
#银行贷款	Lonans	
六、“三同时”项目竣工验收数（个）	**Number of "Three simultaneous"project completion and acceptance (a)**	**6**
七、“三同时”竣工验收项目实际环保投资（万元）	**"Three simultaneous" actual environmental investment completed and accepted (10 000 yuan)**	**3716**
八、“三同时”项目废水治理新增处理能力（万吨/日）	**"Three simultaneous"Add processing capacity of wastewater treatment (10 000 tons / day)**	
九、“三同时”项目废气治理新增处理能力（万立方米/时）	**"Three simultaneous"Add processing capacity of Exhaust treatment (10 000 cu.m/h)**	**74**

注：本表数据来源于市环保局。

“三同时”指建设项目中防治污染的措施，必须与主体工程同时设计，同时施工，同时投产使用。

10-8 各区县、开发区环境保护基本情况（2017年）

区县、开发区	Region	本年完成环保验收项目环保投资额（万元）Investment Completed in accepted Environmental projects this year (10 000 yuan)	工业二氧化硫排放量（吨）Volume of Industrial Sulphur Dioxide Discharged (tons)
全　市	**Total**	**229277.9**	**3904.2**
新城区	Xincheng	579.5	1.4
碑林区	Beilin	9155.0	99.8
莲湖区	Lianhu	3520.0	46.9
灞桥区	Baqiao	11399.5	307.5
未央区	Weiyang	3796.4	74.3
雁塔区	Yanta	6863.0	372.6
阎良区	Yanliang	5640.4	639.9
临潼区	Lintong	9088.0	64.7
长安区	Chang'an	4755.5	481.6
高陵区	Gaoling	2646.4	154.0
鄠邑区	Huyi	1571.7	315.7
蓝田县	Lantian	2111.0	166.3
周至县	Zhouzhi	718.0	5.7
高新开发区	Gaoxinkaifaqu	20196.6	688.9
经济开发区	Jingjikaifaqu	12765.4	208.6
航天基地	Hangtianjidi	8804.4	276.3

注：本表数据来源于市环保局。
　　环境统计中污水处理厂个数包含部分大学园区及部分大型小区的污水处理厂。
　　区县、开发区环保验收项目环保投资额未包括市本级完成数。

Condition of Environment Protection by Regions（2017）

工业化学需氧量排放量（吨）Volume of COD Removed (tons)	垃圾处理站数（座）Number of Rubbish Disposal Works (units)	污水处理厂数（个）Number of Sewage Treatment Works (units)
1246.9	**2**	**37**
45.2		
0.0		
79.2		2
56.0	1	4
45.7		6
12.7		3
48.8		1
73.9		2
28.3		8
87.4	1	1
415.1		3
7.4		3
9.7		1
188.7		1
97.2		2
51.6		

主要统计指标解释

工业用水 指工矿企业在生产过程中用于制造、加工、冷却、空调、净化、洗涤等方面的用水，按新水取用量计，不包括企业内部的重复利用水量。

工业废水排放量 指经过企业厂区所有排放口排到企业外部的工业废水量。包括生产废水、外排的直接冷却水、超标排放的矿井地下水和与工业废水混排的厂区生活污水，不包括外排的间接冷却水（清污不分流的间接冷却水应计算在内）。

直接排入海的 指经企业位于海边的排放口，直接排入海的废水量。直接排放指废水经过工厂的排污口直接排入海，而未经过城市下水道或其他中间体，也不受其他水体的影响。

工业废水排放达标量 指报告期内废水中各项污染物指标都达到国家或地方排放标准的外排工业废水量，包括未经处理外排达标的，经废水处理设施处理后达标排放的，以及经污水处理厂处理后达标排放的。

生活污水排放量 指城镇居民每年排放的生活污水。用人均系数法测算。测算公式为：

$$\text{生活污水排放量} = \text{城镇生活污水排放系数} \times \text{市镇非农业人口} \times 365$$

生活污水中化学需氧量（COD）排放量 指城镇居民每年排放的生活污水中的COD的量。用人均系数法测算。测算公式为：

$$\text{城镇生活污水中COD产生系数} = \text{城镇牛活污水中COD排放量} \times \text{市镇非农业人口} \times 365$$

化学需氧量（COD） 指用化学氧化剂氧化水中有机污染物时所需的氧量。COD值越高，表示水中有机污染物污染越重。

工业废气排放量 指报告期内企业厂区内燃料燃烧和生产工艺过程中产生的各种排入大气的含有污染物的气体的总量，以标准状态（273K，101325Pa）计算。测算公式为：

$$\text{工业废气排放量} = \text{燃料燃烧过程中废气排放量} + \text{生产工艺过程中废气排放量}$$

生活及其他SO_2排放量 以生活及其他煤炭消费量和其含硫量为基础，根据以下公式计算：

$$\text{生活及其他}SO_2\text{排放量} = \text{生活及其他煤炭消费量} \times \text{含硫量} \times 0.8 \times 2$$

工业SO_2排放量 指报告期内企业在燃料燃烧和生产工艺过程中排入大气的SO_2总量，计算公式为：

$$\text{工业}SO_2\text{排放量} = \text{燃料燃烧过程中}SO_2\text{排放量} + \text{生产工艺过程中}SO_2\text{排放量}$$

工业烟尘排放量 指企业厂区内燃料燃烧过程中产生的烟气中夹带的颗粒物排放量。

生活及其他烟尘排放量 指除工业生产活动以外的所有社会、经济活动及公共设施的经营活动中燃烧所排放的烟尘纯重量。以生活及其他煤炭消费量为基础进行测算。

工业粉尘排放量 指企业在生产工艺过程中排放的能在空气中悬浮一定时间的固体颗粒物排放量。如钢铁企业的耐火材料粉尘、焦化企业的筛焦系统粉尘、烧结机的粉尘、石灰窑的粉尘、建材企业的水泥粉尘等。不包括电厂排入大气的烟尘。

工业固体废物产生量 指报告期内企业在生产过程中产生的固体状、半固体状和高浓度液体状废弃物的总量，包括危险废物、冶炼废渣、粉煤灰、炉渣、煤矸石、尾矿、放射性废物和其他废物等；不包括矿山开采的剥离废石和掘进废石（煤矸石和呈酸性或碱性的废石除外）。酸性或碱性废石指采掘的废石其流经水、雨淋水的pH值小于4或pH值大于10.5者。

危险废物 指列入国家危险废物名录或根据国家规定的危险废物鉴别标准和鉴别方法认定的，具有爆炸性、易燃性、易氧化性、毒性、腐蚀性、易传染疾病等危险特性之一的废物。

工业固体废物综合利用量 指报告期内企业通过回收、加工、循环、交换等方式，从固体废物中提取或者使其转化为可以利用的资源、能源和其他原材料的固体废物量（包括当年利用往年的工业固体废物贮存量），如用作农业肥料、生产建筑材料、筑路等。综合利用量由原产生固体废物的单位统计。

工业固体废物综合利用率 指工业固体废物综合利用量占丁业固体废物产生量（包括综合利用往年贮存量）的百分率。计算公式为：

$$\text{工业固体废物综合利用率}=\frac{\text{工业固体废物综合利用量}}{\text{工业固体废物产生量}+\text{综合利用往年贮存量}}\times 100\%$$

工业固体废物贮存量 指报告期内企业以综合利用或处置为目的，将固体废物暂时贮存或堆存在专设的贮存设施或专设的集中堆存场所内的数量。专设的固体废物贮存场所或贮存设施必须有防扩散、防流失、防渗漏、防止污染大气、水体的措施。

工业固体废物处置量 指报告期内企业将固体废物焚烧或者最终置于符合环境保护规定要求的场所，并不再回取的工业固体废物量（包括当年处置往年的工业固体废物贮存量）。处置方式有填埋（其中危险废物应安全填埋）、焚烧、专业贮存场（库）封场处理、深层灌注、回填矿井及海洋处置（经海洋管理部门同意投海处置）等。

工业固体废物排放量 指报告期内企业将所产生的固体废物排到固体废物污染防治设施、场所以外的数量，不包括矿山开采的剥离废石和掘进废石（煤矸石和呈酸性或碱性的废石除外）。

“三废”综合利用产品产值 指报告期内利用“三废”作为主要原料生产的产品价值（现行价）；已经销售或准备销售的应计算产品价值，留作生产自用的不应计算产品价值。

生活垃圾清运量 指报告期内收集和运送到各生活垃圾处理厂（场）和生活垃圾最终消纳点的生活垃圾数量。生活垃圾指城市日常生活或为城市日常生活提供服务的活动中产生的固体废物以及法律行政规定的视为城市生活垃圾的固体废物。包括：居民生活垃圾、商业垃圾、集市贸易市场垃圾、街道清扫垃圾、公共场所垃圾和机关、学校、厂矿等单位的生活垃圾。

生活垃圾无害化处理率 指报告期生活垃圾无害化处理量与生活垃圾产生量的比率。在统计上，由于生活垃圾产生量不易取得，可用清运量代替。计算公式为：

$$\text{生活垃圾无害化处理率}=\frac{\text{生活垃圾无害化处理量}}{\text{生活垃圾产生量}}\times 100\%$$

Explanatory Notes on Main Statistical Indicators

Water Used by Industry refers to new withdrawals of water, excluding reuse of water within enterprises.

Waste Water Discharged by Industry refers to the volume of waste water discharged by industrial enterprises through all their outlets, including waste water from production process, directly cooled water, groundwater from mining wells which does not meet discharge standards and sewage from households mixed with waste water produced by industrial activities, but excluding indirectly cooled water discharged (It should be included if the discharge is not separated from waste water).

Waste Water Directly Discharged into Sea refers to the volume of waste water directly discharged into sea through outlets of enterprises situated by sea without going through municipal sewerage networks or any other intermediates or being affected by any other water bodies.

Industrial Waste Water Meeting Discharge Standards refers to volume of industrial waste water discharge which, with or without treatment, reaches national or local standards with regard to all pollutants.

Urban Non-industrial Waste Water Discharge refers to annual discharge of non-industrial waste water by urban households. It is estimated by per capita coefficient using the formula:

$$\text{Urban non-industrial waste water discharge} = \text{urban non-industrial waste water discharge coefficient} \times \text{urban non-alagricultur population} \times 365$$

Volume of Chemical Oxygen Demand (COD) Generated by Urban Non-industrial Waster Water refers to chemical oxygen demand generated through the annual discharge of non-industrial waste water by urban households. It is estimated as:

$$\text{Volume of chemical oxygen demand (cod) generated by urban non-industrial waster water} = \text{Coefficient of COD generated through urban non-industrial waste water} \times \text{urban non-agricultura l population} \times 365$$

Chemical Oxygen Demand (COD) refers to the amount of oxygen required when chemical oxidants are used to oxidize organic pollutants in water. A higher value of COD corresponds to more serious pollution by organic pollutants.

Industrial Waste Air Emission refers to the discharge into atmosphere of waste air containing pollutants generated from fuel burning and production processes in enterprises within a given period of time. It is calculated at standard status (273K, 101325Pa) as:

$$\text{Industrial waste air emission} = \text{tnoissimehrough fuel burning} + \text{tnoissimehrough production process}$$

SO_2 Emission through Non-industrial and Other Activities is calculated on the basis of consumption of coal by households and other activities and the sulphur content of coal with the following formula:

$$SO_2 \text{ emission through non-industrial and other activities} = \text{of coalby households andother activities} \times \text{sulphur content} \times 0.8 \times 2$$

SO_2 Emission through Industrial Activities refers to volume of sulphur dioxide emission from fuel burning and production process by enterprises during a given period of time. It is calculated as:

$$SO_2 \text{ emission through industrial activities} = SO_2 \text{emIssIon from fuel burning} + SO_2 \text{ emission from production process}$$

Industrial Soot Emission refers to the volume of soot in smoke emitted in the process of fuel burning in the premises of enterprises.

Soot Emission by Consumption and Others refers to the net volume of soot emitted by fuel burning from all social and economic activities and operations of public facilities other than industrial activities. It is calculated on the basis of coal consumption by households and others.

Industrial Dust Emission refers to volume of dust emitted by production process of enterprises and suspended in the air for a given period of time, including dust from refractory material of iron and steel works, dust from coke-screening systems and sintering machines of coke plants, dust from lime kilns and dust from cement production in building material enterprises, but excluding soot and dust emitted from power plants.

Industrial Solid Wastes Produced refers to total volume of solid, semi-solid and high concentration liquid residues produced by industrial enterprises from production process in a given period of time, including hazardous wastes, slag, coal ash, gangue, tailings, radioactive residues and other wastes, but excluding stones stripped or dug out in mining - gangue and acid or alkaline stones not included (a stone is acid or alkaline according to the pH value of the water being below 4 or above 10.5 when the stone is in, or soaked by water).

Hazardous Wastes refers to those included in the national hazardous wastes catalogue or specified as any one of the following properties in the national hazardous wastes identification standards: explosive, ignitable, oxidizable, toxic, corrosive or liable to cause infectious diseases or lead to other dangers.

Industrial Solid Wastes Utilized refers to volume of solid wastes from which useful materials can be extracted or which can be converted into usable resources, energy or other materials by means of reclamation, processing, recycling and exchange (including utilizing in the year the stocks of industrial solid wastes of the previous year). Examples of such utilizations include fertilizers, building materials and road materials. The information shall be collected by the producing units of the wastes.

Rate of Utilization of Industrial Solid Wastes refers to the percentage of industrial solid wastes utilized over industrial solid wastes produced (including stocks of the previous years). It is calculated as:

$$\text{Rate of utilization of industrial solid wastes} = \frac{\text{volume of industrial solid wastes utilized}}{\text{industrial solid wastesproduced+ stock of previous years}} \times 100\%$$

Stock of Industrial Solid Wastes refers to the volume of solid wastes placed in special facilities or special sites for purposes of utilization or disposal. The sites or facilities should take measures against dispersion, loss, seepage, and air and water contamination.

Industrial Solid Wastes Disposed refers to the quantity of industrial solid wastes which are burnt or placed ultimately in the sites meeting the requirements for environmental protection and not salvaged or recycled (including disposition in the year of those wastes of previous years). The disposition includes landfill (Safe landfills should be conducted for hazardous wastes), incineration, containment spaces, deep underground disposal, backfill in mining pits and disposal at sea.

Industrial Solid Wastes Discharged refers to the volume of industrial solid wastes discharged by producing enterprises to disposal facilities or to other sites. The wastes exclude stones stripped or dug from mining (gangue and acid or alkaline waste stones not included).

Output Value of Products Made from Waste Gas, Waste Water and Solid Wastes refers to the current value of products with waste gas, waste water and solid wastes as main materials of production. Products sold and ready to sell shall be included while those produced for own use shall not be included.

Consumption Wastes Transported refers to volume of consumption wastes collected and transported to disposal factories or sites. Consumption wastes are solid wastes produced from urban households or from service activities for urban households, and solid wastes regarded by laws and regulations as urban consumption wastes, including those from households, commercial activities, markets, cleaning of streets, public sites, offices, schools, factories, mining units and other sources.

Ratio of Consumption Wastes Treated refers to consumption wastes treated over that produced. In practical statistics, as it is difficult to estimate, the volume of consumption wastes produced is replaced with that transported. It is calculated as:

$$\text{Ratio of consumption wastes treated} = \frac{\text{consumption wastes treated}}{\text{consumption wastes produced}} \times 100\%$$

11 农 业

AGRICULTURE

资料整理：张喜兰　马秋娟　薛　丰
Data management：Zhang Xilan　Ma Qiujuan　Xue Feng
数据审核：马　琰
Data audit：Ma yan

第十一部分　农业

一、简要说明

本章资料主要包括农村基本情况、农业生产条件与生产情况、耕地、农林牧渔及服务业产值、主要农产品产量以及各区县农业生产和农村经济效益主要指标，由西安市统计局农村处提供。

二、主要指标

年末常用耕地面积（万亩）	374.45	比上年下降	2.2%
农林牧渔及服务业总产值（亿元）	497.39	比上年增长	4.8%
农作物播种面积（万亩）	730.51	比上年下降	2.4%
粮食产量（万吨）	187.87	比上年下降	4.3%

11　AGRICULTURE

Ⅰ.Brief Introduction

Data in this chapter reflects basic condition of agriculture production of Xi'an city. It is primarily consist of basic condition of rural area, condition of agriculture production, plow land, production value of farming, forestry, animal husbandry and fishery, gross yield of primary produce and primary indicators of agriculture production and rural area economic performance. The data are provided and compiled by Rural Area Division of the Xi'an Bureau of Statistics.

Ⅱ.Major Indicators

		Increase over Preceding Year
Cultivated Area Year-end(10 000 mu)	374.45	-2.2%
Gross Output Value of Farming, Forestry, Animal Husbandry, Fishery and Service(100 mil. Yuan)	497.39	4.8%
Sown Area of Crops(10 000 mu)	730.51	-2.4%
Grain Output(10 000 tons)	187.87	-4.3%

11-1 主要年份农村基层组织、乡村户数、人口及劳动力情况

Grassroots Organizations in Rural Areas, Rural Households, Population and Labor Force in Representative Years

指　标	Item	2005	2007	2008	2009	2010	2011
一、乡村户数（万户）	**Rural Households(10000 households)**	**101.50**	**100.85**	**101.02**	**101.00**	**101.43**	**102.59**
二、农村人口和从业人员情况	**Condition of Rural Population and Employment**						
1.乡村劳动力资源总数（万人）	Total Rural Labor Force (10000 persons)	255.93	254.06	256.17	255.00	256.36	260.97
2.乡村从业人员数（万人）	Number of Rural Workers (10000 persons)	223.30	222.09	223.85	223.13	225.04	230.56
#女性	Female	103.22	101.83	103.11	102.76	103.25	109.61
#农业	Agricultural	137.69	131.96	126.46	121.78	116.58	116.15
三、自来水受益村数（个）	**The Number of Tap Water Villages (unit)**	**1756**	**1881**	**1934**	**2058**	**2184**	**2400**
四、通汽车村数（个）	**The Number of Villages with Bus Service (unit)**	**2952**	**2973**	**2996**	**2989**	**2989**	**2978**
五、通电话村数（个）	**The Number of Villages with Telephone Service (unit)**	**3101**	**3129**	**3086**	**3071**	**3052**	**3033**

11-1 续表 continued

指　标	Item	2012	2013	2014	2015	2016	2017
一、乡村户数（万户）	**Rural Households(10000 households)**	**101.92**	**101.37**	**99.26**	**92.77**	**92.63**	**106.28**
二、农村人口和从业人员情况	**Condition of Rural Population and Employment**						
1.乡村劳动力资源总数（万人）	Total Rural Labor Force (10000 persons)	259.06	257.96	252.40	230.21	230.62	262.44
2.乡村从业人员数（万人）	Number of Rural Workers (10000 persons)	226.92	222.67	216.33	200.38	204.11	225.88
#女性	Female	107.63	106.70	104.03	96.46	98.10	107.16
#农业	Agricultural	113.29	108.48	110.30	105.10	102.32	110.38
三、自来水受益村数（个）	**The Number of Tap Water Villages (unit)**	**2545**	**2650**	**2765**	**2718**	**2507**	**2706**
四、通汽车村数（个）	**The Number of Villages with Bus Service (unit)**	**2936**	**2927**	**2186**	**2209**		
五、通电话村数（个）	**The Number of Villages with Telephone Service (unit)**	**2974**	**2966**	**2536**	**2593**		

11-2 各区县乡村从业人员数（2017年）

Number of Rural Employees by Region (2017)

单位：万人　　(10 000 persons)

区　县	Region	乡村劳动力资源总数 Total rural labor force	乡村从业人员数合计 Total number of employees in rural areas	女性从业人员 Female employees	农林牧渔业 Forestry Animal Husbandry and Fishery
合　计	**Total**	**262.44**	**225.88**	**107.16**	**110.38**
新城区	Xingcheng				
碑林区	Beilin				
莲湖区	Lianhu				
灞桥区	Baqiao	18.48	14.64	6.14	4.82
未央区	Weiyang	2.06	0.12	0.04	0.02
雁塔区	Yanta				
阎良区	Yanliang	11.18	10.06	4.69	5.90
临潼区	Lintong	36.57	32.15	15.29	19.18
长安区	Chang'an	38.27	33.55	15.34	16.86
高陵区	Gaoling	9.82	8.16	3.69	2.80
鄠邑区	Huyi	31.40	26.70	12.45	14.54
蓝田县	Lantian	33.16	30.46	19.50	12.92
周至县	Zhouzhi	40.21	32.35	13.65	18.11

11–3 主要年份耕地面积

Area of Cultivated Land in Representative Years

单位：万亩 (10 000 mu)

年 份 Year	年末常用耕地面积 Cultivated Area Year-end	水田 Paddy Field	水浇地 Irrigable Land
1970	554.09	18.20	297.05
1975	538.35	20.34	349.13
1978	530.96	16.70	370.46
1980	526.29	17.45	372.96
1985	508.88	17.63	328.10
1990	495.32	17.97	311.91
1991	492.09	17.03	309.17
1992	485.30	16.44	298.19
1993	479.04	14.36	304.49
1994	471.44	13.98	299.58
1995	463.97	17.04	278.01
1996	451.50	14.21	283.76
1997	456.62	11.90	290.49
1998	455.15	11.18	282.23
1999	450.74	11.31	281.96
2000	443.37	10.26	284.04
2001	431.69	9.00	274.73
2002	424.46	7.98	275.96
2003	413.84	6.65	263.75
2004	404.87	6.59	254.04
2005	400.17	5.55	254.04
2006	395.79	5.33	263.75
2007	391.77	4.80	255.95
2008	390.77	4.64	255.36
2009	387.89	4.39	260.71
2010	383.32	4.03	257.43
2011	377.10	3.80	253.46
2012	369.91	3.32	248.97
2013	366.23	5.33	263.75
2014	360.73	2.42	237.26
2015	356.89	2.37	228.14
2016	346.80	0.96	223.91
2017	374.45	0.62	242.13

11-4　各区县耕地面积（2017年）

单位：亩

区　县	Region	年末常用耕地面积 Cultivated Area Year-end	水田 Paddy Field	旱地 Dry Land	水浇地 Irrigable Land
合　计	**Total**	**3744460**	**6150**	**3738310**	**2421291**
新城区	Xincheng				
碑林区	Beilin				
莲湖区	Lianhu				
灞桥区	Baqiao	72604		72604	50330
未央区	Weiyang	1815		1815	1815
雁塔区	Yanta				
阎良区	Yanliang	229271		229271	221852
临潼区	Lintong	687932		687932	526384
长安区	Chang'an	483227	4180	479047	171258
高陵区	Gaoling	219074		219074	219074
鄠邑区	Huyi	528662	580	528082	470100
蓝田县	Lantian	588718	410	588308	
周至县	Zhouzhi	492603	780	491823	362013

Area of Cultivated Land by Region（2017）

(mu)

当年增加的耕地面积 Area of Newly Increased Cultivated Land	新开荒地面积 Area of Newly Reclamation of Wasteland	当年减少的耕地面积 Decrease in Cultivated Area in the Year	国家基建占地 Capital Construction	退耕改果、茶、桑面积 Area for Change into Fruit, Tea and Mulberry	退耕造林面积 Area for Change into Woods
3075	**15**	**102623**	**36504**	**23091**	**1749**
350		6374	3454	597	1689
		660	660		
		2586	825	20	
		1090	318	772	
25	15	8763	5062	3619	60
		5819	5619	200	
		738		738	
		3862		1623	
2400		12143	821	11322	

11-5 主要年份农业机械拥有量（年末数）

指标	Item	2005	2008	2009
农用机械总动力（千瓦）	Total Power of Agricultural Machinery(kw)	2239001	2712616	2616053
大中型拖拉机（台）	Large and Medium Tractors(unit)	8415	11092	11479
小型拖拉机（台）	Mini-tractors(unit)	26326	19036	18406
大中型拖拉机配套农具（台）	Number of Large and Medium Tractor Towing Farm Machinery(unit)	19334	25125	26575
小型拖拉机配套农具（台）	Mini-Tractor Towing Farm Machinery (unit)	47883	26984	29039
农用排灌柴油机（台）	Agricultural Diesel Engines(unit)	2219	2670	2691
农用排灌电动机（台）	Agricultural Motors(unit)	79666	85349	83243
农用水泵（台）	Agricultural Water Pump(unit)	77567	80462	80174
节水灌溉类机械（套）	Equipment in Water-saving Irrigation(set)	1290	1728	1799
联合收割机（台）	Combine Harvesters(unit)	4802	5390	6155
自走式机动割晒机（台）	Self-propelled Motorized Swather(unit)	4226	2174	1220
机动脱粒机（台）	Motorized Huller (unit)	13870	23781	11960
农用运输车（辆）	Agricultucal Transporter(unit)	47348	54860	50671

注：本表数据来源于市农林委，2017年数据不包含西咸新区。

Possession of Agricultural Machinery

in Representative Years（Number of year-end）

2010	2011	2012	2013	2014	2015	2016	2017
2677334	2890247	2983979	3108354	3203302	3253733	2615435	2543023
14675	12585	12987	12927	9946	9652	10177	9275
14194	13008	11471	8971	7538	8447	9175	8501
29215	36209	32166	32662	31451	32602	38833	31726
24393	29624	27869	25853	21806	21518	20972	18833
3309	2639	2891	2509	2409	2409	1772	1467
79462	87461	87056	86216	85244	84975	84734	80899
77367	75426	80982	80575	79849	79695	79681	76916
1710	1733	2106	2218	2562	2517	2476	2366
6718	7854	8502	9114	7815	8144	8458	7656
208	187						
13231	13407	14493	14700	14749	14504	14272	14169
51665	51838	51850	51710	51410	51365		

11-6 各区县农业机械拥有量（2017年）

指标	Item	西安市 Xi' an	灞桥区 Baqiao	未央区 Weiyang
农用机械总动力（千瓦）	Total Power of Agricultural Machinery(kw)	2543023	142018	46873
大中型拖拉机（台）	Large and Medium Tractors(unit)	9275	58	17
小型拖拉机（台）	Mini-tractors(unit)	8501	56	
大中型拖拉机配套农具（台）	Number of Large and Medium Tractor Towing Farm Machinery(unit)	31726	257	50
小型拖拉机配套农具（台）	Mini-Tractor Towing Farm Machinery (unit)	18833	91	40
农用排灌柴油机（台）	Agricultural Diesel Engines(unit)	1467		
农用排灌电动机（台）	Agricultural Motors(unit)	80899	2458	850
农用水泵（台）	Agricultural Water Pump(unit)	76916	1486	633
节水灌溉类机械（套）	Equipment in Water-saving Irrigation(set)	2366	43	90
联合收割机（台）	Combine Harvesters(unit)	7656	55	6
自走式机动割晒机（台）	Self-propelled Motorized Swather(unit)			
机动脱粒机（台）	Motorized Huller (unit)	14169	40	6

注：本表数据来源于市农林委，2017年数据不包含西咸新区。

Possession of Agricultural Machinery by Region（2017）

雁塔区 Yanta	阎良区 Yanliang	临潼区 Lintong	长安区 Chang'an	高陵区 Gaoling	鄠邑区 Huyi	蓝田县 Lantian	周至县 Zhouzhi
61955	155777	408257	351578	213281	490827	245672	332877
32	809	1145	1495	1484	1647	1165	1253
7	364	212	1109	163	1657	644	4192
70	2427	6535	5374	5770	6071	2421	2101
26	364	3083	201	640	3456	3681	7161
		73	391		56	652	277
520	5954	16974	14440	3760	12735	3147	15156
500	5796	16460	9718	3760	12735	2486	17237
	485	142	936		149	63	227
14	565	1781	1215	684	2557	387	355
	1121	4948	792	545	2381	1815	2431

11-7 主要年份农业机械化、化肥、水利、水电情况

指标	Item	2000	2005	2007
一、农业机械化水平（万亩）	**Statistics on Agricultural Machinery (10 000 mu)**			
当年机械耕地面积（实际）	Area Ploughed by Tractors	366.81	360.68	361.62
当年机械播种面积（作业）	Seeded Area by Tractors	482.74	485.62	521.36
当年机械收获面积（作业）	Harvest Area by Tractors	272.83	271.77	296.06
二、农用化肥施用量（吨）	**Use of Agricultural Fertilizers and Insecticides(ton)**			
1. 按实物量计算合计	Practicality Consumption	697243	749802	762401
氮肥	Nitrogenous Fertilizer	392366	411161	408847
磷肥	Phosphate Fertilizer	155480	161444	160932
钾肥	Potash Fertilizer	31841	34114	34284
复合肥	Compound Fertilizer	78620	115458	124784
2. 按折纯法计算合计	Standard Consumption	196343	211790	220251
氮肥	Nitrogenous Fertilizer	102982	107645	109484
磷肥	Phosphate Fertilizer	18658	19368	19311
钾肥	Potash Fertilizer	15921	17055	17141
复合肥	Compound Fertilizer	39313	57009	62398
三、农用塑料薄膜使用量（公斤）	**Plastic Sheet for Agricultural Use(kg)**	**1622198**	**1855383**	**2096169**
四、农用柴油使用量（吨）	**Diesel Oil for Agricultural Use (ton)**	**52706**	**50832**	**50137**
五、农药使用量（公斤）	**Pesticide (kg)**	**1559333**	**1427879**	**1444867**
六、农村水利化情况（万亩）	**Irrigation and Water Conservancy (10 000 mu)**			
有效灌溉面积	Effective Irrigation Area	335.97	280.1	276.28
旱涝保收面积	Stable-Harvesting Arable Land	294.06	255.37	247.99
机电排灌面积	Electrical Irrigation Area	249.11	223.74	210.51
七、农村电气化情况	**Rural electrization**			
乡村及村以下办水电站（个）	Hydropower Station in Rural Areas(unit)	67	79	76
装机容量（千瓦）	Installed Power Generation Capacity(kw)	7236	13775	24827
发电量（万千瓦小时）	Generating Capacity (10 000 kwh)	1137.95	2239	10085
已配套机电井（眼）	Electricity Powered Well(unit)	50289	46505	45783

注：本表部分数据来源于市农林委。

Agricultural Machinery,Chemical Fertilizers,Water Conservancy, Hydropower in Representative Years

2008	2009	2010	2011	2012	2013	2014	2015	2016	2017
404.42	413.7	367.32	427.03	425.4	425.21	549.07	533.21	518.07	498.57
539.81	544.86	548.28	507.55	529.99	523.15	509.58	492.9	499.36	532.61
313.11	342.82	403.5	413.93	428.28	443.57	466.21	474.1	488.85	470.66
767980	776319	781072	785885	807900	794361	820315	810849	771144	800468
413397	414481	397975	398395	414339	401140	412544	408396	374476	383467
157145	153825	152943	151005	151967	152565	156662	157601	152278	153808
34149	33069	37715	38195	43356	39630	42504	46284	46388	45866
132481	142137	158062	163797	198238	201026	208605	198568	198002	217327
225949	230299	235532	239497	243281	239701	251217	246284	242871	255267
112000	112275	108868	110412	113662	109497	116055	108833	111150	115631
18855	18457	18315	18026	18061	18023	18505	18584	18033	19072
17077	16534	17997	18095	21267	18973	20110	21986	21779	21486
66247	71042	78811	81764	90291	93208	96547	96881	91909	99078
2122310	**2141969**	**2450496**	**2533372**	**2683201**	**2678745**	**2657870**	**2770750**	**2880480**	**3157710**
51097	**51346**	**61917**	**61637**	**57451**	**62563**	**74935**	**59360**	**55982**	**67510**
1465819	**1325459**	**1243105**	**1242773**	**1252490**	**1210060**	**1220638**	**1174883**	**1126305**	**1703736**
274.48	273.17	281.28	262.32	267.84	240.22	248.34	244.72	259.78	256.13
249.31	247.6	234.15	214.62	211.31	196.96	189.69	188.5	201.7	184.91
211.01	213.42	224.6	200.36	198.66	229.29	230.58	239.63		
76	75	44	44	46	46	48	48		
24827	25047	22325	22325	78848	80433	80633	80423		
10477	10678	7268	7268	26447	19613	25526.08			
47032	46790	44310	40345	33959					

11-8 各区县农业机械化、化肥、水利、水电情况（2017年）

指标	Item	西安市 Xi'an	灞桥区 Baqiao	未央区 Weiyang
一、农业机械化水平（万亩）	**Statistics on Agricultural Machinery (10 000 mu)**			
当年机械耕地面积（实际）	Area Ploughed by Tractors	498.57	19.00	
当年机械播种面积（作业）	Seeded Area by Tractors	532.61	14.82	
当年机械收获面积（作业）	Harvest Area by Tractors	470.66	13.80	
二、农用化肥施用量（吨）	**Use of Agricultural Fertilizers and Insecticides(ton)**			
1. 按实物量计算合计	Practicality Consumption	800468	18743	661
氮肥	Nitrogenous Fertilizer	383467	6517	152
磷肥	Phosphate Fertilizer	153808	1271	198
钾肥	Potash Fertilizer	45866	1783	116
复合肥	Compound Fertilizer	217327	9172	195
2.按折纯法计算合计	Standard Consumption	255267	7484	239
氮肥	Nitrogenous Fertilizer	115631	3003	69
磷肥	Phosphate Fertilizer	19072	153	24
钾肥	Potash Fertilizer	21486	887	56
复合肥	Compound Fertilizer	99078	3441	90
三、农用塑料薄膜使用量（公斤）	**Plastic Sheet for Agricultural Use(kg)**	**3157710**	**13030**	**33000**
四、农用柴油使用量（吨）	**Diesel Oil for Agricultural Use (ton)**	**67510**	**356**	**493**
五、农药使用量（公斤）	**Pesticide (kg)**	**1703736**	**22389**	**411**
六、农村水利化情况（万亩）	**Irrigation and Water Conservancy (10 000 mu)**			
有效灌溉面积	Effective Irrigation Area	256.15	9.93	0.60
旱涝保收面积	Stable-Harvesting Arable Land	184.92		0.60
机电排灌面积	Electrical Irrigation Area			

注：本表部分数据来源于市农林委、水务局。

Agricultural Machinery,Chemical Fertilizers,Water Conservancy,Hydropower by Region (2017)

雁塔区 Yanta	阎良区 Yanliang	临潼区 Lintong	长安区 Chang'an	高陵区 Gaoling	鄠邑区 Huyi	蓝田县 Lantian	周至县 Zhouzhi
	38.58	83.97	102.83	35.58	71.39	77.93	61.21
	28.86	108.09	93.15	42.43	85.00	81.30	71.81
	24.79	91.60	90.57	39.51	81.50	65.10	55.26
	77218	152261	60053	60017	105397	122430	149472
	34965	80965	26411	25329	60076	65452	62511
	15489	44783	8311	16892	15810	25453	16003
	6552	2892	5510	2794	6324	8450	9120
	20212	23621	19821	15002	23187	23075	61838
	27921	40008	17602	13885	31960	46769	52752
	13337	21376	7467	4318	16193	28857	15353
	1772	5374	1040	2032	1918	2985	1920
	3195	1446	2556	1420	2769	3732	4560
	9617	11812	6539	6115	11080	11195	30919
	1360000	**231560**	**106050**	**38670**	**582000**	**335000**	**98660**
	3271	**15307**	**7727**	**2554**	**11149**	**9885**	**3335**
	216941	**303059**	**81218**	**178534**	**61070**	**74565**	**165238**
	21.59	53.15	35.30	22.82	45.81	11.82	55.13
	22.56	46.50	19.71	21.20	43.10		31.25

11-9 主要年份农林牧渔及服务业总产值及指数

Gross Output Value of Farming,Forestry,Animal Husbandry,Fishery, Service and Related Indices in Representative Years

单位：万元 (10 000 yuan)

年 份 Year	农林牧渔及服务总产值（现价） Gross Output Value (At current prices)	农业 Farming	林业 Forestry	牧业 Animal Husbandry	渔业 Fishery	农林牧渔服务业 Service of Farming, Forestry, Animal Husbandry and Fishery	指数（上年=100）（可比价） Indices(preceding year= 100) (At cinstant prices)
1970	40617	35965	713	3896	43		111.2
1975	55322	47378	1509	6403	32		93.9
1978	65423	56519	1444	7427	33		104.7
1980	65322	54004	1177	10106	35		85.0
1985	134933	105888	2559	26186	300		106.4
1990	262073	191088	3134	65840	2011		102.5
1991	295620	208324	3362	81070	2864		108.6
1992	321155	219160	4225	94045	3725		108.6
1993	387068	261959	5031	115810	4268		112.8
1994	565056	359609	7819	192140	5488		102.4
1995	754597	513348	7185	228598	5466		106.8
1996	786003	552726	7573	219214	6490		102.1
1997	836201	585973	9226	233623	7379		110.3
1998	853279	625465	8146	212045	7623		107.5
1999	739905	530029	8883	194552	6441		100.7
2000	743712	514845	8482	212612	7773		104.3
2001	767511	527160	8427	223861	8063		102.8
2002	797444	539978	11378	238761	7327		103.0
2003	837857	551398	10550	269610	6299		101.5
2004	967946	580798	12773	314517	6728	53130	108.4
2005	1065437	657262	13086	329856	7340	57893	107.7
2006	1141484	686748	15188	346626	7017	85905	107.2
2007	1341450	798163	15845	410213	9051	108178	105.3
2008	1682725	956549	19031	564095	11084	131966	107.8
2009	1787032	1061756	22663	546191	11830	144592	106.5
2010	2270994	1438934	26787	629376	12830	163067	107.4
2011	2726608	1729295	34453	754593	14856	193411	106.6
2012	3083562	1933149	62291	820392	19877	247853	106.0
2013	3428905	2173363	80199	863902	22773	288668	104.9
2014	3672101	2363649	86889	879515	24030	318018	105.1
2015	3807573	2444234	97776	887325	19519	358719	105.1
2016	4056321	2587519	102222	940934	19640	406006	104.2
2017	4973925	3248677	135570	1045793	22700	521185	104.8

11-10 主要年份农林牧渔及服务业总产值指数

Related Indices of Gross Output Value of Farming,Forestry,Animal Husbandry,Fishery and Service in Representative Years

年 份 Year	农林牧渔及服务业 总产值指数（上年=100） （可比价） Indices(preceding year= 100) (At constant prices)	农业 Farming	林业 Forestry	牧业 Animal Husbandry	渔业 Fishery	农林牧渔服务业 Service of Farming, Forestry, Animal Husbandry and Fishery
2005	107.7	108.0	98.7	107.3	112.6	107.9
2006	107.2	106.0	102.5	109.3	104.5	109.4
2007	105.3	106.4	101.3	102.4	106.3	108.7
2008	107.8	107.9	112.2	106.0	100.5	113.7
2009	106.5	105.4	121.3	106.8	107.4	110.2
2010	107.4	108.7	115.2	104.3	92.7	108.9
2011	106.6	108.2	105.7	102.9	102.1	107.7
2012	106.0	105.6	143.0	104.8	113.4	108.5
2013	104.9	104.3	131.3	104.0	110.1	105.9
2014	105.1	105.8	105.7	103.2	106.0	105.9
2015	105.1	106.7	113.8	100.2	71.2	106.2
2016	104.2	104.8	114.7	100.6	100.1	106.6
2017	104.8	105.0	111.0	103.0	104.3	106.2

11-11 主要年份农林牧渔及服务业总产值构成

Gross Output Value and Its Composition of Farming, Forestry, Animal Husbandry,Fishery and Service at Current Price in Representative Years

年 份 Year	农林牧渔及服务业 总产值(%) Service of Farming, Forestry, Animal Husbandry and Fishery(%)	农业 Farming	林业 Forestry	牧业 Animal Husbandry	渔业 Fishery	农林牧渔服务业 Service of Farming, Forestry, Animal Husbandry and Fishery
2005	100	61.7	1.2	31.0	0.7	5.4
2006	100	60.9	1.3	31.5	0.6	5.7
2007	100	59.5	1.2	30.6	0.7	8.0
2008	100	56.9	1.1	33.5	0.7	7.8
2009	100	59.4	1.3	30.5	0.7	8.1
2010	100	63.3	1.2	27.7	0.6	7.2
2011	100	63.4	1.3	27.7	0.5	7.1
2012	100	62.7	2.0	26.6	0.7	8.0
2013	100	63.4	2.3	25.2	0.7	8.4
2014	100	64.4	2.4	24.0	0.7	8.5
2015	100	64.2	2.6	23.3	0.5	9.4
2016	100	63.8	2.5	23.2	0.5	10.0
2017	100	65.3	2.7	21.0	0.5	10.5

11-12 各区县农林牧渔及服务业总产值（2017年）

Gross Output Value of Farming, Forestry, Animal Husbandry, Fishery and Service by Region （2017）

单位：万元　　　　(10 000 yuan)

区　县	Region	农林牧渔及服务业总产值 Gross Output Value	农业 Farming	林业 Forestry	牧业 Animal Husbandry	渔业 Fishery	农林牧渔服务业 Service of Farming, Forestry, Animal Husbandry and Fishery
合　计	**Total**	**4973925**	**3248677**	**135570**	**1045793**	**22700**	**521185**
新城区	Xincheng						
碑林区	Beilin						
莲湖区	Lianhu						
灞桥区	Baqiao	364717	282115	3755	38876	1096	38875
未央区	Weiyang	13836	2942	1536	6648	677	2033
雁塔区	Yanta						
阎良区	Yanliang	412635	294571	1343	72050	444	44227
临潼区	Lintong	588206	322997	3425	185314	6614	69856
长安区	Chang'an	556509	390500	9681	90148	7462	58718
高陵区	Gaoling	607588	341130	4865	183396	345	77852
蓝田县	Lantian	539025	317923	28004	144572	1993	46533
周至县	Zhouzhi	591455	406244	51788	81623	865	50935
鄠邑区	Huyi	496405	311138	16530	101085	2771	64881

11-13 各区县农林牧渔及服务业总产值指数和构成（2017年）

Gross Output Value and Its Composition of Farming, Forestry, Animal Husbandry,Fishery and Service at Current Price by Region（2017）

单位：%　　(%)

区县	Region	农林牧渔及服务业总产值 Gross Output Value	农业 Farming	林业 Forestry	牧业 Animal Husbandry	渔业 Fishery	农林牧渔服务业 Service of Farming, Forestry, Animal Husbandry and Fishery
全市指数	**Total**	**104.8**	**105.0**	**111.0**	**103.0**	**104.3**	**106.2**
新城区	Xincheng						
碑林区	Beilin						
莲湖区	Lianhu						
灞桥区	Baqiao	105.1	104.3	503.4	105.4	113.9	102.7
未央区	Weiyang	91.0	48.6	380.3	94.1	315.1	153.7
雁塔区	Yanta						
阎良区	Yanliang	105.1	104.1	200.0	107.9	195.3	105.5
临潼区	Lintong	105.2	109.5	122.8	97.3	100.8	110.5
长安区	Chang'an	105.0	109.3	77.9	89.9	92.5	114.0
高陵区	Gaoling	105.3	105.0	325.1	101.0	124.8	114.9
蓝田县	Lantian	105.0	100.8	204.8	108.5	118.9	93.9
周至县	Zhouzhi	104.7	105.1	92.6	108.9	137.0	108.7
鄠邑区	Huyi	104.6	100.3	106.8	117.7	180.8	103.0
全市构成	**Total**	**100.0**	**65.3**	**2.7**	**21.0**	**0.5**	**10.5**
新城区	Xincheng						
碑林区	Beilin						
莲湖区	Lianhu						
灞桥区	Baqiao	100.0	77.3	1.0	10.7	0.3	10.7
未央区	Weiyang	100.0	21.3	11.1	48.0	4.9	14.7
雁塔区	Yanta						
阎良区	Yanliang	100.0	71.4	0.3	17.5	0.1	10.7
临潼区	Lintong	100.0	54.9	0.6	31.5	1.1	11.9
长安区	Chang'an	100.0	70.2	1.7	16.2	1.3	10.6
高陵区	Gaoling	100.0	56.1	0.8	30.2	0.1	12.8
蓝田县	Lantian	100.0	59.0	5.2	26.8	0.4	8.6
周至县	Zhouzhi	100.0	68.7	8.8	13.8	0.1	8.6
鄠邑区	Huyi	100.0	62.6	3.3	20.4	0.6	13.1

11-14 主要年份农林牧渔及服务业增加值

Value-Added of Farming, Forestry, Animal Husbandry, Fishery and Service in Representative Years

单位：万元 (10 000 yuan)

年份 Year	农林牧渔及服务业增加值 Farming,Forestry, Animal Husbandry, Fishery and Service	农业 Farming	林业 Forestry	牧业 Animal Husbandry	渔业 Fishery	农林牧渔服务业 Service of Farming, Forestry, Animal Husbandry and Fishery
1995	413981	329662	4413	76746	3160	
1996						
1997						
1998						
1999						
2000	446481	336777	4323	101353	4028	
2001	458720	342427	4258	108096	3939	
2002	477691	351358	6419	116591	3323	
2003	458378	312849	5473	137236	2820	
2004	582009	393349	6811	164572	2919	14358
2005	660148	444320	6888	169701	3373	35866
2006	704427	465823	8556	177431	3227	49390
2007	825053	538794	8420	210930	4467	62442
2008	1034471	639071	10592	301305	5598	77905
2009	1103793	698043	11958	303594	5913	84285
2010	1400575	935489	14362	349204	6503	95017
2011	1731398	1161249	18807	428169	7679	115494
2012	1955931	1297824	33973	465476	10115	148543
2013	2177588	1459093	43740	490162	11589	173004
2014	2336074	1586842	47388	499021	12229	190594
2015	2416880	1632882	53533	505551	9986	214928
2016	2563772	1718635	56239	535111	10061	243726
2017	3124573	2132397	76489	590546	11740	313401

11-15 主要年份农林牧渔及服务业增加值指数

Indices of Value-Added of Farming, Forestry, Animal Husbandry, Fishery and Service in Representative Years

年 份 Year	农林牧渔及服务业增加值指数（上年=100）（可比价） Farming,Forestry,Animal Husbandry,Fishery and Service	农业 Farming	林业 Forestry	牧业 Animal Husbandry	渔业 Fishery	农林牧渔服务业 Service of Farming, Forestry, Animal Husbandry and Fishery
2008	107.6	107.6	112.0	105.8	100.0	114.0
2009	106.3	103.6	114.6	111.2	106.3	108.8
2010	106.9	107.9	108.7	104.3	94.0	108.9
2011	106.7	108.1	106.1	102.8	102.7	108.1
2012	106.0	105.6	142.8	104.8	113.4	108.5
2013	104.8	104.3	131.3	104.0	110.1	105.9
2014	105.2	105.8	104.1	103.2	106.0	105.9
2015	105.1	106.5	114.0	100.5	71.3	106.2
2016	104.1	104.5	112.6	100.5	100.3	106.9
2017	104.8	105.1	111.0	102.3	104.3	106.2

11-16 各区县农林牧渔及服务业增加值（2017年）

Value-Added of Farming, Forestry, Animal Husbandry, Fishery and Service by Region（2017）

单位：万元 (10 000 yuan)

区 县	Region	农林牧渔及服务业增加值 Farming,Forestry, Animal Husbandry, Fishery and Service	农业 Farming	林业 Forestry	牧业 Animal Husbandry	渔业 Fishery	农林牧渔服务业 Service of Farming, Forestry, Animal Husbandry and Fishery
合 计	**Total**	**3124573**	**2132397**	**76489**	**590546**	**11740**	**313401**
新城区	Xincheng						
碑林区	Beilin						
莲湖区	Lianhu						
灞桥区	Baqiao	241944	192900	2499	22389	435	23721
未央区	Weiyang	7887	2077	803	3514	219	1274
雁塔区	Yanta						
阎良区	Yanliang	269657	199234	756	42108	223	27336
临潼区	Lintong	358616	211636	2023	98076	2771	44110
长安区	Chang'an	373960	287696	6049	40981	4761	34473
高陵区	Gaoling	379723	214434	2825	108842	142	53480
蓝田县	Lantian	328571	197694	16746	86113	875	27143
周至县	Zhouzhi	367857	263329	26811	48446	445	28826
鄠邑区	Huyi	310795	202708	9112	63944	1648	33383

11-17 各区县农林牧渔及服务业增加值指数（2017年）

Indices of Value-Added of Farming, Forestry, Animal Husbandry, Fishery and Service by Region（2017）

（上年=100）（可比价） (preceding year = 100) (At constant prices)

区 县	Region	农林牧渔及服务业增加值指数 Farming,Forestry,Animal Husbandry,Fishery and Service	农业 Farming	林业 Forestry	牧业 Animal Husbandry	渔业 Fishery	农林牧渔服务业 Service of Farming, Forestry, Animal Husbandry and Fishery
合 计	**Total**	**104.8**	**105.1**	**111.0**	**102.3**	**104.3**	**106.2**
新城区	Xincheng						
碑林区	Beilin						
莲湖区	Lianhu						
灞桥区	Baqiao	105.1	105.2	497.7	91.2	127.6	113.2
未央区	Weiyang	91.0	49.0	419.4	98.6	669.0	155.5
雁塔区	Yanta						
阎良区	Yanliang	105.1	104.2	197.2	107.6	197.1	105.3
临潼区	Lintong	105.2	108.9	123.1	96.7	100.5	109.7
长安区	Chang'an	105.0	108.5	82.5	85.6	94.7	112.9
高陵区	Gaoling	105.3	103.9	328.3	102.7	200.0	113.4
蓝田县	Lantian	105.0	101.1	204.4	107.8	102.6	95.4
周至县	Zhouzhi	104.7	104.9	91.0	109.3	137.0	108.6
鄠邑区	Huyi	104.6	101.4	102.2	116.3	200.5	100.1

11-18 主要年份农作物播种面积

Sown Areas of Farm Crops In Representative Years

单位：万亩　　　　(10 000mu)

年　份 Year	总播种面积 Total Sown Area	粮食 Grain Crops	小麦 Wheat	玉米 Corn	油料 Oil-bearing Crops	蔬菜 Vegetables
1980	835.43	706.35	324.17	273.14	10.01	24.02
1985	795.41	704.36	378.20	271.14	8.01	45.03
1990	816.41	731.42	387.20	282.14	12.00	51.03
1991	820.41	731.37	389.19	283.14	13.01	47.03
1992	820.65	715.50	384.60	273.60	16.20	54.60
1993	821.63	713.49	380.40	273.69	14.84	63.90
1994	821.10	719.00	375.90	272.40	13.80	59.90
1995	784.74	690.63	370.41	259.55	18.57	57.59
1996	797.40	709.00	366.30	286.80	18.80	55.50
1997	755.78	670.83	367.71	248.79	15.53	59.36
1998	789.99	705.03	370.17	285.45	14.69	60.95
1999	793.08	709.95	371.94	294.00	12.74	60.68
2000	784.94	697.55	369.89	283.70	13.46	64.35
2001	763.16	678.05	359.19	278.57	11.87	61.77
2002	751.10	655.59	350.64	271.95	11.40	67.71
2003	737.06	632.55	336.05	261.89	11.04	69.44
2004	753.83	630.63	311.52	286.50	9.74	77.55
2005	757.91	642.75	325.10	287.87	9.51	83.33
2006	769.49	648.00	313.23	307.89	8.58	87.03
2007	762.38	637.05	306.98	304.13	7.41	91.07
2008	756.06	630.31	319.39	286.69	8.59	93.02
2009	757.11	628.69	318.36	285.20	8.59	94.83
2010	751.74	621.71	317.18	279.93	8.98	95.71
2011	704.17	573.13	306.39	243.06	8.83	96.97
2012	701.33	572.50	305.34	242.20	7.70	97.82
2013	695.53	567.87	298.93	245.64	7.67	99.89
2014	684.28	551.46	290.53	238.65	7.01	101.56
2015	675.59	537.69	280.73	235.83	6.83	103.49
2016	659.04	527.74	275.66	231.96	6.18	103.01
2017	730.51	569.96	298.74	251.62	6.44	132.29

注：2011年农作物播种面积为陕西省统计局依据（国统字办[2011]68号）文件调整数。

11-19 各区县主要农作物播种面积（2017年）

Sown Areas of Major Farm Crops by Region（2017）

单位：万亩 (10 000 mu)

区　县	Region	总播种面积 Total Sown Area	粮食 Grain Crops	小麦 Wheat	玉米 Corn	油料 Oil-bearing Crops	蔬菜 Vegetables	瓜果类 Fruits Class
合　计	**Total**	**730.51**	**569.96**	**298.74**	**251.62**	**6.44**	**132.29**	**17.30**
新城区	Xincheng							
碑林区	Beilin							
莲湖区	Lianhu							
灞桥区	Baqiao	23.76	15.51	9.54	5.67	0.27	7.40	0.49
未央区	Weiyang	0.08	0.03	0.02	0.01	0.00	0.04	0.01
雁塔区	Yanta							
阎良区	Yanliang	46.23	21.03	11.09	9.92	0.08	18.29	6.83
临潼区	Lintong	114.85	95.54	52.23	39.61	0.98	15.70	1.75
长安区	Chang'an	110.33	79.78	40.89	38.40	1.18	25.60	3.57
高陵区	Gaoling	50.92	38.28	19.31	18.70	0.00	12.12	0.52
鄠邑区	Huyi	89.20	78.63	39.56	38.11	0.30	8.66	1.58
蓝田县	Lantian	107.73	93.31	49.26	32.55	2.14	9.71	1.47
周至县	Zhouzhi	79.84	67.65	34.23	32.02	0.90	9.02	0.13

11-20 主要年份农作物产品产量

Yield of Major Farm Crops in Representative Years

单位：万吨 (10 000 ton)

年份 Year	粮食作物 Grain Crops	夏粮 Summer Grain	小麦 Wheat	秋粮 Autumn Grain	稻谷 Rice	玉米 Corn	油料 Oil-bearing Crops	油菜籽 Rapeseeds	蔬菜 Vegetables
1978	132.80	64.20	58.20	68.70	5.10	55.80	0.09	0.07	45.66
1979	145.70	81.80	74.20	63.90	4.50	53.40	0.33	0.29	49.11
1980	114.40	56.60	52.20	57.80	4.70	47.70	0.54	0.50	40.13
1981	116.10	78.70	74.30	37.40	3.40	31.50	0.76	0.75	34.06
1982	148.90	85.60	82.20	63.30	4.90	55.50	0.51	0.49	53.71
1983	148.10	81.80	79.60	66.30	4.80	58.50	0.36	0.34	46.99
1984	157.60	82.40	81.00	75.20	5.00	66.50	0.46	0.29	75.47
1985	150.10	76.10	74.80	74.00	5.10	65.10	0.75	0.39	86.44
1986	162.40	91.70	90.10	70.70	4.80	61.80	1.25	0.82	85.84
1987	171.20	87.00	85.20	84.20	5.00	74.30	1.57	1.22	95.16
1988	158.00	86.80	84.60	71.10	3.80	61.40	0.89	0.51	113.50
1989	173.60	93.50	91.20	80.20	4.70	70.40	1.33	0.94	129.32
1990	172.40	91.70	89.70	80.80	5.50	70.40	1.35	0.94	119.32
1991	178.80	91.10	89.20	87.70	5.00	77.50	1.20	0.74	117.41
1992	183.40	101.70	99.60	81.70	4.70	72.30	1.49	0.87	128.12
1993	190.00	101.10	99.00	88.90	4.90	78.60	1.40	1.00	145.80
1994	157.40	86.90	84.90	70.50	4.50	61.40	1.08	0.78	135.26
1995	175.30	99.80	97.40	75.50	3.40	67.80	2.17	1.90	133.60
1996	187.50	80.10	78.40	107.40	3.40	95.60	1.83	1.55	138.01
1997	190.50	114.30	112.30	76.30	3.50	69.40	1.86	1.65	142.11
1998	212.70	104.40	104.00	108.30	3.20	99.10	1.67	1.36	148.87
1999	204.40	95.50	94.40	108.90	2.90	99.70	1.30	1.00	153.24
2000	201.90	92.60	91.60	109.30	3.10	100.50	1.34	0.95	162.14
2001	197.10	98.10	97.20	98.90	2.70	91.30	1.23	0.90	152.80
2002	192.40	94.50	93.50	97.90	2.10	91.60	1.22	0.84	169.74
2003	176.30	98.20	96.70	78.20	1.60	72.30	1.13	0.70	169.67
2004	195.80	97.80	96.00	98.00	1.70	91.60	1.14	0.84	180.96
2005	205.50	100.00	99.10	105.50	1.60	99.30	1.16	0.89	195.70
2006	193.50	86.00	85.40	107.40	1.40	101.20	1.08	0.87	189.30
2007	189.10	77.30	76.70	111.80	1.50	105.60	0.96	0.77	204.30
2008	214.40	105.90	105.60	108.50	0.90	103.00	1.15	0.95	221.53
2009	218.20	103.00	102.10	115.20	0.90	109.50	1.12	0.93	242.41
2010	221.70	106.60	105.80	115.10	0.80	108.90	1.20	1.00	253.10
2011	182.04	90.54	89.68	91.49	0.67	85.30	1.17	0.95	261.66
2012	192.55	95.73	94.92	96.82	0.57	89.29	1.02	0.88	277.80
2013	183.12	83.59	82.77	99.52	0.39	91.83	1.00	0.87	298.12
2014	175.61	88.05	87.35	87.56	0.25	83.30	0.98	0.80	316.28
2015	180.86	93.12	92.40	87.74	0.00	84.04	0.95	0.80	332.79
2016	175.33	89.90	89.24	85.43	0.08	81.91	0.86	0.77	336.75
2017	187.87	98.58	97.98	89.29	0.04	85.36	0.93	0.86	445.43

注：2011年农作物产品产量为陕西省统计局依据(国统字办[2011]70号)文件调整数。

11-21 各区县主要农作物产品产量（2017年）

Yield of Major Farm Crops by Region（2017）

单位：万吨 (10 000 tons)

区 县	Region	粮食作物 Grain Crops	夏粮 Summer Grain	小麦 Wheat	秋粮 Autumn Grain	稻谷 Rice	玉米 Corn
合 计	**Total**	**187.87**	**98.58**	**97.98**	**89.29**	**0.04**	**85.36**
新城区	Xincheng						
碑林区	Beilin						
莲湖区	Lianhu						
灞桥区	Baqiao	4.96	3.24	3.24	1.72		1.66
未央区	Weiyang	0.01	0.01	0.01			
雁塔区	Yanta						
阎良区	Yanliang	8.48	4.66	4.66	3.82		3.82
临潼区	Lintong	30.48	16.56	16.56	13.92		12.75
长安区	Chang'an	26.53	13.32	13.32	13.21	0.04	13.09
高陵区	Gaoling	17.92	8.48	8.48	9.44		9.39
鄠邑区	Huyi	26.90	13.75	13.56	13.15		13.11
蓝田县	Lantian	25.38	13.94	13.70	11.44		9.80
周至县	Zhouzhi	20.66	10.76	10.61	9.90		9.77

11-21 续表 continued

单位：万吨 (10 000 tons)

区 县	Region	油料 Oil-bearing Crops	油菜籽 Rapeseeds	蔬菜 Vegetables	瓜果类 Fruits Class
合 计	**Total**	**0.93**	**0.86**	**445.43**	**57.46**
新城区	Xincheng				
碑林区	Beilin				
莲湖区	Lianhu				
灞桥区	Baqiao	0.04	0.03	30.94	1.14
未央区	Weiyang			0.19	0.01
雁塔区	Yanta				
阎良区	Yanliang	0.01	0.01	83.88	24.86
临潼区	Lintong	0.12	0.10	50.44	7.62
长安区	Chang'an	0.21	0.21	56.78	7.37
高陵区	Gaoling	0.00	0.00	54.03	3.73
鄠邑区	Huyi	0.06	0.05	28.31	3.66
蓝田县	Lantian	0.28	0.28	19.17	0.49
周至县	Zhouzhi	0.13	0.10	21.94	4.55

11–22 主要年份农作物单位面积产量

Yield of Farm Crops Per Unit Area in Representative Years

单位：公斤/亩 (kg/mu)

年份 Year	粮食作物 Grain Crops	夏粮 Summer Grain	小麦 Wheat	秋粮 Autumn Grain	玉米 Corn	油料 Oil-bearing Crops	油菜籽 Rapeseeds	蔬菜 Vegetables
1990	236	232	232	241	249	103	101	2349
1991	245	229	229	264	274	94	89	2332
1992	256	259	259	253	264	92	101	2344
1993	266	260	260	274	287	94	107	2282
1994	219	226	226	211	225	79	84	2260
1995	254	263	263	243	261	117	128	2320
1996	265	214	214	321	333	86	100	2489
1997	284	305	306	257	279	76	129	2395
1998	302	278	279	328	347	114	121	2443
1999	288	253	254	327	339	102	106	2526
2000	289	247	248	338	354	102	112	2520
2001	291	270	271	314	328	104	113	2474
2002	293	266	267	326	337	107	115	2507
2003	279	287	288	269	276	102	110	2444
2004	310	308	308	313	320	117	129	2333
2005	320	304	305	336	345	121	132	2349
2006	299	273	273	323	329	125	135	2175
2007	297	250	250	341	347	129	132	2245
2008	340	330	331	350	359	134	137	2382
2009	347	320	321	375	384	131	131	2556
2010	357	333	334	381	389	130	131	2644
2011	318	293	293	347	351	133	134	2698
2012	336	310	311	367	369	132	130	2840
2013	322	277	277	374	374	130	125	2985
2014	318	301	301	339	349	140	130	3114
2015	336	329	329	345	356	139	133	3216
2016	332	323	324	342	353	140	132	3269
2017	330	327	328	332	339	144	139	3367

注：2011年农作物单产为陕西省统计局依据(国统字办[2011]72号)文件调整数。

11-23 各区县主要农作物单位面积产量（2017年）

The Output of Main Crops Per Unit Area by Region（2017）

单位：公斤/亩 (kg/mu)

区 县	Region	粮食作物 Grain Crops	夏粮 Summer Grain	小麦 Wheat	秋粮 Autumn Grain	玉米 Corn
合 计	**Total**	**330**	**327**	**328**	**332**	**339**
新城区	Xincheng					
碑林区	Beilin					
莲湖区	Lianhu					
灞桥区	Baqiao	320	340	340	288	293
未央区	Weiyang	345	344	344	348	348
雁塔区	Yanta					
阎良区	Yanliang	403	420	420	385	385
临潼区	Lintong	319	317	317	321	322
长安区	Chang'an	332	326	326	339	341
高陵区	Gaoling	468	439	439	498	502
鄠邑区	Huyi	342	341	343	344	344
蓝田县	Lantian	272	279	278	264	301
周至县	Zhouzhi	305	309	310	302	305

11-23 续表 continued

单位：公斤/亩 (kg/mu)

区 县	Region	油料 Oil-bearing Crops	油菜籽 Rapeseeds	蔬菜 Vegetables	瓜果类 Fruits Class
合 计	**Total**	**144**	**139**	**3367**	**3321**
新城区	Xincheng				
碑林区	Beilin				
莲湖区	Lianhu				
灞桥区	Baqiao	132	133	4183	2307
未央区	Weiyang			4950	1687
雁塔区	Yanta				
阎良区	Yanliang	130	130	4587	3643
临潼区	Lintong	129	111	3213	4355
长安区	Chang'an	179	179	2218	2061
高陵区	Gaoling			4457	7177
鄠邑区	Huyi	190	191	1974	2495
蓝田县	Lantian	131	131	2433	3851
周至县	Zhouzhi	140	121	3267	2874

11-24　设施农业生产情况（2017年）

Agricultural Production Facilities (2017)

指　标	Item	播种面积（亩）Seeded Area (mu)	产量（吨）output(ton)
一、蔬菜	**Vegetables**	**276248**	**1429393**
其中：芹菜	Celery	89336	396691
油菜	Rape	10630	23340
菠菜	Spinach	22812	51308
黄瓜	Cucumber	26850	167513
西红柿	Tomato	30882	128219
辣椒	Chilli	14066	58324
二、瓜果类	**Fruits class**	**100640**	**367790**
其中：草莓	Strawberry	11637	22765
三、花卉苗木	**Flower seedling wood**	**17354**	
四、食用菌	**Edible Fungi**		15666
五、其他	**Others**	**1018**	
补充资料：　设施数量（个）	Number of Facilities (unit)		135156
设施占地面积（亩）	Area of Facilities(mu)	241619	

11-25　主要年份林业生产情况

Statistics on Forestry in Representative Years

指　标	Item	2000	2010	2012	2013	2014	2015	2016	2017
一、营林情况	**Afforestation**								
当年造林面积合计（万亩）	Build Forestry Areas(10 000 mu)	27.47	16.10	9.08	12.29	14.70	8.28	4.51	4.07
迹地更新面积（万亩）	Reforestation Area (10000 mu)	1.08							
封山育林面积（万亩）	Hill-closeure for Afforestation Areas (10 000 mu)	18.78	55.10	41.90	44.40	42.99	44.00	43.80	28.80
零星四旁植树（万株）	Planting(10 000 plants)	731.0	509.2	579.2	588.3	621.0	516.0	462.0	686.7
育苗面积（万亩）	Raise Seedlings Areas(10 000 mu)	2.05	11.95	11.64	17.37	17.73	19.84	22.78	48.24
#本年新育	New Seedling of Current Year	1.69	1.75	1.98	6.10	2.70	1.00	1.72	
二、主要林产品产量（吨）	**Main Forestry Product(ton)**								
生漆	Lacquer	11	10						
核桃	Walnuts	997	7875	15253	18033	16531	24344	19240	15010
板栗	Chinese Chestnut	744	7736	7654	4379	6922	8225	6694	6751
花椒	Pepper	140	1420	879	319	371	204	402	216
三、村及村以下采伐木材（万立方米）	**Timber Harvested at or below** Village Level (10 000 cu.m)	1.62	3.3	1.04	0.88		0.07	0.28	

注：本表数据来源于市农林委。

11-26 各区县林业生产情况（2017年）

Statistics On Forestry by Region（2017）

区 县 Region	当年造林面积（亩） Build Forestry Areasin in The Year(mu)	零星植树（万株） Planting (10 000 plants)	育苗面积（亩） Raise Seedlings Areas(mu)	核桃产量（吨） Output of Walnuts (ton)	板栗产量（吨） Output of Chinese Chestnut (ton)
合 计 Total	**40650**	**686.67**	**482430**	**15010**	**6751**
新城区 Xincheng					
碑林区 Beilin					
莲湖区 Lianhu					
灞桥区 Baqiao	945	10	915		
未央区 Weiyang		41			
雁塔区 Yanta		1		230	
阎良区 Yanliang	2115	46	2910		
临潼区 Lintong	8910	72	7800	1000	
长安区 Chang'an	3510	170	41220	720	510
高陵区 Gaoling	3555	40	30300		
鄠邑区 Huyi	2085	115	60915	450	21
蓝田县 Lantian	12195	90	150090	8000	5600
周至县 Zhouzhi	7335	90	171135	4146	620

注：本表数据来源于市农林委。

11-27 主要年份果业生产情况

Statistics on Fruits in Representative Years

指标	Item	2000	2005	2010	2013	2014	2015	2016	2017
果园面积合计（万亩）	**Areas of Orchards (10 000 mu)**	**47.86**	**55.55**	**74.95**	**78.06**	**81.23**	**79.21**	**79.76**	**93.97**
苹果园	Apple Orchards	12.15	5.96	3.55	1.28	1.22	1.24	1.19	7.48
梨园	Pears Orchards	5.79	3.01	2.27	1.68	1.61	1.55	1.43	2.15
葡萄园	Grapes Orchards	1.89	3.02	4.83	6.70	9.39	9.50	10.20	11.92
桃园	Peach Orchards	3.47	8.66	7.68	6.49	6.14	6.09	6.05	9.21
猕猴桃园	Chinese Goosebeery Orchards	16.83	4.33	34.92	41.99	42.16	39.62	39.67	39.98
杏园	Apricot Orchards	0.62	2.50	3.62	3.52	3.99	3.96	3.86	4.18
柿子园	Presimmons Orchards	1.96	2.69	3.16	2.78	2.59	3.05	3.13	2.71
石榴园	Pomegranate Orchards			3.43	3.57	3.59	3.59	3.59	3.33
水果产量（吨）	**Output of Fruits (ton)**	**343551**	**512869**	**847821**	**951851**	**996570**	**1052000**	**1077442**	**1347706**
苹果	Apple	89416	53387	39130	25212	26047	31970	30522	131349
梨	Pears	65459	57059	55122	47618	48757	50729	49888	57438
葡萄	Grapes	16647	30951	64885	92380	99889	126625	133627	175293
桃	Peach	27010	89755	142051	122186	125147	131228	132329	217953
猕猴桃	Chinese Goosebeery	96640	137853	296023	395847	410614	425250	441735	456634
杏	Apricot			48544	55330	61145	63726	60877	65923
柿子	Persimmon			35287	41712	43705	39560	38445	48648
石榴	Pomegranate			40211	30642	32793	29840	29859	31257

11-28 各区县果业生产情况（2017年）

Area and Output of Fruits by Region（2017）

区 县	Region	果园面积（万亩） Area of Orchards(10 000 mu)	水果产量（吨） Output of Fruits(ton)
合 计	**Total**	**93.97**	**1347706**
新城区	Xincheng		
碑林区	Beilin		
莲湖区	Lianhu		
灞桥区	Baqiao	7.84	131721
未央区	Weiyang	0.02	73
雁塔区	Yanta		
阎良区	Yanliang	2.76	72358
临潼区	Lintong	6.95	77315
长安区	Chang'an	3.53	53870
高陵区	Gaoling	3.17	74734
鄠邑区	Huyi	7.94	102078
蓝田县	Lantian	7.82	132793
周至县	Zhouzhi	40.65	453345

11-29 果品加工、销售及生产服务情况

指标	Item	西安市 Xi' an	灞桥区 Baqiao	未央区 Weiyang
一、果品加工企业数（个）	**Number of Fruit Processing Enterprises(unit)**	**50**	**1**	
其中：苹果加工企业数量	Number of Apple Processing Enterprises			
猕猴桃加工企业数	Number of Kiwi Processing Enterprises	38		
二、果品加工企业果汁加工能力（吨）	**Processing Ability of Fruit Juice in Fruit Processing Enterprises**	**4660**	**50**	
其中：苹果汁加工能力	Processing Ability of Apple Juice			
三、当年果品加工企业鲜果消耗量（吨）	**Fresh Fruit Consumption of Fruit Processing Enterprise in the Year**	**106034**	**150**	
其中：加工消耗苹果数量	Number of Fresh Apple Consumption	2550		
加工消耗猕猴桃数量	Number of Fresh Kiwi Consumption	100080		
四、仓储能力（吨）	**Storage Capacity(ton)**	**366985**	**2400**	
其中：气调库	Gas Reservoir	132800	2400	
机械库	Machine Shop	234185		
五、果业合作（个）	**Fruit Industry Cooperation(unit)**	**442**	**27**	
六、果苗木繁育中心（个）	**Fruit Seedling Breeding Center(unit)**	**11**		
七、果业服务投入（万元）	**Service Investment in Fruit Industry(10000 yuan)**	**424**	**10**	**2**
1. 技术培训投入	Technical Training Investment	92	5	
2. 科研投入	Scientific Research Investment	47	2	2
3. 生产技术指导投入	Production Technology Guidance Investment	285	3	
八、果品销售方式（吨）	**Fruit Sales Mode(ton)**	**1237641**	**10**	
1. 产品批发市场	Product Wholesale Market	585691	6	
2. 采供商	Supplier	293926	2	
3. 专卖、直销店	Franchised and Direct Outlets	32717		
4. 超级市场	Supermarket	25720		
5. 电子商务	Electronic Commerce	104768	1	
6. 农产品加工厂	Agricultural Product Processing Plant	133531	1	
7. 其它	Others	61288		
九、按销售区域分（吨）	**By the Sales Area(ton)**	**1237641**	**10**	
1. 国内市场	Domestic market	1207641	10	
2. 国际市场	International Market	30000		
附记：累计建成绿色果园面积（亩）	Cumulative Green Orchard Area(mu)	4900	1500	
建成有机果园面积面积（亩）	Construction of Organic Orchard Area(mu)	2210	800	

阎良区 Yanliang	临潼区 Lintong	长安区 Chang'an	高陵区 Gaoling	鄠邑区 Huyi	蓝田县 Lantian	周至县 Zhouzhi
	5			**1**	**3**	**38**
						38
	3000			**550**	**100**	
	2780			**2000**	**550**	**100000**
	2550					
	80					100000
	3065	**1000**		**8220**		**350000**
	1600	1000		5500		120000
	1465			2720		230000
19	**73**	**20**	**13**	**74**	**26**	**178**
	3	**2**		**2**		**3**
5	**240**	**5**	**13**	**50**	**15**	**50**
5		5	9	3	10	40
				40		
	240		4	7	5	10
72358	**96294**	**230**	**73223**	**136000**	**100000**	**520000**
37200	37676		22500	94000	50000	250000
23800	16061		37953	16000	10000	90000
710	907		5050	2800		10000
380				4600		10000
750	33170	230	520	1600	5000	60000
3750	2780			17000	10000	100000
5768	5700		7200		25000	
72358	**96294**	**230**	**73223**	**136000**	**100000**	**520000**
72358	96294	230	73223	136000	100000	490000
						30000
				2520	650	
					60	

11-30 主要年份畜牧业生产情况

Statistics on Livestock Husbandry in Representative Years

指标	Item	2000	2005	2010	2013	2014	2015	2016	2017
一、活牲畜年末存栏（头）	**Live Animals in Stock at Year-end (head)**	**260742**	**322521**	**216043**	**211791**	**217257**	**199438**	**169273**	**184125**
# 役畜	Draught Animals	98130	90717	42243	31510	26760	24412	19161	17866
1. 牛	Cattle	256073	320773	215072	210743	216326	199386	169242	184104
#肉牛	Farm Cattle			65447	60165	64478	65863	72567	70078
#奶牛	Dairy Cattle	48164	96498	118747	120836	126174	109520	77453	96160
2. 马（匹）	Horses	736	559	456	549	513	52	31	21
3. 驴	Donkeys	476	175	67	52	59			
4. 骡	Mules	3457	1014	448	447	359			
二、猪年末存栏（头）	**Pigs in Stock at Year-end**	**1284592**	**1472869**	**943183**	**965683**	**950124**	**924870**	**895272**	**969132**
# 能繁殖的母猪	Female Hogs of Reprductive Ability	93775	123543	106610	103967	99989	94000	85637	94356
三、羊年末存栏（只）	**Sheep and Goats in Stock at Year-end**	**421103**	**532471**	**294539**	**273747**	**279207**	**283334**	**265668**	**310242**
1. 山羊	Goats	397121	520354	288738	267382	271722	273941	258354	299349
# 奶山羊	Milch Goats	266525	358733	246442	222546	224901	208909	185249	255571
2. 绵羊	Sheeps	23982	12117	5801	6365	7485	9393	7314	10893
四、家禽年末存栏（万只）	**Poultry in Stock at Year-end (10 000 heads)**	**1623.81**	**1372.56**	**1034.2**	**1172.61**	**1161.16**	**1183.23**	**1125.25**	**1243.4**
五、年末养蜂箱数（箱）	**Honey (box)**	20408	24287	22984	17415	20663	19536	15031	20607

11-31 各区县畜牧业生产情况（2017年）

Statistics On Livestock, Animal Husbandry by Region（2017）

区 县	Region	活牲畜年末存栏（头）Live Animals In Stock at Year-end (head)	役畜 Draught Animals	牛（头）Cattle (head)	奶牛 Dairy Cattle	马（匹）Horses (head)	驴（头）Donkeys (head)	骡（头）Mutes (head)
合 计	**Total**	**184125**	**17866**	**184104**	**96160**	**21**		
新城区	Xincheng							
碑林区	Beilin							
莲湖区	Lianhu							
灞桥区	Baqiao	6370	30	6349	6098	21		
未央区	Weiyang	21		21	21			
雁塔区	Yanta							
阎良区	Yanliang	18780		18780	18095			
临潼区	Lintong	47093	6222	47093	40871			
长安区	Chang'an	5563		5563	2487			
高陵区	Gaoling	21302		21302	10282			
鄠邑区	Huyi	6940	26	6940	1994			
蓝田县	Lantian	37458	7035	37458	2970			
周至县	Zhouzhi	28815	4553	28815	2630			

11-31 续表 continued

区 县	Region	猪（头）Swine (head)	能繁殖的母猪 breeding sows	羊（只）Sheep and Goats (head)	山羊 Goats	奶山羊 Milch Goats	家禽（万只）Poultry (10 000 head)	蜂（箱）Honey (box)
合 计	**Total**	**969132**	**94356**	**310242**	**299349**	**255571**	**1243.4**	**20607**
新城区	Xincheng							
碑林区	Beilin							
莲湖区	Lianhu							
灞桥区	Baqiao	43332	5143	10323	10323	10323	34.55	330
未央区	Weiyang	1148	358	50	50	50	0.38	
雁塔区	Yanta							
阎良区	Yanliang	38368	4210	53927	53927	53927	63.48	700
临潼区	Lintong	219214	19125	81017	77850	77850	266.12	1681
长安区	Chang'an	107554	9528	16455	16115	9051	238.71	1570
高陵区	Gaoling	51065	3680	26672	24345	24345	164.27	
鄠邑区	Huyi	125360	10760	6620	6620	6620	114.6	7571
蓝田县	Lantian	79505	8054	73750	72700	46115	125	3570
周至县	Zhouzhi	159995	18735	11538	11403	2085	99.8	4955

11-32 主要年份畜产品和水产品产量

单位：吨

年 份 Year	肉类总产量 Output of Meat	猪 肉 Pork	牛 肉 Beef	羊 肉 Mutton	禽 肉 Poultry
1990	63273	50646	4667	1931	5885
1991	72268	55086	5623	2162	9062
1992	88994	68134	6468	2460	11290
1993	93420	71274	7249	2220	12174
1994	106691	79433	8298	2350	15681
1995	127815	86513	11251	3731	23948
1996	91468	63750	5402	2578	19324
1997	106597	75381	6672	3468	20596
1998	134152	98974	8788	4710	21424
1999	130124	93859	9827	4147	21963
2000	147571	106137	12066	4766	23760
2001	157277	113353	11900	5153	20540
2002	161092	118634	11516	5394	20515
2003	165860	122759	13241	5180	19682
2004	171545	126404	13641	5874	18493
2005	182046	136503	14031	6106	18803
2006	108634	81199	8267	2841	13417
2007	102191	73254	8589	3111	14075
2008	115352	84654	9840	3335	16060
2009	126182	94490	10142	3677	17190
2010	136501	102296	10854	3875	18338
2011	144631	104816	11860	3645	19390
2012	151711	110506	12079	3697	20046
2013	157449	114288	12143	4036	20817
2014	161886	118627	12288	4198	20887
2015	161254	115953	12361	4287	21441
2016	156829	112629	12541	4340	20652
2017	183100	130906	13786	5143	24767

注：1.2010年起，根据统计制度要求，水产品产量及养殖面积统计数据取自市水务局。
2.2017年水产品及养殖面积不包含西咸新区。

Output of Livestock Products and Aquatic Products in Representative Years

(ton)

奶类产量 Output of Milk	牛 奶 Cow Milk	禽 蛋 Poultry Eggs	蜂蜜（公斤） Honey(kg)	水产品 Output of Aquatic Products	养殖面积（万亩） Water Raise Areas (10 000 mu)
82017	50528	55938	1035392	4258	2.55
91006	57700	90558	1022797	4949	2.63
100080	63586	104970	739275	6015	2.8
111070	73897	125244	662049	7132	2.97
145412	99025	146503	547808	7900	3.1
132909	85753	141227	535891	8517	3.21
133372	86103	138044	613290	8910	3.51
150964	98078	156066	713918	10054	3.46
174099	119719	142519	537304	10480	3.4
209144	145191	135981	541613	11061	3.38
245913	176155	138305	460598	11384	3.35
255437	179977	132303	479839	12480	3.17
288009	202826	134336	497530	12017	3.31
336296	245407	128833	537805	9967	2.48
384319	289564	117597	449765	9721	2.46
422229	327961	118115	421052	9370	2.38
471438	374813	97816	414271	11937	1.6
528037	428462	98140	401761	12402	1.38
589697	475681	108515	503031	12487	1.4
618186	498394	116685	528731	13044	1.52
633663	509178	123793	436759	11850	2.24
647978	509777	125639	217632	11800	2.2
666439	513337	129970	213174	14010	2.95
657748	512796	135382	219344	14200	2.19
658016	514587	135191	250464	14218	2.31
637340	485640	145470	243198	14190	2.26
562038	420765	140357	219646	13449	1.96
558412	394813	146273	240238	13832	2.24

11-33 各区县主要畜产品和水产品产量（2017年）

Output of Major Livestock Products and Aquatic Products by Region (2017)

单位：吨 (ton)

区县	Region	肉类总产量 Output of Meat	猪肉 Pork	牛肉 Beef	羊肉 Mutton	禽肉 Poultry
合计	**Total**	**183100**	**130906**	**13786**	**5143**	**24767**
新城区	Xincheng					
碑林区	Beilin					
莲湖区	Lianhu					
灞桥区	Baqiao	7820	5725	797	175	932
未央区	Weiyang	2510	2055	409	10	36
雁塔区	Yanta					
阎良区	Yanliang	7734	5107	725	724	1089
临潼区	Lintong	46275	31581	3865	1646	4618
长安区	Chang'an	15072	10437	722	321	3326
高陵区	Gaoling	9512	6209	557	301	1676
鄠邑区	Huyi	17300	14247	602	76	2075
蓝田县	Lantian	21899	10506	2790	1065	6122
周至县	Zhouzhi	25818	22212	1775	171	1657

11-33 续表 continued

区县	Region	奶类产量 Output of Milk	牛奶 Cow Milk	禽蛋 Poultry Eggs	蜂蜜（公斤） Honey(kg)	水产品 Output of Aquatic Products	养殖面积（亩） Water Raise Areas (mu)
合计	**Total**	**558412**	**394813**	**146273**	**240238**	**13832**	**22425**
新城区	Xincheng						
碑林区	Beilin						
莲湖区	Lianhu						
灞桥区	Baqiao	30815	25025	4582	8330	700	1245
未央区	Weiyang	270	265	27		750	585
雁塔区	Yanta						
阎良区	Yanliang	103187	77052	6769	19180	225	180
临潼区	Lintong	211056	160790	38038	42762	3300	4965
长安区	Chang'an	24731	12878	25406	23468	5715	8655
高陵区	Gaoling	55070	40537	18433		235	180
鄠邑区	Huyi	14035	9034	12615	66020	1105	645
蓝田县	Lantian	43297	8642	10519	27576	1302	3660
周至县	Zhouzhi	13676	10282	10057	51016	500	2310

注：1.2010年起，根据统计制度要求，水产品产量及养殖面积统计数据取自市水务局。
2.本表合计数水产品及养殖面积不包含西咸新区。

11-34 农业科技、教育情况（2017年）

Agricultural Science and Technology Education（2017）

指标	Item	2017
农业研究开发机构（个）	Agricultural research and development institutions (unit)	348
农业科技人员（人）	Agricultural scientific and technical personnel(persons)	3535
农业科研成果（个）	Agricultural scientific research achievements (unit)	14
农民技能培训人数（万人）	The number of peasants skills training(10000 persons)	15.6
良种推广面积（万亩）	Thoroughbred promotion area (10000 mu)	758.83
农业信息站（个）	Information station of Agricultural (unit)	3104

注：本表数据来源于市农林委。

11-35 主要年份农产品人均占有量

Per Capita Output of Major Farm Products in Representative Years

单位：公斤/人 (kg/ person)

年份 Year	粮食 Grain	油料 Oil-bearing Crops	猪牛羊肉 Pork Beef and Mutton	禽蛋 Poultry Eggs	奶类 Milk	水果 Fruits	蔬菜 Vegetables
1978	266.7	0.2	5.4	0.9	3.3	6.8	91.7
1979	288.6	0.6	6.7	1.0	4.0	5.1	97.3
1980	223.5	1.1	5.9	1.2	4.1	6.9	78.4
1981	222.9	1.5	6.6	1.7	4.7	5.8	65.4
1982	281.5	1.0	4.9	2.7	5.6	5.9	101.6
1983	276.6	0.7	4.9	3.2	6.5	5.0	87.8
1984	289.4	0.8	4.8	6.2	8.7	4.8	138.6
1985	271.4	1.4	6.8	5.7	10.2	7.6	156.3
1986	288.0	2.2	7.8	6.4	12.1	9.6	152.2
1987	298.0	2.7	7.3	6.8	13.8	10.6	165.6
1988	269.7	1.5	8.0	8.9	15.6	11.1	193.7
1989	290.7	2.2	8.4	7.6	13.1	10.2	216.5
1990	298.7	2.1	9.4	9.2	14.2	11.5	196.0
1991	290.6	2.0	10.2	14.7	14.8	11.7	190.8
1992	294.3	2.4	12.4	16.8	16.2	17.3	205.6
1993	301.2	2.2	12.8	19.9	17.6	25.9	231.1
1994	246.1	1.7	14.1	22.9	22.7	28.0	211.5
1995	270.4	3.4	15.7	21.8	20.5	37.5	206.1
1996	286.3	3.2	11.0	21.1	20.4	43.9	210.8
1997	287.8	2.8	12.9	23.6	22.8	43.3	214.7
1998	318.3	2.5	16.8	21.3	26.1	50.0	222.8
1999	303.0	1.9	16.0	20.2	31.0	52.7	227.2
2000	293.5	1.9	17.9	20.1	35.7	49.9	235.7
2001	283.7	1.8	18.8	19.0	36.8	48.8	219.9
2002	273.8	1.7	19.3	19.1	41.0	53.5	241.6
2003	246.0	1.6	19.7	18.0	46.9	53.6	236.8
2004	270.1	1.6	20.1	16.2	53.0	63.9	249.6
2005	277.1	1.6	21.1	15.9	56.9	69.1	263.8
2006	256.9	1.4	12.3	13.0	62.6	73.5	251.4
2007	247.4	1.3	11.1	12.8	69.1	79.2	267.3
2008	256.0	1.4	11.7	13.0	70.4	85.6	264.5
2009	258.7	1.3	12.8	13.8	73.3	93.6	287.4
2010	261.8	1.4	13.8	14.6	74.8	100.1	298.9
2011	213.8	1.4	14.1	14.8	76.1	107.1	318.9
2012	225.6	1.2	14.8	15.2	78.1	109.2	325.6
2013	213.2	1.2	15.2	15.8	76.6	110.8	347.1
2014	204.0	1.1	15.7	15.7	76.3	115.8	367.5
2015	208.7	1.1	15.3	16.8	73.5	121.4	384.0
2016	200.0	1.0	14.8	16.0	64.1	122.9	384.0
2017	197.1	1.0	15.7	15.3	58.6	144.4	467.2

11-36 主要年份农村经济效益指标

Main Indicators of Rural Economic Benefit in Representative Years

年份 Year	每一劳动力创造的 Average Labor Force Production			每亩耕地种植业总产值（元） Output of Each Unit of Area Planting(yuan)	每百元物耗生产的总产值（元） Output per 100-Yuan of Material Consumed(yuan)
	农林牧渔及服务业总产值（元） Gross Output Value of Farming,Forestry, Animal Husbandry, Fishery and Service (yuan)	粮食（公斤） Grain Crops(kg)	油料（公斤） Oil-bearing Crops(kg)		
1978	504.7	1024.6	0.7	104.3	
1979	549.0	1096.5	2.3	116.0	
1980	483.1	846.1	4.0	99.2	
1981	502.8	840.5	5.5	105.4	
1982	631.5	1058.9	3.6	139.3	
1983	606.5	1053.2	2.6	124.1	
1984	850.7	1154.2	3.4	163.6	
1985	1020.1	1134.6	5.6	183.1	
1986	1132.2	1236.4	9.5	204.6	
1987	1280.3	1277.2	11.7	231.5	
1988	1558.4	1148.0	6.5	273.2	
1989	1605.3	1231.9	9.5	295.0	
1990	1766.3	1279.1	10.0	343.4	233.3
1991	1958.8	1326.6	8.9	380.4	238.4
1992	2093.7	1360.7	11.1	451.6	241.8
1993	2528.9	1409.7	10.4	546.8	240.1
1994	3705.0	1167.8	8.0	762.8	227.6
1995	4953.0	1300.6	16.1	1106.5	225.9
1996	5154.8	1391.2	13.6	1224.2	234.5
1997	5493.0	1413.4	13.8	1283.3	239.2
1998	5615.9	1578.1	12.4	1374.3	247.0
1999	4826.5	1516.6	9.7	1175.9	251.7
2000	5091.5	1498.0	9.9	1161.1	250.2
2001	5328.5	1462.4	9.1	1221.1	248.6
2002	5617.4	1427.5	9.1	1272.0	265.9
2003	5761.2	1308.1	8.4	1332.4	254.3
2004	6885.4	1452.7	8.5	1434.6	261.7
2005	7737.9	1524.7	8.6	1642.3	262.9
2006	8415.5	1435.7	8.0	1756.9	263.1
2007	10165.6	1403.0	7.1	2037.3	259.8
2008	13306.4	1695.4	9.1	2447.9	259.6
2009	14674.3	1791.7	9.2	2737.9	261.6
2010	19480.7	1901.3	10.0	3753.4	260.9
2011	23474.6	1567.2	10.1	4585.8	274.0
2012	27219.4	1699.6	10.1	5175.7	273.5
2013	31608.7	1688.0	9.2	5934.5	274.0
2014	33292.2	1605.0	8.9	6552.4	274.9
2015	36228.8	1720.9	9.0	7069.8	273.8
2016	39643.3	1713.6	8.5	7461.2	271.8
2017	45063.2	1702.1	8.4	8676.0	269.0

主要统计指标解释

农林牧渔业总产值 指以货币表现的农、林、牧、渔业全部产品和对农林牧渔业生产活动进行的各种支持性服务活动的价值总量，它反映一定时期内农林牧渔业生产总规模和总成果。1957年以前的农林牧渔业总产值中包括了厩肥和农民自给性手工业（如农民自制衣服、鞋、袜，自己从事粮食初步加工等）。1958年及以后，林业中增加了村及村以下竹木采伐产值；牧业中取消了厩肥产值；副业中取消了农民自给性手工业产值，增加了村及村以下办的工业产值；渔业中增加了海洋捕捞水产品产值。1980年及以后，在副业中增加了农民家庭兼营工业商品部分的产值。从1984年起村及村以下工业产值划归工业。从1993年起取消副业，将野生动物的捕猎划入牧业，野生植物采集和农民家庭兼营商品性工业划归农业。从2003年起，执行新的国民经济行业分类标准，农林牧渔业总产值中包括了农林牧渔服务业产值。林业中增加了森林采运业产值。农业中取消了家庭兼营商品性工业产值，将野生林产品的采集划归林业。第一次农业普查以后，由于畜牧业产品年报数据与普查数据之间存在一定的差距，根据农业普查结果对畜牧业年报数据进行了修正，对畜牧业产值进行了相应修正。

农林牧渔业总产值的计算方法通常是按农、林、牧、渔业产品及其副产品的产量分别乘以各自单位产品价格求得；少数生产周期较长，当年没有产品或产品产量不易统计的，则采用间接方法匡算其产值；然后将四业产品产值及农林牧渔服务业产值相加即为农林牧渔业总产值。

粮食产量 指全社会的产量。包括国有经济经营的、集体统一经营的和农民家庭经营的粮食产量，还包括工矿企业办的农场和其他生产单位的产量。粮食除包括稻谷、小麦、玉米、高粱、谷子及其他杂粮外，还包括薯类和豆类。其产量计算方法，豆类按去豆荚后的干豆计算；薯类（包括甘薯和马铃薯，不包括芋头和木薯）1963年以前按每4公斤鲜薯折1公斤粮食计算，从1964年开始改为按5公斤鲜薯折1公斤粮食计算。城市郊区作为蔬菜的薯类（如马铃薯等）按鲜品计算，并且不作粮食统计。其他粮食一律按脱粒后的原粮计算。1989年以前全国粮食产量数据主要靠全面报表取得，1989年开始使用抽样调查数据。

棉花产量 指全社会的产量。包括春播棉和夏播棉。产量按皮棉计算。不包括木棉。

油料产量 指全部油料作物的生产量。包括花生、油菜籽、芝麻、向日葵籽、胡麻籽（亚麻籽）和其他油料。不包括大豆、木本油料和野生油料。花生以带壳干花生计算。

水产品产量 指人工养殖的水产品和天然生长的水产品的捕捞量。包括海水的鱼类、虾蟹类、贝类和藻类以及内陆水域的鱼类、虾蟹类和贝类，不包括淡水生植物。水产品产量是通过各级水产和统计部门逐级上报取得数据。1995年及以前，贝类中牡蛎按鲜肉计算；蚶、蛤、蛏按5斤鲜品折1斤计算。1996年以后则统一按鲜品计算。

猪、牛、羊肉产量 指当年出栏并已屠宰、除去头蹄下水后带骨肉（即胴体重）的重量。包括全社会范围内的产量。1996年前为各级逐级上报数据。1996年第一次农业普查以后，由于畜牧业产品年报数据与普查数据之间存在一定的差距，根据普查结果对畜牧业年报数据进行了修正。1999年以后，国家统计局在部分地区开展了猪、牛、羊、禽等主要畜禽品种的抽样调查，并用抽样数据作为国家定案数据使用。未开展抽样调查的地区和品种，仍使用各级统计部门逐级上报数据。2008年，根据第二次农业普查结果，对2006年2007年畜牧业年报数据进行了修正。

畜禽存栏头（只）数 指报告期末农村各种合作经济组织和国营农场、农民个人、机关、团体、学校、工矿企业、部队等单位以及城镇居民饲养的大牲畜、猪、羊、家禽等畜禽的存栏数。

常用耕地 是指耕地总资源中专门种植农作物并经常进行耕种、能够正常收获的土地。包括当年实际耕种的熟地；弃耕、休闲不满三年，随时可以复耕的地；开荒利用三年以上的地。不包括临时种植农作物的坡度在25度以上的陡坡地；在河套、湖畔、库区临时开发的成片或零星土地；也不包括已列为国家和省（区、市）退耕计划但临时耕种的土地。

农作物播种面积 指实际播种或移植有农作物的面积。凡是实际种植有农作物的面积，不论种植在耕地上还是种植在非耕地上，均包括在农作物播种面积中。在播种季节基本结束后，因遭灾而重新改种和补种的农作物面积，也包括在内。它是反映我国耕地面积利用情况的一个重要指标。目前，农作物播种面积主要包括粮食、棉花、油料、糖料、麻类、烟叶、蔬菜和瓜类、药材和其他农作物九大类。

有效灌溉面积 指具有一定的水源，地块比较平整，灌溉工程或设备已经配套，在一般年景下，当年能够进行正常灌溉的耕地面积。在一般情况下，有效灌溉面积应等于灌溉工程或设备已经配备，能够进行正常灌溉的水田和水浇地面积之和。它是反映我国耕地抗旱能力的一个重要指标。

农用化肥施用量 指本年内实际用于农业生产的化肥数量，包括氮肥、磷肥、钾肥和复合肥。化肥施用量要求按折纯量计算数量。折纯量是指把氮肥、磷肥、钾肥分别按含氮、含五氧化二磷、含氧化钾的百分之百成份进行折算后的数量。复合肥按其所含主要成分折算。公式为：

折纯量=实物量×某种化肥有效成份含量的百分比

农业机械总动力 指主要用于农、林、牧、渔业的各种动力机械的动力总和。包括耕作机械、排灌机械、收获机械、农用运输机械、植物保护机械、牧业机械、林业机械、渔业机械和其他农业机械【内燃机按引擎马力折成瓦（特）计算、电动机按功率折成瓦（特）计算】。不包括专门用于乡、镇、村、组办工业、基本建设、非农业运输、科学试验和教学等非农业生产方面用的动力机械与作业机械。这个指标的统计数据主要来源于农机部门。

Explanatory Notes on Main Statistical Indicators

Gross Output Value of Agriculture, Forestry, Animal Husbandry and Fishery refers to the total value of products of agriculture, forestry, animal husbandry and fishery, and total value of services in support of agriculture, forestry, animal husbandry and fishery activities. It reflects the total scale and results of agricultural production during a given period. Prior to 1957, China's gross agricultural output value included barnyard manure and handicraft products for self- consumption (clothes, shoes, stockings, and initial grain processing undertaken by peasants). Since 1958, cutting and felling of bamboo and trees by villages and other cooperative organizations under villages have been included in forestry; value of barnyard manure has been excluded from animal husbandry; self consumed handicrafts have not been included from sideline occupations, while the output value of industries run by villages and cooperative organizations under village has been included in sideline occupations; and the output value of fish catches by motor fishing boats has been added to fishery. Since 1980, the value of handicraft products made for sale by individuals in households has been added to sideline occupations. Since 1984, industries run by villages and under villages have been included in the sector of industry. Since 1993, the subdivision of sideline occupations has been cancelled, and the hunting of wild animals has been classified into animal husbandry, and the gathering of wild plants and commodity industry run by rural household have been included in farming. A new industrial classification of economic activities was introduced in 2003. Under the new classification, value of services to agriculture, forestry, animal husbandry and fishery is included in the gross output value of agriculture, value of wood felling and transport is included in forestry, value of industrial output by rural households is not included in agriculture, and the collection of wild forest products is taken from agriculture and included in forestry. The First Agriculture Census of China revealed some discrepancy between the production of animal products from the annual reports and that from the census. According to the result of the First Agriculture census, efforts were made to adjust the output value of animal husbandry to make the figures from the annual reports consistent with the census data.

Gross output value of agrieulture is obtained by multiplying the output of each product or by-product by its price, resulting in the output value of each single item. For a small number of products, annual output of which is not available or difficult to get due to the long production (growing) process involved, the output value is estimated through an indirect approach. The sum of output values of all products of agriculture, forestry, animal husbandry and fishery and services in support to those industries is then equal to the gross output value of agriculture.

Grain Output refers to the total output in the whole country including grains produced by State farms, collective units, rural households, as well as by farms affiliated to industrial and mining enterprises and other production units. Grain includes rice, wheat, corn, sorghum, millet and other miscellaneous grains as well as tubers and beans. Output of beans refers to dry beans without pods. The output of tubers (sweet potatoes and potatoes, not including taros and cassava) are converted into that of grain at the ratio 4:1, i.e. 4 kilograms of fresh tubers were equivalent to 1 kilogram of grain up to 1963. Since 1964 the ratio for conversion has been 5:1. Tubers supplied as vegetables (such as potatoes) in cities and suburbs are calculated as fresh vegetables and their output is not included in the output of grain. Output of all other grains refers to husked grain. Data on grain production before 1989 were obtained through the Comprehensive Statistical Reporting System. Since 1989, data from sample surveys are used.

Cotton Output refers to cotton production in the whole country including cotton planted in spring and in autumn. Output is measured as the weight of ginned cotton. Ceiba is not included.

Output of Oil–bearing Crops refers to the total production of oil-bearing crops of various kinds, including peanuts (dry, in shell), rapeseeds, sesame, sunflower seeds, flax seeds, and other oil-bearing crops. Soybeans, oil-bearing woody plants, and wild oil-bearing crops are not included.

Output of Aquatic Products refers to catches of both artificially cultured and naturally grown aquatic products, including fish, shrimps, crabs and shellfish in sea and inland water as well as seaweed. Freshwater plants are not included. Data on output of aquatic products are reported by aquatic product and statistical agencies level by level. Before 1995, among the shellfish, oyster was counted as fresh meat; 5 kilograms of ark shell, clams and frogs are equivalent to 1 kilogram of fresh aquatic products; they have all been counted as flesh aquatic products since 1996.

Output of Pork, Beef, and Mutton refers to the meat of slaughtered hogs, cattle, sheep and goats with head, feet, and offal taken away. Data refers to the production of the whole country. The First Agricultural Census of China in 1996 revealed some discrepancy between the production of animal products from the annual reports and that from the census. Efforts were made to adjust the output value of animal husbandry to make the figures from the annual reports consistent with the census data. Since 1999, the NBS conducted sample surveys for the major animal husbandry products, such as hogs, cattle, sheep and goats and fowls, and the data from sample surveys are used as national finalized data. Those products, which are not covered by the sample survey, are still reported by statistical agencies level by level. In 2007. the data on animal husbandry from 2000 to 2006 were revised according to the results of the Second Agriculture Census of China. In 2008, A Monitoring and Survey Program was set up on main livestock, the data on the main livestock such as hog, cattle, sheep and poultry became the official data based on the sampling survey.

Number of Livestock or Poultry in Stock at Beginning (or End) of Period refers to the total number of large animals, pigs, sheep, fowls, etc. raised by rural cooperative organizations, State farms, rural individuals, government agencies, schools, industrial and mining enterprises, army, and urban residents at the beginning (or end) of the reference period.

Regularly Cultivated Land refers to farmland among the total land resources which is exclusively used for farming and is under regular cultivation with harvest in normal years. Included are currently cultivated land, land that has been abandoned or put in idle for less than 3 years and could be re-used for cultivation at any time, and new-claimed land that has been put into cultivation for more than 3 years. Excluded under this category are steep slope land over 25 degrees under temporary cultivation, land (large or small plots) that is claimed along river bends, lake sides or banks of reservoirs, as well as land that has been designated under the "Green for Grain" programmes of the state and provincial governments but is still temporarily under cultivation.

Sown Area of Crops refers to area of transplanted with crops regardless of being land sown or in cultivated area or non-cultivated area. Area of land re-sown due to lso included. This is an important indicator that can reflect the utilization condition of the cultivated land in China. At present, the sown area of crops mainly include the following 9 categories of crops: grain, cotton, oil-bearing crops, sugar crops, flax crops, tobacco, vegetables and melons, medicinal materials and other farm crops.natural disasters is also included. This is an important indicator that can reflect the utilization condition of the cultivated land in China. At present, the sown area of crops mainly include the following 9 categories of crops: grain, cotton, oil-bearing crops, sugar crops, flax crops, tobacco, vegetables and melons, medicinal materials and other farm crops.

Irrigated Area refers to area of land that are effectively irrigated, i.e. relatively level land, where there are water sources or complete sets of irrigation facilities to lift and move adequate water for irrigation purpose under normal conditions. Under normal situations, irrigated area is the sum of watered fields and irrigated fields where irrigation systems or equipment have been installed for regular irrigation purpose. This important indicator reflects drought resistance capacity of the cultivated land in China.

Consumption of Chemical Fertilizers in Agriculture refers to the quantity of chemical fertilizers applied in agriculture in the year, including nitrogenous fertilizer, phosphate fertilizer, potash fertilizer, and compound fertilizer. The consumption of chemical fertilizers is calculated in terms of volume of effective components by means of converting the gross weight of the respective fertilizers into weight containing effective component (e.g. nitrogen content in nitrogenous fertilizer, phosphorous pentoxide contents in phosphate fertilizer, and potassium oxide contents in potash fertilizer). Compound fertilizer is converted in regard to its major components. The formula is:

Volume of effective component= physical quantity × effective component of certain chemical fertilizer (%)

Total Power of Agricultural Machinery refers to total mechanical power of machinery used in agriculture, forestry, animal husbandry and fishery, including machinery for ploughing, irrigation and drainage, harvesting, transport, plant protection, animal husbandry, forestry and fishery and other agricultural machineries. (For the power of internal combustion engines, it is converted from its horsepower into watts while for electric motors the output power is converted into watts.) Machinery employed for non-agricultural purposes, such as the machines used in township-run and village-run industry, construction, non-agricultural transport, scientific experiments and teaching, are not included. Data are mainly from agricultural machinery agencies.

12 工　业

INDUSTRY

资料整理：赵　晖　王凤玲　程雅莉　陈小兵　李　玫　沈佳慧　王　玥
Data management：Zhao Hui Wang Fengling Cheng Yali Chen Xiaobing Li Mei Shen Jiahui Wang Yue
数据审核：丁抗玲
Data audit：Ding Kangling

第十二部分　工业

一、简要说明

本章资料包括规模以上工业企业单位数、总产值、主要经济指标等，由西安市统计局工业处提供。按照国家统计局统一核算的要求，自今年起取消“规模以上工业企业分行业增加值表”。

二、主要指标

规模以上工业企业单位数（个）	1403	比上年增长	15.0%
规模以上工业增加值（亿元）	1579.88	比上年增长	5.8%

12 INDUSTRY

Ⅰ.Brief Introduction

Data in this chapter includes number of industrial enterprises above designated size and gross product, primary economic. Data in this chapter are provided and compiled by Industry Division of the Xi'an Bureau of Statistics.

Ⅱ.Major Indicators

Number of Industrial Enterprises Gross Output Above Designated Size(item)	1403	15.0%
Value Added of Industry Above Designated Size (100 million yuan)	1579.88	5.8%

12-1 主要年份全部工业总产值

Gross Output Value of Industry in Representative Years

单位：万元 (10 000 yuan)

年份 Year	全部工业总产值 Gross Industrial Output Value	工业总产值指数（上年=100） Index of Gross Industry Output Value (Preceding Year=100)	国有经济 State-owned Enterprises	集体经济 Collective-owned Enterprises	其他经济类型 Enterprises of Other Ownership
1952	23512	139.6	9917	464	13131
1962	120833	86.8	102103	17599	1131
1965	200416	132.1	183164	17252	
1970	333386	143.5	305303	28083	
1975	385509	106.1	332982	52527	
1978	483262	116.9	405376	77886	
1979	517483	106.6	438850	78633	
1980	531755	101.8	440139	91577	39
1985	853196	120.4	632702	218893	1601
1986	976326	112.1	706380	267282	2664
1987	1142228	114.2	809186	328701	4341
1988	1429811	116.0	1012268	416217	1326
1989	1653472	106.1	1160877	486754	5814
1990	1771310	107.4	1196777	548605	25928
1991	2002727	110.0	1325242	604495	72990
1992	2300472	112.5	1488541	561369	250562
1993	3045988	121.7	1748145	1071122	226721
1994	3891584	120.6	1960533	1581321	349730
1995	4058952	108.7	2071755	1663536	323661
1996	5338510	133.4	2132140	2836176	370194
1997	5794532	121.8	1915536	2005610	1873386
1998	6738224	117.3	2593405	2077273	2067546
1999	7151528	117.1	2128243	2174220	2849065
2000	6394812	115.3	2749778	2094680	1550354
2001	7361510	116.4	3098431	2380910	1882169
2002	8379363	115.8	3472067	2312923	2594373
2003	9750800	115.1	4149015	1501372	4100413
2004	11853224	118.4	5414952	875412	5562860
2005	13085580	106.3	5916553	674900	6494127
2006	15573516	119.0	7527607	514810	7531099
2007	19798593	122.1	10179303	365329	9253961
2008	23881446	120.6	12479652	441987	10959807
2009	28270652	118.3	14440321	388777	13441554
2010	35628752	126.0	18353877	435206	16839669
2011	40933178	114.9	20654524	377199	19901455
2012	46560824	113.8	24303736	376427	21880661
2013	50426416	108.3	25358096	325004	24743316
2014	56606273	112.3	27352693	332712	28920867
2015	51599121	91.2	25008248	161009	26429864
2016	54624261	105.9	24498532	139018	29986711
2017	62853398	115.1	28750377	200886	33902135

注：2013年数据为全国第三次经济普查数据。

12-1 续表 continued

单位：万元 (10 000 yuan)

年份 Year	轻工业 Light Industry	重工业 Heavy Industry	大型工业 Large-size Industry Enterprises	中型工业 Medium-size Industry Enterprises	小型工业 Small-size Industry Enterprises
1952	20800	2712			
1962	68221	52618			
1965	98631	101785			
1970	124467	208919			
1975	167285	218224	145262	130592	109655
1978	220480	262782	168397	121813	193052
1979	243043	274440	189877	133759	193847
1980	283475	248280	193092	130053	208610
1985	401748	451448	333820	147488	371888
1986	458270	518056	401037	150644	424645
1987	516776	625452	472958	171698	497572
1988	699593	730210	615946	210089	603776
1989	712743	940729	696368	258414	698690
1990	787857	983453	716421	279098	775791
1991	897676	1105051	888052	303151	811524
1992	967104	1333368	988049	311628	1000795
1993	1121957	1924031	1258137	384255	1403596
1994	1578875	2312709	1479613	390233	2021738
1995	1636219	2422733	1575030	371156	2112766
1996	2347887	2990623	1693985	358913	3285612
1997	2700085	3094447	1675521	274888	3844123
1998	3232681	3505543	1821556	308424	4608244
1999	3488547	3662981	1744637	337795	5069096
2000	3121419	3273393	2320973	328494	3745345
2001	3518054	3843456	2656010	368497	4337003
2002	3935764	4443599	3038828	398834	4941701
2003	4028859	5721941	2911821	2217447	4621532
2004	4211592	7641632	3595150	3237701	5020373
2005	4078417	9007163	4640325	3228553	5216702
2006	4510970	11062546	5970535	3414468	6188513
2007	7331719	12466874	8351303	4171131	7276159
2008	6010865	17870581	10472686	5005676	8403084
2009	6636464	21634188	12309192	6186395	9775065
2010	7841869	27786884	15002737	8537140	12088876
2011	8992547	31940631	20882834	6261444	13788900
2012	10218288	36342536	23896868	6243799	16420157
2013	9297919	41128497	17390620	7271086	25764710
2014	10369659	46236614	24880136	8875553	22850583
2015	10089660	41509461	26485412	8432031	16681678
2016	9774967	44849294	28603440	8074967	17945853
2017	10986026	51867372	34454909	10051995	18346494

12-2 主要年份各区县规模以上工业总产值

Gross Output Value of Industry above Designated Size in Representative Years

单位：亿元 (100 million yuan)

区 县	Region	1998	1999	2000	2001	2002	2003	2004	2005	2006	2007
合 计	**Total**	**350.38**	**366.59**	**417.97**	**482.61**	**544.78**	**638.66**	**830.06**	**981.02**	**1187.74**	**1577.05**
新城区	Xincheng	67.19	71.36	78.25	89.87	105.92	137.46	145.61	196.00	135.14	157.18
碑林区	Beilin	20.57	19.48	21.50	23.15	30.32	22.22	15.92	20.13	18.31	19.10
莲湖区	Lianhu	63.24	65.92	75.68	93.78	106.33	124.24	157.67	185.86	200.75	281.57
灞桥区	Baqiao	19.55	19.95	21.35	20.56	22.99	28.80	37.25	42.29	57.11	80.01
未央区	Weiyang	53.31	52.84	61.41	73.63	80.14	93.23	145.63	170.16	220.08	265.93
雁塔区	Yanta	65.00	75.88	94.38	102.58	107.75	113.99	151.61	144.51	167.58	204.70
阎良区	Yanliang	26.54	26.06	27.56	36.22	40.04	40.98	55.86	68.10	75.84	95.29
临潼区	Lintong	8.90	7.55	7.64	9.36	14.14	34.67	53.49	66.91	85.96	114.09
长安区	Chang'an	7.92	7.70	8.70	8.42	9.96	10.81	19.40	26.43	67.19	101.61
高陵区	Gaoling	1.60	1.83	2.58	3.28	3.97	7.09	14.89	16.50	97.94	177.65
鄠邑区	Huyi	12.75	13.24	13.07	15.27	16.58	18.74	24.48	35.28	49.55	61.28
蓝田县	Lantian	2.58	2.37	3.81	4.76	5.12	5.00	5.34	5.69	8.35	13.13
周至县	Zhouzhi	1.24	2.41	2.05	1.73	1.51	1.45	2.92	3.16	3.94	5.52

12-2 续表 continued

单位：亿元 (100 million yuan)

区 县	Region	2008	2009	2010	2011	2012	2013	2014	2015	2016	2017
合 计	**Total**	**2007.85**	**2468.27**	**3130.15**	**3552.21**	**4066.31**	**4436.58**	**4961.12**	**4924.57**	**5266.25**	**6018.79**
新城区	Xincheng	147.54	195.45	272.13	323.64	307.67	344.30	372.75	398.68	401.62	394.86
碑林区	Beilin	48.99	58.60	108.14	138.72	18.46	23.48	27.66	29.59	31.91	31.15
莲湖区	Lianhu	356.90	399.83	458.30	457.96	459.41	419.81	407.16	402.62	405.48	471.67
灞桥区	Baqiao	123.34	178.82	242.15	280.52	278.37	308.04	300.73	175.89	181.17	137.52
未央区	Weiyang	327.65	393.22	499.88	510.39	684.55	733.75	858.40	839.29	959.84	1014.93
雁塔区	Yanta	262.32	249.69	286.19	367.97	587.65	624.55	694.34	677.00	648.80	721.42
阎良区	Yanliang	109.43	128.99	163.55	176.67	219.31	276.71	300.25	321.23	342.53	316.66
临潼区	Lintong	130.93	165.77	222.01	277.75	341.01	404.45	418.75	263.29	204.22	181.43
长安区	Chang'an	154.74	277.98	334.89	350.68	354.65	383.41	346.35	720.87	956.32	1001.19
高陵区	Gaoling	256.55	305.94	402.98	516.33	662.99	741.34	854.73	869.60	835.74	939.03
鄠邑区	Huyi	65.09	81.54	96.89	100.42	93.55	101.40	104.68	135.94	189.31	359.94
蓝田县	Lantian	17.62	23.40	31.93	35.87	41.60	49.33	46.22	49.32	55.47	74.43
周至县	Zhouzhi	6.76	9.03	11.11	15.29	17.08	26.01	29.10	41.25	53.84	65.64

12-3 各区县规模以上工业企业工业总产值（2017年）

单位：亿元

区县	Regin	单位数（个）Number of Enterprises (unit)	工业总产值 Gross Industrial Output Value	国有经济 State-owned Enterprises	集体经济 Collective-owned Enterprises	其他经济类型 Enterprises of Other Ownership
新城区	Xincheng	12	394.86	238.33		156.53
碑林区	Beilin	14	31.15			31.15
莲湖区	Lianhu	30	471.67	214.88		256.79
灞桥区	Baqiao	85	137.52	0.35	7.83	129.34
未央区	Weiyang	193	1014.93	1.06	0.43	1013.44
雁塔区	Yanta	223	721.42	149.13		572.29
阎良区	Yanliang	106	316.66	5.47	4.12	307.07
临潼区	Lintong	72	181.43	2.49		178.94
长安区	Chang'an	143	1001.19	21.77		979.42
高陵区	Gaoling	157	939.03	7.20		931.83
鄠邑区	Huyi	100	359.94	10.12	0.72	349.10
蓝田县	Lantian	44	74.43	1.72		72.71
周至县	Zhouzhi	53	65.64		0.90	64.74

Gross Output Value of Industrial Enterprises above Designated Size by Region（2017）

（100 million yuan）

轻工业 Light Industry	重工业 Heavy Industry	大型工业 Large-size Industry Enterprises	中型工业 Medium-size Industry Enterprises	小型工业 Small-size Industry Enterprises
96.00	298.86	327.34	16.55	50.97
13.53	17.62	9.15	13.97	8.03
45.36	426.31	440.87	20.86	9.94
44.87	92.65	29.70	44.85	62.97
276.10	738.83	358.68	191.12	465.13
88.78	632.64	347.14	195.59	178.69
46.70	269.96	177.47	22.22	116.97
70.43	111.00	65.02	42.75	73.66
54.45	946.74	798.17	99.23	103.79
61.69	877.34	491.41	173.37	274.25
60.50	299.44	160.82	15.06	184.06
34.31	40.12	9.55	6.05	58.83
41.68	23.96		8.81	56.83

12-4 主要年份规模以上工业企业主要经济指标

单位：亿元

年份 Year	企业单位数 （个） Number of Enterprises (unit)	工业总产值 （当年价格） Gross Industrial Output Value (At Current Prices)	从业人员年平均人数 （万人） Annual Average Employers (10 000person)
1998	793	350.38	51.71
1999	770	366.59	45.64
2000	816	417.97	43.25
2001	785	482.61	40.12
2002	771	544.78	38.48
2003	735	638.66	36.55
2004	1066	830.06	38.08
2005	902	981.02	37.92
2006	904	1187.74	37.94
2007	937	1577.05	38.55
2008	1032	2007.85	40.17
2009	1131	2468.27	43.42
2010	1126	3130.15	47.11
2011	891	3552.21	50.42
2012	970	4066.31	49.23
2013	1056	4436.57	44.27
2014	1146	4961.12	49.53
2015	1150	4924.57	50.59
2016	1220	5266.25	49.54
2017	1403	6018.79	51.11

注：2013年数据为全国第三次经济普查数据。

Major Economic Indicators of Industrial Enterprises above Designated Size in Representative Years

(100 million yuan)

资产总计 Total Assets	负债合计 Total Liabilites	所有者权益合计 Total Owners' Equities	主营业务收入 Revenue from Principal Business	利润总额 Total Profits	利税总额 Total Pre-tax Profits
810.56	548.68	261.88	346.84	-1.26	14.82
853.90	577.94	275.96	346.26	8.26	27.30
958.05	622.46	323.72	420.42	16.11	36.29
1054.36	657.88	384.65	451.62	17.97	40.84
1065.76	643.78	412.27	541.64	25.43	51.31
1195.69	733.04	460.97	645.53	33.82	64.99
1333.91	869.30	464.60	812.46	38.57	74.23
1503.85	977.42	508.82	980.97	28.72	67.25
1651.67	1062.11	578.33	1183.51	61.46	110.23
1940.52	1254.01	686.51	1561.25	106.22	168.54
2426.13	1518.86	907.27	1928.05	84.89	168.63
2913.56	1779.38	1130.76	2384.52	177.20	280.68
3592.13	2069.29	1515.65	3011.19	245.37	373.56
3975.38	2295.49	1678.19	3381.27	172.94	312.78
4775.92	2835.55	1926.72	3758.56	167.77	320.57
5127.69	3049.36	2071.72	4171.21	211.26	392.14
6048.34	3607.62	2436.06	4566.20	226.17	401.20
6740.26	3860.55	2926.55	4374.11	206.88	341.40
7473.07	4158.75	3302.36	5028.28	290.96	438.59
7862.59	4162.97	3595.73	5710.70	367.77	532.35

12-5 各区县规模以上工业企业主要经济指标（2017年）

单位：亿元

区县	Region	企业单位数（个）Number of Enterprises (unit)	从业人员年平均人数（万人）Annual Average Employers (10 000 persons)	资产合计（亿元）Total Assets (100 mill yuan)
新城区	Xingcheng	12	3.13	442.03
碑林区	Beilin	14	0.52	89.44
莲湖区	Lianhu	30	5.28	863.71
灞桥区	Baqiao	85	2.14	201.04
未央区	Weiyang	193	6.22	936.10
雁塔区	Yanta	223	8.04	1370.60
阎良区	Yanliang	106	3.54	433.98
临潼区	Lintong	72	1.61	321.63
长安区	Chang'an	143	6.16	1398.93
高陵区	Gaoling	157	4.25	756.88
鄠邑区	Huyi	100	4.26	416.62
蓝田县	Lantian	44	0.60	79.16
周至县	Zhouzhi	53	0.37	45.80

Major Economic Indicators of Industrial Enterprises above Designated Size by Region (2017)

(100 million yuan)

负债合计 Total Liabilites	所有者权益合计 Total Owners' Equities	主营业务收入 Revenue from Principal Business	利润总额 Total Profits	利税总额 Total Pre-tax Profits
291.44	150.59	348.73	11.51	31.84
60.38	29.06	37.85	7.44	10.50
357.89	484.15	427.51	34.34	55.88
128.27	72.77	122.10	4.20	8.22
463.97	470.79	996.94	59.25	86.22
631.33	665.64	703.38	37.71	57.74
289.73	144.02	319.86	6.28	9.99
167.79	153.31	160.93	8.09	13.91
571.68	827.08	897.41	146.59	157.86
522.28	231.43	918.07	31.95	54.58
281.17	135.46	341.39	3.33	13.66
43.48	35.68	70.10	4.34	5.41
20.01	25.80	50.16	3.87	5.18

12-6 规模以上工业企业主要工业产品产量（2017年）

Major Output of Industrial Enterprises above Designated Size (2017)

产品名称	Name of Products	2017	比上年增长(%) Increase over Preceding Year (%)
自来水生产量(亿立方米)	Tap Water Production (100 million cu.m)	4.85	7.3
大米(万吨)	Rice (10 000 ton)	3.46	9.6
小麦粉(万吨)	Wheat Flour (10 000 ton)	104.98	-4.5
精制食用植物油(万吨)	Edible Vegetable Oil (10 000 ton)	24.56	34.0
鲜、冷藏肉（万吨）	Fresh/Frozen Meat(10 000 ton)	4.80	-0.8
饲料（万吨）	Mixed Feed(10 000 ton)	104.50	-4.5
配合饲料	Compound feed	17.25	56.1
混合饲料	Mixed feed	87.15	-11.1
方便面(万吨)	instant Noodle(10 000 ton)	12.65	11.9
乳制品(万吨)	Dairy Products (10 000 ton)	96.22	-1.8
液体乳	Milk	83.54	-3.7
固体及半固体乳制品	Solid and semi-solid dairy products	12.69	12.2
饮料酒(万千升)	Beverage Wine (10 000 kiloliter)	49.70	-10.4
白酒（折65度，商品量）	Liquor (as 65 degree, amount of goods)	0.06	-73.0
啤酒	Beer	49.07	-0.7
葡萄酒	Wine	0.58	-90.1
软饮料(万吨)	Soft Beverage (10 000 ton)	191.11	-9.7
碳酸饮料类（汽水）	Carbonated Beverage	33.92	-19.5
果汁和蔬菜汁饮料	Juice and Fruit Beverage	57.96	-8.9
包装饮用水类	Canned Drinking Water	35.78	3.7
纱(万吨)	Yarn (10 000 ton)	4.74	-23.8
1. 棉纱	Cotton Yarn	3.01	-28.7
2. 棉混纺纱	Blend Fabric	0.56	4.8
3. 化学纤维纱	Pure Chemical-Fibre Yarn	1.17	-20.2
布(亿米)	Cloth (100 million m)	1.27	3.8

12-6 续表1 continued1

产品名称	Name of Products	2017	比上年增长(%) Increase over Preceding Year (%)
1. 棉布	Cotton Cloth	0.46	18.1
2. 棉混纺布	Blend Fabric	0.29	21.4
3. 化学纤维布	Pure Chemical-Fibre Cloth	0.52	-12.6
人造板（万立方米）	Artificial Board (10 000 cu.m)	50.64	8.2
纤维板	Fibre Board	50.64	8.2
家具（万件）	Furniture (10 000unit)	35.99	15.0
木质家具	Wooden Furniture	16.46	22.9
金属家具	Metal furniture	4.59	13.4
软体家具	Soft Furniture (inc.: Sofa ,Mattress etc.)	6.00	-13.4
机制纸及纸板（外购原纸加工除外）（万吨）	Machine Made Paper(not including processing of procured base paper)(10 000 ton)	18.62	-8.0
纸制品（万吨）	Paper-Made Products (10 000 ton)	11.99	-8.7
瓦楞纸箱	Corrugated Paper	9.55	6.5
单色印刷（万令）	Monochrom Printed products(10 000 ream)	58.17	6.2
多色印刷品（万对开色令）	Colored Printed products(10 000 ream)	842.20	19.3
化学农药原药(折有效成分100%)(万吨)	Chemical Pesticide(100% effective content)(10 000 ton)	0.39	-5.1
涂料（万吨）	Construction Paint(10 000 ton)	1.77	-18.1
合成洗涤剂（万吨）	Synthetic Detergents (10 000 ton)	5.52	-15.6
合成洗衣粉（万吨）	Washing Power	1.14	-26.4
液体洗涤剂	Liquid detergent	3.52	-6.6
化学原料药（万吨）	Chemical Medicine (10 000 ton)	0.02	7.1
中成药（万吨）	Traditional Chinese Medicine (10 000 ton)	0.68	4.2
化学纤维（万吨）	Chemical Fiber	1.39	-31.3
人造纤维（纤维素纤维）（万吨）	Man-made Fiber	1.39	-31.3
塑料制品（万吨）	Plastic Product (10 000 ton)	14.25	4.6

12-6 续表2 continued2

产品名称	Name of Products	2017	比上年增长(%) Increase over Preceding Year (%)
水泥（万吨）	Cement (10 000 ton)	216.95	-0.3
硅酸盐水泥熟料（万吨）	Portland Cement Clinker (10 000 ton)	80.55	-4.8
水泥混凝土电杆（万根）	Cement Pole(10 000 unit)	2.72	14.3
商品混凝土(万立方米)	Ready-mixed Concrete (10 000 cu.m)	2359.12	-29.7
沥青和改性沥青防水卷材（万平方米）	Asphalt and Modified Bitumen Membrane(10 000 sq.m)	2636.23	-5.3
钢化玻璃(万平方米)	Toughened Glass(10 000 sq.m)	449.30	32.2
日用玻璃制品（万吨）	Glassware(10 000 ton)	1.29	341.5
钢材（万吨）	Rolled-steel Final Products (10 000 ton)	54.91	-4.9
线材（盘条）	Wire Rod	8.66	-34.4
其他钢材	Other steel	44.51	45.8
铝材(万吨)	Aluminum Material (10 000 ton)	3.97	-0.2
黄金（千克）	Gold (kg)	31.00	-90.5
单晶硅（万千克）	Monocrystalline Silicon (10 000kg)	1629.53	93.3
工业锅炉（蒸发量吨）	industrial Boiler steam(ton)	2646.60	13.4
发动机（万千瓦）	Engine (10 000 kw)	339.93	72.1
汽车发动机（万千瓦）	Motor Engine(10 000 kw)	339.93	72.1
金属切削机床(万台)	Metal-cutting Machines (10 000 unit)	0.73	66.7
泵(万台)	Pump (Liquid pump)(10 000 unit)	1.31	-92.3
风机（万台）	Fan(10 000 unit)	0.84	6.0
气体压缩机（万台）	Gas Compressor(10 000 unit)	31.11	9.5
阀门（万吨）	Valves (10 000 ton)	0.22	-83.1
铸铁件（万吨）	iron Castings (10 000 ton)	1.18	6.0
铸钢件（万吨）	Steel Castings (10 000 ton)	1.56	-65.6
锻件（万吨）	Forgings (10 000 ton)	0.08	-77.3
矿山专用设备（万吨）	Mining Equipment (10 000 ton)	5.97	108.0

12-6 续表3 continued3

产品名称	Name of Products	2017	比上年增长(%) Increase over Preceding Year (%)
炼油、化工生产专用设备（万吨）	Oil Refining and Chemical industry Machine(10 000 ton)	6012.00	54.0
金属冶炼设备（吨）	Metal Smelting Equipments(ton)	4004.10	59.6
金属轧制设备（吨）	Metal-rolling Machine(ton)	1897.10	-33.7
印刷专用设备（吨）	Printing Equipment(ton)	116.00	-4.1
环境污染防治设备(台/套)	Special Equipment for Environment Protection	147.00	-2.6
大气污染防治设备	Equipment for Preventing Atmospheric Pollution	147.00	2.1
汽车（万辆）	Motor Vehicle(10 000unit)	44.52	16.4
基本型乘用车（轿车）	Basic Type Passenger Vehicles(car)	18.14	-7.4
轿车（排量≤1升）	Car0L-1.0L Gas Displacement(1.0L included)	2.19	3.5
轿车（1升＜排量≤1.6升）	Car1.0L-1.6L Gas Displacement(1.6L included)	15.95	-8.7
运动型多用途乘用车（SUV）	Sports Utility Vehicle (SUV)	7.36	7.7
客车	Passenger Vehicles	0.11	-51.5
大型客车（车长>10米）	Large Buses （Length>10m）		
中型客车（7米＜车长≤10米）	Medium Bus 7m-10m Length	0.02	-68.5
轻型客车（车长≤7米）	Light Buses（Length≤7m）	0.09	13.5
载货汽车	Trucks	18.92	63.0
新能源汽车	New Energy Vehicles (10000 unit)	8.15	67.7
改装汽车（万辆）	Refit Trucks (10 000 unit)	0.11	-18.1
铁路货车（万辆）	Freight(10 000 unit)	0.35	167.6
电动机（万千瓦）	Electric motor(Ten thousand kilowatts)	224.00	-35.3
直流电动机	DC motors	18.43	-30.1
交流电动机	Alternating Current Motor(10 000kw)	196.31	-38.3
变压器（万千伏安）	Transformer(10 000KVA)	14204.85	5.4
高压开关板（万面）	High-voltage Switch Panel(10 000 unit)	0.67	-17.1
低压开关板（万面）	Low-voltage Switch Panel(10 000 unit)	0.95	-5.9

12-6 续表4 continued 4

产品名称	Name of Products	2017	比上年增长(%) Increase over Preceding Year (%)
电力电缆(万千米)	Electric Power Cables(10 000 km)	12.88	268.3
通信及电子网络用电缆(万对千米)	Communication Cables(10 000 pair km)	4.07	-10.9
光缆（万芯千米）	Cable (10 000 Core.km)	586.35	16.8
绝缘制品(吨)	Insulating Products(ton)	15159.00	2.0
电子元件（亿只）	Electronic Components(100 million unit)	4.44	-25.8
工业自动化调节仪表与控制系统（万台、套）	Automatization meter and system (10 000 unit)	3.27	13.6
分析仪器及装置（万台、套）	Analysis instruments and Apparatus(10 000 set)	2.36	21.6
化学试剂（万吨）	Chemicals Reagents(10000 ton)	34.62	24.8
十种有色金属（万吨）	Ten kinds of nonferrous metals (10 000ton)	16.13	34.8
锌	Zinc	12.99	42.7
镍	Nickel	3.15	9.7
起重机（吨）	Crane (ton)	298.00	-19.0
减速机（台）	Reducer (a)	9915.00	107.2
模具（万套）	Molds (10 000set)	1.63	-74.8
电动自行车（万辆）	Electric bicycle (10 000car)	74.07	6.6
电力电容器（万千乏）	Power capacitors (10 000kW)	3401.41	5.3
高压开关设备（11万伏以上）（万台）	High Voltage Switchgear (above 110,000 volt) (10 000a)	2.07	-6.3
灯具及照明装置（万套/台/个）	Lamps and lighting equipment (10 000set /a)	1.38	-52.2
半导体分立器件（亿只）	Discrete semiconductor devices (100million unit)	461.82	-6.5
光电子器件（亿只/片）	Optoelectronic devices (100million unit)	22.60	13.4
工业仪表（万台/个）	Industrial Instrumentation (10 000a)	14.30	24.0
环境监测专用仪器仪表（台）	Special equipment for prevention and control of environmental pollution(unit)	30750.00	-23.7
发电量（亿千瓦小时）	Power generation(One hundred million kilowatt-hours)	176.74	-3.9
火力发电量（亿千瓦小时）	Thermal power generation(One hundred million kilowatt-hours	175.81	-4.0
水力发电量（亿千瓦小时）	Hydropower(One hundred million kilowatt-hours)	0.93	14.0
风力发电量（亿千瓦小时）	Wind power generation(One hundred million kilowatt-hours)		

12-7 主要年份规模以上工业企业经济效益指标

Indicators of Economic Performance of Industrial Enterprises above Designated Size in Representative Years

年 份 Year	总资产贡献率 (%) Ratio of Total Assets to Industrial Output Value (%)	资产负债率 (%) Assets-Liability Ratio (%)	流动资产周转次数 (次/年) Rate of Annual Turnover Working Capitals (times/year)	成本费用利润率 (%) Ratio of Profits to Cost (%)	全员劳动生产率 (元/人・年) Overall Labor Productivity (yuan/person・year)	产品销售率 (%) Proportion of Industrial Products Sold (%)
1998		67.7	0.9	-266.1	19185	95.3
1999		67.7	0.9	2.5	22878	95.9
2000		65.0	1.0	4.2	29496	97.1
2001	5.8	62.4	0.9	4.1	38267	96.7
2002	6.2	60.4	1.1	5.1	46940	96.7
2003	7.0	61.3	1.1	5.7	58801	96.3
2004	6.9	65.2	1.2	5.0	66752	97.9
2005	8.4	65.0	1.3	3.1	82815	97.5
2006	7.8	64.3	1.4	5.5	97561	98.2
2007	10.2	64.6	1.6	7.3	129706	96.8
2008	8.6	62.6	1.5	4.6	150641	96.1
2009	11.3	61.1	1.7	8.1	161289	97.6
2010	12.2	57.6	1.7	8.8	188483	97.1
2011	8.6	57.7	1.5	5.2	194105	97.4
2012	7.7	59.4	1.5	4.5	230032	96.7
2013	8.5	59.5	1.5	5.2	264324	95.7
2014	7.4	59.7	1.4	5.2	266789	94.9
2015	5.7	57.3	1.3	4.8	268182	94.5
2016	6.4	55.7	1.3	6.0	277240	96.0
2017	7.2	53.0	1.4	6.6	294393	97.3

12-8 规模以上工业企业主要经济指标（2017年）

单位：万元

分　组	Classify	企业单位数（个） Number of Enterprises (unit)	亏损企业 Loss Making Enterprises	工业总产值（当年价格） Gross Industrial Output Value (At Current Prices)
总计	**Total**	**1403**	**259**	**60187926**
#市区	Urban	1306	252	58787252
#亏损企业	Deficit Enterprises	259	259	8479425
按隶属关系分	**Grouped by Jurisdiction of Management**			
中央企业	Central Enterprises	93	16	12728378
省属企业	Provincial Enterprises	79	22	10835940
市属企业	Municipal Enterprises	1231	221	36623608
按登记注册类型分组	**Grouped by Registion Status**			
内资企业	Domestic Investment Enterprises	1288	233	49701826
国有	State-owned Enterprises	30	6	6550063
集体	Collective-owned Enterprises	7		139955
股份合作	Share-holding Corperative	5		18308
联营	Joint Ownership Enterprises			
国有联营	State Joint Ownership Enterprises			
集体联营	Collective Joint Ownership Enterprises			
国有与集体联营	Joint State-collective Ownership Enterprises			
其他联营	Other Joint Ownership Enterprises			
有限责任公司	Limited Liability Corporations	641	124	29733698
国有独资公司	State Sole Funded Enterprises	50	11	4394661
其他有限责任公司	Other Limited Liability Corporation	591	113	25339038
股份有限公司	Share-holding Corperation Ltd.	114	21	5709311
私营	Private Enterprises	488	81	7542537
私营独资	Private-funded Enterprises	5	1	39858
私营合伙	Private Partnership Enterprises	1		2909
私营有限责任公司	Private Limited Liability Corporations	449	77	7008813
私营股份有限公司	Private Share Holding Corporations	33	3	490957
其他	Other Domestic Funded Enterprises	3	1	7954
港澳台商投资	Enterprises with Funds from Hong Kong,Macao and Taiwan	26	6	3056448
外商投资	Foreign Funded Enterprises	89	20	7429652
按轻重工业分	**Grouped by Light Industry and Heavy Industry**			
轻工业	Light Industry	368	64	9802142
重工业	Heavy Industry	1035	195	50385784

Major Economic Indicators of Industrial Enterprises above Designated Size (2017)

(10 000yuan)

工业销售产值（当年价）Value of Industry Products Sales (At Current Prices)	出口交货值 Export Delivery Value	从业人员年平均人数（人）Annual Average Employers (person)	资产总计 Total Assets	流动资产合计 Total Working Capitals	固定资产合计 Total Fixed Assets	固定资产原价 Origing Value of Fixed Assets	累计折旧 Accumulative Total Depreciation
58536811	**5805239**	**511119**	**78625859**	**42457756**	**22170355**	**38769916**	**18227028**
57213558	5763220	500695	77376212	41811103	21784631	38124051	17950010
8260018	380959	107740	15615663	7264114	3835390	5997919	2338905
12354437	588415	162321	23279174	12298228	7357913	12406424	5920250
10606463	411710	71209	13675644	7525593	2840817	4580477	1980959
35575911	4805114	277589	41671041	22633936	11971626	21783015	10325819
48321803	2143533	436853	65176028	36787563	15960479	27763957	13017999
6374846	271613	88512	12374359	6539447	4772322	7231250	3305634
141473		1342	99771	38007	32430	80203	23998
16741		455	28220	20754	4067	10879	6350
29259917	1200563	251365	35429466	21525115	7440808	13953743	6735563
4242301	105042	50696	9299638	5283147	1776885	3619349	1708842
25017616	1095521	200669	26129829	16241968	5663924	10334394	5026721
5435827	556226	38933	10668068	4927589	2379415	4595224	2331162
7087047	115132	56085	6573920	3735583	1330283	1891325	615116
39432		363	9156	5058	3998	6210	2367
2903		93	1394	926	468	1189	722
6617606	113377	51442	5189480	3329078	1252948	1785387	590022
427106	1755	4187	1373890	400520	72869	98539	22005
5952		161	2224	1070	1154	1335	176
3059042	190340	31706	2499891	1156785	811187	1223616	445596
7155966	3471366	42560	10949939	4513408	5398690	9782343	4763433
9391294	249462	86080	8830253	4812927	2728341	4437680	2140801
49145517	5555776	425039	69795606	37644829	19442014	34332236	16086227

12-8 续表1

单位：万元

分组	Classify	负债合计 Total Liabilites	流动负债合计 Total Working Liabilities	非流动负债 Non-Working Liabilities
总计	**Total**	**41629661**	**33560492**	**6876440**
#市区	Urban	40994794	33101463	6758364
#亏损企业	Deficit Enterprises	10917072	8754550	1816781
按隶属关系分	**Grouped by Jurisdiction of Management**			
中央企业	Central Enterprises	12334563	10113026	2386978
省属企业	Provincial Enterprises	8040731	6939164	867086
市属企业	Municipal Enterprises	21254368	16508302	3622376
按登记注册类型分组	**Grouped by Registion Status**			
内资企业	Domestic Investment Enterprises	35660320	29213226	5351078
国有	State-owned Enterprises	6528837	5459772	1445722
集体	Collective-owned Enterprises	42601	41767	734
股份合作	Share-holding Corperative	12282	10516	1759
联营	Joint Ownership Enterprises			
国有联营	State Joint Ownership Enterprises			
集体联营	Collective Joint Ownership Enterprises			
国有与集体联营	Joint State-collective Ownership Enterprises			
其他联营	Other Joint Ownership Enterprises			
有限责任公司	Limited Liability Corporations	21469678	17940219	2695119
国有独资公司	State Sole Funded Enterprises	4976922	4025006	905690
其他有限责任公司	Other Limited Liability Corporation	16492756	13915213	1789429
股份有限公司	Share-holding Corperation Ltd.	4233584	3149302	867751
私营	Private Enterprises	3372538	2610850	339992
私营独资	Private-funded Enterprises	6029	2378	
私营合伙	Private Partnership Enterprises	763	743	20
私营有限责任公司	Private Limited Liability Corporations	2943359	2508442	317189
私营股份有限公司	Private Share Holding Corporations	422387	99288	22783
其他	Other Domestic Funded Enterprises	801	801	
港澳台商投资	Enterprises with Funds from Hong Kong,Macao and Taiwan	1617854	1300693	317132
外商投资	Foreign Funded Enterprises	4351487	3046574	1208230
按轻重工业分	**Grouped by Light Industry and Heavy Industry**			
轻工业	Light Industry	4885670	4000732	768163
重工业	Heavy Industry	36743991	29559761	6108278

continued1

(10 000yuan)

所有者权益合计 Total Owners' Equities	实收资本 Total Capital Hold	营业收入 Total Revenue	主营业务收入 Revenue from Principal Business	营业成本 Total Cost	主营业务成本 Cost of Principal Business	税金及附加 Taxs and Other Changes	主营业务税金及附加 Taxes and Other Charges on Principal Business
35957256	**15819067**	**58268099**	**57107043**	**49868813**	**48858367**	**374547**	**359915**
35342477	15534241	57062127	55904445	48860767	47854156	369029	354715
3935067	3219962	8519870	8272687	7849837	7624263	89968	89178
10690816	4510429	12923444	12580951	11095480	10866987	82554	78735
5637220	2518862	10996266	10665483	9686733	9375157	52013	50632
19629220	8789777	34348389	33860609	29086600	28616222	239980	230549
28496351	11677092	47921479	46996900	41214391	40399970	266790	252940
5606233	1769645	6537706	6324095	5462568	5339830	50382	47032
57170	9252	144278	99910	128030	89749	1105	1105
15938	9311	16687	15848	12543	12213	117	117
13933487	6892139	29159000	28564761	25668340	25152826	143063	136887
4322716	1577921	4358688	4226025	3637627	3525402	34611	30850
9610771	5314219	24800313	24338736	22030713	21627424	108451	106037
6426264	1887673	5097219	5062930	4039429	4018888	31124	30733
2455836	1106333	6955907	6924739	5893752	5782694	40913	37001
3127	1706	39465	39465	35478	35478	79	79
632	402	2693	2693	2182	2182	18	18
2233241	994192	6401612	6373954	5456730	5347486	38430	34616
218836	110033	512137	508626	399363	397548	2385	2288
1423	2739	10683	4619	9728	3771	87	67
882037	318483	3035820	2916675	2779524	2670930	57144	56552
6578868	3823492	7310800	7193468	5874898	5787467	50613	50423
3916075	1760903	9125892	8994892	7028616	6874757	79987	74284
32041181	14058165	49142207	48112151	42840198	41983610	294560	285631

12-8 续表2

单位：万元

分组	Classify	销售费用 Expenses for Sales	管理费用 Expenses for Management	财务费用 Financial cost
总计	**Total**	**2016852**	**3068312**	**408654**
#市区	Urban	1980055	2992858	401705
#亏损企业	Deficit Enterprises	289967	490383	138483
按隶属关系分	**Grouped by Jurisdiction of Management**			
中央企业	Central Enterprises	256296	900715	112601
省属企业	Provincial Enterprises	450042	398844	34987
市属企业	Municipal Enterprises	1310515	1768752	261066
按登记注册类型分组	**Grouped by Registion Status**			
内资企业	Domestic Investment Enterprises	1543678	2485348	304581
国有	State-owned Enterprises	175363	512571	51735
集体	Collective-owned Enterprises	3596	8173	91
股份合作	Share-holding Corperative	349	1876	327
联营	Joint Ownership Enterprises			
国有联营	State Joint Ownership Enterprises			
集体联营	Collective Joint Ownership Enterprises			
国有与集体联营	Joint State-collective Ownership Enterprises			
其他联营	Other Joint Ownership Enterprises			
有限责任公司	Limited Liability Corporations	872449	1336717	137825
国有独资公司	State Sole Funded Enterprises	120010	377999	20014
其他有限责任公司	Other Limited Liability Corporation	752439	958718	117811
股份有限公司	Share-holding Corperation Ltd.	212066	302835	66620
私营	Private Enterprises	279855	322765	47850
私营独资	Private-funded Enterprises	2010	1289	197
私营合伙	Private Partnership Enterprises	164	195	3
私营有限责任公司	Private Limited Liability Corporations	255005	283686	41396
私营股份有限公司	Private Share Holding Corporations	22676	37595	6255
其他	Other Domestic Funded Enterprises		411	132
港澳台商投资	Enterprises with Funds from Hong Kong,Macao and Taiwan	77434	95650	22995
外商投资	Foreign Funded Enterprises	395740	487313	81079
按轻重工业分	**Grouped by Light Industry and Heavy Industry**			
轻工业	Light Industry	964324	556407	79576
重工业	Heavy Industry	1052528	2511905	329078

continued2

(10 000yuan)

营业利润 Operating Profit	利润总额 Total Profits	亏损企业亏损额 Total Loss of Deficit Enterprises	利税总额 Total Pre-tax Profits	应付职工薪酬 Salary Payable	本年应交增值税 Value Added Tax Payable
3257515	**3677674**	**340185**	**5323543**	**4629768**	**1271323**
3183360	3595541	337133	5217623	4555158	1253054
-374159	-340185	340185	-144409	927621	105808
571283	616786	80957	996408	1900344	297068
321283	343406	39877	670149	648090	274731
2364949	2717482	219352	3656986	2081334	699524
2300432	2493720	252890	3832430	3930826	1071920
323427	351124	12780	600364	768037	198858
1656	2803		5792	8470	1885
1558	1707		2736	1515	912
1089139	1203031	191542	1970630	2427994	624537
272673	300933	61590	488890	643765	153346
816466	902098	129952	1481740	1784229	471191
491604	527856	28237	680612	429001	121632
393011	407163	20093	571717	295550	123641
412	412	31	863	1159	371
132	132		272	340	122
348249	360137	17884	509641	273878	111074
44218	46483	2177	60942	20174	12075
37	37	239	578	260	455
3731	8142	28139	81415	261949	16129
953351	1175812	59156	1409699	436993	183274
482181	536683	72691	971911	675281	355241
2775334	3140991	267495	4351632	3954487	916082

12-8 续表3

单位：万元

分 组	Classify	企业单位数（个） Number of Enterprises (unit)	亏损企业 Loss Making Enterprises	工业总产值（当年价格） Gross Industrial Output Value (At Current Prices)
按企业规模分	**Grouped by Size of Enterprises**			
大型企业	Large-size	64	10	34454909
中型企业	Medium-size	188	35	10051995
小型企业	Small-size	1151	214	15681022
按经济组织类型分组	**Grouped by Economic Type of Orgnization**			
独资企业	Appropratorship	90	16	11740059
合作、合伙企业	Partnership	14	2	87071
股份有限公司	Corporaton	151	24	7170806
有限责任公司	Limited Liability Company	1148	217	41189991
按控股情况分	**Grouped by Cast strand**	1403	259	60187926
国有控股	State owned shares	277	66	28374773
集体控股	Collective shares	25	2	2221280
私人控股	Private holdings	961	163	21550242
港澳台控股	Hong Kong and Macao Holdings	19	2	486271
外商投资	Foreign Investment	61	13	6436563
其他	Others	60	13	1118798
按工业行业大类分	**Grouped by Sector**			
煤炭开采和洗选业	Mining and Washing of Coal			
石油和天然气开采业	Extraction of Petroleum and Natural Gas			
黑色金属矿采选业	Mining and Processing of Ferrous Metal Ores			
有色金属矿采选业	Mining and Processing of Non-ferrous Metal Ores			
非金属矿采选业	Mining and Processing of Nonmetal Ores			
开采辅助活动	Mining Auxiliary Activities	5	1	513271
其他采矿业	Mining of other Ores			
农副食品加工业	Processing of Food from Agricultural Porducts	52	7	1582305
食品制造业	Manufacture of Foods	46	6	1455895
酒、饮料和精制茶制造业	Manufacture of Alcohol,Beverages and Tea	24	3	814304
烟草制品业	Manufacture of Tobacco	2		21483
纺织业	Manufacture of Textile	16	5	216137
纺织服装、服饰业	Textile, apparel industry	4		72956
皮革、毛皮、羽毛及其制品和制鞋业	Manufacture of Leather, Fur, Feather and Related Products, and Shoes	2	1	39575

continued3

(10 000yuan)

工业销售产值（当年价） Value of Industry Products Sales (At Current Prices)	出口交货值 Export Delivery Value	从业人员年平均人数（人） Annual Average Employers (person)	资产总计 Total Assets	流动资产合计 Total Working Capitals	固定资产合计 Total Fixed Assets	固定资产原价 Origing Value of Fixed Assets	累计折旧 Accumulative Total Depreciation
33544187	4527702	286918	46235799	24713414	15383611	27139283	13064957
10127961	409966	111074	15048265	7685973	3474975	6393825	3124321
14864663	867571	113127	17341795	10058369	3311769	5236808	2037750
11505102	3648562	112989	19799276	9091450	9075991	15740199	7529881
82892	2046	1449	93142	56800	24003	40800	19854
6729143	671356	48701	13207808	5866309	2900566	5139838	2538790
40219674	1483275	347980	45525633	27443197	10169796	17849080	8138503
58536811	5805239	511119	78625859	42457756	22170355	38769916	18227028
27920192	1286974	288301	45417516	25231048	12007699	19977734	8976604
2144173	325172	7300	2599308	1243086	740364	2212920	1498693
20668040	609462	162578	18784451	11041201	3729616	6320273	2855468
486561	153979	6208	405636	227319	142575	261710	96714
6231318	3406437	34825	9518648	3690124	5046679	9216911	4531293
1086528	23216	11907	1900300	1024979	503422	780369	268256
517852		5656	758026	520966	135456	343185	205189
1554167	2227	8561	1003998	670096	196040	518196	293904
1382476	7858	13715	795724	354974	269343	470788	216320
983261	112114	7964	1385082	658397	464529	745062	296921
22162		689	67344	34345	22635	39190	6267
206803	12206	8331	375309	148724	185356	305014	134229
66116		1519	108887	78006	17633	21227	4223
39140		744	63458	41734	4223	8569	4346

12-8 续表4

单位：万元

分组	Classify	负债合计 Total Liabilites	流动负债合计 Total Working Liabilities	非流动负债 Non-Working Liabilities
按企业规模分	**Grouped by Size of Enterprises**			
大型企业	Large-size	24009114	18996286	4528571
中型企业	Medium-size	8388670	7179445	1384312
小型企业	Small-size	9231878	7384761	963557
按经济组织类型分组	**Grouped by Economic Type of Orgnization**			
独资企业	Appropratorship	8806601	6728106	2451049
合作、合伙企业	Partnership	34511	30885	1975
股份有限公司	Corporaton	5383013	3777569	1026353
有限责任公司	Limited Liability Company	27405537	23023933	3397062
按控股情况分	**Grouped by Cast strand**	41629661	33560492	6876440
国有控股	State owned shares	25725578	21406519	4125529
集体控股	Collective shares	1033995	824496	201716
私人控股	Private holdings	10189857	8156601	1194672
港澳台控股	Hong Kong and Macao Holdings	167019	151007	15983
外商投资	Foreign Investment	3527999	2260018	1172361
其他	Others	985213	761851	166178
按工业行业大类分	**Grouped by Sector**			
煤炭开采和洗选业	Mining and Washing of Coal			
石油和天然气开采业	Extraction of Petroleum and Natural Gas			
黑色金属矿采选业	Mining and Processing of Ferrous Metal Ores			
有色金属矿采选业	Mining and Processing of Non-ferrous Metal Ores			
非金属矿采选业	Mining and Processing of Nonmetal Ores			
开采辅助活动	Mining Auxiliary Activities	220941	219795	1146
其他采矿业	Mining of other Ores			
农副食品加工业	Processing of Food from Agricultural Porducts	716131	685099	29236
食品制造业	Manufacture of Foods	367660	350442	14176
酒、饮料和精制茶制造业	Manufacture of Alcohol,Beverages and Tea	733324	593407	138179
烟草制品业	Manufacture of Tobacco	11973	11973	
纺织业	Manufacture of Textile	216471	148984	121635
纺织服装、服饰业	Textile, apparel industry	56635	50463	3171
皮革、毛皮、羽毛及其制品和制鞋业	Manufacture of Leather, Fur, Feather and Related Products, and Shoes	27191	21303	5888

continued4

(10 000yuan)

所有者权益合计 Total Owners' Equities	实收资本 Total Capital Hold	营业收入 Total Revenue	主营业务收入 Revenue from Principal Business	营业成本 Total Cost	主营业务成本 Cost of Principal Business	税金及附加 Taxs and Other Changes	主营业务税金及附加 Taxes and Other Charges on Principal Business
22226685	8766886	33587026	32795786	29173624	28578391	220555	215865
6420304	2815456	9815599	9589026	8100797	7862860	67582	63076
7310267	4236726	14865475	14722231	12594392	12417116	86409	80975
10753385	4914274	11724739	11425619	9802005	9602773	87694	83753
58630	47567	86746	77541	73853	66042	544	524
7083909	2060216	6488555	6449110	5002305	4978956	41500	41011
18061332	8797010	39968059	39154773	34990650	34210596	244809	234628
35957256	15819067	58268099	57107043	49868813	48858367	374547	359915
19433686	8438736	29005747	28173472	25429189	24804427	173481	164475
1565313	397661	1757423	1705383	1344392	1301445	6798	6793
7833489	2910793	19602464	19405502	16688073	16416153	139882	135098
238617	151515	488509	478890	393023	385881	5518	4927
5971066	3423362	6322575	6264491	5063579	5011589	43217	43215
915086	496999	1091381	1079305	950558	938871	5650	5408
537085	284175	375593	371330	312126	310105	2381	2257
287867	126493	1382735	1374817	1216790	1213253	4465	4259
428064	211724	1352494	1328451	1070299	1014017	8895	8305
651758	229923	972625	957589	723809	710478	19139	19138
55371	38915	25996	25737	14948	14839	602	602
136332	44043	212743	208261	192343	170453	2031	1038
52252	32628	50340	49694	41349	40510	403	397
36267	21500	68187	38849	60105	33293	419	419

12-8 续表5

单位：万元

分 组	Classify	销售费用 Expenses for Sales	管理费用 Expenses for Management	财务费用 Financial cost
按企业规模分	**Grouped by Size of Enterprises**			
大型企业	Large-size	903877	1614420	184158
中型企业	Medium-size	551244	596451	101203
小型企业	Small-size	561731	857441	123294
按经济组织类型分组	**Grouped by Economic Type of Orgnization**			
独资企业	Appropratorship	318679	826529	104729
合作、合伙企业	Partnership	3327	5712	1105
股份有限公司	Corporaton	415837	421809	99300
有限责任公司	Limited Liability Company	1279010	1814263	203521
按控股情况分	**Grouped by Cast strand**			
国有控股	State owned shares	646644	1607543	166854
集体控股	Collective shares	67303	88753	7535
私人控股	Private holdings	873796	870110	146000
港澳台控股	Hong Kong and Macao Holdings	41510	20945	3000
外商投资	Foreign Investment	364929	426263	80618
其他	Others	22670	54698	4647
按工业行业大类分	**Grouped by Sector**			
煤炭开采和洗选业	Mining and Washing of Coal			
石油和天然气开采业	Extraction of Petroleum and Natural Gas			
黑色金属矿采选业	Mining and Processing of Ferrous Metal Ores			
有色金属矿采选业	Mining and Processing of Non-ferrous Metal Ores			
非金属矿采选业	Mining and Processing of Nonmetal Ores			
开采辅助活动	Mining Auxiliary Activities	1188	30559	-3527
其他采矿业	Mining of other Ores			
农副食品加工业	Processing of Food from Agricultural Porducts	62911	47609	11477
食品制造业	Manufacture of Foods	141205	55638	2004
酒、饮料和精制茶制造业	Manufacture of Alcohol,Beverages and Tea	121676	47632	6340
烟草制品业	Manufacture of Tobacco	1099	4998	-204
纺织业	Manufacture of Textile	4773	12151	1641
纺织服装、服饰业	Textile, apparel industry	3142	5320	757
皮革、毛皮、羽毛及其制品和制鞋业	Manufacture of Leather, Fur, Feather and Related Products, and Shoes	1470	2739	142

continued5

(10 000yuan)

营业利润 Operating Profit	利润总额 Total Profits	亏损企业亏损额 Total Loss of Deficit Enterprises	利税总额 Total Pre-tax Profits	应付职工薪酬 Salary Payable	本年应交增值税 Value Added Tax Payable
2125035	2405365	78908	3210375	3042095	584455
468302	539889	114058	950318	849481	342847
664178	732420	147219	1162850	738192	344021
1098561	1306759	27796	1640873	981829	246420
2003	2184	1458	4742	6304	2014
555944	622486	30415	888269	578968	224283
1601007	1746245	280517	2789660	3062668	798606
1109559	1213709	202667	2055665	3001285	668475
296802	301951	526	338124	164768	29375
892665	973493	79343	1498939	972419	385564
25257	26925	1674	43044	57408	10601
875956	1096778	49924	1295235	358171	155240
57276	64819	6052	92537	75718	22068
30016	26254	40	33734	100575	5100
28825	37403	4431	59604	42362	17737
77045	76723	5697	126916	91824	41297
124099	152753	4155	203062	99748	31171
4676	4680		7940	6894	2659
2302	3507	4614	8400	40496	2862
422	592		3201	3951	2207
3461	3258	137	4385	5488	708

12-8 续表6

单位：万元

分 组	Classify	企业单位数（个）Number of Enterprises (unit)	亏损企业 Loss Making Enterprises	工业总产值（当年价格）Gross Industrial Output Value (At Current Prices)
棕、草制品业	and Straw Products			
家具制造业	Manufacture of Furniture	14	1	143534
造纸及纸制品业	Manufacture of Paper and Paper Products	24	5	225367
印刷和记录媒介复制	Printing,Reproduction of Recording Media	31	5	939938
文教、工美、体育和娱乐用品制造业	Manufacture of Articles For Cultural,Educational and Sports Activities	12	2	312843
石油加工业、炼焦和核燃料加工业	Processing of Petroleum, Cokeing,Processing of Nuclear and Nuclear Fuel	8	3	44015
化学原料及化学制品制造业	Manufacture of Raw Chemical Materials and Chemical Products	84	13	4206545
医药制造业	Manufacture of Medicines	59	12	2378992
化学纤维制造业	Manufacture of Chemical Fibers	3		130884
橡胶和塑料制品业	Manufacture of Rubber and Plastics	37	7	835006
非金属矿物制品业	Manufacture of Non-metallic Mineral Products	147	33	1737897
黑色金属冶炼和压延加工业	Smelting and Pressing of Ferrous Metals	17	5	428633
有色金属冶炼和压延加工业	Smelting and Pressing of Non-ferrous Metals	40	5	2544372
金属制品业	Manufacture of Metal Products	82	17	1457242
通用设备制造业	Manufacture of General Purpose Machinery	85	14	1743176
专用设备制造业	Manufacture of Special Equipment	122	31	2301856
汽车制造业	Manufacture of Motor Vehicle	52	3	10372579
铁路、船舶、航空航天和其他运输设备制造业	Railways,Shipbuilding,Aerospace and Other Transportation Equipment Manufacturing Industry	80	6	5717234
电气机械和器材制造业	Manufacture of Electric Equipment and Machinery	142	29	6767799
计算机、通讯和其他电子设备制造业	Manufacture of Communication Equipment, Computers and other Electronic Equipment	92	17	7561403
仪器仪表制造业	Manufacture of Measuring Instruments and Machinery	55	9	1277538
其他制造业	Manufacture of Other Manufacturing	9	2	81447
废弃资源综合利用业	Recycling and Disposal of Waste	4	1	12530
金属制品、机械和设备修理业	Metal Products,Machinery and Equipment Repair Industry	4	1	19490
电力、热力的生产和供应业	Production and Supply of Electric Power and Heat Power	21	10	2715336
燃气生产和供应业	Gas Mining and Supplying Industry	15	3	1336790
水的生产和供应业	Production and Supply of Water	7	1	123613

continued6

(10 000yuan)

工业销售产值（当年价） Value of Industry Products Sales (At Current Prices)	出口交货值 Export Delivery Value	从业人员年平均人数（人） Annual Average Employers (person)	资产总计 Total Assets	流动资产合计 Total Working Capitals	固定资产合计 Total Fixed Assets	固定资产原价 Origing Value of Fixed Assets	累计折旧 Accumulative Total Depreciation
132621		1933	123082	75451	45300	50522	16175
218844		2643	118397	78268	27635	36179	12255
888614	1219	7676	754762	425180	256920	540880	293516
287320	93890	1143	49506	34348	8837	13533	4776
41281		4995	94104	40799	51615	19793	7209
4055150	563930	24176	5914103	2495040	1532720	3291184	1757401
2113140	12268	17854	2120594	1237443	569171	751700	469602
132306		542	168629	84979	78525	145045	66520
823051	84012	17506	1826742	1046421	420550	492238	154099
1713763	9144	15554	1782305	1111630	481394	890869	426125
426837	4744	2419	261551	179341	48675	115111	46343
2364761	180082	9183	3002597	1087218	481763	811989	324221
1423150	29451	24163	3312406	1580119	625419	1051699	433223
1711777	132527	19276	3814183	2801358	430354	899935	462019
2109338	169096	25561	5238718	3064883	730792	1142930	410654
10469947	279992	66608	7698843	5511717	1571927	2266883	783312
5397381	383263	73911	10044891	5894367	1888331	2971076	1331419
7344625	305774	47971	8596081	5997308	2011869	3176264	1640460
6693946	3349815	50207	9658589	4147655	4440787	8792925	4309421
1083154	62541	16109	2103202	1326520	415445	709952	288608
82396	2351	1182	75834	48978	20643	26973	9933
12229		149	10734	2392	5797	8596	820
17753	6734	264	32303	21563	5923	7532	2585
2716087		21780	4906710	1007496	3592879	6336631	3118520
1335773		6947	1900756	458298	927193	1402656	475275
123613		3392	287149	128913	145239	292727	183670

12-8 续表7

单位：万元

分 组	Classify	负债合计 Total Liabilites	流动负债合计 Total Working Liabilities	非流动负债 Non-Working Liabilities
棕、草制品业	and Straw Products			
家具制造业	Manufacture of Furniture	60860	48575	5779
造纸及纸制品业	Manufacture of Paper and Paper Products	64734	56210	6512
印刷和记录媒介复制	Printing,Reproduction of Recording Media	268857	228701	22371
文教、工美、体育和娱乐用品制造业	Manufacture of Articles For Cultural,Educational and Sports Activities	23380	22288	780
石油加工业、炼焦和核燃料加工业	Processing of Petroleum, Cokeing,Processing of Nuclear and Nuclear Fuel	52934	45135	7799
化学原料及化学制品制造业	Manufacture of Raw Chemical Materials and Chemical Products	3468477	2683797	736492
医药制造业	Manufacture of Medicines	1103431	902315	83819
化学纤维制造业	Manufacture of Chemical Fibers	108786	81456	25922
橡胶和塑料制品业	Manufacture of Rubber and Plastics	1189919	824401	349212
非金属矿物制品业	Manufacture of Non-metallic Mineral Products	1127650	997374	65260
黑色金属冶炼和压延加工业	Smelting and Pressing of Ferrous Metals	160767	132067	12923
有色金属冶炼和压延加工业	Smelting and Pressing of Non-ferrous Metals	894959	426376	76704
金属制品业	Manufacture of Metal Products	1811185	1176602	320284
通用设备制造业	Manufacture of General Purpose Machinery	2050550	1869087	139934
专用设备制造业	Manufacture of Special Equipment	2569198	2230908	279050
汽车制造业	Manufacture of Motor Vehicle	5192599	4772107	412652
铁路、船舶、航空航天和其他运输设备制造业	Railways,Shipbuilding,Aerospace and Other Transportation Equipment Manufacturing Industry	5244466	4482244	1023482
电气机械和器材制造业	Manufacture of Electric Equipment and Machinery	4253429	3675685	443114
计算机、通讯和其他电子设备制造业	Manufacture of Communication Equipment, Computers and other Electronic Equipment	3676006	2425807	1235968
仪器仪表制造业	Manufacture of Measuring Instruments and Machinery	1025997	874169	148815
其他制造业	Manufacture of Other Manufacturing	40988	32091	8897
废弃资源综合利用业	Recycling and Disposal of Waste	7182	3449	870
金属制品、机械和设备修理业	Metal Products,Machinery and Equipment Repair Industry	13357	13357	
电力、热力的生产和供应业	Production and Supply of Electric Power and Heat Power	3574833	2615280	916144
燃气生产和供应业	Gas Mining and Supplying Industry	1027073	690714	144338
水的生产和供应业	Production and Supply of Water	174455	111545	62910

continued7

(10 000yuan)

所有者权益合计 Total Owners' Equities	实收资本 Total Capital Hold	营业收入 Total Revenue	主营业务收入 Revenue from Principal Business	营业成本 Total Cost	主营业务成本 Cost of Principal Business	税金及附加 Taxs and Other Changes	主营业务税金及附加 Taxes and Other Charges on Principal Business
62221	23835	117640	115770	99752	98310	617	540
53663	31395	220650	220330	203387	203362	482	482
485905	241522	891278	884143	745280	740826	4797	4782
26126	17799	316224	316207	308898	307447	276	192
41170	53819	49627	47771	40573	40223	247	245
2445626	1076752	3849476	3790160	3199964	3154971	16498	16375
1011164	279681	1948743	1947736	1071961	1071293	20432	20399
59844	82961	142111	133233	122338	115245	656	656
636823	459212	858489	831407	753303	746932	4027	3840
654653	406932	1743699	1726660	1542465	1523853	8801	8364
100784	70265	432258	423777	401084	392513	1645	1145
2107638	569395	2522390	2480791	2358728	2327356	5836	5536
768554	451494	1483325	1466288	1254526	1240845	8349	8213
1762003	442388	1600156	1580466	1343996	1327887	13207	11896
2641064	1379021	2182598	2161733	1700736	1687432	18441	18234
2506242	843314	10310202	9930966	9422844	9067630	81606	80764
4583597	1779910	6146849	6030823	5379820	5306691	25167	23439
4319327	1686072	6229484	6081297	5095533	4978981	53030	49464
5975060	3326988	6799186	6769854	5848023	5825131	33336	33132
1077205	328981	1242805	1230724	992374	953935	7009	4929
34846	18155	83782	83317	71923	71692	484	484
3552	2007	13981	13851	11869	11465	84	61
18946	24907	17952	17754	13991	13793	127	127
1331877	808850	3005861	2937500	2838824	2791568	21740	21490
873683	343148	1418884	1354879	1251747	1198784	7156	7070
112694	65286	152633	127873	122309	110113	1810	1335

12-8 续表8

单位：万元

分　组	Classify	销售费用 Expenses for Sales	管理费用 Expenses for Management	财务费用 Financial cost
棕、草制品业	and Straw Products			
家具制造业	Manufacture of Furniture	4142	5059	437
造纸及纸制品业	Manufacture of Paper and Paper Products	3301	4935	1186
印刷和记录媒介复制	Printing,Reproduction of Recording Media	26242	60475	3657
文教、工美、体育和娱乐用品制造业	Manufacture of Articles For Cultural,Educational and Sports Activities	1334	3160	350
石油加工业、炼焦和核燃料加工业	Processing of Petroleum, Cokeing,Processing of Nuclear and Nuclear Fuel	1133	4211	76
化学原料及化学制品制造业	Manufacture of Raw Chemical Materials and Chemical Products	73514	196867	39931
医药制造业	Manufacture of Medicines	505668	193069	24833
化学纤维制造业	Manufacture of Chemical Fibers	1104	4975	3640
橡胶和塑料制品业	Manufacture of Rubber and Plastics	30200	35179	13310
非金属矿物制品业	Manufacture of Non-metallic Mineral Products	44312	66162	11668
黑色金属冶炼和压延加工业	Smelting and Pressing of Ferrous Metals	6826	12994	2190
有色金属冶炼和压延加工业	Smelting and Pressing of Non-ferrous Metals	12413	63414	15428
金属制品业	Manufacture of Metal Products	32092	126791	22541
通用设备制造业	Manufacture of General Purpose Machinery	63310	167168	8196
专用设备制造业	Manufacture of Special Equipment	110287	178822	23219
汽车制造业	Manufacture of Motor Vehicle	235853	278601	-3163
铁路、船舶、航空航天和其他运输设备制造业	Railways,Shipbuilding,Aerospace and Other Transportatiòn Equipment Manufacturing Industry	83403	348309	38398
电气机械和器材制造业	Manufacture of Electric Equipment and Machinery	307505	446356	43354
计算机、通讯和其他电子设备制造业	Manufacture of Communication Equipment, Computers and other Electronic Equipment	48362	405165	62765
仪器仪表制造业	Manufacture of Measuring Instruments and Machinery	34815	158713	6980
其他制造业	Manufacture of Other Manufacturing	1957	6779	1532
废弃资源综合利用业	Recycling and Disposal of Waste	1158	964	25
金属制品、机械和设备修理业	Metal Products,Machinery and Equipment Repair Industry	371	4586	377
电力、热力的生产和供应业	Production and Supply of Electric Power and Heat Power	6395	37567	49415
燃气生产和供应业	Gas Mining and Supplying Industry	34695	34774	13703
水的生产和供应业	Production and Supply of Water	7823	13729	3260

continued8

(10 000yuan)

营业利润 Operating Profit	利润总额 Total Profits	亏损企业亏损额 Total Loss of Deficit Enterprises	利税总额 Total Pre-tax Profits	应付职工薪酬 Salary Payable	本年应交增值税 Value Added Tax Payable
7559	7835	7	9987	8467	1536
7360	8084	424	13776	18950	5210
52773	56446	1024	100193	79560	38950
2206	2277	195	3048	3731	495
3386	2494	947	3754	2520	1013
394548	414416	20337	511366	323518	80452
134611	133539	10266	339078	173011	185107
8411	8750		7474	6881	-1932
23231	21137	5895	36848	58793	11684
67885	72872	4019	127525	73017	45852
6054	6213	766	12039	10059	4181
70200	86209	3570	127697	70427	35652
22392	30855	25958	67868	200363	28664
57260	72229	12742	142422	183474	56985
146550	159579	36795	250629	220769	72609
241323	249446	33121	467911	561013	136859
314137	329014	18469	483425	942161	129244
313396	339066	53419	520454	361293	128358
871341	1095707	14651	1165417	349487	36374
82480	97924	33627	136747	132399	31814
995	2172	1246	5376	8767	2720
-119	63	114	336	531	188
-1266	-923	2022	-197	3207	599
70547	85770	33291	215508	341383	107998
85758	86272	7675	111150	65159	17722
4490	4943	48	10676	36523	3923

12-9 规模以上国有及国有控股工业企业主要经济指标（2017年）

单位：万元

分 组	Classify	企业单位数（个） Number of Enterprises (unit)	亏损企业 Loss Making Enterprises	工业总产值（当年价格） Gross Industrial Output Value (At Current Prices)
总计	**Total**	**277**	**66**	**28374773**
#市区	Urban	273	66	28141131
#亏损企业	Deficit Enterprises	66	66	3969305
按隶属关系分	**Grouped by Jurisdiction of Management**			
中央企业	Central Enterprises	93	16	12728378
省属企业	Provincial Enterprises	57	18	9461540
市属企业	Municipal Enterprises	127	32	6184855
按轻重工业分	**Grouped by Light Industry and Heavy Industry**			
轻工业	Light Industry	40	10	1111706
重工业	Heavy Industry	237	56	27263067
按企业规模分	**Grouped by Size of Enterprises**			
大型企业	Large-size	44	8	20332531
中型企业	Medium-size	83	20	4991222
小型企业	Small-size	150	38	3051020
按工业行业大类分	**Grouped by Sector**			
煤炭开采和洗选业	Mining and Washing of Coal			
石油和天然气开采业	Extraction of Petroleum and Natural Gas			
黑色金属矿采选业	Mining and Processing of Ferrous Metal Ores			
有色金属矿采选业	Mining and Processing of Non-ferrous Metal Ores			
非金属矿采选业	Mining and Processing of Nonmetal Ores			
开采辅助活动	Mining Auxiliary Activities	2		475198
其他采矿业	Mining of Other Ores			
农副食品加工业	Processing of Food from Agricultural Porducts	4	3	36353
食品制造业	Manufacture of Foods	6	1	186992
酒、饮料和精制茶制造业	Manufacture of Alcohol,Beverages and Tea	1		117272
烟草制品业	Manufacture of Tobacco	2		21483
纺织业	Manufacture of Textile	5	2	115579
纺织服装、服饰业	Textile, apparel industry			
皮革、毛皮、羽毛及其制品和制鞋业	Leather fur feathers and its products and footwear	1		34262
木材加工和木、竹、藤、棕、草制品业	Processing of Timber, Manufacture of Wood,Plato and Straw Products			

Major Economic Indicators of State-owned and State-holding Share Industrial Enterprises above Designated Size（2017）

(10 000yuan)

工业销售产值（当年价）Value of Industry Products Sales (At Current Prices)	出口交货值 Export Delivery Value	从业人员年平均人数（人）Annual Average Employers (person)	资产总计 Total Assets	流动资产合计 Total Working Capitals	固定资产合计 Total Fixed Assets	固定资产原价 Origing Value of Fixed Assets	累计折旧 Accumulative Total Depreciation
27920192	**1286974**	**288301**	**45417516**	**25231048**	**12007699**	**19977734**	**8976604**
27687443	1280119	285797	44898141	25011133	11842351	19649690	8813042
3965068	259986	56757	9320130	4343642	2362103	3883759	1552490
12354437	588415	162321	23279174	12298228	7357913	12406424	5920250
9367169	376367	62785	12471579	6817494	2509901	4269237	1811012
6198586	322192	63195	9666763	6115326	2139885	3302073	1245342
1248789	14367	21584	1673286	907696	607095	1195822	632025
26671403	1272607	266717	43744230	24323352	11400604	18781912	8344579
20301817	915105	215739	31658009	18444531	9089045	15182980	7079326
4674383	147015	53421	9464042	4297171	2111438	3480766	1405558
2943992	224854	19141	4295465	2489346	807216	1313988	491720
479779		5024	674561	460211	119441	308734	186752
34697	2227	1008	73748	53002	19539	43987	24382
184878		1956	80869	49922	25586	57154	28651
263935		1312	178141	111871	20545	50030	32304
22162		689	67344	34345	22635	39190	6267
116881	6365	7018	305664	108701	167599	222926	66256
34262		591	54333	32741	4145	8279	4133

12-9 续表1

单位：万元

分组	Classify	负债合计 Total Liabilites	流动负债合计 Total Working Liabilities	非流动负债 Non-Working Liabilities
总计	**Total**	**25725578**	**21406519**	**4125529**
#市区	Urban	25455738	21249770	4018238
#亏损企业	Deficit Enterprises	7063486	5775106	1339214
按隶属关系分	**Grouped by Jurisdiction of Management**			
中央企业	Central Enterprises	12334563	10113026	2386978
省属企业	Provincial Enterprises	7370165	6341787	856142
市属企业	Municipal Enterprises	6020850	4951706	882409
按轻重工业分	**Grouped by Light Industry and Heavy Industry**			
轻工业	Light Industry	816958	649645	208370
重工业	Heavy Industry	24908620	20756874	3917159
按企业规模分	**Grouped by Size of Enterprises**			
大型企业	Large-size	18000518	14916301	2924975
中型企业	Medium-size	5192543	4499197	888854
小型企业	Small-size	2532517	1991021	311700
按工业行业大类分	**Grouped by Sector**			
煤炭开采和洗选业	Mining and Washing of Coal			
石油和天然气开采业	Extraction of Petroleum and Natural Gas			
黑色金属矿采选业	Mining and Processing of Ferrous Metal Ores			
有色金属矿采选业	Mining and Processing of Non-ferrous Metal Ores			
非金属矿采选业	Mining and Processing of Nonmetal Ores			
开采辅助活动	Mining Auxiliary Activities	205532	204386	1146
其他采矿业	Mining of Other Ores			
农副食品加工业	Processing of Food from Agricultural Porducts	98195	98195	
食品制造业	Manufacture of Foods	29731	29651	80
酒、饮料和精制茶制造业	Manufacture of Alcohol,Beverages and Tea	82611	81630	981
烟草制品业	Manufacture of Tobacco	11973	11973	
纺织业	Manufacture of Textile	184872	120482	118546
纺织服装、服饰业	Textile, apparel industry			
皮革、毛皮、羽毛及其制品和制鞋业	Leather fur feathers and its products and footwear	24275	18387	5888
木材加工和木、竹、藤、棕、草制品业	Processing of Timber, Manufacture of Wood,Plato and Straw Products			

continued1

(10 000yuan)

所有者权益合计 Total Owners' Equities	实收资本 Total Capital Hold	营业收入 Total Revenue	主营业务收入 Revenue from Principal Business	营业成本 Total Cost	主营业务成本 Cost of Principal Business	税金及附加 Taxs and Other Changes	主营业务税金及附加 Taxes and Other Charges on Principal Business
19433686	**8438736**	**29005747**	**28173472**	**25429189**	**24788279**	**173481**	**164475**
19184151	8331672	28732799	27902730	25204543	24565005	172730	163786
2234818	2154601	4176226	4068959	3917071	3821791	21612	20965
10690816	4510429	12923444	12580951	11095480	10850839	82554	78735
5103721	2348664	9801361	9483223	8913254	8611571	42514	41133
3639149	1579643	6280942	6109298	5420455	5325869	48413	44607
833822	551075	1323538	1253756	1043880	973264	19877	18409
18599864	7887661	27682209	26919716	24385309	23815015	153604	146066
13657491	5169674	20705293	20069803	18055407	17582236	126206	121516
4032209	1835424	5373423	5233842	4773424	4656397	31989	28661
1743986	1433638	2927031	2869827	2600358	2549646	15286	14298
469029	269992	338333	336473	280003	279739	1937	1813
-24447	11253	33667	33535	30671	30552	189	189
51138	26191	191998	185995	161494	155778	766	766
95530	95531	265231	265086	193368	193229	10047	10047
55371	38915	25996	25737	14948	14839	602	602
98287	18696	122411	118486	113163	91273	1575	582
30058	15000	63599	34262	56175	29364	364	364

12-9 续表2

单位：万元

分 组	Classify	销售费用 Expenses for Sales	管理费用 Expenses for Management	财务费用 Financial cost
总计	**Total**	**646644**	**1607543**	**166854**
#市区	Urban	644765	1579722	166206
#亏损企业	Deficit Enterprises	89820	259518	74817
按隶属关系分	**Grouped by Jurisdiction of Management**			
中央企业	Central Enterprises	256296	900715	112601
省属企业	Provincial Enterprises	209306	306160	16259
市属企业	Municipal Enterprises	181042	400668	37994
按轻重工业分	**Grouped by Light Industry and Heavy Industry**			
轻工业	Light Industry	71784	89026	4408
重工业	Heavy Industry	574860	1518517	162446
按企业规模分	**Grouped by Size of Enterprises**			
大型企业	Large-size	497533	1136500	91853
中型企业	Medium-size	101056	283706	54060
小型企业	Small-size	48055	187337	20941
按工业行业大类分	**Grouped by Sector**			
煤炭开采和洗选业	Mining and Washing of Coal			
石油和天然气开采业	Extraction of Petroleum and Natural Gas			
黑色金属矿采选业	Mining and Processing of Ferrous Metal Ores			
有色金属矿采选业	Mining and Processing of Non-ferrous Metal Ores			
非金属矿采选业	Mining and Processing of Nonmetal Ores			
开采辅助活动	Mining Auxiliary Activities	843	27921	-3624
其他采矿业	Mining of Other Ores			
农副食品加工业	Processing of Food from Agricultural Porducts	1751	2762	344
食品制造业	Manufacture of Foods	10279	8018	-2
酒、饮料和精制茶制造业	Manufacture of Alcohol,Beverages and Tea	29110	2286	-1819
烟草制品业	Manufacture of Tobacco	1099	4998	-204
纺织业	Manufacture of Textile	1815	9423	992
纺织服装、服饰业	Textile, apparel industry			
皮革、毛皮、羽毛及其制品和制鞋业	Leather fur feathers and its products and footwear	1102	2499	130
木材加工和木、竹、藤、棕、草制品业	Processing of Timber, Manufacture of Wood,Plato and Straw Products			

continued2

(10 000yuan)

营业利润 Operating Profit	利润总额 Total Profits	亏损企业亏损额 Total Loss of Deficit Enterprises	利税总额 Total Pre-tax Profits	应付职工薪酬 Salary Payable	本年应交增值税 Value Added Tax Payable
1109559	**1213709**	**202667**	**2055665**	**3001285**	**668475**
1091867	1190350	202667	2026926	2962282	663846
-216399	-202667	202667	-114142	578774	66912
571283	616786	80957	996408	1900344	297068
259401	281663	36382	486953	519323	162777
278875	315260	85328	572304	581618	208630
107494	111077	14718	176570	192782	45616
1002065	1102632	187949	1879095	2808503	622859
853045	893070	48749	1453343	2321195	434067
167630	206900	70583	404849	478934	165960
88884	113739	83335	197473	201156	68448
28311	24244		29765	95103	3584
-2065	-1546	4016	-720	5753	637
11363	10858	525	15319	12232	3695
42051	42076		63312	17340	11189
4676	4680		7940	6894	2659
-2057	-1062	3782	1909	35881	1396
3478	3395		4154	4901	395

12-9 续表3

单位：万元

分组	Classify	企业单位数（个） Number of Enterprises (unit)	亏损企业 Loss Making Enterprises	工业总产值（当年价格） Gross Industrial Output Value (At Current Prices)
家具制造业	Manufacture of Furniture			
造纸及纸制品业	Manufacture of Paper and Paper Products			
印刷和记录媒介复制	Printing,Reproduction of Recording Media	4	1	221128
文教、工美、体育和娱乐用品制造业	Manufacture of Articles For Cultural,Educational and Sports Activities			
石油加工业、炼焦和业核燃料加工	Processing of Petroleum, Cokeing,Processing of Nuclear and Nuclear Fuel			
化学原料及化学制品制造业	Manufacture of Raw Chemical Materials and Chemical Products	22	6	1685831
医药制造业	Manufacture of Medicines	3		67597
化学纤维制造业	Manufacture of Chemical Fibers	2		71728
橡胶和塑料制品业	Manufacture of Rubber and Plastics	5	1	615541
非金属矿物制品业	Manufacture of Non-metallic Mineral Products	11	1	210287
黑色金属冶炼和压延加工业	Smelting and Pressing of Ferrous Metals	3		307029
有色金属冶炼和压延加工业	Smelting and Pressing of Non-ferrous Metals	16	2	970649
金属制品业	Manufacture of Metal Products	15	3	849807
通用设备制造业	Manufacture of General Purpose Machinery	15	3	965396
专用设备制造业	Manufacture of Special Equipment	28	11	927875
汽车制造业	Manufacture of Motor Vehicle	17	2	7332498
铁路、船舶、航空航天和其他运输设备制造业	Railways,Shipbuilding,Aerospace and Other Transportation Equipment Manufacturing Industry	31	2	4749297
电气机械和器材制造业	Manufacture of Electric Equipment and Machinery	24	7	2975012
计算机、通讯和其他电子设备制造业	Manufacture of Communication Equipment, Computers and other Electronic Equipment	23	5	906408
仪器仪表制造业	Manufacture of Measuring Instruments and Machinery	8	3	641744
其他制造业	Manufacture of Other Manufacturing	1		40171
废弃资源综合利用业	Recycling and Disposal of Waste			
金属制品、机械和设备修理业	Metal Products,Machinery and Equipment Repair Industry	2	1	14167
电力、热力的生产和供应业	Production and Supply of Electric Power and Heat Power	13	8	2552855
燃气生产和供应业	Gas Mining and Supplying Industry	7	3	1161297
水的生产和供应业	Production and Supply of Water	6	1	121317

continued3

(10 000yuan)

工业销售产值（当年价）Value of Industry Products Sales (At Current Prices)	出口交货值 Export Delivery Value	从业人员年平均人数（人）Annual Average Employers (person)	资产总计 Total Assets	流动资产合计 Total Working Capitals	固定资产合计 Total Fixed Assets	固定资产原价 Origing Value of Fixed Assets	累计折旧 Accumulative Total Depreciation
217631		2599	339128	215068	102938	294276	191372
1611711	169539	17176	2735771	887529	698908	1246727	514739
61611		993	79127	37876	35653	47620	11968
70262		348	60805	38812	19668	70928	51260
616960	83689	14534	1631352	923436	369048	423976	124023
210286	9144	1835	242403	159555	66136	92262	27866
309036	3892	800	145765	105820	28944	85099	37339
873606	31391	4234	2094909	662937	257713	383858	142644
827324	25014	17753	1747793	1036229	473487	844285	373288
965988	12081	10125	2917863	2196454	244800	560801	309672
807260	116825	12507	2684281	1652030	428829	697607	250459
7433028	243225	35210	5038801	4149677	783296	1167809	396500
4545300	357414	68929	9192901	5379136	1722409	2782616	1270273
3002859	150143	28205	5337165	3759498	1316378	1651019	731963
870177	60136	15620	2058791	1213731	354886	666992	280748
473163	6950	9845	1359604	804987	271147	505308	232337
40183	2205	190	9783	8693	590	996	407
12641	6734	140	25517	17260	3854	4316	1438
2552202		20262	4203057	584807	3411955	6085130	3044722
1161053		6041	1793987	419518	892955	1343711	451175
121317		3357	284053	127202	144615	292098	183666

12-9 续表4

单位：万元

分　组	Classify	负债合计 Total Liabilites	流动负债合计 Total Working Liabilities	非流动负债 Non-Working Liabilities
家具制造业	Manufacture of Furniture			
造纸及纸制品业	Manufacture of Paper and Paper Products			
印刷和记录媒介复制	Printing,Reproduction of Recording Media	45479	33781	8
文教、工美、体育和娱乐用品制造业	Manufacture of Articles For Cultural,Educational and Sports Activities			
石油加工业、炼焦和业核燃料加工	Processing of Petroleum, Cokeing,Processing of Nuclear and Nuclear Fuel			
化学原料及化学制品制造业	Manufacture of Raw Chemical Materials and Chemical Products	2060335	1704306	324750
医药制造业	Manufacture of Medicines	32164	32064	100
化学纤维制造业	Manufacture of Chemical Fibers	15234	13546	280
橡胶和塑料制品业	Manufacture of Rubber and Plastics	1098187	755035	343151
非金属矿物制品业	Manufacture of Non-metallic Mineral Products	131698	104713	4249
黑色金属冶炼和压延加工业	Smelting and Pressing of Ferrous Metals	88555	78204	10351
有色金属冶炼和压延加工业	Smelting and Pressing of Non-ferrous Metals	488541	315664	57658
金属制品业	Manufacture of Metal Products	1160677	854643	306034
通用设备制造业	Manufacture of General Purpose Machinery	1634734	1494370	121428
专用设备制造业	Manufacture of Special Equipment	1145096	1045390	89099
汽车制造业	Manufacture of Motor Vehicle	3444274	3349471	89003
铁路、船舶、航空航天和其他运输设备制造业	Railways,Shipbuilding,Aerospace and Other Transportation Equipment Manufacturing Industry	4950240	4208203	1005117
电气机械和器材制造业	Manufacture of Electric Equipment and Machinery	2416829	1993315	304487
计算机、通讯和其他电子设备制造业	Manufacture of Communication Equipment, Computers and other Electronic Equipment	1537306	1214847	340416
仪器仪表制造业	Manufacture of Measuring Instruments and Machinery	661232	568253	92980
其他制造业	Manufacture of Other Manufacturing	2375	2375	
废弃资源综合利用业	Recycling and Disposal of Waste			
金属制品、机械和设备修理业	Metal Products,Machinery and Equipment Repair Industry	9676	9676	
电力、热力的生产和供应业	Production and Supply of Electric Power and Heat Power	3011155	2303156	707998
燃气生产和供应业	Gas Mining and Supplying Industry	980758	649868	138869
水的生产和供应业	Production and Supply of Water	173844	110935	62910

continued4

(10 000yuan)

所有者权益合计 Total Owners' Equities	实收资本 Total Capital Hold	营业收入 Total Revenue	主营业务收入 Revenue from Principal Business	营业成本 Total Cost	主营业务成本 Cost of Principal Business	税金及附加 Taxs and Other Changes	主营业务税金及附加 Taxes and Other Charges on Principal Business
293649	157362	218846	217236	155052	154083	2842	2842
675436	535803	1758256	1700971	1549626	1505519	9895	9776
46963	14377	61673	61611	33416	33413	669	669
45571	61961	71190	71188	61009	61009	438	438
533165	397384	649702	622794	573837	567599	3146	2959
110705	85114	194752	194422	179124	179001	755	570
57210	50236	328812	326739	310813	308505	1327	847
1606368	505506	1057987	1021016	952775	925849	4741	4741
587116	322779	797676	786489	652383	645747	3747	3747
1281499	186495	868458	852614	736039	721967	8710	7539
1534051	953014	865869	855540	732884	725710	8148	8061
1594526	579419	7312300	7057064	6684745	6441900	26609	25776
4025835	1589096	5245640	5129968	4616586	4543496	20562	19014
2905873	955691	2671027	2531716	2092783	1995135	26970	26649
523793	248628	950132	944990	773650	764722	6892	6799
698372	182837	667912	658881	547263	542548	3085	1026
7407	2200	40184	40184	37422	37422	136	136
15841	22519	12839	12641	10404	10206	46	46
1191902	741617	2821751	2797826	2689141	2680165	20623	20373
813229	308337	1219171	1164434	1069906	1041198	6860	6779
110209	62786	150337	125577	120510	108315	1802	1327

12-9 续表5

单位：万元

分 组	Classify	销售费用 Expenses for Sales	管理费用 Expenses for Management	财务费用 Financial cost
家具制造业	Manufacture of Furniture			
造纸及纸制品业	Manufacture of Paper and Paper Products			
印刷和记录媒介复制	Printing,Reproduction of Recording Media	4774	28821	-1836
文教、工美、体育和娱乐用品制造业	Manufacture of Articles For Cultural,Educational and Sports Activities			
石油加工业、炼焦和业核燃料加工	Processing of Petroleum, Cokeing,Processing of Nuclear and Nuclear Fuel			
化学原料及化学制品制造业	Manufacture of Raw Chemical Materials and Chemical Products	27853	98914	24382
医药制造业	Manufacture of Medicines	7916	5684	228
化学纤维制造业	Manufacture of Chemical Fibers	471	3047	23
橡胶和塑料制品业	Manufacture of Rubber and Plastics	22618	23174	11501
非金属矿物制品业	Manufacture of Non-metallic Mineral Products	1636	7361	2823
黑色金属冶炼和压延加工业	Smelting and Pressing of Ferrous Metals	5096	4961	1843
有色金属冶炼和压延加工业	Smelting and Pressing of Non-ferrous Metals	5898	45674	6192
金属制品业	Manufacture of Metal Products	15458	90802	13948
通用设备制造业	Manufacture of General Purpose Machinery	30592	120697	2408
专用设备制造业	Manufacture of Special Equipment	32844	70535	5435
汽车制造业	Manufacture of Motor Vehicle	177363	168993	-26846
铁路、船舶、航空航天和其他运输设备制造业	Railways,Shipbuilding,Aerospace and Other Transportation Equipment Manufacturing Industry	69200	312247	35029
电气机械和器材制造业	Manufacture of Electric Equipment and Machinery	137893	266544	19274
计算机、通讯和其他电子设备制造业	Manufacture of Communication Equipment, Computers and other Electronic Equipment	18910	115402	17767
仪器仪表制造业	Manufacture of Measuring Instruments and Machinery	4891	113778	-408
其他制造业	Manufacture of Other Manufacturing	171	778	62
废弃资源综合利用业	Recycling and Disposal of Waste			
金属制品、机械和设备修理业	Metal Products,Machinery and Equipment Repair Industry	93	3659	314
电力、热力的生产和供应业	Production and Supply of Electric Power and Heat Power	628	24858	42713
燃气生产和供应业	Gas Mining and Supplying Industry	28719	30130	12952
水的生产和供应业	Production and Supply of Water	7622	13578	3233

continued5

(10 000yuan)

营业利润 Operating Profit	利润总额 Total Profits	亏损企业亏损额 Total Loss of Deficit Enterprises	利税总额 Total Pre-tax Profits	应付职工薪酬 Salary Payable	本年应交增值税 Value Added Tax Payable
29943	31343	680	50561	48283	16377
63873	75022	17239	145525	155314	60608
13700	13796		18018	7895	3553
6203	6468		7660	4394	753
16290	13506	2455	24824	48157	8172
1411	2954	680	7442	11338	3734
3607	3513		7988	1817	3148
46457	56432	303	88031	46474	26858
5588	13450	20094	31337	160562	14140
26771	39834	9853	86602	132451	38059
20878	30815	30795	65959	128385	26996
226187	229665	7472	369855	318075	113582
224614	238389	16606	353460	904872	94510
165835	175296	6895	288632	246011	86366
20456	29800	10572	49907	116432	13215
5163	15878	30857	27721	64171	8758
1543	1738		2744	2524	870
-1475	-1419	2022	-1210	1982	164
64015	71551	30100	197703	327225	105529
78362	78212	7675	100761	60372	15689
4380	4822	48	10466	36449	3842

12-10 规模以上外商及港澳台商投资工业企业主要经济指标（2017年）

单位：万元

分组	Classify	企业单位数（个）Number of Enterprises (unit)	亏损企业 Loss Making Enterprises	工业总产值（当年价格）Gross Industrial Output Value (At Current Prices)
总计	**Total**	**115**	**26**	**10486100**
#市区	Urban Area	113	26	10435824
#亏损企业	Deficit Enterprises	26	26	3103776
按隶属关系分	**Grouped by Jurisdiction of Management**			
中央企业	Central Enterprises	3	1	82098
省属企业	Provincial Enterprises	7		1011701
市属企业	Municipal Enterprises	105	25	9392301
按登记注册类型分组	**Grouped by Type of Registration**			
港澳台商投资	Enterprises with Funds from Hong Kong, Macao &Taiwan	26	6	3056448
与港澳台商合资经营	Cooperative Enterprises	14	5	2628777
与港澳台商合作经营	Joint-venture Enterprises	1		2356
港澳台商独资	Enterprises with Sole Investment	9		359076
港澳台商投资股份有限公司	Share-holding Corporations Ltd. With their Investment	1		53041
其他港澳台投资	Other	1	1	13199
外商投资	Foreign Funded Enterprises	89	20	7429652
中外合资经营	Joint-venture Enterprises	44	11	1818702
中外合作经营	Cooperation Enterprises	1		5138
外资企业	Foreign Funded Enterprises	39	9	4651108
外商投资股份有限公司	Share-holding Corporations Ltd. With Foreign Funds	3		917496
其他外商投资	Other	2		37207
按轻重工业分	**Grouped by Light Industry and Heavy Industry**			
轻工业	Light Industry	33	8	2505031
重工业	Heavy Industry	82	18	7981069
按企业规模分	**Grouped by Size of Enterprises**			
大型企业	Large-size	14	2	7561312
中型企业	Medium-size	28	8	1282426
小型企业	Small-size	73	16	1642362
微型企业	Microenterprise			
按工业行业大类分	**Grouped by Sector**			
煤炭开采和洗选业	Mining and Washing of Coal			
石油和天然气开采业	Extraction of Petroleum and Natural Gas			
黑色金属矿采选业	Mining and Processing of Ferrous Metal Ores			
有色金属矿采选业	Mining and Processing of Non-ferrous Metal Ores			
非金属矿采选业	Mining and Processing of Nonmetal Ores			
开采辅助活动	Mining Auxiliary Activities			
其他采矿业	Mining of Other Ores			

Major Economic Indicators of Foreign,Hong Kong,Macao and Taiwan Invested Industrial Enterprises above Designated Size (2017)

(10 000 yuan)

工业销售产值（当年价） Value of Industry Products Sales (At Current Prices)	出口交货值 Export Delivery Value	从业人员年平均人数（人） Annual Average Employers (person)	资产总计 Total Assets	流动资产合计 Total Working Capitals	固定资产合计 Total Fixed Assets	固定资产原价 Origing Value of Fixed Assets	累计折旧 Accumulative Total Depreciation
10215008	**3661706**	**74266**	**13449830**	**5670193**	**6209876**	**11005959**	**5209029**
10167035	3661383	73889	13387895	5651316	6166817	10923789	5160184
3056002	107452	32036	3081251	1403647	1083244	1489021	520008
80632	48	652	126421	66757	27419	89225	63443
889795	1464	5339	777447	476837	251299	167295	102855
9244582	3660194	68275	12545963	5126598	5931158	10749439	5042731
3059042	190340	31706	2499891	1156785	811187	1223616	445596
2630735	41289	26786	2201941	1006756	689743	999399	363980
2740		75	2755	2499	256	935	679
364440	147833	3463	180723	90863	83993	158227	53076
48630	1219	1082	76514	38079	26427	43530	17103
12498		300	37958	18588	10767	21526	10758
7155966	3471366	42560	10949939	4513408	5398690	9782343	4763433
1711415	128047	18387	2704746	1582249	786296	1110550	448938
4977	324	129	6936	4326	2609	2609	825
4584912	3229117	19309	7135266	2418074	4183248	8264310	4144807
817580	112157	4499	1089336	500121	421855	402546	168521
37081	1722	236	13655	8638	4681	2328	343
2360120	195150	17713	2830453	1324315	1139124	1416342	566281
7854888	3466557	56553	10619377	4345878	5070752	9589617	4642748
7423593	3121820	48838	10212208	3747527	5138999	9443236	4594476
1184071	193225	17267	1641809	998700	571924	752188	275094
1607344	346662	8161	1595813	923966	498953	810535	339459

12-10 续表1

单位：万元

分 组	Classify	负债合计 Total Liabilites	流动负债合计 Total Working Liabilities	非流动负债 Non-Working Liabilities
总计	**Total**	**5969341**	**4347267**	**1525362**
#市区	Urban Area	5935224	4314857	1523655
#亏损企业	Deficit Enterprises	2199630	1861658	337056
按隶属关系分	**Grouped by Jurisdiction of Management**			
中央企业	Central Enterprises	29290	26957	2333
省属企业	Provincial Enterprises	444716	379751	2723
市属企业	Municipal Enterprises	5495335	3940559	1520306
按登记注册类型分组	**Grouped by Type of Registration**			
港澳台商投资	Enterprises with Funds from Hong Kong, Macao &Taiwan	1617854	1300693	317132
与港澳台商合资经营	Cooperative Enterprises	1494356	1191077	303279
与港澳台商合作经营	Joint-venture Enterprises	305	305	
港澳台商独资	Enterprises with Sole Investment	90902	77037	13837
港澳台商投资股份有限公司	Share-holding Corporations Ltd. With their Investment	23344	23343	1
其他港澳台投资	Other	8947	8932	15
外商投资	Foreign Funded Enterprises	4351487	3046574	1208230
中外合资经营	Joint-venture Enterprises	1498144	1384195	81475
中外合作经营	Cooperation Enterprises	3526	3526	
外资企业	Foreign Funded Enterprises	2138232	1147153	990756
外商投资股份有限公司	Share-holding Corporations Ltd. With Foreign Funds	703697	505637	135818
其他外商投资	Other	7888	6063	181
按轻重工业分	**Grouped by Light Industry and Heavy Industry**			
轻工业	Light Industry	1736783	1417533	256979
重工业	Heavy Industry	4232558	2929734	1268383
按企业规模分	**Grouped by Size of Enterprises**			
大型企业	Large-size	4133059	2719811	1351006
中型企业	Medium-size	952370	882072	69399
小型企业	Small-size	883912	745385	104958
微型企业	Microenterprise			
按工业行业大类分	**Grouped by Sector**			
煤炭开采和洗选业	Mining and Washing of Coal			
石油和天然气开采业	Extraction of Petroleum and Natural Gas			
黑色金属矿采选业	Mining and Processing of Ferrous Metal Ores			
有色金属矿采选业	Mining and Processing of Non-ferrous Metal Ores			
非金属矿采选业	Mining and Processing of Nonmetal Ores			
开采辅助活动	Mining Auxiliary Activities			
其他采矿业	Mining of Other Ores			

continued 1

(10 000 yuan)

所有者权益合计 Total Owners' Equities	实收资本 Total Capital Hold	营业收入 Total Revenue	主营业务收入 Revenue from Principal Business	营业成本 Total Cost	主营业务收入 Cost of Principal Business	税金及附加 Taxs and Other Changes	主营业务税金及附加 Taxes and Other Charges on Principal Business
7460905	**4141975**	**10346620**	**10110143**	**8654422**	**8458397**	**107757**	**106975**
7433087	4130867	10307031	10070672	8625730	8429705	107239	106458
881621	604808	3054783	2932878	2821824	2706612	54942	54941
97131	93194	80486	80319	68387	68282	593	593
332730	79061	903093	890770	568238	558479	7429	7429
7031044	3969720	9363041	9139054	8017798	7831636	99734	98953
882037	318483	3035820	2916675	2779524	2670930	57144	56552
707585	211850	2613666	2503072	2443369	2341221	52180	52180
2451	714	2740	2729	2137	2133	18	18
89821	62022	362801	356805	287717	282849	4137	3546
53170	15000	43821	43538	35210	35155	522	522
29010	28897	12793	10530	11091	9572	287	287
6578868	3823492	7310800	7193468	5874898	5787467	50613	50423
1187020	698829	1793781	1712986	1422211	1369064	11136	10945
3409	1108	4977	4977	4278	4278	3	3
4997034	3071648	4640490	4605344	3888213	3854868	31991	31991
385639	47510	835379	834017	528303	527365	7469	7469
5767	4397	36173	36144	31893	31893	15	15
1093670	472895	2378767	2339057	1773329	1737275	20975	20385
6367235	3669080	7967853	7771086	6881093	6721122	86782	86591
6079149	3093528	7467031	7272996	6269381	6109589	86836	86836
689439	512912	1172714	1158581	932182	917629	10529	9819
692317	535535	1706875	1678566	1452859	1431178	10392	10321

12-10 续表2

单位：万元

分 组	Classify	销售费用 Expenses for Sales	管理费用 Expenses for Management	财务费用 Financial cost
总计	**Total**	**473174**	**582964**	**104073**
#市区	Urban Area	472995	580761	103090
#亏损企业	Deficit Enterprises	107611	140726	32726
按隶属关系分	**Grouped by Jurisdiction of Management**			
中央企业	Central Enterprises	1213	7109	66
省属企业	Provincial Enterprises	189052	75595	15983
市属企业	Municipal Enterprises	282910	500260	88025
按登记注册类型分组	**Grouped by Type of Registration**			
港澳台商投资	Enterprises with Funds from Hong Kong, Macao &Taiwan	77434	95650	22995
与港澳台商合资经营	Cooperative Enterprises	37752	78592	20713
与港澳台商合作经营	Joint-venture Enterprises	143	236	-28
港澳台商独资	Enterprises with Sole Investment	35803	12701	1641
港澳台商投资股份有限公司	Share-holding Corporations Ltd. With their Investment	2826	2787	270
其他港澳台投资	Other	912	1335	399
外商投资	Foreign Funded Enterprises	395740	487313	81079
中外合资经营	Joint-venture Enterprises	113804	115268	3587
中外合作经营	Cooperation Enterprises	110	387	2
外资企业	Foreign Funded Enterprises	101906	291794	51066
外商投资股份有限公司	Share-holding Corporations Ltd. With Foreign Funds	178269	78593	26155
其他外商投资	Other	1650	1272	270
按轻重工业分	**Grouped by Light Industry and Heavy Industry**			
轻工业	Light Industry	350041	154487	35596
重工业	Heavy Industry	123134	428477	68477
按企业规模分	**Grouped by Size of Enterprises**			
大型企业	Large-size	352831	412194	80050
中型企业	Medium-size	67781	88973	10798
小型企业	Small-size	52563	81796	13226
微型企业	Microenterprise			
按工业行业大类分	**Grouped by Sector**			
煤炭开采和洗选业	Mining and Washing of Coal			
石油和天然气开采业	Extraction of Petroleum and Natural Gas			
黑色金属矿采选业	Mining and Processing of Ferrous Metal Ores			
有色金属矿采选业	Mining and Processing of Non-ferrous Metal Ores			
非金属矿采选业	Mining and Processing of Nonmetal Ores			
开采辅助活动	Mining Auxiliary Activities			
其他采矿业	Mining of Other Ores			

continued 2

(10 000 yuan)

营业利润 Operating Profit	利润总额 Total Profits	亏损企业亏损额 Total Loss of Deficit Enterprises	利税总额 Total Pre-tax Profits	应付职工薪酬 Salary Payable	本年应交增值税 Value Added Tax Payable
957082	**1183954**	**87295**	**1491114**	**698942**	**199403**
950069	1174630	87295	1477665	696214	195796
-105013	-87295	87295	-16190	269015	16164
3650	3661	3164	5400	10976	1145
49767	48697		154601	114227	98474
903666	1131596	84131	1331113	573738	99783
3731	8142	28139	81415	261949	16129
-18597	-15491	26920	43763	212908	7073
235	233		402	514	151
20702	21821		32844	38487	6886
2622	2797		5060	8231	1741
-1231	-1219	1219	-654	1809	278
953351	1175812	59156	1409699	436993	183274
182216	198568	44171	265626	147889	55923
198	198		294	678	93
752365	930599	14985	1001010	165676	38419
17499	45351		141654	121562	88835
1074	1097		1115	1188	3
104606	144248	39591	299071	249883	133848
852476	1039706	47704	1192043	449059	65555
803242	1010729	30160	1231692	492828	134127
52753	67597	42473	112852	123086	34726
101088	105628	14662	146570	83028	30550

12-10 续表3

单位：万元

分组	Classify	企业单位数（个） Number of Enterprises (unit)	亏损企业 Loss Making Enterprises	工业总产值（当年价格） Gross Industrial Output Value (At Current Prices)
农副食品加工业	Processing of Food from Agricultural Porducts	2		20048
食品制造业	Manufacture of Foods	6	1	564651
酒、饮料和精制茶制造业	Manufacture of Alcohol,Beverages and Tea	7	1	517862
烟草制品业	Manufacture of Tobacco			
纺织业	Manufacture of Textile			
纺织服装、服饰业	Textile, apparel industry			
皮革、毛皮、羽毛及其制品和制鞋业	Leather fur feathers and its products and footwear			
木材加工和木、竹、藤、棕、草制品业	Processing of Timber,Manufacture of Wood,Plam and Straw Products			
家具制造业	Manufacture of Furniture			
造纸及纸制品业	Manufacture of Paper and Paper Products	1	1	5354
印刷和记录媒介复制	Printing,Reproduction of Recording Media	2		151566
文教、工美、体育和娱乐用品制造业	Manufacture of Articles For Cultural,Educational and Sports Activities	2		79145
石油加工业、炼焦和核燃料加工业	Processing of Petroleum, Cokeing,Processing of Nuclear and Nuclear Fuel	1		5271
化学原料及化学制品制造业	Manufacture of Raw Chemical Materials and Chemical Products	9	1	187932
医药制造业	Manufacture of Medicines	4	1	886663
化学纤维制造业	Manufacture of Chemical Fibers	2		111863
橡胶和塑料制品业	Manufacture of Rubber and Plastics	3	2	9695
非金属矿物制品业	Manufacture of Non-metallic Mineral Products	6	1	124532
黑色金属冶炼和压延加工业	Smelting and Pressing of Ferrous Metals	2		15583
有色金属冶炼和压延加工业	Smelting and Pressing of Non-ferrous Metals	4	1	136284
金属制品业	Manufacture of Metal Products	3	1	40010
通用设备制造业	Manufacture of General Purpose Machinery	7	1	180198
专用设备制造业	Manufacture of Special Equipment	9	2	273426
汽车制造业	Manufacture of Motor Vehicle	9	2	2719081
铁路、船舶、航空航天和其他运输设备制造业	Railways,Shipbuilding,Aerospace and Other Transportation Equipment Manufacturing Industry	8		261249
电气机械和器材制造业	Manufacture of Electric Equipment and Machinery	12	7	521415
计算机、通讯和其他电子设备制造业	Manufacture of Communication Equipment, Computers and other Electronic Equipment	10	3	3299041
仪器仪表制造业	Manufacture of Measuring Instruments and Machinery	3		85522
其他制造业	Manufacture of Other Manufacturing	1		2356
废弃资源综合利用业	Recycling and Disposal of Waste			
金属制品、机械和设备修理业	Metal Products,Machinery and Equipment Repair Industry	1	1	5663
电力、热力的生产和供应业	Production and Supply of Electric Power and Heat Power			
燃气生产和供应业	Gas Mining and Supplying Industry	1		281694
水的生产和供应业	Production and Supply of Water			

continued 3

(10 000 yuan)

工业销售产值（当年价）Value of Industry Products Sales (At Current Prices)	出口交货值 Export Delivery Value	从业人员年平均人数（人）Annual Average Employers (person)	资产总计 Total Assets	流动资产合计 Total Working Capitals	固定资产合计 Total Fixed Assets	固定资产原价 Origing Value of Fixed Assets	累计折旧 Accumulative Total Depreciation
20087		503	17922	13451	2967	6526	3560
553172		3993	309370	124532	117147	199054	82003
546463	112114	4889	972607	424188	369499	605499	243408
5354		155	6249	4070	711	2359	1648
144369	1219	1204	106419	46571	36284	57753	21469
79135	79135	184	8046	5798	1160	2516	1356
5271		4630	40163	63	40100	2029	744
187655	72464	451	242520	84223	141348	207769	68497
769846	2070	5193	753865	404301	284717	152400	97411
113285		392	151416	79166	69194	134044	64850
9136	324	373	29034	18638	10053	20891	10041
122292		1299	245633	136636	94723	168922	83183
14693	66	164	10235	8426	1805	4778	2973
134605	112972	348	61108	32444	18050	26411	8360
40188	4005	613	60233	24365	32310	50418	18108
159895	14656	1725	177432	122049	35239	83727	52940
273867	48436	2028	376272	267774	56827	102349	49082
2722115	37632	27476	2384833	1140414	751166	1053421	374778
249352	35695	1307	342602	312634	21522	25906	16301
446677	12111	3484	768400	416660	298683	330129	86710
3240984	3082157	10436	5740582	1727534	3637246	7494632	3835034
85399	39917	684	99370	93283	5857	17988	12428
2740		75	2755	2499	256	935	679
6734	6734	65	11251	6385	3618	3618	976
281694		2595	531517	174089	179395	251886	72491

12-10 续表4

单位：万元

分组	Classify	负债合计 Total Liabilites	流动负债合计 Total Working Liabilities	非流动负债 Non-Working Liabilities
农副食品加工业	Processing of Food from Agricultural Porducts	9679	9679	
食品制造业	Manufacture of Foods	155885	154758	1128
酒、饮料和精制茶制造业	Manufacture of Alcohol,Beverages and Tea	553382	416625	136757
烟草制品业	Manufacture of Tobacco			
纺织业	Manufacture of Textile			
纺织服装、服饰业	Textile, apparel industry			
皮革、毛皮、羽毛及其制品和制鞋业	Leather fur feathers and its products and footwear			
木材加工和木、竹、藤、棕、草制品业	Processing of Timber,Manufacture of Wood,Plam and Straw Products			
家具制造业	Manufacture of Furniture			
造纸及纸制品业	Manufacture of Paper and Paper Products	2713	2713	
印刷和记录媒介复制	Printing,Reproduction of Recording Media	44300	43975	325
文教、工美、体育和娱乐用品制造业	Manufacture of Articles For Cultural,Educational and Sports Activities	5468	5439	
石油加工业、炼焦和核燃料加工业	Processing of Petroleum, Cokeing,Processing of Nuclear and Nuclear Fuel	23914	16116	7799
化学原料及化学制品制造业	Manufacture of Raw Chemical Materials and Chemical Products	133151	82451	49056
医药制造业	Manufacture of Medicines	455547	332403	60902
化学纤维制造业	Manufacture of Chemical Fibers	105354	79712	25642
橡胶和塑料制品业	Manufacture of Rubber and Plastics	15209	14616	592
非金属矿物制品业	Manufacture of Non-metallic Mineral Products	145229	126505	18708
黑色金属冶炼和压延加工业	Smelting and Pressing of Ferrous Metals	5287	5157	131
有色金属冶炼和压延加工业	Smelting and Pressing of Non-ferrous Metals	34421	24931	9198
金属制品业	Manufacture of Metal Products	41152	41152	
通用设备制造业	Manufacture of General Purpose Machinery	55702	54942	761
专用设备制造业	Manufacture of Special Equipment	162424	120878	10136
汽车制造业	Manufacture of Motor Vehicle	1627830	1316118	311712
铁路、船舶、航空航天和其他运输设备制造业	Railways,Shipbuilding,Aerospace and Other Transportation Equipment Manufacturing Industry	167892	164317	3396
电气机械和器材制造业	Manufacture of Electric Equipment and Machinery	520006	485133	34874
计算机、通讯和其他电子设备制造业	Manufacture of Communication Equipment, Computers and other Electronic Equipment	1292838	450516	841422
仪器仪表制造业	Manufacture of Measuring Instruments and Machinery	22062	22062	
其他制造业	Manufacture of Other Manufacturing	305	305	
废弃资源综合利用业	Recycling and Disposal of Waste			
金属制品、机械和设备修理业	Metal Products,Machinery and Equipment Repair Industry	3928	3928	
电力、热力的生产和供应业	Production and Supply of Electric Power and Heat Power			
燃气生产和供应业	Gas Mining and Supplying Industry	385662	372837	12825
水的生产和供应业	Production and Supply of Water			

continued 4

(10 000 yuan)

所有者权益合计 Total Owners' Equities	实收资本 Total Capital Hold	营业收入 Total Revenue	主营业务收入 Revenue from Principal Business	营业成本 Total Cost	主营业务收入 Cost of Principal Business	税金及附加 Taxs and Other Changes	主营业务税金及附加 Taxes and Other Charges on Principal Business
8242	1892	18514	18423	13281	13281	196	196
153484	81165	558146	542927	440037	424505	5500	4910
419225	99247	559637	545236	434912	422098	6590	6590
3536	2000	4579	4579	4506	4506	10	10
62119	19540	139561	138937	127222	126863	616	616
2578	845	79135	79135	78771	78771		
16248	33000	5012	5012	4152	4122	36	34
109369	99148	217020	216359	185288	185246	622	622
298317	76747	768716	768306	443941	443716	7254	7254
46062	45800	122163	113285	103626	96532	477	477
13825	11788	9447	9387	8143	8116	102	102
100403	45255	122193	117249	100875	95454	1172	1054
4948	3836	14989	14693	13246	12951	47	47
26687	20662	144236	143993	129861	129744	141	141
19081	19567	56055	55230	49703	49056	786	786
121730	84204	173833	171435	153806	152232	830	830
194265	61129	282892	281014	211436	210413	2634	2575
757004	249550	2711957	2589027	2482748	2370628	53054	53054
174710	49171	248021	247835	185714	185712	2424	2412
248393	305996	433144	431344	381612	377077	1781	1780
4447744	2701385	3245654	3237746	2766563	2760829	19570	19570
77307	10568	86316	85452	51741	51741	545	545
2451	714	2740	2729	2137	2133	18	18
7322	18769	6933	6734	6082	5884		
145855	100000	335727	284073	275022	246787	3353	3353

12-10 续表5

单位：万元

分 组	Classify	销售费用 Expenses for Sales	管理费用 Expenses for Management	财务费用 Financial cost
农副食品加工业	Processing of Food from Agricultural Porducts	368	1594	151
食品制造业	Manufacture of Foods	68235	18335	-300
酒、饮料和精制茶制造业	Manufacture of Alcohol,Beverages and Tea	70287	31625	7764
烟草制品业	Manufacture of Tobacco			
纺织业	Manufacture of Textile			
纺织服装、服饰业	Textile, apparel industry			
皮革、毛皮、羽毛及其制品和制鞋业	Leather fur feathers and its products and footwear			
木材加工和木、竹、藤、棕、草制品业	Processing of Timber,Manufacture of Wood,Plam and Straw Products			
家具制造业	Manufacture of Furniture			
造纸及纸制品业	Manufacture of Paper and Paper Products	69	135	-3
印刷和记录媒介复制	Printing,Reproduction of Recording Media	4067	3687	1031
文教、工美、体育和娱乐用品制造业	Manufacture of Articles For Cultural,Educational and Sports Activities	12	194	3
石油加工业、炼焦和核燃料加工业	Processing of Petroleum, Cokeing,Processing of Nuclear and Nuclear Fuel		603	-144
化学原料及化学制品制造业	Manufacture of Raw Chemical Materials and Chemical Products	6762	9214	2388
医药制造业	Manufacture of Medicines	190448	73554	18367
化学纤维制造业	Manufacture of Chemical Fibers	1011	4363	3632
橡胶和塑料制品业	Manufacture of Rubber and Plastics	364	1052	-88
非金属矿物制品业	Manufacture of Non-metallic Mineral Products	770	7315	-1611
黑色金属冶炼和压延加工业	Smelting and Pressing of Ferrous Metals	259	963	-69
有色金属冶炼和压延加工业	Smelting and Pressing of Non-ferrous Metals	2180	4614	1400
金属制品业	Manufacture of Metal Products	1231	3564	947
通用设备制造业	Manufacture of General Purpose Machinery	5784	7584	696
专用设备制造业	Manufacture of Special Equipment	13557	22840	1265
汽车制造业	Manufacture of Motor Vehicle	50759	97268	23263
铁路、船舶、航空航天和其他运输设备制造业	Railways,Shipbuilding,Aerospace and Other Transportation Equipment Manufacturing Industry	7145	11635	1862
电气机械和器材制造业	Manufacture of Electric Equipment and Machinery	22393	43661	6722
计算机、通讯和其他电子设备制造业	Manufacture of Communication Equipment, Computers and other Electronic Equipment	5532	217127	38017
仪器仪表制造业	Manufacture of Measuring Instruments and Machinery	5626	4258	20
其他制造业	Manufacture of Other Manufacturing	143	236	-28
废弃资源综合利用业	Recycling and Disposal of Waste			
金属制品、机械和设备修理业	Metal Products,Machinery and Equipment Repair Industry		2627	304
电力、热力的生产和供应业	Production and Supply of Electric Power and Heat Power			
燃气生产和供应业	Gas Mining and Supplying Industry	16173	14916	-1515
水的生产和供应业	Production and Supply of Water			

continued 5

(10 000 yuan)

营业利润 Operating Profit	利润总额 Total Profits	亏损企业亏损额 Total Loss of Deficit Enterprises	利税总额 Total Pre-tax Profits	应付职工薪酬 Salary Payable	本年应交增值税 Value Added Tax Payable
2908	3098		4013	4131	719
29608	29326	4511	53263	36691	18436
68630	96452	2081	118453	73811	15410
-138	-138	138	-64	572	63
4118	5561		8706	9454	2529
156	209		269	986	60
365	365		402	721	
12673	13021	687	13928	8131	285
33870	31782	2220	134808	105318	95772
8068	8144		6613	5631	-2008
-125	-114	312	302	1577	314
13672	15938	688	24569	7846	7458
542	633		1008	1487	327
6057	7527	729	11245	3373	3578
-186	-180	2344	1454	5212	849
3915	4057	1219	6443	14145	1556
34385	32215	623	40577	22589	5728
5531	9638	27915	76864	220803	14173
31498	31856		49402	21846	15122
-25571	-12301	40475	-307	39518	10214
669669	849306	1331	869601	80189	725
24126	24071		26651	9294	2036
235	233		402	514	151
-2081	-2022	2022	-2021	1058	1
35156	35276		44533	24047	5905

12-11 规模以上大中型工业企业主要经济指标（2017年）

单位：万元

分 组	Classify	企业单位数（个） Number of Enterprises (unit)	亏损企业 Loss Making Enterprises	工业总产值（当年价格） Gross Industrial Output Value (At Current Prices)
总计	**Total**	**252**	**45**	**44506904**
#市区	Urban	248	45	44262761
#亏损企业	Deficit Enterprises	45	45	670
按隶属关系分	**Grouped by Jurisdiction of Management**			
中央企业	Central Enterprises	50	10	11680099
省属企业	Provincial Enterprises	38	11	10184521
市属企业	Municipal Enterprises	164	24	22642284
按登记注册类型分组	**Grouped by Registion Status**			
内资企业	Domestic Investment Enterprises	210	35	35663165
国有	State-owned Enterprises	21	3	6485605
集体	Collective-owned Enterprises	1		78291
股份合作	Share-holding Corperative			
联营	Joint Ownership Enterprises			
国有联营	State Joint Ownership Enterprises			
集体联营	Collective Joint Ownership Enterprises			
国有与集体联营	Joint State-collective Ownership Enterprises			
其他联营	Other Joint Ownership Enterprises			
有限责任公司	Limited Liability Corporations	131	26	22369897
国有独资公司	State Sole Funded Enterprises	30	6	4149388
其他有限责任公司	Other Limited Liability Corporation	101	20	18220509
股份有限公司	Share-holding Corperation Ltd.	35	5	4326523
私营	Private Enterprises	22	1	2402849
私营独资	Private-funded Enterprises			
私营合伙	Private Partnership Enterprises			
私营有限责任公司	Private Limited Liability Corporations	18	1	2106118
私营股份有限公司	Private Share Holding Corporations	4		296731
其他	Other Domestic Funded Enterprises			
港澳台商投资	Enterprises with Funds from Hong Kong,Macao and Taiwan	10	2	2784949
外商投资	Foreign Funded Enterprises	32	8	6058790
按轻重工业分	**Grouped by Light Industry and Heavy Industry**			
轻工业	Light Industry	67	12	4823342
重工业	Heavy Industry	185	33	39683562
按企业规模分	**Grouped by Size of Enterprises**			
大型企业	Large-size	64	10	34454909

Major Economic Indicators of Large and Medium-sized Industrial Enterprises above Designated Size（2017）

(10 000 yuan)

工业销售产值（当年价） Value of Industry Products Sales (At Current Prices)	出口交货值 Export Delivery Value	从业人员年平均人数（人） Annual Average Employers (person)	资产总计 Total Assets	流动资产合计 Total Working Capitals	固定资产合计 Total Fixed Assets	固定资产原价 Origing Value of Fixed Assets	累计折旧 Accumulative Total Depreciation
43672148	**4937668**	**397992**	**61284064**	**32399388**	**18858586**	**33533108**	**16189278**
43430117	4930813	395058	60749771	32178414	18679372	33185066	16018603
655	33		496	308	664	154	651
11328724	557937	156749	21917270	11533738	7162409	12021073	5724276
9994913	375447	65513	12315460	6707136	2651678	4314408	1892521
22348511	4004284	175730	27051334	14158514	9044499	17197627	8572481
35064484	1622623	331887	49430047	27653161	13147662	23337684	11319708
6310114	271173	86663	12192655	6433735	4728848	7157683	3273408
78291		572	40794	16032	20469	30323	13444
22251727	883223	202113	27550492	16528293	5894519	11411501	5700268
3998229	90912	47840	8189296	4720979	1679581	3398140	1600523
18253498	792311	154273	19361196	11807314	4214938	8013361	4099745
4169162	405909	28120	7701016	3402544	2005382	4073911	2148739
2255190	62318	14419	1945090	1272557	498444	664266	183849
2009958	61313	12934	1812390	1201400	455769	609081	171339
245232	1005	1485	132700	71157	42675	55185	12510
2788699	105990	30218	2341606	1059815	775661	1160722	421051
5818965	3209055	35887	9512411	3686412	4935263	9034702	4448519
4664375	125343	53519	5509422	2974210	1759492	2908814	1515530
39007773	4812325	344473	55774642	29425178	17099094	30624294	14673748
33544187	4527702	286918	46235799	24713415	15383611	27139283	13064957

12-11 续表1

单位：万元

分 组	Classify	负债合计 Total Liabilites	流动负债合计 Total Working Liabilities	非流动负债 Non-Working Liabilities
总计	**Total**	**32397784**	**26175731**	**5912883**
#市区	Urban	32128013	26019052	5805592
#亏损企业	Deficit Enterprises	606	7	18
按隶属关系分	**Grouped by Jurisdiction of Management**			
中央企业	Central Enterprises	11663417	9666903	2313911
省属企业	Provincial Enterprises	7224853	6183419	819981
市属企业	Municipal Enterprises	13509514	10325409	2778991
按登记注册类型分组	**Grouped by Registion Status**			
内资企业	Domestic Investment Enterprises	27312355	22573849	4492478
国有	State-owned Enterprises	6418918	5383148	1412427
集体	Collective-owned Enterprises	34638	34538	
股份合作	Share-holding Corperative			
联营	Joint Ownership Enterprises			
国有联营	State Joint Ownership Enterprises			
集体联营	Collective Joint Ownership Enterprises			
国有与集体联营	Joint State-collective Ownership Enterprises			
其他联营	Other Joint Ownership Enterprises			
有限责任公司	Limited Liability Corporations	16754854	14119707	2221836
国有独资公司	State Sole Funded Enterprises	4400869	3524120	851300
其他有限责任公司	Other Limited Liability Corporation	12353985	10595587	1370536
股份有限公司	Share-holding Corperation Ltd.	2956289	2050699	699074
私营	Private Enterprises	1147656	985757	159141
私营独资	Private-funded Enterprises			
私营合伙	Private Partnership Enterprises			
私营有限责任公司	Private Limited Liability Corporations	1093900	946937	144205
私营股份有限公司	Private Share Holding Corporations	53756	38820	14936
其他	Other Domestic Funded Enterprises			
港澳台商投资	Enterprises with Funds from Hong Kong,Macao and Taiwan	1563600	1253441	310160
外商投资	Foreign Funded Enterprises	3521829	2348441	1110245
按轻重工业分	**Grouped by Light Industry and Heavy Industry**			
轻工业	Light Industry	3072599	2449102	614228
重工业	Heavy Industry	29325185	23726629	5298655
按企业规模分	**Grouped by Size of Enterprises**			
大型企业	Large-size	24009114	18996286	4528571

continued 1

(10 000 yuan)

所有者权益合计 Total Owners' Equities	实收资本 Total Capital Hold	营业收入 Total Revenue	主营业务收入 Revenue from Principal Business	营业成本 Total Cost	主营业务成本 Cost of Principal Business	税金及附加 Taxs and Other Changes	主营业务税金及附加 Taxes and Other Charges on Principal Business
28646989	**11582342**	**43402624**	**42384812**	**37274421**	**36425102**	**288137**	**278941**
28382466	11461278	43120152	42104988	37043399	36195888	287137	278002
30	10						
10014564	3991453	11910880	11586204	10183198	9951163	77525	74022
5090607	2051744	10359105	10062188	9140305	8864912	48212	47167
13541818	5539145	21132639	20736420	17950918	17609027	162400	157752
21878401	7975902	34762879	33953235	30072857	29397883	190772	182286
5534448	1740105	6468691	6258109	5406385	5268286	49729	46379
6156	4860	78291	33923	75572	37291	935	935
10795637	4779251	22168542	21644771	19610371	19157102	108406	103417
3788427	1090435	4127814	4000149	3439728	3335307	32215	28889
7007210	3688816	18040728	17644622	16170643	15821795	76191	74528
4744726	1237593	3823437	3801045	3098225	3087838	22344	22278
797434	214093	2223918	2215387	1882304	1847366	9358	9277
718490	181263	1952068	1944043	1675448	1640688	8561	8480
78944	32830	271850	271344	206856	206678	797	797
778006	242580	2758180	2639762	2519957	2411823	56523	55932
5990582	3363860	5881565	5791815	4681607	4615396	40842	40723
2414317	943252	4571394	4472912	3239172	3141079	45375	43476
26232672	10639090	38831230	37911900	34035249	33284023	242762	235465
22226685	8766886	33587025	32795786	29173624	28562242	220555	215865

12-11 续表2

单位：万元

分 组	Classify	销售费用 Expenses for Sales	管理费用 Expenses for Management	财务费用 Financial cost
总计	**Total**	**1455121**	**2210871**	**285360**
#市区	Urban	1451332	2182237	284605
#亏损企业	Deficit Enterprises			
按隶属关系分	**Grouped by Jurisdiction of Management**			
中央企业	Central Enterprises	242762	852253	105863
省属企业	Provincial Enterprises	422945	359173	27870
市属企业	Municipal Enterprises	789414	999445	151627
按登记注册类型分组	**Grouped by Registion Status**			
内资企业	Domestic Investment Enterprises	1034510	1709703	194512
国有	State-owned Enterprises	173786	501235	51119
集体	Collective-owned Enterprises		2688	-198
股份合作	Share-holding Corperative			
联营	Joint Ownership Enterprises			
国有联营	State Joint Ownership Enterprises			
集体联营	Collective Joint Ownership Enterprises			
国有与集体联营	Joint State-collective Ownership Enterprises			
其他联营	Other Joint Ownership Enterprises			
有限责任公司	Limited Liability Corporations	626348	949266	82558
国有独资公司	State Sole Funded Enterprises	112999	326372	19215
其他有限责任公司	Other Limited Liability Corporation	513349	622894	63343
股份有限公司	Share-holding Corperation Ltd.	142078	194623	49920
私营	Private Enterprises	92298	61891	11113
私营独资	Private-funded Enterprises			
私营合伙	Private Partnership Enterprises			
私营有限责任公司	Private Limited Liability Corporations	77324	44399	9538
私营股份有限公司	Private Share Holding Corporations	14974	17492	1575
其他	Other Domestic Funded Enterprises			
港澳台商投资	Enterprises with Funds from Hong Kong,Macao and Taiwan	72609	89744	22831
外商投资	Foreign Funded Enterprises	348002	411424	68017
按轻重工业分	**Grouped by Light Industry and Heavy Industry**			
轻工业	Light Industry	698548	326187	46709
重工业	Heavy Industry	756573	1884684	238651
按企业规模分	**Grouped by Size of Enterprises**			
大型企业	Large-size	903877	1614420	184157

continued 2

(10 000 yuan)

营业利润 Operating Profit	利润总额 Total Profits	亏损企业亏损额 Total Loss of Deficit Enterprises	利税总额 Total Pre-tax Profits	应付职工薪酬 Salary Payable	本年应交增值税 Value Added Tax Payable
2593337	**2945254**	**192967**	**4160693**	**3891577**	**927302**
2575550	2921793	192967	4130725	3850654	921795
510453	549731	62584	910582	1845916	283326
308216	325836	25432	630593	605741	256546
1774668	2069687	104951	2619518	1439920	387430
1737342	1866928	120334	2816149	3275663	758449
324677	351093	10473	597243	751695	196421
-725	13		1716	5751	767
845569	924005	92902	1485994	2078978	453586
253445	277434	26494	455819	588407	146170
592124	646571	66408	1030175	1490571	307416
369899	391808	16953	488459	348486	74306
197922	200009	6	242737	90753	33369
167862	169439	6	204679	84284	26678
30060	30570		38058	6469	6691
-2825	1108	26868	70033	253958	12402
858820	1077218	45765	1274511	361956	156451
283797	335507	48350	636852	494698	255970
2309540	2609747	144617	3523841	3396879	671332
2125035	2405365	78909	3210375	3042096	584455

12-11 续表3

单位：万元

分 组	Classify	企业单位数（个） Number of Enterprises (unit)	亏损企业 Loss Making Enterprises	工业总产值（当年价格） Gross Industrial Output Value (At Current Prices)
中型企业	Medium-size	188	35	10051995
按经济组织类型分组	**Grouped by Economic Type of Orgnization**			
独资企业	Appropratorship	39	7	10676013
合作、合伙企业	Partnership	1	1	13199
股份有限公司	Corporaton	42	5	5591749
有限责任公司	Limited Liability Company	170	32	28225943
按控股情况分	**Grouped by Cast strand**			
国有控股	State owned shares	127	28	25323752
集体控股	Collective shares	8		2003929
私人控股	Private holdings	78	8	10965935
港澳台控股	Hong Kong and Macao Holdings	9	1	371611
外商投资	Foreign Investment	23	6	5355753
其他	Others	7	2	485924
按工业行业大类分	**Grouped by Sector**			
煤炭开采和洗选业	Mining and Washing of Coal			
石油和天然气开采业	Extraction of Petroleum and Natural Gas			
黑色金属矿采选业	Mining and Processing of Ferrous Metal Ores			
有色金属矿采选业	Mining and Processing of Non-ferrous Metal Ores			
非金属矿采选业	Mining and Processing of Nonmetal Ores			
开采辅助活动	Mining Auxiliary Activities	2		487775
其他采矿业	Mining of other Ores			
农副食品加工业	Processing of Food from Agricultural Porducts	8	1	553669
食品制造业	Manufacture of Foods	14	2	833872
酒、饮料和精制茶制造业	Manufacture of Alcohol,Beverages and Tea	6	1	556517
烟草制品业	Manufacture of Tobacco	1		10859
纺织业	Manufacture of Textile	4	2	115497
纺织服装、服饰业	Textile, apparel industry	1		45171
皮革、毛皮、羽毛及其制品和制鞋业	Manufacture of Leather, Fur, Feather and Related Products, and Shoes	1		34262
木材加工和木、竹、藤、棕、草制品业	Processing of Timber, Manufacture of Wood,Plam and Straw Products	1		44000
家具制造业	Manufacture of Furniture	1		14951

continued 3

(10 000 yuan)

工业销售产值（当年价）Value of Industry Products Sales (At Current Prices)	出口交货值 Export Delivery Value	从业人员年平均人数（人）Annual Average Employers (person)	资产总计 Total Assets	流动资产合计 Total Working Capitals	固定资产合计 Total Fixed Assets	固定资产原价 Origing Value of Fixed Assets	累计折旧 Accumulative Total Depreciation
10127961	409966	111074	15048265	7685973	3474975	6393825	3124321
10452580	3361502	106621	18685630	8538918	8646594	15047711	7275610
12498		300	37958	18588	10767	21526	10758
5278166	520290	35164	8995849	4008185	2496338	4575169	2346872
27928904	1055876	255907	33564627	19833697	7704887	13888702	6556038
24976200	1062120	269160	41122051	22741703	11200483	18663744	8484884
1939089	325172	5381	2348277	1092150	687765	2110720	1464356
10740973	298848	80698	8383526	4948698	1941806	3559341	1751601
371085	69916	5336	333633	174014	131745	241826	88921
5165894	3180424	30288	8409051	3073232	4654935	8612014	4296918
478907	1188	7129	687526	369591	241852	345463	102598
492213		5505	726804	501659	125655	329716	201520
532922	2227	4546	541954	397485	74267	232875	158550
802661		10077	496957	235577	179018	311185	133858
729225	112114	6117	1085787	539820	328525	575102	249320
10859		510	42802	22676	19391	32056	2377
116795	4144	6961	286501	91809	169224	275449	120705
41504		1101	61894	48472	9474	11676	2202
34262		591	54333	32741	4145	8279	4133
34200		495	161343	57310	55286	68536	37042
14867		548	17862	7636	9830	5831	2732

12-11 续表4

单位：万元

分　组	Classify	负债合计 Total Liabilites	流动负债合计 Total Working Liabilities	非流动负债 Non-Working Liabilities
中型企业	Medium-size	8388670	7179445	1384312
按经济组织类型分组	**Grouped by Economic Type of Orgnization**			
独资企业	Appropratorship	8121251	6164905	2332904
合作、合伙企业	Partnership	8947	8932	15
股份有限公司	Corporaton	3733726	2615138	849829
有限责任公司	Limited Liability Company	20533860	17386756	2730135
按控股情况分	**Grouped by Cast strand**			
国有控股	State owned shares	23193061	19415498	3813830
集体控股	Collective shares	955769	755011	200609
私人控股	Private holdings	4940651	3930612	726994
港澳台控股	Hong Kong and Macao Holdings	139755	125888	13867
外商投资	Foreign Investment	2821842	1680202	1079397
其他	Others	346706	268520	78186
按工业行业大类分	**Grouped by Sector**			
煤炭开采和洗选业	Mining and Washing of Coal			
石油和天然气开采业	Extraction of Petroleum and Natural Gas			
黑色金属矿采选业	Mining and Processing of Ferrous Metal Ores			
有色金属矿采选业	Mining and Processing of Non-ferrous Metal Ores			
非金属矿采选业	Mining and Processing of Nonmetal Ores			
开采辅助活动	Mining Auxiliary Activities	210105	208959	1146
其他采矿业	Mining of other Ores			
农副食品加工业	Processing of Food from Agricultural Porducts	436106	407931	28175
食品制造业	Manufacture of Foods	222478	219434	3043
酒、饮料和精制茶制造业	Manufacture of Alcohol,Beverages and Tea	573446	435927	137519
烟草制品业	Manufacture of Tobacco	9227	9227	
纺织业	Manufacture of Textile	170016	109486	114677
纺织服装、服饰业	Textile, apparel industry	42505	39785	2720
皮革、毛皮、羽毛及其制品和制鞋业	Manufacture of Leather, Fur, Feather and Related Products, and Shoes	24275	18387	5888
木材加工和木、竹、藤、棕、草制品业	Processing of Timber, Manufacture of Wood,Plam and Straw Products	89683	55267	32797
家具制造业	Manufacture of Furniture	9664	8610	1054

continued 4

(10 000 yuan)

所有者权益合计 Total Owners' Equities	实收资本 Total Capital Hold	营业收入 Total Revenue	主营业务收入 Revenue from Principal Business	营业成本 Total Cost	主营业务成本 Cost of Principal Business	税金及附加 Taxs and Other Changes	主营业务税金及附加 Taxes and Other Charges on Principal Business
6420304	2815456	9815599	9589026	8100797	7862860	67582	63076
10325089	4643542	10607417	10325468	8836932	8633015	80029	76088
29010	28897	12793	10530	11091	9572	287	287
5262122	1332432	4972050	4947506	3866325	3854767	31127	31061
13030768	5577471	27810364	27101308	24560073	23927748	176694	171505
17689700	7005098	26078716	25303645	22828832	22238633	158196	150178
1392508	336017	1547005	1497309	1167718	1125200	5922	5922
3442874	773556	9752592	9609722	8476434	8306499	81397	80929
193878	122726	367095	358129	276692	269984	5353	4762
5587209	3130802	5179478	5147720	4112024	4080663	34752	34751
340820	214143	477738	468287	412721	404123	2517	2399
516699	271375	349954	347229	290513	289956	2250	2126
105848	46266	440858	439956	393760	393562	776	776
274479	121377	813216	789598	592437	570143	7205	6614
512341	171207	738876	726408	546314	535152	13101	13101
33575	27400	12406	12406	5104	5104	414	414
93980	11006	119326	118418	112469	92704	1495	664
19389	7500	28332	27687	22092	21253	337	332
30058	15000	63599	34262	56175	29364	364	364
71660	12500	33100	33000	28520	14715	299	254
8198	6000	16548	16548	13615	13615	58	58

12-11 续表5

单位：万元

分组	Classify	销售费用 Expenses for Sales	管理费用 Expenses for Management	财务费用 Financial cost
中型企业	Medium-size	551244	596451	101203
按经济组织类型分组	**Grouped by Economic Type of Orgnization**			
独资企业	Appropratorship	292565	766457	92695
合作、合伙企业	Partnership	912	1335	399
股份有限公司	Corporaton	338106	293449	77917
有限责任公司	Limited Liability Company	823538	1149630	114349
按控股情况分	**Grouped by Cast strand**			
国有控股	State owned shares	598590	1420207	145912
集体控股	Collective shares	59332	76401	6843
私人控股	Private holdings	421050	299367	61004
港澳台控股	Hong Kong and Macao Holdings	40486	18608	2946
外商投资	Foreign Investment	323603	371188	69058
其他	Others	12060	25100	-403
按工业行业大类分	**Grouped by Sector**			
煤炭开采和洗选业	Mining and Washing of Coal			
石油和天然气开采业	Extraction of Petroleum and Natural Gas			
黑色金属矿采选业	Mining and Processing of Ferrous Metal Ores			
有色金属矿采选业	Mining and Processing of Non-ferrous Metal Ores			
非金属矿采选业	Mining and Processing of Nonmetal Ores			
开采辅助活动	Mining Auxiliary Activities	696	29463	-3598
其他采矿业	Mining of other Ores			
农副食品加工业	Processing of Food from Agricultural Porducts	18316	11948	6012
食品制造业	Manufacture of Foods	121036	38719	196
酒、饮料和精制茶制造业	Manufacture of Alcohol,Beverages and Tea	100418	28473	5351
烟草制品业	Manufacture of Tobacco	918	2458	-171
纺织业	Manufacture of Textile	1292	7586	835
纺织服装、服饰业	Textile, apparel industry	2187	3648	720
皮革、毛皮、羽毛及其制品和制鞋业	Manufacture of Leather, Fur, Feather and Related Products, and Shoes	1102	2499	130
木材加工和木、竹、藤、棕、草制品业	Processing of Timber, Manufacture of Wood,Plam and Straw Products	488	1929	2612
家具制造业	Manufacture of Furniture	992	1342	34

continued 5

(10 000 yuan)

营业利润 Operating Profit	利润总额 Total Profits	亏损企业亏损额 Total Loss of Deficit Enterprises	利税总额 Total Pre-tax Profits	应付职工薪酬 Salary Payable	本年应交增值税 Value Added Tax Payable
468302	539889	114058	950318	849481	342847
1049048	1253799	21192	1562472	922384	228644
-1231	-1219	1219	-654	1809	278
420007	470453	16953	673149	484667	171569
1125513	1222221	153603	1925726	2482717	526811
1020676	1099969	119332	1858191	2800129	600027
287274	291649		321742	154410	24171
439301	485855	26571	720019	533891	152766
23755	24937	1219	40003	53534	9713
795703	1013367	42709	1181573	304120	133454
26628	29477	3136	39165	45493	7171
27688	24157		30882	99873	4476
9501	15832	1405	22947	22892	6340
56156	55240	5094	92114	70864	29670
110713	141440	2081	181186	87015	26646
3806	3808		5838	4803	1616
-2738	-1754	3782	1404	34187	1664
400	497		2281	2605	1447
3478	3395		4154	4901	395
-748	210		5545	2097	5036
507	749		1292	1864	485

12-11 续表6

单位：万元

分　组	Classify	企业单位数（个）Number of Enterprises (unit)	亏损企业 Loss Making Enterprises	工业总产值（当年价格）Gross Industrial Output Value (At Current Prices)
造纸及纸制品业	Manufacture of Paper and Paper Products	1	1	10112
印刷和记录媒介复制	Printing,Reproduction of Recording Media	8	1	433712
文教、工美、体育和娱乐用品制造业	Manufacture of Articles For Cultural,Educational and Sports Activities			
石油加工业、炼焦和核燃料加工业	Processing of Petroleum, Cokeing,Processing of Nuclear and Nuclear Fuel	1		5271
化学原料及化学制品制造业	Manufacture of Raw Chemical Materials and Chemical Products	14	4	2737270
医药制造业	Manufacture of Medicines	16	1	1844260
化学纤维制造业	Manufacture of Chemical Fibers			
橡胶和塑料制品业	Manufacture of Rubber and Plastics	3	1	600770
非金属矿物制品业	Manufacture of Non-metallic Mineral Products	8		245437
黑色金属冶炼和压延加工业	Smelting and Pressing of Ferrous Metals	2		83726
有色金属冶炼和压延加工业	Smelting and Pressing of Non-ferrous Metals	6		1709738
金属制品业	Manufacture of Metal Products	7	2	763741
通用设备制造业	Manufacture of General Purpose Machinery	11	3	1007891
专用设备制造业	Manufacture of Special Equipment	21	5	1320522
汽车制造业	Manufacture of Motor Vehicle	20	3	9924578
铁路、船舶、航空航天和其他运输设备制造业	Railways,Shipbuilding,Aerospace and Other Transportation Equipment Manufacturing Industry	20	2	4612613
电气机械和器材制造业	Manufacture of Electric Equipment and Machinery	24	7	4745480
计算机、通讯和其他电子设备制造业	Manufacture of Communication Equipment, Computers and other Electronic Equipment	29	4	7011267
仪器仪表制造业	Manufacture of Measuring Instruments and Machinery	7		963403
其他制造业	Manufacture of Other Manufacturing			
废弃资源综合利用业	Recycling and Disposal of Waste			
金属制品、机械和设备修理业	Metal Products,Machinery and Equipment Repair Industry			
电力、热力的生产和供应业	Production and Supply of Electric Power and Heat Power	9	4	2582056
燃气生产和供应业	Gas Mining and Supplying Industry	5	1	1104419
水的生产和供应业	Production and Supply of Water	1		104065

continued 6

(10 000 yuan)

工业销售产值（当年价） Value of Industry Products Sales (At Current Prices)	出口交货值 Export Delivery Value	从业人员年平均人数（人） Annual Average Employers (person)	资产总计 Total Assets	流动资产合计 Total Working Capitals	固定资产合计 Total Fixed Assets	固定资产原价 Origing Value of Fixed Assets	累计折旧 Accumulative Total Depreciation
10112		386	11425	7294	1180	1180	436
409995	1219	4976	510854	299427	183609	407695	232931
5271		4630	40163	63	40100	2029	744
2671475	332148	18753	4739700	1772328	1306539	2876127	1609450
1629806	2070	12460	1501955	862733	411682	542460	383633
603398	83689	14417	1621635	917276	365526	420061	123631
244184		3177	407896	255474	82609	136115	55741
85102	3892	1003	96360	63292	24704	76714	30761
1559643	29779	6026	2503682	783126	358727	650143	263730
776312	24547	16849	1585724	937524	425980	779589	349046
1010349	21836	11719	2950263	2210027	257867	547838	285550
1178292	83584	15954	2495105	1678386	474771	803180	321813
10030418	278279	62815	7257307	5155777	1506856	2171306	748367
4424509	343514	67626	8838676	5240611	1641930	2675165	1234553
5444820	286067	37684	6969896	4782411	1820733	2873542	1531478
6190983	3284957	43336	8891023	3602535	4368422	8661637	4250689
797569	43602	10979	1499635	895334	358432	604532	246306
2582056		20244	3936126	504870	3276329	5904661	3003468
1104281		5844	1768557	407864	883781	1332987	449013
104065		2663	181845	87851	93994	215442	155499

12-11 续表7

单位：万元

分　组	Classify	负债合计 Total Liabilites	流动负债合计 Total Working Liabilities	非流动负债 Non-Working Liabilities
造纸及纸制品业	Manufacture of Paper and Paper Products	6481	4937	1544
印刷和记录媒介复制	Printing,Reproduction of Recording Media	143532	132498	11034
文教、工美、体育和娱乐用品制造业	Manufacture of Articles For Cultural,Educational and Sports Activities			
石油加工业、炼焦和核燃料加工业	Processing of Petroleum, Cokeing,Processing of Nuclear and Nuclear Fuel	23914	16116	7799
化学原料及化学制品制造业	Manufacture of Raw Chemical Materials and Chemical Products	2803940	2153496	650443
医药制造业	Manufacture of Medicines	732786	600685	68684
化学纤维制造业	Manufacture of Chemical Fibers			
橡胶和塑料制品业	Manufacture of Rubber and Plastics	1095260	752108	343151
非金属矿物制品业	Manufacture of Non-metallic Mineral Products	247680	213297	31625
黑色金属冶炼和压延加工业	Smelting and Pressing of Ferrous Metals	55467	45199	10269
有色金属冶炼和压延加工业	Smelting and Pressing of Non-ferrous Metals	582657	164469	40197
金属制品业	Manufacture of Metal Products	1070650	783764	286886
通用设备制造业	Manufacture of General Purpose Machinery	1630016	1509198	119818
专用设备制造业	Manufacture of Special Equipment	1121926	982752	134302
汽车制造业	Manufacture of Motor Vehicle	4963045	4556079	401165
铁路、船舶、航空航天和其他运输设备制造业	Railways,Shipbuilding,Aerospace and Other Transportation Equipment Manufacturing Industry	4856379	4120532	999120
电气机械和器材制造业	Manufacture of Electric Equipment and Machinery	3459692	3045242	414369
计算机、通讯和其他电子设备制造业	Manufacture of Communication Equipment, Computers and other Electronic Equipment	3311768	2113749	1221090
仪器仪表制造业	Manufacture of Measuring Instruments and Machinery	683799	594179	89620
其他制造业	Manufacture of Other Manufacturing			
废弃资源综合利用业	Recycling and Disposal of Waste			
金属制品、机械和设备修理业	Metal Products,Machinery and Equipment Repair Industry			
电力、热力的生产和供应业	Production and Supply of Electric Power and Heat Power	2748239	2161378	586761
燃气生产和供应业	Gas Mining and Supplying Industry	961358	634968	134369
水的生产和供应业	Production and Supply of Water	111690	78072	33618

continued 7

(10 000 yuan)

所有者权益合计 Total Owners' Equities	实收资本 Total Capital Hold	营业收入 Total Revenue	主营业务收入 Revenue from Principal Business	营业成本 Total Cost	主营业务成本 Cost of Principal Business	税金及附加 Taxs and Other Changes	主营业务税金及附加 Taxes and Other Charges on Principal Business
4944	5000	9383	9383	8820	8820	7	7
367322	184798	411723	407133	325598	322386	3840	3840
16248	33000	5012	5012	4152	4122	36	34
1935761	791657	2458886	2413601	2024463	1992230	10437	10318
769169	154094	1563163	1562548	848545	848183	15781	15781
526375	396584	639098	612513	565024	559096	3105	2918
160216	67190	262633	250277	219851	207041	2250	2132
40892	37736	86047	83927	72091	69783	873	393
1921026	405868	1740187	1722197	1639648	1629790	3788	3488
515074	262019	751934	740775	615226	608075	3350	3350
1320247	199486	945055	926710	792147	776427	9463	8295
1373179	712065	1248041	1236040	980914	972966	11620	11564
2294262	745012	9880313	9516049	9065151	8720919	79122	78291
3765513	1418593	5126696	5012497	4530904	4458662	19664	18318
3510203	1204284	4269111	4130141	3446011	3350373	34826	34779
5579254	3046088	6312992	6288771	5477743	5456893	30066	29897
815836	178423	942716	934245	779662	744167	4436	2401
1187887	714477	2843680	2775753	2702248	2655165	20864	20614
807199	297337	1162400	1107663	1011935	983227	6780	6760
70155	39000	127339	104065	103289	91209	1530	1058

12-11 续表8

单位：万元

分 组	Classify	销售费用 Expenses for Sales	管理费用 Expenses for Management	财务费用 Financial cost
造纸及纸制品业	Manufacture of Paper and Paper Products	154	236	152
印刷和记录媒介复制	Printing,Reproduction of Recording Media	11832	35142	-41
文教、工美、体育和娱乐用品制造业	Manufacture of Articles For Cultural,Educational and Sports Activities			
石油加工业、炼焦和核燃料加工业	Processing of Petroleum, Cokeing,Processing of Nuclear and Nuclear Fuel		603	-144
化学原料及化学制品制造业	Manufacture of Raw Chemical Materials and Chemical Products	36819	132617	30582
医药制造业	Manufacture of Medicines	415425	156290	19880
化学纤维制造业	Manufacture of Chemical Fibers			
橡胶和塑料制品业	Manufacture of Rubber and Plastics	22440	22732	11494
非金属矿物制品业	Manufacture of Non-metallic Mineral Products	12784	10416	-1532
黑色金属冶炼和压延加工业	Smelting and Pressing of Ferrous Metals	4565	5789	500
有色金属冶炼和压延加工业	Smelting and Pressing of Non-ferrous Metals	5061	37527	9431
金属制品业	Manufacture of Metal Products	14873	85255	11412
通用设备制造业	Manufacture of General Purpose Machinery	40989	124329	3350
专用设备制造业	Manufacture of Special Equipment	64344	93110	12864
汽车制造业	Manufacture of Motor Vehicle	215240	253963	-4171
铁路、船舶、航空航天和其他运输设备制造业	Railways,Shipbuilding,Aerospace and Other Transportation Equipment Manufacturing Industry	63994	299362	34994
电气机械和器材制造业	Manufacture of Electric Equipment and Machinery	221776	324798	28441
计算机、通讯和其他电子设备制造业	Manufacture of Communication Equipment, Computers and other Electronic Equipment	26989	349302	61462
仪器仪表制造业	Manufacture of Measuring Instruments and Machinery	14616	86922	-352
其他制造业	Manufacture of Other Manufacturing			
废弃资源综合利用业	Recycling and Disposal of Waste			
金属制品、机械和设备修理业	Metal Products,Machinery and Equipment Repair Industry			
电力、热力的生产和供应业	Production and Supply of Electric Power and Heat Power	578	25092	39479
燃气生产和供应业	Gas Mining and Supplying Industry	28402	29091	12689
水的生产和供应业	Production and Supply of Water	6795	10230	2749

continued 8

(10 000 yuan)

营业利润 Operating Profit	利润总额 Total Profits	亏损企业亏损额 Total Loss of Deficit Enterprises	利税总额 Total Pre-tax Profits	应付职工薪酬 Salary Payable	本年应交增值税 Value Added Tax Payable
14	-11	11	62	1021	65
36471	38189	11	65277	66539	23249
365	365		402	721	
296804	309573	14878	370803	278750	50793
109340	109440	391	284520	145260	159299
15202	12417	2455	23498	47293	7975
18347	18627		36112	20395	15236
1878	1807		4780	2790	2100
48802	54571		76035	45253	17677
5517	12365	19653	32858	157768	17143
29169	42164	9777	90789	141803	39162
101856	106309	12504	157959	147609	40030
215955	222821	33120	426120	539904	124173
171160	182179	16606	292164	889786	90321
242085	267093	38910	395053	290299	93133
844309	1061157	3703	1114598	299115	23375
94267	102852		128116	67337	20828
69140	75434	23887	202502	328585	106204
81289	81188	4699	103610	58452	15642
2604	3140		7792	31796	3122

12-12 规模以上高技术产业工业企业主要经济指标（2017年）

单位：万元

行业	Sector	企业单位数（个） Number of Enterprises (unit)	亏损企业 Loss Making Enterprises
总计	**Total**	**287**	**51**
一、医药制造业	**Pharmaceutical Manufacturing**	**59**	**12**
（一）化学药品制造	Chemical manufacturing	20	3
化学药品原料药制造	Chemical raw materials Medicine manufacturing	6	
化学药品制剂制造	Chemical preparations manufacturing	14	3
（二）中药饮片加工	Chinese medicine Pieces processing	2	
（三）中成药生产	Chinese medicine production	24	6
（四）兽用药品制造	Veterinary pharmaceutical manufacturing	3	1
（五）生物药品制造	Biopharmaceutical manufacturing	6	1
（六）卫生材料及医药用品制造	Sanitary materials and medical supplies manufacturing	4	1
二、航空航天器制造业	**Aerospace & aviation industry**	**52**	**4**
（一）飞机制造	Aircraft Manufacturing	13	1
（二）航天器制造	Spacecraft Manufacturing	4	
（三）航空、航天相关设备制造	Aviation and aerospace-related equipment manufacturing	27	2
（四）其他航空航天器制造	Other aerospace manufacturing	5	
（五）航空航天器修理	Aerospace vehicle repair	3	1
三、电子及通讯设备制造业	**Electronic and communication equipment manufacturing**	**94**	**17**
（一）电子工业专用设备制造	Electronic equipment manufacturing	4	
（二）光纤、光缆制造	Optical fiber, cable manufacturing	2	
（三）锂离子电池制造	Lithium-ion battery manufacturing	3	2
（四）通信设备制造	Communications equipment manufacturing	17	5
通信系统设备制造	Communications system equipment	14	4
通信终端设备制造	Communication Terminal Equipment	3	1
（五）广播电视设备制造	Broadcasting and TV Equipment	2	
广播电视节目制作及发射设备制造	Radio and television program production and transmission equipment		
广播电视接收设备及器材制造	Radio and television reception apparatus and equipment manufacturing	1	
应用电视设备及其他广播电视设备制造	Application television equipment and other radio and television equipment manufacturing	1	
（六）雷达及配套设备制造	Radar and ancillary equipment manufacturers	3	1
（七）视听设备制造	Audiovisual equipment manufacturing	1	
电视机制造	TV manufacturing	1	
音响设备制造	Audio Equipment manufacturing		
影视录放设备制造	Video recording equipment manufacturing		
（八）电子器件制造	Electronic device manufacturing	27	4
电子真空器件制造	Electronic vacuum device manufacturing		
半导体分立器件制造	Discrete semiconductor device manufacturing	10	2
集成电路制造	Semiconductor Manufacturing	8	1
光电子器件及其他电子器件制造	Optoelectronic devices and other electronic device manufacturing	9	1
（九）电子元件制造	Electronics Manufacturing	27	3
电子元件及组件制造	Electronic components and component manufacturing	25	3
印刷电路板制造	Printed circuit board manufacturing	2	
（十）其他电子设备制造	Other electronic equipment manufacturing	8	2

Major Economic Indicators of High Technology Industry Industrial Enterprises above Designated Size (2017)

(10 000 yuan)

工业总产值（当年价格）Gross Industrial Output Value (At Current Prices)	工业销售产值（当年价）Value of Industry Products Sales (At Current Prices)	出口交货值 Export Delivery Value	从业人员年平均人数（人）Annual Average Employers (person)	资产总计 Total Assets	流动资产合计 Total Working Capitals	固定资产合计 Total Fixed Assets	固定资产原价 Origing Value of Fixed Assets	累计折旧 Accumulative Total Depreciation
18592860	**16875798**	**4161144**	**157314**	**26695722**	**13201813**	**8291302**	**15234955**	**7529962**
2378992	**2113140**	**12268**	**17854**	**2120594**	**1237443**	**569171**	**751700**	**469602**
1317882	1157332	3300	8437	1109798	646031	347408	242364	134829
41391	27580	1269	585	52784	26635	21688	27307	6007
1276491	1129752	2031	7852	1057014	619396	325720	215057	128823
13136	12764	8591	81	6186	4505	124	231	108
791060	701695	39	6231	648031	415112	125070	376856	280963
13748	13323		1089	93300	65105	24601	12623	6434
214027	199497	88	1477	237988	93637	65864	110554	44224
29139	28530	251	539	25292	13055	6104	9071	3044
4736457	**4431827**	**381381**	**65267**	**8752550**	**4991130**	**1752862**	**2722161**	**1207381**
3469415	3356263	354129	51877	6704101	3863625	1241674	2063814	927910
467171	461595	11257	6809	1135411	610490	313585	405702	192410
725188	546181	9260	5535	738252	415999	175527	233824	79074
58006	52847		849	145442	82353	16211	11466	5521
16677	14941	6734	197	29344	18662	5865	7354	2464
7846541	**6908944**	**3353476**	**52180**	**10196748**	**4383742**	**4732835**	**9097642**	**4373967**
24167	26849	92	482	66113	51668	12012	15847	3836
140889	105991		654	72321	55516	12866	30593	17727
175735	138366	3569	1303	468126	185974	270417	262389	45257
2635613	2018207	197710	15179	1028442	816282	157402	251577	98587
509163	483742	197710	11372	648090	447058	148522	239468	94229
2126451	1534466		3807	380352	369224	8881	12109	4358
15326	15086	9810	295	18991	17708	1206	3168	1963
3088	3088		37	13536	12869	667	2047	1380
12238	11998	9810	258	5455	4839	539	1121	582
418814	310856	28122	5651	1063055	575193	248443	386883	139713
25154	23642	1048	136	7819	1848	5824	9676	3852
25154	23642	1048	136	7819	1848	5824	9676	3852
3814666	3686146	3030565	16620	6514951	2059089	3887422	7865267	3978524
311008	258772	81084	2494	393327	208732	83600	155548	72243
3432552	3363788	2946469	12374	6039519	1800251	3788979	7685950	3897092
71106	63586	3012	1752	82105	50106	14843	23768	9190
555034	545693	82246	11171	876822	556261	130664	262829	80436
474919	465925	13549	10084	806190	516979	99409	183393	53469
80115	79768	68697	1087	70632	39283	31255	79437	26967
41142	38108	313	689	80110	64204	6580	9412	4073

12-12 续表1

单位：万元

行业	Sector	负债合计 Total Liabilites	流动负债合计 Total Working Liabilities
总计	**Total**	**12779715**	**10044941**
一、医药制造业	**Pharmaceutical Manufacturing**	**1103431**	**902315**
（一）化学药品制造	Chemical manufacturing	563852	432822
化学药品原料药制造	Chemical raw materials Medicine manufacturing	21324	19310
化学药品制剂制造	Chemical preparations manufacturing	542529	413512
（二）中药饮片加工	Chinese medicine Pieces processing	3151	3151
（三）中成药生产	Chinese medicine production	402500	349480
（四）兽用药品制造	Veterinary pharmaceutical manufacturing	35326	33260
（五）生物药品制造	Biopharmaceutical manufacturing	86113	73211
（六）卫生材料及医药用品制造	Sanitary materials and medical supplies manufacturing	12489	10392
二、航空航天器制造业	**Aerospace & aviation industry**	**4590425**	**3865860**
（一）飞机制造	Aircraft Manufacturing	3644794	3132508
（二）航天器制造	Spacecraft Manufacturing	541817	374837
（三）航空、航天相关设备制造	Aviation and aerospace-related equipment manufacturing	340642	298953
（四）其他航空航天器制造	Other aerospace manufacturing	51557	47947
（五）航空航天器修理	Aerospace vehicle repair	11616	11616
三、电子及通讯设备制造业	**Electronic and communication equipment manufacturing**	**4109560**	**2823829**
（一）电子工业专用设备制造	Electronic equipment manufacturing	33164	31908
（二）光纤、光缆制造	Optical fiber, cable manufacturing	36617	36117
（三）锂离子电池制造	Lithium-ion battery manufacturing	381866	344481
（四）通信设备制造	Communications equipment manufacturing	585045	556281
通信系统设备制造	Communications system equipment	308479	283020
通信终端设备制造	Communication Terminal Equipment	276566	273262
（五）广播电视设备制造	Broadcasting and TV Equipment	13675	13675
广播电视节目制作及发射设备制造	Radio and television program production and transmission equipment		
广播电视接收设备及器材制造	Radio and television reception apparatus and equipment manufacturing	10328	10328
应用电视设备及其他广播电视设备制造	Application television equipment and other radio and television equipment manufacturing	3346	3346
（六）雷达及配套设备制造	Radar and ancillary equipment manufacturers	725671	594119
（七）视听设备制造	Audiovisual equipment manufacturing	3936	3936
电视机制造	TV manufacturing	3936	3936
音响设备制造	Audio Equipment manufacturing		
影视录放设备制造	Video recording equipment manufacturing		
（八）电子器件制造	Electronic device manufacturing	1670774	746789
电子真空器件制造	Electronic vacuum device manufacturing		
半导体分立器件制造	Discrete semiconductor device manufacturing	184687	146697
集成电路制造	Semiconductor Manufacturing	1457971	577640
光电子器件及其他电子器件制造	Optoelectronic devices and other electronic device manufacturing	28116	22452
（九）电子元件制造	Electronics Manufacturing	634024	472742
电子元件及组件制造	Electronic components and component manufacturing	603613	442789
印刷电路板制造	Printed circuit board manufacturing	30411	29954
（十）其他电子设备制造	Other electronic equipment manufacturing	24789	23782

continued 1

(10 000 yuan)

非流动负债 Non-Working Liabilities	所有者权益合计 Total Owners' Equities	实收资本 Total Capital Hold	营业收入 Total Revenue	主营业务收入 Revenue from Principal Business	营业成本 Total Cost	主营业务成本 Cost of Principal Business	税金及附加 Taxs and Other Changes	主营业务税金及附加 Taxes and Other Charges on Principal Business
2860997	**13685658**	**6146316**	**17405419**	**17231114**	**14423066**	**14274370**	**83221**	**79051**
83819	**1011164**	**279681**	**1948743**	**1947736**	**1071961**	**1071293**	**20432**	**20399**
68788	545945	134916	1166440	1166006	668855	668426	12234	12234
2014	31460	11530	28031	28031	13721	13721	343	343
66774	514485	123386	1138409	1137975	655135	654705	11891	11891
	3035	3500	12764	12764	11670	11670	11	11
12136	241893	79995	604789	604342	314409	314305	6648	6648
250	57974	5960	12004	12004	8127	8127	103	74
548	149515	44430	128011	127885	49890	49756	1280	1277
2097	12802	10880	24735	24735	19010	19010	155	155
987750	**3945299**	**1474602**	**5157140**	**5047953**	**4599875**	**4531720**	**15628**	**13911**
785039	2842523	1161276	3890629	3802082	3538494	3479438	11555	10947
166980	593594	76337	557862	539212	459809	452003	959	959
32121	397611	192354	630311	628520	546910	545815	2417	1309
3610	93843	20228	63200	63198	42286	42286	606	606
	17729	24407	15139	14941	12376	12178	90	90
1271687	**6079666**	**3464176**	**7014069**	**6981127**	**6053494**	**6027888**	**34234**	**34030**
1256	32949	14420	27608	25891	19348	18738	395	395
500	35704	23825	96137	94683	76122	74938	374	374
37386	86259	131150	138857	137316	142510	141214	324	324
6951	444053	181287	2071427	2060637	1902421	1897008	4165	4094
8143	340266	146287	540733	530384	410512	405099	2255	2185
-1191	103787	35000	1530694	1530253	1491909	1491909	1910	1910
	5316	3600	15224	15086	11042	11042	40	40
	3208	2400	3215	3088	2431	2431	34	34
	2108	1200	12010	11998	8610	8610	6	6
130162	337384	66647	411375	410370	336578	335922	1886	1886
	3883	3883	16379	16379	13275	13275	103	103
	3883	3883	16379	16379	13275	13275	103	103
899723	4836000	2901085	3682903	3673966	3129033	3117280	21454	21425
18952	208639	58261	254965	254021	217978	211021	1476	1447
879430	4581549	2816288	3365105	3357113	2866774	2861978	19521	19521
1341	45812	26537	62833	62833	44281	44281	457	457
195012	242798	101050	514655	508759	395540	391571	5115	5010
194555	202577	70246	431718	428667	328929	327206	4750	4646
457	40221	30804	82937	80092	66612	64365	365	365
697	55321	37229	39504	38040	27625	26901	379	378

12-12 续表2

单位：万元

行业	Sector	销售费用 Expenses for Sales	管理费用 Expenses for Management
总计	**Total**	**694488**	**1116721**
一、医药制造业	**Pharmaceutical Manufacturing**	**505668**	**193069**
（一）化学药品制造	Chemical manufacturing	257109	121950
化学药品原料药制造	Chemical raw materials Medicine manufacturing	5150	5361
化学药品制剂制造	Chemical preparations manufacturing	251959	116588
（二）中药饮片加工	Chinese medicine Pieces processing	534	321
（三）中成药生产	Chinese medicine production	195362	55101
（四）兽用药品制造	Veterinary pharmaceutical manufacturing	1264	1103
（五）生物药品制造	Biopharmaceutical manufacturing	49161	12319
（六）卫生材料及医药用品制造	Sanitary materials and medical supplies manufacturing	2238	2276
二、航空航天器制造业	**Aerospace & aviation industry**	**60002**	**277251**
（一）飞机制造	Aircraft Manufacturing	48816	188588
（二）航天器制造	Spacecraft Manufacturing	3413	46657
（三）航空、航天相关设备制造	Aviation and aerospace-related equipment manufacturing	5083	31906
（四）其他航空航天器制造	Other aerospace manufacturing	2503	6009
（五）航空航天器修理	Aerospace vehicle repair	188	4091
三、电子及通讯设备制造业	**Electronic and communication equipment manufacturing**	**62651**	**426709**
（一）电子工业专用设备制造	Electronic equipment manufacturing	2074	3578
（二）光纤、光缆制造	Optical fiber, cable manufacturing	4406	4951
（三）锂离子电池制造	Lithium-ion battery manufacturing	9593	19200
（四）通信设备制造	Communications equipment manufacturing	8628	30196
通信系统设备制造	Communications system equipment	7790	27318
通信终端设备制造	Communication Terminal Equipment	838	2878
（五）广播电视设备制造	Broadcasting and TV Equipment	1459	1935
广播电视节目制作及发射设备制造	Radio and television program production and transmission equipment		
广播电视接收设备及器材制造	Radio and television reception apparatus and equipment manufacturing	106	356
应用电视设备及其他广播电视设备制造	Application television equipment and other radio and television equipment manufacturing	1353	1579
（六）雷达及配套设备制造	Radar and ancillary equipment manufacturers	3321	41580
（七）视听设备制造	Audiovisual equipment manufacturing	2295	287
电视机制造	TV manufacturing	2295	287
音响设备制造	Audio Equipment manufacturing		
影视录放设备制造	Video recording equipment manufacturing		
（八）电子器件制造	Electronic device manufacturing	9520	259345
电子真空器件制造	Electronic vacuum device manufacturing		
半导体分立器件制造	Discrete semiconductor device manufacturing	4284	18577
集成电路制造	Semiconductor Manufacturing	3889	233400
光电子器件及其他电子器件制造	Optoelectronic devices and other electronic device manufacturing	1347	7367
（九）电子元件制造	Electronics Manufacturing	18642	57418
电子元件及组件制造	Electronic components and component manufacturing	15687	55988
印刷电路板制造	Printed circuit board manufacturing	2955	1431
（十）其他电子设备制造	Other electronic equipment manufacturing	2712	8219

continued 2

(10 000 yuan)

财务费用 Financial cost	营业利润 Operating Profit	利润总额 Total Profits	亏损企业亏损额 Total Loss of Deficit Enterprises	利税总额 Total Pre-tax Profits	应付职工薪酬 Salary Payable	本年应交增值税 Value Added Tax Payable
146014	**1504861**	**1775196**	**112957**	**2239262**	**1673107**	**380846**
24833	**134611**	**133539**	**10266**	**339078**	**173011**	**185107**
20053	85421	83951	4018	223476	124024	127291
293	3160	3472		6020	2508	2205
19760	82261	80479	4018	217456	121516	125086
169	60	25		42	267	6
2406	32034	31981	5597	87028	33827	48399
338	1070	1101	233	1598	1127	394
1530	15307	15576	391	25566	10434	8710
337	719	905	27	1368	3331	307
36032	**163423**	**179027**	**19732**	**272208**	**833491**	**77553**
29784	66163	75007	9280	134637	671162	48075
1155	45733	49270		54414	102115	4185
4562	41678	43186	8430	66643	52471	21039
179	11573	12946		17497	5285	3945
353	-1724	-1381	2022	-983	2458	308
69743	**836587**	**1072644**	**43656**	**1147316**	**370080**	**40439**
270	4297	4492		6799	3793	1911
532	9842	10066		13489	7167	3048
6296	-42864	-30222	30274	-29828	13778	70
325	122350	154493	6955	175568	100624	16911
244	89289	116429	6488	125520	81404	6836
81	33061	38064	467	50049	19221	10075
198	346	409		741	2073	292
178	109	161		480	232	285
20	237	248		261	1841	7
5657	19723	21465	208	26000	63139	2649
102	318	328		561	1174	131
102	318	328		561	1174	131
43390	697512	881822	1475	905250	119069	1974
4268	14749	18055	565	20504	16009	973
38792	673948	854320	789	874555	92660	713
330	8814	9447	121	10192	10400	289
12507	24587	29157	2867	46394	53211	12122
12309	13210	17619	2867	33976	44378	11608
197	11376	11539		12418	8833	514
468	477	635	1878	2343	6052	1330

12-12 续表3

单位：万元

行 业	Sector	企业单位数（个） Number of Enterprises (unit)	亏损企业 Loss Making Enterprises
四、计算机及办公设备制造业	**Computer and office equipment manufacturing**	**7**	**2**
（一）计算机整机制造	Computer machine manufacturing		
（二）计算机零部件制造	Computer parts manufacturing		
（三）计算机外围设备制造	Computer peripheral equipment manufacturing	3	1
（四）其他计算机制造	Other computer manufacturing	4	1
（五）办公设备制造	Office Equipment manufacturing		
复印和胶印设备制造	Photocopying and offset printing equipment manufacturing		
计算器及货币专用设备制造	Calculator and money and special equipment manufacturing		
五、医疗设备及仪器仪表制造业	**Medical equipment and instrumentation manufacturing**	**69**	**13**
（一）医疗仪器设备及器械制造	Medical equipment and device manufacturing	14	4
医疗诊断、监护及治疗设备制造	Medical diagnosis, monitoring and treatment equipment manufacturing	4	2
口腔科用设备及器具制造	Stomatology manufacture equipment and appliances		
医疗实验室及医用消毒设备和器具制造	Medical laboratory and medical sterilization equipment and equipment manufacturing		
医疗、外科及兽医用器械制造	Medical, surgical and veterinary instruments manufacturing	2	
机械治疗及病房护理设备制造	Mechanical treatment and ward care equipment manufacturing	2	1
假肢、人工器官及植（介）入器械制造	Prostheses, artificial organs and implantable(interventional) device manufacturing	1	
其他治疗设备及器械制造	Other treatment equipment and equipment manufacturing	5	1
（二）仪器仪表制造	Instruments manufacturing	55	9
工业自动控制系统装置制造	Manufacture of industrial automation control system devices manufacturing	12	3
电工仪器仪表制造	Electrical Instruments manufacturing	4	2
绘图、计算及测量仪器制造	Drawings, calculation and measurement equipment manufacturing	1	
实验分析仪器制造	Experimental analysis equipment manufacturing	1	
试验机制造	Testing Machine Manufacturing		
供应用仪表及其他通用仪器制造	Supply of manufacturing devices and other general instrument Manufacturing	11	1
环境检测专用仪器仪表制造	Environmental testing special Instruments Manufacturing	4	
运输设备及生产用计数仪表制造	Transport equipment and manufacturing with the counting instrument manufacturing		
导航、气象及海洋专用仪器制造	Navigation, meteorological and oceanographic special equipment manufacturing	1	
农林牧渔专用仪器仪表制造	Agriculture, forestry, animal husbandry and fishery special Instruments manufacturing		
地质勘探和地震专用仪器制造	Geological exploration and seismic special equipment manufacturing	3	1
教学专用仪器制造	Teaching special equipment manufacturing		
核子及核辐射测量仪器制造	Nucleon and nuclear radiation measuring instruments manufacturing	2	
电子测量仪器制造	Electronic Measuring Instruments Manufacturing	2	
其他专用仪器制造	Other special equipment manufacturing	4	1
光学仪器制造	Optical Instruments Manufacturing	5	1
其他仪器仪表制造业	Other instrumentation manufacturing	5	
六、信息化学品制造业	**Information chemicals manufacturing**	**6**	**3**
（一）信息化学品制造	Information Chemical Manufacturing	6	3

continued 3

(10 000 yuan)

工业总产值（当年价格） Gross Industrial Output Value (At Current Prices)	工业销售产值（当年价） Value of Industry Products Sales (At Current Prices)	出口交货值 Export Delivery Value	从业人员年平均人数（人） Annual Average Employers (person)	资产总计 Total Assets	流动资产合计 Total Working Capitals	固定资产合计 Total Fixed Assets	固定资产原价 Origing Value of Fixed Assets	累计折旧 Accumulative Total Depreciation
55655	**56207**		**466**	**68399**	**57070**	**3246**	**4113**	**2273**
42351	43233		318	55957	47695	2780	3320	1942
13303	12974		148	12443	9374	466	792	331
1358646	**1161308**	**62929**	**17495**	**2259723**	**1434385**	**436670**	**738586**	**298084**
81108	78154	388	1386	156520	107864	21225	28634	9475
26350	22586	289	469	45023	29483	10481	12979	4461
4323	5442		133	4424	3687	300	349	151
4123	4054		193	9648	5198	3369	5137	1768
11521	11346	100	92	12037	6226	2701	3556	856
34792	34727		499	85389	63270	4374	6613	2238
1277538	1083154	62541	16109	2103202	1326520	415445	709952	288608
383593	363686	3265	1815	299632	150293	97089	132304	34246
18457	17561	1223	380	33599	25142	3466	4854	1388
11016	10550	700	175	26769	21567	1289	2596	1321
1794	2134		52	4098	2287	1093	1865	772
76726	68206	750	1452	92479	74346	13415	20489	6712
113396	113409	36652	1027	117806	110211	6875	18147	11538
14093	14093		136	15037	14142	843	1983	1140
15580	14486	5047	244	60729	47465	813	3234	2421
31176	35263	10	963	90862	51690	4489	12227	7678
12833	12153	3	155	11854	10985	599	1893	1165
38800	27577	7898	516	94060	80364	5040	12418	2073
522030	363438	6993	8441	1175366	692675	267532	478212	210693
38045	40599		753	80912	45355	12902	19731	7463
2216570	**2204371**	**351090**	**4052**	**3297707**	**1098043**	**796517**	**1920754**	**1178656**
2216570	2204371	351090	4052	3297707	1098043	796517	1920754	1178656

12-12 续表4

单位：万元

行业	Sector	负债合计 Total Liabilites	流动负债合计 Total Working Liabilities
四、计算机及办公设备制造业	**Computer and office equipment manufacturing**	**18093**	**14483**
（一）计算机整机制造	Computer machine manufacturing		
（二）计算机零部件制造	Computer parts manufacturing		
（三）计算机外围设备制造	Computer peripheral equipment manufacturing	11889	8579
（四）其他计算机制造	Other computer manufacturing	6204	5904
（五）办公设备制造	Office Equipment manufacturing		
复印和胶印设备制造	Photocopying and offset printing equipment manufacturing		
计算器及货币专用设备制造	Calculator and money and special equipment manufacturing		
五、医疗设备及仪器仪表制造业	**Medical equipment and instrumentation manufacturing**	**1116532**	**945587**
（一）医疗仪器设备及器械制造	Medical equipment and device manufacturing	90535	71419
医疗诊断、监护及治疗设备制造	Medical diagnosis, monitoring and treatment equipment manufacturing	28090	10158
口腔科用设备及器具制造	Stomatology manufacture equipment and appliances		
医疗实验室及医用消毒设备和器具制造	Medical laboratory and medical sterilization equipment and equipment manufacturing		
医疗、外科及兽医用器械制造	Medical, surgical and veterinary instruments manufacturing	2493	2493
机械治疗及病房护理设备制造	Mechanical treatment and ward care equipment manufacturing	3447	2647
假肢、人工器官及植（介）入器械制造	Prostheses, artificial organs and implantable(interventional) device manufacturing	764	764
其他治疗设备及器械制造	Other treatment equipment and equipment manufacturing	55741	55356
（二）仪器仪表制造	Instruments manufacturing	1025997	874169
工业自动控制系统装置制造	Manufacture of industrial automation control system devices manufacturing	252218	186347
电工仪器仪表制造	Electrical Instruments manufacturing	19917	19882
绘图、计算及测量仪器制造	Drawings, calculation and measurement equipment manufacturing	12785	12785
实验分析仪器制造	Experimental analysis equipment manufacturing	378	378
试验机制造	Testing Machine Manufacturing		
供应用仪表及其他通用仪器制造	Supply of manufacturing devices and other general instrument Manufacturing	37399	34100
环境检测专用仪器仪表制造	Environmental testing special Instruments Manufacturing	26955	25962
运输设备及生产用计数仪表制造	Transport equipment and manufacturing with the counting instrument manufacturing		
导航、气象及海洋专用仪器制造	Navigation, meteorological and oceanographic special equipment manufacturing	6323	6323
农林牧渔专用仪器仪表制造	Agriculture, forestry, animal husbandry and fishery special Instruments manufacturing		
地质勘探和地震专用仪器制造	Geological exploration and seismic special equipment manufacturing	30094	26584
教学专用仪器制造	Teaching special equipment manufacturing		
核子及核辐射测量仪器制造	Nucleon and nuclear radiation measuring instruments manufacturing	40363	40152
电子测量仪器制造	Electronic Measuring Instruments Manufacturing	3279	3279
其他专用仪器制造	Other special equipment manufacturing	55178	38238
光学仪器制造	Optical Instruments Manufacturing	512603	452634
其他仪器仪表制造业	Other instrumentation manufacturing	28505	27505
六、信息化学品制造业	**Information chemicals manufacturing**	**1841674**	**1492867**
（一）信息化学品制造	Information Chemical Manufacturing	1841674	1492867

continued 4

(10 000 yuan)

非流动负债 Non-Working Liabilities	所有者权益合计 Total Owners' Equities	实收资本 Total Capital Hold	营业收入 Total Revenue	主营业务收入 Revenue from Principal Business	营业成本 Total Cost	主营业务成本 Cost of Principal Business	税金及附加 Taxs and Other Changes	主营业务税金及附加 Taxes and Other Charges on Principal Business
3423	**50306**	**32207**	**47719**	**46617**	**32509**	**32133**	**197**	**197**
3123	44067	28396	34302	33271	22209	21862	150	150
300	6239	3811	13416	13346	10300	10271	47	47
167132	**1143190**	**365380**	**1321811**	**1309606**	**1029386**	**990854**	**7644**	**5547**
18317	65985	36399	79006	78883	37012	36919	636	618
17932	16933	13494	23511	23482	15611	15599	123	123
	1931	1330	5442	5442	2750	2750	78	78
	6201	3000	4054	4054	2148	2148	39	21
	11272	3475	11346	11346	4239	4239	126	126
385	29648	15100	34653	34559	12264	12184	270	270
148815	1077205	328981	1242805	1230724	992374	953935	7009	4929
64559	47414	55681	318027	316946	299195	266831	1993	1970
35	13681	17208	17643	17438	14990	14750	187	187
	13984	5900	10550	9727	6470	6233	47	39
	3720	1688	2395	2134	1412	1412	19	19
3299	55080	31934	69117	68651	44207	44196	673	673
993	90851	14375	114268	113404	74372	74372	682	669
	8714	1303	14093	14091	9994	9994	189	189
3510	30635	7940	13828	13811	7395	7395	100	100
212	50499	10211	33123	31728	19959	19698	596	280
	8575	1800	12332	12153	8107	8054	96	96
16923	38882	17520	33842	33735	18536	17486	343	343
58284	662763	144523	561815	555299	456608	452437	1850	131
1000	52408	18899	41773	41607	31130	31079	234	234
347187	**1456033**	**530270**	**1915936**	**1898076**	**1635842**	**1620483**	**5087**	**4968**
347187	1456033	530270	1915936	1898076	1635842	1620483	5087	4968

12-12 续表5

单位：万元

行　业	Sector	销售费用 Expenses for Sales	管理费用 Expenses for Management
四、计算机及办公设备制造业	**Computer and office equipment manufacturing**	**1784**	**6185**
（一）计算机整机制造	Computer machine manufacturing		
（二）计算机零部件制造	Computer parts manufacturing		
（三）计算机外围设备制造	Computer peripheral equipment manufacturing	981	4712
（四）其他计算机制造	Other computer manufacturing	803	1473
（五）办公设备制造	Office Equipment manufacturing		
复印和胶印设备制造	Photocopying and offset printing equipment manufacturing		
计算器及货币专用设备制造	Calculator and money and special equipment manufacturing		
五、医疗设备及仪器仪表制造业	**Medical equipment and instrumentation manufacturing**	**50176**	**169274**
（一）医疗仪器设备及器械制造	Medical equipment and device manufacturing	15360	10561
医疗诊断、监护及治疗设备制造	Medical diagnosis, monitoring and treatment equipment manufacturing	3351	3930
口腔科用设备及器具制造	Stomatology manufacture equipment and appliances		
医疗实验室及医用消毒设备和器具制造	Medical laboratory and medical sterilization equipment and equipment manufacturing		
医疗、外科及兽医用器械制造	Medical, surgical and veterinary instruments manufacturing	1034	759
机械治疗及病房护理设备制造	Mechanical treatment and ward care equipment manufacturing	1023	928
假肢、人工器官及植（介）入器械制造	Prostheses, artificial organs and implantable(interventional) device manufacturing	2390	2237
其他治疗设备及器械制造	Other treatment equipment and equipment manufacturing	7563	2707
（二）仪器仪表制造	Instruments manufacturing	34815	158713
工业自动控制系统装置制造	Manufacture of industrial automation control system devices manufacturing	5748	39205
电工仪器仪表制造	Electrical Instruments manufacturing	460	1727
绘图、计算及测量仪器制造	Drawings, calculation and measurement equipment manufacturing	1696	1488
实验分析仪器制造	Experimental analysis equipment manufacturing	119	805
试验机制造	Testing Machine Manufacturing		
供应用仪表及其他通用仪器制造	Supply of manufacturing devices and other general instrument Manufacturing	6201	10039
环境检测专用仪器仪表制造	Environmental testing special Instruments Manufacturing	7720	6721
运输设备及生产用计数仪表制造	Transport equipment and manufacturing with the counting instrument manufacturing		
导航、气象及海洋专用仪器制造	Navigation, meteorological and oceanographic special equipment manufacturing	52	1335
农林牧渔专用仪器仪表制造	Agriculture, forestry, animal husbandry and fishery special Instruments manufacturing		
地质勘探和地震专用仪器制造	Geological exploration and seismic special equipment manufacturing	1541	2577
教学专用仪器制造	Teaching special equipment manufacturing		
核子及核辐射测量仪器制造	Nucleon and nuclear radiation measuring instruments manufacturing	1879	7306
电子测量仪器制造	Electronic Measuring Instruments Manufacturing	382	1142
其他专用仪器制造	Other special equipment manufacturing	2966	5702
光学仪器制造	Optical Instruments Manufacturing	2525	76596
其他仪器仪表制造业	Other instrumentation manufacturing	3528	4072
六、信息化学品制造业	**Information chemicals manufacturing**	**14207**	**44234**
（一）信息化学品制造	Information Chemical Manufacturing	14207	44234

continued 5

(10 000 yuan)

财务费用 Financial cost	营业利润 Operating Profit	利润总额 Total Profits	亏损企业亏损额 Total Loss of Deficit Enterprises	利税总额 Total Pre-tax Profits	应付职工薪酬 Salary Payable	本年应交增值税 Value Added Tax Payable
120	**6029**	**7399**	**1268**	**8561**	**4145**	**965**
68	5284	6625	1214	7495	3096	720
52	745	775	55	1066	1050	245
7871	**98179**	**114096**	**34738**	**160012**	**141573**	**38272**
892	15699	16172	1111	23265	9174	6458
687	-191	-72	885	3744	3706	3693
22	799	863		1585	956	644
67	-152	-89	172	305	739	355
2	2339	2463		3233	945	644
113	12904	13006	54	14398	2828	1122
6980	82480	97924	33627	136747	132399	31814
657	3410	6292	29507	20098	66732	11813
63	265	398	171	803	2498	219
-48	712	817		1099	1144	236
1	39	382		565	340	163
444	7390	8393	761	12655	8112	3588
125	24981	25049		29214	11246	3483
-5	3533	3538		4585	2141	858
3903	-1688	-1323	1789	-711	2212	512
472	10364	10662		13645	9548	2386
-14	2623	2713		3542	1013	733
2211	4038	5124	33	5965	2848	498
-1324	24171	32744	1367	39696	19731	5101
495	2642	3136		5592	4833	2222
7414	**266033**	**268491**	**3296**	**312088**	**150808**	**38510**
7414	266033	268491	3296	312088	150808	38510

12-13 规模以上工业企业主要经济效益指标（2017年）

行　业	Sector	总资产贡献率（%） Ratio of Total Assets to Industrial Output Value (%)	资产负债率（%） Assets-Liability Ratio (%)
总计	**Total**	**7.2**	**53.0**
按工业行业大类分	**Grouped by Sector**		
煤炭开采和洗选业	Mining and Washing of Coal		
石油和天然气开采业	Extraction of Petroleum and Natural Gas		
黑色金属矿采选业	Mining and Processing of Ferrous Metal Ores		
有色金属矿采选业	Mining and Processing of Non-ferrous Metal Ores		
非金属矿采选业	Mining and Processing of Nonmetal Ores		
开采辅助活动	Mining Auxiliary Activities	3.9	29.2
其他采矿业	Mining of Other Ores		
农副食品加工业	Processing of Food from Agricultural Porducts	6.9	71.3
食品制造业	Manufacture of Foods	16.5	46.2
酒、饮料和精制茶制造业	Manufacture of Alcohol,Beverages and Tea	15.7	52.9
烟草制品业	Manufacture of Tobacco	11.5	17.8
纺织业	Manufacture of Textile	2.7	57.7
纺织服装、服饰业	Textile, Garments industry	3.6	52.0
皮革、毛皮、羽毛及其制品和制鞋业	Manufacture of Leather, Fur, Feather and Related Products	7.2	42.9
木材加工和木、竹、藤、棕、草制品业	Processing of Timber, Manufacture of Wood,Plam and Straw Products	4.6	54.5
家具制造业	Manufacture of Furniture	8.4	49.5
造纸及纸制品业	Manufacture of Paper and Paper Products	12.3	54.7
印刷和记录媒介复制	Printing,Reproduction of Recording Media	13.8	35.6
文教、工美、体育和娱乐用品制造业	Manufacture of Articles For Cultural,Educational and Sports Activities	6.3	47.2

Major Indicators of Economic Performance of Industrial Enterprises above Designated Size (2017)

流动资产周转率（次） Rate of Annual Turnover Working Capitals (times)	成本费用利润率（%） Ratio of Profits to Cost (%)	工业产品销售率（%） Proportion of Industrial Products Sold (%)	产值利税率（%） Ratio of Output Value to Profits and Tax (%)	每百元固定资产实现利税（元） Profit and Tax per 100 yuan of Fixed Assets (yuan)	每百元销售收入实现利税（元） Profit and Tax per 100 yuan of Sales Revenue (yuan)
1.4	**6.6**	**97.3**	**8.8**	**24.0**	**9.3**
0.7	7.7	100.9	6.6	24.9	9.1
2.1	2.8	98.2	3.8	30.4	4.3
3.8	6.1	95.0	8.7	47.1	9.6
1.5	17.0	120.8	24.9	43.7	21.2
0.8	22.5	103.3	36.7	35.0	30.7
1.4	1.7	95.7	3.9	4.5	4.0
0.7	1.2	90.5	4.4	18.2	6.4
1.6	5.1	98.7	11.1	104.8	11.3
0.8	0.3	82.3	10.4	9.8	12.3
1.6	7.2	92.4	7.0	22.1	8.6
2.8	3.8	97.1	6.1	50.0	6.3
2.1	6.8	94.5	10.7	39.0	11.3
9.2	0.7	91.8	1.0	34.1	0.9

12-13 续表1

行 业	Sector	总资产贡献率（%） Ratio of Total Assets to Industrial Output Value (%)	资产负债率（%） Assets-Liability Ratio (%)
石油加工业、炼焦和核燃料加工业	Processing of Petroleum, Cokeing,Processing of Nuclear and Nuclear Fuel	2.0	56.3
化学原料及化学制品制造业	Manufacture of Raw Chemical Materials and Chemical Products	9.2	58.7
医药制造业	Manufacture of Medicines	16.2	52.0
化学纤维制造业	Manufacture of Chemical Fibers	6.6	64.5
橡胶和塑料制品业	Manufacture of Rubber and Plastics	2.7	65.1
非金属矿物制品业	Manufacture of Non-metallic Mineral Products	7.7	63.3
黑色金属冶炼和压延加工业	Smelting and Pressing of Ferrous Metals	5.4	61.5
有色金属冶炼和压延加工业	Smelting and Pressing of Non-ferrous Metals	4.6	29.8
金属制品业	Manufacture of Metal Products	2.8	54.7
通用设备制造业	Manufacture of General Purpose Machinery	3.9	53.8
专用设备制造业	Manufacture of Special Equipment	5.1	49.0
汽车制造业	Manufacture of Motor Vehicle	6.1	67.5
铁路、船舶、航空航天和其他运输设备制造业	Railways, Shipbuilding,Aerospace and Other Transportation Equipment Manufacturing Industry	5.2	52.2
电气机械和器材制造业	Manufacture of Electric Equipment and Machinery	6.4	49.5
计算机、通讯和其他电子设备制造业	Manufacture of Communication Equipment, Computers and other Electronic Equipment	12.5	38.1
仪器仪表制造业	Manufacture of Measuring Instruments and Machinery	6.6	48.8
其他制造业	Manufacture of Other Manufacturing	8.2	54.1
废弃资源综合利用业	Recycling and Disposal of Waste	3.1	66.9
金属制品、机械和设备修理业	Metal Products,Machinery and Equipment Repair Industry	-0.4	41.4
电力、热力的生产和供应业	Production and Supply of Electric Power and Heat Power	5.4	72.9
燃气生产和供应业	Gas Mining and Supplying Industry	5.3	54.0
水的生产和供应业	Production and Supply of Water	4.9	60.8

continued 1

流动资产周转率（次） Rate of Annual Turnover Working Capitals (times)	成本费用利润率（%） Ratio of Profits to Cost (%)	工业产品销售率（%） Proportion of Industrial Products Sold (%)	产值利税率（%） Ratio of Output Value to Profits and Tax (%)	每百元固定资产实现利税（元） Profit and Tax per 100 yuan of Fixed Assets (yuan)	每百元销售收入实现利税（元） Profit and Tax per 100 yuan of Sales Revenue (yuan)
1.2	5.4	93.9	8.6	7.4	7.9
1.5	11.8	96.4	12.2	33.4	13.5
1.6	7.4	88.8	14.3	59.6	17.4
1.7	6.6	101.1	5.7	9.6	5.6
0.8	2.5	98.6	4.4	8.7	4.4
1.6	4.4	98.6	7.3	26.5	7.4
2.4	1.5	99.6	2.8	24.6	2.8
2.3	3.5	92.9	5.0	26.5	5.1
0.9	2.2	97.7	4.7	10.9	4.6
0.6	4.6	98.2	8.2	33.1	9.0
0.7	7.9	91.6	10.9	34.3	11.6
1.9	2.5	100.9	4.5	29.8	4.7
1.0	5.6	94.4	8.5	25.6	8.0
1.0	5.8	108.5	7.7	25.9	8.6
1.6	17.2	88.5	15.4	26.2	17.2
0.9	8.2	84.8	10.7	32.9	11.0
1.7	2.6	101.2	6.6	26.2	6.5
5.9	0.5	97.6	2.4	5.2	2.2
0.8	-4.8	91.3	-1.0	-3.4	-1.1
3.0	2.9	100.0	7.9	6.0	7.3
3.1	6.5	99.9	8.3	12.0	8.2
1.2	3.4	100.0	8.7	7.4	8.4

12-14 规模以上大中型工业企业主要经济效益指标（2017年）

行　业	Sector	总资产贡献率（%） Ratio of Total Assets to Industrial Output Value (%)	资产负债率%） Assets-Liability Ratio (%)
总计	**Total**	**7.1**	**52.9**
按国民经济行业分	**Grouped by Sector**		
煤炭开采和洗选业	Mining and Washing of Coal		
石油和天然气开采业	Extraction of Petroleum and Natural Gas		
黑色金属矿采选业	Mining and Processing of Ferrous Metal Ores		
有色金属矿采选业	Mining and Processing of Non-ferrous Metal Ores		
非金属矿采选业	Mining and Processing of Nonmetal Ores		
开采辅助活动	Mining Auxiliary Activities	3.7	28.9
其他采矿业	Mining of other Ores		
农副食品加工业	Processing of Food from Agricultural Porducts	5.2	80.5
食品制造业	Manufacture of Foods	19.3	44.8
酒、饮料和精制茶制造业	Manufacture of Alcohol,Beverages and Tea	18.0	52.8
烟草制品业	Manufacture of Tobacco	13.2	21.6
纺织业	Manufacture of Textile	0.9	59.3
纺织服装、服饰业	Textile, apparel industry	4.9	68.7
皮革、毛皮、羽毛及其制品和制鞋业	Leather fur feathers and its products and footwear	8.0	44.7
木材加工和木、竹、藤、棕、草制品业	Processing of Timber,Manufacture of Wood,Plam and Straw Products	4.8	55.6
家具制造业	Manufacture of Furniture	7.4	54.1
造纸及纸制品业	Manufacture of Paper and Paper Products	1.9	56.7
印刷和记录媒介复制业	Printing,Reproduction of Recording Media	12.8	28.1
文教、工美、体育和娱乐用品制造业	Manufacture of Articles For Cultural,Educational and Sports Activities		

Major Economic Indicators of Large and Medium-sized Industrial Enterprises above Designated Size（2017）

流动资产周转率（次）Rate of Annual Turnover Working Capitals (times)	成本费用利润率（%）Ratio of Profits to Cost (%)	工业产品销售率（%）Proportion of Industrial Products Sold (%)	产值利税率（%）Ratio of Output Value to Profits and Tax (%)	每百元固定资产实现利税（元）Profit and Tax per 100 yuan of Fixed Assets (yuan)	每百元销售收入实现利税（元）Profit and Tax per 100 yuan of Sales Revenue (yuan)
1.3	**7.1**	**98.1**	**9.3**	**22.1**	**9.8**
0.7	7.6	100.9	6.3	24.6	8.9
1.1	3.7	96.2	4.1	30.8	5.2
3.5	7.3	96.3	11.0	51.5	11.7
1.4	20.8	131.0	32.6	55.2	24.9
0.6	45.8	100.0	53.2	29.9	46.8
1.3	-1.4	101.1	1.2	0.8	1.2
0.6	1.7	91.8	5.1	24.2	8.3
1.9	5.7	100.0	12.2	102.4	12.2
0.6	0.6	77.7	12.5	9.9	16.7
2.2	4.7	99.3	8.7	13.3	7.9
1.3	-0.1	100.0	1.0	8.3	1.1
1.4	10.3	94.5	15.1	35.6	16.0

12-14 续表1

行 业	Sector	总资产贡献率（%） Ratio of Total Assets to Industrial Output Value (%)	资产负债率%） Assets-Liability Ratio (%)
石油加工、炼焦和核燃料加工业	Processing of Petroleum, Cokeing,Processing of Nuclear and Nuclear Fuel	-3.9	59.5
化学原料和化学制品制造业	Manufacture of Raw Chemical Materials and Chemical Products	8.4	59.2
医药制造业	Manufacture of Medicines	19.1	48.8
化学纤维制造业	Manufacture of Chemical Fibers		
橡胶和塑料制品业	Manufacture of Rubber and Plastics	2.1	67.5
非金属矿物制品业	Manufacture of Non-metallic Mineral Products	8.8	60.7
黑色金属冶炼和压延加工业	Smelting and Pressing of Ferrous Metals	5.4	57.6
有色金属冶炼和压延加工业	Smelting and Pressing of Non-ferrous Metals	3.3	23.3
金属制品业	Manufacture of Metal Products	2.9	67.5
通用设备制造业	Manufacture of General Purpose Machinery	3.1	55.3
专用设备制造业	Manufacture of Special Equipment	6.7	45.0
汽车制造业	Manufacture of Motor Vehicle	5.8	68.4
铁路、船舶、航空航天和其他运输设备制造业	Railways,Shipbuilding,Aerospace and Other Transportation Equipment Manufacturing Industry	3.7	54.9
电气机械和器材制造业	Manufacture of Electric Equipment and Machinery	6.0	49.6
计算机、通信和其他电子设备制造业	Manufacture of Communication Equipment, Computers and other Electronic Equipment	13.0	37.3
仪器仪表制造业	Manufacture of Measuring Instruments and Machinery	8.4	45.6
其他制造业	Manufacture of Other Manufacturing		
废弃资源综合利用	Recycling and Disposal of Waste		
金属制品、机械和设备修理业	Metal Products,Machinery and Equipment Repair Industry		
电力、热力生产和供应业	Production and Supply of Electric Power and Heat Power	6.2	69.8
燃气生产和供应业	Gas Mining and Supplying Industry	5.2	54.4
水的生产和供应业	Production and Supply of Water	5.8	61.4

continued 1

流动资产周转率（次） Rate of Annual Turnover Working Capitals (times)	成本费用利润率（%） Ratio of Profits to Cost (%)	工业产品销售率（%） Proportion of Industrial Products Sold (%)	产值利税率（%） Ratio of Output Value to Profits and Tax (%)	每百元固定资产实现利税（元） Profit and Tax per 100 yuan of Fixed Assets (yuan)	每百元销售收入实现利税（元） Profit and Tax per 100 yuan of Sales Revenue (yuan)
79.6	7.9	100.0	7.5	1.0	8.0
1.4	13.9	97.6	13.5	28.4	15.4
1.8	7.6	88.4	15.4	69.1	18.2
0.7	2.0	100.4	3.9	6.4	3.8
1.0	7.7	99.5	14.7	43.7	14.4
1.4	2.2	101.7	5.7	19.4	5.7
2.2	3.2	91.2	4.4	21.2	4.4
0.8	1.7	101.6	4.3	7.7	4.4
0.4	4.4	100.2	9.0	35.2	9.8
0.7	9.2	89.2	12.0	33.3	12.8
1.9	2.3	101.1	4.3	28.3	4.5
1.0	3.7	95.9	6.3	17.8	5.8
0.9	6.6	114.7	8.3	21.7	9.6
1.8	17.9	88.3	15.9	25.5	17.7
1.1	11.7	82.8	13.3	35.7	13.7
5.6	2.7	100.0	7.8	6.2	7.3
2.9	7.5	100.0	9.4	11.7	9.4
1.5	2.6	100.0	7.5	8.3	7.5

12-15　规模以上工业主要产品生产能力（2017年）

Production Capacity of Major Products of Industrial Enterprises above Designated Size（2017）

指　标	Item	2017
棉纺锭/纺纱量（锭/吨）	Cotton spindles / spinning volume(ingot/ton)	2000409
气流纺锭/纺纱量（头/吨）	Rotor spinning / spinning volume(head/ton)	1856
棉布织机/布（台/万米）	Cotton loom / cloth (unit/10000 meter)	2838
化学纤维（吨）	Chemical Fibre (ton)	24000
硅酸盐水泥熟料（吨）	Portland Cement Clinker (ton)	2700000
水泥（吨）	Cement(ton)	5300000
平板玻璃（重量箱）	Plate Glass(weight case)	6370000
钢材（吨）	Rolled Steel (ton)	921366
铁合金（吨）	Ferroalloy (ton)	11075
金属切削机床（台）	Metal-cutting Machine Tools（unit）	8420
汽车（辆）	Motor Vehicles（unit）	543000
其中：乘用车（辆）	Passenger Vehicles（unit）	303000
新能源乘用车（辆）	New energy passenger car(unit)	70000
商用汽车（辆）	Commercial vehicle(unit)	240000
太阳能电池（千瓦）	Solar cell （KW）	650000
微型计算机设备（台）	Micro Computer Equipment（unit）	211200
移动通信手持机（台）	Mobile Handset（unit）	37280000
彩色电视机（台）	Color TV Set（unit）	60000
发电设备容量总计/发电量（万千瓦/万千瓦小时）	Total capacity of power generation equipment / generation capacity (10000 KW/10000 KWh)	355
其中：火电设备容量（万千瓦）	Thermal Power（10 000kw）	353
水电设备容量（万千瓦）	Hydropower（10 000kw）	2

主 要 统 计 指 标 解 释

工业 指从事自然资源的开采，对采掘品和农产品进行加工和再加工的物质生产部门。具体包括：（1）对自然资源的开采，如采矿、晒盐等（但不包括禽兽捕猎和水产捕捞）；（2）对农副产品的加工、再加工，如粮油加工、食品加工、缫丝、纺织、制革等；（3）对采掘品的加工、再加工，如炼铁、炼钢、化工生产、石油加工、机器制造、木材加工等，以及电力、自来水、煤气的生产和供应等；（4）对工业品的修理、翻新，如机器设备的修理、交通运输工具（如汽车）的修理等。

工业统计调查单位为独立核算法人工业企业。

独立核算法人工业企业指从事工业生产经营活动的单位。独立核算法人工业企业应同时具备以下条件：①依法成立，有自己的名称、组织机构和场所，能够承担民事责任；②独立拥有和使用资产，承担负债，有权与其他单位签订合同；③独立核算盈亏，并能够编制资产负债表。

国有及国有控股企业 指国有企业加上国有控股企业。国有企业（即原全民所有制工业或国营工业）指企业全部资产归国家所有，并按《中华人民共和国企业法人登记管理条例》规定登记注册的非公司制的经济组织。包括国有企业、国有独资公司和国有联营企业。1957年以前的公私合营和私营工业，后均改造为国营工业，1992年改为国有工业，这部分工业的资料不单独分列时，均包括在国有企业内。国有控股企业是对混合所有制经济的企业进行的“国有控股”分类。它是指这些企业的全部资产中国有资产（股份）相对其他所有者中的任何一个所有者占资（股）最多的企业。该分组反映了国有经济控股情况。

本篇涉及的其他企业登记注册类型的解释详见综合篇。

轻工业 指主要提供生活消费品和制作手工工具的工业。按其所使用的原料不同，可分为两大类：（1）以农产品为原料的轻工业，是指直接或间接以农产品为基本原料的轻工业。主要包括食品制造、饮料制造、烟草加工、纺织、缝纫、皮革和毛皮制作、造纸以及印刷等工业；（2）以非农产品为原料的轻工业，是指以工业品为原料的轻工业。主要包括文教体育用品、化学药品制造、合成纤维制造、日用化学制品、 日用玻璃制品、日用金属制品、手工工具制造、医疗器械制造、文化和办公用机械制造等工业。

重工业 指为国民经济各部门提供物质技术基础的主要生产资料的工业。按其生产性质和产品用途，可以分为下列三类：（1）采掘（伐）工业，是指对自然资源的开采，包括石油开采、煤炭开采、金属矿开采、非金属矿开采等工业；（2）原材料工业，指向国民经济各部门提供基本材料、动力和燃料的工业。包括金属冶炼及加工、炼焦及焦炭、化学、化工：原料、水泥、人造板以及电力、石油和煤炭加工等工业；（3）加工工业，是指对工业原材料进行再加工制造的工业。包括装备国民经济各部门的机械设备制造工业、金属结构、水泥制品等工业，以及为农业提供的生产资料如化肥、农药等工业。

根据上述划分原则，修理业中以重工业产品为修理作业对象的划为重工业，反之划为轻工业。

工业总产值

（1）定义：

工业总产值是工业企业在一定时期内生产的以货币形式表现的工业最终产品和提供工业性劳务活动的总价值量。它反映一定时间内工业生产的总规模和总水平。

（2）计算原则：

工业生产的原则，即凡是企业在报告期生产的经检验合格的产品，不管是否在报告期销售，均包括在内。

最终产品的原则，即凡是计入工业总产值的产品，必须是本企业生产的经检验合格的，不需要再进行任何加工的最终产品。如果企业有中间产品（半成品）对外销售，则对外销售的中间产品应视为企业的最终产品。

工厂法原则，即工业总产值是以下业企业作为基本计算（核算）单位，即按企业的最终产品计算工业总产值。按这种方法计算的工业总产值，不允许同一产品价值在企业内部重复计算，不能把企业内部各个车间（分厂）生产的成果相加，但允许企业间的重复计算。

（3）内容及计算方法：

1995年全国工业普查对工业总产值（原规定）的内容及计算原则和方法做了某些修订，修订后的工业总产值（新规定）包括三项内容：即本期生产成品价值、对外加工费收入、在制品半成品期末期初差额价值三部分。

本期生产成品价值指企业本期生产，并在报告期内不再进行加工，经检验、包装入库的全部工业成品（半成品）价值合计，包括企业生产的自制设备及提供给本企业在建工程、其他非工业部门和福利部门等单位使用的成品价值。本期生产成品价值为按自备原材料生产的产品的数量乘以本期不含增值税（销项税额）的产品实际销售平均单价计算；会计核算中按成本价格转帐的自制设备和自产自用的成品，按成本价格计算生产成品价值。生产成品价值中不包括用定货者来料加工的成品（半成品）价值。

对外加工费收入指企业在报告期内完成的对外承接的工业品加工（包括用定货者来料加工产品）的加工费收入和对外工业修理作业所取得的加工费收入。对外加工费收入按不含增值税（销项税额）的价格计算，可根据会计“产品销售收入”科目的有关资料取得。

对于本企业对内非工业部门提供的加工修理、设备安装的劳务收入，如果企业会计核算基础较好，能取得这部分资料，而且这部分价值所占比重较大，应包括在对外加工费收入中。

自制半成品在制品期末期初差额价值指企业报告期在制品期末减期初的差额价值，本指标一般可以从会计核算资料中取得。如果会计产品成本核算中不计算半成品、在制品的成本，则总产值中也不包括这部分价值，反之则包括。

（4）工业总产值统计范围变化和计算方法修订情况：

1984年以前工业总产值不包括村办工业，村办工业总产值划归农业。1984年以后工业总产值包括村办工业。

1995年工业普查对工业总产值计算方法做了修订，即从1995年始按新修订（新规定）方法计算工业总产值。新规定与原规定的区别如下：

全价与加工费的计算原则不同：新规定为凡自备原材料，不论其生产繁简程度如何，一律按全价计算工业总产值；凡来料加工，允许按加工费计算工业总产值。原规定则视生产加工的繁简程度不同，规定哪些行业按全价，哪些行业按加工费计算工业总产值。

自制半成品、在产品期末期初差额价值的计算原则不同：新规定要求，凡会计产品成本核算时计算了成本的差额价值，总产值中就应包括，否则可不包括；原规定则按生产周期六个月的界限区分，凡生产周期六个月以上的企业，总产值计算中应包括这部分差额价值，否则可不包括。

计算价格不同：新规定按不含增值税（销项税额）的价格计算；原规定则按含增值税（销项税额）的价格计算。

工业增加值 指工业企业在报告期内以货币表现的工业生产活动的最终成果。

工业增加值有两种计算方法：一是生产法，即工业总产出减去工业中间投入加上应交增值税；二是收入法，即从收入的角度出发，根据生产要素在生产过程中应得到的收入份额计算，具体构成项目有固定资产折旧、劳动者报酬、生产税净额、营业盈余，这种方法也称要素分配法。本年鉴中的工业增加值是以收入法计算的。

生产法工业增加值的计算方法为：

工业增加值＝工业总产出-工业中间投入+应交增值税

（1）工业总产出：指工业企业在一定时期内工业生产活动的总成果。工业总产出包括：成品生产价值，对外加工费收入，自制半成品、在产品期末期初差额价值。1995年后用新规定计算的工业总产值代替。

（2）工业中间投入：指工业企业在工业生产活动中消耗的外购物质产品和对外支付的服务费用。服务费用包括支付给物质生产部门（工业、农业、批发零售贸易业、建筑业、运输邮电业）的服务费用和支付给非物质生产部门（如保险、金融、文化教育、科学研究、医疗卫生、行政管理等）的服务费用。工业中间投入的确定须遵循以下原则：必须从外部购入的，并已计入工业总产出的产品和服务价值；必须是本期投入生产，并一次性消耗掉（包括本期摊销的低值易耗品等）的产品和服务价值。

工业中间投入包括直接材料费用、制造费用中的工业中间投入、管理费用中的工业中间投入、销售费用中的工业中间投入和利息支出五部分。

资产总计 指企业拥有或控制的能以货币计量的经济资源，包括各种财产、债权和其他权利。资产按流动性分为流动资产、长期投资、固定资产、无形资产、递延资产和其他资产。该指标根据企业会计“资产负债表”中“资产总计”项目的期末数增列。

流动资产 指企业可以在一年内或者超过一年的一个生产周期内变现或者耗用的资产，包括现金及各种存款、短期投资，应收及预付款项、存货等。

固定资产原价 指企业在建造、购置、安装、改建、扩建、技术改造某项固定资产时所支出的全部货币总额。它一般包括买价、包装费、运杂费和安装费等。

固定资产净值 指固定资产原价减去历年已提折旧额后的净额。计算公式为：

固定资产净值=固定资产原价-累计折旧

负债合计 指企业所承担的能以货币计量，将以资产或劳务偿付的债务，偿还形式包括货币、资产或提供劳务。负债一般按偿还期长短分为流动负债和长期负债。根据会计“资产负债表”中“负债合计”的年末数填列。

所有者权益合计 指企业投资人对企业净资产的所有权。企业净资产为企业全部资产与企业全部负债的差额，包括实收资本、资本公积、盈余公积、未分配利润等。根据会计“资产负债表”中“所有者权益”项的期末数填列。

主营业务收入 指会计“利润表”中对应指标的本年累计数。未执行2001年《企业会计制度》的企业，用“产品销售收入”的本期累计数代替。

主营业务成本 指会计“利润表”中对应指标的本年累计数。未执行2001年《企业会计制度》的企业，用“产品销售成本”的本期累计数代替。

主营业务税金及附加 指会计“利润表”中对应指标的本年累计数。未执行2001年《企业会计制度》的企业，用“产品销售税金及附加”的本期累计数代替。

利润总额 指企业在生产经营过程中各种收入扣除各种耗费后的盈余，反映企业在报告期内实现的盈亏总额，包括营业利润、补贴收入、投资净收益和营业外收支净额。根据会计“利润表”中的对应指标的本期累计数填列。

本年应交增值税 指企业按税法规定，从事货物销售或提供加工、修理修配劳务等增加货物价值的活动本期应交纳的税金。指企业在报告期应交增值税额。计算公式为：

本年应交增值税=销项税额-（进项税额-进项税额转出）-出口抵减内销产品应纳税额-减免税款+出口退税

本年进项税额 指工业企业在报告期内购入货物或接受应税劳务而支付的、准予从销项税额中抵扣的增值税额。

本年销项税额 指工业企业在报告期内销售货物或提供应税劳务应收取的增值税额。

从业人员平均人数 是指报告期内每天拥有的从业人员人数。其计算公式为：

月平均人数=报告月内每天实有人数之和／报告月日历日数

季平均人数=季内各月平均人数之和／3

年平均人数=年内各月平均人数之和／12

总资产贡献率 反映企业全部资产的获利能力，是企业经营业绩和管理水平的集中体现，是评价和考核企业盈利能力的核心指标。计算公式为：

总资产贡献率（%）=（利润总额+税金总额+利息支出）／平均资产总额×100%

公式中：税金总额为产品销售税金及附加与应交增值税之和；平均资产总额为期初期末资产之和的算术平均值。

资产负债率 该指标既反映企业经营风险的大小，也反映企业利用债权人提供的资金从事经营活动的能力。计算公式为：

资产负债率（%）=负债总额／资产总额×100%

资产与负债均为报告期期末数。

流动资产周转次数 指一定时期内流动资产完成的周转次数，反映投入工业企业流动资金的周转速度。计算公式为：

流动资产周转次数：产品销售收入／全部流动资产平均余额

公式中：全部流动资产平均余额为期初和期末的流动资产之和的算术平均值。

成本费用利润率 反映企业投入的生产成本及费用的经济效益，同时也反映企业降低成本所取得的经济效益。计算公式为：

成本费用利润率（%）=利润总额／成本费用总额×100%

公式中：成本费用总额为产品销售成本、销售费用、管理费用、财务费用之和。

产品销售率 该指标反映工业产品已实现销售的程度，是分析工业产销衔接情况，研究工业产品满足社会需求的指标。计算公式为：

产品销售率（%）=工业销售产值／工业总产值（现价）×100%

Explanatory Notes on Main Statistical Indicators

Industry refers to the material production sector which is engaged in the extraction of natural resources and processing and reprocessing of minerals and agricultural products, including (1) extraction of natural resources, such as mining, salt production (but not including hunting and fishing); (2) processing and reprocessing of farm and sideline produces, such as rice husking, flour milling, wine making, oil pressing, silk reeling, spinning and weaving, and leather making; (3) manufacture of industrial products, such as steel making, iron smelting, chemicals manufacturing, petroleum processing, machine building, timber processing; water and gas production and electricity generation and supply; (4)repairing of industrial products such as the repairing of machinery and means of transport (including cars).

In industrial statistics surveys, the units of enquiry are corporate industrial enterprises with independent accounting systems.

Corporate industrial enterprises with independent accounting systems refer to enterprises engaging in industrial production activities, which meet the following requirements: (1) They are established legally, having their own names, organizations, location and able to take civil liability; (2) They possess and use their assets independently, assume liabilities and are entitled to sign contracts with other units; (3) They are financially independent and compile their own balance sheets.

State–owned and State–holding Enterprises refer to state-owned enterprises plus State-holding enterprises. State-owned enterprises (originally known as State-run enterprises with ownership by the whole society) are non-corporate economic entities registered in accordance with the Regulation of the People's Republic of China on the Management of Registration of Legal Enterprises, where all assets are owned by the State. Included in this category are State-owned enterprises, State-funded corporations and State-owned joint-operation enterprises. Joint State- private industries and private industries, which existed before 1957, were transformed into state-run industries since 1957, and into State-owned industries after 1992. Statistics on those enterprises are included in the State- owned industries instead of being grouped them separately. State-holding enterprises are a sub- classification of enterprises with mixed ownership, referring to enterprises where the percentage of State assets (or shares by the State) is larger than any other single share holder of the same enterprise. This sub- classification illustrates the control of the State over a particular industry.

For explanation of enterprises of other types of registration covered in this chapter, please refer to General Survey.

Light Industry refers to the industry that produces consumer goods and hand tools. It consists of two categories, depending on the materials used:

(1) Industries using farm products as raw materials. These are the branches of light industry which directly or indirectly use farm products as basic raw materials, including the manufacture of food and beverages, tobacco processing, textile, clothing, fur and leather manufacturing, paper making, printing, etc.

(2) Industries using non-farm products as raw materials. These are the branches of light industry which use manufactured goods as raw materials, including the manufacture of cultural, educational articles and sports goods, chemicals, synthetic fibre, chemical products for daily use, glass products for daily use, metal products for daily use, hand tools, medical apparatus and instruments, and the manufacture of cultural and office machinery.

Heavy Industry refers to the industry which produces capital goods, and provides various sectors of the national economy with necessary material and technical basis for production. It consists of the following three branches according to the purpose of production or the use of products:

(1) Mining, quarrying and logging industry, which refers to the industry that extracts natural resources, including extraction of petroleum, coal, metal and non-metal ores.

(2) Raw materials industry refers to the industry that provides various sectors of the national economy with raw materials, fuels and power. It includes smelting and processing of metals, coking and coke chemistry, chemical materials and building materials such as cement, plywood, and power, petroleum refining and coal dressing

(3) Manufacturing industry which refers to the industry that processes raw materials. It includes machine-building industries which equip sectors of the national economy; industries producing metal structure and cement products; and industries producing means of agricultural production, such as chemical fertilizers and pesticides.

In accordance with the above principles of classification, the repairing trades, which are engaged primarily in repairing products of heavy industry, are classified as heavy industry while those which are engaged in repairing products of light industry are classified as light industry.

Gross Industrial Output Value

(1) Definition: Gross industrial output value is the total volume of final industrial products produced and industrial services provided during a given period in monetary terms. It reflects the total achievements and overall scale of industrial production during a given period.

(2) Principles for calculation:

Statistics on industrial production follow the principle that all products produced by the enterprises and accepted through quality check during the reference period are to be included no matter whether they are sold or not during the reference period.

Determination of final products follows the principle that all products that are included in the calculation of gross industrial output value are the final products of the enterprise which have been accepted through quality check and require no further processing. If an enterprise has intermediate (semi-finished) products to sell, these intermediate products are considered as the final products of the enterprise.

Gross industrial output value is calculated following the principle of factory approach, i.e. industrial enterprise is used as the basic accounting unit in calculating the gross industrial output value. By this approach, value of the same product is not to be double-counted, and the output value of different workshops (branch factories) within the enterprise should not be added. However, this approach allows the possibility of double counting between enterprises.

(3) Content and method of calculation: The old definition of gross industrial output value was modified during the 1995 National Industrial Census. The revised (new) definition of gross industrial output value consists of 3 components: value of the finished products during the reference period, income from processing for external parties, and value of change in semi-finished products between the end and the beginning of the reference period.

Value of finished products during the reference period: refers to the value of all finished (semi-finished) industrial products that are produced during the reference period without the need for further processing, checked for acceptance, packed and put into the warehouse of the enterprise, including the value of own-produced equipment and the value of products provided to the projects under construction of the enterprise, and to other non-industrial or welfare units. Value of finished products during the reference period is calculated by the quantity of products produced using own materials multiplied by the average unit prices at which products are sold (excluding value-added tax). Own-produced equipment and products produced for own use are valued at cost prices as in the case of enterprise accounting. Value of finished products does not include the value of finished products (semi-finished products) that are produced using the materials from the clients who place the orders.

Income from external processing: refers to income from contracted external processing of industrial products (including processing of industrial products using materials from the clients), and the income from industrial repairing work provided to other parties. Income from external processing is calculated using information from the item "products sales income" in the enterprise accounting at the prices with value-added tax excluded.

For income from services such as processing, repairing and installation of equipment provided to non- industrial units within the enterprise, if the accounting work of the enterprise is good enough to separate it from other records, and the share of such services is significant, it should also be included in the income from external processing.

Value of change in semi-finished products between the end and the beginning of the reference period: refers to the value of change in semi-finished products between the end and the beginning of the reference period, which generally can be obtained from accounting records of enterprises. If the enterprise accounting excludes the cost of semi-finished products, then it should not be included in the gross industrial output value, and the reverse if otherwise.

(4) Changes in the scope and method of calculation of the gross industrial output value

Prior to 1984, the value of rural industry run by villages was classified into agriculture instead of industry Since 1984, it has been included in the gross industrial output value. Method of calculation for the gross industrial output value was modified in the industriaLcensus in 1995. The difference in the new method as compared with the old one is outlined below:

Principle in using full value vs. processing fee: The new method stipulates that all products produced using own materials are to be calculated with full value in reporting the gross industrial output value irrespective of the complexity of production, and for external processing, it allows calculation using processing fee. In the old method, however, the use of full value or processing fee was determined by the degree of complexity of production in different branches of industries.

Principle in determining the value of change in semi-finished products: The new method requires that value of change in semi-finished products should be included in the gross industrial output value if it is included in the accounting record of the enterprise, otherwise it should not be included. In the old method, it is determined by the type of enterprises in terms of production cycle. If the production cycle is over 6 months, the value of change in semi-finished products is included in the gross industrial output value, otherwise it is not.

Difference in prices: The new method uses prices excluding value-added tax in the calculation of gross industrial output value, while the old method used prices including value-added tax.

Value–added of Industry refers to the final results of industrial production of industrial enterprises in money terms during the reference period.

Industrial value-added can be calculated by two approaches: the production approach, i.e. gross industrial output value minus intermediate input plus value-added tax, and the income approach, i.e. income for various factors used in the course of production, including depreciation of fixed assets, remuneration of labourers, net of production tax, and operating surplus. Value-added of industry in the Yearbook is calculated by the income approach as follows:

Value-added of industry = gross industrial output - industrial intermediate input + value-added tax

(1) Gross industrial output: refers to the total achievements of industrial production activities during a given period. Gross industrial output includes value of finished products, income from external processing, and value of change in semi-finished products between the end and the beginning of the reference period. Since 1995, the gross industrial output value obtained by the new method is used in the calculation.

(2) Industrial intermediate input: refers to purchased goods and paid services consumed during the industrial production of enterprises. Fees paid for services include fees paid for the services provided by material production sectors (industry, agriculture, wholesale and retail trade, construction, transport, post and telecommunications) and by non-material production sectors (insurance, banking, culture, education, scientific research, health and medical care, public administration, etc.). The determination of industrial intermediate input follows the principle that the goods and services must be purchased from outside and included in the gross industrial output, and that the goods and services are inputted into production and consumed (include low-value consumables) during the reference period.

Industrial intermediate input includes 5 components, namely direct consumption of materials, industrial intermediate input in manufacturing cost, industrial intermediate input in management cost, industrial intermediate input in marketing cost and expenditure on interest.

Total Assets refer to all economic resources, in monetary term, these are owned or controlled by enterprises, including properties, creditor's equity and other economic rights of all forms. Classified by the degree of liquidity, total assets include working capitals, long-term investment, fixed assets, intangible assets, deferred assets and other assets. Data on this indicator can be obtained by the year-end figures of total assets in the Assets and Liability Table of accounting records of enterprises.

Working Capital refers to capital that an enterprise can cash or use during one year or one production cycle that may exceed one year, including cash and savings deposits of various forms, short-term investment, money receivable and prepaid money, inventories, etc.

Original Value of Fixed Assets refers to the total value, in monetary terms, that an enterprise spent on fixed assets, through construction, purchase, installation, transformation, expansion or technical upgrading. Generally, it covers cost of purchase, packing, transportation and installation, etc.

Net Value of Fixed Assets refers to the original value of fixed assets minus depreciation over the years, i.e.:

Net value of fixed assets = original value of fixed assets - cumulative depreciation

Total Liabilities refer to payable liabilities of enterprises that have to be repaid in terms of money, assets or labour services. In terms of payment, it can be divided into liquid liabilities and long-term liabilities. Data on this item is obtained from the ending figures on total liabilities from the Assets and Liability Table from the enterprises.

Total Equity refers to the ownership of net assets of enterprise by its investors. Net assets equal total assets minus total liabilities of the enterprise, including the paid-in capital, accumulation of capital and operating surplus and non-distributed profits. Data are obtained from the ending figures on "total equity" from the "balance sheets" .

Revenue from Principal Business refers to the annual accumulation of the corresponding item in the "profit table" of the accountant. For enterprises that do not follow the 2001 Enterprise Accounting Standards, the year-end accumulation of revenue from the sales of products is used as a substitute.

Cost of Principal Business refers to the annual accumulation of the corresponding item in the "profit table" of the accountant. For enterprises that do not follow the 2001 Enterprise Accounting Standards, theyear-end accumulation of cost for the sales of products is used as a substitute.

Tax and Extra Charges from Principal Bosiness refer to the annual accumulation of the corresponding item in the "profit table" of the accountant. For enterprises that do not follow the 2001 Enterprise Accounting Standards, the year-end accumulation of tax and extra charges from the sales of products is used as a substitute.

Total Profits refers to the balance of various incomes minus various spendings in the course of operation, reflecting the total profits and losses of enterprises in reporting period. It includes: operating profits, income from subsidies, net investment income and net income from activities other than operation. Data are obtained from the annual accumulation of the corresponding item in the "profit table" of the accountant.

Value-added Tax Payable in the Current Year refers to the payable tax of enterprises which engaged in selling of goods or providing services that bring added value to the goods, such as processing, repairing, fitting and other activities should be paid according to Tax Law. It refers to the amount of the value-added tax which should be paid by the enterprises during the reference period. The formula is as tollows:

Value-added Tax Payable in the Current Year = tax on sales-(tax on purchase-transferred tax on purchase)- exports deduct tax payable on domestic sales-tax relief+the export tax rebate.

Tax on Purchase in Current Year refers to goods purchased by industrial enterprises or value added tax that should be paid but being granted the right to deduct from the tax on sales.

Tax on Sales in Current Year refers to value added tax on industrial enterprises from sales of goods or taxable services that should be charged value added tax.

Average number of employed persons refers to the number of employee everyday during the reference period, calculated with the following formula:

$$\text{Monthly average Number} = \frac{\text{sum of actual employees everyday in reference month}}{\text{number of calendar dates in reference month}}$$

$$\text{Quarterly average number} = \frac{\text{sum of monthly average number in reference quarter}}{3}$$

$$\text{Annual average number} = \frac{\text{sum of monthly average number in reference year}}{12}$$

Ratio of Profits, Taxes and Interests to Average Assets reflects the profit-making capability of all assets of the enterprise and is a key indicator manifesting the performance and management and evaluating the profit-making potential of the enterprise. It is calculated as

$$\text{Ratio of Profits, Taxes and Interests toAverageAssets(\%)} = \frac{\text{otal profits+ total taxes+ interest payment}}{\text{average assets}} \times 100\%$$

In the above formula, total taxes is the sum of tax and extra charges on the sales of products and value-added tax payable; and average assets is the arithmetic mean of the sum of beginning assets and ending assets.

Ratio of Debts to Assets reflects both the operation risk and the capability of the enterprise in making use of the capital from the creditors. It is calculated as follows:

$$\text{Ratio of Debts toAssets(\%)} = \frac{\text{total debts}}{\text{total assets}} \times 100\%$$

Both assets and debts are figures at the end of the reference period.

Turnover of Working Capital refers to the number of times of turnover of working capital in a given period of time, which reflects the speed of the turnover of working capital of industrial enterprises, and is calculated as follows:

$$\text{Turnover of Working Capital} = \frac{\text{sales revenue of products}}{\text{average balance of total working capital}}$$

In the above formula, average balance of total working capital refers to the arithmetic mean of the sum of working capital at the beginning and at the end of the reference period.

Ratio of Profits to Total Industrial Costs refers to the ratio of profits realized in a given period to the total costs in the same period, which reflects the economic efficiency of input cost and is calculated as follows:

$$\text{Ratio of Profits to Total Industrial Cost (\%)} = \frac{\text{total profits}}{\text{total costs}} \times 100\%$$

Total costs in the above formula are the sum of cost of products sold, marketing cost, management cost and financial cost.

Sales Ratio of Products is an indicator reflecting the actual sale of industrial products, analyzing the production-selling and supply-demand relations. It is calculated as:

$$\text{Sales Ratio of Products (\%)} = \frac{\text{value of industrial sales}}{\text{gross industrial output value (current prices)}} \times 100\%$$

13 能　源

ENERGY

资料整理：于元英　张　育　李　婷
Data management：Yu Yuanying　Zhang Yu　Li Ting
数据审核：马建华
Data audit：Ma Jianhua

第十三部分　能源

一、简要说明

本章资料包括规模以上工业能源购销存情况、全市单位GDP能耗、规模以上工业企业用水情况等，由西安市统计局能源与环境处提供。

二、主要指标

规模以上工业综合能源消费量（万吨标准煤）	698.92	比上年下降	2.1%
单位GDP能耗（吨标准煤/万元）	0.384	比上年下降	4.61%

13 ENERGY

Ⅰ.Brief Introduction

Data in this chapter reflects energy purchases consumption and inventory of industrial enterprises above designated size,energy consumption per unit of GDP in whole city, and statistics on water use of industrial enterprises above designated size. data in this chapter are provided and compiled by Energy and Environment Division of the Xi'an Bureau of Statistics.

Ⅱ.Major Indicators

		Increase over Preceding Year
Comprehensive Energy Consumption Above Designated Size(10 000 Tons of Standard Coal)	698.92	-2.1%
Energy Consumption of GDP per Unit (Tons of Standard Coal /10 000 yuan)	0.384	-4.61%

13-1 全市及各区县单位GDP能耗

Energy Consumption per Unit of GDP by Region

单位：吨标准煤 / 万元 (ton of SCE/10 000 yuan)

地 区	Region	单位GDP能耗 Energy Consumption Per Unit of GDP														
		GDP按2005年价格计算 GDP are calculated at 2005 constant prices						GDP按2010年价格计算 GDP are calculated at 2010 constant prices						GDP按2015年价格计算 GDP are calculated at 2015 constant prices		
		2005	2006	2007	2008	2009	2010	2010	2011	2012	2013	2014	2015	2015	2016	2017
西安市	**Xi'an**	**0.911**	**0.873**	**0.823**	**0.768**	**0.726**	**0.711**	**0.575**	**0.555**	**0.535**	**0.516**	**0.486**	**0.470**	**0.410**	**0.394**	**0.384**
新城区	Xincheng	0.783	0.751	0.708	0.667	0.629	0.621	0.563	0.544	0.525	0.506	0.479	0.463	0.416	0.401	0.378
碑林区	Beilin	0.640	0.613	0.580	0.547	0.514	0.510	0.438	0.421	0.406	0.392	0.368	0.356	0.287	0.277	0.258
莲湖区	Lianhu	0.766	0.735	0.701	0.646	0.609	0.587	0.521	0.501	0.483	0.466	0.430	0.416	0.372	0.359	0.330
灞桥区	Baqiao	1.194	1.163	1.091	1.023	0.964	0.923	0.663	0.638	0.615	0.592	0.562	0.543	0.517	0.497	0.426
未央区	Weiyang	1.122	1.078	1.019	0.951	0.894	0.882	0.680	0.655	0.632	0.609	0.563	0.539	0.444	0.427	0.376
雁塔区	Yanta	0.884	0.842	0.795	0.749	0.703	0.674	0.512	0.494	0.476	0.459	0.441	0.425	0.362	0.349	0.313
阎良区	Yanliang	0.825	0.778	0.740	0.695	0.656	0.652	0.533	0.515	0.497	0.480	0.444	0.430	0.364	0.352	0.311
临潼区	Lintong	0.940	0.912	0.860	0.790	0.753	0.717	0.676	0.652	0.629	0.607	0.558	0.541	0.502	0.484	0.427
长安区	Chang'an	1.059	0.994	0.939	0.890	0.841	0.824	0.642	0.619	0.596	0.575	0.555	0.532	0.460	0.443	0.345
高陵区	Gaoling	0.892	0.848	0.790	0.747	0.704	0.677	0.487	0.467	0.451	0.435	0.403	0.391	0.345	0.333	0.310
鄠邑区	Huyi	1.411	1.367	1.287	1.188	1.123	1.089	0.978	0.940	0.906	0.873	0.844	0.811	0.791	0.761	0.657
蓝田县	Lantian	1.727	1.673	1.606	1.517	1.444	1.414	1.083	1.047	1.011	0.978	0.924	0.895	0.771	0.742	0.680
周至县	Zhouzhi	1.502	1.465	1.386	1.309	1.237	1.212	0.959	0.928	0.897	0.867	0.801	0.778	0.649	0.626	0.567

13-1 续表 continude

地 区	Region	比上年增长(%) Growth Rates over Preceding Year(%)											
		2006	2007	2008	2009	2010	2011	2012	2013	2014	2015	2016	2017
西安市	**Xi'an**	**-4.15**	**-5.75**	**-6.65**	**-5.56**	**-2.06**	**-3.56**	**-3.51**	**-3.57**	**-5.89**	**-3.20**	**-3.83**	**-4.61**
新城区	Xincheng	-4.15	-5.67	-5.79	-5.80	-1.15	-3.51	-3.50	-3.50	-5.39	-3.27	-3.58	-3.27
碑林区	Beilin	-4.18	-5.44	-5.65	-5.95	-0.91	-3.89	-3.50	-3.50	-6.06	-3.20	-3.66	-3.65
莲湖区	Lianhu	-4.07	-4.60	-7.93	-5.65	-3.58	-3.84	-3.60	-3.61	-7.76	-3.14	-3.58	-5.93
灞桥区	Baqiao	-2.54	-6.20	-6.24	-5.80	-4.20	-3.81	-3.62	-3.64	-5.20	-3.30	-3.75	-6.95
未央区	Weiyang	-3.97	-5.44	-6.63	-6.05	-1.31	-3.60	-3.60	-3.60	-7.60	-4.16	-3.86	-4.49
雁塔区	Yanta	-4.71	-5.64	-5.80	-6.08	-4.18	-3.61	-3.61	-3.60	-3.89	-3.58	-3.55	-6.36
阎良区	Yanliang	-5.77	-4.80	-6.08	-5.62	-0.61	-3.38	-3.50	-3.50	-7.59	-3.00	-3.46	-3.99
临潼区	Lintong	-3.03	-5.73	-8.16	-4.58	-4.81	-3.52	-3.51	-3.51	-8.07	-3.00	-3.46	-6.29
长安区	Chang'an	-6.15	-5.53	-5.22	-5.50	-2.08	-3.60	-3.63	-3.63	-3.40	-4.10	-3.56	-5.10
高陵区	Gaoling	-4.85	-6.85	-5.50	-5.70	-3.82	-3.93	-3.52	-3.54	-7.32	-3.00	-3.52	-4.00
鄠邑区	Huyi	-3.07	-5.85	-7.70	-5.50	-2.99	-3.85	-3.60	-3.62	-3.40	-3.82	-3.84	-3.89
蓝田县	Lantian	-3.13	-4.01	-5.50	-4.84	-2.06	-3.39	-3.40	-3.30	-5.48	-3.17	-3.84	-3.27
周至县	Zhouzhi	-2.46	-5.43	-5.51	-5.50	-2.06	-3.30	-3.30	-3.30	-7.63	-2.90	-3.50	-3.64

注：能源消耗按等价值计算；2013年以前数据，根据第三次经济普查结果进行了调整。

13-2 主要年份全社会用电量

单位：万千瓦时

行 业	Sector	2008	2009
总 计	**Total**	**1605089**	**1724067**
#行业用电量合计	Total of Industry of Electricity	1293574	1358483
1. 第一产业	Primary Industry	127054	99083
2. 第二产业	Secondary Industry	724852	766029
3. 第三产业	Tertiary Industry	441668	493371
一、农、林、牧、渔、水利业	Agriculture ,Forestry,Animal Husbandry and Fishery	127054	99083
二、工业	Industry	696291	724920
1. 轻工业	Light Industry	182176	167144
2. 重工业	Heavy Industry	514115	557776
三、建筑业	Construction	28561	41108
四、交通运输、仓储及邮政业	Traffic,Transport, Storage and Post	56614	62031
五、信息传输、计算机服务和软件业	Information Transmission,Computer Service and Software	26680	29328
六、商业、住宿和餐饮业	Commercial,Hotels and Catering Services	111676	122203
七、金融、房地产、商务及居民服务业	Finance,Real Estate,Business Affairs and Households Services	81674	102400
八、公共事业及管理组织	Public Utilities and Management Organization	165024	177409
九、城乡居民生活用电	Electricity Consumption of Urban and Rural Residents	311515	365585
1. 乡村	Rural	63072	99941
2. 城市	City	248443	265644

注：1.本表数据来源于国网陕西省供电公司西安供电公司和国网陕西电力公司西咸供电公司。
2.2017年为包含西咸新区数据。

Electricity Consumption of the Whole Society in Representative Years

(10 000 kw. h)

2010	2011	2012	2013	2014	2015	2016	2017
1993751	**2167453**	**2352571**	**2554679**	**2753213**	**2844836**	**3120582**	**3613693**
1499903	1590486	1706859	1854696	2002503	2049492	2216797	2586468
108720	117984	109086	110405	95997	89970	87825	102033
883259	910360	932622	991202	1086105	1088866	1147294	1388903
507924	562142	665151	753089	820401	870656	981678	1095531
108720	117984	109086	110405	95997	89970	87825	102033
838317	859796	875018	920024	998132	997115	1062188	1287836
177362	183766	175392	170246	165933	165290	170735	183582
660955	676030	699626	749778	832199	831826	891453	1104254
44942	50564	57605	71179	87973	91750	85106	101068
58509	66684	69633	78722	88805	90914	109911	128970
30760	33191	37444	39551	42662	46203	61950	77104
148418	166558	199970	228117	253199	277248	301414	334387
116163	131236	150832	165833	180824	185329	212666	232317
154074	164473	207271	240866	254911	270962	295737	322753
493848	576966	645713	699982	750710	795344	903785	1027226
142059	169898	197937	216148	235938	241920	263871	288571
351789	407068	447776	483834	514773	553424	639914	738655

13-3 规模以上工业企业能源购进、消费及库存（2017年）

能源名称	Name	年初库存量 Stock (year-beginning)	购进量/实物量 Purchases	其中：购自省外 Wherein: purchased from outside the province
原煤(吨)	Raw Coal (ton)	883018	11966566	76575
洗精煤(吨)	Washed Coal(ton)			
其他洗煤(吨)	Other Washed Coals(ton)	29975	188768	
煤制品（吨）	Briquettes(ton)	164	1403	
焦炭(吨)	Coke(ton)	8	98	
其他焦化产品(吨)	Other Coking Products(ton)			
焦炉煤气(万立方米)	Coke Oven Gas(10000 cu.m)			
高炉煤气(万立方米)	Blast Furnace Gas(10000 cu.m)			
转炉煤气(万立方米)	Converter Gas(10000 cu.m)			
发生炉煤气(万立方米)	Producer Gas(10000 cu.m)			
天然气（气态）（万立方米）	Natural Gas(10 000cu.m)	1781	41879	
液化天然气（液态）（吨）	Liquefied Natural Gas (Liquid)(ton)		2328	58
煤层气(万立方米)	Voalbed Gas(10000 cu.m)			
原油(吨)	Crude Oil(ton)			
汽油(吨)	Gasoline(ton)	72	21067	1178
煤油(吨)	Kerosene(ton)	38	162	1
柴油(吨)	Diesel Oil(ton)	1077	64669	917
燃料油(吨)	Fuel Oil(ton)	80	1383	502
液化石油气(吨)	LPG(ton)		525	
炼厂干气(吨)	Refinery Gas(ton)			
石脑油(吨)	Naphtha(ton)			
润滑油（吨）	Lubricating Oil (ton)		545	
石蜡(吨)	Paraffin(ton)			
溶剂油（吨）	Solvent Oil (ton)	2	408	
石油焦(吨)	Petrol Coke(ton)			
石油沥青(吨)	Petroleum Asphalt(ton)	6813	9274	
其它石油制品(吨)	Other Petroleum Products(ton)	12204	1987	
热力(百万千焦)	Heat (1 million kilo-joule)		4747509	
电力(万千瓦时)	Electricity(10 000kwh)		851782	
煤矸石(用于燃料)(吨)	Coal Gangue(used for fuel)(ton)		413	
城市生活垃圾(用于燃料)(吨)	City Domestic Waste(used for fuel)(ton)			
生物燃料（吨标准煤）	Biofuel(tons of SCE)		12736	
余热余压（百万千焦）	Residual Heat and Pressure(million of KJ)			
工业废料(用于燃料)(吨)	Industrial Waste(used for fuel)(ton)			
其他燃料（吨标准煤）	Other Fuels(ton of SCE)	2	991	
能源合计(吨标准煤)	Total Energy(ton of SCE)			

Energy Purchases, Consumption and Inventory of Industrial Enterprises above Designated Size (2017)

消费量 合计 Consumption Total	工业 生产消费 Industrial Production Consume	用于 原材料 as Raw Material	非工业 生产消费 Non-industrial Production Consume	期末库存量 Stock (year-end)
11948837	11945308	1056672	3529	894564
151775	151775			66968
1504	1115		389	22
106	106			1
42389	41793	1141	596	1204
2313	2308		5	15
21011	17120	394	3892	56
156	156	1		40
64518	61837	3922	2682	1173
1451	1442		9	12
527	525		3	
545	545			
408	408	403		1
9428	9428			5865
1987	1987			71
6789274	6761870		27404	
1003889	995808		8081	
399	399			15
12669	12652		17	66
995	994		1	
10719278	10688097		31181	

13-4 规模以上工业企业分行业主要能源品种消费量（2017年）

Major Energy Consumption above Designated Size by Industry（2017）

行 业	Sector	原煤 (吨) Raw Coal (ton)	天然气 (万立方米) Natural Gas(10 000 cu.m)
总 计	**Total**	**11948837**	**42389**
煤炭开采和洗选业	Coal Mining and Dressing		
石油和天然气开采业	Petroleum and Natural Gas Extraction		
黑色金属矿采选业	Ferrous Metals Mining and Dressing		
有色金属矿采选业	Nonferrous Metals Mining and Dressing		
非金属矿采选业	Nonmetal Minerals Mining and Dressing		
开采辅助活动	Ancillary activities for mining	314	391
其他采矿业	Other Mining Industry		
农副食品加工业	Agricultural Products and Non-stable Food Processing Industry	223244	703
食品制造业	Food Production	13852	3459
酒、饮料和精制茶制造业	Wine, soft drinks and refined tea industry	57239	832
烟草制品业	Tobacco Processing	4460	48
纺织业	Textile Industry	776	243
纺织服装、服饰业	Textile, apparel industry		45
皮革、毛皮、羽毛及其制品和制鞋业	Leather, Fur, Feather (eiderdown) and Their Products Industry	5	
木材加工和木、竹、藤、棕、草制品业	Timber Processing,Bamboo,Cane,Palm Fiber and Straw Products		
家具制造业	Furniture Manufacturing		
造纸及纸制品业	Papermaking and Paper products	4205	536
印刷和记录媒介复制业	Printing,Record Medium Reproduction	65	435
文教、工美、体育和娱乐用品制造业	Culture, education, Craft art, sports and entertainment goods manufacturing industry		
石油加工、炼焦和核燃料加工业	Petroleum Refining, Ccoke Making and Nuclear Fuel Processing Industry	696	182
化学原料和化学制品制造业	Raw Chemical Materials and Chemical Products	1442677	2626
医药制造业	Medical and Pharmaceutical Products	2723	1945
化学纤维制造业	Chemical Fiber		
橡胶和塑料制品业	Rubber and plastic products industry	125749	3203
非金属矿物制品业	Nonmetal Mineral Products	123722	1201
黑色金属冶炼和压延加工业	Smelting and Pressing of Ferrous Metals	3293	33
有色金属冶炼和压延加工业	Smelting and Pressing of Nonferrou Metals	269	845
金属制品业	Metal Products	2031	351
通用设备制造业	General Equipment Manufacturing Industry	63	613
专用设备制造业	Special Purpose Equipment	21	423
汽车制造业	Automotive Manufacturing	7533	4718
铁路、船舶、航空航天和其他运输设备制造业	Railroad, marine, aerospace and other transportation equipment manufacturing	158	189
电气机械和器材制造业	Electric Equipment and Machinery	321	2981
计算机、通信和其他电子设备制造业	Communication Equipment, Computer and Other Electronic Equipment Manufacturing Industry		3254
仪器仪表制造业	Instrument manufacturing industry		30
其他制造业	Other manufacturing	51	7
废弃资源综合利用	Comprehensive utilization of waste resources		
金属制品、机械和设备修理业	Metal products, machinery and equipment repair industry		7
电力、热力生产和供应业	Electric Power, Heating Power Generating and Supplying Industry	9935369	12613
燃气生产和供应业	Gas Mining and Supplying Industry		227
水的生产和供应业	Water Processing and Supplying Industry		248

13-4 续表 continued

行 业	Sector	汽油 (吨) Gasoline (ton)	柴油 (吨) Diesel Oil (ton)	热力 (百万千焦) Heat (million kilo joule)	电力 (万千瓦时) Electricity (10 000 kwh)
总 计	**Total**	**21011**	**64518**	**6789274**	**1003889**
煤炭开采和洗选业	Coal Mining and Dressing				
石油和天然气开采业	Petroleum and Natural Gas Extraction				
黑色金属矿采选业	Ferrous Metals Mining and Dressing				
有色金属矿采选业	Nonferrous Metals Mining and Dressing				
非金属矿采选业	Nonmetal Minerals Mining and Dressing				
开采辅助活动	Ancillary activities for mining	654	6564		2316
其他采矿业	Other Mining Industry				
农副食品加工业	Agricultural Products and Non-stable Food Processing Industry	969	713	1988805	22840
食品制造业	Food Production	899	650	398570	18582
酒、饮料和精制茶制造业	Wine, soft drinks and refined tea industry	540	1320	164069	16717
烟草制品业	Tobacco Processing	37	52	3887	1004
纺织业	Textile Industry	58		119719	22334
纺织服装、服饰业	Textile, apparel industry	52	2		135
皮革、毛皮、羽毛及其制品和制鞋业	Leather, Fur, Feather (eiderdown) and Their Products Industry	40		11964	278
木材加工和木、竹、藤、棕、草制品业	Timber Processing,Bamboo,Cane,Palm Fiber and Straw Products	9	20		4179
家具制造业	Furniture Manufacturing	204	134		2316
造纸及纸制品业	Papermaking and Paper products	110	99	52314	4966
印刷和记录媒介复制业	Printing,Record Medium Reproduction	325	86	55469	7365
文教、工美、体育和娱乐用品制造业	Culture, education, Craft art, sports and entertainment goods manufacturing industry	25	30		767
石油加工、炼焦和核燃料加工业	Petroleum Refining, Ccoke Making and Nuclear Fuel Processing Industry	1258	616		2755
化学原料和化学制品制造业	Raw Chemical Materials and Chemical Products	434	739	9615	132026
医药制造业	Medical and Pharmaceutical Products	1033	195	189294	13245
化学纤维制造业	Chemical Fiber	7	7	1156094	5948
橡胶和塑料制品业	Rubber and plastic products industry	379	3956	2205	13515
非金属矿物制品业	Nonmetal Mineral Products	982	38047	1102	43768
黑色金属冶炼和压延加工业	Smelting and Pressing of Ferrous Metals	26	28		5707
有色金属冶炼和压延加工业	Smelting and Pressing of Nonferrou Metals	390	102	880209	62687
金属制品业	Metal Products	656	275	7370	9323
通用设备制造业	General Equipment Manufacturing Industry	1016	196	3692	11025
专用设备制造业	Special Purpose Equipment	3089	1013	28668	19661
汽车制造业	Automotive Manufacturing	2318	7089	333239	120031
铁路、船舶、航空航天和其他运输设备制造业	Railroad, marine, aerospace and other transportation equipment manufacturing	647	374	60234	16062
电气机械和器材制造业	Electric Equipment and Machinery	1616	578	903762	62278
计算机、通信和其他电子设备制造业	Communication Equipment, Computer and Other Electronic Equipment Manufacturing Industry	590	62	210490	201747
仪器仪表制造业	Instrument manufacturing industry	588	19	5893	2306
其他制造业	Other manufacturing	95	85		580
废弃资源综合利用	Comprehensive utilization of waste resources	2	110		151
金属制品、机械和设备修理业	Metal products, machinery and equipment repair	58	37		113
电力、热力生产和供应业	Electric Power, Heating Power Generating and Supplying Industry	1051	1216	202610	160920
燃气生产和供应业	Gas Mining and Supplying Industry	526	79		6673
水的生产和供应业	Water Processing and Supplying Industry	328	22		9567

13-5 规模以上工业企业分行业综合能源消费量（2017年）

Comprehensive Energy Consumption by Sector above Designated Size（2017）

单位：吨标准煤 (ton of SCE)

行业	Scetor	2017	比上年增长(%) Increase over Preceding Year (%)
总计	**Total**	**6989190**	**-2.1**
煤炭开采和洗选业	Coal Mining and Dressing		
石油和天然气开采业	Petroleum and Natural Gas Extraction		
黑色金属矿采选业	Ferrous Metals Mining and Dressing		
有色金属矿采选业	Nonferrous Metals Mining and Dressing		
非金属矿采选业	Nonmetal Minerals Mining and Dressing		
开采辅助活动	Ancillary activities for mining	18816	19.6
其他采矿业	Other Mining Industry		
农副食品加工业	Agricultural Products and Non-stable Food Processing Industry	194530	3.1
食品制造业	Food Production	93320	-4.0
酒、饮料和精制茶制造业	Wine, soft drinks and refined tea industry	80245	-10.3
烟草制品业	Tobacco Processing	5037	-2.0
纺织业	Textile Industry	32918	-9.9
纺织服装、服饰业	Textile, apparel industry	832	289.7
皮革、毛皮、羽毛及其制品和制鞋业	Leather, Fur, Feather (eiderdown) and Their Products Industry	812	1.1
木材加工和木、竹、藤、棕、草制品业	Timber Processing,Bamboo,Cane,Palm Fiber and Straw Products	9453	-8.0
家具制造业	Furniture Manufacturing	3334	81.5
造纸及纸制品业	Papermaking and Paper products	24718	-15.6
印刷和记录媒介复制业	Printing,Record Medium Reproduction	17080	-9.1
文教、工美、体育和娱乐用品制造业	Culture, education, Craft art, sports and entertainment goods manufacturing industry	1089	78.8
石油加工、炼焦和核燃料加工业	Petroleum Refining, Ccoke Making and Nuclear Fuel Processing Industry	9862	1.9
化学原料和化学制品制造业	Raw Chemical Materials and Chemical Products	1203039	-3.1
医药制造业	Medical and Pharmaceutical Products	52231	-18.3
化学纤维制造业	Chemical Fiber	46754	-6.2
橡胶和塑料制品业	Rubber and plastic products industry	39945	-17.6
非金属矿物制品业	Nonmetal Mineral Products	316519	0.0
黑色金属冶炼和压延加工业	Smelting and Pressing of Ferrous Metals	10116	-34.9
有色金属冶炼和压延加工业	Smelting and Pressing of Nonferrou Metals	119178	1.8
金属制品业	Metal Products	19167	-6.5
通用设备制造业	General Equipment Manufacturing Industry	20526	-15.3
专用设备制造业	Special Purpose Equipment	32943	-0.9
汽车制造业	Automotive Manufacturing	206285	15.3
铁路、船舶、航空航天和其他运输设备制造业	Railroad, marine, aerospace and other transportation equipment manufacturing	23229	-1.8
电气机械和器材制造业	Electric Equipment and Machinery	149585	-0.2
计算机、通信和其他电子设备制造业	Communication Equipment, Computer and Other Electronic Equipment Manufacturing Industry	297702	8.1
仪器仪表制造业	Instrument manufacturing industry	4054	-1.6
其他制造业	Other manufacturing	1058	-15.5
废弃资源综合利用	Comprehensive utilization of waste resources	349	28.3
金属制品、机械和设备修理业	Metal products, machinery and equipment repair industry	338	-31.4
电力、热力生产和供应业	Electric Power, Heating Power Generating and Supplying Industry	3928627	-2.8
燃气生产和供应业	Gas Mining and Supplying Industry	11967	-12.9
水的生产和供应业	Water Processing and Supplying Industry	13531	1.1

13-6 规模以上工业企业用水情况（2017年）

Statistics on Water Use of Industrial Enterprises above Designated Size（2017）

指 标	Item	取水量（万立方米）Water Use (10 000 cu.m)	外供水量（万立方米）Outward Water Supply (10 000 cu.m)
合 计	**Total**	**70242**	**57140**
地表淡水	Surface fresh water	44791	168
地下淡水	Underground fresh water	13960	1018
自来水	Tap Water	10132	55954
陆地苦咸水	Land lake Salt water	5	
矿井水	Mine Water	5	
雨水	Rain Water	25	
再生水	Reclaimed Water	1323	
其他水	Other Water	1	
外排水量	Efflux capacity	5487	
重复用水量	Repeated water consumption	168850	

13-7 规模以上工业企业分行业用水情况（2017年）

Volume of Water Use of Industrial Enterprises above Designated Size by Industry (2017)

行　业	Sector	取水量（万立方米） Water Use (10 000 cu.m)
总　计	**Total**	**70242**
煤炭开采和洗选业	Coal Mining and Dressing	79
石油和天然气开采业	Petroleum and Natural Gas Extraction	
黑色金属矿采选业	Ferrous Metals Mining and Dressing	
有色金属矿采选业	Nonferrous Metals Mining and Dressing	
非金属矿采选业	Nonmetal Minerals Mining and Dressing	
开采辅助活动	Ancillary activities for mining	
其他采矿业	Other Mining Industry	
农副食品加工业	Agricultural Products and Non-stable Food Processing Industry	263
食品制造业	Food Production	436
酒、饮料和精制茶制造业	Wine, soft drinks and refined tea industry	654
烟草制品业	Tobacco Processing	3
纺织业	Textile Industry	90
纺织服装、服饰业	Textile, apparel industry	20
皮革、毛皮、羽毛及其制品和制鞋业	Leather, Fur, Feather (eiderdown) and Their Products Industry	1
木材加工和木、竹、藤、棕、草制品业	Timber Processing,Bamboo,Cane,Palm Fiber and Straw Products	2
家具制造业	Furniture Manufacturing	15
造纸及纸制品业	Papermaking and Paper products	18
印刷和记录媒介复制业	Printing,Record Medium Reproduction	57
文教、工美、体育和娱乐用品制造业	Culture, education, Craft art, sports and entertainment goods manufacturing industry	4
石油加工、炼焦和核燃料加工业	Petroleum Refining, Ccoke Making and Nuclear Fuel Processing Industry	79
化学原料和化学制品制造业	Raw Chemical Materials and Chemical Products	1319
医药制造业	Medical and Pharmaceutical Products	304
化学纤维制造业	Chemical Fiber	51
橡胶和塑料制品业	Rubber and plastic products industry	299
非金属矿物制品业	Nonmetal Mineral Products	409
黑色金属冶炼和压延加工业	Smelting and Pressing of Ferrous Metals	3
有色金属冶炼和压延加工业	Smelting and Pressing of Nonferrou Metals	189
金属制品业	Metal Products	52
通用设备制造业	General Equipment Manufacturing Industry	74
专用设备制造业	Special Purpose Equipment	163
汽车制造业	Automotive Manufacturing	762
铁路、船舶、航空航天和其他运输设备制造业	Railroad, marine, aerospace and other transportation equipment manufacturing	115
电气机械和器材制造业	Electric Equipment and Machinery	620
计算机、通信和其他电子设备制造业	Communication Equipment, Computer and Other Electronic Equipment Manufacturing Industry	1502
仪器仪表制造业	Instrument manufacturing industry	117
其他制造业	Other manufacturing	9
废弃资源综合利用	Comprehensive utilization of waste resources	
金属制品、机械和设备修理业	Metal products, machinery and equipment repair industry	3
电力、热力生产和供应业	Electric Power, Heating Power Generating and Supplying Industry	4905
燃气生产和供应业	Gas Mining and Supplying Industry	24
水的生产和供应业	Water Processing and Supplying Industry	57601

13-7 续表 continude

行　业	Sector	外供水量（万立方米）Outward Water Supply (10 000 cu.m)
总　计	**Total**	**57140**
煤炭开采和洗选业	Coal Mining and Dressing	
石油和天然气开采业	Petroleum and Natural Gas Extraction	
黑色金属矿采选业	Ferrous Metals Mining and Dressing	
有色金属矿采选业	Nonferrous Metals Mining and Dressing	
非金属矿采选业	Nonmetal Minerals Mining and Dressing	
开采辅助活动	Ancillary activities for mining	
其他采矿业	Other Mining Industry	
农副食品加工业	Agricultural Products and Non-stable Food Processing Industry	
食品制造业	Food Production	
酒、饮料和精制茶制造业	Wine, soft drinks and refined tea industry	
烟草制品业	Tobacco Processing	
纺织业	Textile Industry	
纺织服装、服饰业	Textile, apparel industry	
皮革、毛皮、羽毛及其制品和制鞋业	Leather, Fur, Feather (eiderdown) and Their Products Industry	
木材加工和木、竹、藤、棕、草制品业	Timber Processing,Bamboo,Cane,Palm Fiber and Straw Products	
家具制造业	Furniture Manufacturing	
造纸及纸制品业	Papermaking and Paper products	
印刷和记录媒介复制业	Printing,Record Medium Reproduction	
文教、工美、体育和娱乐用品制造业	Culture, education, Craft art, sports and entertainment goods manufacturing industry	
石油加工、炼焦和核燃料加工业	Petroleum Refining, Ccoke Making and Nuclear Fuel Processing Industry	
化学原料和化学制品制造业	Raw Chemical Materials and Chemical Products	
医药制造业	Medical and Pharmaceutical Products	
化学纤维制造业	Chemical Fiber	
橡胶和塑料制品业	Rubber and plastic products industry	
非金属矿物制品业	Nonmetal Mineral Products	
黑色金属冶炼和压延加工业	Smelting and Pressing of Ferrous Metals	
有色金属冶炼和压延加工业	Smelting and Pressing of Nonferrou Metals	
金属制品业	Metal Products	
通用设备制造业	General Equipment Manufacturing Industry	
专用设备制造业	Special Purpose Equipment	3
汽车制造业	Automotive Manufacturing	
铁路、船舶、航空航天和其他运输设备制造业	Railroad, marine, aerospace and other transportation equipment manufacturing	
电气机械和器材制造业	Electric Equipment and Machinery	
计算机、通信和其他电子设备制造业	Communication Equipment, Computer and Other Electronic Equipment Manufacturing Industry	
仪器仪表制造业	Instrument manufacturing industry	
其他制造业	Other manufacturing	
废弃资源综合利用	Comprehensive utilization of waste resources	
金属制品、机械和设备修理业	Metal products, machinery and equipment repair industry	
电力、热力生产和供应业	Electric Power, Heating Power Generating and Supplying Industry	
燃气生产和供应业	Gas Mining and Supplying Industry	
水的生产和供应业	Water Processing and Supplying Industry	57137

13-8 分区县规模以上工业企业综合能源消费量（2017年）

Comprehensive Energy Consumption above Designated Size by Region（2017）

单位：吨标准煤 (ton of SCE)

区　县	Region	综合能源消费量 Comprehensive Energy Consumption	增速（%） Growth Rate (%)
全　市	**Total**	**6989190**	**-2.1**
新城区	Xincheng	342933	12.6
碑林区	Beilin	47716	75.7
莲湖区	Lianhu	179799	12.5
灞桥区	Baqiao	869429	0.2
未央区	Weiyang	242847	-9.7
雁塔区	Yanta	307075	1.4
阎良区	Yanliang	38308	-23.9
临潼区	Lintong	69640	-3.6
长安区	Chang'an	498986	8.3
高陵区	Gaoling	193295	2.1
鄠邑区	Huyi	875158	3.2
蓝田县	Lantian	116021	0.2
周至县	Zhouzhi	16011	-14.8

主要统计指标解释

单位生产总值能耗 指一定时期内，一个国家或地区每生产一个单位的生产总值所消耗的能源。计算公式为：

单位生产总值能耗=能源消费总量/生产总值

工业企业能源消费量 指工业企业在工业生产活动和非工业生产活动中消费的能源，包括工业生产活动中作为燃料、动力、原料、辅助材料使用的能源，生产工艺中使用的能源，用于能源加工转换的能源；非工业生产活动中使用的能源。具体包括：

（1）用于本企业产品生产、工业性作业和其他生产性活动的能源；

（2）用于技术更新改造措施、新技术研究和新产品试制以及科学试验等方面的能源；

（3）用于经营维修、建筑及设备大修理、机电设备和交通运输工具等方面的能源；

（4）用于劳动保护的能源；

（5）生产交通运输工具的企业（如造船厂、汽车制造厂），向成品轮船、汽车中添加动力用油，应算作企业的能源消费，但不作为工业生产消费，应作为非工业生产消费和交通运输工具消费。

（6）其他非生产消费的能源。

工业生产能源消费量 指工业企业为进行工业生产活动所消费的能源。主要包括：

（1）用于本企业产品生产、工业性作业的能源，包括用作原料、材料、燃料、动力的能源；作为能源加工转换企业，还包括用作加工转换的能源（这部分能源不能理解为用作原材料，用作原材料的概念见后面的解释）；

（2）产品生产过程中作为辅助材料使用的能源；

（3）生产工艺过程使用的能源；

（4）新技术研究、新产品试制、科学试验使用的能源；

（5）为了工业生产活动而在进行的各种修理过程中使用的能源；

（6）生产区内的劳动保护用能等。

用于原材料的能源消费量 指能源产品不作能源使用，即不作燃料、动力使用，而作为生产另外一种产品（非能源产品）的原料或作为辅助材料使用，作原料使用时通常构成这种产品的实体。它与用作加工转换的区别是：用作加工转换，投入的是能源，产出的主要产品还是能源（或产出的产品属于加工转换过程中产生的不作能源使用的其他副产品和联产品）。而用作原材料时，投入的是能源，产出的主要产品是能源范畴以外的产品，包括产出的某种产品在广义上可以用作能源（比如可以燃烧以提供热量），但通常意义上不作能源使用的产品。

非工业生产能源消费量 指在工业企业能源消费中，除“工业生产能源消费”以外的能源消费，即非工业生产用能和工业企业附属的不从事工业生产活动的非独立核算单位用能。比如本企业施工单位进行技术更新改造、维修等过程用能，非生产区的劳动保护用能，科研单位、农场、车队、学校、医院、食堂、托儿所等单位用能。但是必须注意，上述单位如果是独立核算的，其用能既不能包括在“工业企业能源消费”中，亦不能包括在“非工业生产能源消费”中。

生产交通运输工具的企业（如造船厂、汽车制造厂），向成品轮船、汽车中添加动力用油，应算作企业的非工业生产消费。

综合能源消费量 指企业（单位）在报告期内工业生产实际消费的各种能源（扣除能源加工转换和能源回收利用等重复因素）的总和。计算综合能源消费量时，需要将各种能源品种的消费量换算成按照标准计量单位（如：吨标准煤）计量的消费量。不同工业法人单位的计算方法见《能源购进、消费与库存》（205-1表）的说明。

取水量 指企业从各种水源直接提取或者从市场购买的用于厂区、办公区内工业生产活动的水量，以实际获得的新水量为准。

外供水量 指企业外供给其他单位的水或水产品的量，以离厂水量为准。包括外供给其他企业或市场的原水、自来水、海水淡化水、矿泉水、纯净水等。不包括直流冷却水量、再生水（中水）、未利用直接排放的矿井水和雨水量、北方地区供暖企业供给城镇热力网内循环的热水量、进入城镇污水管网和直接排到自然环境中的水量。

Explanatory Notes on Main Statistical Indicators

Energy Consumption per Unit of GDP refers to the energy consumption per unit of Gross Domestic Product in a country or the Gross Regional Product in a region in the same reference period. The formula is:

Energy Consumption per Unit of GDP= Total Energy Consumption/Gross Domestic Product

Energy Consumption of Industrial Enterprises refers to the energy consumed by industrial enterprises in industrial production activities and non-industrial production activities, including energy used as fuel, power, raw materials and auxiliary materials in industrial production activities, energy used in production processes, energy for processing and conversion, and energy in the course of use of non-industrial production activities. Specifically, it includes:

(1)Energy used for the production, industrial operation and other productive activities of the enterprise;

(2)Energy for technological upgrading, new technology research and trial production of new products and scientific experiments.

(3) Energy for maintenance, construction and equipment repair, electrical and mechanical equipment and transportation.

(4) Energy for labor protection;

(5)Enterprises manufactured means of conveyance (such as making shipyards and automobile manufacturers), adding power oil to the finished product ships and cars, should be used as the energy consumption of the enterprises, but not as industrial production and consumption, it should be included in the consumption of non-industrial production and transportation means.

(6)Other non-productive energy sources.

Energy Consumption of Industrial Production refers to the energy consumed by industrial enterprises in industrial production activities. It mainly includes:

(1)Energy for the production and industrial operation of the products of the enterprise, including energy for raw materials, materials, fuel and power; as energy processing and conversion enterprises, including energy for processing and conversion (this part of the energy cannot be understood as raw materials, the concept of raw material is explained later)

(2)Energy used as auxiliary material during the production of products;

(3)Energy used in the production process;

(4)Energy for new technology research, trial production of new products and scientific test;

(5)Energy used in various repair processes for industrial production activities;

(6)Labor protection energy in the production area.

Energy Consumption for Raw Materials refers the energy products are not used for energy use, that is, not to be used as fuel and power, but as raw materials for the production of another product (non-energy products) or as auxiliary materials, which usually constitute the entity of this product when used as a raw material. The difference between it and the conversion of processing is that it is used as a process conversion, which is invested in energy, the main product of the output still is energy (or the produced product belongs to other by-products and associated products that are not used for energy use in the process of processing and conversion). When used as raw materials, energy is invested, and the main product is beyond the energy category, including a product that can be used as a source of energy in the broad sense (for example, to be burned to provide heat), but in general, it is not used for energy use.

Non-industry Consumption Energy refers to the energy consumed by industrial enterprises except for industrial production activities, means that energy consumed by non-industry production and it is not independent accounting units which was engaged in industrial production activities affiliated to industrial enterprises. For example, the energy consumption of technical renovation, maintenance and other processes carried out by construction units of this enterprise, labor protection for non-production areas, energy consumption of scientific research units, farms, motorcade, schools, hospitals, canteens, nursery schools and other units. However, it must be noted that if the above-mentioned units are independently accounted, their use can neither be included in the "industrial energy consumption" nor in the "non-industrial production energy consumption".

Enterprises manufactured means of conveyance(such as making shipyards and automobile manufacturers) adding power oil to finished ships and cars, should be regarded as non-industrial production and consumption of enterprises.

Comprehensive Energy Consumption refers to the sum of the various energy sources for the actual consumption of industrial production during the reporting period (the repeating factors of the conversion of energy processing and energy recovery and utilizationhave been deducted). When calculating the comprehensive energy consumption, it is necessary to convert the consumption of various types of energy into the consumption measured in accordance with the standard unit of measurement (e.g. tons of standard coal). The calculation methods of different industrial legal entities are described in terms of energy purchase, consumption and inventory (205-1 table).

Water Intake refers to the amount of water directly extracted from a variety of water sources or purchased from the market for industrial production activities in the factory and office areas, which is based on the actual new amount of water.

External Water Supply refers to the quantity of water or aquatic products supplied to other units by the enterprises, taking the quantity of water away from the plant as the criterion. It includes raw water, tap water, desalination water, mineral water, purified water, etc., which are supplied to other enterprises or markets. Direct current cooling water, reclaimed water (water), unused mine water and rain water, the hot water in the urban heat network supplied by the heating enterprises in the north are not included.

14 建筑业

CONSTRUCTION

资料整理：杨雪峰
Data management: Yang Xuefeng
数据审核：席锋旭
Data audit: Xi Fengxu

第十四部分　建筑业

一、简要说明

本章资料主要包括建筑业基本情况、建筑业施工企业生产情况和财务状况，由西安市统计局固定资产投资处提供。

二、主要指标

企业个数（个）	1055	比上年增长	15.3%
建筑业总产值（亿元）	3304.54	比上年增长	13.7%
#国有及国有控股企业	2588.18	比上年增长	13.1%
房屋建筑竣工面积（万平方米）	2553.10	比上年增长	7.3%
房屋建筑面积竣工率(%)	18.9	比上年提高	0.2个百分点

14 CONSTRUCTION

Ⅰ.Brief Introduction

This chapter consists of basic situation of the construction industry, production and financial situation of the construction enterprises, provided by Fixed Asset Investment Division of the Xi'an Bureau of Statistics.

Ⅱ.Major Indicators

		Increase over Preceding Year
Number of Enterprises(item)	1055	15.3%
Total Output Value of Construction(100 mil. yuan)	3304.54	13.7%
State-owned or State Holding Majority Shares	2588.18	13.1%
Floor Space of Buildings Completed(10 000 sq.m)	2553.10	7.3%
Rate of Floor Space of Buildings Completed(%)	18.9	0.2 percentage points

14-1 主要年份建筑业总产值

Total Output Value of Construction in Representative Years

单位：亿元 (100mil. yuan)

年份 Year	单位数（个） Number of Enterprises (unit)	建筑业总产值 Total Output Value of Construction	国有及国有控股 State-owned or State Holding Majority Shares	集体企业 Collective-owned Enterprises
2000	184	105.93	78.87	14.87
2001	205	114.81	91.82	15.47
2002	223	133.47	85.03	15.35
2003	204	177.11	119.99	13.40
2004	244	244.42	201.68	16.59
2005	235	326.65	276.68	19.61
2006	217	416.48	348.20	23.65
2007	279	604.75	432.63	32.67
2008	328	915.12	676.12	460.14
2009	326	1074.55	875.19	47.15
2010	324	1334.00	1034.04	58.39
2011	336	1619.09	1278.33	79.42
2012	396	1874.23	1364.70	96.83
2013	420	2228.41	1702.08	154.87
2014	539	2586.33	1981.24	95.02
2015	706	2650.41	2044.05	69.73
2016	893	2897.55	2288.23	63.35
2017	1055	3304.54	2588.18	70.56

注：1、1996年以后建筑业年报统计范围由往年的县及县以上（含县级建制镇）各种经济类型的建筑企业，改为具有建筑业资质等级三级及三级以上的各种经济类型的建筑施工企业；2002年改为具有建筑业资质等级的各种经济类型的建筑施工企业。

2、本表资料含劳务分包企业。

3、由于统计口径变化，对部分年份建筑业总产值相关数据进行了修订。

14-2 全市建筑施工总承包企业基本情况（2017年）

Basic Situation of Construction General Contracting Contractors in Whole City（2017）

指　标	Item	合计 Total	国有及国有控股 State-owned or State Holding Majority Shares
企业单位数（个）	Number of Enterprises (unit)	661	109
#二级以上企业	Special and First and Second Class Enterprise	535	97
计算劳动生产率的平均人数（万人）	Average Number of Employed Persons in Calculation of Labor Productivity (10 000 persons)	71.90	52.66
#二级以上企业	Special and First and Second Class Enterprise	69.16	51.66
建筑业总产值（亿元）	Total Output Value of Construction(100 million yuan)	2971.18	2416.26
#二级以上企业	Special and First and Second Class Enterprise	2893.14	2385.16
全员劳动生产率 按总产值计算(万元/人)	Overall Labor Productivity Calculated by Total Output Value(10 000yuan/person)	41.32	45.88

14-3 施工总承包和专业承包建筑企业生产情况（2017年）

分 组	Classify	签订的合同额（万元） Contract Value (10 000 yuan)	建筑业总产值（万元） Total Output Value of Constrution (10 000 yuan)
总计	**Total**	**90857399**	**33045416**
#国有及国有控股	State-owned and State Holding Majority Shares	77745015	25881768
一、按登记注册类型分	**Grouped by Registion Status**		
内资	Domestic Investment Enterprises	90856428	33034000
国有企业	State-owned Enterprises	4762815	2106676
集体企业	Collective-owned Enterprises	941688	705610
股份合作企业	Share-holding Corperative Enterprises	6463	6080
联营企业	Joint Ownership Enterprises	19080	18316
国有独资公司	State-owned Company	11236979	5133110
其他有限责任公司	Limited Liability Corporations	62288631	19093650
股份有限公司	Share-holding Corperation Ltd.	1620080	608191
私营企业	Private Enterprises	9980692	5362367
其他企业	Others		
港澳台商投资企业	Enterprises with Funds from Hong Kong,Macao and Taiwan	432	11197
外商投资企业	Enterprises with Foreign Investment	539	219
二、按国民经济行业分	**Grouped by Sector**		
房屋建筑业	Building Engineering Construction	30459979	12107500
土木工程建筑业	Civil Engineering Construction	55186112	17886526
建筑安装业	Installation of Construction	3805901	2082062
建筑装饰和其他建筑业	Architectural Decoration and Other Construction	1405407	969328
三、按隶属关系分	**Grouped by Administrative Relationship**		
中央	Central	56116582	16239841
地方	Region	34740817	16805575
四、按企业资质等级分	**Grouped by Class of Enterprises**		
1. 施工总承包	Overall Contractor for Construction	85881955	29711840
#特级	Special Class	28548018	7848546
一级	First Class	50331032	18208120
二级	Second Class	5138457	2874770
2. 专业承包	Special Contractor	4975444	3333576
#一级以上	First Class	3612373	2320644
二级	Second Class	990119	825790

Main Indicators on General Constructing Contractors and Professional Contractors（2017）

在外省完成的产值 Output Value in Other Provinces	建筑工程产值 Output Value of Constrution	安装工程产值 Output Value of Installation	其他产值 Others	竣工产值（万元） Completed Output Value (10 000 yuan)	房屋建筑施工面积（平方米） Number of Projects under Constrution (sq.m)	本年新开工 Beginning Projects in This Year
14890215	**29713956**	**2445590**	**885870**	**11411172**	**134914909**	**44327939**
14210996	24176287	1255798	449684	8289396	106394438	31629594
14890215	29713304	2434826	885870	11410597	134914909	44327939
795300	1904505	187861	14311	726788	7067609	1108432
34056	549219	119947	36445	449057	3794898	1963055
	6080					
2963	18316			14818	166328	134908
2113821	4921977	149003	62130	2218554	22077086	8297452
11230442	17506201	1165767	421682	5216627	75442045	22156426
214505	583131	21659	3401	365386	2809609	485187
499128	4223875	790589	347901	2419367	23557334	10182479
	432	10764		355		
	220			220		
2648140	11071418	829227	206855	5817985	121527277	40793760
11126789	16738755	624485	523286	4392771	9113178	1925412
966461	1156260	833346	92456	697185	4009472	1588749
148825	747523	158532	63273	503231	264982	20018
11922387	15452898	414712	372230	4202747	39753504	10026987
2967828	14261058	2030878	513640	7208425	95161405	34300952
14151794	27336202	1618507	757132	10040902	133387281	43236411
3982878	7712491	63772	72284	2168512	35597649	9327739
9529590	16639726	1210576	357818	6211815	83356416	28086464
463649	2395295	241443	238032	1381578	12952889	4842329
738421	2377754	827083	128738	1370270	1527628	1091528
661167	1893450	327461	99733	1125530	972431	592942
32035	368142	434245	23402	222320	544084	490773

14-3 续表

分组	Classify	房屋建筑竣工面积（平方米）Floor Space of Buildings Completed (sq.m)	房屋竣工价值（万元）Housing Completion Value (10 000 yuan)
总计	**Total**	**25530994**	**5024277**
#国有及国有控股	State-owned and State Holding Majority Shares	15835150	3375874
一、按登记注册类型分	**Grouped by Registion Status**		
内资	Domestic Investment Enterprises	25530994	5024277
国有企业	State-owned Enterprises	933625	169047
集体企业	Collective-owned Enterprises	2401622	364591
股份合作企业	Share-holding Corperative Enterprises		
联营企业	Joint Ownership Enterprises	14784	1042
国有独资公司	State-owned Company	3922556	998774
其他有限责任公司	Limited Liability Corporations	10862849	2140718
股份有限公司	Share-holding Corperation Ltd.	529725	134189
私营企业	Private Enterprises	6865833	1215916
其他企业	Others		
港澳台商投资企业	Enterprises with Funds from Hong Kong,Macao and Taiwan		
外商投资企业	Enterprises with Foreign Investment		
二、按国民经济行业分	**Grouped by Sector**		
房屋建筑业	Building Engineering Construction	24706309	4835478
土木工程建筑业	Civil Engineering Construction	618090	143445
建筑安装业	Installation of Construction	186905	44389
建筑装饰和其他建筑业	Architectural Decoration and Other Construction	19690	965
三、按隶属关系分	**Grouped by Administrative Relationship**		
中央	Central	3497406	833671
地方	Region	22033588	4190606
四、按企业资质等级分	**Grouped by Class of Enterprises**		
1. 施工总承包	Overall Contractor for Construction	24680550	4925987
#特级	Special Class	7119356	1662469
一级	First Class	13977114	2582439
二级	Second Class	2633816	550905
2. 专业承包	Special Contractor	850444	98290
#一级以上	First Class	480960	31156
二级	Second Class	359484	66805

continued

计算劳动生产率的平均人数（人） Average Number of Employed Persons in Calculation of Labour Productivity(person)	建筑业企业期末从业人员数（人） The Number of Employees in Construction Enterprises at the end of Period (person)	工程技术人员 Technical Personnel	自有机械设备年末净值（万元） The Net Value of Machinery and Equipment Owned at the end of the Year (10 000 yuan)	自有机械设备年末总台数（台） The Total Number of Machinery and Equipment Owned owned (stand)	自有机械设备年末总功率（千瓦） Total Power of Machinery and Equipment Owned at the end of the Year (kw)	企业总产值（万元） Gross Output Value of Enterprises (10 000 yuan)
802677	**703169**	**106644**	**706736**	**100599**	**3189805**	**35799830**
556255	492421	65700	490797	34259	2408592	28099047
802425	702871	106619	706476	100374	3189524	35788414
64288	64238	5957	22947	4443	107002	2138549
26999	24128	4050	13968	5001	32499	711671
275	229	33				6080
884	887	252	6318	31	1982	19553
107139	80480	16387	101533	9608	540657	5240983
390392	352899	46358	380042	22119	1835592	21263026
16565	16136	1562	6069	1012	5707	611609
195883	163874	32020	175599	58160	666085	5796943
218	264	4	1	5	1	11197
34	34	21	259	220	280	219
332059	269892	47300	153350	60278	678158	12364112
401339	369174	46705	496689	30055	2264063	20196546
35335	33424	8539	42547	6494	152012	2239350
33944	30679	4100	14150	3772	95572	999822
379576	350754	38263	386949	20143	1921065	18409153
423101	352415	68381	319787	80456	1268740	17390677
719006	632497	92889	627869	91381	2837836	32388178
140958	120034	19442	135080	6054	573903	9875501
445396	396017	49781	354476	66187	1784358	18550010
105244	89120	19226	117291	16263	432351	3152145
83671	70672	13755	78867	9218	351969	3411652
47893	38555	8690	61010	5614	181212	2376361
28145	27395	3946	15342	3061	125120	839149

14-4 施工总承包和专业承包建筑业企业主要指标（2017年）

指　标	Item	企业数（个） Number of Enterprises (unit)	总产值（万元） Total Output Value (10 000 yuan)	直接从事生产经营活动的平均人数（人） Directly Engaged in the Production and Business Activities of the Average Number of People (person)
总计	**Total**	**1042**	**33045416**	**802677**
#国有及国有控股	State-owned and State Holding Majority Shares	153	25881768	556255
一、按登记注册类型分	**Grouped by Registion Status**			
内资	Domestic Investment Enterprises	1039	33034000	802425
国有企业	State-owned Enterprises	26	2106676	64288
集体企业	Collective-owned Enterprises	43	705610	26999
股份合作企业	Share-holding Corperative Enterprises	1	6080	275
联营企业	Joint Ownership Enterprises	2	18316	884
国有独资公司	State-owned Company	38	5133110	107139
有限责任公司	Limited Liability Corporations	115	19093650	390392
股份有限公司	Share-holding Corperation Ltd.	10	608191	16565
私营企业	Private Enterprises	804	5362367	195883
其他企业	Others			
港澳台商投资企业	Enterprises with Funds from Hong Kong,Macao and Taiwan	1	11197	218
外商投资企业	Enterprises with Foreign Investment	2	219	34
二、按国民经济行业分	**Grouped by Sector**			
房屋建筑业	Building Engineering Construction	410	12107500	332059
土木工程建筑业	Civil Engineering Construction	292	17886526	401339
建筑安装业	Installation of Construction	168	2082062	35335
建筑装饰和其他建筑业	Architectural Decoration and Other Construction	172	969328	33944
三、按隶属关系分	**Grouped by Administrative Relationship**			
中央	Central	49	16239841	379576
地方	Region	993	16805575	423101
四、按企业资质等级分	**Grouped by Class of Enterprises**			
1. 施工总承包	Overall Contractor for Construction	666	29711840	719006
#特级	Special Class	14	7848546	140958
一级	First Class	169	18208120	445396
二级	Second Class	361	2874770	105244
2. 专业承包	Special Contractor	376	3333576	83671
#一级以上	First Class	149	2320644	47893
二级	Second Class	170	825790	28145

Major Indicators of General Construction Contractors and Professional Contractors（2017）

建筑业企业期末从业人员数（人）The Number of Employees in Construction Enterprises at the End of Period (person)	利润总额（万元）Total Profit (10000 yuan)	利税总额（万元）Total Profits and Taxes (10000 yuan)	按总产值计算劳动生产率（万元/人）Productivity by Gross Output Value (10000 yuan/person)	产值利润率（%）Profit Rate of Output Value (%)	产值利税率（%）Profit and Tax Rate of Output Value (%)	资产总计（万元）Total Assets (10000 yuan)	负债总计（万元）Total Liabilities (10000 yuan)	资产负债率（%）Asset Liability Ratio (%)
703169	**936441**	**1793413**	**41.17**	**2.8**	**5.4**	**42391102**	**32200146**	**76.0**
492421	689420	1262249	46.53	2.7	4.9	32301510	26425797	81.8
702871	936517	1793398	41.17	2.8	5.4	42387709	32198803	76.0
64238	54474	126184	32.77	2.6	6.0	2137390	1705805	79.8
24128	29108	64837	26.13	4.1	9.2	569546	279761	49.1
229	160	574	22.11	2.6	9.4	7717	6368	82.5
887	6334	6970	20.72	34.6	38.1	31535	6883	21.8
80480	184232	310770	47.91	3.6	6.1	6777121	5165401	76.2
352899	442120	826161	48.91	2.3	4.3	24465976	20479131	83.7
16136	14709	36021	36.72	2.4	5.9	925387	781807	84.5
163874	205380	421881	27.38	3.8	7.9	7473037	3773647	50.5
264	30	45	51.36	0.3	0.4	435	580	133.3
34	-106	-30	6.44	-48.4	-13.7	2958	763	25.8
269892	274513	623213	36.46	2.3	5.1	12593154	8784374	69.8
369174	551394	960584	44.57	3.1	5.4	26508596	21231711	80.1
33424	74814	136751	58.92	3.6	6.6	2317341	1605510	69.3
30679	35720	72865	28.56	3.7	7.5	972011	578551	59.5
350754	501011	848073	42.78	3.1	5.2	22096476	18652703	84.4
352415	435430	945340	39.72	2.6	5.6	20294626	13547443	66.8
632497	805661	1567765	41.32	2.7	5.3	39037259	30057042	77.0
120034	279745	511315	55.68	3.6	6.5	17779196	14734328	82.9
396017	372657	734687	40.88	2.0	4.0	15404916	12044775	78.2
89120	121258	259672	27.32	4.2	9.0	4713239	2512025	53.3
70672	130780	225648	39.84	3.9	6.8	3353843	2143104	63.9
38555	78972	143142	48.45	3.4	6.2	2209522	1537548	69.6
27395	42447	68008	29.34	5.1	8.2	828824	407390	49.2

14-5 施工总承包和专业承包建筑业企业财务状况（2017年）

单位：万元

指　标	Item	资产总计 Total Assets	流动资产合计 Total Current Assets	固定资产合计 Total Fixed Assets
总计	**Total**	**42391102**	**35134017**	**2096191**
#国有及国有控股	State-owned and State Holding Majority Shares	32301510	26570613	1359538
一、按登记注册类型分	**Grouped by Registion Status**			
内资	Domestic Investment Enterprises	42387709	35130936	2096177
国有企业	State-owned Enterprises	2137390	1824458	83203
集体企业	Collective-owned Enterprises	569546	472307	68248
股份合作企业	Share-holding Corperative Enterprises	7717	7434	78
联营企业	Joint Ownership Enterprises	31535	28432	980
国有独资公司	State-owned Company	6777121	5472379	381020
有限责任公司	Limited Liability Corporations	24465976	20256359	914763
股份有限公司	Share-holding Corperation Ltd.	925387	813649	29323
私营企业	Private Enterprises	7473037	6255918	618562
其他企业	Others			
港澳台商投资企业	Enterprises with Funds from Hong Kong, Macao and Taiwan	435	432	3
外商投资企业	Enterprises with Foreign Investment	2958	2649	11
二、按国民经济行业分	**Grouped by Sector**			
房屋建筑业	Building Engineering Construction	12593154	11042424	534097
土木工程建筑业	Civil Engineering Construction	26508596	21202574	1396380
建筑安装业	Installation of Construction	2317341	2090225	89060
建筑装饰和其他建筑业	Architectural Decoration and Other Construction	972011	798794	76654
三、按隶属关系分	**Grouped by Administrative Relationship**			
中央	Central	22096476	17783976	904184
地方	Region	20294626	17350041	1192007
四、按企业资质等级分	**Grouped by Class of Enterprises**			
1. 施工总承包	Overall Contractor for Construction	39037259	32274038	1864754
#特级	Special Class	17779196	14102483	421010
一级	First Class	15404916	13514138	849454
二级	Second Class	4713239	3828287	430084
2. 专业承包	Special Contractor	3353843	2859979	231437
#一级	First Class	2209522	1972601	130866
二级	Second Class	828824	649035	51561

Financial Status of General Constructing Contractors and Professional Contractors (2017)

(10 000yuan)

固定资产原价 Original Value of Fixed Assets	累计折旧 Accumulated Depreciation		负债合计 Total Liabilities	流动负债合计 Total Current Liabilities	非流动负债 Non Current Liabilities	所有者权益合计 Total Owners' Equity	实收资本 Paid in Capital
		本年折旧 Depreciation of This Year					
3773236	**2054279**	**388456**	**32200146**	**30307823**	**1699863**	**10190955**	**6952213**
2851574	1656306	327892	26425797	24901748	1507149	5875713	3596634
3773158	2054211	388425	32198803	30306542	1699863	10188906	6949613
165006	94792	19299	1705805	1615594	90191	431586	149472
77478	26759	3917	279761	247771	17016	289785	270132
1285	1207		6368	6242	125	1349	847
1437	1275	177	6883	5662		24652	13847
902616	605704	91503	5165401	4944924	205171	1611721	905580
1834618	987799	220645	20479131	19253274	1224283	3986845	2723128
51730	24011	2086	781807	745168	36639	143580	65105
738988	312664	50798	3773647	3487907	126438	3699388	2821502
31	28		580	580		-145	661
47	40	31	763	701		2194	1939
702622	329158	71966	8784374	8426955	276086	3808780	2555165
2826140	1605745	293854	21231711	19810111	1328370	5276886	3627802
136183	74317	16532	1605510	1528123	67164	711832	489558
108291	45059	6104	578551	542634	28243	393457	279688
2219542	1343826	250913	18652703	17601722	1050981	3443773	2146459
1553694	710453	137543	13547443	12706101	648882	6747182	4805754
3466396	1898137	365144	30057042	28282192	1598093	8980218	6156851
777682	377898	95302	14734328	13746411	987916	3044869	1705532
1935594	1185363	218984	12044775	11630995	377702	3360140	2314143
498524	236713	36832	2512025	2202833	179617	2201215	1784406
306840	156142	23312	2143104	2025631	101770	1210737	795362
220408	118943	13362	1537548	1488965	39548	671975	443862
70266	32126	8276	407390	375530	27793	421434	253767

14-5 续表

单位：万元

指 标	Item	营业收入 Total Revenue	主营业务收入 Main Business Income
总计	**Total**	**39511747**	**39326479**
#国有及国有控股	State-owned and State Holding Majority Shares	31956033	31843266
一、按登记注册类型分	**Grouped by Registion Status**		
内资	Domestic Investment Enterprises	39509103	39323835
国有企业	State-owned Enterprises	2143358	2135943
集体企业	Collective-owned Enterprises	748855	748469
股份合作企业	Share-holding Corperative Enterprises	4745	4745
联营企业	Joint Ownership Enterprises	31143	31143
国有独资公司	State-owned Company	5980154	5952808
有限责任公司	Limited Liability Corporations	24091571	24001817
股份有限公司	Share-holding Corperation Ltd.	597012	559392
私营企业	Private Enterprises	5912266	5889518
其他企业	Others		
港澳台商投资企业	Enterprises with Funds from Hong Kong, Macao and Taiwan	434	434
外商投资企业	Enterprises with Foreign Investment	2210	2210
二、按国民经济行业分	**Grouped by Sector**		
房屋建筑业	Building Engineering Construction	12070814	12028130
土木工程建筑业	Civil Engineering Construction	24268746	24171398
建筑安装业	Installation of Construction	2141594	2100294
建筑装饰和其他建筑业	Architectural Decoration and Other Construction	1030593	1026657
三、按隶属关系分	**Grouped by Administrative Relationship**		
中央	Central	21916806	21847250
地方	Region	17594941	17479229
四、按企业资质等级分	**Grouped by Class of Enterprises**		
1. 施工总承包	Overall Contractor for Construction	36376125	36239148
#特级	Special Class	16761227	16725700
一级	First Class	15273290	15186744
二级	Second Class	3379306	3366114
2. 专业承包	Special Contractor	3135622	3087331
#一级以上	First Class	2318294	2314610
二级	Second Class	621476	585132

continued 1

(10 000yuan)

营业成本 Total Cost	主营业务成本 Main Business Costs	税金及附加 Taxs and Other Charges	主营业务税金及附加 The Main Business Tax and Surcharges	管理费用 Management Costs	营业利润 Operating Profit	利润总额 Total Profit	应付职工薪酬 Payable to Employees	应交增值税 Value Added Tax Payable
37034011	**36822769**	**218032**	**212120**	**1159650**	**933877**	**936441**	**5126495**	**638940**
30279737	30144249	105819	103181	829952	684987	689420	4057524	467010
37031551	36820310	218019	212107	1159400	933960	936517	5126163	638862
1999221	1993530	11912	11852	58925	53691	54474	336304	59798
641723	630477	18560	18505	22211	30044	29108	130571	17169
4405	4405	46	46	135	160	160	1313	368
23392	23392	306	306	1084	6353	6334	3096	330
5538970	5476111	28648	27703	180187	180666	184232	949848	97890
22944684	22869289	73033	71399	640531	442528	442120	2767627	311008
557958	531459	1694	1268	15909	14047	14709	89249	19618
5321199	5291647	83819	81028	240418	206471	205380	848155	132681
354	354	2	2	32	41	30	20	13
2105	2105	11	11	218	-124	-106	312	65
11280219	11189832	113295	110529	259094	286624	274513	2069243	235405
22879600	22793716	79110	76552	768754	538277	551394	2714926	330080
1935654	1904834	12377	11964	96764	73579	74814	205479	49560
938538	934387	13249	13075	35038	35397	35720	136847	23895
20763073	20708666	54005	52894	625935	484556	501011	2657741	293057
16270938	16114103	164027	159226	533715	449321	435430	2468754	345882
34229974	34058376	192317	187482	1021654	804385	805661	4796137	569787
16239676	16212594	45535	45075	278114	267736	279745	1685229	186035
14172958	14102064	76238	74501	520784	384730	372657	2559141	285792
2965580	2897976	61080	58649	164438	120105	121258	435599	77334
2804037	2764393	25715	24638	137996	129492	130780	330358	69153
2109622	2104516	14229	13379	89852	78070	78972	211172	49941
525753	500315	10047	9854	35414	42577	42447	92024	15514

14-6 劳务分包建筑业企业生产经营情况（2017年）

单位：万元

指 标	Item	固定资产原价 Original Value of Fixed Assets	本年折旧 Depreciation of this year
总计	**Total**	**586**	**282**
#国有及国有控股	State-owned and State Holding Majority Shares		
一、按登记注册类型分	**Grouped by Registion Status**		
内资	Domestic Investment Enterprises	586	282
国有企业	State-owned Enterprises		
集体企业	Collective-owned Enterprises		
股份合作企业	Share-holding Corperative Enterprises		
联营企业	Joint Ownership Enterprises		
国有独资公司	State-owned Company		
其他有限责任公司	Limited Liability Corporations	3	
股份有限公司	Share-holding Corperation Ltd.		
私营企业	Private Enterprises	583	282
其他企业	Others		
港澳台商投资企业	Enterprises with Funds from Hong Kong,Macao and Taiwan		
外商投资企业	Enterprises with Foreign Investment		
二、按国民经济行业分	**Grouped by Sector**		
房屋建筑业	Building Engineering Construction	459	228
土木工程建筑业	Civil Engineering Construction	46	14
建筑安装业	Installation of Construction		
建筑装饰和其他建筑业	Architectural Decoration and Other Construction	81	40
三、按隶属关系分	**Grouped by Administrative Relationship**		
中央	Central		
地方	Region	586	282

Production and Management Situation of Subcontractor Construction Enterprises（2017）

（10 000yuan）

资产总计 Total Assets	负债合计 Total Liabilities	实收资本 Paid in Capital	营业收入 Total Revenue	主营业务收入 Main Business Income	营业成本 Total Cost	主营业务成本 Main Business Cost
65102	**57357**	**5084**	**95530**	**95530**	**87661**	**83934**
65102	57357	5084	95530	95530	87661	83934
1803	1715		3314	3314	3235	3235
63299	55642	5084	92216	92216	84426	80699
54422	49471	2409	65564	65564	58477	58477
1996	1131	1005	4121	4121	3796	69
8684	6755	1670	25845	25845	25388	25388
65102	57357	5084	95530	95530	87661	83934

14-6 续表

单位：万元

指标	Item	营业税金及附加 Taxs and Other Charges	主营业务税金及附加 Taxs and Other Charges on Principal Business
总计	**Total**	**425**	**411**
#国有及国有控股	State-owned and State Holding Majority Shares		
一、按登记注册类型分	**Grouped by Registion Status**		
内资	Domestic Investment Enterprises	425	411
国有企业	State-owned Enterprises		
集体企业	Collective-owned Enterprises		
股份合作企业	Share-holding Corperative Enterprises		
联营企业	Joint Ownership Enterprises		
国有独资公司	State-owned Company		
其他有限责任公司	Limited Liability Corporations	12	12
股份有限公司	Share-holding Corperation Ltd.		
私营企业	Private Enterprises	413	399
其他企业	Others		
港澳台商投资企业	Enterprises with Funds from Hong Kong,Macao and Taiwan		
外商投资企业	Enterprises with Foreign Investment		
二、按国民经济行业分	**Grouped by Sector**		
房屋建筑业	Building Engineering Construction	304	304
土木工程建筑业	Civil Engineering Construction	14	
建筑安装业	Installation of Construction		
建筑装饰和其他建筑业	Architectural Decoration and Other Construction	107	107
三、按隶属关系分	**Grouped by Administrative Relationship**		
中央	Central		
地方	Region	425	411

continued 1

(10 000yuan)

销售费用 Sale Expenses	管理费用 Management Costs	财务费用 Financial Expenses	营业利润 Operating Profit	利润总额 Total Profit	应付职工薪酬 Payable to Employees	应交增值税 Value Added Tax Payable
9	**5810**	**129**	**1455**	**1452**	**50031**	**2423**
9	5810	129	1455	1452	50031	2423
	61		6	6	3220	101
9	5749	129	1449	1446	46811	2322
	5477	129	1187	1189	46733	2197
	164		93	93	10	121
9	169		175	170	3288	105
9	5810	129	1455	1452	50031	2423

14-7 各区县建筑业主要经济指标（2017年）

Major Indicators of Construction Enterprises by Region（2017）

区 县	Region	企业个数 (个) Number of Enterprises (unit)	总产值 (亿元) Total Output Value (100 million yuan)	计算劳动生产率的平均人数(万人) Average Number of Employed Persons in Calculation of Labor Productivity(10 000person)	全员劳动生产率 (万元/人) Overall Labor Productivity (10 000 yuan/person)	利税总额 (亿元) Total Pre-tax Profits (100 million yuan)
全 市	**Total**	**1042**	**3304.54**	**80.27**	**41.17**	**179.34**
新城区	Xincheng	57	347.67	5.46	63.68	11.73
碑林区	Beilin	152	784.72	13.5	58.13	32.74
莲湖区	Lianhu	81	271.29	6.52	41.61	11.21
灞桥区	Baqiao	39	139.92	5.06	27.65	9.56
未央区	Weiyang	179	669.51	20.50	32.66	28.92
雁塔区	Yanta	348	812.49	20.09	40.44	63.37
阎良区	Yanliang	24	13.04	0.49	26.61	0.63
临潼区	Lintong	29	11.18	0.75	14.91	0.89
长安区	Chang'an	50	162.56	3.34	48.67	8.91
高陵区	Gaoling	13	29.88	2.13	14.03	3.87
鄠邑区	Huyi	9	21.07	0.68	30.99	1.49
蓝田县	Lantian	11	15.07	0.5	30.14	1.55
周至县	Zhouzhi	14	10.00	0.66	15.15	0.82

注：本表数据依据施工总承包和专业承包企业数据加工整理。

14-8 各区县建筑业房屋施工及竣工面积（2017年）

Floor Space of Buildings under Construction & Completed by Region（2017）

区 县	Region	房屋建筑施工面积（万平方米）Floor Space under Construction (10 000sq.m)	本年新开工面积 Newly Started This Year	房屋建筑竣工面积（万平方米）Floor Space of Buildings Completed (10 000sq.m)	竣工房屋价值（亿元）Value of Buildings Completed (100 million yuan)
全 市	**Total**	**13491.49**	**4432.79**	**2553.10**	**502.43**
新城区	Xincheng	1290.28	339.88	288.03	62.60
碑林区	Beilin	4222.08	1956.11	812.57	152.62
莲湖区	Lianhu	1820.99	748.72	410.44	104.42
灞桥区	Baqiao	142.67	70.10	50.83	7.85
未央区	Weiyang	3078.31	503.06	239.07	46.23
雁塔区	Yanta	2077.88	402.66	353.21	68.08
阎良区	Yanliang	54.31	14.42	17.36	3.47
临潼区	Lintong	66.74	40.23	19.91	3.57
长安区	Chang'an	175.16	38.50	39.85	6.04
高陵区	Gaoling	119.00	48.85	70.98	10.15
鄠邑区	Huyi	104.77	51.67	67.99	13.94
蓝田县	Lantian	114.55	96.33	87.90	9.54
周至县	Zhouzhi	74.42	31.18	27.69	4.75

14-9 各区县建筑业企业主要经济效益指标（2017年）

Major Economic Performance Indicators on Construction Enterprises by Region（2017）

区 县	Region	人均利润总额（元/人）Per Profit (yuan/person)	人均利税（元/人）Per Pre-Tax Profits (yuan/person)	人均竣工产值（元/人）Per Output Value of Buildings Completed (yuan/person)	人均施工面积（平方米/人）Per Floor Space of Buildings Under Construcyion (sq.m/person)	人均竣工面积（平方米/人）Per Floor Space of Buildings Completed (sq.m/person)
全 市	**Total**	**11666**	**22343**	**142164**	**168**	**32**
新城区	Xincheng	10368	21461	325671	236	53
碑林区	Beilin	11563	24241	221742	313	60
莲湖区	Lianhu	7682	17186	227826	279	63
灞桥区	Baqiao	11350	18910	250389	28	10
未央区	Weiyang	7478	14108	49729	150	12
雁塔区	Yanta	17523	31537	94189	103	18
阎良区	Yanliang	4613	12912	228783	111	35
临潼区	Lintong	2635	11940	86908	89	27
长安区	Chang'an	14453	26699	74722	52	12
高陵区	Gaoling	9899	18231	51898	56	33
鄠邑区	Huyi	5163	21851	223374	153	99
蓝田县	Lantian	12931	30846	213014	228	175
周至县	Zhouzhi	3575	12493	94887	113	42

14-9 续表 continued

区 县	Region	产值利润率（%）Ratio of Profits to Output Value（%）	产值利税率（%）Ratio of Pre-tax Profits to Output Value (%)	资产利润率（%）Ratio of Profits to Assets (%)	资产利税率（%）Ratio of Pre-tax Profits to Assets（%）	资产负债率（%）Ratio of Debts to Assets（%）
全 市	**Total**	**2.8**	**5.4**	**2.2**	**4.2**	**76.0**
新城区	Xincheng	1.6	3.4	2.0	4.2	82.9
碑林区	Beilin	2.0	4.2	1.7	3.5	81.2
莲湖区	Lianhu	1.8	4.1	1.5	3.3	70.5
灞桥区	Baqiao	4.1	6.8	2.3	3.8	77.5
未央区	Weiyang	2.3	4.3	1.6	3.0	80.0
雁塔区	Yanta	4.3	7.8	3.0	5.3	73.0
阎良区	Yanliang	1.7	4.9	1.0	2.9	58.2
临潼区	Lintong	1.8	8.0	1.6	7.0	47.8
长安区	Chang'an	3.0	5.5	3.9	7.2	72.5
高陵区	Gaoling	7.0	13.0	4.2	7.7	18.2
鄠邑区	Huyi	1.7	7.1	3.2	13.6	63.7
蓝田县	Lantian	4.3	10.3	10.9	25.9	46.6
周至县	Zhouzhi	2.3	8.2	3.4	11.9	44.1

主要统计指标解释

建筑业统计单位 指从事房屋、构筑物建造和设备安装活动的法人企业。建筑业法人企业应具有建筑业资质并能够独立核算，同时其应具备以下条件：①依法成立，有自己的名称、组织机构和场所，能够承担民事责任；②独立拥有和使用资产，承担负债，有权与其他单位签订合同；③独立核算盈亏，能够编制资产负债表。

建筑业总产值 是以货币形式表现的建筑业企业在一定时期内生产的建筑业产品和提供的服务的总和。建筑业总产值包括：

（1）建筑工程产值：指列入建筑工程预算内的各种工程价值。

（2）安装工程产值：指设备安装工程价值，不包括被安装设备本身的价值。

（3）其他产值：建筑业总产值中除建筑工程、安装丁程以外的产值。包括房屋构筑物修理产值、非标准设备制造产值、总包企业向分包企业收取的管理费以及不能明确划分的施工活动所完成的产值。

a. 房屋构筑物修理产值：指房屋和构筑物修理所完成的产值，但不包括被修理房屋、构筑物本身价值和生产设备的修理价值。

b. 非标准设备制造产值：指加工制造没有定型的非标准生产设备的加了费和原材料价值（如化工厂、炼油厂用的各种罐、槽，矿井生产统一使用的各种漏斗、三角槽、阀门等）以及附属加工厂为本企业承建工程制作的非标准设备的价值。

建筑业增加值 指建筑业企业在报告期内以货币形式表现的建筑业生产经营活动的最终成果。

从2004年第一次全国经济普查开始，建筑业现价增加值按生产法和分配法（收入法）两种方法计算，以收入法的计算结果为准，即从收入的角度出发，根据生产要素在生产过程中应得的收入份额计算。具体计算方法：经济普查年度建筑业增加值按照《经济普查年度GDP核算方案》计算，非经济普查年度建筑业增加值按照们≥经济普查年度GDP核算方案》计算。

房屋建筑施工面积 指在报告期内施过工的全部房屋建筑面积，包括本期新开工的房屋面积、上期施工跨入本期继续施工的房屋面积、上期停缓建在本期恢复施工的房屋面积、本期竣工的房屋面积及本期施丁后又停缓建的房屋面积。

房屋建筑竣工面积 指在报告期内房屋建筑按照设计要求全部完工，达到了使用条件，经验收鉴定合格，正式移交使用单位的房屋建筑面积。

Explanatory Notes on Main Statistical Indicators

Statistical Unit in the Construction Industry refers to a corporate enterprise engaged in the construction of buildings and structures and in the installation of equipment. A corporate construction enterprise should have qualification certificates with independent accounting system, and should meet the following 3 requirements: a) being set up in line with relevant legal basis, having its full name, organization and location, and capable of taking civil liabilities; b) independently possessing and using its assets and assuming its liabilities, and entitled to sign contracts with other institutions; and c) making independent accounts of its profits and losses, and capable of compiling its own balance sheet.

Gross Output Value of Construction refers to total of construction products and services, expressed in money terms, produced or rendered by construction and installation enterprises during a given period of time. It includes:

(1)Output value of construction projects: the value of projects covered by the project budgets;

(2) Output value of installation projects: the value of the installation of equipment, (excluding the value of the equipment to be installed);

(3)Other output values: the output value of construction industry apart from that of construction projects and installation projects. It includes: output value of repair of buildings and structures; output value of non-standard equipment manufacturing; overhead expenses received by contracted enterprises from the sub-contracted enterprises and the completed output value of construction activities for which there is no clear definition.

a. Output value of repair of buildings and structures: the value created through the repairs of buildings or structures. It does not include the value of buildings or structures being repaired and the value of the repair of production equipment;

b. Output value of manufactured non-standard equipment: the value of non-standard production equipment, including raw materials and manufacturing cost, made for the construction project (i.e., chemical plant; kettles or tanks used by refineries; various fillers, triangle tanks, valves used by mines). It also includes the output value of equipment manufactured by subsidiary workshops.

Value-added of Construction refers to the final result of the activities of production and operation of enterprises of the construction industry in monetary terms during the reference period.

Starting from the 2004 economic census, value-added of construction is calculated by both production approach and income approach, with the figures from the income approach as the final figures. Under the income approach, calculation starts from the perspective of income and is based on the share of income derived from the production process by the relevant factors of production. Specifically, value-added of construction for the Census years is calculated in accordance with the Programme of Compilation of GDP and National Accounts for the Year of Economic Census, and value-added of construction for other years is calculated in accordance with the Programme of Compilation of GDP and National Accounts for the Non Economic Census Years.

Floor Space of Buildings Under Construction refers to floor space of buildings under construction during the reference period, including the floor space of buildings for which construction has newly started; buildings for which construction has started earlier and is continuing during the reference period; and buildings for which construction has been suspended earlier but has restarted during the reference period; buildings completed during the reference period; and buildings under construction but construction has subsequently been during the reference period.

Floor Space of Buildings Completed refers to the floor space of buildings that are completed in the reference period in accordance with the requirements of the design, up to the standard for being put into use, and having been checked and accepted by departments concerned as qualified ones.

15 运输邮电和信息化

TRANSPORT,POSTAL TELECOMMUNICATION SERVICE AND INFORMATIZATION

资料整理：齐昆峰
Data management：Qi Kunfeng
数据审核：王金桂
Data audit：Wang Jingui

第十五部分　运输邮电和信息化

一、简要说明

本章资料包括交通运输业和邮电通信业的基本情况，主要是交通运输工具、货物和旅客运输量、邮电业务、邮政局所及服务点等基本情况以及一套表单位信息化情况。资料由西安市统计局服务业和社会科技处根据有关部门提供资料整理。2017年运输邮电数据为西安原口径数据，信息化数据为包含西咸新区数据。

二、主要指标

邮电业务总量（亿元）	439.85	比上年增长	14.8%
全社会车辆数（万辆）	288.56	比上年增长	11.5%
#民用小轿车	161.85	比上年增长	10.8%

15　TRANSPORT, POSTAL TELECOMMUNICATION SERVICE AND INFORMATIZATION

Ⅰ.Brief Introduction

Data in this chapter consists of primarily basic data of communication, transportation and postal service industry, transportation facility, amount of goods and passenger transportation, basic data of postal service, post offices and service establishments of Xi'an City. Data in this chapter is compiled by Tertiary Industry and Social & Science and Technology Division of the Xi'an Bureau of Statistics according to the data provided by department concerned of the municipal government.

Ⅱ.Major Indicators

		Increase over Preceding Year
Amount of Postal and Telecommunication Service(100 mil. yuan)	439.85	14.8%
Number of Vehides in the whole Sciety(10 000 unit)	288.56	11.5%
Civil Car	161.85	10.8%

15-1 主要年份各种交通线路和桥梁

Transportation Routes and Bridges in Representative Years

年 份 Year	公路里程 （公里） Length of Highways (km)	桥 梁 （座） Bridges (seat)	桥梁长度 （米） Length of Bridge (m)
1978			
1979			
1980			
1981			
1982			
1983			
1984			
1985			
1986			
1987			
1988			
1989	2563		
1990	2586		
1991	2785		
1992	2786		
1993	2801		
1994	2830		
1995	2852		
1996	2877		
1997	3026		
1998	3047		
1999	2789		
2000	3010		
2001	3298		
2002	7862	629	29799
2003	8360	629	29799
2004	8360	629	29799
2005	8500	634	46973
2006	9530	634	46973
2007	9672	1319	91412
2008	11895	1710	151996
2009	12378	1856	154866
2010	12378	1856	154866
2011	12599	1863	149743
2012	13127	2190	214978
2013	13135	2213	224962
2014	13251	2213	224949
2015	13328	2323	250910
2016	13356	2423	256058
2017	13383	2435	286841

注：本表数据来自市交通局、民航通航里程2013年统计口径发生较大变化。
2017年数据为西安原口径数据。

15-1 续表 continued

年　份 Year	永久式桥梁 （座） Permanent Bridges (seat)	永久式桥梁长度 （米） Length of Permanent Bridges (m)	民航通航里程 （重复航线）（公里） Length of Total Civil Aviation Routes(km)
1978			
1979			
1980			
1981			
1982			
1983			
1984			
1985			
1986			
1987			
1988			
1989			
1990			
1991			
1992			65007
1993			83215
1994			100800
1995			119753
1996			126433
1997			173010
1998			180000
1999			141284
2000			139764
2001			154614
2002	629	29799	211000
2003	629	29799	381800
2004	629	29799	386953
2005	632	46915	485749
2006	632	46915	418852
2007	1275	90716	553355
2008	1657	150980	515524
2009	1803	153850	587904
2010	1803	153850	742375
2011	1811	148810	898628
2012	2138	213985	981450
2013	2161	223970	70643568
2014	2171	224165	78626210
2015	2286	250175	93375419
2016	2386	255322	92561215
2017	2399	286164	113501600

15-2 各种交通线路里程和桥梁数（2017年）

Length of Transportation Routes and Number of Bridges (2017)

指　标	Item	2017
公路里程（公里）	**Length of Highways (km)**	**13383**
等级公路	Expressways and Class I to IV Highways	12884
高速	Expressway	572
一级	First Class	325
二级	Second Class	1404
三级	Third Class	1232
四级	Forth Class	9351
等外公路	Highways below Class IV	499
桥梁	Bridges	
永久式桥梁	Permanent	
座（座）	Seat (seat)	2399
长度（米）	Length (m)	286164
民航通航里程(公里)(重复航线)	**Length of Total Civil Aviation Routes(km)**	**113501600**
民航航线条数（条）	**Length of Civil Aviation routes(Article)**	**337**
国际航线	International routes	57

注：本表数据来自市交通局。
本表数据为西安原口径数据。

15-3 主要年份全社会车辆数

Possession of Civil Vehicles in Representative Years

单位：辆、台 (unit)

年 份 Year	合计 Total	汽车 Motor	载客汽车 Passenget Vehicles	载货汽车 Ordinary Trucks	摩托车 Motorcycles	拖拉机 Tractors
1999	**279335**	133192	63772	44348		38023
2000	**310252**	138318	89783	44974		37177
2001	**369988**	172436	110744	55453		31355
2002	**454998**	206653	134527	64623	176960	36083
2003	**516719**	242599	163872	70781	191834	34733
2004	**512802**	276012	195524	74557	156709	34755
2005	**544586**	377628	240923	82463	131440	34741
2006	**608155**	393778	296078	89772	131449	33236
2007	**840376**	522616	360081	97614	284594	32028
2008	**875005**	595735	430472	89093	247079	30176
2009	**1012937**	754803	567326	113430	224121	31347
2010	**1253461**	961283	739038	145740	259239	29151
2011	**1445811**	1174874	928669	171649	241132	25600
2012	**1633257**	1380125	1123105	186412	224279	24458
2013	**1862063**	1634885	1372371	207058	200419	21898
2014	**2139024**	1926012	1658714	224409	190625	17484
2015	**2394052**	2191023	1929195	224322	179619	18099
2016	**2588479**	2444000	2191862	226915	119771	19352
2017	**2885557**	2716361	2451906	243998	145207	17776

注：本表数据来自市车管所。
2017年数据为西安原口径数据。

15-4 全社会车辆数（2017年）

Possession of Civil Vehicles（2017）

指　标	Item	2017
合计（辆）	**Total (unit)**	**2885557**
民用汽车（辆）	Motor(unit)	2716361
#私人汽车拥有量	Possession of Private Vehicles	2466623
载客汽车	Passenger Vehicles	2451906
#大　型	Large	17612
轿　车	Car	1618522
普通载货汽车	Ordinary Trucks	243998
#重、中型	Heavy and Medium	63240
其他汽车	Others	20457
#三　轮	Three Wheelers	4462
拖拉机（台）	Tractors(unit)	17776
# 大中型	Large and Medium	
小　型	Small-sized	
摩托车（辆）	Motorcycle (unit)	145207
普通摩托车	Bicycle Motor	141961
挂车（辆）	Articulated Trailers (unit)	6213
其他类型车（辆）	Others (unit)	

注：本表数据来自市车管所。
　　本表数据为西安原口径数据。

15-5 主要年份交通运输量及周转量

Passenger Traffic and Kilometers and Freight Traffic and Ton-kilometers in Representative Years

年 份 Year	客运量 （万人次） Passenger Traffic (10 000 person-times)	旅客周转量 （万人公里） Passenger-Km (10 000 person-Km)	货运量 （万吨） Freight Traffic (10 000 tons)	货物周转量 （万吨公里） Freight Ton-Km (10 000 ton-Km)
1978	1334		3723	
1979	1420		3919	
1980	1508		3655	
1981	1839		3379	
1982	2340		4067	
1983	3054		4225	
1984	2899		4966	
1985	2404		5681	
1986	2186		5409	
1987	3781		6294	
1988	5721		6968	
1989	6092		8742	
1990	5748		6980	
1991	4193		3389	
1992	4368		8233	
1993	8036		8406	
1994	8321		8754	
1995	9069		9590	
1996	9854		10577	
1997	8922		9358	
1998	9223		9429	
1999	10311	2130383	9766	3452383
2000	8068	2507896	6999	3691963
2001	9078	2658037	7728	4229430
2002	12399	2524444	9482	4544040
2003	11413	2596402	9392	5037684
2004	10832	3112374	14845	5850029
2005	10479	1607568	12051	1249525
2006	11245	1721217	11832	1354318
2007	12466	1753464	15124	1473182
2008	26501	2529007	27560	3490707
2009	28693	2582025	30606	3766806
2010	30294	2942957	34323	4301680
2011	33375	3223544	39239	5212010
2012	36154	3387448	44924	5958742
2013	38289	3634915	50119	6471497
2014	25719	3091147	42039	6234128
2015	26904	3241463	46270	6430083
2016	23671	2909172	23888	5521252
2017	24287	3267158	25497	5979131

注：本表数据由市交通局、西安铁路局、咸阳机场、长安航空公司、东方航空公司西北分公司提供。
2016年陕西省公路运输统计计算系数变化，因此与往年数据不可比。
2017年数据为西安原口径数据。

15-6 交通运输量及运输周转量（2017年）

Passenger Traffic and Kilometers and Freight Traffic and Ton-kilometers (2017)

指　标	Item	2016	2017
一、客运量合计（万人次）	**Passenger Traffic(10 000 person-times)**	**23671**	**24287**
铁路	Railway	4199	4500
公路	Highway	15773	15601
民航	Civil Aviation	3699	4186
二、旅客周转量合计（万人公里）	**Passenger-Km (10 000 person-Km)**	**2909172**	**3267158**
铁路	Railway	676528	680961
公路	Highway	908379	900328
民航	Civil Aviation	1324265	1685869
三、货运量合计（万吨）	**Freight Traffic(l0 000 tons)**	**23888**	**25497**
铁路	Railway	854	994
公路	Highway	23011	24477
民航	Civil Aviation	23	26
四、货物周转量（万吨公里）	**Freight Ton-Kin (10 000 ton-Km)**	**5521252**	**5979131**
铁路	Railway	2270502	2459206
公路	Highway	3240829	3509694
民航	Civil Aviation	9920	10232

注：本表数据由市交通局、西安铁路局、咸阳机场、长安航空公司、东方航空公司西北分公司提供。
2016年由于公路统计计算系数变化，与上年数据不可比。
2017年数据为西安原口径数据。

15-7 主要年份邮政电信情况

年份 Year	邮电业务总量（万元） Business Volume of Postal and Telecommunication Services(10 000 yuan)	电信业务总量 Business Volume of Telecommunication Services	邮政业务总量 Business Volume of Postal Services
1978	1420		
1979	1616		
1980	1640		
1981	1713		
1982	2154		
1983	2250		
1984	2484		
1985	2972		
1986	3244		
1987	3911		
1988	5327		
1989	5973		
1990	7843		
1991	5700		
1992	6610		
1993	36581		
1994	54034		
1995	76450		
1996	104566		
1997	124601		
1998	204927		
1999	306457		
2000	461628		
2001	367620		
2002	515259	470492	44767
2003	820943	770673	50270
2004	1027415	975045	52370
2005	1320447	1261033	59414
2006	1867560	1796533	71027
2007	2267633	2191250	76383
2008	2646662	2564524	82138
2009	2989246	2900836	88410
2010	3231059	3167750	63309
2011	2005025	1944329	60696
2012	2162035	2098273	63762
2013	2479430	2313630	165800
2014	2922011	2695332	226679
2015	3315324	2983024	332300
2016	3831119	3299859	531260
2017	4398547	3728783	669764

注：2002年及以后，邮政电信机构分离；2001—2010年邮电业务总量按2000年不变价格计算；2011年后邮电业务总量按2010年不变价格计算，故与以往年份不可比。
2017年数据为西安原口径数据。

Basic Statistic on Postal and Telecommunication Service in Representative Years

固定电话年末用户数（户） Number of Immobile Telephone at Year-end (subscriber)	农村电话用户数 Number of Telephone in Rural Areas at Year-end	移动电话用户年末数（户） Number of Mobile Phone at Year-end (subscriber)	互联网年末宽带用户数（户） Number of Broad Band Net User (subscriber)
12828	1062		
13487	1052		
14024	1086		
14497	1125		
15357	1129		
16922	1156		
18611	1203		
21624	1239		
26373	1235		
30200	1290		
34265	1357		
39506	1498		
45267	1668		
49516	2479		
60727	2613		
101327	2671		
197398	5067		
299485	8386		
430270	13654		
573244	21202		
736998	37863		
874586	74761		
1242637	170199		
1711500	259374	1277400	17183
2095230	358803	1964200	35230
2538393	415593	2412392	160900
2934424	480276	3500900	243448
3214806	500847	4199570	339280
3159639	467526	5510720	508775
3145819	419446	6645863	586213
3068807	383869	7377575	813987
2891009	358238	11200566	1167916
2617691	335048	14230800	1461804
2703640	320189	16141463	1841027
3110176	335864	18035397	2023059
3191112	330602	21606662	2670473
3066575	372823	20253157	2779458
2920773	306336	17669953	2899714
2843336	314457	17395026	3358343
2732174	294055	18542137	3467859

注：本表数据由市邮政管理局、市邮政局，中国联通、中国电信、中国移动等西安分公司提供。

15-8 邮政业务及服务网点

Postal Service and Branch Post Office

指 标	Item	2010	2013	2014	2015	2016	2017
一、邮政业务总量（万元）	**Business Volume of Postal Services(10 000 yuan)**	63309	165800	226679	332300	531260	669764
二、邮政业务收入（万元）	**Gross Income of Post Services (10 000 yuan)**	58831	177100	213893	307008	439867	544555
其中：快递业务收入（万元）	Express Delivery Business Income (10 000 yuan)		97100	134306	207451	331605	413699
三、函件（万件）	**Number of Letters (10 000 pcs)**	8176	2856	2112	1707	1367	1360
四、包件（万件）	**Parcels (10 000 pcs)**	59	89	71	69	51	48
五、汇票（万张）	**Money Order (10 000 pcs)**	123	148	81	48	17	15
六、报纸订销累计份数（万份）	**Accumulated Newspaper Prescribing and Sales Volume (10 000 pcs)**	11724	14495	14338	14457	14395	14744
七、杂志订销累计份数（万份）	**Accumulated Magazine Prescribing and Sales Volume (10 000 pcs)**	550	1628	1572	1285	1155	956
八、特快专递类业务（万件）	**Express Mail Service Volume (10 000 pcs)**	582	138	107	61	63	63
九、集邮业务量（万枚）	**Stamps For Collection (10 000 pcs)**	860	1431	1477	1920	1607	1687
十、邮政营销网点（处）	**Number of Post Office Branch Establishments (unit)**	305	269	280	299	297	297
#设在农村的局所	In it: Number of Post Offices in Rural Area	20	110	123	140	149	149
十一、邮政信筒信箱（个）	**Number of Mailboxes(unit)**	1108	1108	1170	1170	422	422

注：本表数据来自市邮政管理局和邮政局，2013年邮政数据统计口径变化。
本表2017年数据未包含西咸新区。

15-9 电信业务情况

Telecommunication Service

指　标	Item	2010	2012	2013	2014	2015	2016	2017
一、电信业务总量（万元）	**Business Volume of Telecommunication Services (10 000 yuan)**	**3167750**	**2098273**	**2313630**	**2695332**	**2983024**	**3299859**	**3728783**
二、电信业务总收入（万元）	**Gross Income of Telecommunication Services (10 000 yuan)**	**1038865**	**1162257**	**1316435**	**1356705**	**1338203**	**1420708**	**1451625**
三、固定电话年末用户数（万户）	**Number of Immobile Telephone at Year-end(10 000 subscribers)**	**261.77**	**311.02**	**319.11**	**306.66**	**292.08**	**284.33**	**273.22**
#农村电话年末户数	Number of Telephone in Rural Areas at Year-end	33.50	33.59	33.06	37.28	30.63	31.45	29.41
四、电话交换机总容量（万门）	**Capacity (number) of Telephone Switchboard (10 000 lines)**	**449.05**	**420.38**	**378.02**	**230.01**	**145.08**	**75.92**	
五、移动电话用户年末数（万户）	**Number of Mobile Phone at Year-end (10 000 subscribers)**	**1423.08**	**1803.54**	**2160.67**	**2025.32**	**1767.00**	**1739.50**	**1854.21**
#4G电话用户数	4G Mobile Phone Subscribers						1113.03	1369.00
六、互联网年末用户数（万户）	**Number of Broad Band Net User (10 000 subscribers)**	**146.18**	**202.31**	**267.05**	**277.95**	**289.97**	**335.83**	**346.79**

注：本表数据由中国联通、中国电信、中国移动等西安分公司提供。
2017年数据为西安原口径数据。

15-10 一套表单位信息化基本情况（2017年）

单位：个

指　标	Item	企业数 Number of Enterprises	使用计算机的企业 Computer-used Enterprise
总计	**Total**	**6818**	**6803**
按国民经济门类分	**According To the Categories of National Economy**		
采矿业	Mining Industry	5	5
制造业	Manufacturing Industry	1305	1305
电力、热力、燃气及水生产和供应业	Electricity, Heat, Gas and Water Production and Supply	41	41
建筑业	Construction Business	1046	1044
批发和零售业	Wholesale and Retail Trade	1256	1255
交通运输、仓储和邮政业	Transportation, Warehousing and Postal Services	194	193
住宿和餐饮业	Accommodation and Catering Industry	659	658
信息传输、软件和信息技术服务业	Information Transmission, Software and Information Technology	208	208
房地产业	Estate	1180	1170
租赁和商务服务业	Leasing and Business Services	297	297
科学研究和技术服务业	Scientific Eesearch and Eechnical Services	251	251
水利、环境和公共设施管理业	Management of Water Wonservancy, Environment and Public Facilities	64	64
居民服务、修理和其他服务业	Services of Households, Repairs and Other Services	59	59
教育	Education	18	18
卫生和社会工作	Health and Social Service	65	65
文化、体育和娱乐业	Culture, Sports and Entertainment	170	170

注：一套表单位包括规模以上工业企业、限额以上批零住餐企业、资质以内建筑业企业、规模以上服务业企业、房地产开发经营企业。

Basic Statistics on Informatization of "One Sheet" Units (2017)

(unit)

有信息技术人员的企业 Enterprises with Information Technology Personnel	有局域网的企业 LAN Enterprises	使用信息化管理的企业 Enterprises Managed by Information Technology	有信息化投入的企业 Enterprises with Informatization Input	使用互联网的企业 Enterprises Using the Internet
5734	**5251**	**6613**	**5644**	**6794**
4	5	5	3	5
1213	1112	1280	1186	1300
38	35	41	39	41
871	738	1002	807	1043
1035	975	1222	1015	1252
145	131	190	154	193
545	483	636	595	657
206	199	206	195	208
882	839	1134	874	1172
244	230	286	242	296
227	207	248	224	251
51	47	60	52	64
48	44	57	52	59
16	15	18	15	18
64	56	64	58	65
145	135	164	133	170

15-11 一套表单位信息化设施及投入情况（2017年）

指 标	Item	期末使用计算机数量（台）Computers Used at the End of Period（unit）
总计	**Total**	**585466**
按国民经济门类分	**According To the Categories of National Economy**	
采矿业	Mining Industry	3879
制造业	Manufacturing Industry	133375
电力、热力、燃气及水生产和供应业	Electricity, Heat, Gas and Water Production and Supply	6096
建筑业	Construction Business	72156
批发和零售业	Wholesale and Retail Trade	61953
交通运输、仓储和邮政业	Transportation, Warehousing and Postal Services	24583
住宿和餐饮业	Accommodation and Catering Industry	16434
信息传输、软件和信息技术服务业	Information Transmission, Software and Information Technology	141223
房地产业	Estate	34118
租赁和商务服务业	Leasing and Business Services	15584
科学研究和技术服务业	Scientific Eesearch and Eechnical Services	50899
水利、环境和公共设施管理业	Management of Water Wonservancy, Environment and Public Facilities	4522
居民服务、修理和其他服务业	Services of Households, Repairs and Other Services	1471
教育	Education	2416
卫生和社会工作	Health and Social Service	8091
文化、体育和娱乐业	Culture, Sports and Entertainment	8666

注：一套表单位包括规模以上工业企业、限额以上批零住餐企业、资质以内建筑业企业、规模以上服务业企业、房地产开发经营企业。

Information Technology Facilities and Investment of "One Sheet" Units (2017)

信息技术人员（人）Information Technology Personnel（Person）	拥有网站个数（个）Number of Websites Owned（unit）	信息化投入（万元）Informatization Input (10 000 yuan)	一次性投入（万元）Disposable Input (10 000 yuan)	运营维护投入（万元）Operation and Maintenance Input (10 000 yuan)
28574	**4616**	**420305**	**269527**	**150778**
23	3	240	88	152
6531	1206	143844	108225	35619
161	23	4866	4467	399
4024	653	20782	15742	5040
3823	761	72313	20541	51772
1033	90	39907	25614	14293
1301	311	11825	6374	5451
5723	222	68477	43400	25077
2293	604	17782	13891	3891
935	216	10923	8247	2676
1611	224	20011	16079	3932
159	48	2432	1894	538
98	44	666	425	241
91	16	437	276	161
233	63	3504	2885	619
535	132	2296	1379	917

15-12 一套表单位信息化管理情况（2017年）

单位：个

指　标	Item	企业数 Number of Enterprises	使用信息化管理的企业 Number of Enterprises Managed by Information Technology
总计	**Total**	**6818**	**6613**
按国民经济门类分	**According To the Categories of National Economy**		
采矿业	Mining Industry	5	5
制造业	Manufacturing Industry	1305	1280
电力、燃气及水的生产供应业	Electricity, Heat, Gas and Water Production and Supply	41	41
建筑业	Construction Business	1046	1002
批发和零售业	Wholesale and Retail Trade	1256	1222
交通运输、仓储和邮政业	Transportation, Warehousing and Postal Services	194	190
住宿和餐饮业	Accommodation and Catering Industry	659	636
信息传输、软件和信息技术服务业	Information Transmission, Software and Information Technology	208	206
房地产业	Estate	1180	1134
租赁和商务服务业	Leasing and Business Services	297	286
科学研究和技术服务业	Scientific Eesearch and Eechnical Services	251	248
水利、环境和公共设施管理业	Management of Water Wonservancy, Environment and Public Facilities	64	60
居民服务、修理和其他服务业	Services of Households, Repairs and Other Services	59	57
教育	Education	18	18
卫生和社会工作	Health and Social Service	65	64
文化、体育和娱乐业	Culture, Sports and Entertainment	170	164

注：一套表单位包括规模以上工业企业、限额以上批零住餐企业、资质以内建筑业企业、规模以上服务业企业、房地产开发经营企业。

Information Management Situation of "One Sheet" Units (2017)

(unit)

财务管理 Financial Management	购销存管理 Purchase and Sale Management	生产制造管理 Manufacturing Management	物流配送管理 Logistics Distribution Management	客户关系管理 Customer Relationship Management	人力资源管理 Human Resource Management	其他 Others
5899	**2823**	**985**	**647**	**1937**	**2573**	**1422**
5	3	1		2	3	2
1180	805	599	234	408	519	179
40	16	15	2	11	20	9
883	202	91	23	226	411	266
1041	863	79	249	451	371	202
162	33	14	45	36	62	55
542	301	28	28	161	180	161
196	82	30	18	77	116	51
1022	261	45	18	315	484	261
264	54	12	13	84	130	66
232	55	42	6	69	129	74
54	15	4	1	7	22	16
48	22	5	2	20	26	15
17	3	1		6	6	7
58	43	2	1	22	24	18
155	65	17	7	42	70	40

15-13 一套表单位电子商务交易情况（2017年）

指 标	Item	企业数（个）Number of Enterprises (unit)
总计	**Total**	**6818**
按国民经济门类分	**According To the Categories of National Economy**	
采矿业	Mining Industry	5
制造业	Manufacturing Industry	1305
电力、燃气及水的生产供应业	Electricity, Heat, Gas and Water Production and Supply	41
建筑业	Construction Business	1046
批发和零售业	Wholesale and Retail Trade	1256
交通运输、仓储和邮政业	Transportation, Warehousing and Postal Services	194
住宿和餐饮业	Accommodation and Catering Industry	659
信息传输、软件和信息技术服务业	Information Transmission, Software and Information Technology	208
房地产业	Estate	1180
租赁和商务服务业	Leasing and Business Services	297
科学研究和技术服务业	Scientific Eesearch and Eechnical Services	251
水利、环境和公共设施管理业	Management of Water Wonservancy, Environment and Public Facilities	64
居民服务、修理和其他服务业	Services of Households, Repairs and Other Services	59
教育	Education	18
卫生和社会工作	Health and Social Service	65
文化、体育和娱乐业	Culture, Sports and Entertainment	170

注：一套表单位包括规模以上工业企业、限额以上批零住餐企业、资质以内建筑业企业、规模以上服务业企业、房地产开发经营企业。

E-commerce Transactions of “One Sheet” Units (2017)

有电子商务交易的企业（个）Enterprises with Ecommerce Transactions（unit）	有电子商务销售的企业 Ecommerce Sales Enterprises	有电子商务采购的企业 E-Commerce Purchases Enterprises	拥有电子商务交易平台的企业（个）With Ecommerce Trading Platform Enterprises（unit）	全年电子商务销售金额（万元）Sales of Ecommerce (10 000 yuan)	全年电子商务采购金额（万元）Purchases of Ecommerce (10 000 yuan)
853	**626**	**401**	**111**	**5793477**	**4060154**
134	87	85	27	169264	33272
2		2			20003
58	7	53	3	1230	567627
167	144	66	39	4065310	3006657
21	13	11	6	70968	1909
290	281	66	6	143348	1543
45	19	29	12	155734	3945
33	2	31		90	50763
30	20	19	7	1134021	338333
13	4	11		152	34498
11	8	7	3	3607	225
6	3	3	1	200	51
2	1	2		20521	359
5	3	4	1	760	92
36	34	12	6	28272	877

主要统计指标解释

公路里程　指在一定时期内实际达到《公路工程技术标准JTJ01-88》规定的等级公路，并经公路主管部门正式验收交付使用的公路里程数。包括大中城市的郊区公路以及通过小城镇街道部分的公路里程和桥梁、隧道渡口的长度，不包括大中城市的街道、厂矿、林区生产用道和农业生产用道的里程。两条或多条公路共同经由同一路段，只计算一次，不得重复计算里程长度。它是反映公路建设发展规模的重要指标，也是计算运输网密度等指标的基础资料。

民用航空航线里程　指民航运输定期班机飞行的航线长度的总和。航线长度按机场之间的距离计算，通常有两种计算方法：一是将每条航线长度相加称为重复计算航线里程；一是将两线或两条以上航线经过同一区段里程，只计算一次航线长度称为不重复计算航线里程。一般常用的是后者，它能确切反映民航运输网的规模，是表明民航事业为国民经济服务和方便人民生活程度的主要指标。

货（客）运量　指在一定时期内，各种运输工具实际运送的货物（旅客）数量。它是反映运输业为国民经济和人民生活服务的数量指标，也是制定和检查运输生产计划、研究运输发展规模和速度的重要指标。货运按吨计算，客运按人计算。货物不论运输距离长短、货物类别，均按实际重量统计。旅客不论行程远近或票价多少，均按一人一次客运量统计；半价票、小孩票也按一人统计。

货物（旅客）周转量　指在一定时期内，由各种运输工具运送的货物（旅客）数量与其相应运输距离的乘积之总和。它是反映运输业生产总成果的重要指标，也是编制和检查运输生产计划，计算运输效率、劳动生产率以及核算运输单位成本的主要基础资料。计算货物周转量通常按发出站与到达站之间的最短距离，也就是计费距离计算。计算公式为：

货物（旅客）周转量=Σ货物（旅客）运输量×运输距离

民用汽车拥有量　指报告期末，在公安交通管理部门按照《机动车注册登记工作规范》，已注册登记领有民用车辆牌照的全部汽车数量。汽车拥有量统计的主要分类：根据汽车结构分为载客汽车、载货汽车及其他汽车；根据汽车所有者不同分为个人（私人）汽车、单位汽车；根据汽车的使用性质分为营运汽车、非营运汽车；根据汽车大小规格不同载客汽车分为大型、中型、小型和微型，载货汽车分为重型、中型、轻型和微型。

邮电业务总量　指以价值量形式表现的邮电通信企业为社会提供各类邮电通信服务的总数量。邮电业务量按专业分类包括函件、包件、汇票、报刊发行、邮政快件、特快专递、邮政储蓄、集邮、公众电报、用户电报、传真、长途电话、出租电路、无线寻呼、移动电话、分组交换数据通信、出租代维等。计算方法为各类产品乘以相应的平均单价（不变价）之和，再加上出租电路和设备、代用户维护电话交换机和线路等的服务收入。它综合反映了一定时期邮电业务发展的总成果，是研究邮电业务量构成和发展趋势的重要指标。计算公式为：

邮电业务总量=Σ（各类邮电业务量×不变单价）+出租代维及其他业务收入

移动电话用户　是指通过移动电话交换机进入移动电话网、占用移动电话号码的电话用户。用户数量以报告期末在移动电话营业部门实际办理登记手续进入移动电话网的户数进行计算，一部移动电话统计为一户。

电话用户　指接入国家公众固定电话网，并按固定电话业务进行经营管理的电话用户。1997年以前，电话用户分为市内电话用户和农村电话用户。“市内电话用户”是指接入县城及县以上城市的电话网上的电话用户；“农村电话用户”是指接入县邮电局农话台及县以下农村电话交换点，以县城为中心（除市活用户外）联通县、乡（镇）、行政村、村民小组的用户。从1997年起，电话用户数分组调整为以用户所在区域划分为“城市电话用户”和“乡村电话用户”，与过去的按市内电话和农村电话划分方法不同。而电话用户总数、电话机总部数统计范围不变。

农村电话用户　指县城关区以下的集镇和农村接入局用交换机的电话用户数。

局用交换机容量　是指安装在本地电信运营商内用于接续本地固定电话的电话交换机容量，有倍增设备按倍增后的数量计数。包括现用和备用的人工或自动交换机的全部容量。

计算机数　指报告期末企业（单位）使用的计算机数量，包括台式机、笔记本电脑和平板电脑。

信息技术人员　指专职从事信息技术系统的制定、设计、开发、安装、操作、维护、管理和评估的人员。

信息化投入　包括企业（单位）一次性投入和运

营维护投入。

一次性投入 包括企业（单位）购置各类硬件和软件的实际支出。

运营维护投入 包括企业（单位）更新维护各类信息通信硬件和软件的实际支出。

互联网 指在世界范围内的公共计算机网络。它提供一系列通信服务（包括万维网）的接入，并传送电子邮件、新闻、娱乐和数据文件等。

全年电子商务销售金额 指报告期内企业（单位）借助网络订单而销售的商品和服务总额。借助网络订单指通过网络接受订单，付款和配送可以不借助于网络。

全年电子商务采购金额 指报告期内企业（单位）借助网络订单而采购的商品和服务总额。借助网络订单指通过网络发送订单，付款和配送可以不借助于网络。

Explanatory Notes on Main Statistical Indicators

Length of Highways refers to the length of highways which are built in conformity with the grades specified by the highway engineering standard formulated by the Ministry of Communications, and have been formally checked and accepted by the departments of highways and put into use. The length of highways includes that of the suburb highways at large and medium- sized cities,highways passing through streets at small cities and towns,and also the length of bridges, tunnel and ferries. It does not include the length of streets in big and medium-sized cities and highways built for the production purpose at factories, mines, forest areas and agricultural areas. If two or more highways go the same section of the way, the length of the section is only calculated for once and no duplication is allowed. The length of highways is an important indicator to show the development of the highway construction and to provide essential information to calculate the transport network density.

Length of Civil Aviation Routes refers to the length of all routes for regular civil aviation flights. There are usually two ways to calculate the distance between airports connected by the route length: one is to put the length of all air routes together, called duplicated calculation of the length of the routes; the other is not to allow the duplication in calculation when two or more routes passing the same section of aviation routes. The latter is usually used, as it can precisely show the size of the civil aviation network and indicate the extent of civil aviation serving the national economy and the people.

Freight (Passenger) Traffic refers to the volume of freight (passenger) transported with various means. Freight transport is calculated in tons and passenger traffic is calculated in the number of persons. Despite the type of freight and travelling distance, the freight transport is calculated in the actual weight of the goods: and despite the travelling distance and ticket price, the passenger traffic is calculated by the principle that one person can be counted only once in one travel. The passenger who travel with a half price ticket or a child ticket is also calculated as one person. The freight (passenger) traffic provides a quantitative measure to show how the transport industry serves the national economy and people, and is also an important indicator for planning the transport industry and for studying the development scale and speed of the transport industry.

Freight Ton-kilometers(Passenger-kilometers) refer to the sum of the products of the volume of transported cargo (passengers) multiplying by the transport distance, usually using ton-kilometer and passenger-kilometer as units for measurement. Normally, the shortest distance between the departure station and the destination station (i.e., the payable distance) is the basis to calculate the freight ton-kilometers. This is an important indicator to show the total results of the transport industry, to prepare and examine the transport plan and to measure the efficiency, the labour productivity and the unit cost of transport.

The formula is as follows:

Freight Ton-kilometers(Passenger-kilometers)=Σ {Freight (Passenger) Traffic × Distance of Transportation }

Measuring unit: ton-kilometer (person-kilometer)

Possession of Civil Motor Vehicles refer to the total numbers of vehicles that are registered and received vehicles license tags according to the Work Standard for Motor Vehicles Registration formulated by the Transport Management Office under the department of public security at the end of the reference period. They are divided into categories. According to the structure of motor vehicles, they are divided into passenger vehicles, trucks and others; according to ownership into private vehicles and vehicles for the unit' s use; according to kind of usage into working vehicles and non-working vehicles; and according to size of vehicles into large passenger vehicles, medium-sized passenger vehicles, small passenger vehicles and mini passenger vehicles, heavytrucks, light-heavy trucks, light trucks and mini-trucks.

Business Volume of Post and Telecommunications refers to the total amount of post and telecommunications services, expressed in value terms, provided by the post and telecommunications departments for the society. Post and telecommunication services can be classified asletters, parcels, remittance, issue of newspapers and magazines, fast mail service, express mail service, savings deposits, stamps for collection, public and individual telegraph service, facsimiles, long-distance telephone service,leasing of telephone lines, urban paging service, mobile telephone service, data transfer and transmission, etc. The accounting approach is to multiply the service products of all types with their average unit price (constant price) to get sum of business value, plus income from other services such as leasing of telephone lines and equipment, maintenance of telephone switchboards and lines on behalf of customers. This indicator reflects the overall results of post and telecommunications service during a given period, and is important to study the composition of business service and the development of post and telecommunications service.

The formula is as follows:

Business Volume of Post and Telecommunications=Σ (Transaction of Post and Telecommunication Service x Constant Price) + Income from Leasing, Maintenance and other Services

Mobile Telephone Subscribers refer to the persons who own mobile telephone numbers and are connected with the mobile telephone communication network through the mobile telephone switchboards. The number of subscribers is calculated by the subscribers who have completed registration at mobile communication business centers and entered into the mobile telephone network. One mobile telephone is taken as a subscriber.

Telephone Subscribers refer to subscribers that are connected to the public line telephone network provided with telephone services. Before 1997, telephone subscribers were classified as city subscribers and village subscribers. City subscribers referred to those connected to city telephone networks in county towns and cities, while village subscribers referred to those connected to village telephone stations at and below counties. Since 1997, the classification of telephone subscribers was modified on the basis of physical location of the subscribers as Urban telephone subscribers and rural telephone subscribers , which is different from the previous classification of categorizing local telephones and rural telephones , while the definition of total subscribers and total number of telephones remain unchanged.

Rural Telephone Subscribers refer to telephone subscribers, located at towns under county town and country, that are connected to the public line telephone network.

Capacity of Office Telephone Exchanges refers to the capacity (measured in gate) of telephone exchanges installed in the offices of local telecommunication service providers for communication between fixed telephones. It includes the capacity of both manual and automatic exchanges in use and for stand-by purpose. Equipment with expansion function is to be counted by the expanded capacity.

The number of computer srefers to the number of computers used in an enterprise or a company at the end of the reporting period, including desktops, laptops, and tablet computers.

Information technology personnel refers topeople who is engaged in the formulation, design, development, installation, operation, maintenance, management and evaluation of an information technology system.

Informatization Input includes the One-time investment input and operation maintenance investment of an enterprise or a company.

One-time Investment Input includes the actual expenditure in purchasing all kinds of hardware and software of an enterprise or a company.

Operation and Maintenance Input includesthe actual expenditure inupdating and maintenance of all kinds of information communication hardware and software of anenterprise or a company.

The Internet refers to the public computer network around the world. It provides access to a range of communications services including the world wide web, and transmits e-mail, news, entertainment, and data files,etc.

The amount of E-commerce sales during the whole year the total amount of goods and services sold by means of network orders of an enterprise or a company during the reporting period.By means of network ordersmeans that the orders are received over the network, but the payment and distribution can be made without the network.

The amount of E-commerce purchases during the whole yearrefers to the total amount of goods and services purchased by means of network orders of an enterprise or a company during the reporting period.

By means of network orders means that the orders are sent over the network, but the payment and distribution can be made without the network.

16 国内贸易

DOMESTIC TRADE

资料整理：马晓庆　杨　骏　左　宇　赵琳瑛　胡树建
Data management: Ma Xiaoqing　Yang Jun　Zuo Yu　Zhao Linying　Hu Shujian
数据审核：黄小丹
Data audit:Huang Xiaodan

第十六部分　国内贸易

一、简要说明

本章资料主要包括社会消费品零售总额，批发零售贸易业商品购、销等情况，限额以上批发零售贸易业主要商品销售情况，限额以上批发零售贸易和住宿餐饮企业财务状况、经济效益，以及交易市场情况，由西安市统计局贸易外经处提供。

二、主要指标

社会消费品零售总额（亿元）	4249.81	比上年增长	8.5%

16 DOMESTIC TRADE

Ⅰ.Brief Introduction

Content of this chapter consists of total retail sales of consumer goods, sails data on commodity purchasing and sails of wholesale and retail trade, sales data on primary goods exceeds quotation, financial, economic performance and market data on wholesale and retail trade and food services industry exceeds quotation. Data in this chapter is compiled and provided by Trade and Foreign Economy Division of the Xi'an Bureau of Statistics.

Ⅱ.Maior Indicators

		Increase over Preceding Year
Total Retail Sales of Consumer Goods (100 mil. yuan)	4249.81	8.5%

16-1 主要年份社会消费品零售额

Total Retail Sales of Consumer Goods in Representative Years

单位：亿元 (100 million yuan)

年 份 Year	社会消费品零售总额 Total Retail Sales of Consumer Goods	城镇 Urban	乡村 Village	批发和零售业 Wholesale Trades and Retail Trades	住宿和餐饮业 Accommodation and Catering Trade	其他行业 Others
1978	12.70	8.82	3.88	11.01	0.53	0.21
1979	13.94	9.88	4.06	11.88	0.60	0.21
1980	15.88	11.53	4.35	13.05	0.80	0.20
1981	17.41	12.85	4.56	14.31	0.80	0.19
1982	18.54	13.79	4.75	15.25	0.88	0.27
1983	20.82	15.14	5.68	16.95	1.03	0.32
1984	24.87	19.13	5.74	19.47	1.29	0.46
1985	32.92	26.09	6.83	25.04	1.69	0.48
1986	37.50	29.25	8.25	28.88	1.97	0.64
1987	43.86	34.62	9.24	33.32	2.50	0.49
1988	59.65	47.74	11.91	44.84	2.97	0.78
1989	68.05	54.60	13.45	54.41	2.98	0.76
1990	72.77	59.42	13.35	57.46	3.79	0.90
1991	81.04	66.93	14.11	60.35	4.43	1.26
1992	100.84	89.17	11.67	71.86	6.13	2.30
1993	115.38	104.41	10.97	75.99	7.49	2.71
1994	144.64	131.56	13.08	89.79	9.12	3.43
1995	186.60	165.98	20.62	115.46	11.97	3.73
1996	222.94	198.19	24.75	145.05	15.83	4.02
1997	264.47	238.17	26.30	169.08	22.12	4.17
1998	291.45	257.39	34.06	183.43	30.97	4.27
1999	323.37	283.32	40.05	207.96	34.78	4.85
2000	360.42	317.12	43.30	232.89	41.42	5.43
2001	406.21	358.97	47.24	265.25	48.87	5.86
2002	459.76	409.86	49.90	309.36	51.42	6.45
2003	502.65	449.62	53.03	440.28	53.30	9.07
2004	578.55	520.89	57.66	509.55	56.87	12.13
2005	670.56	604.63	65.93	592.77	63.59	14.20
2006	784.95	708.31	76.64	694.03	74.77	16.15
2007	936.21	845.59	90.62	828.63	89.32	18.26
2008	1176.58	1063.93	112.65	1033.00	122.90	20.68
2009	1398.37	1336.41	61.96	1250.41	147.96	
2010	1678.01	1610.88	67.13	1497.71	180.30	
2011	2039.24	1968.41	70.83	1825.79	213.45	
2012	2400.67	2326.84	73.83	2156.49	244.18	

年 份 Year	社会消费品零售总额 Total Retail Sales of Consumer Goods	按销售单位所在地分 By Location of Establishments			按消费形态分By Consumption Patterns	
		城镇零售额 Urban Areas	城区 Urban District	乡村零售额 Rural Areas	商品零售 Retail Sales	餐饮收入 Catering income
2013	2742.89	2657.49	2124.72	85.40	2526.10	216.79
2014	3093.89	2996.43	2596.00	97.46	2865.07	228.82
2015	3405.38	3292.83	2832.66	112.55	3146.45	258.93
2016	3767.20	3639.32	3266.69	127.88	3486.21	280.99
2017	4249.81	4098.00	3524.33	151.81	3916.20	333.61

注：依据2008年第二次经济普查数据，对2005-2007年数据进行调整。
依据2013年第三次经济普查数据，对2009年—2013年数据进行调整。
2009年以前按经营单位所在地分为市和县及县以下。
2002年以前按行业分组中不包括制造业零售额和农业对非农业居民零售额。
2016年数据根据第三次农业普查结果及有关制度规定进行了修订。

16-2 社会消费品零售总额

Total Retail Sales of Consumer Goods

单位：亿元 (100 million yuan)

分 类	Classify	2016	2017
社会消费品零售总额	**Total Retail Sales of Consumer Goods**	**3767.20**	**4249.81**
（一）按销售单位所在地分	Grouped by Region		
（1）城镇	Urban	3639.32	4098.00
#城区	District	3266.69	3524.33
（2）乡村	Village	127.88	151.81
（二）按消费形态分	Grouped by Consumption Patterns		
（1）商品零售	Retail Sales	3486.21	3916.20
（2）餐饮收入	Catering Income	280.99	333.61

注：2016年数据根据第三次农业普查结果及有关制度规定进行了修订。

16-3 各区县社会消费品零售总额

Total Retail Sales of Consumer Goods by Region

单位：亿元 (100 million yuan)

区 县	Region	2005	2007	2008	2009	2010	2011	2012	2013	2014	2015	2016	2017
全 市	**Toatl**	670.56	936.21	1176.58	1398.37	1678.01	2039.24	2400.67	2742.89	3093.89	3405.38	3767.20	4249.81
新城区	Xincheng	129.00	169.95	207.01	241.56	285.41	342.48	397.08	446.06	499.78	557.59	607.98	667.03
碑林区	Beilin	131.09	172.55	206.80	241.48	285.45	342.56	395.07	445.11	505.87	561.46	610.53	625.92
莲湖区	Lianhu	116.34	144.57	169.62	198.10	234.84	282.08	325.93	368.62	413.00	451.82	491.72	503.68
灞桥区	Baqiao	17.89	22.79	27.01	36.26	50.18	68.02	95.43	132.26	154.28	173.26	200.82	232.31
未央区	Weiyang	64.38	114.53	164.14	200.54	245.41	301.10	361.75	423.72	480.79	515.21	586.17	558.35
雁塔区	Yanta	104.87	167.18	225.95	272.35	327.95	401.56	472.92	534.30	596.50	656.47	714.37	782.59
阎良区	Yanliang	8.25	11.29	13.85	16.41	19.67	23.91	27.87	31.37	34.93	37.90	41.22	45.59
临潼区	Lintong	20.37	25.04	29.02	34.29	40.95	49.72	57.75	64.08	72.63	77.99	84.66	96.47
长安区	Chang'an	37.36	52.44	64.67	76.80	91.86	111.41	130.09	144.94	164.00	183.37	202.49	231.40
高陵区	Gaoling	4.75	7.24	9.48	11.51	14.09	17.53	22.43	25.01	28.40	31.73	44.54	51.78
鄠邑区	Huyi	14.18	19.12	23.21	27.31	32.63	39.38	45.49	50.97	57.52	63.71	69.98	77.75
蓝田县	Lantian	13.53	17.83	21.44	25.00	29.70	35.64	41.18	45.74	51.57	56.40	62.08	70.42
周至县	Zhouzhi	8.54	11.69	14.38	16.75	19.86	23.84	27.68	30.71	34.63	38.47	50.64	57.08

注：2016年数据根据第三次农业普查结果及有关制度规定进行了修订。

16-4 限额以上批发零售贸易企业财务状况（2017年）

单位：万元

分类	Classify	单位数（个）Number (unit)	资产总计 Total Assets	流动资产合计 Circulating Funds	固定资产合计 Total Fixed Assets
总计	**Total**	**1261**	**25589191.1**	**18901353.5**	**1870625.6**
一、批发企业	**Wholesale Enterprises**	**519**	**14713846.9**	**11337805.0**	**759351.9**
1. 按登记注册类型分组	Grouped by Category of Commodities				
内资企业	Domestic Funded Enterprises	502	13481571.3	10508958.7	740093.6
国有	State-owned Enterprises	21	944392.6	812501.8	87471.6
集体	Collective-owned Enterprises	3	13638.4	13159.6	474.3
股份合作	Corperative Enterprises				
联营	Joint Ownership Enterprises				
国有联营	State Joint Ownership Enterprises				
集体联营	Collective Joint Ownership Enterprises				
国有与集体联营	Joint State-collective Enterprises				
其他联营	Others Joint Ownership Enterprises				
有限责任公司	Limited Liability Corporations	260	8800994.1	6856409.9	487694.0
国有独资公司	State Funded Corporations	15	1634953.0	1471508.1	14606.6
其他有限责任公司	Other Limited Liability Corporations	245	7166041.1	5384901.8	473087.4
股份有限公司	Share-holding Corporations Ltd.	16	1834217.2	1098596.5	80062.4
私营	Private Enterprises	199	1886689.9	1727848.4	83194.7
私营独资	Private-funded Enterprises	1	1296.8	1208.9	87.9
私营合伙	Private Partnership Enterprises				
私营有限责任公司	Private Limited Liability Corporations	192	1737422.1	1599869.5	81217.2
私营股份有限公司	Private Share-holding Corporations Ltd.	6	147971.0	126770.0	1889.6
其他	Other Enterprises	3	1639.1	442.5	1196.6
港澳台商投资	Enterprises with Funds from Hong Kong, Macao &Taiwan	4	80646.3	73305.3	6828.7
外商投资	Foreign Funded Enterprises	13	1151629.3	755541.0	12429.6
2. 按国民经济行业分组	Grouped by Sector				

Financial Status of Wholesale and Retail Enterprises above Designated Size (2017)

(10 000 yuan)

固定资产原价 Original Value of Fixed Assets	累计折旧 Accumulated Depreciation	负债合计 Total Liabilities	流动负债合计 Circulating Liabilities	非流动负债合计 Non-Circulating Liabilities	所有者权益合计 Total Owners' Equities	实收资本 Paid in Capital	营业收入 Total Revenue	主营业务收入 Revenue from Principal Business
2702465.8	**952677.5**	**18433898.9**	**17045360.9**	**1389439.5**	**7155292.2**	**5375537.7**	**64274134.7**	**63723015.3**
1109844.2	**389057.9**	**10925428.1**	**9875871.4**	**1049556.7**	**3788418.8**	**3362867.4**	**44654832.1**	**44402824.1**
1079326.1	377746.0	9942887.8	9111618.4	831269.4	3538683.5	3171823.9	39038936.6	38788363.7
142115.4	66963.9	490407.3	485294.6	5112.7	453985.3	61259.4	2374871.2	2367086.5
529.5	67.0	13048.0	12455.1	592.9	590.4	613.3	41402.6	41402.6
646375.4	175972.5	6661780.4	5950516.9	711263.5	2139213.7	1598265.3	24014174.5	23820303.5
30862.6	16302.2	1459279.1	1446625.1	12654.0	175673.9	106665.4	5306493.1	5295762.4
615512.8	159670.3	5202501.3	4503891.8	698609.5	1963539.8	1491599.9	18707681.4	18524541.1
169567.7	95952.8	1301678.2	1267305.1	34373.1	532539.0	190972.1	7379162.4	7338908.1
118845.7	38088.5	1475572.8	1395645.6	79927.2	411117.1	1319623.2	5211858.9	5203196.0
201.5	113.6	1246.1	1227.4	18.7	50.7	50.0	5023.3	5023.3
114696.2	35707.6	1362877.8	1285926.9	76950.9	374544.3	1297247.0	4638281.1	4631463.0
3948.0	2267.3	111448.9	108491.3	2957.6	36522.1	22326.2	568554.5	566709.7
1892.4	701.3	401.1	401.1		1238.0	1090.6	17467.0	17467.0
9377.1	2548.4	63110.0	63110.0		17536.3	5635.7	158476.5	158142.9
21141.0	8763.5	919430.3	701143.0	218287.3	232199.0	185407.8	5457419.0	5456317.5

16-4 续表1

单位：万元

分类	Classify	营业成本 Total Cost	主营业务成本 Cost of Principal Business	税金及附加 Taxs and Other Changes	主营业务税金及附加 Taxs and Other Changes on Principal Business
总计	**Total**	**59294701.5**	**59020312.4**	**382069.4**	**374967.9**
一、批发企业	**Wholesale Enterprises**	**42489019.8**	**42250167.6**	**226272.3**	**221000.9**
1. 按登记注册类型分组	Grouped by Category of Commodities				
内资企业	Domestic Funded Enterprises	36976084.1	36737883.0	225058.4	219831.2
国有	State-owned Enterprises	2003470.7	1998833.2	160433.6	159122.2
集体	Collective-owned Enterprises	40071.6	40071.6	31.2	31.2
股份合作	Corperative Enterprises				
联营	Joint Ownership Enterprises				
国有联营	State Joint Ownership Enterprises				
集体联营	Collective Joint Ownership Enterprises				
国有与集体联营	Joint State-collective Enterprises				
其他联营	Others Joint Ownership Enterprises				
有限责任公司	Limited Liability Corporations	22867612.8	22715006.4	47799.8	47430.1
国有独资公司	State Funded Corporations	4894857.0	4890922.0	6883.5	6555.6
其他有限责任公司	Other Limited Liability Corporations	17972755.8	17824084.4	40916.3	40874.5
股份有限公司	Share-holding Corporations Ltd.	7104004.9	7051432.0	8761.6	5237.0
私营	Private Enterprises	4946005.9	4917621.6	8032.2	8010.7
私营独资	Private-funded Enterprises	4824.3	4824.3	3.1	3.1
私营合伙	Private Partnership Enterprises				
私营有限责任公司	Private Limited Liability Corporations	4399320.5	4371696.4	6509.4	6487.9
私营股份有限公司	Private Share-holding Corporations Ltd.	541861.1	541100.9	1519.7	1519.7
其他	Other Enterprises	14918.2	14918.2		
港澳台商投资	Enterprises with Funds from Hong Kong, Macao &Taiwan	119552.9	119552.0	555.7	555.7
外商投资	Foreign Funded Enterprises	5393382.8	5392732.6	658.2	614.0
2. 按国民经济行业分组	Grouped by Sector				

continued 1

(10 000 yuan)

销售费用 Sale Expenses	管理费用 Management Expenses	财务费用 Financial Expenses	营业利润 Business Profits	利润总额 Total Profits	应付职工薪酬 Salary Payable	所得税费用 Income Tax Expenses	应交增值税 Value Added Tax Payable
2290297.8	**869587.8**	**245462.2**	**1225792.4**	**1261716.7**	**918092.8**	**226748.8**	**535142.2**
986120.9	**308955.8**	**154043.4**	**472082.1**	**503820.0**	**368261.2**	**88866.4**	**258767.7**
949046.0	289983.2	90581.3	475010.5	490115.7	342772.2	85679.5	251297.9
51415.8	37648.8	2579.9	119210.2	127671.1	52071.4	34525.1	58208.1
559.1	752.6	-21.0	9.1	-1.6	628.0	25.1	187.2
589242.8	180276.7	68508.8	226084.1	228613.3	180499.9	37024.4	122725.8
359201.8	23904.0	4354.3	-6527.4	-7245.8	30323.3	1762.6	37009.3
230041.0	156372.7	64154.5	232611.5	235859.1	150176.6	35261.8	85716.5
178142.0	17694.8	6629.6	64873.4	66193.2	56509.8	2385.3	41104.2
129525.7	53480.6	12826.0	62633.2	65439.2	52418.1	11719.6	29072.6
133.1	24.2	38.1	0.5	0.5	49.8		30.7
124910.9	50298.4	10553.9	47364.2	50141.5	42736.8	11538.5	28035.3
4481.7	3158.0	2234.0	15268.5	15297.2	9631.5	181.1	1006.6
160.6	129.7	58.0	2200.5	2200.5	645.0		
24625.1	9483.8	15.8	4243.2	4272.4	17753.8	548.8	4803.8
12449.8	9488.8	63446.3	-7171.6	9431.9	7735.2	2638.1	2666.0

16-4 续表2

单位：万元

分 类	Classify	单位数（个） Number (unit)	资产总计 Total Assets	流动资产合计 Circulating Funds	固定资产合计 Total Fixed Assets
农、林、牧产品批发	Wholesale of Agricultural,Forestry and Animal Husbandry Products	4	74573.9	32760.5	12701.1
食品、饮料及烟草制品批发	Wholesale of food Beverages and Tobaccos	61	994455.2	845329.1	86937.9
纺织、服装及家庭服务器批发	Wholesale of Textiles, Garments and Daily Articles	30	630922.1	574674.2	29718.6
文化、体育用品及器材批发	Wholesale of Culture, Sports Appliances and Equipments	31	305356.4	231003.6	13843.8
医药及医疗器材批发	Wholesale of Medicines and Medical Appliances	105	2388215.2	2274923.4	43272.1
矿产品、建材及化工产品批发	Wholesale of Mineral Products, Building Materials and Chemical Products	177	9042056.7	6219560.7	499983.5
机械设备、五金产品及电子产品批发	Wholesale of Machinery, Hardware, and Electronic Equipment	103	1242964.1	1129660.2	70782.8
贸易经纪与代理	Trade Broker and Agency	2	17953.1	17276.6	366.3
其他批发	Other wholesale not Classified Elsewhere	6	17350.2	12616.7	1745.8
二、零售企业	**Retail Trade**	**742**	**10875344.2**	**7563548.5**	**1111273.7**
1. 按登记注册类型分组	Grouped by Category of Commodities				
内资	Domestic Funded Enterprises	694	7504175.7	5410309.1	867362.9
国有	State-owned Enterprises	8	401143.3	353965.9	44662.3
集体	Collective-owned Enterprises	17	11536.5	3807.9	5665.5
股份合作	Corperative Enterprises				
联营	Joint Ownership Enterprises				
国有联营	State Joint Ownership Enterprises				
集体联营	Collective Joint Ownership Enterprises				
国有与集体联营	Joint State-collective Enterprises				
其他联营	Others Joint Ownership Enterprises				
有限责任公司	Limited Liability Corporations	338	4404475.6	3066359.0	600125.0
国有独资公司	State Funded Corporations	9	186269.9	104645.0	56787.4

continued 2

(10 000 yuan)

固定资产原价 Original Value of Fixed Assets	累计折旧 Accumulated Depreciation	负债合计 Total Liabilities	流动负债合计 Circulating Liabilities	非流动负债合计 Non-Circulating Liabilities	所有者权益合计 Total Owners' Equities	实收资本 Paid in Capital	营业收入 Total Revenue	主营业务收入 Revenue from Principal Business
17809.8	5108.7	65248.8	37514.6	27734.2	9325.1	13002.8	41946.0	41549.4
144077.7	65868.9	354390.8	345426.3	8964.5	640064.4	86404.3	3078231.3	3076425.1
59871.5	32977.6	545755.0	539975.0	5780.0	85167.1	56495.7	3325688.8	3320880.6
23455.0	10690.5	192792.3	181854.2	10938.1	112564.1	1060592.2	524363.4	522640.8
61546.6	23420.6	2090245.4	1952783.8	137461.6	297969.8	255477.5	3892116.4	3884353.1
697986.2	215767.9	6592644.3	5772886.6	819757.7	2449412.4	1769122.8	31872492.4	31649045.8
101408.0	33613.7	1059010.3	1020752.6	38257.7	183953.8	114351.3	1869403.5	1857339.2
405.8	72.2	16730.5	16410.2	320.3	1222.6	419.8	36480.0	36479.8
3283.6	1537.8	8610.7	8268.1	342.6	8739.5	7001.0	14110.3	14110.3
1592621.6	**563619.6**	**7508470.8**	**7169489.5**	**339882.8**	**3366873.4**	**2012670.3**	**19619302.6**	**19320191.2**
1224954.3	424637.4	5245460.9	4986812.5	259549.8	2258714.8	1498089.0	13733005.4	13512855.9
59817.6	19785.7	307903.0	304950.5	2952.5	93240.3	3822.3	735348.6	729553.2
6542.1	1027.3	9400.1	8567.2	832.9	2136.4	1534.1	30180.5	30180.5
827230.9	268760.0	3146905.0	3073575.0	74122.9	1257570.6	851087.9	8493518.5	8331040.5
72522.6	18845.1	124838.0	119177.8	5660.2	61431.9	27248.3	196584.5	192769.0

16-4 续表3

单位：万元

分 类	Classify	营业成本 Total Cost	主营业务成本 Cost of Principal Business	税金及附加 Taxs and Other Changes	主营业务税金及附加 Taxs and Other Changes on Principal Business
农、林、牧产品批发	Wholesale of Agricultural,Forestry and Animal Husbandry Products	39604.3	39589.6	22.7	22.7
食品、饮料及烟草制品批发	Wholesale of food Beverages and Tobaccos	2628177.4	2607467.9	160062.1	158855.2
纺织、服装及家庭服务器批发	Wholesale of Textiles, Garments and Daily Articles	3181517.6	3180842.8	11405.2	11405.2
文化、体育用品及器材批发	Wholesale of Culture, Sports Appliances and Equipments	484863.1	483105.8	868.8	638.9
医药及医疗器材批发	Wholesale of Medicines and Medical Appliances	3604069.8	3581902.9	7093.5	7087.6
矿产品、建材及化工产品批发	Wholesale of Mineral Products, Building Materials and Chemical Products	30768684.2	30586337.4	43718.1	40007.5
机械设备、五金产品及电子产品批发	Wholesale of Machinery, Hardware, and Electronic Equipment	1737188.5	1726006.3	3075.8	2957.7
贸易经纪与代理	Trade Broker and Agency	32408.1	32408.1	1.1	1.1
其他批发	Other wholesale not Classified Elsewhere	12506.8	12506.8	25.0	25.0
二、零售企业	**Retail Trade**	**16805681.7**	**16770144.8**	**155797.1**	**153967.0**
1. 按登记注册类型分组	Grouped by Category of Commodities				
内资	Domestic Funded Enterprises	11896798.4	11875572.6	126023.0	125222.2
国有	State-owned Enterprises	667305.2	667093.5	1680.6	1680.6
集体	Collective-owned Enterprises	26652.1	26652.1	474.2	474.2
股份合作	Corperative Enterprises				
联营	Joint Ownership Enterprises				
国有联营	State Joint Ownership Enterprises				
集体联营	Collective Joint Ownership Enterprises				
国有与集体联营	Joint State-collective Enterprises				
其他联营	Others Joint Ownership Enterprises				
有限责任公司	Limited Liability Corporations	7389445.3	7372883.6	75049.5	74786.0
国有独资公司	State Funded Corporations	165924.4	165585.1	521.3	507.7

continued 3

(10 000 yuan)

销售费用 Sale Expenses	管理费用 Management Expenses	财务费用 Financial Expenses	营业利润 Business Profits	利润总额 Total Profits	应付职工薪酬 Salary Payable	所得税费用 Income Tax Expenses	应交增值税 Value Added Tax Payable
1620.9	771.4	208.6	-282.0	255.4	712.3	7.9	9.7
91833.7	52764.3	-2880.5	152616.3	155107.6	63285.2	35862.6	64398.9
63129.1	26851.2	1114.2	41677.9	42010.5	45767.4	5560.1	11904.0
18869.4	12494.0	472.8	6674.7	6967.0	10785.2	1029.5	1677.1
94654.3	65205.2	29834.4	87356.2	88121.1	56251.1	8759.7	38562.5
663971.6	108320.1	115145.8	159119.2	183025.4	151267.9	29936.5	126723.9
48722.0	41428.4	10252.0	23544.4	26636.0	39066.9	7628.4	15296.8
2546.1	430.7	-183.1	1310.5	1417.6	515.3	4.3	122.8
773.8	690.5	79.2	64.9	279.4	609.9	77.4	72.0
1304176.9	**560632.0**	**91418.8**	**753710.3**	**757896.7**	**549831.6**	**137882.4**	**276374.5**
759822.3	415206.9	69706.7	478094.0	486985.9	391502.9	80366.4	199118.2
30121.6	20377.1	2454.2	16437.0	16483.9	22577.0	3711.8	15540.7
1348.5	1443.1	104.4	158.4	131.5	1714.4		137.0
475061.2	234673.8	36375.8	284678.6	290456.7	241644.5	54916.7	119042.2
16680.9	10583.3	628.9	2375.3	3686.6	17173.4	724.1	1236.7

16-4 续表4

单位：万元

分 类	Classify	单位数（个） Number (unit)	资产总计 Total Assets	流动资产合计 Circulating Funds	固定资产合计 Total Fixed Assets
其他有限责任公司	Other Limited Liability Corporations	329	4218205.7	2961714.0	543337.6
股份有限公司	Share-holding Corporations Ltd.	12	657277.6	412928.0	37434.8
私营	Private Enterprises	315	2025349.0	1571341.4	178345.4
私营独资	Private-funded Enterprises	6	2622.9	1414.1	840.7
私营合伙	Private Partnership Enterprises	2	1011.3	859.7	118.7
私营有限责任公司	Private Limited Liability Corporations	298	1942917.7	1506173.8	167194.0
私营股份有限公司	Private Share-holding Corporations Ltd.	9	78797.1	62893.8	10192.0
其他	Other Enterprises	4	4393.7	1906.9	1129.9
港澳台商投资	Enterprises with Funds from Hong Kong, Macao &Taiwan	29	1961147.6	1199024.5	118263.6
外商投资	Foreign Funded Enterprises	19	1410020.9	954214.9	125647.2
2. 按国民经济行业分组	Grouped by Sector				
综合零售	Integrated Retail	115	3553432.0	2060220.3	422351.6
食品、饮料及烟草制品专门零售	Food, Beverages and Tobaccos Special Retail Trade	66	223181.1	130037.7	53900.2
纺织、服装及日用品专门零售	Special Retail of Textiles,Garments and Daily Consumer Articles	52	424328.2	303541.2	28207.3
文化、体育用品及器材专门零售	Retail of Culture,Sports Appliances and Equipments	38	433861.5	299661.2	84697.8
医药及医疗器材专门零售	Retail of Medicines and Medical Appliances	32	217811.8	193187.3	10155.5
汽车、摩托车、燃料及零配件专门零售	Retail of Motor Vehicles,Motorcycles, Fuel and Parts	286	4007666.1	2918092.9	389217.7
家用电器及电子产品专门零售	Special Retail of Household Electric Appliances and Electronic Products	69	749236.5	579993.4	29044.8
五金、家具及室内装饰材料专门零售	Special Retail of Hardware,Furniture and Decoration Materials	46	573684.0	407967.4	76689.5
货摊、无店铺及其他零售业	Non-shop and Other Retail	38	692143.0	670847.1	17009.3

continued 4

(10 000 yuan)

固定资产原价 Original Value of Fixed Assets	累计折旧 Accumulated Depreciation	负债合计 Total Liabilities	流动负债合计 Circulating Liabilities	非流动负债合计 Non-Circulating Liabilities	所有者权益合计 Total Owners' Equities	实收资本 Paid in Capital	营业收入 Total Revenue	主营业务收入 Revenue from Principal Business
754708.3	249914.9	3022067.0	2954397.2	68462.7	1196138.7	823839.6	8296934.0	8138271.5
84024.7	50394.5	273900.9	254261.7	19639.2	383376.7	352216.3	460764.9	443511.0
245846.4	84287.6	1505800.3	1344433.3	161475.5	519548.7	287225.3	4004438.5	3969816.3
1079.5	238.9	247.3	234.2	13.1	2375.6	657.8	18481.1	18480.1
229.9	111.2	1124.3	1017.8	106.5	-113.0	130.0	9759.1	9759.1
234273.7	79197.9	1445533.1	1285335.8	160305.8	497384.6	276117.5	3804195.3	3770809.3
10263.3	4739.6	58895.6	57845.5	1050.1	19901.5	10320.0	172003.0	170767.8
1492.6	382.3	1551.6	1024.8	526.8	2842.1	2203.1	8754.4	8754.4
185165.6	75287.7	1274038.4	1232208.5	41829.9	687109.2	248039.1	2343610.8	2280087.9
182501.7	63694.5	988971.5	950468.5	38503.1	421049.4	266542.2	3542686.4	3527247.4
632288.4	229310.5	2291283.3	2174303.9	116979.5	1262148.7	829608.0	3288031.4	3087196.0
61677.0	9378.2	135222.3	121020.5	14201.8	87958.8	90106.8	219627.3	214797.3
52659.1	27300.6	221964.2	219046.8	3025.9	202364.0	111763.6	616324.2	610216.2
101821.6	18702.4	290645.5	236588.4	54057.1	143216.0	79075.5	766623.1	762695.8
15434.5	6115.7	171967.4	171760.4	207.0	45844.4	24826.4	322900.4	313521.9
539147.8	189964.2	3010251.6	2915416.5	95644.6	997414.5	695442.2	8188720.7	8129345.0
52145.3	23333.4	367000.7	361338.9	5645.2	382235.8	79668.0	2582956.9	2568433.8
113720.0	49240.3	385560.6	337221.1	48339.5	188123.4	59926.3	1635011.9	1634894.9
23727.9	10274.3	634575.2	632793.0	1782.2	57567.8	42253.5	1999106.7	1999090.3

16-4 续表5

单位：万元

分　类	Classify	营业成本 Total Cost	主营业务成本 Cost of Principal Business	税金及附加 Taxs and Other Changes	主营业务税金及附加 Taxs and Other Changes on Principal Business
其他有限责任公司	Other Limited Liability Corporations	7223520.9	7207298.5	74528.2	74278.3
股份有限公司	Share-holding Corporations Ltd.	404636.9	404172.4	1723.9	1723.9
私营	Private Enterprises	3400782.9	3396795.0	47035.4	46498.1
私营独资	Private-funded Enterprises	17491.8	17466.8	128.8	128.8
私营合伙	Private Partnership Enterprises	8512.2	8512.2	26.3	26.3
私营有限责任公司	Private Limited Liability Corporations	3218230.7	3214274.4	46567.6	46030.6
私营股份有限公司	Private Share-holding Corporations Ltd.	156548.2	156541.6	312.7	312.4
其他	Other Enterprises	7976.0	7976.0	59.4	59.4
港澳台商投资	Enterprises with Funds from Hong Kong, Macao &Taiwan	1893403.2	1882279.3	14277.7	13980.6
外商投资	Foreign Funded Enterprises	3015480.1	3012292.9	15496.4	14764.2
2. 按国民经济行业分组	Grouped by Sector				
综合零售	Integrated Retail	2674307.3	2661185.1	23717.5	22645.4
食品、饮料及烟草制品专门零售	Food, Beverages and Tobaccos Special Retail Trade	183550.5	177651.1	1160.2	1157.1
纺织、服装及日用品专门零售	Special Retail of Textiles,Garments and Daily Consumer Articles	477060.9	476567.9	3001.1	3001.1
文化、体育用品及器材专门零售	Retail of Culture,Sports Appliances and Equipments	553293.6	552915.9	3829.9	3648.7
医药及医疗器材专门零售	Retail of Medicines and Medical Appliances	234516.0	233532.0	2841.1	2837.8
汽车、摩托车、燃料及零配件专门零售	Retail of Motor Vehicles,Motorcycles, Fuel and Parts	7443782.3	7430417.9	24392.2	23966.6
家用电器及电子产品专门零售	Special Retail of Household Electric Appliances and Electronic Products	2208344.7	2207348.8	42974.0	42853.0
五金、家具及室内装饰材料专门零售	Special Retail of Hardware,Furniture and Decoration Materials	1238188.3	1237981.6	48457.5	48437.6
货摊、无店铺及其他零售业	Non-shop and Other Retail	1792638.1	1792544.5	5423.6	5419.7

continued 5

(10 000 yuan)

销售费用 Sale Expenses	管理费用 Management Expenses	财务费用 Financial Expenses	营业利润 Business Profits	利润总额 Total Profits	应付职工薪酬 Salary Payable	所得税费用 Income Tax Expenses	应交增值税 Value Added Tax Payable
458380.3	224090.5	35746.9	282303.3	286770.1	224471.1	54192.6	117805.5
35839.5	18518.3	3169.8	3712.7	4720.0	25316.1	668.9	16588.5
216989.0	139938.1	27594.9	173115.2	175201.7	99994.0	21068.9	47809.4
343.8	269.5	14.0	183.9	184.4	366.2	27.4	81.8
743.7	391.0	0.2	85.8	91.4	560.5		75.5
210353.2	133825.3	27116.7	169108.1	170494.8	96728.0	21002.6	47375.0
5548.3	5452.3	464.0	3737.4	4431.1	2339.3	38.9	277.1
462.5	256.5	7.6	-7.9	-7.9	256.9	0.1	0.4
257686.5	88162.3	16673.3	111874.0	107292.8	88039.3	20258.1	15476.0
286668.1	57262.8	5038.8	163742.3	163618.0	70289.4	37257.9	61780.3
363401.1	168731.6	9667.3	97193.0	95715.2	190124.0	18801.3	
17516.5	12229.1	1938.2	3778.0	4699.5	18930.6	837.9	918.5
83046.3	22119.7	2313.2	31206.4	30388.5	35255.1	6131.7	12171.7
121601.7	41666.5	11759.3	33952.9	36697.7	28484.7	2181.8	3715.7
55707.5	13310.4	1613.7	15750.7	15258.0	29951.1	1598.9	7360.4
300669.7	141430.7	47012.4	229864.4	230584.2	174264.4	67349.7	93797.3
151370.6	74208.4	6205.9	100581.5	100163.8	38996.9	23382.3	48851.4
49579.1	62420.7	10833.4	226251.1	226732.2	13266.5	17788.5	28520.5
161284.4	24514.9	75.4	15132.3	17657.6	20558.3	-189.7	24338.5

16-5 限额以上住宿和餐饮企业财务状况（2017年）

单位：万元

分　类	Classify	单位数（个）Number (unit)	资产总计 Total Assets	流动资产合计 Circulating Funds	固定资产合计 Total Fixed Assets
总计	**Total**	**671**	**2830690.3**	**1067943.0**	**1237909.1**
一、住宿业	**Hotel Services**	**303**	**2065723.1**	**667201.5**	**1070538.5**
1.按登记注册类型分组	Grouped by Type of Registration				
内资	Domestic Funded Enterprises	288	1786077.1	552949.4	931207.1
国有	State-owned Enterprises	19	146719.3	26855.4	95579.2
集体	Collective-owned Enterprises	1	55.0	55.0	
股份合作	Cooperative Enterprises				
联营	Joint Ownership Enterprises				
国有联营	State Joint Ownership Enterprises				
集体联营	Collective Joint Ownership Enterprises				
国有与集体联营	Joint State-collective Enterprises				
其他联营	Others Joint Ownership Enterprises				
有限责任公司	Limited Liability Corporations	134	1272314.4	369176.5	738744.8
国有独资公司	State Sole Funded Corporations	8	142474.7	28385.5	100180.9
其他有限责任公司	Other Limited Liability Corporations	126	1129839.7	340791.0	638563.9
股份有限公司	Share-holding Corporations Ltd.	2	11352.9	665.0	10678.5
私营	Private Enterprises	132	355635.5	156197.5	86204.6
私营独资	Private-funded Enterprises	2	2057.1	1359.0	698.1
私营合伙	Private Partnership Enterprises				
私营有限责任公司	Private Limited Liability Corporations	128	353005.7	154440.8	85487.3
私营股份有限公司	Private Share-holding Corporations Ltd.	2	572.7	397.7	19.2
其他	Other Enterprises				
港澳台商投资	Enterprises with Funds from Hong Kong, Macao &Taiwan	6	161693.1	66208.6	75140.8
外商投资	Foreign Funded Enterprises	9	117952.9	48043.5	64190.6
2.按国民经济行业分组	Grouped by Sector				
旅游饭店	Tourist Hotel	182	1727476.5	568815.1	938686.8
一般旅馆	Normal Hotel	111	274045.0	91594.3	102904.8
其他住宿业	Others	10	64201.6	6792.1	28946.9

Finacial Status of Hotels and Catering Eenterprises above Designated Size（2017）

(10 000 yuan)

固定资产原价 Original Value of Fixed Assets	累计折旧 Accumulated Depreciation	负债合计 Total Liabilities	流动负债合计 Circulating Liabilities	非流动负债合计 Non-Circulating Liabilities	所有者权益合计 Total Owners' Equities	实收资本 Paid in Capital	营业收入 Total Revenue	主营业务收入 Revenue from Principal Business
2049499.9	**836355.9**	**2282080.3**	**1808125.9**	**473807.7**	**548610.0**	**1069594.1**	**1214557.8**	**1199171.7**
1753981.9	**699662.5**	**1707207.0**	**1285103.0**	**422104.0**	**358516.1**	**827122.2**	**572999.1**	**565777.7**
1461286.0	545270.0	1464466.7	1125107.9	339358.8	321610.4	664382.8	489841.7	484405.0
145805.9	53479.8	79870.4	48015.3	31855.1	66848.9	52381.0	39204.2	38189.4
					55.0	15.0	355.0	355.0
1127664.5	396900.1	1156403.5	893878.4	262525.1	115910.9	415647.3	308417.8	304689.5
169120.2	71471.2	179644.3	123865.9	55778.4	-37169.6	57520.7	38112.3	37412.4
958544.3	325428.9	976759.2	770012.5	206746.7	153080.5	358126.6	270305.5	267277.1
17283.6	6605.1	5919.7	5919.7		5433.2	5433.2	3291.2	3291.2
170532.0	88285.0	222273.1	177294.5	44978.6	133362.4	190906.3	138573.5	137879.9
1055.6	357.5	1451.9	1451.9		605.2	1500.0	981.5	981.5
169412.5	87882.8	220739.8	175779.7	44960.1	132265.9	188956.3	136856.4	136162.8
63.9	44.7	81.4	62.9	18.5	491.3	450.0	735.6	735.6
162362.9	87254.3	132447.1	101716.4	30730.7	29246.0	110715.5	34482.3	34467.5
130333.0	67138.2	110293.2	58278.7	52014.5	7659.7	52023.9	48675.1	46905.2
1592320.4	664034.5	1516951.4	1100483.7	416467.7	210525.1	676494.0	452354.8	446690.1
124887.6	27791.0	162601.2	156964.9	5636.3	111443.8	138248.2	99624.5	98442.7
36773.9	7837.0	27654.4	27654.4		36547.2	12380.0	21019.8	20644.9

16-5 续表1

单位：万元

分 类	Classify	营业成本 Total Cost	主营业务成本 Cost of Principal Business
总计	**Total**	**532760.4**	**528209.4**
一、住宿业	**Hotel Services**	**215778.7**	**213863.2**
1.按登记注册类型分组	Grouped by Type of Registration		
内资	Domestic Funded Enterprises	186368.4	184911.9
国有	State-owned Enterprises	13105.7	12977.1
集体	Collective-owned Enterprises	280.0	280.0
股份合作	Cooperative Enterprises		
联营	Joint Ownership Enterprises		
国有联营	State Joint Ownership Enterprises		
集体联营	Collective Joint Ownership Enterprises		
国有与集体联营	Joint State-collective Enterprises		
其他联营	Others Joint Ownership Enterprises		
有限责任公司	Limited Liability Corporations	122953.4	122420.9
国有独资公司	State Sole Funded Corporations	11896.4	11896.4
其他有限责任公司	Other Limited Liability Corporations	111057.0	110524.5
股份有限公司	Share-holding Corporations Ltd.	1894.2	1894.2
私营	Private Enterprises	48135.1	47339.7
私营独资	Private-funded Enterprises	361.6	361.6
私营合伙	Private Partnership Enterprises		
私营有限责任公司	Private Limited Liability Corporations	47119.9	46324.5
私营股份有限公司	Private Share-holding Corporations Ltd.	653.6	653.6
其他	Other Enterprises		
港澳台商投资	Enterprises with Funds from Hong Kong, Macao &Taiwan	12936.9	12936.9
外商投资	Foreign Funded Enterprises	16473.4	16014.4
2.按国民经济行业分组	Grouped by Sector		
旅游饭店	Tourist Hotel	171764.3	170375.9
一般旅馆	Normal Hotel	39993.7	39466.6
其他住宿业	Others	4020.7	4020.7

continued 1

(10 000 yuan)

税金及附加 Taxs and Other Changes	主营业务税金及附加 Taxs and Other Changes on Principal Business	销售费用 Sale Expenses	管理费用 Management Expenses	财务费用 Financial Expenses	营业利润 Business Profits	利润总额 Total Profits	应付职工薪酬 Salary Payable	所得税费用 Income Tax Expenses	应交增值税 Value Added Tax Payable
16386.8	**15399.7**	**403482.3**	**261489.7**	**22915.3**	**-22645.7**	**-21547.6**	**313746.6**	**9565.3**	**25063.9**
10443.3	**9554.1**	**179161.6**	**180761.9**	**16956.7**	**-30370.0**	**-30436.5**	**160797.3**	**3896.0**	**15746.3**
8366.8	8009.3	155723.9	158017.5	15735.0	-34660.0	-34613.3	139055.4	1666.2	12838.3
630.1	589.7	11645.1	11291.1	1674.2	820.7	-906.9	14101.9	169.1	1195.3
5.5	5.5	40.0	31.8	0.2	-2.5	-2.5	84.0		10.6
6222.9	5923.0	98200.5	101984.4	9372.5	-30853.3	-30316.7	91224.9	918.7	8100.0
748.6	748.6	12024.7	12370.4	957.2	-12.8	-3.3	10559.4		331.0
5474.3	5174.4	86175.8	89614.0	8415.3	-30840.5	-30313.4	80665.5	918.7	7769.0
229.3	229.3	1007.4	85.4	1.7	77.1	85.2	1526.0		135.6
1279.0	1261.8	44830.9	44624.8	4686.4	-4702.0	-3472.4	32118.6	578.4	3396.8
15.6	15.6	560.8	182.9	0.4	-139.9	-139.9	326.1		7.4
1258.5	1241.3	44266.5	44411.5	4685.6	-4604.8	-3374.5	31618.8	574.2	3372.3
4.9	4.9	3.6	30.4	0.4	42.7	42.0	173.7	4.2	17.1
1016.8	1016.8	10286.9	11001.9	1466.5	-2191.3	-2127.3	10538.9	226.0	1833.6
1059.7	528.0	13150.8	11742.5	-244.8	6481.3	6304.1	11203.0	2003.8	1074.4
9110.2	8281.0	139677.9	142846.9	16043.1	-27342.9	-27542.0	133812.8	3611.3	12847.3
1045.0	1030.1	31639.2	27464.2	666.9	-1045.8	-991.3	23375.2	321.4	2556.5
288.1	243.0	7844.5	10450.8	246.7	-1981.3	-1903.2	3609.3	-36.7	342.5

16-5 续表2

单位：万元

分 类	Classify	单位数（个） Number (unit)	资产总计 Total Assets	流动资产合 计 Circulating Funds	固定资产合 计 Total Fixed Assets
二、餐饮业	**Catering Trade**	**368**	**764967.2**	**400741.5**	**167370.6**
1.按登记注册类型分组	Grouped by Type of Registration				
内资	Domestic Funded Enterprises	356	686166.1	370242.9	147002.6
国有	State-owned Enterprises	3	4807.5	1507.3	3141.2
集体	Collective-owned Enterprises				
股份合作	Cooperative Enterprises				
联营	Joint Ownership Enterprises				
国有联营	State Joint Ownership Enterprises				
集体联营	Collective Joint Ownership Enterprises				
国有与集体联营	Joint State-collective Enterprises				
其他联营	Others Joint Ownership Enterprises				
有限责任公司	Limited Liability Corporations	138	298712.4	172572.0	78817.9
国有独资公司	State Sole Funded Corporations	2	11430.5	3335.9	7777.4
其他有限责任公司	Other Limited Liability Corporations	136	287281.9	169236.1	71040.5
股份有限公司	Share-holding Corporations Ltd.	5	172917.3	84679.7	24424.5
私营	Private Enterprises	208	209430.8	111283.1	40521.7
私营独资	Private-funded Enterprises	13	4091.7	1926.7	1452.4
私营合伙	Private Partnership Enterprises				
私营有限责任公司	Private Limited Liability Corporations	192	204766.5	108923.7	39050.0
私营股份有限公司	Private Share-holding Corporations Ltd.	3	572.6	432.7	19.3
其他	Other Enterprises	2	298.1	200.8	97.3
港澳台商投资	Enterprises with Funds from Hong Kong, Macao &Taiwan	7	24221.3	7594.8	8362.3
外商投资	Foreign Funded Enterprises	5	54579.8	22903.8	12005.7
2.按国民经济行业分	Grouped by Sdctor				
正餐服务	Dinner	355	677915.9	369226.1	141365.9
快餐服务	Fast Food	10	77038.6	27998.5	23296.4
饮料及冷饮服务	Beverages and Cold Drinks	1			
其他餐饮业	Other Catering Services	2	10012.7	3516.9	2708.3

continued 2

(10 000 yuan)

固定资产原价 Original Value of Fixed Assets	累计折旧 Accumulated Depreciation	负债合计 Total Liabilities	流动负债合计 Circulating Liabilities	非流动负债合计 Non-Circulating Liabilities	所有者权益合计 Total Owners' Equities	实收资本 Paid in Capital	营业收入 Total Revenue	主营业务收入 Revenue from Principal Business
295518.0	**136693.4**	**574873.3**	**523022.9**	**51703.7**	**190093.9**	**242471.9**	**641558.7**	**633394.0**
254907.4	116279.1	520168.2	479747.3	40274.2	165997.9	222393.3	493124.9	491013.4
4608.1	1466.9	3387.2	762.9	2624.3	1420.3	2067.0	7222.4	7222.4
131214.4	56767.4	277585.3	264419.7	13018.9	21127.1	83425.8	182144.0	180917.9
12832.7	5055.3	8251.9	7924.3	327.6	3178.6	3923.2	6293.9	6160.6
118381.7	51712.1	269333.4	256495.4	12691.3	17948.5	79502.6	175850.1	174757.3
41107.5	17022.3	66540.2	51550.4	14989.8	106377.1	60445.6	80743.0	80630.7
77507.2	40639.3	171614.3	161973.1	9641.2	37816.5	76359.0	222252.6	221479.5
2218.9	784.6	3174.7	3167.3	7.4	917.0	1729.4	6249.7	6216.9
75090.9	39676.5	168073.8	158440.0	9633.8	36692.7	74379.6	214387.5	213647.2
197.4	178.2	365.8	365.8		206.8	250.0	1615.4	1615.4
470.2	383.2	1041.2	1041.2		-743.1	95.9	762.9	762.9
15178.3	6981.4	28901.3	23763.7	5137.6	-4680.0	11931.0	38337.2	38337.2
25432.3	13432.9	25803.8	19511.9	6291.9	28776.0	8147.6	110096.6	104043.4
251399.7	118076.3	527876.5	484037.4	43692.4	150039.4	220772.7	493882.2	491586.5
41194.6	18059.8	41895.3	34024.0	7871.3	35143.3	16635.8	144327.4	138458.4
2923.7	557.3	5101.5	4961.5	140.0	4911.2	5063.4	3349.1	3349.1

16-5 续表3

单位：万元

分 类	Classify	营业成本 Total Cost	主营业务成本 Cost of Principal Business
二、餐饮业	**Catering Trade**	**316981.7**	**314346.2**
1.按登记注册类型分组	Grouped by Type of Registration		
内资	Domestic Funded Enterprises	249665.5	248765.4
国有	State-owned Enterprises	5942.2	5942.2
集体	Collective-owned Enterprises		
股份合作	Cooperative Enterprises		
联营	Joint Ownership Enterprises		
国有联营	State Joint Ownership Enterprises		
集体联营	Collective Joint Ownership Enterprises		
国有与集体联营	Joint State-collective Enterprises		
其他联营	Others Joint Ownership Enterprises		
有限责任公司	Limited Liability Corporations	90790.5	90165.3
国有独资公司	State Sole Funded Corporations	2551.9	2447.6
其他有限责任公司	Other Limited Liability Corporations	88238.6	87717.7
股份有限公司	Share-holding Corporations Ltd.	37713.7	37713.7
私营	Private Enterprises	114828.9	114554.0
私营独资	Private-funded Enterprises	3943.8	3938.4
私营合伙	Private Partnership Enterprises		
私营有限责任公司	Private Limited Liability Corporations	110139.4	109869.9
私营股份有限公司	Private Share-holding Corporations Ltd.	745.7	745.7
其他	Other Enterprises	390.2	390.2
港澳台商投资	Enterprises with Funds from Hong Kong, Macao &Taiwan	16986.4	16963.3
外商投资	Foreign Funded Enterprises	50329.8	48617.5
2.按国民经济行业分	Grouped by Sdctor		
正餐服务	Dinner	246060.1	245086.3
快餐服务	Fast Food	68874.0	67212.3
饮料及冷饮服务	Beverages and Cold Drinks		
其他餐饮业	Other Catering Services	2047.6	2047.6

continued 3

(10 000 yuan)

税金及附加 Taxs and Other Changes	主营业务税金及附加 Taxs and Other Changes on Principal Business	销售费用 Sale Expenses	管理费用 Management Expenses	财务费用 Financial Expenses	营业利润 Business Profits	利润总额 Total Profits	应付职工薪酬 Salary Payable	所得税费用 Income Tax Expenses	应交增值税 Value Added Tax Payable
5943.5	**5845.6**	**224320.7**	**80727.8**	**5958.6**	**7724.3**	**8888.9**	**152949.3**	**5669.3**	**9317.6**
5699.4	5620.6	171507.9	63457.3	5586.3	-2259.5	-720.2	126210.6	3206.8	8096.3
354.3	354.3	934.8	239.4	2.4	-250.7	-146.7	704.6		372.9
1859.1	1859.0	63188.5	29895.9	3413.1	-7044.3	-6850.8	46406.0	851.2	1680.4
110.1	110.1	1267.3	2521.2	191.2	-347.8	-353.6	2692.7		176.0
1749.0	1748.9	61921.2	27374.7	3221.9	-6696.5	-6497.2	43713.3	851.2	1504.4
580.6	580.6	30616.1	6839.0	363.9	5213.7	5703.1	25240.7	988.3	832.3
2899.4	2820.7	76389.2	26472.9	1805.6	-154.2	598.2	53536.3	1367.3	5188.7
132.1	122.2	1320.6	689.5	17.3	146.4	161.4	1513.9	20.5	136.3
2759.1	2690.3	74332.3	25676.7	1785.7	-316.5	420.9	51637.4	1346.8	4997.6
8.2	8.2	736.3	106.7	2.6	15.9	15.9	385.0		54.8
6.0	6.0	379.3	10.1	1.3	-24.0	-24.0	323.0		22.0
73.9	73.9	18558.3	2406.7	423.9	-106.9	-332.2	6804.4		779.4
170.2	151.1	34254.5	14863.8	-51.6	10090.7	9941.3	19934.3	2462.5	441.9
5652.3	5573.5	177677.4	63202.7	5561.7	-3734.9	-2217.6	128355.5	2965.1	9533.1
264.9	245.8	46355.5	17097.2	386.4	10910.2	10557.5	24453.2	2472.6	1298.0
26.3	26.3	287.8	427.9	10.5	549.0	549.0	140.6	231.6	-1513.5

16-6 限额以上批发零售贸易业商品购进、销售、库存总额（2017年）

单位：个、万元

分 类	Classify	单位数 Number of Enterprises	商品购进额 Total Purchases	进口 Imports
总计	**Total**	**1288**	**64684429.9**	**734851.0**
一、批发企业	**Wholesale Enterprises**	**521**	**45988718.2**	**248972.3**
1.按登记注册类型分组	Grouped by Type of Registration			
内资企业	Domestic Funded Enterprises	504	40494862.2	225540.4
国有	State-owned Enterprises	21	2264945.3	641.7
集体	Collective-owned Enterprises	3	48086.3	
股份合作	Cooperative Enterprises			
联营	Joint Ownership Enterprises			
国有联营	State Joint Ownership Enterprises			
集体联营	Collective Joint Ownership Enterprises			
国有与集体联营	Joint State-collective Enterprises			
其他联营	Others Joint Ownership Enterprises			
有限责任公司	Limited Liability Corporations	260	23751857.4	136270.9
国有独资公司	State Sole Funded Corporations	15	4964064.8	2944.3
其他有限责任公司	Other Limited Liability Corporations	245	18787792.6	133326.6
股份有限公司	Share-holding Corporations Ltd.	18	9311503.7	
私营	Private Enterprises	199	5106069.5	88627.8
私营独资	Private-funded Enterprises	1	4804.8	
私营合伙	Private Partnership Enterprises			
私营有限责任公司	Private Limited Liability Corporations	192	4520019.3	88627.8
私营股份有限公司	Private Share-holding Corporations Ltd.	6	581245.4	
其他	Other Enterprises	3	12400.0	
港澳台商投资	Enterprises with Funds from Hong Kong, Macao &Taiwan	4	134304.8	
外商投资	Foreign Funded Enterprises	13	5359551.2	23431.9
个体经营户	Individusl Enterprises			
2.按国民经济行业分组	Grouped by Economic Sector			
农、林、牧产品批发	Wholesale of Agricultural,Forestry and Animal Husbandry Products	4	35665.5	

Total Purchases,Sales and Inventories of Wholesale and Retail Enterprises above Designated Size（2017）

(unit，10 000 yuan)

商品销售额 Sales Value	公共网络商品销售额 Public Network Sales	银行卡支付商品销售额 Bank Card Paid Sales	批发额 Wholesale Trade	出口 Exports	零售额 Retail Trade	期末商品库存额 Value of Stock at Final goods
73486810.1	**8468962.9**	**5882683.4**	**47630423.2**	**786397.2**	**25856386.9**	**3148171.2**
50546632.6	**5709785.1**	**1848708.3**	**46649546.3**	**757257.9**	**3897086.3**	**1334181.4**
44729137.0	5709600.1	1822139.4	40917821.1	757257.9	3811315.9	1242475.1
2919104.5	1788748.9	1346451.6	2812094.0	25550.7	107010.5	88242.4
47188.6		11293.5	42819.3		4369.3	2270.3
26073238.4	586177.5	294838.8	23622110.9	413582.4	2451127.5	695027.9
5397018.6			4604831.5	20740.1	792187.1	70781.6
20676219.8	586177.5	294838.8	19017279.4	392842.3	1658940.4	624246.3
9834132.7	3247380.1	26781.8	8846295.9	220681.8	987836.8	93796.5
5838005.8	87293.6	142773.7	5578695.1	97443.0	259310.7	363042.0
5876.8			5876.8			407.9
5244777.7	87293.6	120878.0	5059263.8	97443.0	185513.9	345910.2
587351.3		21895.7	513554.5		73796.8	16723.9
17467.0			15805.9		1661.1	96.0
184812.5		3224.6	102879.6		81932.9	32737.4
5632683.1	185.0	23344.3	5628845.6		3837.5	58968.9
41557.1			39669.6		1887.5	2436.8

16-6 续表1

单位：个、万元

分　类	Classify	单位数 Number of Enterprises	商品购进额 Total Purchases	进口 Imports
食品、饮料及烟草制品批发	Wholesale of Food, Beverages and Tobacco Products	61	2516341.8	9112.3
纺织、服装及家庭服务器批发	Wholesale of Textiles, Garments and Daily Articles	31	3953968.1	
文化、体育用品及器材批发	Wholesale of Culture, Sports Articles and Equipments	31	498161.2	
医药及医疗器材批发	Wholesale of Medicines and Medical Appliances	105	3497966.6	11736.3
矿产品、建材及化工产品批发	Wholesale of Mineral Products, Building Materials and Chemical Products	177	33529792.8	144818.0
机械设备、五金产品及电子产品批发	Wholesale of Machinery, Hardwares, Transport Means and Electronic Products	104	1912492.9	82659.0
贸易经纪与代理	Trade Manage and Agent	2	31811.3	641.7
其他批发	Other Wholesales	6	12518.0	5.0
3.按经营形式分组	Grouped by Means of Operation			
独立门店	Independent Shop	364	27862110.8	166703.0
连锁总店	Headquarter of Chain Store	2	110579.9	
连锁门店	Chain Store			
其他	Other	155	18016027.5	82269.3
二、零售企业	**Retail Trade**	**767**	**18695711.7**	**485878.7**
1.按登记注册类型分组	Grouped by Registration Status			
内资	Domestic Funded Enterprises	697	12646710.3	313205.0
国有	State-owned Enterprises	10	801918.9	
集体	Collective-owned Enterprises	17	30331.1	
股份合作	Cooperative Enterprises			
联营	Joint Ownership Enterprises			
国有联营	State Joint Ownership Enterprises			
集体联营	Collective Joint Ownership Enterprises			
国有与集体联营	Joint State-collective Enterprises			

continued 1

(unit，10 000 yuan)

商品销售额 Sales Value	公共网络商品销售额 Public Network Sales	银行卡支付商品销售额 Bank Card Paid Sales	批发额 Wholesale Trade	出口 Exports	零售额 Retail Trade	期末商品库存额 Value of Stock at Final goods
3388189.2	1321110.3	1356359.1	3139640.6	7032.5	248548.6	135114.1
4074778.0	424546.5	127019.6	2755106.8	164339.4	1319671.2	157206.4
575196.5	9565.7	927.5	560024.0	7756.4	15172.5	53058.4
4344415.9	49156.5	135053.8	4034130.0	3732.8	310285.9	337519.8
35972369.6	3861899.5	131431.8	34054621.4	54445.1	1917748.2	510640.7
2097478.3	43506.6	71458.5	2013955.9	494401.0	83522.4	130598.9
36480.0		26458.0	36230.0	25550.7	250.0	5652.9
16168.0			16168.0			1953.4
30779593.3	651940.5	290869.1	27180662.5	485066.7	3598930.8	776488.8
108009.0			31489.0		76520.0	3379.0
19659030.3	5057844.6	1557839.2	19437394.8	272191.2	221635.5	553853.5
22940177.5	**2759177.8**	**4033975.1**	**980876.9**	**29139.3**	**21959300.6**	**1813989.8**
15680007.4	602276.1	3239531.6	717710.2	29139.3	14962297.2	1393855.6
857755.2	99.1	520284.0	122959.4		734795.8	155678.8
31919.2		1179.1	1648.9		30270.3	1843.1

16-6 续表2

单位：个、万元

分类	Classify	单位数 Number of Enterprises	商品购进额 Total Purchases	进口 Imports
其他联营	Others Joint Ownership Enterprises			
有限责任公司	Limited Liability Corporations	339	7508847.9	178986.8
国有独资公司	State Sole Funded Corporations	9	197361.4	5268.4
其他有限责任公司	Other Limited Liability Corporations	330	7311486.5	173718.4
股份有限公司	Share-holding Corporations Ltd.	12	428663.1	32407.4
私营	Private Enterprises	315	3871630.6	101810.8
私营独资	Private-funded Enterprises	6	20634.1	
私营合伙	Private Partnership Enterprises	2	10468.6	
私营有限责任公司	Private Limited Liability Corporations	298	3660965.9	69063.9
私营股份有限公司	Private Share-holding Corporations Ltd.	9	179562.0	32746.9
其他	Other Enterprises	4	5318.7	
港澳台商投资	Enterprises with Funds from Hong Kong, Macao &Taiwan	29	2029374.6	172673.7
外商投资	Foreign Funded Enterprises	19	3479745.9	
个体经营户	Individusl Enterprises	22	539880.9	
2.按国民经济行业分组	Grouped by Registered Kind			
综合零售	General Retail Sales Trade	121	2635551.8	859.5
食品、饮料及烟草制品专门零售	Retail of Food, Beverage and Tobaccos	67	223157.3	451.5
纺织、服装及日用品专门零售	Retail of Textiles, Garments and Daily Articles	54	509132.7	1127.6
文化、体育用品及器材专门零售	Retail of Culture, Sports Articles and Equipments	39	650360.8	5268.4
医药及医疗器材专门零售	Retail of Medicines and Medical Appliances	32	306554.8	
汽车、摩托车、燃料及零配件专门零售	Retail of Motor Vehicles, Motorcycles, Feuls and Parts	292	8273241.4	469835.2
家用电器及电子产品	Retail of Household Electronic Equipments	72	2441418.3	2852.0

continued 2

(unit，10 000 yuan)

商品销售额			批发额		零售额	期末商品库存额
	公共网络商品销售额	银行卡支付商品销售额		出口		Value of
Sales Value	Public Network Sales	Bank Card Paid Sales	Wholesale Trade	Exports	Retail Trade	Stock at Final goods
9718895.4	253666.0	1863876.4	383593.5	28913.3	9335301.9	861095.1
202474.9		28638.3	2658.4	275.3	199816.5	47784.2
9516420.5	253666.0	1835238.1	380935.1	28638.0	9135485.4	813310.9
583861.6	59374.1	107289.6			583861.6	30032.4
4478803.5	289136.9	746902.5	209096.4	226.0	4269707.1	344988.5
20939.8	315.1	1071.8			20939.8	484.7
10823.5					10823.5	611.8
4260809.6	282773.8	688190.0	203694.6	226.0	4057115.0	324378.1
186230.6	6048.0	57640.7	5401.8		180828.8	19513.9
8772.5			412.0		8360.5	217.7
2634751.8	53466.3	750892.7	200945.5		2433806.3	323995.4
4092333.3	2103435.4	43550.8	41504.9		4050828.4	84182.1
533085.0			20716.3		512368.7	11956.7
4030428.2	13700.1	569328.3	9879.1		4020549.1	227932.9
260391.6	11083.1	51600.1	58389.3		202002.3	33528.8
763512.5	62324.0	27971.8	35408.0		728104.5	118310.7
911683.0	2053.6	157890.9	254069.1	275.3	657613.9	207264.4
333057.5	3224.1	4314.8	16244.2		316813.3	51654.6
9286743.5	233054.4	2158889.6	285854.5		9000889.0	1001381.5
3158223.3	216396.0	274480.9	221869.9		2936353.4	124958.6

16-6 续表3

单位：个、万元

分　类	Classify	单位数 Number of Enterprises	商品购进额 Total Purchases	进口 Imports
专门零售	and Products			
五金、家具及室内装饰材料	retail of Hardwares, Furniture and Room	52	1632796.8	5096.6
专门零售	Decorative Building			
货摊、无店铺及其他零售业	No Fixed Stores and Other Retails	38	2023497.8	387.9
3.按经营形式分组	Grouped by Means of Operation			
独立门店	Independent Shop	639	13731355.7	485217.7
连锁总店	Headquarter of Chain Store	33	810554.1	
连锁门店	Chain Store	8	121085.8	273.1
其他	Other	87	4032716.1	387.9
4.按零售业态分组	Grouped by Retail Size			
有店铺	Retail of Shop	708	16417602.5	479942.7
食杂店	Grocery Store	2	3942.7	
便利店	Convenience Store	10	74830.0	
折扣店	Dime Store			
超市	Supermarket	60	299611.9	436.4
大型超市	Larget Supermarket	15	939010.6	
仓储会员店	Warehouse Club	4	7069.1	
百货店	Department Store	62	1516811.3	423.1
专业店	Special Store	274	5541639.9	252216.4
专卖店	Monopoly Store	230	5062077.8	226866.8
家居建材商店	Home-building Material Store	24	1276193.5	
购物中心	Shopping Center	9	1526958.7	
厂家直销中心	Factory Outlet Center	18	169457.0	
无店铺零售	Retail of No-shop	59	2278109.2	5936.0
电视购物	TV Shopping	1	49479.0	
邮购	Mail Order	1	813.6	451.5
网上商店	Online Stores	34	2013343.0	387.9
自动售货亭	Vending Machine			
电话购物	Tele Shopping			

continued 3

(unit, 10 000 yuan)

商品销售额 Sales Value	公共网络商品销售额 Public Network Sales	银行卡支付商品销售额 Bank Card Paid Sales	批发额 Wholesale Trade	出口 Exports	零售额 Retail Trade	期末商品库存额 Value of Stock at Final goods
1893339.0	9083.5	725055.7	78641.0	28638.0	1814698.0	37852.5
2302798.9	2208259.0	64443.0	20521.8	226.0	2282277.1	11105.8
16738948.9	451343.2	3223942.0	538338.7	28913.3	16200610.2	1375122.8
1115034.9	57741.3	83205.5	21817.7		1093217.2	118150.6
557294.2	12769.3	271076.4	35096.2		522198.0	18504.8
4528899.5	2237324.0	455751.2	385624.3	226.0	4143275.2	302211.6
20359687.7	480592.0	3964146.8	865893.6	275.3	19493794.1	1780650.9
5338.4					5338.4	95.5
84386.7		8690.6	9266.3		75120.4	6164.0
358208.4	2128.4	47367.2	31492.8		326715.6	57781.5
1384361.3	3296.8	192892.0			1384361.3	122101.2
8730.7					8730.7	702.9
2430715.0	11724.4	375852.4	4975.9		2425739.1	58800.4
6778491.0	278968.8	1451096.3	287254.3	275.3	6491236.7	603866.8
5868398.8	171610.9	1169268.4	397033.3		5471365.5	846500.6
1524125.2	4862.7	717320.2	1550.9		1522574.3	21630.1
1728668.7		759.7	92075.4		1636593.3	45969.1
188263.5	8000.0	900.0	42244.7		146018.8	17038.8
2580489.8	2278585.8	69828.3	114983.3	28864.0	2465506.5	33338.9
55637.8		53844.0			55637.8	1041.2
1162.1	713.9		365.3		796.8	714.3
2293310.4	2266108.9	8952.4	24714.4	226.0	2268596.0	11774.6

16-7 限额以上住宿和餐饮业经营情况（2017年）

单位：个、万元

分 类	Classify	单位数 Number of Enterprises	营业额 Business Revenue	银行卡支付营业额 Bank Card Paid Turnover
总计	**Total**	**716**	**1423905.5**	**249822.5**
一、住宿业	**Lodging Services**	**319**	**680430.7**	**140883.6**
1. 按国民经济行业分组	Grouped by Economic Sector			
旅游饭店	Tour Restaurant	193	542606.0	113471.7
一般旅馆	Common Hotel	116	116143.1	24599.3
其他住宿业	Others	10	21681.6	2812.6
2. 按登记注册类型分组	Grouped by Registration Status			
内资企业	Domestic Funded Enterprises	301	576096.3	119280.6
国有	State-owned Enterprises	25	57685.3	11920.0
集体	Collective-owned Enterprises	1	385.0	
股份合作	Cooperative Enterprises			
联营	Joint Ownership Enterprises			
国有联营	State Joint Ownership Enterprises			
集体联营	Collective Joint Ownership Enterprises			
国有与集体联营	Joint State-collective Ownership Enterprises			
其他联营	Other Joint Ownership Enterprises			
有限责任公司	Limited Liability Corporations	138	350190.8	70195.6
国有独资公司	State-funded Corporations	8	38730.7	18637.9
其他有限责任公司	Other Limited Liability Corporations	130	311460.1	51557.7
股份有限公司	Stock Limited Corporation	4	19215.0	489.5
私营	Private Enterprises	133	148620.2	36675.5
私营独资	Private-funded Enterprises	2	995.3	
私营合伙	Private Partnership Enterprises			
私营有限责任公司	Private Limited Liability Corporations	129	146867.0	36640.7
私营股份有限公司	Private Share Holding Corporations	2	757.9	34.8
其他	Others			
港澳台商投资	Enterprises Funded by Hong Kong, Macao and Taiwan	7	52104.2	12138.2
外商投资	Foreign Funded Enterprises	9	51395.8	9464.8
个体经营	Individual Enterprises	2	834.4	

Statistic on Hotel Services and Catering Services above Designed Size (2017)

(unit, 10 000 yuan)

客房收入 From Hotel Room	公共网络客房收入 Public Network Room Revenue	餐费收入 From Meals	公共网络餐费收入 Public Network Catering Revenue	商品销售收入 From Commodities
409373.0	**54886.6**	**887598.2**	**27153.5**	**48315.9**
366469.1	**48682.5**	**245611.9**	**3930.4**	**15912.0**
277637.8	37371.6	202901.3	3502.7	13917.6
77611.3	11299.4	33132.7	427.7	1871.9
11220.0	11.5	9577.9		122.5
311971.5	39299.3	209385.0	3348.5	14597.0
25448.2	2041.1	25781.9	23.8	1840.6
139.5		146.3		99.2
175353.6	14625.3	140755.0	1579.2	4979.9
18308.1	1810.3	18159.2	88.3	512.6
157045.5	12815.0	122595.8	1490.9	4467.3
5739.7	21.9	4714.8	0.5	6619.8
105290.5	22611.0	37987.0	1745.0	1057.5
368.4		215.3		34.7
104173.6	22079.1	37762.3	1745.0	1022.8
748.5	531.9	9.4		
24047.1	3068.6	17999.1	296.3	850.2
29656.2	6314.6	18187.7	285.6	464.8
794.3		40.1		

16-7 续表1

单位：个、万元

分类	Classify	单位数 Number of Enterprises	营业额 Business Revenue	银行卡支付营业额 Bank Card Paid Turnover
二、餐饮业	**Catering Trade**	**397**	**743474.8**	**108938.9**
1. 按国民经济行业分	Grouped by Economic Sector			
正餐服务	Dinner Services	384	587396.7	108938.9
快餐服务	Fast Food Services	10	152486.2	
其他餐饮业	Other Catering Services	3	3591.9	
2. 按登记注册类型分	Grouped by Registration Status			
内资	Domestic Funded Enterprises	364	563981.7	105330.1
国有	State-owned Enterprises	4	10313.9	365.7
集体	Collective-owned Enterprises			
股份合作	Cooperative Enterprises			
联营	Joint Ownership Enterprises			
国有联营	State Joint Ownership Enterprises			
集体联营	Collective Joint Ownership Enterprises			
国有与集体联营	Joint State-collective Ownership Enterprises			
其他联营	Other Joint Ownership Enterprises			
有限责任公司	Limited Liability Corporations	144	223558.7	37836.0
国有独资公司	State-funded Corporations	2	6686.3	2496.6
其他有限责任公司	Other Limited Liability Corporations	142	216872.4	35339.4
股份有限公司	Stock Limited Corporation	5	85829.6	33311.3
私营	Private Enterprises	208	233079.2	33817.1
私营独资	Private-funded Enterprises	13	6537.4	479.1
私营合伙	Private Partnership Enterprises			
私营有限责任公司	Private Limited Liability Corporations	192	224860.2	33338.0
私营股份有限公司	Private Share Holding Corporations	3	1681.6	
其他	Others	3	11200.3	
港澳台商投资	Enterprises Funded by Hong Kong, Macao and Taiwan	7	39737.2	1387.1
外商投资	Foreign Funded Enterprises	5	116626.5	2179.8
个体经营	Individual Enterprises	21	23129.4	41.9

continued 1

(unit, 10 000 yuan)

客房收入 From Hotel Room	公共网络客房收入 Public Network Room Revenue	餐费收入 From Meals	公共网络餐费收入 Public Network Catering Revenue	商品销售收入 From Commodities
42903.9	**6204.1**	**641986.3**	**23223.1**	**32403.9**
42903.9	6204.1	492624.5	21680.3	31878.0
		146037.4	1542.8	258.4
		3324.4		267.5
42465.3	6204.1	471954.4	20882.1	30470.2
1084.0		6813.1		1449.8
28344.8	4782.3	178840.1	4434.6	6360.1
461.1		5168.6	121.1	912.8
27883.7	4782.3	173671.5	4313.5	5447.3
3554.8	1043.8	58932.7	5462.4	17856.5
3722.7	378.0	222319.7	10985.1	4757.3
		6378.1	217.3	159.3
3722.7	378.0	214303.0	10767.8	4555.0
		1638.6		43.0
5759.0		5048.8		46.5
393.5		38335.9	1206.7	186.9
		110254.8	1130.0	103.7
45.1		21441.2	4.3	1643.1

16-8 限额以上批发和零售业主要商品分类销售额（2017年）

Sale Values of Wholesale and Retail Enterprises above Designated Size by Category of Main Commodities (2017)

单位：万元 (10 000 yuan)

分类	Classify	销售合计 Total Sales Value	批发 Wholesale Value	零售 Retail Value
总计	**Total**	**68188477.4**	**43820458.9**	**24368018.5**
其中：通过公共网络实现的商品销售	Sales Achieved through the Public Network	3749920.9	1344410.9	2405510.0
粮油、食品类	Cereals, Oils and Foodstuffs	2731554.1	1513732.8	1217821.3
粮油类	Grain and Oil	532930.5	90514.6	442415.9
肉禽蛋类	Meat, Poultry and Eggs	243043.2	43501.3	199541.9
水产品类	Aquatic Products	52010.7	28213.7	23797.0
蔬菜类	Vegetables	844857.0	786951.9	57905.1
干鲜果品类	Fresh and Dried Fruit Category	659343.9	506033.9	153310.0
饮料类	Beverages	510141.5	193516.8	316624.7
烟酒类	Tobacco and Liquor	1967568.3	1644007.1	323561.2
服装、鞋帽、针、纺织品类	Clothing, Shoes, Hats and Textiles	6403014.3	3133403.7	3269610.6
#服装类	Clothing	5488838.1	2989592.7	2499245.4
鞋帽类	Shoes and Hats	610482.5	123595.9	486886.6
针、纺织品类	Knitwear and Textiles	303693.7	20215.1	283478.6
化妆品类	Cosmetics	486145.3	40060.7	446084.6
金银珠宝类	Gold,Silver and Jewelry	600890.3	202245.9	398644.4
日用品类	Articles for Daily Use	873687.0	111716.7	761970.3
#儿童玩具类	Children's Toys	99488.7		99488.7
五金、电料类	Hardwear and Electrical Materials	312758.2	100210.8	212547.4
体育、娱乐用品类	Sports and Recreation Articles	908362.0	13062.1	895299.9
#照相器材类	Photography Equipment	94452.7		94452.7
书报杂志类	Newspapers and Magazines	286006.8	165674.5	120332.3
电子出版物及音像制品类	E-journal and Video Products	67070.8		67070.8
家用电器和音像器材类	Household Appliances and Video Products	2449529.9	649628.5	1799901.4
中西药品类	Traditional Chinese and Western Medicine	3923116.2	3600318.7	322797.5
#西药	Western Medicine	3114365.8	2891862.8	222503.0
中草药及中成药	Chinese Herbal Medicine and Traditional Chinese Medicine	227161.6	168381.0	58780.6
文化办公用品类	Cultural and Official Goods	1053597.6	242634.3	810963.3
#计算机及其配套产品	Among Them: Computers and Ancillary Products	342957.7	119336.7	223621.0
家具类	Furniture	1126758.8	53.4	1126705.4
通讯器材类	Communication Appliances	1182562.6	254516.7	928045.9
煤炭及制品类	Coal and Related Products	5772258.1	5772258.1	
木材及制品类	Wood and Wooden Products	56632.5	56632.5	
石油及制品类	Petroleum and Related Products	14189916.3	12064614.4	2125301.9
化工材料及制品类	Raw Chemical Materials	1944496.6	1943413.8	1082.8
#化肥类	Chemical Fertilizers	59905.6	58860.3	1045.3
金属材料类	Metal Materials	9196748.4	9196748.4	
建筑及装潢材料类	Buildings and Decoration Materials	1210376.2	349624.1	860752.1
机电产品及设备类	Mechanical and Electrical Products	747513.3	737025.7	10487.6
#农机类	Agricultural Machinery			
汽车类	Automobile	8721883.9	812528.6	7909355.3
种子饲料类	Seeds and Feedstuff	19882.8	19869.8	13.0
棉麻类	Cotton,Hemp	21567.4	21567.4	
其他类	Others	1424438.2	981393.4	443044.8

16-9 亿元以上商品交易市场成交情况（2017年）

Basic Statistics on Commodity Exchange Markets of Transaction Value over 100 Million Yuan（2017）

分　类	Classify	年末出租摊位数（个）Number of Rental Booths at Year-end (unit)	成交额（万元）Turnover (10 000 yuan)
1. 粮油、食品类	Cereals, Oils and Foodstuffs	4417	1307734
#粮油类	Grain and Oil	683	329188
肉禽蛋类	Meat, Poultry and Eggs	608	178031
水产品类	Aquatic Products	531	32653
蔬菜类	Vegetables	1224	214679
干鲜果品类	Fresh and Dried Fruit Category	1348	552656
2. 饮料类	Beverages	507	9776
3. 烟酒类	Tobacco and Liquor	255	4807
4. 服装、鞋帽、针纺织品类	Clothing, Shoes, Hats and Textiles	6816	3588497
#服装类	Clothing	3894	1886846
鞋帽类	Shoes and Hats	1827	1628651
针纺织品类	Knitwear and Textiles	1095	73000
5. 化妆品类	Cosmetics	31	1031
6. 金银珠宝类	Gold,Silver and Jewelry		
7. 日用品类	Articles for Daily Use	589	32184
#洗涤用品类	Bathing and Washing		
儿童玩具类	Children's Toys		
8. 五金、电料类	Hardwear and Electrical Materials	911	27037
9. 体育、娱乐用品类	Sports and Recreation Articles	400	16957
10. 书报杂志类	Newspapers and Magazines		
11. 电子出版物及音像制品类	E-journal and Video Products		
12. 家用电器和音像器材类	Household Appliances and Video Products	20	741
13. 中西药品类	Traditional Chinese and Western Medicine		
#西药	Western Medicine		
中草药及中成药	Chinese Herbal Medicine and Traditional Chinese Medicine		
14. 文化办公用品类	Cultural and Official Goods	802	295691
#计算机及其配套产品	Computer and Related Products	590	238407
15. 家具类	Furniture	441	36320
16. 通讯器材类	Communication Appliances	1264	229175
17. 煤炭及制品类	Coal and Related Products		
18. 木材及制品类	Wood and Wooden Products		
19. 石油及制品类	Petroleum and Related Products		
20. 化工材料及制品类	Raw Chemical Materials	36	150000
#化肥类	Chemical Fertilizers		
21. 金属材料类	Metal Materials	95	170000
22. 建筑及装潢材料类	Buildings and Decoration Materials	4868	509873
23. 机电产品及设备类	Mechanical and Electrical Products	1060	150261
#农机类	Agricultural Machinery		
24. 汽车类	Automobile	1662	258642
25. 种子饲料类	Seeds and Feedstuff		
26. 棉麻类	Cotton,Hemp		
27. 其他类	Others	104	16885

16-10 批发和零售业连锁经营情况（2017年）

Basic Statistics on Chain Business of Wholesale and Retail Trades（2017）

指 标	Item	本年合计 Total	上年合计 Total Last Year	本年直营店 Regular Chain
一、门店总数（个）	**Number of Stores(unit)**	**1524**	**1392**	**1281**
二、年末从业人员数（人）	**Employees at Year-end(person)**	**19720**	**19763**	**18709**
三、年末零售营业面积（平方米）	**Operating Area of Retail at Year-end(sq.m)**	**1010549**	**1015157**	**990339**
四、连锁门店商品购进额（万元）	**Purchases Value of Chain Stores(10 000 yuan)**	**2803649**	**2854190**	**2758870**
其中：统一配送商品购进额	Centralized Purchases and Delivery	2359644	2271332	2314865
其中：自有配送中心配送商品购进额	Self Centralized Purchases and Delivery	2146342	2058438	2116243
非自有配送中心配送商品购进额	Non-self Centralized Purchases and Delivery	59612	90620	59612
五、连锁门店商品销售额（万元）	**Sales Value of Chain Store(10 000 yuan)**	**3540051**	**3477116**	**3493168**
其中：零售额	Retail Value	1410525	1414545	1363642

16-10 续表 continued

指 标	Item	上年直营店 Regular Chain Last Year	本年加盟店 Franchise	上年加盟店 Franchise Last Year
一、门店总数（个）	**Number of Stores(unit)**	**1160**	**243**	**232**
二、年末从业人员数（人）	**Employees at Year-end(person)**	**18873**	**1011**	**890**
三、年末零售营业面积（平方米）	**Operating Area of Retail at Year-end(sq.m)**	**995743**	**20210**	**19414**
四、连锁门店商品购进额（万元）	**Purchases Value of Chain Stores(10 000 yuan)**	**2822721**	**44779**	**31469**
其中：统一配送商品购进额	Centralized Purchases and Delivery	2239863	44779	31469
其中：自有配送中心配送商品购进额	Self Centralized Purchases and Delivery	2036484	30099	21954
非自有配送中心配送商品购进额	Non-self Centralized Purchases and Delivery	90620		
五、连锁门店商品销售额（万元）	**Sales Value of Chain Store(10 000 yuan)**	**3437387**	**46883**	**39729**
其中：零售额	Retail Value	1374816	46883	39729

16-11 住宿和餐饮业连锁经营情况（2017年）

Basic Statistics on Chain Business of Hotels and Catering Services（2017）

指　标	Item	本年合计 Total	上年合计 Total Last Year
一、门店总数（个）	**Number of Stores(unit)**	**282**	**225**
二、年末从业人员数（人）	**Employees at Year-end(person)**	**11571**	**10021**
三、年末餐饮营业面积（平方米）	**Operating Area of Retail at Year-end(sq.m)**	**126332**	**102826**
四、客房总数（间）	**Guest Rooms(room)**		
五、床位数（张）	**Guest Beds(bed)**		
六、餐位数（位）	**Dining Seats(set)**	**75214**	**66078**
七、连锁门店商品购进额（万元）	**Operating Area of Catering Services at Year end(room)(10 000yuan)**	**72150**	**61837**
其中：统一配送商品购进额	Centralized Purchases and Delivery	68798	57750
其中：自有配送中心配送商品购进额	Self Centralized Purchases and Delivery	53602	50090
非自有配送中心配送商品购进额	Non-self Centralized Purchases and Delivery	6612	4655
八、连锁门店商品营业额（万元）	**Sales Value of Chain Store(10 000 yuan)**	**178215**	**138498**
其中：餐费收入	Catering Revenues	177343	137655
商品销售额	Sales Value	872	843

16-11 续表 continued

指　标	Item	本年直营店 Regular Chain	上年直营店 Regular Chain Last Year
一、门店总数（个）	**Number of Stores(unit)**	**277**	**220**
二、年末从业人员数（人）	**Employees at Year-end(person)**	**11248**	**9698**
三、年末餐饮营业面积（平方米）	**Operating Area of Retail at Year-end(sq.m)**	**125632**	**102126**
四、客房总数（间）	**Guest Rooms(room)**		
五、床位数（张）	**Guest Beds(bed)**		
六、餐位数（位）	**Dining Seats(set)**	**75048**	**65912**
七、连锁门店商品购进额（万元）	**Operating Area of Catering Services at Year end(room)(10 000yuan)**	**71126**	**60813**
其中：统一配送商品购进额	Centralized Purchases and Delivery	68798	57750
其中：自有配送中心配送商品购进额	Self Centralized Purchases and Delivery	53602	50090
非自有配送中心配送商品购进额	Non-self Centralized Purchases and Delivery	6612	4655
八、连锁门店商品营业额（万元）	**Sales Value of Chain Store(10 000 yuan)**	**176583**	**136866**
其中：餐费收入	Catering Revenues	175711	136023
商品销售额	Sales Value	872	843

16-12 限额以上住宿和餐饮业经营情况（2017年）

单位：个、亿元

分 类	Classify	2014	
		单位数 Number of Enterprises	营业额 Business Revenue
总计	**Total**	**602**	**141.65**
一、住宿业	**Lodging Services**	**237**	**63.05**
1. 按登记注册类型分组	Grouped by Registration Status		
内资企业	Domestic Funded Enterprises	220	51.51
国有	State-owned Enterprises	32	7.38
集体	Collective-owned Enterprises	2	0.24
股份合作	Cooperative Enterprises		
联营	Joint Ownership Enterprises		
国有联营	State Joint Ownership Enterprises		
集体联营	Collective Joint Ownership Enterprises		
国有与集体联营	Joint State-collective Ownership Enterprises		
其他联营	Other Joint Ownership Enterprises		
有限责任公司	Limited Liability Corporations	119	31.79
国有独资公司	State-funded Corporations	4	1.62
其他有限责任公司	Other Limited Liability Corporations	115	30.17
股份有限公司	Stock Limited Corporation	4	1.49
私营	Private Enterprises	63	10.61
私营独资	Private-funded Enterprises	3	0.14
私营合伙	Private Partnership Enterprises	1	0.06
私营有限责任公司	Private Limited Liability Corporations	57	10.30
私营股份有限公司	Private Share Holding Corporations	2	0.11
其他	Others		
港澳台商投资	Enterprises Funded by Hong Kong, Macao and Taiwan	7	5.25
外商投资	Foreign Funded Enterprises	10	6.29
个体经营	Individual Enterprises		
2. 按国民经济行业分组	Grouped by Economic Sector		
旅游饭店	Tour Restaurant	181	55.93
一般旅馆	Common Hotel	51	5.93
其他住宿业	Others	5	1.19

Statistic on Hotel Services and Catering Services above Designed Size（2017）

（100 million yuan)

2015		2016		2017	
单位数 Number of Enterprises	营业额 Business Revenue	单位数 Number of Enterprises	营业额 Business Revenue	单位数 Number of Enterprises	营业额 Business Revenue
567	**127.75**	**604**	**127.53**	**716**	**142.39**
239	**57.99**	**258**	**60.08**	**319**	**68.04**
221	47.30	242	50.55	301	57.61
29	6.48	30	6.45	25	5.77
2	0.18	1	0.04	1	0.04
119	30.21	126	31.67	138	35.02
4	1.32	7	2.84	8	3.87
115	28.89	119	28.83	130	31.15
5	1.74	4	1.72	4	1.92
66	8.69	81	10.67	133	14.86
3	0.12	3	0.18	2	0.10
62	8.54	77	10.45	129	14.68
1	0.03	1	0.04	2	0.08
8	5.17	7	4.25	7	5.21
10	5.52	9	5.27	9	5.14
				2	0.08
176	50.12	184	50.88	193	54.26
56	6.15	65	7.34	116	11.61
7	1.72	9	1.85	10	2.17

16-12 续表1

单位：个、亿元

分 类	Classify	2014	
		单位数 Number of Enterprises	营业额 Business Revenue
二、餐饮业	**Catering Trade**	**365**	**78.60**
1. 按登记注册类型分	Grouped by Registration Status		
内资	Domestic Funded Enterprises	310	53.41
国有	State-owned Enterprises	5	1.14
集体	Collective-owned Enterprises		
股份合作	Cooperative Enterprises		
联营	Joint Ownership Enterprises		
国有联营	State Joint Ownership Enterprises		
集体联营	Collective Joint Ownership Enterprises		
国有与集体联营	Joint State-collective Ownership Enterprises		
其他联营	Other Joint Ownership Enterprises		
有限责任公司	Limited Liability Corporations	177	33.13
国有独资公司	State-funded Corporations	2	0.38
其他有限责任公司	Other Limited Liability Corporations	175	32.75
股份有限公司	Stock Limited Corporation	3	4.28
私营	Private Enterprises	121	14.18
私营独资	Private-funded Enterprises	12	0.63
私营合伙	Private Partnership Enterprises		
私营有限责任公司	Private Limited Liability Corporations	106	13.32
私营股份有限公司	Private Share Holding Corporations	3	0.23
其他	Others	4	0.68
港澳台商投资	Enterprises Funded by Hong Kong, Macao and Taiwan	7	6.88
外商投资	Foreign Funded Enterprises	7	10.04
个体经营	Individual Enterprises	41	8.27
2. 按国民经济行业分	Grouped by Economic Sector		
正餐服务	Dinner Services	351	69.48
快餐服务	Fast Food Services	7	7.74
饮料及冷饮服务	Beverage and Cold Beverage Services		
其他餐饮业	Other Catering Services	7	1.38

continued 1

(100 million yuan)

2015		2016		2017	
单位数 Number of Enterprises	营业额 Business Revenue	单位数 Number of Enterprises	营业额 Business Revenue	单位数 Number of Enterprises	营业额 Business Revenue
328	**69.76**	**346**	**67.46**	**397**	**74.35**
284	50.46	321	49.87	364	56.40
4	1.10	4	1.06	4	1.03
167	31.89	166	26.02	144	22.36
1	0.12	1	0.11	2	0.67
166	31.77	165	25.91	142	21.69
1	3.53	2	6.22	5	8.58
108	12.58	146	15.49	208	23.31
9	0.46	12	0.56	13	0.65
97	11.97	131	14.73	192	22.49
2	0.15	3	0.20	3	0.17
4	1.36	3	1.08	3	1.12
7	4.28	6	3.97	7	3.97
6	9.94	5	10.13	5	11.66
31	5.08	14	3.48	21	2.31
315	63.80	335	61.68	384	58.74
7	4.71	8	4.82	10	15.25
6	1.25	3	0.96	3	0.36

主要统计指标解释

批发业 指批发商向批发、零售单位及其他企事业、机关单位批量销售生活用品和生产资料的活动，以及从事进出口贸易和贸易经纪与代理的活动。批发商可以对所批发的货物拥有所有权，并以本单位、公司的名义进行交易活动；也可以不拥有货物的所有权，而以中介身份做代理销售商。还包括各类商品批发市场中固定摊位的批发活动。

零售业 指百货商店、超级市场、专门零售商店、品牌专卖店、售货摊等主要面向最终消费者（如居民等）的销售活动。包括以互联网、邮政、电话、售货机等方式的销售活动，还包括在同地点，后面加工生产，前面销售的店铺（如前店后厂的面包房）。不包括：谷物、种子、饲料、牲畜、矿产品、生产用原料、化工原料、农用化工产品、机械设备（用车、计算机及通信设备等除外）等生产资料的销售（批发业）；非零售单位附带的零售活动（如汽车修理单位销售汽车零件）；商业零售单位所在商厦的物业管理（物业管理）；商业零售单位所在的商品市场、商业大厦的市场管理活动（市场管理）。

住宿业 指有偿为顾客提供临时住宿的服务活动，不包括提供长期住宿场所的活动（如出租房屋、公寓等）。

餐饮业 指在一定场所，对食物进行现场烹饪、调制，并出售给顾客主要供现场消费的服务活动。

社会消费品零售总额 指批发和零售业、餐饮业、新闻出版业、邮政业和其他服务业等，售予城乡居民用于生活消费的商品和社会集团用于公共消费的商品之总量。社会消费品零售总额包括：

一、批发和零售业企业（单位）售予城乡居民用于生活消费和社会集团用于公共消费的商品。包括：

1. 售予城乡居民的各种生活消费品；

2. 售予入境旅游的外国人、华侨、港澳台同胞的各类商品；

3. 售予行政事业单位、社会团体、军队和武警等机构的商品，以及以零售方式售予各类企业的商品。具体包括：用于非生产和社会交往的办公用品，如通讯设备、计算器具和设备、电讯网络设备、文印设备、音像视听器材和设备、纸张、本册、文具及装订文印材料、家具、日用电器、针纺织品、清洁卫生用品、文体用品、奖品、纪念品、礼品等；供内部人员乘坐的交通工具和燃料；用于办公设施修缮的各类配件、材料、工具等；用于取暖和防暑降温的设备、燃料、材料及食品等；专用于教学的用品和设备；非营利医疗机构的中、西药品、中药材和医疗设备器材；非专用的劳动保护用品；不对外营业的内部食堂用的餐具、炊具、设备、清洁卫生工具和食品、燃料等；军队、武警用于其人员生活的衣着品和个人用品；其他各类非生产性设备和用品。

二、餐饮业出售的主食、菜肴、烟酒饮料和其他商品。

三、新闻出版业、邮政业售予城乡居民、企事业单位、军队和武警等机构的书报杂志、音像制品、邮品等。

四、其他服务业出售的食品、烟酒饮料、服装鞋帽、日常生活用品、医药保健用品、艺术品、工艺美术品、玩具、殡葬用品以及其他消费品。

批发和零售业商品购进、销售、库存总额 指各种登记注册类型的批发和零售业企业（单位）以本企业（单位）为总体的，从国内、国外市场购进的商品总量，销售和出口的商品总量、库存的商品总量等情况。该指标可以反映商品流转过程中商品的购进、销售、库存之间的比例关系和存在的问题。

购进总额 指从本企业（单位）以外的单位和个人购进（包括从境外直接进口）作为转卖或加工后转卖的商品总额。它反映批发和零售业从国内、国外市场上购进商品的总量。商品购进包括：（1）从工农业生产者购进的商品；（2）从出版社、报社的出版发行部门购进的图书、杂志和报纸；（3）从各种登记注册类型的批发和零售业企业（单位）购进的商品；（4）从其他单位购进的商品，如从机关、团体、企业等单位购进的剩余物资，从住宿和餐饮业、其他服务业购进的商品，从海关、市场管理部门购进的缉私和没收的商品，从居民手中收购的废旧商品等；（5）从国（境）外直接进口的商品。不包括企业（单位）为自身经营用和未通过买卖行为而收入的商品以及销售退回、商品升溢等。

销售总额 指对本企业（单位）以外的单位和个人出售（包括对境外直接出口）的商品总额。它反映批发和零售业在国内市场上销售商品以及出口商品的总量。商品销售包括：（1）售给城乡居民和社会集团消费用的商品；（2）售给工业、农业、建筑业、运输邮电业、批发和零售业、住宿和餐饮业、其他服务业等作为生产、经营使用的商品；（3）售给批发和零售业作为转卖或加工后转卖的商品；（4）对国（境）外直接出口的商品。不包括出售本企业（单位）自用的废旧包装用品，未通过买卖行为付出的商品，经本单位介绍、由买卖双方直接结算、本单位只收取手续费的业务，购货退出的商品以及商品损耗和损失等。

库存总额 指报告期末各种登记注册类型的批发和零售业企业（单位）已取得所有权的商品。它反映批发和零售业企业（单位）的商品库存情况和对市场商品供应的保证程度。商品库存包括：（1）存放在批发和零售业经营单位（如门市部、批发站、经营处）仓库、货场、货柜和货架中的商品；（2）挑选、整理、包装中的商品；（3）已记入购进而尚未运到本单位的商品，即发货单或银行承兑凭证已到而货未到的商品；（4）寄放他处的商品，如因购货方拒绝承付而暂时存放在购货方的商品和已办完加工成品收回手续而未提回的商品；（5）委托其他单位代销（未作销售或调出）尚未售出的商品；（6）代其他单位购进尚未交付的商品。不包括所有权不属于本单位的商品、委托外单位加工生产尚未收回成品的商品、外贸企业代理其他单位从国外进口尚未付给订货单位的商品、代国家物资储备部门保管的商品等。

住宿和餐饮业营业额 指住宿和餐饮业法人企业（单位）在经营活动中因提供服务或销售商品等取得的收入。包括：客房收入、餐费收入、商品销售额和其他收入。客房收入指住宿和餐饮业法人企业（单位）在经营活动中因提供住宿服务取得的收入。餐费收入指住宿和餐饮业法人企业（单位）因为顾客提供就餐服务取得的收入，包括经烹饪、调制加工后出售的各种食品，如主食、炒菜、凉拌菜等的收入。商品销售额指住宿和餐饮业法人企业（单位）伴随服务而出售商品所取得的收入（含增值税）。其他收入指营业收入中除客房收入、餐费收入、商品销售额以外的其他收入，包括娱乐、健身和商务服务等。

连锁企业（或称连锁店、连锁公司） 指在核心企业或总店的领导下，由分散的、经营同类商品或服务的企业或活动单位，采取共同方针，实行集中采购和分散销售的有机结合，通过规范化经营，实现规模效益的经济联合组织形式。一般连锁店应由若干个分店组成。其经营特征：（1）经营同类商品；（2）使用统一商号；（3）统一采购配送，采购与销售相分离（部分商品可根据物流合理和保质保鲜原则，由供应商直接送货到门店，其余均由总部统一配送）。

连锁门店的形式分为直营连锁和加盟连锁。

直营连锁也叫正规连锁。指连锁门店均由总部独资或控股开设，在总部的直接领导下统一经营。总部采取纵深似的管理方式，直接下令掌管所有的零售门店，零售门店也必须完全接受总部指挥。这是大型垄断商业资本通过吞并、兼并或独资、控股等途径，发展壮大自身实力和规模的一种形式。

加盟连锁包括特许连锁和自由连锁两种形式。

特许连锁指各连锁门店（被特许人）通过合同形式，取得使用总部（特许人）商标、商号、经营技术和销售总部开发的商品的特许权，各加盟连锁门店为独立法人，在总部指导下统一经营。

自由连锁也称自愿连锁。指连锁公司的门店均为独立法人，各自的资产所有权关系不变，在公司总部的指导下共同经营。各成员店使用共同的店名，与总部订阅有关购、销、宣传等方面的合同，并按合同开展经营活动。在合同规定的范围之外，各成员店可以自由活动。根据自愿原则，各成员店可自由加入连锁体系，也可自由退出。

Explanatory Notes on Main Statistical Indicators

Wholesale Trade refers to the activities of wholesaler selling at wholesale commodities for daily use and capital goods to enterprises of wholesale and retail trades and other enterprises, institutions and government offices, including the activities of wholesaler engaged in import and export and acting as a trade agent. The wholesaler may have the right of ownership over the commodities of wholesale and trade in the name of its own or a company, the wholesaler may not have the right of ownership, only acts an agent. The wholesale trade also include the activities of wholesaler at the fixed stalls of the wholesale market of different commodities.

Retail Trade refers to the activities of department store,supermarket, franchised store, brand store, retail stall and on-the-spot-making-selling store selling commodities to the final consumers (citizens) by any means including internet, post, telephone, sales machine. Retail trade excludes the activities of sales of capital goods such a grain, seed, feed, livestock, mineral products, raw material for production, industrial chemicals, chemical products for farm, machine and equipment (vehicle, computer and communication equipment), and the activities of supplementary sales of non-retailer such as the sales of spare parts of car repair business

Hotel Services refer to the activities of enterprises providing paid services of lodging to the customer, excluding the activities of providing long period of services of lodging (such as leased house and apartments).

Catering Services refer to the activities of enterprises providing on-the-spot services of selling food cooked and prepared to the customer in certain sites

Total Retail Sales of Consumer Goods refer to the sum of retail sales of commodities sold by wholesale and retail trades, catering services, publishing, post and telecommunications and other service industries to urban and rural households for household consumption and to social institutions for public consumption. Retail sales of consumer goods include:

1) Sales sold by wholesale and retail trades to urban~thA and rural households for household consumption and to social institutions for public consumption.

a) of commodities to urban and rural households;

b) of commodities to foreigners, overseas Chinese and Chinese compatriots from Hong Kong, Macao and Taiwan visiting China;

c) of commodities to government agencies, institutions, social organizations, military and armed police units, and commodities to enterprises in the form of retail sales. More specifically, they include: office facilities and articles for non-production purposes such as communications equipment, computing equipment and instruments, TV and network equipment, printing and copying equipment, audio-visual equipment and instruments, paper, notebooks, stationeries, furniture, electric appliances, knitwear, sanitation and cleaning articles, cultural and sport articles, articles for prizes, souvenirs, etc.; transport vehicles and fuels for employees; materials, spare parts and tools for the maintenance of office facilities; equipment, fuels, materials and food for winter heating or summer cooling purposes; articles and equipment for teaching purpose; Chinese and western medicines and medical equipment and facilities purchased by non profit-making medical institutes; non- specialized work safety articles; cooking utensils, tableware, equipment, cleaning articles, food and fuels purchased by in-house cafeterias; clothes and personal articles purchased by military or armed police units for their officials and soldiers; and other equipment and articles for non-production purposes.

2) Sales of stable food, cooked dishes, beverages, tobaccos and other articles by catering units.

3) Sales of books, newspapers, magazines, audio-visual products and post products by publishing, post and telecommunications departments to urban and rural households and to enterprises, institutions, military and armed police units.

4) Sales of food, beverages, tobaccos, clothing, hats, footwear, articles for daily use, medicines, medical and health articles, work of art, handicrafts, toys, funeral articles and other articles by other service industries.

Purchase, Sales and Stock of Commodities by Wholesale and Retail Trades refer to the total volume of commodities purchased, total volume of sales and exports, and the stock of commodities by wholesale and retail enterprises (establishments) of different status of registration from domestic and overseas markets. This indicator reflects the relationship among purchase, sales and stock of commodities in the circulation of goods and reveals the existing problems.

Total Purchases of Commodities refer to the total value of purchases of commodities by enterprises (establishments)from other establishments or individuals (including direct import from abroad) for the purpose of re-selling, either with or without further processing of the commodities purchased. The commodities include: (1) commodities purchased from agricultural and industrial producer, wholesaler, retailer, publishing house and other service business; (2) commodities purchased from institutions and government departments; (3) confiscated goods purchased from the customs authorities or market management agencies; (4) second-hand goods and wastes purchased from residents; The commodities exclude 1 commodities purchased by enterprises (establishments) for use in their own business operation, commodities obtained without buying or selling procedures such as materials, consumable goods of low value, office appliances, etc. 2 received goods without trading, such as goods handed over from others, borrowed goods, preserved goods for others, donated goods from others, processed and retrieved goods, etc. 3. goods of direct settlement between buyer and seller with handling fees introduced by others, 4. goods returned or refused to pay by the buyer, 5. excessive goods.

Total Sales of Commodities refer to value of commodities sold by the establishments to other establishments and individuals (including goods sold for self consumption, including the value-added tax). The commodities include: (1) commodities sold to urban and rural residents and social groups for their consumption; (2) commodities sold to establishments in all industries for their production and operation, including agriculture, industry, construction, transportation, post and telecommunications, catering services, and public utility including commodities sold to wholesale and retail establishments for re-selling, with or without further processing; and (3) commodities for direct export to abroad.Excluded are (1) extended commodities without trading, such as goods handed over to other enterprises and institutions because of the change of organizations, lent goods, returned goods preserved for others, extended processing materials and samples donated to others, (2) goods of direct settlement between buyer and seller with handling fees introduced by others, (3)goods returned after purchase, (4) damaged and spoiled goods, (5) waste and used goods of selfuse,

Total Stock of Commodities refers to total commodities possessed by wholesaler and retailer of various types of registration status at the end of the reference period, reflecting the commodity stock level of various wholesaler and retailer and the potential for market supply. It includes: (1) commodities located in storage, garages, counters, and shelves of operating places (such as sale stores, wholesale centres, and operating offices) ; (2) commodities in the process of being selected, sorted, and packed; (3) commodities not arrived but recorded as purchase in the account, i.e. commodities not arrived but payment receipts for the commodities from the sellers or the banks arrived; (4) commodities deposited in other places rather than places mentioned above, for instance: commodities in the hold of purchasers temporarily due to the refusal of payment and commodities not taken back after going through the formalities; (5) commodities entrusted to other units to sell but not sold yet; (6) commodities purchased for other units but not delivered yet. Commodities not included as stock are those not owned by the enterprises (units), commodities on commission for processing but not yet delivered, imported commodities of agency of foreign trade enterprise but not yet delivered to ordering units and finally those put in stock on behalf of the state material reserves units.

Business Revenue of Hotels and Catering Services refers to revenue received from providing services or selling commodities by corporate enterprises and establishments engaged in hotels and catering services, including income from hotels, from catering services, from selling of commodities and from other services. Income from hotels refers to income of corporate enterprises and establishments engaged in hotels and catering services by providing lodging services. Income from catering services refers to income of corporate enterprises and establishments engaged in hotels and catering services by providing catering services, including selling of cooked or prepared foods such as staple food, cooked dishes or cold dishes. Income from selling of commodities refers to income of corporate enterprises and establishments engaged in hotels and catering services by selling commodities (including value-added tax) that accompany the services they provide. Income from other activities refers to income received other than income from hotels, catering services or selling of commodities, such as income from providing recreation, fitness or business services.

Chain Head Stores (headquarter) refer to the core leading stores responsible for development, allocation, administration and utilization of resources (name of stores, brand of stores, operation model, service standard, management way, ect.) of chain stores. Chain stores refers to the stores engaged in providing homogeneous commodities or services, with the central leadership of head store and guided by common policies, conduct centralized purchase and distributed selling of commodities, in order to gain better efficiency through standardized operation. The chain stores include regular chain stores, franchise chain stores and voluntary chain stores.

Regular Chain store refers to chain stores that are invested or controlled by the headquarters. They operate under direct and unified management from the headquarters.

Franchise chain store refers to the chain stores (franchisees) which are franchised with operation resources such as trade marks, names, patent and operation know-how by the franchisors in form of contract and pay the operation fees to the franchisors.

Voluntary chain store refers the stores operate jointly on the voluntary bases while maintaining their status of independent legal entities with full ownership of their assets. They sell goods of same brand from same channel of resource to the consumers.

17 对外经济贸易和旅游

FOREIGN TRADE AND ECONOMIC COOPERATION TOURISM

资料整理：马晓庆
Data management: Ma Xiaoqing
数据审核：黄小丹
Data audit: Huang Xiaodan

第十七部分　对外经济贸易和旅游

一、简要说明

本章资料包括对外经济贸易、利用外资和旅游等方面资料，由西安市统计局贸易外经处根据西安市商务局、投资委海关和旅发委提供资料整理。

二、主要指标

进出口总值（亿元）	2545.08	比上年增长	39.1%
#出 口	1552.22	比上年增长	63.9%
实际利用外资（亿美元）	53.07	比上年增长	17.8%

17 FOREIGN TRADE AND ECONOMIC COOPERATION TOURISM

Ⅰ.Brief Introduction

Data in this chapter consists of data on foreign trade, using of foreign capital and fund and tourism. Data on foreign economy and trade and tourism are compiled and provided by Foreign Economy Division of the Xi'an Bureau of Statistics according to the data from Xi'an Bureau of Commerce, Xi'an Invesrment Committee, Xi'an Custom Office and Xi'an Tourism Development Committee.

Ⅱ.Major Indicators

		Increase over Preceding Year
Total Imports and Exports (100 mil.yuan)	2545.08	39.1%
#Exports	1552.22	63.9%
Actual Utilized Foreign Investments (USD 100 mil.)	53.07	17.8%

17-1 主要年份外资、外贸基本情况

Main Indicators on Foreign Investments and International Trading in Representative Years

指　标	Item	1990	1995	2000	2005	2010	2011
一、利用外资签定协议项目(个)	**Number of Projects of Foreign Capital Used through the Signed Agreements and Contracts (unit)**	**11**	**184**	**135**	**157**	**82**	**99**
合同外资（万美元）	Contracted Foreign Investments (USD 10 000)	415	28956	54123	121499	119689	120083
实际利用外资（万美元）	Actual Utilized Foreign Investments (USD 10 000)	1154	18653	15633	57113	156653	200522
二、进出口总值（万美元）	**Total Imports and Exports (USD 10 000)**	**38229**	**137510**	**173696**	**390146**	**1039273**	**1260179**
#进口总值	Total Imports	9939	27347	67634	126705	507544	677517
出口总值	Total Exports	28290	110163	106062	263441	531729	582662
进出口差额(出口-进口)	Balance of Imports and Exports	18351	82816	38428	136736	24185	-94855
三、国际旅游者人数总计（万人次）	**Total Number of International Tourists (10 000 person-times)**	**25.88**	**41.35**	**65.03**	**77.56**	**84.18**	**100.23**
#外国人	Foreigners	15.40	37.11	54.65	65.86	73.21	88.63
港、澳、台同胞	Chinese Compatriot From Hong Kong, Macao and Taiwan	10.07	4.16	10.38	11.70	10.97	11.60
四、国际旅游者人天数总计（万人天）	**Total Number of Days of International Tourists (10 000 person/day)**	**55.03**	**84.44**	**162.69**	**224.93**	**241.67**	**287.09**
#外国人	Foreigners	33.48	75.71	131.44	190.99	211.48	254.78
港、澳、台同胞	Chinese Compatriot From Hong Kong, Macao and Taiwan	21.55	8.56	31.15	33.94	30.19	32.31
五、国际旅游收入（亿元）	**Earning of International Tourism (100 millon yuan)**	**1.96**	**10.38**	**22.41**	**33.54**	**42.40**	**51.28**
#商品收入	Income from Mercantile	0.44	2.57	7.71	11.25	11.87	11.38
劳务收入	Income from Labour Service	1.52	7.81	14.70	22.29	30.53	39.90
六、国际旅游者在西安人均停留天数（天）	**Number of Days of Average Tourists Staying in Xi'an (day)**	**2.1**	**2.0**	**2.5**	**2.9**	**2.9**	**2.9**

注：1.2014年起市旅发委未发布国际旅游统计数据。
2.本表来源于市商务局、西安海关、市旅发委、市投资委。2017年利用外资不包含西咸新区、进出口总值为西安原口径数据。
3.合同外资2016年前名称为“利用外资签订协议金额”，实际利用外资2016年前名称为“外商实际直接投资额”。下同。

17-1 续表 continued

指 标	Item	2012	2013	2014*	2015*	2016*	2017*
一、利用外资签定协议项目(个)	**Number of Projects of Foreign Capital Used through the Signed Agreements and Contracts (unit)**	**87**	**152**	**103**	**73**	**72**	**143**
合同外资（万美元）	Contracted Foreign Investments (USD 10 000)	360264	251874	255321	193684	102103	464954
实际利用外资（万美元）	Actual Utilized Foreign Investments (USD 10 000)	247800	312994	370310	400833	450466	530680
二、进出口总值（万美元）	**Total Imports and Exports (USD 10 000)**	**1301446**	**1798534**	**15321514**	**17616896**	**18299476**	**25450843**
#进口总值	Total Imports	571568	950715	7974693	9418142	8826392	9928641
出口总值	Total Exports	729878	847819	7346822	8198754	9473084	15522202
进出口差额(出口-进口)	Balance of Imports and Exports	158310	-102896	-627871	-1219388	646692	5593561
三、国际旅游者人数总计（万人次）	**Total Number of International Tourists (10 000 person-times)**	**115.34**	**121.11**				
#外国人	Foreigners	101.40	106.89				
港、澳、台同胞	Chinese Compatriot From Hong Kong, Macao and Taiwan	13.94	14.22				
四、国际旅游者人天数总计（万人天）	**Total Number of Days of International Tourists (10 000 person/day)**	**334.44**	**351.11**				
#外国人	Foreigners	294.90	310.26				
港、澳、台同胞	Chinese Compatriot From Hong Kong, Macao and Taiwan	39.54	40.85				
五、国际旅游收入（亿元）	**Earning of International Tourism (100 millon yuan)**	**59.89**	**64.16**				
#商品收入	Income from Mercantile	14.19	14.69				
劳务收入	Income from Labour Service	45.70	49.47				
六、国际旅游者在西安人均停留天数 （天）	**Number of Days of Average Tourists** Staying in Xi'an (day)	**2.9**	**2.9**				

注：2014年以后进出口数据计量单位为万元。

17-2 主要年份利用外资情况

Utilization of Foreign Capital in Representative Years

单位：万美元 (USD 10 000)

年 份 Year	合同外资 Contracted Foreign Investments	实际利用外资 Actual Utilized Foreign Investments
1983	3500	800
1984	8	
1985	8361	1106
1986	19919	4010
1987	3218	5552
1988	2423	6758
1989	1645	11632
1990	415	1154
1991	591	1094
1992	24165	5200
1993	57289	8996
1994	20321	15240
1995	28956	18653
1996	35978	20510
1997	27214	22057
1998	40034	22286
1999	40390	13801
2000	54123	15633
2001	60736	17687
2002	70692	20281
2003	96380	25557
2004	78312	27595
2005	121499	57113
2006	182525	82463
2007	143978	111567
2008	118230	114738
2009	60027	121872
2010	119689	156653
2011	120083	200522
2012	360264	247800
2013	251874	312994
2014	255321	370310
2015	193684	400833
2016	102103	450466
2017	464954	530680

注：本表数据来源于市投资委。2017年数据不包含西咸新区。

17-3 外国和港澳台地区在西安投资情况（2017年）

Foreign, Hong Kong, Macao and Taiwan Investment Situation in Xi'an (2017)

单位：万美元 (USD 10 000)

指 标	Item	项目数（个）Number of Projects (unit)	合同外资 Contracted Foreign Investments	实际利用外资 Actual Utilized Foreign Investments
合计数	**Total**	**143**	**464954.24**	**530680.00**
一、按企业类别分组	By Enterprise Category			
1. 中外合资经营企业	Joint-venture Enterprises	72	100426.40	73430.50
2. 中外合作经营企业	Cooperation Enterprises			102.00
3. 外资企业	Wholly Foreign-owned Enterprises	69	364059.50	456696.40
4. 外商投资股份制	FDI Shareholding Inc.	2	468.30	451.10
二、按国民经济行业分组	Grouped by Sector			
（一）农、林、牧、渔业	Agriculture, Forestry, Animal Husbandry and Fishery	1	5000.00	7.87
（二）采矿业	Mining			38.23
（三）制造业	Manufacturing	14	251753.57	394817.18
（四）电力、燃气及水的生产供应业	Generation and Supply of Electricity, Production and Supply of Gas and Water	3	533.71	10935.12
（五）建筑业	Construction	3	4153.82	
（六）批发和零售业	Wholesale and Retail Trades	29	1696.90	28995.18
（七）交通运输、仓储和邮政业	Transportation, Storage and Post	5	10170.01	12070.22
（八）住宿和餐饮业	Hotels and Catering Services	3	4354.03	4190.78
（九）信息传输、软件和信息技术服务业	Information Transmission, Computer Service and Software	5	13643.29	4094.05
（十）金融业	Financial Intermediation	27	44814.40	9362.99
（十一）房地产业	Real Estate	6	72788.51	59720.90
（十二） 租赁和商务服务业	Leasing and Business Services	31	54555.18	4172.08
（十三）科学研究和技术服务业	Scientific Research and Technical Service	9	819.92	1539.62
（十四）水利、环境和公共设施管理业	Management of Water Conservancy, Environment and Public Facilities	1	504.54	622.62

注：本表数据来源于西安海关。本表数据不包含西咸新区。

17-3 续表1

单位：万美元 (USD 10 000)

指　标	Item	项目数（个）Number of Projects (unit)	合同外资 Contracted Foreign Investments	实际利用外资 Actual Utilized Foreign Investments
（十五）居民服务、修理和其他服务业	Services to Households, repairs and other services	2	34.50	13.16
（十六）教育	Education			
（十七）卫生和社会工作	Health and social work			
（十八）文化、体育和娱乐业	Culture, Sports and Entertainment	4	131.86	100.00
（十九）公共管理、社会保障和社会组织	Public administration, social security and social organizations			
（二十）国际组织	International Organizations			
三、按投资国别、地区分组	By Country(Region)			
香港	Hong Kong,China	68	157530.16	202593.80
澳门	Macao,China			438.50
台湾省	Taiwan,China	7	294.09	8204.40
日本	Japan	1	38.80	5876.10
马来西亚	Malaysia			35.80
新加坡	Singapore	2	14389.62	28401.50
韩国	Korea Rep.	12	248443.23	226679.40
德国	Germany	1	948.02	2497.40
意大利	Italy	1	18.58	
法国	France	1	18.13	49.20
英国	United Kingdom	2	232.71	20129.80
瑞士	Switzerland			816.30
丹麦	Denmark	1	25614.41	10723.40
加拿大	Canada	5	2123.59	80.00
美国	United States	8	1116.21	1363.50
澳大利亚	Australia	2	1943.65	0.10
维尔京群岛	Virgin Is.(E)		364.88	1151.60
其它	Others	32	11878.16	21639.20

17-4 各区县、开发区实际利用外资

Actual Utilized Investment by Foreign Entrepreneurs by Region and Development Zone

单位：万美元 (USD 10 000)

区县及开发区	Region and Economic Zone	2010	2012	2013	2014	2015	2016	2017
区县合计	**Sum of Region**	**38855**	**58119**	**45164**	**51423**	**59765**	**67874**	**72527**
新城区	Xincheng	4900	7800	5012	6500	7775	8768	10340
碑林区	Beilin	5150	7800	5103	5871	6873	9360	9941
莲湖区	Lianhu	5471	7800	5100	5843	6873	7532	8656
灞桥区	Baqiao	5215	7397	6124	6933	8148	9056	9601
未央区	Weiyang	5023	7800	6000	6834	7870	8614	9433
雁塔区	Yanta	5488	8190	6179	6847	8074	8907	9843
阎良区	Yanliang	1208	2200	2200	2346	2555	2801	3000
临潼区	Lintong	1200	2400	2400	2504	2765	3031	1102
长安区	Chang'an	1680	2768	3003	3360	3961	4440	4762
高陵区	Gaoling	950	1100	1100	1182	1478	1621	1740
鄠邑区	Huyi	1050	1115	1173	1288	1339	1479	1700
蓝田县	Lantian	550	650	660	707	1283	1401	1490
周至县	Zhouzhi	970	1100	1110	1210	773	864	920
开发区合计	**Sum of Development Zones**	**117798**	**189681**	**267830**	**318887**	**311265**	**381023**	**458153**
高新区	GaoXin	51130	81776	132632	149387	167112	203870	260293
经开区	JingKai	42608	68202	81423	103009	114538	129186	145000
曲江新区	Qujiang	17187	26433	33870	41436		20588	24212
浐灞生态区	Chanba Eco-District	3070	4837	7266	8453	9800	10833	12402
航空基地	Aviation Industry Base	1239	2072	2640	3082	3636	4186	2045
航天基地	Aerospace Base	1554	2403	3000	3501	3980	4567	5117
国际港务区	International Trade&Logistic Park	1010	2082	3469	5050	6429	7793	9083
沣东新城	FengDongXinCheng		1876	3530	4970	5770		

注：本表数据来源于市投资委。2017年数据不包含西咸新区。

17-5 主要年份进出口总值

Total Imports and Exports in Representative Years

单位：万美元 (USD 10 000)

年 份 Year	进出口总值 Total Imports and Exports	出口总值 Total Exports	进口总值 Total Imports
1987	13596	7540	6056
1988	36750	24632	12118
1989	32715	21564	11151
1990	38229	28290	9939
1991	55356	41511	13845
1992	70467	53060	17407
1993	93330	62393	30937
1994	104752	76897	27855
1995	137510	110163	27347
1996	143187	91745	51442
1997	150668	107753	42915
1998	180589	100492	80097
1999	172919	94495	78424
2000	173696	106062	67634
2001	169914	87948	81966
2002	186966	112479	74487
2003	230932	140327	90605
2004	309295	203539	105756
2005	390146	263441	126705
2006	415403	272862	142541
2007	536162	347133	189029
2008	704029	447113	256916
2009	724618	333114	391504
2010	1039273	531729	507544
2011	1260179	582662	677517
2012	1301446	729878	571568
2013	1798534	847819	950715
2014*	15321514	7346822	7974693
2015*	17616896	8198754	9418142
2016*	18299476	9473084	8826392
2017*	25450843	15522202	9928641

注：本表数据来源于西安海关。2014年及以后数据计量单位为万元。2017年数据为西安原口径数据。

17-6 外贸商品进出口总值分国别和地区（2017年）

Total Value of Imports and Exports by Country and Region（2017）

单位：万元 (10 000 yuan)

国别和地区	Country and Region	进出口总值 Total Imports and Exports	出口 Exports
亚洲	**Asia**	**18005507**	**10485335**
#香港	Hong kong	4186558	4185182
台湾省	Taiwan	4968794	748759
日本	Japan	1503965	562455
菲律宾	Phiilippines	89127	58075
马来西亚	Malaysia	274729	233519
韩国	Korea	4915544	3000087
非洲	**Africa**	**327724**	**271241**
#埃及	Egypt	33149	33015
突尼斯	Tunisia	2005	1853
埃塞俄比亚	Ethiopia	794	794
博茨瓦纳	Botswana	728	472
南非	South Africa	101355	56689
欧洲	**Europe**	**2667463**	**1744088**
#德意志联邦国	Germany	526146	205155
法国	France	526628	481679
意大利	Italy	170540	51149
荷兰	Netherland	268056	237136
英国	England	283775	236213
瑞士	Switzerland	53021	4273
西班牙	Spain	35151	29273
俄罗斯联邦	Russia	140783	108999
拉丁美洲	**Latin America**	**520092**	**236212**
#哥伦比亚	Colombia	6157	6157
巴西	Brazil	182647	31669
阿根廷	Argentina	9879	9276
北美洲	**North America**	**3451407**	**2712177**
加拿大	Canada	122711	69455
美国	America	3328695	2642721
大洋洲及太平洋岛屿	**Oceanic and Pacific Islands**	**478631**	**73148**
#澳大利亚	Australia	470971	66679
新西兰	New Zealand	6484	5293

注：本表数据来源于西安海关，为西安原口径数据。

17-7 主要商品分大类出口金额

Export Value of Major Merchandise by Type

单位：万美元 (USD 10 000)

商品分类	HS Section and Division	2000	2002
食用蔬菜、根及块茎	Edible Vegetables, Certain,Roots amd Tubers	1095	1275
蔬菜、水果、坚果或植物其他部分的制品	Vegetables, Fruits, Nuts, or Products Made of Other Parts of Plants	2076	3470
矿砂、矿渣及矿灰	Ores,Slags and Ash	4083	8714
无机化学品；贵金属、稀土金属、放射性元素及其同位素的有机及无机化合物	Inorganic Chemicals,Organic or Inorganic Compounds of Precious Metals,of Rare Earth Metals,of Radioactive Elements or of Isotopes	3714	4141
有机化学品	Organic Chemicals	2367	4883
羊毛、动物细毛或粗毛、马毛纱线及其机织物	Wool ,Fine or Coarse Animal Hair; Horsehair Yarn and Woven Fabric	810	1313
棉花	Cotton	3197	3826
化学纤维短纤	Short Staple Chemical' Fibers	5061	2512
针织或钩编的服装及衣着附件	Articles of Apparel and Clothing Accessories, Knitted or Crocheted	6753	2660
非针织或非钩编的服装及衣着附件	Articles of Apparel and Clothing Accessories, not Knitted or Crocheted	7269	3629
其它纺织制成品；成套物品；旧衣着及旧纺织品	Other Made Up Textile Articles;Sets;Worn Clothing and Worn Textile Articles;Rags Articles	1649	1432
鞋靴、护膝和类似品及其零件	Footwear,Gaiters and The Like;Parts of Such Articles Headgear and Parts Thereof	1347	296
玻璃及其制品	Glass and Glassware	3376	5542
钢铁	Iron and Steel	3534	2167
钢铁制品	Articles of Iron or Steel	5535	7414
铅及制品	Lead Areticles Thereof	1371	444
锌及制品	Zinc Areticles Thereof	4031	1895
其他贱金属、金属陶瓷及其制品	Other Base Metals,Germets;Areticles Thereof	1066	1546
贱金属工具、器具、利口器、餐匙、餐叉及其零件	Tools,Implements,Cutlery,Spons and Forks, of Base Metal;Parts Thereof of Base Metal	2933	2613
核反应堆、锅炉、机器、机械器具及其零件	Nuclear Reactors ,Boilers, Machinery and Mechanical Appliances; and Parts Thereof	10915	16140
电机、电气设备及其零件；录音机及放声机、电视图象、声音的录制和重放设备及其零件、附件	Electrical Machinery and Equipment and Parts Thereof;Sound Recorders and Repreducers, Television Image and Sound Recordes and Repreducers, and Parts and Accessories of Such Articles	8339	8962
光学、照相、电影、计量、检验、医疗或外科仪器及设备、精密仪器及设备；上述物品的零配件、附件	Optical,Photographic,Cinematographic,Measuring, Checking,Precision Medical or Surgical Instruments and Apparatus;Parts and Accessories Thereof	2020	5395
家具、寝具、褥垫、弹簧床垫、软床垫及类似的填充制品；未列名灯具及照明装置；发光标志、发光名牌及类似品；活动房屋	Mattresses,Mattress Supports,Cushions and Similar Stuffed Furnishings;Lamps and Lighting Fittings, not Elsewhere Spcified or Included;Illumihated Signs,Illuminated	2587	2715

注：本表数据来源于西安海关。2014年及以后数据计量单位为万元。2017年数据为西安原口径数据。

17-7 续表1

单位：万美元

商品分类	HS Section and Division	2003	2004
食用蔬菜、根及块茎	Edible Vegetables, Certain,Roots amd Tubers	1379	1386
蔬菜、水果、坚果或植物其他部分的制品	Vegetables, Fruits, Nuts, or Products Made of Other Parts of Plants	4490	7786
矿砂、矿渣及矿灰	Ores,Slags and Ash	11224	30590
无机化学品；贵金属、稀土金属、放射性元素及其同位素的有机及无机化合物	Inorganic Chemicals,Organic or Inorganic Compounds of Precious Metals,of Rare Earth Metals,of Radioactive Elements or of Isotopes	5814	5806
有机化学品	Organic Chemicals	4757	4837
羊毛、动物细毛或粗毛、马毛纱线及其机织物	Wool ,Fine or Coarse Animal Hair; Horsehair Yarn and Woven Fabric	1600	1640
棉花	Cotton	3984	3133
化学纤维短纤	Short Staple Chemical' Fibers	2120	1987
针织或钩编的服装及衣着附件	Articles of Apparel and Clothing Accessories, Knitted or Crocheted	341	7465
非针织或非钩编的服装及衣着附件	Articles of Apparel and Clothing Accessories, not Knitted or Crocheted	4981	5543
其它纺织制成品；成套物品；旧衣着及旧纺织品	Other Made Up Textile Articles;Sets;Worn Clothing and Worn Textile Articles;Rags Articles	2203	2667
鞋靴、护膝和类似品及其零件	Footwear,Gaiters and The Like;Parts of Such Articles Headgear and Parts Thereof	585	2687
玻璃及其制品	Glass and Glassware	6667	8083
钢铁	Iron and Steel	2779	5244
钢铁制品	Articles of Iron or Steel	8474	10398
铅及制品	Lead Areticles Thereof	232	43
锌及制品	Zinc Areticles Thereof	2200	522
其他贱金属、金属陶瓷及其制品	Other Base Metals,Germets;Areticles Thereof	3150	6419
贱金属工具、器具、利口器、餐匙、餐叉及其零件	Tools,Implements,Cutlery,Spons and Forks, of Base Metal;Parts Thereof of Base Metal	3232	3406
核反应堆、锅炉、机器、机械器具及其零件	Nuclear Reactors ,Boilers, Machinery and Mechanical Appliances; and Parts Thereof	21281	24696
电机、电气设备及其零件；录音机及放声机、电视图象、声音的录制和重放设备及其零件、附件	Electrical Machinery and Equipment and Parts Thereof;Sound Recorders and Repreducers, Television Image and Sound Recordes and Repreducers, and Parts and Accessories of Such Articles	15106	19812
光学、照相、电影、计量、检验、医疗或外科仪器及设备、精密仪器及设备；上述物品的零配件、附件	Optical,Photographic,Cinematographic,Measuring, Checking,Precision Medical or Surgical Instruments and Apparatus;Parts and Accessories Thereof	3339	1847
家具、寝具、褥垫、弹簧床垫、软床垫及类似的填充制品；未列名灯具及照明装置；发光标志、发光名牌及类似品；活动房屋	Mattresses,Mattress Supports,Cushions and Similar Stuffed Furnishings;Lamps and Lighting Fittings, not Elsewhere Spcified or Included;Illumihated Signs,Illuminated	3994	4955

continued 1

(USD 10 000)

2005	2006	2007	2008	2009	2010	2011	2012	2013	2014*	2015*	2016*	2017*
1190	1136	1232	1374	803	4740	2016	1961	2699	2686	2039	2555	1129
10531	15374	37426	29270	21920	41289	36763	2576	49361	132663	112701	102768	149311
63247	52046	47378	40502	6141	325	4709	1679	1686	14977	96	178	346
10997	10916	16508	15882	9774	24875	11735	8911	12588	67764	44508	49950	52192
8569	11923	11182	13954	16294	982	20067	17890	28694	109986	109654	117162	148719
903	1400	1065	720	460	10133	796	562	2433	15782	3005	5648	3153
3240	3808	3255	3213	2346	98	2628	2185	5827	9252	14309	6429	5301
1471	1556	1767	1181	2217	479	2586	2375	8245	13685	11581	11178	14502
5736	5332	5345	4371	3617	3209	3366	12316	6491	29551	37030	31646	36441
5068	4078	3875	3623	2919	3394	3262	7050	4861	33872	23610	19393	40633
3000	3342	3090	3187	2813	544	2838	4412	4471	18906	15677	15187	26219
1368	216	348	380	367	150	1003	5252	6293	20186	5032	2292	18614
8576	8272	6246	6538	5574	928	8073	10995	13856	54453	45991	46764	46059
5314	4900	11366	11966	4254	18549	16681	8407	6730	31854	20390	27589	28467
13959	16903	17329	26568	11943	5998	25319	24259	33546	102720	88740	100956	164963
12	158	1650	2	1	10	2	4913	16	3		26	19
135	4119	2470	46	78	28545	10	11	59	109	93	20	334
11233	17695	23414	27576	11276	3556	28092	21397	24030	106691	95442	83309	103608
3052	3607	3917	4083	2777	2893	3641	5176	5992	30653	25321	24868	33582
30832	36174	47381	75911	52372	130296	99631	127795	211009	1929864	2744726	3431041	6147739
23605	22801	33393	56758	53355	136	137105	183536	327931	3113155	3625079	4264312	7044093
2341	3521	4230	6348	5255	196	11066	14908	17879	112646	119117	107892	108613
4773	5086	8301	8296	4769	5328	3860	25644	23595	52352	42140	40142	77439

17-8 主要商品分大类进口金额

Import Value of Major Merchandise by Type

单位：万美元 (USD 10 000)

商品分类	HS Section and Division	2000	2005	2008	2009	2010	2011
无机化学品；贵金属、稀土金属、放射性元素及其同位素的有机及无机化合物	Inorganic Chemicals,Organic or Inorganic Compounds of Precious Metals,of Rare Earth Metals,of Radioactive Elements or of Isotopes	1467	317	6001	5040	7513	19766
有机化学品	Organic Chemicals	7257	15237	15692	14186	13949	18100
塑料及其制品	Plastic and Articles Thereof	2559	4317	2553	3134	4091	3250
钢铁	Iron and Steel	2467	752	3888	2537	10949	10643
铜及制品	Copper and Articles Thereof	2367	689	11097	41195	43343	78482
铝及制品	Aluminium and Articles Thereof	2652	3627	4767	6505	3116	5913
核反应堆、锅炉、机器、机械器具及其零件	Nuclear Reactors ,Boilers, Machinery and Mechanical Appliances; and Parts Thereof	12990	38050	68504	87493	134753	135240
电机、电气设备及其零件；录音机及放声机、电视图象、声音的录制和重放设备及其零件、附件	Electrical Machinery and Equipment and Parts Thereof;Sound Recorders and Repreducers, Television Image and Sound Recordes and Repreducers,and Parts and Accessories of Such Articles	5911	23337	48008	113034	207937	230957
车辆及其零件、附件、铁道及电车道车辆除外	Vehicles Other Than Railway or Tramway Rolling- and Rarts and Accessories Thereof	1530	1387	3789	1798	3109	1527
航空器、航天器及其零配件	Aircraft, Spacecraft and Parts Thereof	10443	8800	26148	13057	3620	4654
光学、照相、电影、计量、检验、医疗或外科仪器及设备、精密仪器及设备；上述物品的零配件、附件	Optical,Photographic,Cinematographic,Measuring, Checking,Precision Medical or Surgical	3673	10424	17737	24210	37414	39317

17-8 续表 continued

单位：万美元 (USD 10 000)

商品分类	HS Section and Division	2012	2013	2014*	2015*	2016*	2017*
无机化学品；贵金属、稀土金属、放射性元素及其同位素的有机及无机化合物	Inorganic Chemicals,Organic or Inorganic Compounds of Precious Metals,of Rare Earth Metals,of Radioactive Elements or of Isotopes	13329	11869	166549	185175	299328	246352
有机化学品	Organic Chemicals	12331	12504	98293	86359	154656	123439
塑料及其制品	Plastic and Articles Thereof	3107	8014	37082	54103	76182	103008
钢铁	Iron and Steel	5928	1802	11893	17403	16093	16567
铜及制品	Copper and Articles Thereof	11857	65170	169061	484480	224287	240188
铝及制品	Aluminium and Articles Thereof	8649	11758	45295	43935	34384	32032
核反应堆、锅炉、机器、机械器具及其零件	Nuclear Reactors ,Boilers, Machinery and Mechanical Appliances; and Parts Thereof	98802	186974	2017587	2021311	990108	926081
电机、电气设备及其零件；录音机及放声机、电视图象、声音的录制和重放设备及其零件、附件	Electrical Machinery and Equipment and Parts Thereof;Sound Recorders and Repreducers, Television Image and Sound Recordes and Repreducers,and Parts and Accessories of Such	257444	444407	3919650	5011437	5272203	6510729
车辆及其零件、附件、铁道及电车道车辆除外	Vehicles Other Than Railway or Tramway Rolling- and Rarts and Accessories Thereof	2222	2966	17521	19700	22697	26662
航空器、航天器及其零配件	Aircraft, Spacecraft and Parts Thereof	8516	9179	43191	35164	31933	101247
光学、照相、电影、计量、检验、医疗或外科仪器及设备、精密仪器及设备；上述物品的零配件、附件	Optical,Photographic,Cinematographic,Measuring, Checking,Precision Medical or Surgical	48206	61727	452559	542812	521411	307404

注：本表数据来源于西安海关。2014年以后数据计量单位为万元。2017年数据为西安原口径数据。

17-9 按贸易方式分外贸出口总值

Total Value of Exports in Foreign Trade by Type of Trade

单位：万元 (10 000 yuan)

指　标	Item	2017	2017年比2016年增长（%） Growth Rate in 2017 over 2016(%)
出口总值	**Total Exports**	**15522202**	**63.9**
1.一般贸易	General Trade	2985895	33.8
2.国家间、国际组织无偿援助	Between Countries, International Organizations	4964	297.8
和赠送的物资	Aid and Donated Materials		
3.来料加工装配贸易	Assembly Processing Trade	33523	-10.3
4.进料加工贸易	Processing With Imported Trade	10433351	49.8
5.对外承包工程出口货物	Exports Contracted Projects	392859	222.6
6.租赁贸易	Lease Trade		
7.易货贸易	Barter		
8.出料加工贸易	Material Processing		
9.保税监管场所进出境货物	Inward and Outward Goods of Free	112	-58.0
(保税仓库进出境货物)	(Trade Storehouse)		
10.海关特殊监管区域物流货物	Re-export Goods of Free Trade Zone	1666547	1370.6
11.其他	Others	4951	164.4

注：本表数据来源于西安海关。本表数据为西安原口径数据。

17-10 按贸易方式分外贸进口总值

Total Value of Imports in Foreign Trade by Type of Trade

单位：万元 (10 000 yuan)

指标名称	Item	2017	2017年比2016年增长（%） Growth Rate in 2017 over 2016(%)
进口总值	**Total Imports**	**9928641**	**12.5**
1.一般贸易	General Trade	2348802	19.0
2.国家间、国际组织无偿援助和赠送的物资	Between Countries, Internationals Organization Aid and Donated Materials		
3.华侨、港澳台同胞、外籍华人捐赠物资	The overseas Chinese, Hong Kong, Macao, Taiwan,Chinese of foreign Donated Materials		
4.来料加工装配贸易	Assembly Processing Trade	30507	-20.2
5.进料加工贸易	Processing With Imported Trade	6630465	19.3
6.来料加工装配进口的设备	Assembly Processing Trade Equipment	657	
7.租赁贸易	Lease Trade	67783	275730.6
8.外商投资企业作为投资进口的设备、物品	Foreign-invested Enterprises as the Import Investment of Equipment, Goods	21120	-54.1
9.出料加工贸易	Material Processing		
10.易货贸易	Barter		
11.保税监管场所进出境货物（保税仓库进出境货物）	Inward and Outward Goods of Free (Trade Storehouse)	31478	125.1
12.海关特殊监管区域物流货物（保税区仓储转口货物）	Re-export Goods of Free Trade Zone (Re-exports)	274303	-20.1
13.海关特殊监管区域进口设备（出口加工区进口设备）	Export Processing Zones Imported (Equipment)	511874	-38.9
14.其他	Other	11652	-22.9

注：本表数据来源于西安海关。本表数据为西安原口径数据。

17-11 主要年份旅游人数及收入

Number of Tourists and Tourism Earnings in Representative Years

年 份 Year	接待旅游者人数（万人次） Number of Tourists (10 000 person-times)	国际旅游人数 Number of International Tourists	旅游总收入（万元） Total Tourism Earnings (10 000 yuan)	国际旅游收入 Earning of International Tourists	国际旅游者在西安人均停留天数（天） Number of Days of Average International Tourists Staying in Xi'an(day)
1980	4.00	4.00	1757	1757	3.8
1985	21.15	21.15	7029	7029	2.2
1990	25.88	25.88	19628	19628	2.1
1995	791.35	41.35	440000	103818	2.0
1996	925.39	45.39	470000	149400	2.6
1997	1010.53	48.53	510000	166359	2.6
1998	1105.80	47.98	560000	160244	2.6
1999	1260.40	55.41	830000	186282	2.5
2000	1567.00	65.03	1050000	224100	2.5
2001	1752.20	67.20	1130000	240700	2.4
2002	1984.13	74.13	1310000	260000	2.2
2003	1647.67	33.66	1064200	121200	2.5
2004	2149.03	65.03	1544000	273900	2.9
2005	2423.60	77.56	1785000	335380	2.9
2006	2738.70	86.73	2043000	378270	2.9
2007	3118.01	100.01	2372000	424263	2.9
2008	3232.20	63.20	2435200	287200	2.6
2009	3929.29	67.29	2974000	310500	2.9
2010	5285.18	84.18	4051800	424000	2.9
2011	6653.23	100.23	5301500	512800	2.9
2012	7978.35	115.35	6543900	598900	2.9
2013	10130.00	121.11	8114400	641600	2.9
2014	12000.00		9500000		
2015	13600.80		10736900		
2016	15012.56		12138100		
2017	18093.14		16333000		

注：本表数据来源于市旅发委。2014年以后市旅发委未发布国际旅游统计数据。

17-12 主要年份旅行社及A级景点

Statistics of Travel Agencies and Level-A Scenic Spots in Representative Years

项 目	Item	2005	2010	2012	2013	2014	2015	2016	2017
旅行社数（个）	Number of Travel Agencies (unit)	221	334	344	360	385	353	410	452
旅行社营业收入（亿元）	Revenue of Travel Agencies (100 million yuan)	17.82	31.22	49.49	57.93	45.70	59.54	66.68	79.39
旅游A级景点数（个）	Number of Level-A Scenic Spots(unit)	18	34	55	61	67	74	72	77
旅游A级景点年接待游客人次（万人次）	Number of Tourists Received at Level-A Scenic Spots (10 000 person times)	930	2726	5306	7163	7462	8553	10454	18120

注：本表数据来源市旅发委。2017年数据不包含西咸新区。

主要统计指标解释

进出口总额 指实际进出我国国境的货物总金额。包括对外贸易实际进出口货物，来料加工装配进出口货物，国家间、联合国及国际组织无偿援助物资和赠送品，华侨、港澳台同胞和外籍华人捐赠品，租赁期满归承租人所有的租赁货物，进料加工进出口货物，边境地方贸易及边境地区小额贸易进出口货物（边民互市贸易除外），中外合资企业、中外合作经营企业、外商独资经营企业进出口货物和公用物品，到、离岸价格在规定限额以上的进出口货样和广告品（无商业价值、无使用价值和免费提供出口的除外），从保税仓库提取在中国境内销售的进口货物，以及其他进出口货物。该指标可以观察一个国家在对外贸易方面的总规模。我国规定出口货物按离岸价格统计，进口货物按到岸价格统计。

商品经营单位所在地进、出口额 指在所在地海关注册登记的有进出口经营权的企业实际进、出口额。

商品目的地进口额和商品货源地出口额 目的地进口额指进口货物的消费、使用或最终抵运地的实际进口额；货源地出口额指出口货物的产地或原始发货地的实际出口额。

利用外资 指我国各级政府、部门、企业和其他经济组织通过对外借款、吸收外商直接投资以及用其他方式筹措的境外现汇、设备、技术等。

外商直接投资 指外国企业和经济组织或个人（包括华侨、港澳台胞以及我国在境外注册的企业）按我国有关政策、法规，用现汇、实物、技术等在我国境内开办外商独资企业、与我国境内的企业或经济组织共同举办中外合资经营企业、合作经营企业或合作开发资源的投资（包括外商投资收益的再投资），以及经政府有关部门批准的项目投资总额内企业从境外借入的资金。

旅游人数：

（1）入境旅游人数：指报告期内来我国观光、度假、探亲访友、就医疗养、购物、参加会议或从事经济、文化、体育、宗教活动的外国人、港澳台同胞等入境游客。统计时，外国人、港澳台同胞每入境一次统计1人次。

（2）出境人数：指中国（大陆）居民因公或因私出境前往其他国家、中国香港特别行政区、澳门特别行政区和台湾省观光、度假、探亲访友、就医疗养、购物、参加会议或从事经济、文化、体育、宗教活动的人数，即出境游客。统计时，按每出境一次统计1人次。

（3）国内旅游人数：指在报告期内在中国（大陆）观光游览、度假、探亲访友、就医疗养、购物、参加会议或从事经济、文化、体育、宗教活动的中国（大陆）居民人数，其出游的目的不是通过所从事的活动谋取报酬。统计时，国内游客按每出游一次统计1人次。

国际旅游（外汇）收入 指入境游客在中国（大陆）境内旅行、游览过程中用于交通、参观游览、住宿、餐饮、购物、娱乐等全部花费。

国内旅游收入 又称旅游总花费指国内游客在国内旅行、游览过程中用于交通、参观游览、住宿、餐饮、购物、娱乐等全部花费。

国际旅行社 指经营业务范围包括入境旅游业务、出境旅游业务和国内旅游业务的旅行社。

国内旅行社 指经营范围仅限于国内旅游业务的旅行社。

星级饭店 指设备、设施、服务符合《旅游饭店星级的划分与评定》（CB／T14308—2003），通过相关旅游管理部门评定，并取得星级饭店称号的饭店（含预备星级饭店）。

Explanatory Notes on Main Statistical Indicators

Total Imports and Exports at Customs refer to the real value of commodities imported and exported across the border of China. They include the actual imports and exports through foreign trade, imported and exported goods under the processing and assembling trades and materials, supplies and gifts as aid given gratis between governments and by the United Nations and other international organizations, and contributions donated by overseas Chinese, compatriots in Hong Kong and Macao and Chinese with foreign citizenship, leasing commodities owned by tenant at the expiration of leasing period, the imported and exported commodities processed with imported materials, commodities trading in border areas (excluding mutual exchange goods), the imported and exported commodities and articles for public use of the Sino-foreign joint ventures, cooperative enterprises and ventures with sole foreign investment. Also included is import or export of samples and advertising goods for which CIF or FOB value are beyond the permitted ceiling (excluding goods of no trading or use value and free commodities for export), imported goods sold in China from bonded warehouses and other imported or exported goods. The indicator of the total imports and exports at customs can be used to observe the total size of external trade in a country. In accordance with the stipulation of the Chinese government, imports are calculated at CIF, while exports are calculated at FOB.

Import Export Value by Location of China's Foreign Trade Managing Units refers to actual value of imports and exports carried out by corporations which have been registered by the local Customs house and are vested with right to run import export business.

Import Value of Commodities by Place of Destination and Export Value of Commodities by Place of Origin in China The former indicator refers to the value of import commodities of the places of their consumption, utilization or the places of their final destination. The latter indicator refers to the value of export commodities of the places of their origin or the places of the commodities dispatched.

Utilization of Foreign Capitals refers to remittance, equipment and technology financed from abroad, by loans, foreign direct investment and other forms undertaken by the Chinese governments at all levels, by various departments, enterprises and other economic units.

Foreign Borrowings refer to funds borrowed from abroad through formal signing of borrowing agreements with foreign institutions, including loans of foreign governments, loans of international financial institutions, commercial loans of foreign banks, export credit, and funds raised by Chinese bonds (and shares before 1996) issued abroad. It is an important part of China's utilization of foreign capitals.

Foreign Direct Investment refers to the investments inside China by foreign enterprises and economic organizations or individuals (including overseas Chinese, compatriots from Hong Kong, Macao and Taiwan, and Chinese enterprises registered abroad), following the relevant policies and laws of China, for the establishment of ventures exclusively with foreign own investment, Sino-foreign joint ventures and cooperative enterprises or for co-operative exploration of resources with enterprises or economic organizations in China.

Number of Tourists

(1) Visitor arrivals refer to the number of foreigners,Chinese compatriots from Hong Kong, Macao and Taiwan Chinese (mainland) who come to China (mainland) for sight-seeing,vacation,visiting relatives, medical treatment, shopping, attending conference, or to engage in economic, cultural, sports and religious activities. In compiling statistics, each time of entering China is counted as one person-time.

(2) Number of Chinese residents going abroad refer to the number of Chinese (mainland) residents going to other countries, Hong Kong Special Administrative region, Macao Special Administrative region and Taiwan for on official or private purposes, for sight-seeing, vacation, visiting relatives, medical treatment, shopping, attending conference, or to engage in economic, cultural, sports and religious

activities. In compiling statistics, each time of leaving is counted as one person-time.

(3) Number of domestic tourists refers to the number of Chinese (mainland) residents who travel within China (mainland) for sight-seeing, vacation, visiting relatives, medical treatment, shopping, attending conference, or to engage in economic, cultural, sports and religious activities. In compiling statistics, each time of travelling is counted as one person-time.

Foreign Exchange Earnings from International Tourism refer to the total expenditure of foreigners, overseas Chinese,Chinese compatriots from Hong Kong,Macao and Taiwan during their stay in the mainland of China on transportation,sighting,accommodation, food,shopping and entertainment.

Income from Domestic Tourism refer to expenditure of domestic tourists on transportation,sighting, accommodation, food, shopping and entertainment while they travel.

International Travel Agencies refer to travel agencies engaged in tourism entering China, Chinese residents going abroad and domestic tourism.

Domestic Travel Agencies refer to travel agencies only engaged in domestic tourism.

Star–rated Hotels refer to hotels rated with stars as assessed by the relevant tourism authorities according to GB/T14308-2003 standard with reference to their infrastructure, facilities and service levels.

18 服务业

SERVICE INDUSTRY

资料整理：王家峰
Data management：Wang Jiafeng
数据审核：王金桂
Data audit：Wang Jingui

第十八部分　服务业

一、简要说明

本资料主要包括规模以上服务业（九个门类、四个中类）单位个数及主要经济指标，由西安市统计局服务业和社科处提供。

二、主要指标

单位数（个）	1546		
资产总计（亿元）	8117.27	比上年增长	9.8%
营业收入（亿元）	2114.65	比上年增长	16.8%
利润总额（亿元）	170.14	比上年增长	17.9%

18　SERVICE　INDUSTRY

Ⅰ.Brief Introduction

The data in this chapter consists of the number of service units and main economic indicators of Service enterprises above designated size (Including nine categories, four Class) , data in this chapter is provided by Tertiary Industry and Social Science&Technology Division of Xi'an Bureau of Statistice.

Ⅱ.Major Indicators

		Increase over Preceding Year
Number of Units(units)	1546	
Total Assets (100 mil. yuan)	8117.27	9.8%
Operating Income(100 mil. yuan)	2114.65	16.8%
The total Profit (100 mil. yuan)	170.14	17.9%

18-1 规模以上服务业按登记注册类型分主要经济指标（2017年）

Main Economic Indicators for Services above the Designated Size grouped by Registration Type（2017）

单位：万元 (10 000 yuan)

指 标	Item	企业单位数（个） Number of Enterprises (unit)	资产总计 Total Assets	固定资产原价 Original Value of Fixed Assets
总计	**Total**	**1546**	**81172689.4**	**42493526.7**
按登记注册类型分组	**Grouped by Registration Type**			
内资企业	Domestic Funded Enterprises	1480	78786389.3	41345243.9
国有	State-owned Enterprises	95	3205991.8	1294058.5
集体	Collective-owned Enterprises	17	66835.6	23060.7
股份合作	Corperative Enterprises	4	12345.3	3416.4
联营	Joint Ownership Enterprises	1	1685.2	542.5
国有联营	State Joint Ownership Enterprises			
集体联营	Collective Joint Ownership Enterprises			
国有与集体联营	Joint State-collective Enterprises			
其他联营	Others Joint Ownership Enterprises	1	1685.2	542.5
有限责任公司	Limited Liability Corporrations	766	66712861.5	36103470.2
国有独资公司	State Funded Corporations	81	34366262.7	18906723.6
其他有限责任公司	Other Limited Liability Corporrations	685	32346598.8	17196746.6
股份有限公司	Other Limited Liability Corporrations	64	4860595.4	3086434.0
私营	Other Limited Liability Corporrations	511	3723586.8	785420.7
私营独资	Private-funded Enterprises	13	11931.3	3716.8
私营合伙	Private Partnership Enterprises	7	69566.0	15916.3
私营有限责任公司	Private Limited Liability Corporations	461	3454637.4	737735.2
私营股份有限公司	Private Share-holding Corporations Ltd.	30	187452.1	28052.4
其他	Other Enterprises	22	202487.7	48840.9
港澳台商投资	Enterprises with Funds from Hong Kong, Macao &Taiwan	28	823485.5	972092.9
与港澳台商合资经营	Joint Ventures	14	352052.7	135211.8
与港澳台商合作经营	Cooperation Enterprises	1	31253.0	2821.7
港澳台商独资经营	Enterprises with Sole Investment from Hong Kong Macau and Taiwan	12	435721.8	833473.9
港澳台商投资股份有限公司	Share-holding Corporations Ltd. with funds from Hong Kong, Macao & Taiwan			
其他港澳台投资	Other Hong Kong, Macao and Taiwan Investment	1	4458.0	585.5
外商投资	Foreign Funded Enterprises	38	1562814.6	176189.9
中外合资经营企业	Sino-foreign Joint Ventures Enterprises	11	900165.3	21329.6
中外合作经营企业	Sino-Foreign Cooperation Enterprises	1	3832.3	3946.8
外资企业	Foreign Owned Enterprises	21	633713.6	144114.3
外商投资股份有限公司	Limited Company Funded by Foreign Investment	2	3389.0	1199.7
其他外商投资	Other Foreign Funded Enterprises	3	21714.4	5599.5

18-1 续表1

单位：万元

指　标	Item	负债合计 Total Liabilities	所有者权益合计 Total Owners' Equities	营业收入 Paid in Capital
总计	**Total**	**50412896.1**	**30759793.3**	**21146457.1**
按登记注册类型分组	**Grouped by Registration Type**			
内资企业	Domestic Funded Enterprises	48766641.0	30019748.3	19758816.7
国有	State-owned Enterprises	2290329.2	915662.6	2134635.9
集体	Collective-owned Enterprises	40009.6	26826.0	53136.3
股份合作	Corperative Enterprises	7359.4	4985.9	3765.5
联营	Joint Ownership Enterprises	1271.0	414.2	158.3
国有联营	State Joint Ownership Enterprises			
集体联营	Collective Joint Ownership Enterprises			
国有与集体联营	Joint State-collective Enterprises			
其他联营	Others Joint Ownership Enterprises	1271.0	414.2	158.3
有限责任公司	Limited Liability Corporrations	42708663.3	24004198.2	13513997.9
国有独资公司	State Funded Corporations	22838645.5	11527617.2	2507131.4
其他有限责任公司	Other Limited Liability Corporrations	19870017.8	12476581.0	11006866.5
股份有限公司	Other Limited Liability Corporrations	1359513.3	3501082.1	1856036.4
私营	Other Limited Liability Corporrations	2230900.9	1492685.9	2053960.2
私营独资	Private-funded Enterprises	7622.6	4308.7	12170.8
私营合伙	Private Partnership Enterprises	36776.2	32789.8	69976.5
私营有限责任公司	Private Limited Liability Corporations	2114524.5	1340112.9	1848123.0
私营股份有限公司	Private Share-holding Corporations Ltd.	71977.6	115474.5	123689.9
其他	Other Enterprises	128594.3	73893.4	143126.2
港澳台商投资	Enterprises with Funds from Hong Kong, Macao &Taiwan	544960.9	278524.6	443684.0
与港澳台商合资经营	Joint Ventures	125999.4	226053.3	102453.9
与港澳台商合作经营	Cooperation Enterprises	21620.1	9632.9	1633.4
港澳台商独资经营	Enterprises with Sole Investment from Hong Kong Macau and Taiwan	396897.2	38824.6	337070.3
港澳台商投资股份有限公司	Share-holding Corporations Ltd. with funds from Hong Kong, Macao & Taiwan			
其他港澳台投资	Other Hong Kong, Macao and Taiwan Investment	444.2	4013.8	2526.4
外商投资	Foreign Funded Enterprises	1101294.2	461520.4	943956.4
中外合资经营企业	Sino-foreign Joint Ventures Enterprises	760679.1	139486.2	72802.5
中外合作经营企业	Sino-Foreign Cooperation Enterprises	262.1	3570.2	2103.6
外资企业	Foreign Owned Enterprises	326008.2	307705.4	840935.5
外商投资股份有限公司	Limited Company Funded by Foreign Investment	2709.0	680.0	10175.0
其他外商投资	Other Foreign Funded Enterprises	11635.8	10078.6	17939.8

continued1

(10 000 yuan)

主营业务收入 Revenue from Principal Business	营业成本 Total Cost	主营业务成本 Cost of Principal Business	销售费用 Sale Expenses
20736664.7	**15282402.8**	**15049646.5**	**1206035.9**
19366881.7	14326383.8	14107401.5	1141298.2
2061865.3	1953483.6	1914973.2	33862.1
50703.2	23662.6	23515.5	8251.3
3506.3	520.4	513.6	121.1
158.3	155.3	155.3	
158.3	155.3	155.3	
13269057.0	9657093.9	9516128.8	783944.5
2446472.6	1449412.9	1419449.2	77354.3
10822584.4	8207681.0	8096679.6	706590.2
1816990.0	1178367.3	1171005.6	127351.3
2021785.7	1407454.5	1376205.3	181324.9
10191.7	7942.5	7509.0	1641.8
68625.8	41481.9	39954.9	1547.9
1820472.2	1276716.7	1247759.4	171782.2
122496.0	81313.4	80982.0	6353.0
142815.9	105646.2	104904.2	6443.0
426773.9	261063.7	247837.4	44723.2
100879.3	70713.0	70332.4	2375.1
1610.3			
321757.9	189624.2	176778.5	40904.9
2526.4	726.5	726.5	1443.2
943009.1	694955.3	694407.6	20014.5
71871.0	49396.6	48848.9	2860.5
2103.6	538.1	538.1	
840919.7	622599.9	622599.9	16843.3
10175.0	8247.0	8247.0	83.4
17939.8	14173.7	14173.7	227.3

18-1 续表2

单位：万元

指标	Item	管理费用 Management Expenses	财务费用 Financial Expenses	投资收益 Investment Income
总计	**Total**	**2104498.2**	**1191706.4**	**286218.3**
按登记注册类型分组	**Grouped by Registration Type**			
内资企业	Domestic Funded Enterprises	1921161.4	1170799.5	285974.2
国有	State-owned Enterprises	240664.7	10458.8	7450.6
集体	Collective-owned Enterprises	17322.0	-63.9	-99.0
股份合作	Corperative Enterprises	3241.3	-67.2	262.9
联营	Joint Ownership Enterprises	383.9	51.3	
国有联营	State Joint Ownership Enterprises			
集体联营	Collective Joint Ownership Enterprises			
国有与集体联营	Joint State-collective Enterprises			
其他联营	Others Joint Ownership Enterprises	383.9	51.3	
有限责任公司	Limited Liability Corporrations	1197876.5	1103407.0	202770.9
国有独资公司	State Funded Corporations	183461.7	851520.3	106109.2
其他有限责任公司	Other Limited Liability Corporrations	1014414.8	251886.7	96661.7
股份有限公司	Other Limited Liability Corporrations	145963.2	22291.9	64480.8
私营	Other Limited Liability Corporrations	293582.6	33301.2	11108.0
私营独资	Private-funded Enterprises	2562.8	74.8	
私营合伙	Private Partnership Enterprises	14703.9	1523.7	
私营有限责任公司	Private Limited Liability Corporations	256336.7	31276.9	10948.9
私营股份有限公司	Private Share-holding Corporations Ltd.	19979.2	425.8	159.1
其他	Other Enterprises	22127.2	1420.4	
港澳台商投资	Enterprises with Funds from Hong Kong, Macao &Taiwan	52893.8	13311.3	47.2
与港澳台商合资经营	Joint Ventures	14763.2	746.2	38.4
与港澳台商合作经营	Cooperation Enterprises	739.6	716.7	
港澳台商独资经营	Enterprises with Sole Investment from Hong Kong Macau and Taiwan	37066.0	11828.1	8.8
港澳台商投资股份有限公司	Share-holding Corporations Ltd. with funds from Hong Kong, Macao & Taiwan			
其他港澳台投资	Other Hong Kong, Macao and Taiwan Investment	325.0	20.3	
外商投资	Foreign Funded Enterprises	130443.0	7595.6	196.9
中外合资经营企业	Sino-foreign Joint Ventures Enterprises	7160.4	533.9	122.4
中外合作经营企业	Sino-Foreign Cooperation Enterprises	149.0	-11.8	
外资企业	Foreign Owned Enterprises	119236.4	7007.7	72.8
外商投资股份有限公司	Limited Company Funded by Foreign Investment	1917.7	27.0	1.7
其他外商投资	Other Foreign Funded Enterprises	1979.5	38.8	

continued2

(10 000 yuan)

营业利润 Business Profits	利润总额 Total Profits	应付职工薪酬 Salary Payable	从业人员平均人数（人） Annual Average Employed Persons (person)
1616118.6	**1701396.9**	**4228194.3**	**406270**
1467549.4	1549702.1	3676287.4	381752
3076.7	17339.6	493732.1	52080
3642.0	3662.6	28245.8	7039
119.5	271.6	1456.1	298
-432.2	-423.2	206.3	60
-432.2	-423.2	206.3	60
878491.9	942987.9	2385739.8	211138
62666.2	87732.2	413764.9	41289
815825.7	855255.7	1971974.9	169849
448664.9	438843.3	324546.5	32727
126895.5	139172.3	403175.8	72475
-63.8	-69.7	3782.9	918
10473.1	10450.4	16298.1	1917
102406.3	111859.6	346850.8	64574
14079.9	16932.0	36244.0	5066
7091.1	7848.0	39185.0	5935
65617.0	65383.3	52213.9	5882
12357.6	12786.2	19013.6	2358
165.7	165.7	133.2	9
53086.9	52423.0	32224.4	3330
6.8	8.4	842.7	185
82952.2	86311.5	499693.0	18636
12509.8	12926.5	11535.3	1107
1414.6	1414.6	270.7	60
67077.3	69778.5	469785.5	16071
-123.5	0.6	7445.8	455
2074.0	2191.3	10655.7	943

18-2 规模以上服务业按规模分主要经济指标（2017年）

单位：万元

指标	Item	企业单位数（个） Number of Enterprises (unit)	资产总计 Total Assets	固定资产原价 Original Value of Fixed Assets
总计	**Total**	**1546**	**81172689.4**	**42493526.7**
按企业规模分组	**Grouped by Size of Enterprises**			
大型企业	Large-size	146	43034546.9	33124844.6
中型企业	Medium-size	321	12450421.5	3000715.2
小型企业	Small-size	894	22909001.8	6133447.6
微型企业	Microenterprise	185	2778719.2	234519.3

18-2 续表1

单位：万元

指标	Item	销售费用 Sale Expenses	管理费用 Manangement Expenses	财务费用 Financial Expenses
总计	**Total**	**1206035.9**	**2104498.2**	**1191706.4**
按企业规模分组	**Grouped by Size of Enterprises**			
大型企业	Large-size	838334.6	1167818.2	861906.6
中型企业	Medium-size	195811.3	447940.3	49589.9
小型企业	Small-size	160432.9	450222.7	271373.9
微型企业	Microenterprise	11457.1	38517.0	8836.0

Main Economic Indicators for Services above the Designated Size grouped by Size of Enterprises（2017）

（10 000 yuan)

负债合计 Total Liabilities	所有者权益合计 Total Owners' Equities	营业收入 Paid in Capital	主营业务收入 Revenue from Principal Business	营业成本 Total Cost	主营业务成本 Cost of Principal Business
50412896.1	**30759793.3**	**21146457.1**	**20736664.7**	**15282402.8**	**15049646.5**
28041672.7	14992874.2	12915931.8	12744175.8	9118385.6	9021830.9
6751960.7	5698460.8	3709453.6	3629218.3	2805647.5	2749383.9
14586007.2	8322994.6	4184098.5	4084649.5	3107259.4	3075244.9
1033255.5	1745463.7	336973.2	278621.1	251110.3	203186.8

continued 1

（10 000 yuan)

投资收益 Investment Income	营业利润 Business Profits	利润总额 Total Profits	应付职工薪酬 Salary Payable	从业人员平均人数（人） Annual Average Employed Persons (person)
286218.3	**1616118.6**	**1701396.9**	**4228194.3**	**406270**
56405.9	995117.8	1040033.7	3025638.3	229415
89573.9	293656.3	316067.2	705452.2	90207
101844.8	252666.3	269588.4	461222.4	79527
38393.7	74678.2	75707.6	35881.4	7121

18-3 规模以上服务业按行业分主要经济指标（2017年）

单位：万元

指标	Item	企业单位数（个）Number of Enterprises (unit)	资产总计 Total Assets	固定资产原价 Original Value of Fixed Assets
总计	**Total**	**1546**	**81172689.4**	**42493526.7**
按国民经济行业大类分组	**Grouped by sector categories**			
铁路运输业	Railway transport industry	4	4906852.8	4818339.0
道路运输业	The road transport industry	117	25206132.3	18479691.3
水上运输业	Water transportation			
航空运输业	The air transport industry	12	3595228.5	1822262.9
管道运输业	Pipeline transportation	1	48378.2	15151.9
装卸搬运和运输代理业	Handling and transport industry	24	151499.8	56435.1
仓储业	Warehousing industry	32	851567.7	160117.6
邮政业	The postal service	10	647669.6	456058.0
电信、广播电视和卫星传输服务业	Telecommunication, broadcasting and satellite transmission services	16	8926349.7	12408150.1
互联网和相关服务	The Internet and related services	23	262282.0	12400.0
软件和信息技术服务业	Software and information technology services	174	2887163.1	439936.4
物业管理	Property management	159	754791.7	165281.3
房地产中介服务	Real estate intermediary service	7	20242.4	4056.4
其他房地产业	Other Real Estate	1	3709.0	540.0
自有房地产经营活动	Owned Real Estate Business Activities	18	555204.5	210729.6
租赁业	Leasing industry	11	887594.1	53597.1
商务服务业	Business services	293	17158144.8	843703.1
研究和试验发展	Research and development	23	1060867.4	388586.8
专业技术服务业	Professional and technical services	222	5317867.2	659384.4
科技推广和应用服务业	Promotion and application of science and technology services	22	855359.8	158883.7
水利管理业	Water resources management industry	3	4499.5	1300.6
生态保护和环境治理业	Ecological protection and environmental control industries	6	137641.6	75088.8
公共设施管理业	Public facilities management industry	53	1957921.7	357830.4
居民服务业	Resident services	24	159964.2	81446.2
机动车、电子产品和日用产品修理业	Motor vehicles, electronics and household goods-repairing	20	157726.8	22081.0
其他服务业	Other service industries	15	20534.2	4572.4
教育	Education	18	81324.6	18650.0
卫生	Health	66	530175.2	256587.8
社会工作	Social work	1	31.7	3.5
新闻出版业	Press and publishing industry	29	465069.4	79171.5
广播、电视、电影和影视录音制作业	Radio, television, film and video recordings	70	693982.8	86212.4
文化艺术业	Culture and arts	47	2602578.4	258848.8
体育	Physical education	10	107272.1	31257.0
娱乐业	The entertainment industry	15	157062.6	67171.6

Main Economic Indicators for Services above the Designated Size grouped by Industry（2017）

（10 000 yuan)

负债合计 Total Liabilities	所有者权益合计 Total Owners' Equities	营业收入 Paid in Capital	主营业务收入 Revenue from Principal Business	营业成本 Total Cost	主营业务成本 Cost of Principal Business
50412896.1	**30759793.3**	**21146457.1**	**20736664.7**	**15282402.8**	**15049646.5**
3334211.7	1572641.1	554345.5	553990.9	401444.1	401417.2
18750378.4	6455753.9	1807603.2	1775293.8	1134269.9	1107417.4
994582.5	2600646.0	443961.3	400525.2	384663.2	363125.0
28690.9	19687.3	35535.3	28474.0	34836.4	29118.4
76489.7	75010.1	146562.5	146481.9	122157.7	122097.7
681984.8	169582.9	427596.3	422408.8	399067.9	394600.7
440696.6	206973.0	699076.6	675493.7	573996.0	572067.7
3488765.9	5437583.8	4366171.4	4309628.7	2884482.1	2826277.0
96906.2	165375.8	385141.8	381520.0	254147.1	254129.5
1550584.0	1336579.1	2957475.5	2919939.4	1998522.1	1990883.4
607321.1	147470.6	555703.9	522704.9	440511.4	417389.8
9790.6	10451.8	19975.4	19975.4	5931.1	5931.1
1846.2	1862.8	7255.5	6674.0	3221.4	2853.4
358374.4	196830.1	96825.9	80327.8	32754.0	32227.2
692337.1	195257.0	103149.8	102288.0	87963.5	87059.3
10640155.7	6517989.1	2253800.7	2184410.4	1690790.2	1669423.9
381155.3	679712.1	610305.3	600881.2	460177.1	456661.9
3430823.5	1887043.7	3663011.3	3635108.5	2935937.8	2908086.3
518635.4	336724.4	135988.5	132966.9	103721.1	102998.1
3478.1	1021.4	6714.0	6642.7	5737.8	5687.3
76922.3	60719.3	32777.5	32051.4	17762.6	17639.6
1396017.2	561904.5	489515.4	484649.9	373683.5	370490.3
158018.7	1945.5	49763.0	49623.6	36640.0	36630.2
130219.2	27507.6	48581.3	47872.7	41873.2	41326.4
9480.8	11053.4	23257.9	23257.9	18097.3	18097.3
57912.9	23411.7	99938.1	99569.8	63021.2	62986.8
304101.7	226073.5	372331.0	367577.8	254040.0	243750.9
1242.9	-1211.2	512.9	512.9	454.6	454.6
263106.2	201963.2	269320.7	262128.2	205001.1	201023.6
410776.1	283206.7	298994.6	290134.5	211705.3	204670.9
1320244.7	1282333.7	132042.1	121856.7	71181.3	69071.6
45804.0	61468.1	27721.8	27070.1	17938.6	17743.0
151841.3	5221.3	25501.1	24623.0	16672.2	16309.0

18-3 续表1

单位：万元

指标	Item	销售费用 Sale Expenses	管理费用 Managenment Expenses	财务费用 Financial Expenses
总计	**Total**	**1206035.9**	**2104498.2**	**1191706.4**
按国民经济行业大类分组	**Grouped by sector categories**			
铁路运输业	Railway transport industry	3.4	6842.1	120115.3
道路运输业	The road transport industry	19329.0	115924.7	785827.9
水上运输业	Water transportation			
航空运输业	The air transport industry	7785.0	41671.7	9290.8
管道运输业	Pipeline transportation		1844.8	72.2
装卸搬运和运输代理业	Handling and transport industry	4927.8	13539.7	398.4
仓储业	Warehousing industry	10780.0	21050.6	13411.8
邮政业	The postal service	2465.4	102351.7	1850.5
电信、广播电视和卫星传输服务业	Telecommunication, broadcasting and satellite transmission services	558187.2	234025.3	33237.8
互联网和相关服务	The Internet and related services	14070.6	36042.2	1839.7
软件和信息技术服务业	Software and information technology services	159621.7	534618.2	10184.6
物业管理	Property management	22224.7	71346.9	7847.8
房地产中介服务	Real estate intermediary service	1847.4	5893.4	-26.3
其他房地产业	Other Real Estate		3115.8	-3.8
自有房地产经营活动	Owned Real Estate Business Activities	890.9	20515.6	8480.6
租赁业	Leasing industry	3723.7	4198.2	2405.7
商务服务业	Business services	106870.9	222548.4	122808.0
研究和试验发展	Research and development	9404.9	73458.7	2173.7
专业技术服务业	Professional and technical services	102876.3	317345.8	481.0
科技推广和应用服务业	Promotion and application of science and technology services	4893.9	19044.0	9358.2
水利管理业	Water resources management industry	65.5	883.4	9.6
生态保护和环境治理业	Ecological protection and environmental control industries	6691.1	4161.8	868.2
公共设施管理业	Public facilities management industry	22338.3	52031.5	14114.2
居民服务业	Resident services	4819.3	7762.4	405.2
机动车、电子产品和日用产品修理业	Motor vehicles, electronics and household goods-repairing	1902.3	4238.0	1522.3
其他服务业	Other service industries	1095.6	2878.9	-39.8
教育	Education	7482.6	17945.1	453.7
卫生	Health	30919.1	58616.6	4729.0
社会工作	Social work	103.5	310.8	0.2
新闻出版业	Press and publishing industry	22167.9	38308.3	-734.5
广播、电视、电影和影视录音制作业	Radio, television, film and video recordings	32177.0	34192.0	8830.3
文化艺术业	Culture and arts	34223.1	29979.9	26286.2
体育	Physical education	4176.8	3474.0	110.1
娱乐业	The entertainment industry	7971.0	4337.7	5397.8

continued 1

(10 000 yuan)

投资收益 Investment Income	营业利润 Business Profits	利润总额 Total Profits	应付职工薪酬 Salary Payable	从业人员平均人数（人） Annual Average Employed Persons (person)
286218.3	**1616118.6**	**1701396.9**	**4228194.3**	**406270**
-20.0	24100.2	19729.6	4120.5	133
24287.1	-58872.0	-45944.9	454749.8	52779
10120.3	4979.1	17541.8	145542.3	8619
	-1325.5	-1381.9	7664.6	593
6.0	5286.6	6628.0	22744.7	3111
-1757.5	-22996.2	538.6	19582.7	3019
	6936.0	6395.0	189676.3	26790
4733.5	611237.4	558724.0	603037.4	44649
-134.3	75910.2	77338.2	29461.5	3161
1484.8	214904.5	278617.1	1186704.6	53642
2168.3	10772.1	11419.1	186533.1	42974
718.1	6778.3	7190.3	6437.0	671
	871.0	319.3	710.2	130
4864.3	34797.8	8506.0	12650.9	1299
59.4	4545.3	5008.5	3370.3	451
138248.3	237535.9	245728.4	273000.8	46630
14412.2	72078.3	77012.3	127743.5	9598
55050.7	328491.7	334231.8	538047.6	44488
1840.8	-622.0	747.2	19077.5	1837
	-11.5	-13.4	742.2	133
8.1	2551.1	4728.9	6696.1	845
166.0	35235.8	35866.5	89380.7	15415
-17.0	-280.3	46.3	17753.5	4841
1900.0	667.1	2005.0	5825.8	1074
	958.9	967.6	11918.6	3424
14.9	10606.1	10469.6	29657.6	4659
2804.8	25088.5	25913.0	102564.6	15001
	-355.6	-350.9	239.7	75
999.6	1642.0	9888.7	41582.6	3950
678.6	5717.3	12136.7	36258.3	4545
23068.5	-14227.4	-2098.5	39921.6	5193
222.6	2039.3	2030.9	4745.6	1020
290.2	-8921.4	-8541.9	10052.1	1521

18-4 规模以上服务业按隶属关系分主要经济指标（2017年）

单位：万元

指标	Item	企业单位数（个） Number of Enterprises (unit)	资产总计 Total Assets	固定资产原价 Original Value of Fixed Assets
总计	**Total**	**1546**	**81172689.4**	**42493526.7**
按隶属关系分	**Grouped by affiliation**			
中央	Central	72	13953390.8	12873308.3
省（自治州、直辖市）	Province (autonomous prefectures, municipalities)	173	31089164.5	20379342.8
地（区、市、州、盟）	Land (District, municipal, State, Union)	214	16094044.4	5852022.3
县（区、市、旗）	Counties (districts, cities, flags)	39	2035968.2	142604.3
街道	Street			
镇	Town			
乡	Township			
（社区）居委会	(Community) neighborhood			
村委会	Village			
其他	Others	1048	18000121.5	3246249.0

18-4 续表1

单位：万元

指标	Item	销售费用 Sale Expenses	管理费用 Management Expenses	财务费用 Financial Expenses
总计	**Total**	**1206035.9**	**2104498.2**	**1191706.4**
按隶属关系分	**Grouped by affiliation**			
中央	Central	394551.4	441550.1	152554.1
省（自治州、直辖市）	Province (autonomous prefectures, municipalities)	297179.3	338359.6	679797.4
地（区、市、州、盟）	Land (District, municipal, State, Union)	138849.3	464400.3	196249.1
县（区、市、旗）	Counties (districts, cities, flags)	4545.8	22122.8	6013.3
街道	Street			
镇	Town			
乡	Township			
（社区）居委会	(Community) neighborhood			
村委会	Village			
其他	Others	370910.1	838065.4	157092.5

Main Economic Indicators for Services above the Designated Size grouped by Affiliation（2017）

(10 000 yuan)

负债合计 Total Liabilities	所有者权益合计 Total Owners' Equities	营业收入 Paid in Capital	主营业务收入 Revenue from Principal Business	营业成本 Total Cost	主营业务成本 Cost of Principal Business
50412896.1	**30759793.3**	**21146457.1**	**20736664.7**	**15282402.8**	**15049646.5**
7933120.1	6020270.7	6274959.6	6181095.8	4783157.5	4735402.6
18068453.7	13020710.8	5123885.0	5002602.6	3291717.7	3222584.9
11435840.7	4658203.7	2693082.0	2641126.3	2133336.3	2101774.4
1388666.9	647301.3	111807.9	105249.4	88326.4	86860.3
11586814.7	6413306.8	6942722.6	6806590.6	4985864.9	4903024.3

continued 1

(10 000 yuan)

投资收益 Investment Income	营业利润 Business Profits	利润总额 Total Profits	应付职工薪酬 Salary Payable	从业人员平均人数（人） Annual Average Employed Persons (person)
286218.3	**1616118.6**	**1701396.9**	**4228194.3**	**406270**
20870.1	463103.1	432061.9	895273.0	63511
93785.4	554981.9	555160.0	745305.0	76991
28804.5	-45457.3	1217.8	815390.4	87897
1868.2	-7249.8	-2361.4	29233.2	6322
140890.1	650740.7	715318.6	1742992.7	171549

主要统计指标解释

国家统计局规模以上服务业单位统计标准：辖区内年营业收入1000万元及以上，或年末从业人员50人及以上服务业法人单位。包括：交通运输、仓储和邮政业，信息传输、软件和信息技术服务业，租赁和商务服务业，科学研究和技术服务业，水利、环境和公共设施管理业，教育，卫生和社会工作；以及物业管理、房地产中介服务、自有房地产经营活动和其他房地产业等行业。

辖区内年营业收入500万元及以上，或年末从业人员50人及以上服务业法人单位。包括：居民服务、修理和其他服务业，文化、体育和娱乐业。

固定资产原价 指固定资产的成本，包括企业在购置、自行建造、安装、改建、扩建、技术改造某项固定资产时所发生的全部支出总额。根据会计“固定资产”科目的期末借方余额填报。

资产总计 指企业过去的交易或者事项形成的、由企业拥有或者控制的、预期会给企业带来经济利益的资源。资产一般按流动性（资产的变现或耗用时间长短）分为流动资产和非流动资产。其中流动资产可分为货币资金、交易性金融资产、应收票据、应收账款、预付款项、其他应收款、存货等；非流动资产可分为长期股权投资、固定资产、无形资产及其他非流动资产等。根据会计“资产负债表”中“资产总计”项目的期末余额数填报。

执行《企业会计准则》或《小企业会计准则》的企业：资产总计=流动资产合计+非流动资产合计；执行其他企业会计制度的企业资产包括流动资产、长期投资、固定资产、无形资产和其他资产等。

负债合计 指企业过去的交易或者事项形成的，预期会导致经济利益流出企业的现时义务。负债一般按偿还期长短分为流动负债和非流动负债。根据会计“资产负债表”中“负债合计”项目的期末余额数填报。

执行《企业会计准则》或《小企业会计准则》的企业：负债合计=流动负债合计+非流动负债合计；执行其他企业会计制度的企业负债包括流动负债和长期负债。

所有者权益合计 指企业资产扣除负债后由所有者享有的剩余权益。公司的所有者权益又称股东权益。包括实收资本、资本公积、盈余公积、未分配利润等。根据会计“资产负债表”中“所有者权益合计”项目的期末余额数填报。

营业收入 指企业经营主要业务和其他业务所确认的收入总额。营业收入合计包括“主营业务收入”和“其他业务收入”。根据会计“利润表”中“营业收入”项目的本期金额数填报。

主营业务收入 指企业确认的销售商品、提供劳务等主营业务的收入。根据会计“主营业务收入”科目的期末贷方余额（结转前）填报。执行《企业会计准则》或《小企业会计准则》的企业，如未设置该科目，以“营业收入”代替填报。

营业成本 指企业经营主要业务和其他业务所发生的成本总额。包括企业（单位）在报告期内从事销售商品、提供劳务等日常活动发生的各种耗费。包括“主营业务成本”和“其他业务成本”。根据会计“利润表”中“营业成本”项目的本期金额数填报。

主营业务成本 指企业经营主要业务所发生的成本总额。根据会计“主营业务成本”科目的期末借方余额（结转前）填报。执行《企业会计准则》或《小企业会计准则》的企业，如未设置该科目，以“营业成本”代替填报。

销售费用 指企业在销售商品和材料、提供劳务的过程中发生的各种费用，包括保险费、包装费、展览费和广告费、商品维修费、预计产品质量保证损失、运输费、装卸费等以及为销售本企业商品而专设的销售机构（含销售网点、售后服务网点等）的职工薪酬、业务费、折旧费等经营费用。建筑业企业销售费用指企业从事施工生产活动过程中发生的各项费用，包括应由企业负担的运输费、装卸费、包装费、保险费、维修费、展览费、差旅费、广告费和其他经费。房地产企业销售费用指企业在从事主要经营业务过程中所发生的各项销售费用，包括转让、销售、结算和出租开发产品等。执行《企业会计准则》或《小企业会计准则》的企业，根据会计“利润表”中“销售费用”项目的本期金额数填报。执行其他企业会计制度的企业，根据会计“利润表”中“营业费用（或经营费用）”项目的本期金额数填报。

管理费用 指企业为组织和管理企业生产经营所发生的费用，包括企业在筹建期间内发生的开办费、董事会和行政管理部门在企业经营管理中发生的，或者应当由企业统一负担的公司经费等。根据会计“利润表”中“管理费用”项目的本期金额数填报。

财务费用 指企业为筹集生产经营所需资金等而发生的筹资费用，包括企业生产经营期间发生的利息支出（减利息收入）、汇兑损失（减汇兑收益）以及相关的手续费等。根据会计“利润表”中“财务费用”项目的本期金额数填报。

投资收益 指企业确认的投资收益或投资损失，反映企业以各种方式对外投资所取得的收益。根据会计

“利润表”中“投资收益”项目的本期金额数填报。如为投资损失以“-”号记。

营业利润 指企业从事生产经营活动所取得的利润。执行《企业会计准则》的企业，营业利润为营业收入减去营业成本、营业税金及附加、销售费用、管理费用、财务费用、资产减值损失，再加上公允价值变动收益和投资收益。执行《小企业会计准则》的企业，营业利润为营业收入减去营业成本，营业税金及附加、销售费用、管理费用、财务费用，再加上投资收益后的金额；执行其他企业会计制度的企业，营业利润为主营业务收入减去主营业务成本、主营业务税金及附加，加上其他业务利润后，再减去销售费用、管理费用、财务费用后的金额。根据会计“利润表”中“营业利润”项目的本期金额数填报。

利润总额 指企业在一定会计期间的经营成果，是生产经营过程中各种收入扣除各种耗费后的盈余，反映企业在报告期内实现的盈亏总额。根据会计“利润表”中“利润总额”项目的本期金额数填报。执行《企业会计准则》或《小企业会计准则》的企业，利润总额为营业利润加上营业外收入，减去营业外支出后的金额；执行其他企业会计制度的企业，利润总额为营业利润加上投资收益、政府补助、营业外收入，再减去营业外支出后的金额。

应付职工薪酬 指企业为获得职工提供的服务而给予各种形式的报酬以及其他相关支出。包括职工工资、奖金、津贴和补贴，职工福利费，医疗保险费、养老保险费、失业保险费、工伤保险费和生育保险费等社会保险费，住房公积金，工会经费和职工教育经费，非货币性福利，因解除与职工的劳动关系给予的补偿，其他与获得职工提供的服务相关的支出。执行《企业会计准则》或《小企业会计准则》的企业，根据会计科目“应付职工薪酬”的本年贷方累计发生额填报；执行其他企业会计制度的企业，应将本年上述职工薪酬包含的科目归并填报。

从业人员平均人数 指报告期内(年度、月度)平均拥有的人员数。按“谁用工，谁统计”的原则，包括正式人员，劳务派遣人员和临时聘用人员。

Explanatory Notes on Main Statistical Indicators

Statistical standard of the services unit above the designated size of the National Bureau of Statistics: The legal entitiesof the area whoseannual revenues are10 million yuan and above, or at the end of the service sector whose employees are more than 50 people.Including: transportation, storage and postal services, information transmission, software and information technology services, leasing and business services, scientific research and technological services, water conservancy, environment and public facilities management industry, education, health and social work as well as property management and real estate services industries.The legal entitiesof the area whoseannual revenues are5 million yuan and above, or at the end of the service sector whose employees are more than 50 people.Including: service, repair and other services, cultural, sports and entertainment.

Original value of fixed assets: It refers to the cost of fixed assets, including the enterprise itself costs on the acquisition, construction, installation, alteration, expansion, technological innovation of an asset for all expenditure. Depending on the "fixed assets" account debit balance at the end of filling.

Total assets: It refers to the resourcesformed bypast transactions or events, thatthe enterprise owns or controls, is expected to bring economic benefits to the enterprise. Asset is classified into current assets and non-current assets by its liquidity (realization of assets or spent time). Current assets can be divided into currency, tradable financial assets, notes receivable, accounts receivable, prepayments, other receivables and inventory; and non-current assets can be classified as equity investments, fixed assets, intangible assets and other non-current assets. It depends on the "balance sheet" of "total assets" closing balance number of items.

For business enterprisesthat implemented the 2006 accounting standard: total assets= total current assets +total non-current assets; for those who didn't implement the accounting standards, assets for business enterprises include current assets, long-term investments, fixed assets, intangible assets and other assets.

Total liabilities: It refers tothe present obligations of the enterprisethat formed by past transactions or events and are expected to lead to an outflow of economic benefits. Liability is divided into current and non-current liabilities according to the length of the repayment period. It depends onthe "balance sheets" in the "total" closing balance number of items.

For business enterprises that implemented the 2006 accounting standard: total liabilities = total current liabilities+ total non-current liabilities; for those who didn't implement the accounting standards, liabilities include current liabilities and long-term liabilities.

Totalowners ' equity: It refers to the residual rights and interests enjoyed by the owner after deducting the liabilities of an enterprise. The owner of the company is also called the shareholder's right. It includes the paid in capital, capital reserves, surplus reserves, undistributed profit and so on. According to the accounting "balance sheet", "the owner's equity total", the final balance of the project is reported.

Operating income: It refers to the total revenue recognized by the business and other business operations of the enterprise. Total operating income includes "main business income" and "other business income". It's reported according to the "business income" project of the "business income" in the accounting "profit statement".

The main business income: It refers to the income of the business of the main business, such as the sale of goods, services, etc..It's reported in accordance with the final credit balance of the accounts of the subject's "main business income" (before the transfer). For business enterprises that didn't implement the accounting standard, if not set up the subject, should fill the forms instead of the "operating income".

Operating cost: Itrefers to the total cost incurred by the business and other business of the enterprise. It includes a variety of costsof enterprises (units) in the reporting period to engage in sales of goods, services and other daily activities provided.It includes"the main business costs" and "other business costs". According to the "operating cost" of the "business cost" of the project in accordance with the accounting statement.

The main business cost: Itrefers to the total cost of the main business. It's reported in accordance with the final debit balance of the subject of accounting "main business cost". For business enterprises that didn't implement the accounting standard, if not set up the subject, should fill the forms instead of the "operating costs".

Selling expenses: It refers to the expenses of the enterprisein sales of goods and materials and providing services, including insurance, packing, exhibition fees and advertising fees, maintenance of commodity, expected to ensure product quality loss, transportation, loading and unloading charges and sales of the enterprise products and dedicated sales organizations (including sales network and after-sales service network) employee compensation, business expenses, depreciation charges and operating expenses. Construction enterprises selling expenses refers to expenses occurring in the process of production enterprises engaged in construction activities, including transportation fee shall be borne by the enterprise, handling, packing, insurance, maintenance, exhibition fees, poor travel costs, advertising costs and other expenses. Real estate enterprise sales cost refers to the business in the main business process of the sales costs, including transfer, sales, settlement and rental development products, etc.. According to the "sales expense" in accounting "profit statement", the amount of the item in this period of the project is reported. For business enterprises that didn't implement the 2006 accounting standard, according to the number of "operating expenses (or operating expenses)" of the project in accordance with the "profit statement".

Management expenses: Itrefers to the expenses for the organization and management of enterprise production and management of the enterprises, including costs in construction occurred during the start-up costs, the board of directors and administrative departments in enterprise management, or shall be made by the enterprise unified burden of company funds. According to the "management fee" in the accounting "profit table", the amount of this period of the project is reported.

Financial expenses: Itrefers tothe costsof the enterprise to raise the production and business operation required capital and funding, including occurred during the production and operation of enterprises interest payments (a reduction in interest income), exchange loss (less exchange gains) and related fees. It is reportedaccording to the amount of the "financial expense" in the project of "financial expense" in the accounting "profit statement".

Investment income: Itrefers to the enterprise confirming the investment income or investment losses, reflecting the foreign investment income of the enterprise in various ways. According to the "investment income" in the accounting "profit statement", the amount of this period of the project is reported. Such as investment losses to "-".

Operating profit: Itrefers tothe profits made by the enterprises in the production and operation activities. For business enterprises that implemented the 2006 accounting standard, operating profit is revenues minus operating costs, business taxes and surcharges, sales, management costs, financial costs, asset impairment loss and plus fair value changes in income and investment income. Without executing the "accounting standards for business enterprises" enterprises, operating profit equals the main business income minus the cost of major business, main business tax and surcharges, and plus profit from other operations, then minus the cost of sales and management costs, financial costs. It is reported according to the number of "operating profit" items in the accounting "profit table".

Total profit: Itrefers tothe business results of the enterprise in a certain accounting period, and it is the production and operation of various kinds of income after deducting the cost of earnings, reflecting the enterprise in the reporting period to achieve total profit and loss. According to the amount of the total amount of the total profit of the project in accordance with the accounting profit table. For business enterprises that implemented the 2006 accounting standard, the total profit is operating profit plus operating income, andminus operating expenses; while who didn't execute the " accounting standards for business enterprises", a total profit is operating profit plus return on investment, income subsidies, camp outside the industry income, andminus operating expenses.

Employee compensation: Itrefers tovarious forms of remuneration and other related expenses paid by the company for the services provided by the staff and workers. It includes wages, bonuses, allowances and subsidies, employee welfare benefit expenses, medical insurance, endowment insurance, unemployment insurance, work-related injury insurance premiums and maternity insurance fees social insurance, housing provident fund, the trade union funds and employee education funds, non-monetary benefits, for the solution in addition to give labor relations and workers compensation, and obtain a worker to provide other services related expenditure. For business enterprises that implemented the accounting standard, according to accounting subjects "to deal with workers' compensation" this year, the accumulated credits is filled; those who didn't execute the "accounting standards for business enterprises", it should be the employee compensation including the amalgamative course reportingthis year.

Average number of persons engaged in service

activities: It refers to the number of persons engaged in the service industry in the reporting period (annual, monthly). The principles of statistics is implemented according to the principle that "who labor, who statistics," including the official personnel, labor sent contingent personnel and temporaryemployeeswho take part in the enterprise service activities. And itdon't include employeeswho receive wages, dividends, bonusas well as not participate in the service activities of the enterprise.

19 金融业

FINANCIAL INTERMEDIATION

资料整理：罗延庆
Data management: Luo Yanqing
数据审核：陈　英
Data audit：Chen Ying

第十九部分　金融业

一、简要说明

本章资料包括金融、证券和保险业情况，由西安市统计局综合处根据人民银行西安分行营业管理部和市金融办提供资料整理。本部分2017年数据为西安原口径数据。

二、主要指标

金融机构人民币（含外资）存款余额（亿元）	20047.62	比上年增长	5.1%
金融机构人民币（含外资）贷款余额（亿元）	16954.81	比上年增长	10.9%
保费收入（亿元）	421.10	比上年增长	21.8%

19　FINANCIAL INTERMEDIATION

Ⅰ.Brief Introduction

This chapter includes information of the financial, securities and insurance, compiled by Integration Division of the Xi'an Bureau of Statistics, according to data from Xi'an Branch Management Department of the People's Bank of China, Provincial Banking Bureau and Xi'an Financial Office.

Ⅱ.Major Indicators

		Increase over Preceding Year
Deposits in Financial Institution(100 mil. yuan)	20047.62	5.1%
Loans in Financial Institutions(100 mil.yuan)	16954.81	10.9%
Premiums(100 mil. yuan)	421.10	21.8%

19-1 西安银行系统机构、人员数

Number of Institution and Employed Person in Finance System in Xi'an

机构名称	Name of Institution	2016		2017	
		机构数（个）Number of Institution (unit)	年末人数（人）Number of Staff and Workers (person)	机构数（个）Number of Institution (unit)	年末人数（人）Number of Staff and Workers (person)
合计	**Total**	**2095**	**39936**	**2132**	**39628**
1. 人民银行西安分行营业管理部	Management Department of the People's Bank of China Xi'an Branch	1	365	1	360
2. 国家开发银行	National Development Bank	1	189	1	193
3. 中国进出口银行	Export Import Bank of China	1	69	1	71
4. 中国工商银行	Industrial and Commercial Bank of China	189	4931	184	4727
5. 中国农业银行	Agricultural Bank of China	175	3208	176	3134
6. 中国银行	Bank of China	126	3457	133	3525
7. 中国建设银行	Construction Bank of China	200	4362	204	4332
8. 交通银行	Bank of Communication	57	1221	58	1212
9. 中国邮政储蓄银行	The Postal Savings Bank of China	280	873	275	858
10. 中国农业发展银行	Agricultural Development Bank of China	11	281	11	283
11. 中信银行	CITIC Bank	29	926	29	883
12. 中国光大银行	China Everbright Bank	41	954	44	920
13. 华夏银行	China Huaxia Bank	20	789	20	857
14. 广发银行	China Guangfa Bank	1	148	2	192
15. 平安银行	Pingan Bank	12	411	12	384
16. 招商银行	China Merchants Bank	55	1569	55	1571
17. 上海浦东发展银行	Pufa Bank	19	690	39	684
18. 兴业银行	Fujian Industrial Bank	70	870	70	837
19. 中国民生银行	China Minsheng Banking	21	1090	21	1008
20. 恒丰银行	Evergrowing Bank	15	427	17	441
21. 浙商银行	China Zheshang Bank	8	400	8	456
22. 渤海银行	China Bohai Bank	1	100	1	124
23. 北京银行	Bank of Beijing	19	815	22	836
24. 齐商银行	Qi Commercial Bank	8	243	8	229
25. 成都银行	Bank of Chengdu	5	184	6	184
26. 重庆银行	Bank of Chongqing	4	256	6	275
27. 宁夏银行	Bank of Ningxia	6	233	7	236
28. 昆仑银行	Bank of Kunlun	13	440	15	436
29. 西安银行	Bank of Xi'an	145	2587	145	2586
30. 长安银行	Bank of Changan	52	765	59	761
31. 农村商业银行	Rural Commercial Bank	235	3377	343	4632
其中：秦农银行	Qinnong Bank	235	3377	235	3448
32. 农村信用社	Rural Credit Cooperatives	251	3091	136	1808
33. 村镇银行	Village Bank	11	247	11	266
34. 香港汇丰银行	Huifeng Bank of Hong Kong	3	45	3	41
35. 香港东亚银行	Dongya Bank of Hong Kong	7	256	6	217
36. 新加坡星展银行	DBS Bank	1	14	1	13
37. 英国标准渣打银行	British Standard Chartered Bank	1	20	1	22
38. 韩亚银行	Hana Bank	1	33	1	34

注：本表数据来源于人民银行西安营管部，2017年数据为西安原口径数据。下同。

19-2 金融机构（含外资）本外币存贷款年末余额（2017年）

Deposits and Loans of Local Currency and Foreign Currency in Financial Institution (Including Foreign-Funded Institution)at Year-end（2017）

单位：万元 (10 000 yuan)

指 标	Item	2017	比年初增减额 Increase or Decrease Compared with The Beginning of The Year
一、各项存款	**All Deposits**	**203781107**	**8897260**
（一）境内存款	Domestic Deposits	203512023	8939846
1. 住户存款	Household Deposits	75970594	4544389
（1）活期存款	Demand Deposits	30145541	1875891
（2）定期及其他存款	Time and Other Deposits	45825053	2668498
2. 非金融企业存款	Non Financial Enterprises Deposits	84087234	3560857
（1）活期存款	Demand Deposits	44075535	2167122
（2）定期及其他存款	Time and Other Deposits	40011699	1393735
3. 广义政府存款	General Government Deposits	36172439	3752419
（1）财政性存款	Fiscal Deposits	3148850	1172585
（2）机关团体存款	Institution Deposits	33023588	2579834
4. 非银行业金融机构存款	Non Banking Financial Institution Deposits	7281756	-2917819
（二）境外存款	Foreign Deposits	269084	-42586
二、各项贷款	**All Loans**	**171551072**	**16127199**
（一）境内贷款	Domestic Loans	171405738	16218680
1. 住户贷款	Household loans	40202701	7016238
（1）短期贷款	Short-term Loans	4337665	504517
消费贷款	Consumer loans	2382965	1000252
经营贷款	Business loans	1954700	-495735
（2）中长期贷款	Medium-term and Long-term loans	35865035	6511722
消费贷款	Consumer loans	32755079	6530828
经营贷款	Business loans	3109957	-19106
2. 非金融企业及机关团体贷款	Non Financial Enterprises and Institution Loans	131201082	9202441
（1）短期贷款	Short-term Loans	26934019	642851
（2）中长期贷款	Medium-term and Long-term loans	98576729	11393232
（3）票据融资	Bill Financing	5539970	-2773755
（4）融资租赁	Financial Leasing	14485	-6871
（5）各项垫款	Various Advance Funds	135879	-53016
3. 非银行业金融机构贷款	Non Banking Financial Institution Loans	1955	
（二）境外贷款	**Foreign Loans**	**145335**	**-91481**

注：本表数据来源于人民银行西安营管部。

19-3 金融机构（不含外资）本外币存贷款年末余额（2017年）

Deposits and Loans Domestic Funded Financial Institution of Local Currency and Foreign Currency at Year-end（2017）

单位：万元 (10 000 yuan)

指　标	Item	2017	比年初增减额 Increase or Decrease Compared with The Beginning of The Year
一、各项存款	**All Deposits**	**202576682**	**8965735**
（一）境内存款	Domestic Deposits	202336689	9010988
1. 住户存款	Household Deposits	75765760	4482758
（1）活期存款	Demand Deposits	30086540	1877330
（2）定期及其他存款	Time and Other Deposits	45679220	2605428
2. 非金融企业存款	Non Financial Enterprises Deposits	83246131	3461464
（1）活期存款	Demand Deposits	43827294	2154229
（2）定期及其他存款	Time and Other Deposits	39418837	1307235
3. 广义政府存款	General Government Deposits	36113042	3794584
（1）财政性存款	Fiscal Deposits	3148850	1172585
（2）机关团体存款	Institution Deposits	32964192	2621999
4. 非银行业金融机构存款	Non Banking Financial Institution Deposits	7211756	-2727818
（二）境外存款	Foreign Deposits	239993	-45253
二、各项贷款	**All Loans**	**170309965**	**16140294**
（一）境内贷款	Domestic Loans	170168005	16231248
1. 住户贷款	Household loans	40103641	7033751
（1）短期贷款	Short-term Loans	4337300	504152
消费贷款	Consumer loans	2382965	1000252
经营贷款	Business loans	1954335	-496100
（2）中长期贷款	Medium-term and Long-term loans	35766341	6529599
消费贷款	Consumer loans	32680339	6539736
经营贷款	Business loans	3086002	-10137
2. 非金融企业及机关团体贷款	Non Financial Enterprises and Institution Loans	130062409	9197497
（1）短期贷款	Short-term Loans	26781152	669995
（2）中长期贷款	Medium-term and Long-term loans	97599456	11369634
（3）票据融资	Bill Financing	5531459	-2782266
（4）融资租赁	Financial Leasing	14485	-6871
（5）各项垫款	Various Advance Funds	135857	-52995
3. 非银行业金融机构贷款	Non Banking Financial Institution Loans	1955	
（二）境外贷款	**Foreign Loans**	**141960**	**-90954**

注：本表数据来源于人民银行西安营管部。

19-4 主要年份金融机构（含外资）人民币存贷款年末余额

Deposits and Loans in Financial Institutions (Including Foreign-funded) in Representative Years

单位：亿元 (100million yuan)

年 份 Year	存款年末余额（亿元） Balance of Deposit at Year-end	非金融企业存款 Non Financial Enterprises Deposits	住户存款 Household Deposits	贷款年末余额 Balance of Loan at Year-end
1978	11.66		2.57	21.72
1980	17.02		4.22	23.08
1985	40.64		14.26	49.08
1990	146.17	31.10	77.09	152.77
1995	471.89	114.54	291.46	403.16
1996	619.98	199.85	394.02	477.97
1997	686.72	227.61	433.56	503.32
1998	799.54	245.44	499.68	597.34
1999	1014.27	347.49	586.40	786.20
2000	1335.63	540.19	675.83	972.51
2001	1629.72	674.49	800.86	1185.97
2002	2191.47	884.69	988.04	1598.42
2003	2665.87	1041.43	1210.56	1954.18
2004	3061.66	1159.98	1432.86	2052.33
2005	3599.70	1237.37	1716.76	2158.10
2006	4066.16	1374.91	1950.53	2344.77
2007	4582.71	1702.12	2002.38	2683.77
2008	5749.37	2213.67	2513.70	3275.12
2009	7522.08	3077.99	3084.20	4482.63
2010	8933.23	3556.78	3641.09	6482.28
2011	10430.27	5997.60	4155.65	7564.93
2012	12125.53	6927.84	4787.03	8635.22
2013	13763.19	7759.61	5357.05	10023.63
2014	15166.78	8604.03	5698.15	11668.14
2015	17796.38	7031.75	6571.18	13714.02
2016	19073.96	7788.07	7035.81	15282.65
2017	20047.62	8203.27	7497.30	16954.81

注：本表数据来源于人民银行西安营管部，对部分历史年份数据进行了修订。

19-5 金融机构（含外资）人民币存贷款年末余额（2017年）

Loans in Financial Institutions (Including Foreign-funded) in Representative Years（2017）

单位：亿元 （100 million yuan）

指　标	Item	2017	比年初增减额 Increase or Decrease Compared with The Beginning of The Year
一、各项存款	**All Deposits**	**200476162**	**9736546**
（一）境内存款	Domestic Deposits	200374414	9760937
1. 住户存款	Household Deposits	74972963	4612124
（1）活期存款	Demand Deposits	29625463	1951438
（2）定期及其他存款	Time and Other Deposits	45347499	2660686
2. 非金融企业存款	Non Financial Enterprises Deposits	82032714	4176998
（1）活期存款	Demand Deposits	42943023	2935351
（2）定期及其他存款	Time and Other Deposits	39089691	1241647
3. 广义政府存款	General Government Deposits	36141275	3743332
（1）财政性存款	Fiscal Deposits	3148850	1172585
（2）机关团体存款	Institution Deposits	32992424	2570747
4. 非银行业金融机构存款	Non Banking Financial Institution Deposits	7227462	-2771517
（二）境外存款	Foreign Deposits	101749	-24391
二、各项贷款	**All Loans**	**169548127**	**16721676**
（一）境内贷款	Domestic Loans	169539278	16753888
1. 住户贷款	Household loans	40201079	7016848
（1）短期贷款	Short-term Loans	4336095	504965
消费贷款	Consumer loans	2381394	1000700
经营贷款	Business loans	1954700	-495735
（2）中长期贷款	Medium-term and Long-term loans	35864985	6511883
消费贷款	Consumer loans	32755028	6530839
经营贷款	Business loans	3109957	-18956
2. 非金融企业及机关团体贷款	Non Financial Enterprises and Institution Loans	129336244	9737040
（1）短期贷款	Short-term Loans	26014372	795155
（2）中长期贷款	Medium-term and Long-term loans	97636237	11720807
（3）票据融资	Bill Financing	5539970	-2773755
（4）融资租赁	Financial Leasing	14485	-6871
（5）各项垫款	Various Advance Funds	131180	1704
3. 非银行业金融机构贷款	Non Banking Financial Institution Loans	1955	
（二）境外贷款	**Foreign Loans**	**8848**	**-32212**

注：本表数据来源于人民银行西安营管部。

19-6 金融机构（不含外资）人民币存贷款年末余额（2017年）

Year-end Balance of RMB Deposits and Loans in Financial Institutionst（Not Including Foreign-funded）(2017)

单位：万元 (10 000 yuan)

指　标	Item	2017	比年初增减额 Increase or Decrease Compared with The Beginning of The Year
一、各项存款	**All Deposits**	**199434111**	**9858586**
（一）境内存款	Domestic Deposits	199338104	9883896
1. 住户存款	Household Deposits	74804999	4554440
（1）活期存款	Demand Deposits	29581448	1951382
（2）定期及其他存款	Time and Other Deposits	45223551	2603058
2. 非金融企业存款	Non Financial Enterprises Deposits	81293766	4125475
（1）活期存款	Demand Deposits	42772685	2964455
（2）定期及其他存款	Time and Other Deposits	38521081	1161020
3. 广义政府存款	General Government Deposits	36081878	3785497
（1）财政性存款	Fiscal Deposits	3148850	1172585
（2）机关团体存款	Institution Deposits	32933027	2612912
4. 非银行业金融机构存款	Non Banking Financial Institution Deposits	7157462	-2581517
（二）境外存款	Foreign Deposits	96007	-25309
二、各项贷款	**All Loans**	**168314817**	**16720803**
（一）境内贷款	Domestic Loans	168306823	16752875
1. 住户贷款	Household loans	40102020	7034360
（1）短期贷款	Short-term Loans	4335729	504600
消费贷款	Consumer loans	2381394	1000701
经营贷款	Business loans	1954335	-496100
（2）中长期贷款	Medium-term and Long-term loans	35766290	6529760
消费贷款	Consumer loans	32680289	6539747
经营贷款	Business loans	3086002	-9987
2. 非金融企业及机关团体贷款	Non Financial Enterprises and Institution Loans	128202848	9718515
（1）短期贷款	Short-term Loans	25866781	822635
（2）中长期贷款	Medium-term and Long-term loans	96658965	11683294
（3）票据融资	Bill Financing	5531459	-2782266
（4）融资租赁	Financial Leasing	14485	-6871
（5）各项垫款	Various Advance Funds	131158	1724
3. 非银行业金融机构贷款	Non Banking Financial Institution Loans	1955	
（二）境外贷款	**Foreign Loans**	**7994**	**-32072**

注：本表数据来源于人民银行西安营管部。

19-7 保险业务情况

Indicators of Insurance Business

指　标	Item	2013	2014	2015	2016	2017
保险金额（亿元）	**Amount Insured(100 million yuan)**	**42596**	**51454**	**62319**	**108296**	**151617**
保费收入（万元）	**Premiums(10 000 yuan)**	**2024067**	**2194924**	**2630158**	**3458459**	**4211039**
一、财产险（万元）	**Property Insurance(10 000 yuan)**	**629947**	**741762**	**835526**	**933181**	**1037060**
（一）财产保险	Property Insurance	576666	668574	746317	833296	916524
1. 机动车辆及第三者责任	Motor Vehicle and Outside Person Liability	513634	602904	674555	738965	821186
2. 企业财产险	Enterprise Property Insurance	41140	41996	49949	64568	62226
3. 货物运输险	Freight Transport Insurance	3944	4427	5497	4814	5314
4. 家庭财产险	Family Property Insurance	296	584	754	981	1385
5. 建工及安工保险及其责任险	Construction and Installation Projects Insurance and Related Liability Insurance	16133	16893	12325	18368	20001
6. 其他	Others	1519	1770	3237	5600	6412
（二）责任保险	Liability Insurance	13393	16328	23096	26922	32136
（三）信用保险	Export Credit Insurance	8648	8401	10449	17563	14733
（四）保证保险	Guarantee Insurance	21588	36868	45472	42665	60814
（五）农业保险	Agriculture Insurance	9652	11591	10192	12735	12853
二、人身险（万元）	**Personnel Insurance(10 000 yuan)**	**1394120**	**1453162**	**1794632**	**2525278**	**3173979**
（一）人寿保险	Life Insurance	1221975	1238142	1506062	2158260	2625509
1. 非分红保险	Non Dividend Insurance	109810	444520	681952	1261138	1554807
2. 分红保险	Dividend Insurance	1099986	780652	810889	882110	1055099
3. 投资连接保险	Insurance Connection Insurance	330	316	286	236	217
4. 万能保险	Universal Insurance	11849	12654	12935	14776	15386
（二）意外伤害险	Unforeseen Injury Insurance	49541	52963	63450	71888	84603
（三）健康保险	Health Insurance	122604	162057	225120	295130	463867
赔款支出和各项给付	**Indemnity and Other Expenditure**	**664905**	**807652**	**876182**	**1159143**	**1187057**
一、财产险（万元）	**Property Insurance(10 000 yuan)**	**339005**	**372906**	**406530**	**422765**	**489353**
（一）财产保险	Property Insurance	325128	360385	375449	393905	452892
1. 机动车辆及第三者责任	Motor Vehicle and Outside Person Liability	291390	327319	348185	359288	393011
2. 企业财产险	Enterprise Property Insurance	24870	22257	16753	22038	30811
3. 家庭财产保险	Family Property Insurance	93	107	112	324	757
4. 货物运输保险	Freight Transport Insurance	1224	2429	999	1341	2427
5. 建工及安工保险及其责任险	Construction and Installation Projects Insurance and Related Liability Insurance	6480	6719	8023	9741	12471
6. 其他	Others	1071	1554	1377	1173	13414
（二）责任保险	Liability Insurance	5192	5695	6300	11030	12703
（三）信用保险	Export Credit Insurance	5414	1668	7884	3287	3346
（四）保证保险	Guarantee Insurance	1450	2752	13129	10690	11597
（五）农业保险	Agriculture Insurance	1821	2406	3768	3853	8816
二、人身险（万元）	**Personnel Insurance(10 000 yuan)**	**325900**	**434746**	**469652**	**736378**	**697704**
（一）人寿保险	Life Insurance	268455	360895	379370	637444	557798
1. 非分红保险	Non Dividend Insurance	48680	44359	56908	82635	136279
2. 分红保险	Dividend Insurance	216911	313706	318993	551206	418013
3. 投资连接保险	Insurance Connection Insurance	32	33	48	485	162
4. 万能保险	Universal Insurance	2832	2797	3421	3118	3344
（二）意外伤害险	Unforeseen Injury Insurance	10685	11438	16796	15577	19939
（三）健康保险	Health Insurance	46760	62413	73486	83357	119967
退保金（万元）	**Withdrawal(10 000 yuan)**	**167446**	**405676**	**433227**	**482983**	**682534**
#人寿保险	Life Insurance	165303	403099	414260	459733	659965
1. 非分红保险	Non Dividend Insurance	6192	20818	195551	276544	524211
2. 分红保险	Dividend Insurance	159078	382274	218693	183191	135723
3. 投资连接保险	Insurance Connection Insurance	9				
4. 万能保险	Universal Insurance	24	7	16	-2	31

注：本表数据来源于市金融办。

19-8 西安地区证券期货系统机构、人员数

Number of Institution and Employed Person in Securities and Futures System in Xi'an

机构名称	Name of Institution	2016		2017	
		机构数（个） Number of Institution (unit)	年末人数（人） Number of Staff and Workers (person)	机构数（个） Number of Institution (unit)	年末人数（人） Number of Staff and Workers (person)
证券经营机构	**Securities Company and the Sales Department**	**331**	**8444**	**376**	**8961**
一、证券公司	**Securities Company**	**181**	**4464**	**209**	**5238**
西部证券股份有限公司	Western Securities Company Ltd.	104	2476	116	2693
陕西开源证券经纪有限责任公司	KaiYuan Securities Company Ltd.	54	1440	67	1883
中邮证券有限公司	China Post Securities	23	548	26	662
二、证券营业部（含外地公司在西安营业部）	**Sales Department (include Xi'an) departments of nonlocal companies.)**	**150**	**3980**	**167**	**3723**
期货经纪公司	**Futures Company**	**27**	**492**	**30**	**526**
迈科期货经纪有限公司	Maike Futures Company Ltd.	10	216	10	211
陕西长安期货经纪有限公司	Shanxi ChangAn Futures Company Ltd.	9	103	11	128
西部期货经纪有限公司	Western Futures Brokerage Co., Ltd.	8	173	9	187

注：1.本表数据来源于市金融办。

2.证券公司包括三家公司及其在西安和外地的营业部。

3.中邮证券有限公司原为西安华弘证券经纪有限责任公司。

19-9 证券期货市场基本情况（2017年）

Basic Facts on Securities and Futures Markets（2017）

指 标	Item	2017
一、上市公司情况	**Listed Securities Companies**	
拥有上市股份公司（个）	Number of Listed Share-holding Companies(unit)	33
上市股份公司总股本（亿股）	Total Capital of Listed Share-holding Companies (100 millon shares)	517.32
#流通股(亿股)	Negotiable Shares(100 million shares)	448.21
总市值（亿元）	Total Market Capitalization(100 million yuan)	5154.09
累计证券市场筹措资金（亿元）	Accumulated Capital Raised by Securities Markets(100 millon yuan)	1507.47
二、证券经营机构情况	**Securities Trading Organizations**	
拥有证券公司（个）	Number of Securities Companies(unit)	3
证券营业部（个）（含外地公司在西安营业部）	Number of Securities Business Departments(unit)	153
投资者开户数（万户）	Number of Investors Who have Opened an Account(10 000 accounts)	378.83
证券交易总额（亿元）	Total Turnover(100 million yuan)	15721.58
三、期货市场情况	**Futures Market**	
拥有期货经纪公司（个）	Number of Futures Business Management Companies(unit)	3
期货营业部（个）	Number of Futures Business Departments(unit)	52
期货代理交易额（亿元）	Total Transaction Value in Futures Commissioning (100 million yuan)	55859.29
每个经纪公司平均拥有注册资金（万元）	Average Registered Capital of Each Business Management Company(10 000 yuan)	27600

注：本表数据来源于市金融办。

主要统计指标解释

信贷资金 指金融机构以信用方式积聚和分配的货币资金。金融机构信贷资金的来源有各项存款、金融债券、对国际金融机构负债、流通中现金、其他项目等；信贷资金的运用有各项贷款、有价证券及投资、金银占款、外汇占款、财政借款及在国际金融机构中的资产等。

存款 指企业、机关、团体或居民根据资金必须收回的原则，把货币资金存入银行或其他信贷机构保管并取得一定利息的一种信用活动形式。根据存款对象或性质的不同可划分为企业存款、财政存款、机关团体存款、城乡储蓄存款、农业存款、信托及委托类存款、其他存款等科目。它是银行信贷资金的主要来源。

贷款 指银行或其他信贷机构根据资金必须归还的原则，按一定利率，为企业、个人等提供资金的一种信用活动形式。我国银行贷款分为短期贷款、委托及信托类贷款、其他类贷款等。

保险公司 在中国境内的、经过保险监督管理部门批准设立，并依法登记注册的各类商业保险公司。

保险金额 指保险人承担赔偿或者给付保险金责任的最高限额。

保费 指投保人为取得保险人在约定范围内所承担赔偿责任而支付给保险人的费用。

赔款 指保险人根据保险合同的规定，向被保险人支付的赔偿保险责任损失的金额。

给付 包括死伤医疗给付和满期给付。死伤医疗给付是指保险人根据人寿保险及长期健康保险合同的规定，因被保险人在保险期内发生保险责任范围内的保险事故支付给被保险人（或受益人）的金额。满期给付是指被保险人生存期满，保险人按人寿保险合同规定支付给被保险人的满期保险金额。

Explanatory Notes on Main Statistical Indicators

Credit Funds refer to the monetary funds accumulated and distributed in the means of credit by the financial institutions. The sources of credit funds include various deposits, financial bonds, liabilities to international financial institutions, currency in circulation, other items. The uses of credit funds include loans, securities and investment, position for bullion and silver purchase, position for foreign exchange purchase, advances to treasury, and assets with international financial institutions..

Deposit is a form of credit by which enterprises, institutions, organizations or households can put money into banks and other credit institutions for safekeeping and interest earning under the principle of free withdrawal. According to different depositors, deposits are divided into enterprise deposits, fiscal deposits, deposits of government agencies and organizations, savings deposits of rural and urban households, agricultural savings deposits, entrusted deposits and other deposits. Deposits are major sources of the credit funds of banks.

Loan is a form of credit by which banks and other credit institutions provide funds at certain interest rate to enterprises and individuals in the light of the principle of unconditional repayment. Loans from Chinese banks include short-term loan, medium- term and long-term loans, entrusted loans, and other loans.

Insurance Companies refer to commercial insurance companies of various forms registered by law and established in China with the approval of insurance regulatory agencies.

Amount Insured refers to the maximum that the insurant will get for the claim of the case insured.

Premium is the fee paid by the insurant to the insurer to obtain the obligation of compensation from the insurance within the agreed terms.

Settled Claim is the compensation paid by the insurer to the insurant in accordance with the insurance contract.

Payment includes payment for death, injury or medical treatment and payment at maturity. Payment for death, injury or medical treatment refers to the money paid to the insurant (or the beneficiary) in accordance with the life or health insurance contract when the insurant encounters accidents within the insured period covered in the contract. Payment at maturity refers to the payment to the insurant in accordance with the life insurance contract at the end of the insured period.

20 教育和科技

EDUCATION,SCIENCE AND TECHNOLOGY

资料整理：郝　静　陈春光
Data management：Hao Jing Chen Chunguang
数据审核：王金桂
Data audit：Wang Jingui

第二十部分　教育和科技

一、简要说明

本章资料包括教育事业、科技事业基本情况，由西安市统计局服务业和社会科技处根据西安市教育局等有关部门提供资料整理。科技部分表式依据部门统计制度进行了重新设计调整。

二、主要指标

普通高等学校数（所）	63	与上年	持平
普通高等学校（本专科）在校学生（万人）	72.68	比上年减少	1.00万人
高等学校研究生在校人数（万人）	10.35	比上年增加	0.94万人

20　EDUCATION,SCIENCE AND TECHNOLOGY

Ⅰ.Brief Introduction

Data in this chapter consists of primarily data of educational undertakings, science and technology activities of Xi'an city, compiled by Tertiary Industry and Social & Science and Technology Division of the Xi'an Bureau of Statistics according to data from Xi'an Bureau of Education concerned.

Ⅱ Major Indicators

		Increase over Preceding Year
Number of Regular Institutions of Higher Education(unit)	63	essentially on a par with last year's
Student Enrollment of Regular Institutions of Higher Education (Universities and colleges) (10 000 persons)	72.68	-1.00
Postgraduates Enrollment of Regular Institutions of Higher Education (10 000 persons)	10.35	0.94

20-1 主要年份各类普通教育基本情况

Basic Statistics on Regular Eduction in Representative Years

指　标	Item	2010	2011	2012	2013	2014	2015	2016	2017
学校数（所）	**Number of Schools (units)**								
普通高等学校	Regular Institutions of Higher Educatior	50	61	62	63	63	63	63	63
普通中等专业学校	Regular Specialized Secondary Schools	28	24	24	22	22	20	20	16
普通中学	Regular Secondary School	436	423	419	418	421	422	422	448
小学	Primary Schools	1531	1424	1322	1291	1257	1234	1190	1125
幼儿园	Kindergarten	1004	1122	1239	1295	1343	1417	1475	1605
毕业生人数（万人）	**Graduates (10 000 persons)**								
普通高等学校	Regular Institutions of Higher Educatior	18.3	19.7	20.9	20.17	21.27	23.23	24.06	23.07
普通中等专业学校	Regular Specialized Secondary Schools	2.5	2.3	2.1	1.93	1.76	1.32	1.25	1.06
普通中学	Regular Secondary School	17.0	16.4	15.6	15.24	14.54	13.92	13.96	13.89
小学	Primary Schools	9.6	8.9	8.9	8.51	8.29	7.85	8.46	9.06
幼儿园	Kindergarten	5.4	6.4	7.6	8.42	8.90	10.01	9.81	10.79
招生数（万人）	**New Enrollment (10 000 persons)**								
普通高等学校	Regular Institutions of Higher Educatior	21.7	23.1	25.2	23.88	23.58	23.41	23.08	23.70
普通中等专业学校	Regular Specialized Secondary Schools	2.1	2.0	1.7	1.35	1.25	0.95	0.88	0.96
普通中学	Regular Secondary School	16.2	15.4	15.0	14.47	13.97	13.41	13.72	14.08
小学	Primary Schools	8.6	8.8	8.9	9.56	10.13	10.51	11.65	13.13
幼儿园	Kindergarten	8.4	10.0	11.6	11.00	9.55	11.96	13.65	13.98
在校学生数（万人）	**Total Enrollment (10 000 persons)**								
普通高等学校	Regular Institutions of Higher Educatior	73.3	76.6	80.7	83.83	85.42	84.83	83.10	83.02
普通中等专业学校	Regular Specialized Secondary Schools	6.8	6.1	5.4	4.66	4.07	3.47	3.11	2.74
普通中学	Regular Secondary School	48.9	47.2	45.3	43.73	42.57	41.37	40.70	41.74
小学	Primary Schools	51.6	51.4	50.9	51.95	53.79	56.62	59.79	66.68
幼儿园	Kindergarten	18.4	24.0	27.1	28.56	28.95	30.90	31.80	34.81
教职工数（人）	**Staff and Teachers (persons)**								
普通高等学校	Regular Institutions of Higher Educatior	72247	72739	74041	74993	74954	74857	73686	74218
普通中等专业学校	Regular Specialized Secondary Schools	3249	2868	2733	2599	2315	1991	1917	1556
普通中学	Regular Secondary School	39207	41135	41197	41003	40576	40689	41352	44546
小学	Primary Schools	34118	32457	32208	31863	32162	32585	34646	38494
幼儿园	Kindergarten	18710	23680	27735	31989	33062	36004	39753	44895
专任教师（人）	**Number of Full-time Teachers (persons)**								
普通高等学校	Regular Institutions of Higher Educatior	42098	42734	44487	46436	46766	47768	47158	47917
普通中等专业学校	Regular Specialized Secondary Schools	1845	1723	1595	1474	1346	1228	1210	998
普通中学	Regular Secondary School	31506	31675	31526	31419	32615	33014	33962	36565
小学	Primary Schools	29944	29900	29651	29421	28395	28748	30941	34163
幼儿园	Kindergarten	10638	12577	14293	16238	17337	19096	21395	23789

注：1.本表数据来源于市教育局。

2.本表中普通高等学校毕业生、招生、在校生数含研究生及普通高等学校中普通本、专科学生数。

3.本表中小学的学校数是指独立小学个数，其在校生、教职工等指标均为普通初等教育；幼儿园的校数是指独立的幼儿园个数，其在校生、教职工等指标均为学前教育。（下表同）

4.本表中普通中学学生数据为普通中等教育口径，小学学生数为普通初等教育口径，幼儿园学生数为学前教育口径。

5.本表2017年数据包含西咸新区。

20-2 各级各类学校、教职工情况（2017年）

Situation of All Kinds of Schools and Staff Members at All Levels （2017）

指　标	Item	学校数（所）Number of Schools (units)	教职工数（人）Number of Staff and Teachers (persons)	专任教师数（人）Full-time Teachers (persons)
一、高等教育	**Higher education**	**76**	**76710**	**49233**
（一）研究生培养机构	Postgraduate training institutions	(43)		
1、高等学校	Institutions of Higher Schools	(22)		
2、科研机构	Scientific Research Institution	(21)		
（二）普通高等学校	Regular Institutions of Higher Schools	63	74218	47917
1、本科院校	Universities and Colleges of Undergraduate Course	42	63993	40933
其中：独立学院	Non-university Tertiary	11	5959	3733
2、专科院校	Higher Vocational Colleges	21	10225	6984
其中：高等职业学校	Higher Vocational College	19	8748	6183
（三）成人高等学校	Adult Higher Schools	13	2492	1316
二、中等职业教育	**Secondary Occupation Education**	**163**	**13123**	**11002**
(一)普通中等专业学校	Regular Specialized Secondary Schools	16	1556	998
(二)成人中等专业学校	Adult Secondary Specialized Schools	2	157	74
其中：市属	Municipal schools			
(三)职业高中学校	Vocational Hight Schools	62	3318	2405
其中：市属	Municipal schools	61	3318	2405
(四)技工学校	Technical Schools	83	8092	7525
其中：市属	Municipal schools	31	2020	1695
三、基础教育	**Elementary Education**	**3188**	**128364**	**94822**
（一）普通中等教育	Regular Institutions Education	448	44546	36565
1、高中	Senior High Schools	160		19821
完全中学	Complete Secondary Schools	99	13655	11346
高级中学	Senior Secondary Schools	48	7446	6127
十二年一贯制学校	Twelve-year Consistency Schools	13	3029	2348
2、初中	Junior Middle Schools	288		16744
初级中学	Junior Middle Schools	238	16069	13179
九年一贯制学校	Nine-year Consistency Schools	50	4347	3565
完全中学	Complete Secondary school	(99)		
十二年一贯制学校	Twelve-year Consistency schools	(13)		
附设普通初中班的学校	Senior Secondary Schools with Regular Junior Secondary Classes	(1)		
（二）普通初等教育	Regular Primary Education	1125	38494	34163
独立小学	Independent Primary Schools	1125		32497
教学点	Teaching Points	(308)		1666
九年一贯制学校	Nine-year Consistency schools	(45)		
十二年一贯制学校	Twelve-year Consistency schools	(11)		
附设小学班的学校	Schools with Primary Classes	(4)		
（三）特殊教育	Special Education Schools	9	386	272
特殊教育学校	Special Education Schools	9	386	272
附设特教班的学校	Schools with Special Edution Classes	(1)		
（四）工读学校	Reformatory Schools	1	43	33
（五）学前教育	Preschool Education	1605	44895	23789
幼儿园	Kindergarten	1605	44895	23789
附设幼儿班的学校	Schools with Nursery Classes	(87)		
另有：技术培训机构	Technique Training Institution	1787	19142	13029

注：1.本表数据来源于市教育局。
2.本表为西安市行政区划内各级各类学校全口径数据（不含军事院校、党校）。
3.技工学校数据由西安市人力资源和社会保障局提供。
4.按照事业统计主体校原则，完全中学、十二年一贯制学校的学校数计入普通高中，九年一贯制学校的校数计入普通初中。
5.教职工数按照办学类型划分，为使用方便，专任教师同时按照办学层次列出。
6.( ) 内数据不计入总计，下表同。
7.本表数据包含西咸新区。

20-3 各级各类教育学生情况（2017年）

Basic Facts on Education Student by School Type（2017）

单位：人 (person)

指 标	Item	毕业生数 Number of Graduates	招生数 New Enrollment	在校学生数 Total Enrollment	女生 Female Students
一、高等教育	**Higher education**	**356206**	**437637**	**1224995**	**585495**
(一)研究生	Postgraduates	25808	36296	104092	48473
1、高等学校	Institutions of Higher Schools	25616	36084	103458	48317
2、科研机构	Scientific Research Institution	192	212	634	156
(二）普通高等教育	Regular Institutions of Higher Schools	205041	200954	726752	356345
1、本科	Universities Course Schools	128379	126114	501248	251312
2、专科	Junior Colleges	76662	74840	225504	105033
(三）成人高等教育	Higher Vocational Colleges	52839	45114	113724	57153
其中：成人高等学校	Contains:Adult Higher Education	5021	7057	18066	8514
(四）网络本专科生	Network Undergraduate and clooege students	72518	155273	280427	123524
1、本科	Universities Course Schools	32321	61306	109718	50416
2、专科	Junior Colleges	40197	93967	170709	73108
二、中等职业教育	**Secondary Occupation Education**	**49115**	**74551**	**190624**	**33298**
1、普通中等专业学校	Regular Specialized Secondary Schools	10587	9604	27392	12112
2、成人中等专业学校	Adult Secondary Specialized Schools	92	106	274	133
3、职业高中学校	Vocational high Schools	14325	17080	45145	21053
其中：市属	Municipal schools	14325	17080	45145	21053
4、技工学校	Technical Schools	24111	47761	117813	
其中：市属	Municipal schools	5860	14464	32049	
三、基础教育	**Elementary Education**	**337679**	**412764**	**1434895**	**676557**
(一)普通中等教育	Regular Institutions Education	138948	140824	417436	196048
1、高中	Senior High Schools	55159	51768	158173	77438
完全中学	Complete Secondary Schools	24857	25500	76126	37682
高级中学	Senior Secondary Schools	27781	23782	74812	36258
十二年一贯制学校	Twelve-year Consistency schools	2521	2486	7235	3498
2、初中	Junior Middle Schools	83789	89056	259263	118610
初级中学	Junior Middle Schools	45801	45930	136039	61567
九年一贯制学校	Nine-year Consistency Schools	5852	6597	19210	8894
十二年一贯制学校	Twelve-year Consistency Schools	3602	4825	12431	5550
完全中学	Complete Secondary school	28534	31704	91583	42599
(二)普通初等教育	Regular Primary Education	90592	131313	666824	312843
小学	Pricmary Schools	83588	119935	610923	286943
九年一贯制学校	Nine-year Consistency schools	4914	8771	41498	19328
十二年一贯制学校	Twelve-year Consistency Schools	2090	2607	14403	6572
(三）特殊教育	Special Education Schools	237	774	2498	932
1、特殊教育学校	Special Education Schools	95	416	1155	430
2、小学附设特教班	Primary Schools with Special Education Classes			8	2
3、小学随班就读	Elementary Inclusive	98	195	888	348
4、初中随班就读	Junior Mainstreaming	44	112	324	112
5、小学送教上门	Primary School Delivery		37	94	30
6、初中送教上门	Junior High School Delivery		14	29	10
(四）工读学校	Reformatory Schools	14	15	27	4
(五）学前教育	Preschool Education	107888	139838	348110	166730
1、独立幼儿园	Independent Kindergartens	106410	138570	346219	165799
2、附设幼儿园	Attached Kindergartens	1478	1268	1891	931
另有：职业技术培训机构	Vocational and Technical Institutions	498447		634088	341067

注：1.本表数据来源于市教育局。
2.本表数据包含西咸新区。

20-4 主要年份普通高等学校和科研机构研究生情况

Basic Statistics of Postgraduates on Regular Institutions of Higher Education and Scientific Research Institution in Representative Years

单位：人 (person)

年 份 Year	毕业生数 Number of Graduates	高等学校 Higher Schools	招生数 New Enrollment	高等学校 Higher Schools	在校学生数 Total Enrollment	高等学校 Higher Schools
1978			232	232	232	232
1980			127	127	651	651
1985	754	754	2819	2819	4799	4799
1990	2051	2051	1662	1662	5275	5275
1995	1769	1769	2712	2712	7974	7974
1998	2316	2316	3888	3888	10833	10833
1999	2903	2903	5020	5020	12986	12986
2000	3236	3236	6924	6924	16620	16620
2001	3881	3770	9274	8966	22564	21855
2002	4103	3952	11282	10882	28446	27471
2003	5971	5765	14322	13882	36936	35790
2004	8384	8127	17310	16871	45402	44169
2005	10416	10127	18583	18106	52699	51310
2006	12914	12552	19581	19105	58433	56951
2007	15506	15124	20570	20167	64137	62801
2008	17234	16788	21892	21443	67296	65834
2009	19025	18574	24879	24400	72366	70908
2010	19526	19129	25971	25477	76993	75483
2011	20965	20605	26686	26256	81696	80332
2012	22963	22578	28065	27618	84712	83306
2013	24778	24385	28786	28333	87002	85570
2014	24092	23881	28636	28436	88518	87826
2015	25322	25104	29487	29293	91448	90790
2016	24779	24562	30263	30079	94720	94102
2017	25808	25616	36296	36084	104092	103458

注：1.本表数据来源于市教育局。
2.本表2017年数据包含西咸新区。

20-5 主要年份普通高等学校基本情况（本专科）

Basic Statistics on Regular Institution of Higher Education in Representative Years

单位：所、万人 (units 10 000 persons)

年份 Year	学校数 Number of Schools	毕业生数 Number of Graduates	招生数 New Enrollment	在校学生数 Total Enrollment	教职工数 Number of Staff and Teachers	专任教师数 Full-time Teachers
1978	21	0.60	1.31	2.88	2.24	0.87
1980	24	0.21	1.08	4.17	2.55	0.97
1985	28	1.17	2.28	6.49	3.40	1.28
1990	31	2.11	2.00	7.50	4.15	1.56
1995	32	2.87	3.13	10.07	4.21	1.59
1998	29	2.61	3.30	11.58	3.91	1.50
1999	29	2.84	5.12	13.79	3.95	1.52
2000	25	2.71	6.79	17.75	3.81	1.57
2001	32	3.31	8.31	23.24	4.30	1.75
2002	35	3.82	10.75	30.15	4.67	2.06
2003	37	5.89	12.21	36.42	4.92	2.21
2004	41	7.66	13.17	40.29	5.45	2.69
2005	44	10.08	14.68	47.79	5.73	2.95
2006	47	11.75	15.15	51.40	6.14	3.29
2007	48	14.33	16.96	56.03	6.56	3.67
2008	48	15.82	19.31	60.10	6.90	3.89
2009	49	15.04	18.84	63.22	7.08	4.06
2010	50	16.33	19.16	65.74	7.22	4.21
2011	61	17.68	20.52	68.52	7.27	4.27
2012	62	18.64	22.46	72.40	7.40	4.45
2013	63	17.73	21.05	75.27	7.50	4.64
2014	63	18.88	20.74	76.64	7.50	4.68
2015	63	20.72	20.49	75.75	7.49	4.78
2016	63	21.60	20.07	73.68	7.37	4.72
2017	63	20.50	20.10	72.68	7.42	4.79

注：1.本表数据来源于市教育局。
2.本表2017年数据包含西咸新区。

20-6 主要年份普通中等专业学校基本情况

Basic Statistics on Regular Specialized Secondary Schools in Representative Years

年 份 Year	学校数（所） Number of Schools (units)	毕业生数 （万人） Number of Graduates (10 000 persons)	招生数 （万人） New Enrollment (10 000 persons)	在校学生数 （万人） Total Enrollment (10 000 persons)	教职工数（人） Number of Staff and Teachers(person)	专任教师数 （人） Full-time Teachers(person)
1978	19	0.19	0.45	0.82	3937	1110
1980	31	0.18	0.42	1.50	3895	1474
1985	37	0.43	0.76	1.70	6071	2363
1990	44	0.56	0.68	2.09	7136	2891
1995	46	0.97	1.37	3.74	5903	2533
1996	47	1.15	1.61	4.18	5940	2573
1997	47	1.20	1.65	4.63	6124	2731
1998	47	1.26	1.62	5.08	6181	2840
1999	46	1.42	2.11	5.75	6385	2865
2000	47	1.63	1.90	6.02	6964	3172
2001	47	1.70	1.58	5.63	5252	2467
2002	46	1.60	1.69	5.57	5170	2508
2003	34	1.62	1.80	5.28	4562	2302
2004	35	1.40	2.09	5.71	4676	2388
2005	32	1.44	2.26	6.16	3924	2130
2006	31	1.84	2.61	7.30	3621	2014
2007	30	2.03	2.91	7.97	3548	2011
2008	29	2.58	2.55	8.06	3278	1814
2009	28	2.70	2.15	7.44	2965	1720
2010	28	2.45	2.08	6.75	3249	1845
2011	24	2.34	1.96	6.11	2868	1723
2012	24	2.15	1.67	5.43	2733	1595
2013	22	1.93	1.35	4.66	2599	1474
2014	22	1.76	1.25	4.07	2315	1346
2015	20	1.32	0.95	3.47	1991	1228
2016	20	1.25	0.88	3.11	1917	1210
2017	16	1.06	0.96	2.74	1556	998

注：1.本表数据来源于市教育局。
2.本表2017年数据包含西咸新区。

20-7 主要年份普通中等教育基本情况

Basic Situation of General Secondary Education in Major Years

年 份 Year	学校数（所） Number of Schools (units)	毕业生数（万人） Number of Graduates (10 000 persons)	招生数（万人） New Enrollment (10 000 persons)	在校学生数（万人） Total Enrollment (10 000 persons)	教职工数（人） Number of Staff and Teachers(person)	专任教师数（人） Full-time Teachers(person)
1978	962	10.85		44.16	27380	20660
1980	1002	12.33	14.03	44.08	29867	22530
1985	563	10.72	13.05	38.24	30063	22050
1990	518	9.11	10.49	30.03	30739	22386
1995	485	8.13	12.40	32.32	30423	21984
1996	462	8.67	13.03	35.25	30902	22478
1997	466	9.96	13.83	37.16	31682	23129
1998	467	10.64	15.00	39.79	32371	23884
1999	469	11.21	16.58	43.49	33387	25114
2000	466	12.01	17.88	48.31	34385	26230
2001	470	13.85	18.98	52.50	35442	27190
2002	467	15.76	19.68	55.36	36706	28335
2003	467	16.76	18.78	56.44	38252	29887
2004	461	18.01	18.85	56.54	39121	30600
2005	460	18.82	18.83	55.74	39456	31094
2006	457	18.04	18.61	56.11	39341	31203
2007	453	18.37	17.96	54.68	39171	31373
2008	442	17.99	17.16	52.83	39088	31425
2009	439	17.80	16.57	50.63	39002	31415
2010	436	17.01	16.15	48.89	39207	31506
2011	423	16.44	15.42	47.20	41135	31675
2012	419	15.64	14.98	45.33	41197	31526
2013	418	15.24	14.47	43.73	41003	31419
2014	421	14.54	13.97	42.57	40576	32615
2015	422	13.92	13.41	41.37	40689	33014
2016	422	13.96	13.72	40.70	41352	33962
2017	448	13.89	14.08	41.74	44546	36565

注：1.本表数据来源于市教育局。
2.本表2017年数据包含西咸新区。

20-8 各区县普通中等教育基本情况（2017年）

Basic Situation of Ordinary Secondary Education in Various Districts and Counties（2017）

单位：所、人 (unit, person)

区 县	Region	学校数 Number of Schools	毕业生数 Number of Graduates	高中 Senior	招生数 New Enrollment	高中 Senior	在校学生数 Total Enrollment	女生 Female Students	高中 Senior	教职工数 Number of Staff and Teachers	专任教师数 Full-time Teachers
合 计	**Total**	**448**	**138948**	**55159**	**140824**	**51768**	**417436**	**196048**	**158173**	**44546**	**36565**
新城区	Xincheng	25	11657	3920	10956	3852	32904	15838	11699	2730	2299
碑林区	Beilin	36	16034	6610	17363	6909	50425	23161	20457	3958	3147
莲湖区	Lianhu	20	10600	3576	10933	3797	32189	15276	11090	2896	2323
灞桥区	Baqiao	26	7702	2315	8024	2213	23341	11003	6394	2844	2270
未央区	Weiyang	32	9582	4070	11478	4075	33614	16057	12603	4088	3351
雁塔区	Yanta	47	15881	5458	17717	5984	50403	24027	17462	5489	4528
阎良区	Yanliang	12	3559	1530	3203	1147	9870	5004	3788	1136	1009
临潼区	Lintong	33	10075	4454	8794	3553	28196	14039	11923	3293	2764
长安区	Chang'an	48	12973	5667	13204	5265	39558	18703	16460	4011	3576
高陵区	Gaoling	15	3449	1287	3623	1227	10571	5243	3778	977	803
鄠邑区	Huyi	34	9404	4609	8290	3818	25362	11268	12027	2913	2544
蓝田县	Lantian	45	10065	4549	8528	3705	26684	12988	11230	3260	2544
周至县	Zhouzhi	35	9967	4632	9304	3838	28880	11980	12414	3186	2311

注：1.本表数据来源于市教育局。
2.本表合计栏数据包含西咸新区。

20-9 主要年份职业高中基本情况

Basic Statistics on Vocational Secondary Schools in Representative Years

单位：所、人 (unit, person)

年 份 Year	学校数 Number of Schools	毕业生数 Number of Graduates	招生数 New Enrollment	在校学生数 Total Enrollment	教职工数 Number of Staff and Teachers	专任教师数 Full-time Teachers
1985	40	1661	8346	17621	1375	868
1990	58	5936	8095	20151	2674	1574
1995	71	8976	12490	32673	2394	1877
1996	67	9235	10563	25955	3098	1735
1997	73	8756	13390	29068	2993	1709
1998	89	7753	13949	31264	3152	1823
1999	91	8480	13062	31973	3217	1908
2000	95	9949	13903	32188	3311	1997
2001	85	10300	15591	34336	3517	2113
2002	78	8659	17231	39428	3461	2192
2003	87	10755	17310	44033	4036	2458
2004	83	12177	17865	46358	4101	2515
2005	91	15092	20603	51766	4750	2892
2006	96	14887	21158	53828	5193	3126
2007	86	14881	24434	56012	4899	3064
2008	84	15813	30201	62963	4878	3008
2009	84	14691	31042	72388	5129	3179
2010	84	18100	30042	78244	5222	3178
2011	78	22493	27641	75108	4849	3173
2012	77	24048	24995	67969	4775	3148
2013	74	21243	23043	61968	4699	3085
2014	81	19156	19508	60024	4860	3186
2015	80	18565	15060	49092	3239	2214
2016	64	17773	14305	43576	3126	2275
2017	62	14325	17080	45145	3318	2405

注：1.本表数据来源于市教育局。
2.本表2017年数据包含西咸新区。

20-10 各区县职业高中基本情况（2017年）

Basic Statistics on Vocational Secondary Schools by Region（2017）

单位：所、人 (unit, person)

区 县	Region	学校数 Number of Schools	毕业生数 Number of Graduates	招生数 New Enrollment	在校学生数 Total Enrollment	女生 Female Students	教职工数 Number of Staff and Teachers	专任教师数 Full-time Teachers
合 计	**Total**	**62**	**14325**	**17080**	**45145**	**21053**	**3318**	**2405**
新城区	Xincheng	9	3278	5551	13588	6124	583	380
碑林区	Beilin	7	1309	2745	5080	1895	342	178
莲湖区	Lianhu	5	2047	1296	4633	2812	284	193
灞桥区	Baqiao	7	634	555	1704	1192	160	126
未央区	Weiyang	3	864	414	1596	751	128	94
雁塔区	Yanta	10	1769	1430	4177	1961	381	282
阎良区	Yanliang	2	801	609	1988	1064	183	124
临潼区	Lintong	5	892	850	2549	972	242	179
长安区	Chang'an	4	1241	1585	4033	1902	449	363
高陵区	Gaoling	1	408	327	1047	449	90	83
鄠邑区	Huyi	2	317	552	1525	479	210	197
蓝田县	Lantian	1	220	630	1631	632	112	91
周至县	Zhouzhi	3	503	411	1317	707	119	90

注：1.本表数据来源于市教育局。
2.本表仅包括市属部分。
3.本表合计栏数据包含西咸新区。

20-11 主要年份普通初等教育基本情况

Basic Situation of General Primary Education in Major Years

年份 Year	学校数（所） Number of Schools (units)	毕业生数（万人） Number of Graduates (10 000 persons)	招生数（万人） New Enrollment (10 000 persons)	在校学生数（万人） Total Enrollment (10 000 persons)	教职工数（人） Number of Staff and Teachers(person)	专任教师数（人） Full-time Teachers(person)
1978	2667	13.07	14.10	74.03	29744	26428
1980	2337	11.91	12.57	73.36	31770	28360
1985	2337	11.21	9.57	62.16	31075	26430
1990	2343	8.67	10.85	61.87	33788	29090
1995	2360	9.93	14.09	79.36	35568	30270
1996	2362	10.48	13.63	81.81	35821	30267
1997	2368	10.98	12.48	82.67	35767	30117
1998	2361	12.18	11.88	82.03	35576	30089
1999	2354	13.65	11.61	79.81	35639	30196
2000	2323	13.83	11.51	77.81	35336	30215
2001	2277	14.20	11.07	74.51	34257	29281
2002	2137	13.89	10.13	70.78	34143	29428
2003	2084	12.97	9.28	66.78	34080	29531
2004	2016	12.37	9.12	63.75	33794	29367
2005	1980	11.92	8.47	60.47	33907	29674
2006	1929	11.53	9.16	59.33	34460	30018
2007	1872	11.38	8.67	56.83	34901	30533
2008	1781	10.58	8.33	54.66	34653	30382
2009	1666	9.96	7.84	52.52	34389	30334
2010	1531	9.61	8.64	51.56	34118	29944
2011	1424	8.92	8.77	51.39	32457	29900
2012	1322	8.88	8.88	50.85	32208	29651
2013	1291	8.51	9.56	51.95	31863	29421
2014	1257	8.29	10.13	53.79	32162	28395
2015	1234	7.85	10.51	56.62	32585	28748
2016	1190	8.46	11.65	59.79	34646	30941
2017	1125	9.06	13.13	66.68	38494	34163

注：1.本表数据来源于市教育局。
2.本表2017年数据包含西咸新区。

20-12 各区县普通初等教育基本情况（2017年）

Basic Situation of General Primary Education in Various Districts and Counties（2017）

单位：所、人 (unit, person)

区 县	Region	学校数 Number of Schools	毕业生数 Number of Graduates	招生数 New Enrollment	在校学生数 Total Enrollment	女生 Female Students	教职工数 Number of Staff and Teachers	专任教师数 Full-time Teachers
合 计	**Total**	**1125**	**90592**	**131313**	**666824**	**312843**	**38494**	**34163**
新城区	Xincheng	35	6031	6114	36566	17069	2169	1944
碑林区	Beilin	43	6795	8081	45394	21123	2529	2112
莲湖区	Lianhu	47	8015	9559	54505	25714	2602	2323
灞桥区	Baqiao	78	6231	10868	52254	24809	2781	2462
未央区	Weiyang	68	9171	18759	84098	39127	3607	3194
雁塔区	Yanta	79	12460	20974	101663	47542	4836	4315
阎良区	Yanliang	23	2268	3001	15702	7637	1010	933
临潼区	Lintong	104	5825	7253	38944	18463	2812	2572
长安区	Chang'an	131	7842	12727	62789	29660	3586	3179
高陵区	Gaoling	71	2551	4240	20856	10137	1509	1266
鄠邑区	Huyi	101	4652	5127	28852	13199	2046	1820
蓝田县	Lantian	85	4987	4810	28001	13201	2601	2393
周至县	Zhouzhi	123	5461	6633	34485	15806	2432	2137

注：1.本表数据来源于市教育局。
2.本表合计栏数据包含西咸新区。

20-13 主要年份学前教育基本情况

Basic Conditions of Pre-school Education in Representative Years

年　份 Year	幼儿园（个） Number of Kindergartens (unit)	班数（个） Number of Class (unit)	在园幼儿数（万人） Student Enrollment (10000 persons)	教职工数（人） Number of Staff and Teachers(person)	专任教师数（人） Full-time Teachers(person)
1978	191		4.44	3568	1315
1980	186		9.61	5525	2657
1985	310	3135	9.71	6887	2770
1990	256	3816	14.04	6123	2058
1995	257	4464	16.40	6173	2659
1996	244	4313	15.44	5918	2661
1997	228	4243	14.72	6065	2748
1998	235	4195	13.44	6272	2910
1999	234	4222	13.34	6329	2982
2000	367	4142	12.85	6346	2995
2001	366	4306	11.97	6224	3069
2002	378	4186	11.53	6541	3397
2003	610	4470	12.39	8959	4853
2004	660	4507	12.16	9870	5577
2005	737	4712	12.75	10528	5959
2006	863	5037	13.00	12335	7106
2007	830	5081	14.00	13468	7951
2008	905	5506	15.00	14932	8704
2009	896	5710	16.00	15928	9240
2010	1004	6420	18.00	18710	10638
2011	1122	8010	24.00	23680	12577
2012	1239	8729	27.10	27735	14293
2013	1295	9408	28.56	31989	16238
2014	1343	9782	28.95	33062	17337
2015	1417	10457	30.90	36004	19096
2016	1475	11090	31.80	39753	21395
2017	1605	12234	34.81	44895	23789

注：1.本表数据来源于市教育局。
　　2.幼儿园在园人数中包括学前班。
　　3.本表2017年数据包含西咸新区。

20-14 主要年份特殊教育基本情况

Basic Statistics on Special Education in Representative Years

单位：所、人 (unit, person)

年份 Year	学校数 Number of Schools	毕业生数 Number of Graduates	招生数 New Enrollment	在校学生数 Total Enrollment	教职工数 Number of Staff and Teachers	专任教师数 Full-time Teachers
1980	1	48	64	315	66	43
1985	2	14	36	318	94	59
1990	5	35	111	451	142	96
1995	5	27	147	1363	204	141
1996	5	60	164	1520	210	150
1997	5	153	164	1655	210	148
1998	5	266	140	2145	232	157
1999	5	349	115	1912	235	160
2000	5	269	145	1880	230	156
2001	5	237	209	1915	238	162
2002	5	216	148	1661	232	157
2003	5	156	161	1380	237	166
2004	5	137	142	1290	236	167
2005	5	184	182	1445	240	169
2006	6	171	143	1425	254	178
2007	6	169	114	1342	259	190
2008	6	83	96	1286	259	190
2009	7	311	202	1523	335	234
2010	8	214	402	1529	340	235
2011	8	280	222	1393	343	231
2012	8	197	220	1392	352	248
2013	8	194	212	1174	338	243
2014	8	172	222	1225	345	238
2015	8	168	338	1373	352	240
2016	8	214	327	1604	359	246
2017	9	237	774	2498	386	272

注：1.本表数据来源于市教育局。
2.包括盲、聋、哑、弱智儿童教育。
3.本表2017年数据包含西咸新区。

20-15 基础教育监测评价情况（2017年）

Monitoring and Evaluation of Basic Education（2017）

指　标	Item	2017
入学率(%)	Enrollment Rate(%)	
小学	Primary Schools	99.99
初中	Junior Middle Schools	99.98
巩固率(%)	The Consolidation Rate (%)	
小学(六年)	Primary Schools (six years)	98.69
初中(三年)	Junior Middle Schools (three years)	96.2
毕业率(%)	The Graduate Rate(%)	
小学	Primary school	99.76
初中	Junior middle school	98.28
专任教师学历合格率(%)	Qualified Rate Of Full-time Teacher Education (%)	
小学	Primary Schools	99.99
初中	Junior Middle Schools	99.99
高中	Senior Middle Schools	98.63
幼儿园	Kindergartens	98.63
小学教师专科以上学历达到率(%)	Rate of Primary School Teachers with College degree or Above (%)	98.48
初中教师本科以上学历达到率(%)	Rate of Junior Middle SchoolTeachers with Bachelor degree or Above (%)	92.39
高中教师研究生以上学历达到率(%)	Rate of Senior Middle School Teachers with Postgraduate degree or Above (%)	16.82

注：1.本表数据来源于市教育局。
　　2.本表数据包含西咸新区。

20-16 主要年份平均每万人口在校学生数及构成

单位：人、%

年 份 Year	平均每万人 高等学校在校学生 Per 10000 people on average Hight Education Students in the school	平均每万人 高中阶段在校学生 Per 10000 people on average Number of Senior high School Students in the school	平均每万人 初中在校学生 Per 10000 people on average Number of Junior Secondary School Students in the school
1978	58		
1980	84		
1985	117		
1990	123		
1995	168		
1996	177		
1997	180		
1998	189		
1999	224		
2000	282		
2001	366		
2002	470		
2003	560		
2004	618	463	517
2005	715	492	489
2006	760	534	484
2007	817	543	466
2008	863	571	444
2009	901	619	413
2010	939	635	361
2011	1090	576	337
2012	1132	541	319
2013	1146	448	307
2014	1157	414	301
2015	1125	374	286
2016	1080	360	280
2017	982	363	270

注：1.本表数据来源于市教育局。
2.2011年起，参与计算的学生总数含成人教育及网络教育数据。
3.本表2017年数据含西咸新区。

The Average Number of Students in the School every 10000 Individuals in Representative Years

(persons,%)

平均每万人 小学在校学生 Per 10000 people on average Number of Primary School Students in the school	普通高等学校在校学生 占学生总数比重 Senior high School Students in the school in accounting for the proportion of the total number of students	中等学校在校学生 占学生总数比重 Junior Secondary School students in the school in accounting for the proportion of the total number of students	小学在校学生 占学生总数比重 Primary School students in the school in accounting for the proportion of the total number of students
1486	2.3	34.9	58.6
1434	3.1	33.2	55.3
1124	5.3	31.3	50.9
1016	6.7	25.1	51.7
1224	7.3	28.0	53.6
1249	7.6	28.8	53.5
1249	7.6	29.8	53.1
1228	8.0	31.3	52.0
1183	9.3	33.2	49.2
1131	11.5	34.8	46.0
1072	14.6	35.9	42.6
1007	18.2	36.4	39.0
932	20.1	33.8	33.5
879	22.2	35.2	31.6
815	26.4	36.2	30.1
788	27.7	37.1	28.7
744	29.3	36.3	26.7
708	30.8	36.1	25.2
672	31.8	36.5	23.7
660	33.0	35.0	23.2
604	29.8	30.1	19.9
595	31.0	28.2	19.5
605	32.6	25.3	20.2
626	33.2	23.8	20.9
650	32.8	22.2	21.9
641	31.4	21.4	22.6
693	29.1	21.3	23.4

20-17 民办教育情况（2017年）

单位：所、人

指 标	Item	学校数 Number of Schools	毕业生数 Number of Graduates
一、民办高等教育(民办高校）	**Private higher Education (Institutions)**	**16**	**78400**
二、民办中等教育	**Private Secondary Education**	**94**	**40322**
民办普通高中	Ordinary High School	29	6946
民办普通中等专业学校	Civilian run ordinary secondary vocational school	1	961
民办职业高中	Vocational high school	37	8363
民办普通初中	Ordinary Junior middle school	27	20728
民办的附设中职班	Private primary school class	(10)	3324
三、民办普通小学	**Private Primary School**	**73**	**10604**
四、民办幼儿园	**Private kindergarten**	**999**	**75751**
另有：民办培训机构	Private Training Institutions	574	256729

注：1.本表数据来源于市教育局。
2.毕业生数中幼儿园为离园人数。
3.民办高等教育在校生为民办高校普通、成人本专科学生数。
4.聘请校外教师中，小学、中学、幼儿园为代课教师和兼任教师之和。
5.按照教育报表制度，民办的附设中职班教职工计入基础教育主体校教职工总数，专任教师为中职层次，故单独统计。
6.本表数据含西咸新区。

Private Education Situation（2017）

(unit, person)

招生数 New Enrollment	在校学生数 Total Enrollment	教职工数 Number of Teachers and Staff	专任教师 Full-time Teachers	聘请外校教师 Teachers hired from Outside Schools
74096	**254991**	**19590**	**12854**	
41904	**119364**	**10130**	**7745**	**16**
7380	20896	5108	3995	
557	2302	235	160	
10690	27240	1374	820	16
21490	63499	3413	2770	
1787	5427			
20772	**96959**	**4561**	**3859**	
101193	**247724**	**31737**	**15736**	**3**
	395084	11852	7825	7026

20-18 全市科技活动情况（2017年）

Scientific and Technological Activizies in the Whole City（2017）

指 标	Item	2017
一、单位数（个）	**Number of Units(unit)**	**2320**
#有R&D活动单位数	The Number of R&D active units	680
二、R&D人员（人）	**Personnel Eagaged in R&D（person）**	**107874**
三、R&D人员折合全时当量（人年）	**R&D Stuff Equivalent to Full Time equivalent （person year）**	**74423.8**
四、R&D经费内部支出（万元）	**R&D Internal Expenditure（10000 yuan）**	**3601731.2**
五、R&D项目(课题）（项）	**R&D Project（Issue）**	**42577**

注：本表数据来源于省统计局反馈。

20-19 规模以上重点行业企业研究与试验发展（R&D）情况（2017年）

R&D Project Status of Key Enterprises above Designated Size（2017）

指 标	Item	2017
一、企业数（个）	**Number of Enterprises(unit)**	**2093**
工业	Industry	1404
非工业	Non-industry	689
#有R&D活动的单位数	The Number of R&D active units	506
工业	Industry	435
非工业	Non-industry	71
二、R&D人员（人）	**Personnel Eagaged in R&D(person)**	**53282**
工业	Industry	39953
非工业	Non-industry	13329
三、R&D人员折合全时当量（人年）	**R&D Stuff Equivalent to Full Time equivalent (person year)**	**35003**
工业	Industry	27259
非工业	Non-industry	7744
四、R&D经费内部支出（万元）	**R&D Internal Expenditure(10000 yuan)**	**1477649**
工业	Industry	1104702
非工业	Non-industry	372947
五、R&D项目（课题）（项）	**Project(Issue)**	**3369**
工业	Industry	2690
非工业	Non-industry	679

20-20 规模以上工业企业研究与试验发展（R&D）基本情况（2017年）

R&D Project Status of Industrial Enterprises above Designated Size（2017）

指　标	Item	企业数（个）Number of enterprises (unit)	有R&D活动的企业数 The Number of R&D enterprises
总计	**Total**	**1404**	**435**
按企业规模分	**Grouped by Size of Enterprises**		
大型企业	Large-size	68	49
中型企业	Medium-size	186	97
小型企业	Small-size	1110	284
微型企业	Microenterprise	40	5
按登记注册类型分	**Grouped by Registered Status**		
内资企业	Domestic Investment Enterprises	1289	403
国有企业	State-owned Enterprises	35	25
集体企业	Collective-owned Enterprise	7	
股份合作企业	Stock Cooperative Enterprises	5	
联营企业	Affiliated Enterprise		
有限责任公司	Limited Liability Corporations	637	211
股份有限公司	Share-holding Corporation Ltd	115	75
私营企业	Private Enterprise	488	92
其他	Other Domestic Funded Enterprises	2	
港、澳、台商投资企业	Enterprises with Funds from Hong Kong, Macao And Taiwan	26	5
外商投资企业	Foreign Funded Enterprises	89	27
按国民经济行业分	**Grouped by Sector**		
采矿业	Mining	7	2
煤炭开采和洗选业	Mining and Washing of Coal		
石油和天然气开采业	Extraction of Petroleum and Natural Gas	1	1

20-20 续表1 continued 1

指 标	Item	企业数（个）Number of enterprises (unit)	有R&D活动的企业数 The Number of R&D enterprises
黑色金属矿采选业	Mining of Ferrous Metal Ores		
有色金属矿采选业	Mining of Non-ferrous Metal Ores		
非金属矿采选业	Mining and Processing of Nonmetal Ores		
开采辅助活动	Mining Other Ores	6	1
制造业	Manufacturing Industry	1354	430
农副食品加工业	Processing of Food from Agriculture Products	51	1
食品制造业	Manufacture of Food	46	7
酒、饮料和精制茶制造业	Manufacture of Beverages	24	5
烟草制品业	Manufacture of Tobacco	3	1
纺织业	Manufacture of Textile	16	3
纺织服装、服饰业	Manufacture of Textile Wearing, Apparel	4	
皮革、毛皮、羽毛及其制品和制鞋业	Manufacture of Leather, Furs, Feather, Related Products and Footware	2	1
木材加工和木、竹、藤、棕、草制品业	Processing of Timber,Manufacture of Wood, Bamboo, Rattan, Palm and Straw Products	6	
家具制造业	Manufacture of Furniture	14	
造纸及纸制品业	Manufacture of Paper And Paper Products	24	
印刷和记录媒介复制业	Printing and Reproduction of Recording Media	31	5
文教、工美、体育和娱乐用品制造业	Education, Art, Sports And Entertainment Products Manufacturing	12	
石油加工、炼焦和核燃料加工业	Processing of Petroleum,Coking and Processing of Nuclear Fuel	8	
化学原料和化学制品制造业	Manufacture of Raw Chemical Materials and Chemical Products	84	37

20-20 续表2 continued 2

指　标	Item	企业数（个）Number of enterprises (unit)	有R&D活动的企业数 The Number of R&D enterprises
医药制造业	Manufacture of Medicines	59	32
化学纤维制造业	Manufacture of Chemical Fiber	3	1
橡胶和塑料制品业	Manufacture of Rubber and Manufacture of Plastic	37	6
非金属矿物制品业	Manufacture of Non-metallic Mineral Products	147	5
黑色金属冶炼和压延加工业	Smelting and Pressing of Ferrous Metals	16	1
有色金属冶炼和压延加工业	Smelting and Pressing of Non-ferrous Metals	40	20
金属制品业	Manufacture of Metal Products	82	18
通用设备制造业	Manufacture of General Purpose Machinery	84	23
专用设备制造业	Manufacture of Special Equipment	122	62
汽车制造业	Manufacture of Motor Vehicle	53	18
铁路、船舶、航空航天和其他运输设备制造业	Railways, Ships, Aerospace And Other Transportation Equipment Manufacturing Industry	80	41
电气机械和器材制造业	Manufacture of Electric Equipment and Machinery	142	50
计算机、通信和其他电子设备制造业	Manufacture of Communication Equipment, Computers and Other Electronic Equipment	91	51
仪器仪表制造业	Manufacture of Measuring Instruments and Machinery	56	35
其他制造业	Other Manufacturing	9	5
废弃资源综合利用业	Comprehensive Utilization Of Waste Resources	4	1
金属制品、机械和设备修理业	Metal Products, Machinery and Equipment Repair Industry	4	1
电力、热力、燃气及水的生产供应业	Production and Supply of Electric Power,Heat,Gas and Water	43	3
电力、热力生产和供应业	Production and Supply of Electric Power and Heat Power	21	3
燃气生产和供应业	Production and Supply of Gas	15	
水的生产和供应业	Production and Supply of Water	7	

20-21 规模以上工业企业研究与试验发展（R&D）人员和经费支出情况（2017年）

指标	Item	R&D人员（人）R&D personnel（person）	研究人员 Researchers
总计	**Total**	**39953**	**17153**
按企业规模分	**Grouped by Size of Enterprises**		
大型企业	Large-size	26674	11129
中型企业	Medium-size	7477	3399
小型企业	Small-size	5761	2606
微型企业	microenterprise	41	19
按登记注册类型分	**Grouped by Registion Status**		
内资企业	Domestic Investment Enterprises	36092	15556
国有企业	State-owned Enterprises	10636	4542
集体企业	Collective-owned Enterprises		
股份合作企业	Stock cooperative enterprises		
联营企业	Affiliated companies		
有限责任公司	Limited Liability Corporations	19583	8296
股份有限公司	Share-holding Corperation Ltd.	3869	1783
私营企业	Private Enterprises	2004	935
其他	Other Domestic Funded Enterprises		
港、澳、台商投资企业	Enterprises with Funds from Hong Kong,Macao and Taiwan	1437	457
外商投资企业	Foreign Funded Enterprises	2424	1140
按国民经济行业分	**Grouped by Sector**		
采矿业	Mining	1466	777
煤炭开采和洗选业	Mining and Washing of Coal		
石油和天然气开采业	Extraction of Petroleum and Natural Gas	879	466
黑色金属矿采选业	Mining of Ferrous Metal Ores		
有色金属矿采选业	Mining of Non-ferrous Metal Ores		
非金属矿采选业	Mining and Processing of Nonmetal Ores		
开采辅助活动	Mining of Other Ores	587	311
制造业	Mannfacturing Industry	37223	15844
农副食品加工业	Processing of Food from Agricultural Products	15	6
食品制造业	Manufacture of Foods	122	28
酒、饮料和精制茶制造业	Manufacture of Beverages	109	58
烟草制品业	Manufacture of Tobacco	50	20
纺织业	Manufacture of Textile	183	90
纺织服装、服饰业	Manufacture of Textile Wearing Apparel		
皮革、毛皮、羽毛及其制品和制鞋业	Manufacture of Leather, Fur, Feather and Related Products and Footwear	51	10

R&D Personnel and Expenditure Conditions of Industrial Enterprises above Designated Size（2017）

R&D经费内部支出（万元） R&D Intramural Expenditure (10000 yuan)	政府资金 Government funds	企业资金 Enterprise funds	境外资金 Foreign funds
1104702	**306292**	**790980**	**1491**
832146	284371	546442	666
156801	13524	138673	465
115124	8387	105244	360
631	10	621	
929142	305844	617198	824
312687	112565	199113	530
484619	181665	301437	283
100345	9351	88174	11
31491	2263	28474	
22445	205	22240	
153115	243	151542	667
19196	3967	15229	
5958	3806	2152	
13238	161	13077	
1081869	302225	772214	1491
56		56	
1104	1	937	
1037		1037	
584		584	
4135	30	4105	
1882		1882	

指标	Item	R&D人员（人）R&D personnel（person）	研究人员 Researchers
木材加工和木、竹、藤、棕、草制品业	Processing of Timber,Manufacture of Wood, Bamboo,Rattan,aplam and Straw Products		
家具制造业	Manufacture of Furniture		
造纸及纸制品业	Manufacture of Paper and Paper Products		
印刷和记录媒介复制业	Printing,Reproduction of Recording Media	366	122
文教、工美、体育和娱乐用品制造业	Manufacture of Articles For Culture, Education and Sport Activities		
石油加工业、炼焦和核燃料加工业	Processing of Petroleum, Coking, Processing of Nuclear Fuel		
化学原料及化学制品制造业	Manufacture of Raw Chemical Materials and Chemical Products	2523	1152
医药制造业	Manufacture of Medicines	1263	596
化学纤维制造业	Manufacture of Chemical Fibers	18	7
橡胶和塑料制品业	Manufacture of Rubber and Manufacture of Plastics	301	136
非金属矿物制品业	Manufacture of Non-metallic Mineral Products	171	86
黑色金属冶炼和压延加工业	Smelting and Pressing of Ferrous Metals	12	6
有色金属冶炼和压延加工业	Smelting and Pressing of Non-ferrous Metals	967	304
金属制品业	Manufacture of Metal Products	2230	765
通用设备制造业	Manufacture of General Purpose Machinery	915	441
专用设备制造业	Manufacture of Special Equipment	2484	1210
汽车制造业	Manufacture of Motor Vehicle	3774	1232
铁路、船舶、航空航天和其他运输设备制造业	Railways,Shipbuilding,Aerospace and Other Transportation Equipment Manufacturing Industry	11796	4923
电气机械和器材制造业	Manufacture of Electric Equipment and Machinery	3062	1301
计算机、通讯和其他电子设备制造业	Manufacture of Communication Equipment, Computers and other Electronic Equipment	4786	2335
仪器仪表制造业	Manufacture of Measuring Instruments and Machinery	1913	963
其他制造业	Other Manufacturing	101	48
废弃资源综合利用业	Comprehensive Utilization Of Waste Resources	3	1
金属制品、机械和设备修理业	Metal Products,Machinery and Equipment Repair Industry	8	4
电力、热力、燃气及水生产和供应业	Production and Distribution of Electricity,Heat,Gas and Water	1264	532
电力、热力的生产和供应业	Production and Supply of Electric Power and Heat Power	1264	532
燃气生产和供应业	Gas mining and supplying industry		
水的生产和供应业	Production and Supply of Water		

continued 1

R&D经费内部支出（万元） R&D Intramural Expenditure (10000 yuan)	政府资金 Government funds	企业资金 Enterprise funds	境外资金 Foreign funds
2481		2481	
71558	8678	62593	
39390	164	38897	
620		620	
11757	1504	10182	
4369	56	4314	
310	6	304	
20392	3452	16810	
44524	10322	34041	146
22367	1229	20641	350
44655	6671	37740	12
123927	1368	120240	16
334144	252017	82127	
101822	3512	96317	967
186677	11792	174697	
62684	1320	60319	
1059	102	956	
4		4	
332		332	
3637	100	3537	
3637	100	3537	

20-22 规模以上工业企业研究和试验发展（R&D）项目情况（2017年）

指标	Item	项目数（项）The number of items（item）
总计	**Total**	**2690**
按企业规模分	**Grouped by Size of Enterprises**	
大型企业	Large-size	1118
中型企业	Medium-size	739
小型企业	Small-size	821
微型企业	microenterprise	12
按登记注册类型分	**Grouped by Registion Status**	
内资企业	Domestic Investment Enterprises	2565
国有企业	State-owned Enterprises	599
集体企业	Collective-owned Enterprises	
股份合作企业	Stock cooperative enterprises	
联营企业	Affiliated companies	
有限责任公司	Limited Liability Corporations	1208
股份有限公司	Share-holding Corperation Ltd.	492
私营企业	Private Enterprises	266
其他	Other Domestic Funded Enterprises	
港澳台商投资	Enterprises with Funds from Hong Kong,Macao and Taiwan	10
外商投资企业	Foreign Funded Enterprises	115
按国民经济行业分	**Grouped by Sector**	
采矿业	Mining	142
煤炭开采和洗选业	Mining and Washing of Coal	
石油和天然气开采业	Extraction of Petroleum and Natural Gas	67
黑色金属矿采选业	Mining of Ferrous Metal Ores	
有色金属矿采选业	Mining of Non-ferrous Metal Ores	
非金属矿采选业	Mining and Processing of Nonmetal Ores	
开采辅助活动	Mining of Other Ores	75
制造业	Mannfacturing Industry	2462
农副食品加工业	Processing of Food from Agricultural Products	1
食品制造业	Manufacture of Foods	12
酒、饮料和精制茶制造业	Manufacture of Beverages	11
烟草制品业	Manufacture of Tobacco	8
纺织业	Manufacture of Textile	14
纺织服装、服饰业	Manufacture of Textile Wearing Apparel	
皮革、毛皮、羽毛及其制品和制鞋业	Manufacture of Leather, Fur, Feather and Related Products and Footwear	17

R&D Project Status of Industrial Enterprises above Designated Size（2017）

参加项目人员（人） Personnel participating in the project（person）	项目经费内部支出（万元） Intramural Expenditure（10 000 yuan）
34506	**1099864**
23268	827724
6162	156472
5038	115037
38	631
30730	924540
9219	309386
16653	483433
3113	100257
1745	31464
1437	22445
2339	152879
1039	19196
578	5958
461	13238
32418	1077040
15	56
117	1103
106	1036
50	573
110	4135
48	1882

20-22 续表1

指标	Item	项目数（项）The number of items（item）
木材加工和木、竹、藤、棕、草制品业	Processing of Timber,Manufacture of Wood, Bamboo,Rattan,aplam and Straw Products	
家具制造业	Manufacture of Furniture	
造纸及纸制品业	Manufacture of Paper and Paper Products	
印刷和记录媒介复制业	Printing,Reproduction of Recording Media	17
文教、工美、体育和娱乐用品制造业	Manufacture of Articles For Culture, Education and Sport Activities	
石油加工业、炼焦和核燃料加工业	Processing of Petroleum, Coking, Processing of Nuclear Fuel	
化学原料及化学制品制造业	Manufacture of Raw Chemical Materials and Chemical Products	354
医药制造业	Manufacture of Medicines	170
化学纤维制造业	Manufacture of Chemical Fibers	1
橡胶和塑料制品业	Manufacture of Rubber and Manufacture of Plastics	26
非金属矿物制品业	Manufacture of Non-metallic Mineral Products	19
黑色金属冶炼和压延加工业	Smelting and Pressing of Ferrous Metals	1
有色金属冶炼和压延加工业	Smelting and Pressing of Non-ferrous Metals	142
金属制品业	Manufacture of Metal Products	113
通用设备制造业	Manufacture of General Purpose Machinery	108
专用设备制造业	Manufacture of Special Equipment	276
汽车制造业	Manufacture of Motor Vehicle	122
铁路、船舶、航空航天和其他运输设备制造业	Railways,Shipbuilding,Aerospace and Other Transportation Equipment Manufacturing Industry	348
电气机械和器材制造业	Manufacture of Electric Equipment and Machinery	392
计算机、通讯和其他电子设备制造业	Manufacture of Communication Equipment, Computers and other Electronic Equipment	177
仪器仪表制造业	Manufacture of Measuring Instruments and Machinery	116
其他制造业	Other Manufacturing	15
废弃资源综合利用业	Comprehensive Utilization Of Waste Resources	1
金属制品、机械和设备修理业	Metal Products,Machinery and Equipment Repair Industry	1
电力、热力、燃气及水生产和供应业	Production and Distribution of Electricity,Heat,Gas and Water	86
电力、热力的生产和供应业	Production and Supply of Electric Power and Heat Power	86
燃气生产和供应业	Gas mining and supplying industry	
水的生产和供应业	Production and Supply of Water	

continued 1

参加项目人员（人） Personnel participating in the project（person）	项目经费内部支出（万元） Intramural Expenditure（10 000 yuan）
148	2479
2164	71493
1143	39332
15	620
233	11744
149	4369
6	310
927	20392
2077	44524
744	22359
2055	44642
3650	123246
10033	333015
2780	101481
4216	186614
1541	60239
80	1059
3	4
8	332
1049	3628
1049	3628

20-23 规模以上工业企业新产品开发、生产及销售情况（2017年）

指标	Item	新产品开发项目数（项） Number of new product development projects（item）
总计	**Total**	**2713**
按企业规模分	**Grouped by Size of Enterprises**	
大型企业	Large-size	987
中型企业	Medium-size	777
小型企业	Small-size	927
微型企业	microenterprise	22
按登记注册类型分	**Grouped by Registion Status**	
内资企业	Domestic Investment Enterprises	2556
国有企业	State-owned Enterprises	613
集体企业	Collective-owned Enterprises	
股份合作企业	Stock cooperative enterprises	
联营企业	Affiliated companies	
有限责任公司	Limited Liability Corporations	1184
股份有限公司	Share-holding Corperation Ltd.	460
私营企业	Private Enterprises	299
其他	Other Domestic Funded Enterprises	
港、澳、台商投资企业	Enterprises with Funds from Hong Kong,Macao and Taiwan	16
外商投资企业	Foreign Funded Enterprises	141
按国民经济行业分	**Grouped by Sector**	
采矿业	Mining	36
煤炭开采和洗选业	Mining and Washing of Coal	
石油和天然气开采业	Extraction of Petroleum and Natural Gas	1
黑色金属矿采选业	Mining of Ferrous Metal Ores	
有色金属矿采选业	Mining of Non-ferrous Metal Ores	
非金属矿采选业	Mining and Processing of Nonmetal Ores	
开采辅助活动	Mining of Other Ores	35
制造业	Mannfacturing Industry	2654
农副食品加工业	Processing of Food from Agricultural Products	4
食品制造业	Manufacture of Foods	21
酒、饮料和精制茶制造业	Manufacture of Beverages	12
烟草制品业	Manufacture of Tobacco	18
纺织业	Manufacture of Textile	20
纺织服装、服饰业	Manufacture of Textile Wearing Apparel	
皮革、毛皮、羽毛及其制品和制鞋业	Manufacture of Leather, Fur, Feather and Related Products and Footwear	19

注：本表数据由省统计局、市科技局、市工商局、市中级人民法院等提供。

New Product Development, Production and Sales of Above-scale Industrial Enterprises (2017)

新产品开发经费支出（万元） New Product Development Expenditure （10 000 yuan）	新产品产值 （万元） New product output value （10 000 yuan）	新产品销售收入 （万元） Sales of new products （10 000 yuan）
1194082	**11257678**	**8827778**
879340	9450455	7117592
175294	1010014	922065
138073	794980	786081
1375	2229	2040
1017323	10423365	8218086
364036	1271383	1331512
	3320	2302
533375	8466762	6180878
81219	559238	574195
38693	122662	129199
3054	596080	412561
173705	238233	197131
7719	2400	2235
260		
7460	2400	2235
1185148	11252755	8817013
643	346	482
3446	14321	22677
1347	2967	2629
2808	157377	118966
4964	15793	15780
2305	9264	17816

20-23 续表1

指标	Item	新产品开发项目数（项）Number of new product development projects（item）
木材加工和木、竹、藤、棕、草制品业	Processing of Timber,Manufacture of Wood, Bamboo,Rattan,aplam and Straw Products	
家具制造业	Manufacture of Furniture	
造纸及纸制品业	Manufacture of Paper and Paper Products	
印刷和记录媒介复制业	Printing,Reproduction of Recording Media	16
文教、工美、体育和娱乐用品制造业	Manufacture of Articles For Culture, Education and Sport Activities	
石油加工业、炼焦和核燃料加工业	Processing of Petroleum, Coking, Processing of Nuclear Fuel	
化学原料及化学制品制造业	Manufacture of Raw Chemical Materials and Chemical Products	328
医药制造业	Manufacture of Medicines	142
化学纤维制造业	Manufacture of Chemical Fibers	1
橡胶和塑料制品业	Manufacture of Rubber and Manufacture of Plastics	24
非金属矿物制品业	Manufacture of Non-metallic Mineral Products	13
黑色金属冶炼和压延加工业	Smelting and Pressing of Ferrous Metals	1
有色金属冶炼和压延加工业	Smelting and Pressing of Non-ferrous Metals	127
金属制品业	Manufacture of Metal Products	104
通用设备制造业	Manufacture of General Purpose Machinery	102
专用设备制造业	Manufacture of Special Equipment	298
汽车制造业	Manufacture of Motor Vehicle	148
铁路、船舶、航空航天和其他运输设备制造业	Railways,Shipbuilding,Aerospace and Other Transportation Equipment Manufacturing Industry	348
电气机械和器材制造业	Manufacture of Electric Equipment and Machinery	541
计算机、通讯和其他电子设备制造业	Manufacture of Communication Equipment, Computers and other Electronic Equipment	205
仪器仪表制造业	Manufacture of Measuring Instruments and Machinery	149
其他制造业	Other Manufacturing	11
废弃资源综合利用业	Comprehensive Utilization Of Waste Resources	
金属制品、机械和设备修理业	Metal Products,Machinery and Equipment Repair Industry	2
电力、热力、燃气及水生产和供应业	Production and Distribution of Electricity,Heat,Gas and Water	23
电力、热力的生产和供应业	Production and Supply of Electric Power and Heat Power	23
燃气生产和供应业	Gas mining and supplying industry	
水的生产和供应业	Production and Supply of Water	

continued 1

新产品开发经费支出（万元） New Product Development Expenditure （10 000 yuan）	新产品产值 （万元） New product output value （10 000 yuan）	新产品销售收入 （万元） Sales of new products （10 000 yuan）
3740	2590	2590
57736	339130	325399
48153	415891	306407
1125		
10515	54800	48871
3917	5332	5565
313	980	980
22909	141170	229798
43435	208105	205293
25983	101266	145634
54369	314044	299927
118135	6448362	3670146
369845	1376485	1771614
133025	892741	916124
202646	542002	495546
72402	206727	207957
1141	3050	6805
	12	8
248		
1215	2523	8530
1215	2523	8530

20-24 规模以上非工业重点行业企业研究与试验发展（R&D）基本情况（2017）

R&D Project Status of Non-Industrial Key Enterprises above Designated Size（2017）

指标	Item	单位数（个）Number of Units (unit)	#有R&D活动单位数（个）The Number of R&D active units (unit)
总计	**Total**	**689**	**71**
按企业规模分	**Grouped by Size of Enterprises**		
大型企业	Large-size	157	43
中型企业	Medium-size	399	27
小型企业	Small-size	124	1
微型企业	Microenterprise	9	
按登记注册类型分	**Grouped by Registered Status**		
内资企业	Domestic Investment Enterprises	662	66
港、澳、台商投资企业	Enterprises with Funds from Hong Kong, Macao And Taiwan	7	
外商投资企业	Foreign Funded Enterprises	20	5
按国民经济行业分	**Grouped by Sector**		
建筑业	Construction	332	27
交通运输、仓储和邮政业	Traffic, Transport, Storage and Post	40	1
信息传输、软件和信息技术服务业	Information Transmission, Computer Services and Software	93	15
租赁和商务服务业	Leasing and Business Services	37	2
科学研究和技术服务业	Scientific Research, Technical Sevice	115	25
水利、环境和公共设施管理业	Management of Water Conservancy, Environment and Public Facilities	31	
卫生和社会工作	Health, Social Security		
文化、体育和娱乐业	Culture, Sports and Entertainment	41	1

20-25 规模以上非工业重点行业企业研究与试验发展（R&D）人员和经费支出情况（2017年）

R&D Personnel and Expenditure of Non-Industrial Key Enterprises above Designated Size（2017）

指标	Item	R&D人员（人）R&D personnel（person）	#研究人员 #Researchers
总计	**Total**	13329	6124
按企业规模分	**Grouped by Size of Enterprises**		
大型企业	Large-size	12200	5612
中型企业	Medium-size	1117	506
小型企业	Small-size	12	6
微型企业	Microenterprise		
按登记注册类型分	**Grouped by Registered Status**		
内资企业	Domestic Investment Enterprises	12666	5793
港、澳、台商投资企业	Enterprises with Funds from Hong Kong, Macao And Taiwan		
外商投资企业	Foreign Funded Enterprises	663	331
按国民经济行业分	**Grouped by Sector**		
建筑业	Construction	4767	1771
交通运输、仓储和邮政业	Traffic, Transport, Storage and Post	43	23
信息传输、软件和信息技术服务业	Information Transmission, Computer Services and Software	4470	2248
租赁和商务服务业	Leasing and Business Services	33	18
科学研究和技术服务业	Scientific Research, Technical Sevice	3992	2053
水利、环境和公共设施管理业	Management of Water Conservancy, Environment and Public Facilities		
卫生和社会工作	Health, Social Security		
文化、体育和娱乐业	Culture, Sports and Entertainment	24	11

20-25 续表1 continued 1

指标	Item	R&D经费内部支出（万元）R&D Intramural Expenditure (10000 yuan)	#政府资金 # Government funds
总计	**Total**	372947	7154
按企业规模分	**Grouped by Size of Enterprises**		
大型企业	Large-size	328206	6843
中型企业	Medium-size	44686	256
小型企业	Small-size	55	55
微型企业	Microenterprise		
按登记注册类型分	**Grouped by Registered Status**		
内资企业	Domestic Investment Enterprises	334811	7038
港、澳、台商投资企业	Enterprises with Funds from Hong Kong, Macao And Taiwan		
外商投资企业	Foreign Funded Enterprises	38136	116
按国民经济行业分	**Grouped by Sector**		
建筑业	Construction	139630	242
交通运输、仓储和邮政业	Traffic, Transport, Storage and Post	87	40
信息传输、软件和信息技术服务业	Information Transmission, Computer Services and Software	176199	1000
租赁和商务服务业	Leasing and Business Services	4287	
科学研究和技术服务业	Scientific Research, Technical Sevice	52447	5872
水利、环境和公共设施管理业	Management of Water Conservancy, Environment and Public Facilities		
卫生和社会工作	Health, Social Security		
文化、体育和娱乐业	Culture, Sports and Entertainment	297	

20-25 续表2 continued 2

指标	Item	#企业资金 # Enterprise funds	#境外资金 # Foreign funds
总计	**Total**	360945	3112
按企业规模分	**Grouped by Size of Enterprises**		
大型企业	Large-size	319702	135
中型企业	Medium-size	41243	2977
小型企业	Small-size		
微型企业	Microenterprise		
按登记注册类型分	**Grouped by Registered Status**		
内资企业	Domestic Investment Enterprises	326036	
港、澳、台商投资企业	Enterprises with Funds from Hong Kong, Macao And Taiwan		
外商投资企业	Foreign Funded Enterprises	34909	3112
按国民经济行业分	**Grouped by Sector**		
建筑业	Construction	139384	
交通运输、仓储和邮政业	Traffic, Transport, Storage and Post	47	
信息传输、软件和信息技术服务业	Information Transmission, Computer Services and Software	175003	
租赁和商务服务业	Leasing and Business Services	1301	2977
科学研究和技术服务业	Scientific Research, Technical Sevice	44914	135
水利、环境和公共设施管理业	Management of Water Conservancy, Environment and Public Facilities		
卫生和社会工作	Health, Social Security		
文化、体育和娱乐业	Culture, Sports and Entertainment	297	

20–26 规模以上非工业重点行业企业研究与试验发展（R&D）项目情况（2017年）

The Situation of Non-Industrial Key Enterprises above Designated Size Projects（2017）

指标	Item	合计 Total	参加项目人员（人） Personnel participating in the project（person）	项目经费内部支出（万元） Intramural Expenditure（10 000 yuan）
总计	**Total**	679	11546	372771
按企业规模分	**Grouped by Size of Enterprises**			
大型企业	Large-size	587	10476	328079
中型企业	Medium-size	91	1060	44637
小型企业	Small-size	1	10	55
微型企业	Microenterprise			
按登记注册类型分	**Grouped by Registered Status**			
内资企业	Domestic Investment Enterprises	655	10899	334723
港、澳、台商投资企业	Enterprises with Funds from Hong Kong, Macao And Taiwan			
外商投资企业	Foreign Funded Enterprises	24	647	38048
按国民经济行业分	**Grouped by Sector**			
建筑业	Construction	222	4392	139548
交通运输、仓储和邮政业	Traffic, Transport, Storage and Post	2	19	87
信息传输、软件和信息技术服务业	Information Transmission, Computer Services and Software	56	3863	176152
租赁和商务服务业	Leasing and Business Services	2	31	4287
科学研究和技术服务业	Scientific Research, Technical Sevice	391	3217	52400
水利、环境和公共设施管理业	Management of Water Conservancy, Environment and Public Facilities			
卫生和社会工作	Health, Social Security			
文化、体育和娱乐业	Culture, Sports and Entertainment	6	24	297

20–27 主要年份知识产权情况

Intellectual Property Rights in Major Years

指 标	Item	2015	2016	2017
一、专利申请合计数（件）	**Patents Application Accepted(unit)**	60986	46103	81110
发明专利	Inventions	14024	18569	40439
实用新型专利	Utility Models	15735	18369	22461
外观专利	Designs	31227	9165	18210
二、授权专利合计（件）	**Patents Application Granted(unit)**	25103	38279	25042
发明专利	Inventions	5873	6686	7902
实用新型专利	Utility Models	12030	12344	11595
外观专利	Designs	7200	19249	5545
三、注册商标（件）	**Registered Trade Mark(unit)**	9600	35391	28448

注：1.本表数据由市科技局和市工商局提供。
　　2.本表2017年数据为原西安口径数据。

20–28 主要年份民事知识产权维权情况

Protection of Civil Intellectual Property Rights in Major Years

指 标	Item	2015	2016	2017
1、专利纠纷	Patent controversies	130	95	112
2、商标纠纷	Trade mark controversies	277	353	404
3、著作权纠纷	Copyright controversies	327	404	190
4、技术合同纠纷	Technological contract controversies	12	10	36
5、其他知识产权纠纷	Others IPR controversies	67	25	110

注：本表数据由市中级人民法院提供。

20-29 规模以上工业企业自主知识产权情况（2017年）

The Independent Intellectual Property Rights of Industrial Enterprises above Designated Size（2017）

指 标	Item	专利申请数（件）Number of Patent Applications (piece)	#发明专利 Invention Patent of	期末有效发明专利数（件）Number of Valid Invention Patents At the End of the Term (piece)
总计	**Total**	**5686**	**2575**	**10551**
按企业规模分	**Grouped by Size of Enterprises**			
大型企业	Large-size	2855	1539	4163
中型企业	Medium-size	1059	370	2426
小型企业	Small-size	1730	640	3891
微型企业	Microenterprise	42	26	71
按登记注册类型分	**Grouped by Registered Status**			
内资企业	Domestic Investment Enterprises	5522	2506	9960
国有企业	State-owned Enterprises	1182	680	2002
集体企业	Collective-owned Enterprise			
股份合作企业	Stock Cooperative Enterprises			6
联营企业	Affiliated Enterprise			
有限责任公司	Limited Liability Corporations	2546	1186	4478
股份有限公司	Share-holding Corporation Ltd	1124	424	2551
私营企业	Private Enterprise	670	216	923
其他	Other Domestic Funded Enterprises			
港、澳、台商投资企业	Enterprises with Funds from Hong Kong, Macao And Taiwan	13	9	63
外商投资企业	Foreign Funded Enterprises	151	60	528
按国民经济行业大类分	**Grouped by Sector**			
采矿业	Mining	337	207	379
煤炭开采和洗选业	Mining and Washing of Coal			
石油和天然气开采业	Extraction of Petroleum and Natural Gas	303	182	274
黑色金属矿采选业	Mining of Ferrous Metal Ores			
有色金属矿采选业	Mining of Non-ferrous Metal Ores			
非金属矿采选业	Mining and Processing of Nonmetal Ores			
开采辅助活动	Mining Other Ores	34	25	105
制造业	Manufacturing Industry	5122	2234	9971
农副食品加工业	Processing of Food from Agriculture Products			
食品制造业	Manufacture of Food	2		29
酒、饮料和精制茶制造业	Manufacture of Beverages	11	5	32
烟草制品业	Manufacture of Tobacco	35	7	13
纺织业	Manufacture of Textile	15	4	15
纺织服装、服饰业	Manufacture of Textile Wearing, Apparel			
皮革、毛皮、羽毛及其制品和制鞋业	Manufacture of Leather, Furs, Feather, Related Products and Footware	16	4	3

20-29 续表1 continued 1

指 标	Item	专利申请数（件）Number of Patent Applications (piece)	#发明专利 Invention Patent of	期末有效发明专利数（件）Number of Valid Invention Patents At the End of the Term (piece)
木材加工和木、竹、藤、棕、草制品业	Processing of Timber,Manufacture of Wood, Bamboo, Rattan, Palm and Straw Products			
家具制造业	Manufacture of Furniture			
造纸及纸制品业	Manufacture of Paper And Paper Products			
印刷和记录媒介复制业	Printing and Reproduction of Recording Media	22	19	99
文教、工美、体育和娱乐用品制造业	Education, Art, Sports And Entertainment Products Manufacturing			
石油加工、炼焦和核燃料加工业	Processing of Petroleum,Coking and Processing of Nuclear Fuel			
化学原料和化学制品制造业	Manufacture of Raw Chemical Materials and Chemical Products	380	220	759
医药制造业	Manufacture of Medicines	83	34	350
化学纤维制造业	Manufacture of Chemical Fiber			
橡胶和塑料制品业	Manufacture of Rubber and Manufacture of Plastic	32	8	90
非金属矿物制品业	Manufacture of Non-metallic Mineral Products	39	9	148
黑色金属冶炼和压延加工业	Smelting and Pressing of Ferrous Metals	10		15
有色金属冶炼和压延加工业	Smelting and Pressing of Non-ferrous Metals	168	118	605
金属制品业	Manufacture of Metal Products	205	121	395
通用设备制造业	Manufacture of General Purpose Machinery	218	84	593
专用设备制造业	Manufacture of Special Equipment	824	260	1065
汽车制造业	Manufacture of Motor Vehicle	646	157	532
铁路、船舶、航空航天和其他运输设备制造业	Railways, Ships, Aerospace And Other Transportation Equipment Manufacturing Industry	870	629	2023
电气机械和器材制造业	Manufacture of Electric Equipment and Machinery	590	183	1146
计算机、通信和其他电子设备制造业	Manufacture of Communication Equipment, Computers and Other Electronic Equipment	627	262	1142
仪器仪表制造业	Manufacture of Measuring Instruments and Machinery	285	106	769
其他制造业	Other Manufacturing	44	4	148
废弃资源综合利用业	Comprehensive Utilization Of Waste Resources			
金属制品、机械和设备修理业	Metal Products, Machinery and Equipment Repair Industry			
电力、燃气及水的生产供应业	Production and Supply of Electric Power,Gas and Water	227	134	201
电力、热力生产和供应业	Production and Supply of Electric Power and Heat Power	222	134	201
燃气生产和供应业	Production and Supply of Gas	2		
水的生产和供应业	Production and Supply of Water	3		

20-30 规模以上非工业重点行业企业知识产权（2017年）

Intellectual Property Rights of Non-Industrial Key Enterprises above Designated Size（2017）

指 标	Item	专利申请数（件）Number of Patent Applications (piece)	#发明专利 Invention Patent of	有效发明专利数（件）Number of Valid Invention Patents At the End of the Term (piece)
总计	**Total**	**2233**	**834**	**3231**
按企业规模分	**Grouped by Size of Enterprises**			
大型企业	Large-size	2040	750	3011
中型企业	Medium-size	185	79	219
小型企业	Small-size	8	5	1
微型企业	Microenterprise			
按登记注册类型分	**Grouped by Registered Status**			
内资企业	Domestic Investment Enterprises	2220	833	3187
港、澳、台商投资企业	Enterprises with Funds from Hong Kong, Macao And Taiwan			
外商投资企业	Foreign Funded Enterprises	13	1	44
按国民经济行业分	**Grouped by Sector**			
建筑业	Construction	579	159	671
交通运输、仓储和邮政业	Traffic, Transport, Storage and Post			
信息传输、软件和信息技术服务业	Information Transmission, Computer Services and Software	670	245	335
租赁和商务服务业	Leasing and Business Services	1	1	1
科学研究和技术服务业	Scientific Research, Technical Sevice	983	429	2211
水利、环境和公共设施管理业	Management of Water Conservancy, Environment and Public Facilities			
卫生和社会工作	Health, Social Security			
文化、体育和娱乐业	Culture, Sports and Entertainment			13

主要统计指标解释

普通高等学校 指按国家规定的设置标准和审批程序批准举办的，通过全国普通高等学校统一招生考试，招收高中毕业生为主要培养对象，实施高等学历教育的全日制大学、独立设置的学院和高等专科学校、高等职业学校及其他机构（独立学院和分校、大专班）。

大学、独立设置的学院主要实施本科层次以上教育。高等专科学校、高等职业学校实施专科层次教育。其他机构是承担国家普通招生计划任务不计校数的机构，包括独立学院、普通高等学校分校、大专班和批准筹建的普通高等学校等。独立学院指由普通本科高校按新机制、新模式举办的本科层次的二级学院，一些普通本科高校按公办机制和模式建立的二级学院，“分校”或其他类似的二级办学机构不属此范畴。

成人高等学校 指按照国家规定的设置标准和审批程序批准举办的，通过全国成人高等教育统一招生考试，招收具有高中毕业或同等学历的人员为主要培养对象，利用函授、业余、脱产等多种形式对其实施高等学历教育的学校。包括职工高等学校、农民高等学校、管理干部学院、教育学院、独立函授学院、广播电视大学、其他机构等。其他机构是承担国家成人招生计划任务不计校数的机构。

小学学龄儿童净入学率 指调查范围内已入小学学习的学龄儿童占校内外学龄儿童总数（包括弱智儿童，不包括盲聋哑儿童）的比重。计算公式为：

小学学龄儿童净入学率（%）=已入学的小学学龄儿童数／校内外小学学龄儿童总数×100%

研究与试验发展（R&D） 指在科学技术领域，为增加知识总量，以及运用这些知识去创造新的应用进行的系统的创造性的活动，包括基础研究、应用研究、试验发展三类活动。国际上通常采用R&D活动的规模和强度指标反映一国的科技实力和核心竞争力。

基础研究 指为了获得关于现象和可观察事实的基本原理的新知识（揭示客观事物的本质、运动规律，获得新发现、新学说）而进行的实验性或理论性研究，它不以任何专门或特定的应用或使用为目的。其成果以科学论文和科学著作为主要形式。用来反映知识的原始创新能力。

应用研究 指为获得新知识而进行的创造性研究，主要针对某一特定的目的或目标。应用研究是为了确定基础研究成果可能的用途，或是为达到预定的目标探索应采取的新方法（原理性）或新途径。其成果形式以科学论文、专著、原理性模型或发明专利为主。用来反映对基础研究成果应用途径的探索。

试验发展 指利用从基础研究、应用研究和实际经验所获得的现有知识，为产生新的产品、材料和装置，建立新的工艺、系统和服务，以及对已产生和建立的上述各项作实质性的改进而进行的系统性丁作。其成果形式主要是专利、专有技术、具有新产品基本特征的产品原型或具有新装置基本特征的原始样机等。在社会科学领域，试验发展是指把通过基础研究、应用研究获得的知识转变成可以实施的计划（包括为进行检验和评估实施示范项目）的过程。人文科学领域没有对应的试验发展活动。主要反映将科研成果转化为技术和产品的能力，是科技推动经济社会发展的物化成果。

R&D人员 指参与研究与试验发展项目研究、管理和辅助工作的人员，包括项目（课题）组人员，企业科技行政管理人员和直接为项目（课题）活动提供服务的辅助人员。反映投入从事拥有自主知识产权的研究开发活动的人力规模。

R&D人员全时当量 指全时人员数加非全时人员按工作量折算为全时人员数的总和。例如：有两个全时人员和三个非全时人员（工作时间分别为20%、30%和70%），则全时当量为2+0.2+0.3+0.7=3.2人年。为国际上比较科技人力投入而制定的可比指标。

R&D经费内部支出 合计指调查单位用于内部开展R&D活动（基础研究、应用研究和试验发展）的实际支出。包括用于R&D项目（课题）活动的直接支出，以及间接用TR&D活动的管理费、服务费、与R&D有关的基本建设支出以及外协加工费等。不包括生产性活动支出、归还贷款支出以及与外单位合作或委托外单位进行R&D活动而转拨给对方的经费支出。

R&D经费内部支出中政府资金 指R&D经费内部支出中来自各级政府部门的各类资金，包括财政科学技术拨款、科学基金、教育等部门事业费以及政府部门预算外资金的实际支出。

R&D经费内部支出中企业资金 指R&D经费内部支出中来自本企业的自有资金和接受其他企业委托而获得的经费，以及科研院所、高校等事业单位从企业获得的资金的实际支出。

R&D项目（课题）数 指在当年立项并开展研究工作、以前年份立项仍继续进行研究的研发项目（课题）数，包括当年完成和年内研究：工作已告失败的研发项目（课题），但不包括委托外单位进行的研发项目（课题）数。

R&D项目（课题）人员全时当量 指实际参加研发项目（课题）活动人员折合的全时当量。

R&D项目（课题）经费内部支出 指调查单位内部在报告年度进行研发项目（课题）研究和试制等的实际支出。包括劳务费、其他日常支出、固定资产购建费、外协加工费等，不包括委托或与外单位合作进行项目（课题）研究而拨付给对方使用的经费。

新产品产值 指报告期企业生产的新产品的产值。新产品是指采用新技术原理、新设计构思研制、生产的全新产品，或在结构、材质、工艺等某一方面比原有产品有明显改进，从而显著提高了产品性能或扩大了使用功能的产品。新产品产值、新产品销售收入既包括经政府有关部门认定并在有效期内的新产品，也包括企业自行研制开发，未经政府有关部门认定，从投产之日起一年之内的新产品。

新产品销售收入 指报告期企业销售新产品实现的销售收入。

专利 是专利权的简称，是对发明人的发明创造经审查合格后，由专利局依据专利法授予发明人和设计人对该项发明创造享有的专有权。包括发明、实用新型和外观设计。反映拥有自主知识产权的科技和设计成果情况。

发明（专利） 指对产品、方法或者其改进所提出的新的技术方案。是国际通行的反映拥有自主知识产权技术的核心指标。

Explanatory Notes on Main Statistical Indicators

Regular Institutions of Higher Education refer to educational establishments set up according to the government evaluation and approval procedures, recruiting graduates from senior secondary schools as the main target by National Matriculation TEST. They include full-time universities, colleges, institutions of higher professional education, institutions of higher vocational education, institutions of higher vocational education and others (non-university tertiary, branch schools and undergraduate classes) .

Universities and colleges primarily provide undergraduate courses; institutions of higher professional education and institutions of higher vocational education primarily provide professional trainings; and others refer to educational establishments, which are responsible for enrolling higher education students under the State Plan but not enumerated in the total number of schools, including: branch schools of universities and colleges, and universities and colleges that have been approved and under plan for construction. Non-university tertiary refers to the regular undergraduate branch college which is running in new mechanism and mode, excluding the branch schools and other similar branches of educational institutions.

Institutions of Higher Education for Adults refer to educational establishments, set up in line with relevant rules approved by the government, enrolling staff and workers with senior secondary school or equivalent education, and providing higher education courses in many forms of correspondence, spare time, or full time for adults. Professionals thus trained receive a qualification equivalent to graduates studying regular courses at regular universities, colleges and professional colleges. Institutions of higher learning for adults include schools of higher education for staff and workers, schools of higher education for peasants, colleges for management cadres, pedagogical colleges, independent correspondence colleges, Radio and TV universities and other educational establishments. Other educational establishments have undertakings to enrol adult students but not enumerated in the schools under the State Plan.

Net Enrolment Ratio of Primary Schools refers to the proportion of school age children enrolled at schools to the total number of school age children both in and outside schools (including retarded children, but excluding blind, deaf and mute children) . The formula is:

$$\text{Net Enrolment Ratio Of Primary Schools} = \frac{\text{Total Primary School-age Children at Schools}}{\text{Total Primary School-age WnerdlihChether or Not Attending School}} \times 100\%$$

Research and Development (R&D) refers to systematic and creative activities in the field of science and technology aiming at increasing the knowledge and using the knowledge for new application. R&D includes 3 categories of activities: basic research, applied research and experimentation for development. The scale and intensity of R&D are widely used internationally to reflect the strength of S&T and the core competitiveness of a country in the world.

Basic Research refers to empirical or theoretical research aiming at obtaining new knowledge on the fundamental principles regarding phenomena or observable facts to reveal the intrinsic nature and underlying laws and to acquire new discoveries or new theories. Basic research takes no specific or designated application as the aim of the research. Results of basic research are mainly released or disseminated in the form of scientific papers or monographs. This indicator reflects the innovation capacity for original knowledge.

Applied Research refers to creative research aiming at obtaining new knowledge on a specific objective or target. Purpose of the applied research is to identify the possible uses of results from basic research, or to explore new (fundamental) methods or new approaches. Results of applied research are expressed in the form of scientific papers, monographs, fundamental models or invention patents. This indicator reflects the exploration of ways to apply the results of basic research.

Experiments and Development refer to systematic activities aiming at using the knowledge from basic and applied researches or from practical experience to develop new products, materials and equipment, to establish new production process, systems and services, or to make substantial improvement on the existing products, process or services. Results of experiment and development activities are embodied in patents, exclusive technology, and monotype of new products or equipment. In social sciences, experiment and development activities refer to the process of converting the knowledge from basic or applied researches into feasible programmes (including conduct of demonstration projects for assessment and evaluation) . There are no experiment and development activities in the science of humanities. This indicator reflects the capability of transferring the results of S&T into technique and products, and measures the realization of S&T in spearheading the economic and social development.

R&D Personnel refer to persons engaged in research, management and supporting activities ofR & D, including persons in the project teams, persons engaged in the management of S&T activities of enterprises and supporting staff providing direct service to the research projects. This indicator reflects the size of personnel engaged in R&D activities with independent intellectual property.

Full-time Equivalent of R&D Personnel refers to the sum of the full-time persons and the full-time equivalent of part-time persons converted by workload. For instance, if there are 2 full-time persons and 3 part-time workers (20%, 30% and 70% of working hours respectively on R&D activities) , the full-time equivalent are 2+0.2+0.3+0.7=3.2 person-years. This is an internationally comparable indicator of S&T manpower input.

Total Internal Expenditure of Funds on R&D refers to the real expenditure of surveyed units on their own R&D activities (basic research, application study, test and development) including direct expenditure on R&D activities, indirect expenditure of management and services on R&D activities, expenditure on capital construction and material processing by others. Excluding the expenditure on production activities, return of loan, and fees transferred to cooperated and entrusted agencies on R&D activities.

Internal Expenditure of Government Funds refersto the expenditure of funds on R&D activities from government agencies at different levels, including appropriate funds on science and technology from financial departments, scientific funds, operating expenses from education departments and the real expenditure of extra budgetary funds from government agencies.

Internal Expenditure of Funds of Enterprises refers to the expenditure of funds on R&D activities from self-raised funds of enterprises and funds from other enterprises through entrustment, and the expenditure of funds of institutions, such as institution of scientific research and universities, from enterprises.

Number of R&D Projects (subjects) refers to the number of R&D projects (subjects) set up and implemented at the reference year, and the number of R&D projects (subjects) set up in former years and under implementation, including the projects (subjects) finished and failed at the reference year, excluding the projects (subjects) implemented by others through entrustment.

Full-time Equivalent of R&D Personnel refers to the full-time equivalent of persons actually engaged in R&D projects. (subjects)

Internal Expenditure of Funds on R&D Projects (subjects) refers to the real expenditure of internal funds of the surveyed units on research and test of R&D projects (subjects) at the reference year, including service fee, other daily expenditure, cost for capital goods, cost of external process; excluding expenditure of funds transferred to other cooperated and entrusted units of the projects.

Output Value of New Products refers to the output value of new products during the reporting period. The new products refer to brand new products produced with new technology and new design, or product that represent noticeable improvement in terms of structure, material, or production process for improving significantly the character of function of the older versions. The output value and sales income of the new products include those of new products certified by relevant government agencies within the period of certification, as well as new products designed and produced by enterprises within a year without certification by government agencies.

Sales Income of New Products refers to the real sales income of new products of the enterprises at the reporting period.

Patent is an abbreviation for the patent right and refers to the exclusive right of ownership by the inventors or designers for the creation or inventions, given from the patent offices after due process of assessment and approval in accordance with the Patent Law. Patents are granted for inventions, utility models and designs. This indicator reflects the achievements of S&T and design with independent intellectual property.

Patented Inventions refer to new technical proposals to the products or methods or their modifications. This is universal core indicator reflecting the technologies with independent intellectual property.

21 文化、体育、卫生、社会福利和其他

CULTURE,SPORTS,PUBLIC HEALTH,SOCIAL WELFARE INSTITUTIONS AND OTHER SOCIAL ACTIVITIES

资料整理：郝　静
Data management：Hao Jing
数据审核：王金桂
Data audit：Wang Jingui

第二十一部分　文化、体育、卫生、社会福利和其他

一、简要说明

本章资料主要包括文化、卫生、民政、体育、计划生育、共青团、妇联以及公检法等方面的内容，由西安市统计局服务业和社会科技处根据西安市文广新局、卫计委、民政局、体育局、妇联、团市委以及公安局、检察院、法院等部门提供资料整理。其中：依据市文广新局、体育局部门报表制度变化，调整了部分表式。

二、主要指标

公共图书馆藏量（千册件）	7340	比上年增加	383
医院数（个）	329	比上年增加	37
医院床位数（万张）	5.82	比上年增加	6711（张）

21　CULTURE,SPORTS,PUBLIC HEALTH,SOCIAL WELFARE INSTITUTIONS AND OTHER SOCIAL ACTIVITIES

Ⅰ.Brief Introduction

Data in this chapter primarily consists of data of culture, sanitation, civil administration, physical education, family planning, Communist Youth League, the Women's Federation, public security organs, procuratorial organs and people's court, compiled by Tertiary Industry and Social Science & Technology Division of Xi'an Bureau of Statistics according to data from Xi'an Bureau of Cuture, health and Family Planning Commision, Bureau of Civial Adnimistration, Bureau of PE, the Women's Federation, Municipal Committee of Communist Youth League, Bureau of Public Security, Procuratorate, People's Court and other department concerned.

Ⅱ.Major Indicators

		Increase over Preceding Year
Number of Collections in Libraries（1000 volume-times）	7340	383
Number of Hospitals(unit)	329	37
Number of Beds(10 000 units)	5.82	6711(unit)

21-1 电影基本情况（2017年）

The Basic Situation of Film（2017）

指 标	Item	2017
电影制片厂（个）	Film Studio(unit)	1
电影制片厂从业人员（人）	Film Studio Employees(person)	900
电影发行放映管理机构（个）	Film Projection and Publication Administrating Institutions(unit)	2
电影发行放映管理机构从业人员（人）	Film Projection and Publication Administrating Institution Staff(person)	8
电影放映单位（个）	Unit of Film Shows(unit)	228
#电影院	Cinema	96
影剧院	Theaters	5
放映队	File Projection Team	127
电影放映单位从业人员（人）	Staff of Unit of Film Shows(person)	2616
#电影院	Cinema	2400
影剧院	Theaters	69
放映队	File Projection Team	147
电影放映场数（千场）	Number of Film Shows（1000 shows）	1247
电影观众人数（千人次）	Number of Spectators(1000 person-times)	32579
电影票房收入（万元）	Box-office Receipts(10 000yuan)	90500
平均每一放映场次的观众人次（人次）	Average Audience of Each Projection(person-times)	26
平均每一放映场次的放映收入（元）	Average Income of Each Projcetion(yuan)	726

注：本表数据来源于市文广新局。
　　本表数据含西咸新区。

21-2 图书馆基本情况（2017年）

The Basic Situation of Library（2017）

指　标	Item	2017
公共图书馆个数（个）	Number of Public Libraries(unit)	13
公共图书馆从业人员（人）	Public Library Practitioners (person)	442
公共图书馆藏量（千册件）	Public Library Reserves(1 000 volume -times)	7340
电子图书（千册）	E-books(1 000 volumes)	5004
阅览室坐席（个）	Number of Seatings in Reading Room(unit)	5123
书刊文献外借人次（千人次）	Number of Books and literature Borrowed by Readers (1 000 person-times)	1181
书刊文献外借册次（千册件）	Volumes of Books and literature Lent to Readers(1 000 volume -times)	3173
图书流通人次（千人次）	Book Circulation Person-time (1 000 person-times)	6786
县以上公共图书馆购书经费（万元）	Book-purchase Fund of Public Library above the County Level(10 000 yuan)	1500
公共图书馆建筑面积（万平方米）	Building Area of Public Library (10 000 sq.m)	9.15

注：本表数据来源于市文广新局。
　　本表数据含西咸新区。

21-3 艺术表演基本情况（2017年）

The Basic Situation of Art Performance（2017）

指　标	Item	2017
艺术表演团体机构数（个）	Number of Organization of Art Performance Troupes(unit)	18
艺术表演团体从业人员（人）	Art Performance Troupes Practitioners (person)	2387
艺术表演团体演出场次（场）	Number of Performances by Art Performance Troupes(show)	5350
#国内演出场次	Domestic Performance	5280
艺术表演观众人次（千人次）	Audience for the Art Performance(1 000 person-times)	6355
艺术表演团体本年创作首映剧目（个）	Art Performance Troupes Creative Premieres of the Year (unit)	13
艺术表演场馆数（个）	Number of Art Performance Places(unit)	16
艺术表演场馆从业人员（人）	Art Performance Place Practitioners (person)	239
艺术表演场馆坐席（个）	Art Performance Place Seatings(unit)	9940
艺术科研机构（个）	Art and Research Institutions(unit)	2
艺术科研机构从业人员（人）	Art and Research Institutions Practitioners(person)	52

注：本表数据来源于市文广新局。
　　本表数据含西咸新区。

21-4 主要年份群众艺术馆、文化馆（站）活动情况

Basic Statistics on Activities of Mass Art Centers and Cultural Centers in Representative Years

指 标	Item	2011	2012	2013	2014	2015	2016	2017
机构数（个）	Number of Insititutions (unit)	196	197	198	199	199	190	202
举办展览个数（个）	Number of Exhibitions (unit)	592	652	658	627	606	562	649
举办展览参观人次（千人次）	Number of Exhibition Visitors(1 000 person-times)	375	416	301	326	289	287	418
组织文艺活动次数（次）	Art Performances and Story-telling Sessions (times)	4544	3273	4114	3617	3811	4246	5498
组织文艺活动参加人次（千人次）	Number of Culture Activities attendees (1 000 person-times)	1778	1377	1633	1576	1574	1688	2631
举办训练班班次（个）	Number of Training Courses (unit)	2224	1798	1616	1872	2126	1906	2597
举办训练班结业人次（千人次）	Number of Certificate Trained Persons (1 000 person-times)	115	143	155	156	207	149	188
组织各类理论研讨和讲座次数（次）	Number of Theoretical Discussion and Seminars(times)	106	78	122	254	216	189	101
组织各类理论研讨和讲座参加人次（千人次）	Number of Persons in Theoretical Discussion and Seminars(1 000 person-times)	15	14	19	28	25	18	17
本年收入（千元）	Income of this year (1 000 yuan)	55367	88475	101365	89520	102567	103706	133378
本年支出（千元）	Expenditure of this year (1 000 yuan)	62368	84522	93485	84827	100749	111942	141012

注：本表数据来源于市文广新局。
本表2017年数据含西咸新区。

21-5 文物保护业基本情况（2017年）

Basic Statistics on Cultural Relics Protection（2017）

指 标	Item	机构（个）Insititution (unit)	人员（人）Personnel (person)	文物藏品 实际数量（件）Factual Number of Collections (piece)	文物藏品 一级品（件）Grade One (piece)	举办陈列展览次数(次) Times of exhibition (times)	参观人员（千人次）Number of Visitors (1000 person-times)
文物保护管理机构	Cultural Relics administrative Departments	28	591	28845	36	17	3160
其他文物机构	Other Agencies	5	150	40899			
博物馆	Museums	101	4401	1884567	3849	551	28594
#免费开放馆	Museums Open Free	97	3611	1860330	2090	515	19378
文物科研机构	Scientific Research of Historical Relics Preservation	2	167	36814	186		

注：本表数据来源于市文物局。
本表数据为西安原口径数据。

21-6 主要年份广播电台及节目制作情况

Basic Statistics of Broadcasting Stations and Program Production in Representative Years

指 标	Item	2011	2012	2013	2014	2015	2016	2017
省、地广播电台（座）	Broadcasting Stations at the Province and District Level(set)	1	1					
省、地广播电视台（座）	Broadcasting Station at Province and District Level(set)	1	1	2	2	2	2	2
县级广播电视台（座）	Number of Wire Broadcasting Stations and TV Relaying Stations(set)	6	6	6	6	6	6	6
中、短波转播发射台（座）	Medium and Short Wave Broadcast Transmitting Station (base)	54	59	57	57	13	13	13
节目套数（套）	Number of Programs(set)	19	20	20	20	20	20	20
全年播出时间(时：分)	Broadcasting Hours annually(hour)	121723	129856	138278	143873	137075	139159	132252
广播节目综合人口覆盖率（%）	Broadcasts comprehensive population coverage	99.42	99.45	99.47	99.49	99.55	99.62	99.65
制作广播节目(时：分)	Productions of Broadcasting(hour)	83368	104300	106554	104459	116603	119424	100169
#新闻资讯类	News Programs	13821	14025	14355	13208	12208	7590	6362
专题服务类	Special Subject Programs	16318	21891	30181	26884	21864	26957	26907
综艺类	Variety Programs	28679	28096	24516	27148	37885	39735	25793
广播剧类	Literature Programs	2014	1720	3083	3712	6674	3990	4680
广告类	Advertisements	14202	19547	20552	18465	15777	18363	15968
其他类	Service Programs	8334	19021	13867	15042	22195	22787	20459

注：本表数据来源于市文广新局。
中、短波转播发射台2014年之前统计口径为中短波、调频发射台及转播台。数据变化因指标含义变化所致。
本表2017年数据含西咸新区。

21-7 主要年份电视台及节目制作情况

Basic Statistics of TV Stations and Production of TV Program in Representative Years

指 标	Item	2011	2012	2013	2014	2015	2016	2017
调频电视转播发射台（座）	FM Television Relay Station (base)	10	11	11	11	48	48	47
无线电视节目（套）	Program Productions of Non-cable television Stations (set)	6	6	6	6	6	2	2
有线电视节目（套）	Program Productions of cable television Stations (set)	16	16	16	16	16	20	20
全年播出时间（时：分）	Broadcasting Hours annually(hour)	147003	137936	140927	143000	141839	140312	136960
电视节目综合人口覆盖率（%）	TV shows comprehensive population coverage(%)	98.60	98.83	98.84	98.96	99.01	99.11	99.13
制作电视节目（时：分）	Earth Stations of Satellite TV (set)	43925	30091	46614	35182	43563	54200	49001
#新闻资讯类	News and Information Programs	10656	11169	13360	11797	11839	12891	10517
专题服务类	Special Subject Programs	19192	7689	7751	8289	8073	9346	9769
综艺类	Variety Programs	5202	5458	6508	5014	6242	7883	9080
影视剧类	Film and Television Drama	3781	113	1820	110	462	490	870
广告类	Advertisement	3200	3663	8066	3491	7921	6198	6493
其他类	Service Programs	1894	1997	9109	6479	9026	17390	12272

注：本表数据来源于市文广新局。
调频电视转播发射台2014年之前统计口径为发射台及转播台。数字变化因指标含义变化所致。
本表2017年数据含西咸新区。

21-8 竞技体育情况（2017年）

The Situation of Competitive Sports (2017)

指 标	Item	2017
奥运会获得奖牌(枚)	Number of Medals Won in the Olympic Games(unit)	
金牌数	Gold	
银牌数	Silver	
铜牌数	Bronze	
全运会获得奖牌(枚)	Number of Medals Won in the National Games(unit)	
金牌数	Gold	4
银牌数	Silver	2
铜牌数	Bronze	1
省运会获得奖牌(枚)	Number of Medals Won in the Provincial Games(unit)	
金牌数	Gold	
银牌数	Silver	
铜牌数	Bronze	
其他国际、国内赛事	Other International and Domestic Events	
金牌数(枚)	Gold(unit)	29
银牌数(枚)	Silver(unit)	25
体育传统项目学校(个)	Sports Traditional Project School(unit)	125
体育传统项目学校在校训练学生数(人)	Number of Students in the Sports Traditional Project School (person)	6750
高水平体育后备人才基地(个)	High Level Sports Reserve Base(unit)	5
省级示范性体校(个)	Provincial Demonstration Sports School(unit)	
等级教练员人数(人)	Number of Graded Coaches (person)	76
国家级	National Level	1
高 级	Senior Level	15
一 级	One Level	27
二 级	Two Level	22
三 级	Three Level	11
二级运动员人数(人)	Second Grade Athletes (person)	242

注：本表数据来源于市体育局。
备战2018年第16届省运会、2019年第二届青运会、2020年第31届东京奥运会。
本表数据不含西咸新区，且仅包括市本级。

21-9 群众体育情况（2017年）

The Situation of Mass Sports (2017)

指　标	Item	2017
全年承办的县级以上群众性体育赛事（个）	Mass Sports Events Held throughout the Year(unit)	260
国家级	National Level	1
省　级	Provincial Level	4
市　级	City Level	27
县　级	County Level	228
全年举办的社会体育指导员培训班（期）	Training Course for Social Sports Instructors Held throughout the Year（time）	15
社会体育指导员人数（名）	Social Sports Instructor（person）	20803
体育先进社区（个）	Advanced Sports Community(unit)	
#国家级	National Level	
省　级	Provincial Level	
群众体育先进单位（个）	Advanced Unit of Mass Sports(unit)	11
#国家	National Level	
省　级	Provincial Level	11
晨晚健身站点（个）	Morning and Evening Fitness sites(unit)	1600
全民健身活动中心（个）	National Fitness Center(unit)	5
乡镇体育健身工程（个）	Township Sports Fitness Project(unit)	5
村级农民体育健身工程（个）	Village Level Farmers' Sports Fitness Project(unit)	70
体育人口（万人）	Sports Population(10 000 person)	420

注：本表数据来源于市体育局。
　　本表数据不含西咸新区。

21-10 体育产业情况（2017年）

The Situation of Sport Industry (2017)

指　标	Item	2017
全市县级标准公共体育场地建设情况	Construction of Standard Public Sports Venues in the County Level	
已建场地个数（个）	Number of Built Sites(units)	3
在建场地个数（个）	Number of Sites in Construction(units)	2
全市全民健身设施建设情况	Construction of National Fitness Facilities in the City	
全民健身长廊（个）	National Fitness Corridor(units)	3
全民健身园区（个）	National Fitness Park(units)	21
多功能运动场（个）	Multifunction Playground(units)	31
户外营地（个）	Outdoor Camps(units)	
全民健身室内健身房（个）	Fitness Indoor Gymnasium(units)	5
健身步道（千米）	Fitness Footpath(km)	14.4
自行车专用道（千米）	Bicycle Special Road(km)	22
全市体育彩票销售情况	Sales of Sports Lottery in the City	
体育彩票销售网点数量（个）	Number of Sales Outlets of Sports Lottery (units)	1836
体育彩票销售网点数量占全省的比重（%）	Proportion of Sports Lottery Sales Outlets Accounts for the Proportion of the Whole Province（%）	35.66
本年体育彩票销售金额（万元）	Sales Amount of Sports Lottery in this Year (10 000 yuan)	28.13
本年体育彩票销售金额占全省的比重（%）	Sales Amount of Sports Lottery in this year Accounts for the Proportion of the Whole Province（%）	42.74
全市体育产业单位数量（个）	Number of Sports Industrial Units in the City (units)	497

注：本表数据来源于市体育局。
　　本表数据不含西咸新区。

21-11 主要年份医疗卫生机构、床位、人员情况

Number of Health Care Institutions, Beds and Personnel in Health Care Institutions in Representative Years

年份 Year	医疗卫生机构数（个） Number of Health Care Institutions (unit)	医院数（个） Number of Health Care Hospital (unit)	医疗卫生机构床位数（张） Number of Health Care Bed (unit)	医院床位数（张） Number of Hospital Bed (unit)	卫生技术人员数（人） Number of Medical Technical Personnel (person)
2008	2239	276	34618	30582	47433
2009	5284	261	36849	32371	52620
2010	5632	258	39407	34274	57756
2011	5554	268	41010	35976	61281
2012	5576	276	44239	39213	66899
2013	5503	281	47867	42753	71134
2014	5554	281	51065	45561	76005
2015	5802	295	54708	49830	81462
2016	5869	292	56332	51508	86258
2017	6376	329	63942	58219	94221

注：本表数据来源于市卫计委。
　　2008年以前数据不含卫生室。
　　本表2017年数据含西咸新区。

21-12　医疗卫生机构、床位及人员情况（2017年）

卫生机构	Health Care Institutions	机构数（个）Number of Institutions (unit)	床位数（张）Number of Beds (unit)
总计	**Total**	**6376**	**63942**
一、医院	**Hospitals**	**329**	**58219**
综合医院	General Hospitals	216	42004
中医医院	Hospitals Specialized in Traditional Chinese Medicine	46	6168
中西医结合医院	Hospitals Integrating Traditional Chinese Medicine with Western Therapeutics in Practice	3	558
民族医院	Nationalities Hospitals		
专科医院	Specialized Hospitals	63	9439
护理院	Nursing centers	1	50
二、基层医疗卫生机构	**Commuting Health Hare Service Centre**	**5948**	**3986**
社区卫生服务中心(站)	Community Health Care Center(Station)	221	1669
社区卫生服务中心	Community Health Care Center	119	1669
社区卫生服务站	Community Health Care Station	102	
卫生院	Health Center	119	2294
街道卫生院	Urban Health-center	2	130
乡镇卫生院	Rural Health-center	117	2164
村卫生室	Village Clinics	3392	
门诊部	Outpatient Department	246	23
诊所、卫生所、医务室	Clinic, Health Center, Infirmary	1970	
三、专业公共卫生机构	**College of Public Health Institutions**	**72**	**1507**
疾病预防控制中心	Center for Disease Control and Prevention	16	
专科疾病防治院（所、站）	Specialized Disease Prevention and Cure Center (Place, Station)	1	800
健康教育所（站、中心）	Health Education Institute (Station, Center)	2	
妇幼保健院（所、站）	Maternal and Child Health Hospital (Station)	13	707
急救中心（站）	Emergency Center	1	
采供血机构	Blood Collection Agencies	1	
卫生监督所（中心）	Health Supervision Agencies (Center)	14	
计划生育技术服务机构	Institutions of Technical Service for Family Planning	24	
四、其他卫生机构	**Other Health Institution**	**27**	**230**
疗养院	Nursing Centres	1	230
卫生监督检验(监测、检测)所(站)	Health Supervision and Inspection Agencies		
医学科学研究机构	Medical Scientific Research Institutions	3	
医学在职培训机构	Medical Training Institutions	5	
临床检验中心（所、站）	Clinical Testing Center (Place, Station)	3	
统计信息中心	Statistical Information Center	1	
其他	Other	14	

注：本表数据来源于市卫计委。
本表人员合计中包括乡村医生3481人和卫生员216人，不含乡镇卫生院在村卫生室工作的执业（助理）医师、注册护士。
本表数据含西咸新区。

Number of Health Care Institutions, Beds and Personnel in Health Care Institutions (2017)

人员合计（人） Total Number of Employed Persons (person)	卫生技术人员 Medical Technical Personnel	执业（助理）医师数 Licensed (Assistant) Doctors	#执业医师 Chartered Doctors
116939	**94221**	**30820**	**27683**
85736	**70319**	**20938**	**19958**
64083	53187	15984	15280
8141	6578	2027	1884
459	386	131	119
13019	10139	2789	2669
34	29	7	6
25815	**20066**	**8833**	**6788**
5791	4879	1518	1215
4878	4069	1227	957
913	810	291	258
3870	3313	859	567
211	175	61	44
3659	3138	798	523
4989	1292	1054	383
4009	3565	1616	1368
7156	7017	3786	3255
4442	**3336**	**892**	**791**
1104	836	337	307
506	399	84	80
73	27		
1647	1318	378	325
129	67	34	32
148	99	12	10
553	421		
282	169	47	37
946	**500**	**157**	**146**
76	41	14	11
127	80	46	45
195	81	6	6
210	56	1	1
6			
332	242	90	83

21-12 续表1

卫生机构	Health Care Institutions	人员合计（人）	
		卫生技术人员中	
		注册护士 Registered Nurses	药师（士） Junior Paramedics
总计	**Total**	**41603**	**4280**
一、医院	**Hospitals**	**33847**	**3068**
综合医院	General Hospitals	25642	2215
中医医院	Hospitals Specialized in Traditional Chinese Medicine	2930	430
中西医结合医院	Hospitals Integrating Traditional Chinese Medicine with Western Therapeutics in Practice	202	15
民族医院	Nationalities Hospitals		
专科医院	Specialized Hospitals	5058	406
护理院	Nursing centers	15	2
二、基层医疗卫生机构	**Commuting Health Hare Service Centre**	**6776**	**1095**
社区卫生服务中心(站)	Community Health Care Center(Station)	1696	375
社区卫生服务中心	Community Health Care Center	1345	310
社区卫生服务站	Community Health Care Station	351	65
卫生院	Health Center	905	223
街道卫生院	Urban Health-center	60	5
乡镇卫生院	Rural Health-center	845	218
村卫生室	Village Clinics	238	
门诊部	Outpatient Department	1349	185
诊所、卫生所、医务室	Clinic, Health Center, Infirmary	2588	312
三、专业公共卫生机构	**College of Public Health Institutions**	**876**	**106**
疾病预防控制中心	Center for Disease Control and Prevention	58	14
专科疾病防治院（所、站）	Specialized Disease Prevention and Cure Center (Place, Station)	210	19
健康教育所（站、中心）	Health Education Institute (Station, Center)		
妇幼保健院（所、站）	Maternal and Child Health Hospital (Station)	524	55
急救中心（站）	Emergency Center	17	2
采供血机构	Blood Collection Agencies	27	7
卫生监督所（中心）	Health Supervision Agencies (Center)		
计划生育技术服务机构	Institutions of Technical Service for Family Planning	40	9
四、其他卫生机构	**Other Health Institution**	**104**	**11**
疗养院	Nursing Centres	15	5
卫生监督检验(监测、检测)所(站)	Health Supervision and Inspection Agencies		
医学科学研究机构	Medical Scientific Research Institutions	9	3
医学在职培训机构	Medical Training Institutions	1	
临床检验中心（所、站）	Clinical Testing Center (Place, Station)		
统计信息中心	Statistical Information Center		
其他	Other	79	3

continued 1

Total Number of Employed Persons (person)				
Among:Medical Technical Personnel		其他技术人员 Other Technical Personnel	管理人员 Administrative Personnel	工勤技能人员 Logistics Technical Workers
技师（士） Technicians	其他 Others			
5593	**11925**	**839**	**9003**	**9179**
4119	**8347**	**592**	**7279**	**7549**
3027	6319	420	5238	5241
418	773	94	674	795
27	11	19	34	20
645	1241	58	1330	1492
2	3	1	3	1
951	**2411**	**78**	**928**	**1043**
386	904	31	400	481
345	842	21	344	444
41	62	10	56	37
284	1042	12	261	284
5	44	1	4	31
279	998	11	257	253
235	180	21	244	179
46	285	14	23	99
411	**1051**	**94**	**580**	**432**
217	210	38	131	99
39	47	3	58	46
	27	28	17	1
119	242	5	167	157
	14	1	35	26
20	33	2	40	7
	421	5	70	57
16	57	12	62	39
112	**116**	**75**	**216**	**155**
3	4		15	20
17	5	12	19	16
3	71	51	47	16
55		7	65	82
			6	
34	36	5	64	21

21-13 各区县医疗卫生机构、床位及人员情况（2017年）

Number of Health Care Institutions, Beds and Employed Persons in Health Care Institutions By Region（2017）

区 县	Region	机构（个）Number of Health Care Institutions (unit)	床位（张）Number of Beds (unit)	人员合计（人）Total Number of Employed Persons (person)	#卫生技术人员 Total Number of Medical Technical Personnel
合 计	**Total**	**6376**	**63942**	**116939**	**94221**
新城区	Xincheng	248	7424	14753	11862
碑林区	Beilin	400	8781	15910	13332
莲湖区	Lianhu	326	7860	13848	11454
灞桥区	Baqiao	466	2852	5179	4258
未央区	Weiyang	347	5674	11167	9229
雁塔区	Yanta	503	9582	19439	16108
阎良区	Yanliang	172	1463	2828	2208
临潼区	Lintong	528	2756	4020	3043
长安区	Chang'an	726	6021	9583	7429
高陵区	Gaoling	218	1999	3393	2848
鄠邑区	Huyi	567	3080	5510	4143
蓝田县	Lantian	619	1528	3085	2391
周至县	Zhouzhi	534	2185	3891	2735

注：本表数据来源于市卫计委。
本表合计栏数据含西咸新区。

21-14 各区县农村村级卫生组织情况（2017年）

Village Level Health Organization in the Rural Area by Region（2017）

区 县	Region	村卫生室（个） Village Health Room（unit）	乡村医生和卫生员（人） Rural Doctors and Health Workers（person）	#乡村医生 Rural Doctors	#卫生员 Health Workers
全 市	**Total**	**3392**	**3697**	**3481**	**216**
新城区	Xincheng				
碑林区	Beilin				
莲湖区	Lianhu				
灞桥区	Baqiao	215	260	258	2
未央区	Weiyang	58	38	38	
雁塔区	Yanta	59	70	61	9
阎良区	Yanliang	80	109	108	1
临潼区	Lintong	349	380	325	55
长安区	Chang'an	499	433	432	1
高陵区	Gaoling	123	186	175	11
鄠邑区	Huyi	476	495	487	8
蓝田县	Lantian	527	405	404	1
周至县	Zhouzhi	461	701	583	118

注：本表数据来源于市卫计委。
本表合计栏数据含西咸新区。

21-15 各区县社区卫生服务中心（站）情况（2017年）

Situations of Community Health Service Center (Station) by Region (2017)

区 县 Region	社区卫生服务中心（站）（个） Community Health Care Center(Station) (unit)	床位数（张） Number of Beds (unit)	人员数（人） Personnel Number (person)	卫生技术人员（人） Medical Technical Personnel (person)	执业（助理）医师 Licensed (Assistant) Doctors	注册护士 Registered Nurses
全 市 Total	**221**	**1669**	**5791**	**4879**	**1518**	**1696**
新城区 Xincheng	15	38	323	260	87	96
碑林区 Beilin	18	60	382	298	134	90
莲湖区 Lianhu	16	170	652	574	204	225
灞桥区 Baqiao	24	143	526	443	140	152
未央区 Weiyang	31	77	610	514	157	208
雁塔区 Yanta	35	30	1072	915	253	338
阎良区 Yanliang	8	76	170	151	43	61
临潼区 Lintong	28	587	688	584	141	143
长安区 Chang'an	23	420	926	763	246	213
高陵区 Gaoling	8		113	98	16	58
鄠邑区 Huyi						
蓝田县 Lantian						
周至县 Zhouzhi						

注：本表数据来源于市卫计委。
本表合计栏数据含西咸新区。

21-16 主要年份医疗卫生机构各类人员情况

Number of Personnel in Health Care Institutions in Representative Years

单位：人 (person)

指 标	Item	2011	2012	2013	2014	2015	2016	2017
人员合计	**Total**	79999	86096	90129	95633	102684	107906	116939
卫生技术人员	Medical Technical Personnel	61281	66899	71134	76005	81462	86258	94221
执业（助理）医师	Licensed (Assistant) Doctors	21551	23051	23885	24820	26626	27864	30820
#执业医师	Chartered Doctors	18904	20414	21205	22145	23818	25023	27683
注册护士	Registered Nurses	25043	27837	29967	32136	34819	37518	41603
药师(士)	Junior Paramedics	3127	3380	3551	3709	3957	4075	4280
技师（士）	Technicians	3622	3953	4089	4276	4690	5058	5593
其他	Other	7938	8678	9642	11064	11370	11743	11925
其他技术人员	Other Technical Personnel	895	633	590	621	816	835	839
管理人员	Administrative Personnel	6769	6939	7160	7355	8248	8470	9003
工勤技能人员	Logistics Technical Workers	6789	7555	7437	7944	8326	8913	9179

注：本表数据来源于市卫计委。
本表2011年及以后合计栏数据含乡村医生和卫生员。
本表2017年数据含西咸新区。

21-17 医疗卫生机构门诊、住院及病床使用情况（2017年）

指　标	Item	总诊疗人次数 总计 Total
总计	**Total**	**60932059**
一、医院	**Hospitals**	**35156796**
综合医院	General Hospitals	26094117
中医医院	Hospitals Specialized in Traditional Chinese Medicine	2965007
中西医结合医院	Hospitals Integrating Traditional Chinese Medicine with Western Therapeutics in Practice	106696
民族医院	Nationalities Hospitals	
专科医院	Specialized Hospitals	5990691
护理院	Nursing Centers	285
二、基层医疗卫生机构	**Commuting Health Care Service Centre**	**24599853**
社区卫生服务中心（站）	Community Health Care Center(Station)	4353963
社区卫生服务中心	Community Health Care Center	3522045
社区卫生服务站	Community Health Care Station	831918
卫生院	Health Center	1931523
街道卫生院	Urban Health-center	98475
乡镇卫生院	Rural Health-center	1833048
村卫生室	Village Clinics	11259445
门诊部	Outpatient Department	1955270
诊所、卫生所、医务室	Clinic, Health Center, Infirmary	5099652
三、专业公共卫生机构	**College of Public Health Institutions**	**1145644**
专科疾病防治院（所、站）	Specialized Disease Prevention and Cure Center (Place, Station)	46997
妇幼保健院（所、站）	Maternal and Child Health Hospital (Station)	934467
急救中心（站）	Emergency Center	164180
四、其他卫生机构	**Other Health Institution**	**29766**
疗养院	Sanatorium	29766

注：本表数据来源于市卫计委。
本表数据含西咸新区。

Medical and Health Institutions Outpatient, Inpatient and Utilization of Beds (2017)

Total Number of Clinics (person time)				观察室 Observation Room	
门、急诊人次数合计 Total Number of People In Outpatient and Emergency Department	门诊人次数(人次) Number of Outpatients (person time)	急诊人次数小计(人次) The Number of Emergency Subtotal (person time)	死亡人数（人） Number of Deaths (person)	留观病例数 (人次) Number of Patients Receiving (person times)	死亡人数 （人） Number of Deaths (persons)
60147197	**56553870**	**3593327**	**3163**	**39988**	**8**
34980649	**31744921**	**3235728**	**3156**	**39781**	**8**
25979901	23404779	2575122	3040	35364	8
2951530	2846282	105248	78	569	
106584	93757	12827	6	90	
5942349	5399818	542531	32	3758	
285	285				
23991138	**23919533**	**71605**	**7**	**104**	
4222319	4172246	50073	7	10	
3403554	3360486	43068	7		
818765	811760	7005		10	
1927887	1906355	21532		94	
98475	95915	2560			
1829412	1810440	18972		94	
10815286	10815286				
1949593	1949593				
5076053	5076053				
1145644	**860045**	**285599**		**103**	
46997	46744	253			
934467	813301	121166		103	
164180		164180			
29766	**29371**	**395**			
29766	29371	395			

21-17 续表1

指 标	Item	急诊死亡率（%）Emergency Mortality (%)	入院人数合计（人）Total Number of Admission Patients (person)
总计	**Total**	**0.09**	**2115116**
一、医院	**Hospitals**	**0.10**	**2013398**
综合医院	General Hospitals	0.12	1565269
中医医院	Hospitals Specialized in Traditional Chinese Medicine	0.07	170492
中西医结合医院	Hospitals Integrating Traditional Chinese Medicine with Western Therapeutics in Practice	0.05	16470
民族医院	Nationalities Hospitals		
专科医院	Specialized Hospitals	0.01	259810
护理院	Nursing Centers	0.01	1356
二、基层医疗卫生机构	**Commuting Health Care Service Centre**	**0.01**	**58324**
社区卫生服务中心（站）	Community Health Care Center(Station)		30966
社区卫生服务中心	Community Health Care Center		30966
社区卫生服务站	Community Health Care Station		
卫生院	Health Center		27050
街道卫生院	Urban Health-center		952
乡镇卫生院	Rural Health-center		26908
村卫生室	Village Clinics		6751
门诊部	Outpatient Department		308
诊所、卫生所、医务室	Clinic, Health Center, Infirmary		
三、专业公共卫生机构	**College of Public Health Institutions**		**39635**
专科疾病防治院（所、站）	Specialized Disease Prevention and Cure Center (Place, Station)		6893
妇幼保健院（所、站）	Maternal and Child Health Hospital (Station)		32742
急救中心（站）	Emergency Center		
四、其他卫生机构	**Other Health Institution**		**3759**
疗养院	Sanatorium		3759

continued 1

出院人数合计（人） Total Number of Discharge Patients (person)	死亡人数（人） Number of Hospital Csualty (person)	病床周转次数（次） Nnumber of Bed Remover (times)	病床使用率（%） Bed occupancy rate (%)	出院者平均住院日（天） Average Stay Days in Hospital (day)
2099522	**9885**	**34**	**83.47**	**8.88**
1998583	**9878**	**36**	**87.19**	**8.86**
1554374	8809	38	87.93	9.37
169447	425	28	85.01	10.84
15931	69	29	69.74	8.81
257586	575	29	86.59	10.53
1345		27	49.51	6.68
57841	**4**	**15**	**32.32**	**7.91**
30591	3	19	39.02	7.35
30591	3	19	39.02	7.35
26942	1	12	28.03	8.64
981		8	53.50	25.64
25961	1	12	26.19	8.00
6752		6	33.35	20.74
308				
39651		**27**	**83.91**	**11.38**
6678		8	92.29	40.25
32673		49	73.80	5.48
3747	**3**	**16**	**42.49**	**9.47**
3747	3	16	42.49	9.47

21-18 提供住宿的社会服务机构（2017年）

Social Welfare Insititutions Providing Accommodation (2017)

指 标	Item	机构数（个）Number of Institutions	年末职工人数（人）Number of Staff and Workers at the End of Year	#女性 Female	床位数（张）Number of Beds	年末在院人数（人）Number of Persons Housed at the Year-end
1、养老服务机构	Pension Service Institutions	140	3189	2088	27365	12951
2、儿童福利院	Baby Welfare Homes	1	72	46	900	611
3、社会福利医院	Social Welfare Hospitals	1	147	56	650	422
4、救助站	Rescue Station	8	114	43	853	167
5、军事供应站	Military Supply Station	1	19	3	1	

注：本表数据来源于市民政局。
本表数据含西咸新区。

21-19 主要年份社会福利事业单位机构及人员情况

Number of Social Welfare Institutions and Personnel

单位：个、人 (unit, person)

指 标	Item	2011	2012	2013	2014	2015	2016	2017
一、机构	**Insititutions**							
烈士纪念建筑物管理单位	Institutions Managing Memorial Buildings of Martyrs	2	2	2	2	2	2	2
救助类单位	Units Providing Assistance	8	8	8	9	9	9	9
殡仪服务单位	Funeral Service Units	21	22	25	26	26	25	27
殡仪馆	Funeral Homes	5	4	4	3	3	3	3
公墓	Cemeteries	12	12	15	16	16	16	19
殡葬管理单位	Funeral Management Units	4	6	6	7	7	6	5
二、人员	**Staff**							
烈士纪念建筑物管理单位	Institutions Managing Memorial Buildings of Martyrs	38	40	42	44	42	42	44
救助类单位	Units Providing Assistance	119	130	137	139	119	121	114
殡仪服务单位	Funeral Service Units	1313	1400	1430	1392	1510	1510	1518
殡仪馆	Funeral Homes	408	442	491	470	497	481	484
公墓	Cemeteries	838	869	855	838	929	953	959
殡葬管理单位	Funeral Management Units	67	89	84	84	84	76	75

注：本表数据来源于市民政局。
本表2017年数据含西咸新区。

21-20 社会保障基本情况（2017年）

Basic Situation of Social Security（2017）

单位：万人、万户 （10 000 persons、10 000 households）

指 标	Item	2017
基本养老保险参保人数	Number of Basic Old-age Insurance	630.76
1. 城镇企业职工养老保险参保人数	Number of Town Enterprise Worker Old-age Insurance	360.45
其中：离退休人员	Retired Personnel	67.06
2. 机关事业单位养老保险参保人数	Number of Institution Old-age Insurance	28.67
其中：离退休人员	Retired Personnel	9.69
3. 城乡居民养老保险参保人数	Number of Rural Residents Old-age Insurance	241.64
城镇基本医疗保险参保人数	Number of urban basic medical insurance	467.33
失业保险参保人数	Number of unemployed insurance	154.96
生育保险参保人数	Number of Maternity insurance	151.16
工伤保险参保人数	Number of industrial injury insurance	172.04
城镇居民最低生活保障户数	The Number of Minimum Living Guarantee for Urban Resident Households	1.93
城镇居民最低生活保障人数	The Number of Minimum Living Guarantee for Urban Residents	3.10
农村居民最低生活保障户数	The Number of Minimum Living Guarantee for Rural Resident Households	2.63
农村居民最低生活保障人数	The Number of Minimum Living Guarantee for Rural Residents	7.43

注：本表数据来源于市人社局、市民政局。
本表中"基本养老保险参保人数"部分不含西咸新区，其他指标均含西咸新区。

21-21 全市及各区县新型农村合作医疗情况（2017年）

Situation of the New Rural Cooperative Medical Care of the Whole City and Area County (2017)

区 县	Region	参加新型农村合作医疗人数（万人）Participate in The New Rural Cooperative Medical Population（10 000 persons）	新型农村合作医疗参合率（%）Participate in The New Rural Cooperative Medical Care Ration（%）
合 计	**Total**	**393.65**	**99.72**
新城区	Xincheng		
碑林区	Beilin		
莲湖区	Lianhu		
灞桥区	Baqiao	29.25	99.56
未央区	Weiyang	6.83	100.00
雁塔区	Yanta	5.71	100.00
阎良区	Yanliang	16.76	99.87
临潼区	Lintong	56.61	100.00
长安区	Chang'an	73.48	99.38
高陵区	Gaoling	23.49	100.00
鄠邑区	Huyi	47.95	99.20
蓝田县	Lantian	56.79	99.71
周至县	Zhouzhi	58.74	100.00
沣东新城	Fengdongxincheng	18.04	98.68

注：本表数据来源于市卫计委。
本表数据为西安原口径数据。

21-22 全市及各区县优抚对象人员情况（2017年）

Statistics on Persons Enjoying Favoured Treatment by Region（2017）

单位：人 (person)

区 县	Region	伤残人员 Number of Disabled Veterans	烈军属人员 Number of Family Members of Martyrs and Soldiers	在乡复员军人 Demobilized Soldiers in Hometown	带病回乡退伍军人 Veterans Returning Home in Sick
合 计	**Total**	**5150**	**888**	**2517**	**1072**
市本级	City Level	48			
新城区	Xincheng	600	31	8	
碑林区	Beilin	622	47	5	1
莲湖区	Lianhu	719	47	22	2
灞桥区	Baqiao	269	50	152	154
未央区	Weiyang	225	58	77	3
雁塔区	Yanta	712	52	53	7
阎良区	Yanliang	110	51	175	59
临潼区	Lintong	270	77	430	226
长安区	Chang'an	359	84	309	105
高陵区	Gaoling	144	65	193	123
鄠邑区	Huyi	250	61	237	82
蓝田县	Lantian	215	67	287	165
周至县	Zhouzhi	320	92	227	100

注：本表数据来源于市民政局。
本表合计栏数据含西咸新区。

21-23 全市及各区县计划生育和婚姻登记情况（2017年）

Conditions of Birth Control and Marriage Registration by Region（2017）

区 县	Region	计划生育率（%）Family Planning Rate(%)	节育率(%) Birth control Rate(%)
合 计	**Total**	**99.5**	**80.8**
新城区	Xincheng	100.0	76.6
碑林区	Beilin	100.0	80.9
莲湖区	Lianhu	100.0	83.2
灞桥区	Baqiao	99.7	84.7
未央区	Weiyang	99.9	58.2
雁塔区	Yanta	99.9	80.2
阎良区	Yanliang	99.5	86.3
临潼区	Lintong	99.4	78.2
长安区	Chang'an	99.7	77.3
高陵区	Gaoling	99.6	88.1
鄠邑区	Huyi	98.9	91.6
蓝田县	Lantian	97.9	85.0
周至县	Zhouzhi	98.8	90.3

注：本表数据来源于市计生委、市民政局、市法院。
本表数据为西安原口径数据。

21-23 续表1 continued 1

区 县	Region	结婚对数（对）Marriages (couple)	再婚人数（人）Remarriages (person)	离婚对数（对）Divorced Couple (couple)
合 计	**Total**	**70954**	**29604**	**28811**
新城区	Xincheng	4275	2007	2107
碑林区	Beilin	7592	2578	2018
莲湖区	Lianhu	5549	2684	2645
灞桥区	Baqiao	5774	2846	2096
未央区	Weiyang	4818	2175	2258
雁塔区	Yanta	9005	3715	4173
阎良区	Yanliang	2453	1256	1072
临潼区	Lintong	5630	2199	2416
长安区	Chang'an	9080	4134	4338
高陵区	Gaoling	2907	1626	1208
鄠邑区	Huyi	4689	1664	1592
蓝田县	Lantian	5049	1521	1509
周至县	Zhouzhi	4133	1199	1379

21-24 全市及各区县妇幼卫生保健情况（2017年）

Care Health Conditions of Women and Child by Region（2017）

区 县	Region	5岁以下儿童死亡率（‰）Mortality rate of Children under 5-year-old（‰）	新生儿死亡率（‰）Infant Mortality Ratio in 2012（‰）	婴儿死亡率（‰）Neonatal Mortality Ratio （‰）
合 计	**Total**	**3.61**	**1.56**	**2.72**
新城区	Xincheng	1.60	0.53	1.07
碑林区	Beilin	2.02	0.76	0.76
莲湖区	Lianhu	7.71	0.86	5.14
灞桥区	Baqiao	2.92	1.36	2.14
未央区	Weiyang	1.71	1.37	1.54
雁塔区	Yanta	4.22	2.82	3.80
阎良区	Yanliang	4.81	2.88	3.52
临潼区	Lintong	4.15	1.04	2.59
长安区	Chang'an	3.49	1.46	2.52
高陵区	Gaoling	3.61	2.84	1.29
鄠邑区	Huyi	3.60	1.14	2.46
蓝田县	Lantian	4.38	1.64	3.10
周至县	Zhouzhi	4.04	2.15	3.77

注：本表数据来源于市卫计委。
本表数据为西安原口径数据。

21-24 续表1 continued 1

区 县	Region	孕产妇死亡率（1/10万）Maternal Mortality Ratio (one in hundred thousandth)	产妇住院分娩比例（%）Proportion of maternal Hospital Births (%)
合 计	**Total**	**12.18**	**99.99**
新城区	Xincheng		100
碑林区	Beilin	25.20	100
莲湖区	Lianhu		100
灞桥区	Baqiao		100
未央区	Weiyang		100
雁塔区	Yanta		100
阎良区	Yanliang	32.04	99.97
临潼区	Lintong	69.13	100
长安区	Chang'an		100
高陵区	Gaoling	25.79	100
鄠邑区	Huyi		100
蓝田县	Lantian	18.24	99.93
周至县	Zhouzhi		100

21-25 主要年份律师、公证及调解情况

Basic Statistics on Lawyer, Notaries and Mediation in Representative Years

指 标	Item	2011	2012	2013	2014	2015	2016	2017
一、律师工作	**Lawyers**							
律师事务所（个）	Number of Law Offices (unit)	97	105	116	122	149	176	200
律师（人）	Lawyers(person)	1347	1522	1639	1846	2198	2462	2836
#专职	Full-time	1275	1439	1560	1738	2092	2337	2716
兼职	Part-time	68	73	77	88	91	84	120
刑事诉讼辩护及代理（件）	Criminal Litigation Defense and Agency（case)		2438	3267	3118	3524	3260	5872
民事诉讼代理（件）	Civil Litigation Agency（case）		8848	10754	9985	15308	16743	24593
行政诉讼代理（件）	Administrative Litigation Agency（case）		170	319	374	532	601	1584
非诉讼法律事务（件）	Nonlitigious Legal Matters（case)		1965	2265	2352	2780	2840	4981
二、公证工作	**Notarization**							
公证处（个）	Number of Notary Offices (unit)	14	14	14	14	14	14	14
公证人员（人）	Notarial Personnel (person)	233	235	222	298	307	293	285
#公证员	Notaries	118	116	115	118	121	115	116
办理公证件数（件）	Number of Notarized Documents Issued (case)	108120	119605	136471	135413	135622	144662	150300
国内	Domestic	68239	79167	98572	90171	86589	95194	95444
涉外	Foreign-related	39545	39888	37444	44773	49033	49468	54215
港澳台	Hong Kong. Macao and Taiwan related	336	550	455	469	373	512	641
三、人民调解工作	**Number of People Mediations**							
已建调委会数（个）	Number of Mediation Committees (unit)	4031	4053	4040	4059	4052	4062	3903
调解人员数（人）	Number of Mediators (person)	12848	15080	15240	15793	14838	14888	14295
调解纠纷数（件）	Number of Civil Disputes Mediated (case)	33851	39230	33651	33641	31696	27455	48690
#调解成功数	Number of Cases Successfully Mediated	32109	37510	32368	32537	30590	26426	47921

注：本表数据来源于市司法局。

2015年开始统计上将港澳台并入国内，表中2015-2016年办理公证件数中港澳台所列数据为其中数，2014年及以前年份港澳台数据与国内、涉外数据为并列关系。

本表2017年数据含西咸新区。

21-26 主要年份共青团组织情况

Basic Facts on Communist Youth League in Representative Years

单位：个、人 (unit, person)

指 标	Item	2011	2012	2013	2014	2015	2016	2017
一、基层团组织	**Grass-root Youth League Organisations**	**11248**	**9097**	**10770**	**10152**	**10074**	**10530**	**10237**
二、共青团员	**Youth League Members**	**345682**	**336156**	**344096**	**343121**	**331261**	**251706**	**201789**
#女团员	Female Youth League Members	159725	157924	158287	153212	146213	110092	88182
三、专职团干部	**Full-time Youth League Cadre**	**270**	**680**	**737**	**659**	**496**	**165**	**158**

注：本表数据来源于共青团西安市委员会。
本表数据不含西咸新区。

21-27 妇联组织及工作情况（2017年）

The Basic Situation of Women's Federation（2017）

指 标	Item	2017
一、妇联组织	**Women's Organizations**	
市级妇联（个）	Municipal Women's Federation(unit)	1
街道妇联（个）	Street Women's Federation(unit)	110
社区妇联（个）	Community Women's Federation(unit)	835
县（区）妇联（个）	County (district) Women's Federation(unit)	13
乡（镇）妇联（个）	Township (town) Women's Federation(unit)	52
村妇联	Village Women's Representative Conference	2409
二、妇联工作		
巾帼建功标兵（个）	Women Business Model(unit)	67
巾帼建功集体（个）	Group of Women Business Model(unit)	171
巾帼文明岗（个）	Women's Civilized Model Post(unit)	67
三八红旗手标兵（人）	Models of "March 8 Red-Banner Holders" (person)	5
三八红旗手（人）	March 8 Red-Banner Holders (person)	146
三八红旗集体（个）	March 8 Red-Banner Groups(unit)	60
五好家庭（户）	Five-virtue Family	278
本级最美家庭（户）	The Most Beautiful Family at the Present Level	379
乡镇最美家庭（户）	The Most Beautiful Family in the Town	190
街道最美家庭（户）	The Most Beautiful Family in the Street	448
村最美家庭（户）	The Most Beautiful Family in the Village	1372
社区最美家庭（户）	The Most Beautiful Family in the Community	529

注：本表数据来源于市妇联。
本表数据为西安原口径数据。

21-28 主要年份交通、火灾及安全生产情况

Transportation, Fire and Safety Production in Representative Years

指　标	Item	2011	2012	2013	2014	2015	2016	2017
道路交通事故	**Road Accidents**							
事故数(起)	Number of Traffic Accident (case)	2264	2446	2252	1970	2392	2943	2858
死亡人数（人）	Number of Deaths (person)	531	516	460	483	481	476	453
受伤人数（人）	Number of Injuries (person)	2260	2486	2217	1832	2318	3012	2856
损失（万元）	Economic Loss (10 000 yuan)	611.9	1011.1	1143.9	1264	1470.2	1653.7	1777.3
火灾事故	**Fire Accidents**							
事故数(起)	Number of Cases (case)	1920	2568	4062	3199	2590	3434	2353
死亡人数（人）	Number of Deaths (person)	8	16	26	17	20	16	8
受伤人数（人）	Number of Injuries (person)	3	4	6	5	7	7	2
损失（万元）	Economic Loss (10 000 yuan)	1587.2	2793.7	3011.9	4381.1	2401.5	1901.1	1659.1
农机事故	**Farm Machinery Accidents**							
事故数(起)	Number of Cases (case)		2	1	24	47	4	2
死亡人数（人）	Number of Deaths (person)		2	1	1	1	1	
工矿商贸事故	**Accidents in Industry, Mine,Business and Trade**							
事故数(起)	Number of Cases (case)	15	13	14	10	10	33	33
死亡人数（人）	Number of Deaths (person)	27	19	18	15	11	35	41

注：本表数据来源于市公安局及安监局。其中交通、火灾数据2011年及以前年份来自于市安监局，2012年以后数据来自于市公安局。
2014年农机及工矿商贸事故发生起数统计口径变化，数据与以前年份不可比。
本表中2017年交通火灾数据为西安原口径，农机和工矿商贸事故含西咸新区。

21-29 主要年份刑事案件情况

Data on Criminal Cases in Representative Years

指　标	Item	2011	2012	2013	2014	2015	2016	2017
一、案件数情况	**Data on Number of Cases**							
立案数（起）	Number of Registered Cases(case)	71499	61071	72611	77051	108955	98056	79828
破案数（起）	Number of Cleared up Cases(case)	17585	20788	26587	25830	28629	30730	33128
破案率（%）	Percent of Cleared up Cases(%)	24.6	34.0	36.6	33.5	26.3	31.3	41.5
抓获作案成员(人)	Number of Criminals Caught(person)	14672	16980	14255	14184	12827	11982	12848
二、查获犯罪集团情况	**Data on Hunted down and Seized Criminal Gangs**							
查获犯罪集团个数（个）	Number of Hunted down and Seized Criminal Gangs (person)	209	853	695	359	153	119	97
查获犯罪集团人数（人）	Number of Members of Hunted down and Seized Criminal Gangs (person)	970	3332	2632	1508	680	492	418
涉及案件（起）	Number of Cases Involved(case)	485	2039	2439	1111	291	242	303
三、涉枪案件情况	**Data on Cases with Guns Involved**							
立案数（起）	Number of Registered Cases(case)	13	30	17	13	9	21	22
破案数（起）	Number of Cleared up Cases(case)	10	25	16	8	6	17	17
破案率（%）	Percent of Cleared up Cases(%)	76.9	83.3	94.1	61.5	66.7	81.0	77.3

注：本表数据来源于市公安局。
　　本表数据为西安原口径数据。

21-30 主要年份治安案件情况

Data on Public Order Cases in Representative Years

指　标	Item	2011	2012	2013	2014	2015	2016	2017
受理数（起）	Number of Accepted Cases(case)	63289	60747	94853	108780	104553	109124	95821
查处数（起）	Number of Investigated and Prosecuted Cases(case)	62647	59949	93546	106811	100954	106999	93634
查处率（%）	Percent of Investigated and Prosecuted Cases(%)	99.0	98.7	98.6	98.2	96.6	98.1	97.7
查处违法人数（人）	Number of Investigated and Prosecuted Law-breakers and Crime Committer(person)	44199	34346	46253	52922	40838	40126	34625

注：本表数据来源于市公安局。
　　本表数据为西安原口径数据。

21-31 主要年份西安市人民检察院案件办理情况

Data on Acceptance of Cases of Xi'an People's Procuratorate

指 标	Item	2011	2012	2013	2014	2015	2016	2017
一、贪污贿赂案件立案人数（人）	**Number of Persons Invovled in Case about Corporation and Bribery(person)**	**166**	**175**	**172**	**207**	**220**	**218**	**248**
二、渎职侵权案件立案人数（人）	**Number of Persons Invovled in Case about Misprison and Toetious(person)**	**33**	**38**	**42**	**56**	**46**	**67**	**75**
三、审查逮捕案件受理件数（件）	**Examination and Arresting(case)**	**5741**	**5024**	**5748**	**6443**	**6545**	**7381**	**7184**
四、逮捕各类案件人数（人）	**Arresting of Criminals of each kind(person)**	**8787**	**7168**	**7177**	**7534**	**6692**	**7763**	**7511**
决定逮捕贪污贿赂犯罪嫌疑人（人）	Suspects of Corporation and Bribery to be Arrested (person)	34	43	49	64	100	26	27
决定逮捕渎职、侵权犯罪嫌疑人（人）	Suspects of Misprision and Tortious to be Arrested (person)		6		18	4		22
批准逮捕刑事犯罪嫌疑人（人）	Suspects of Criminal to be Arrested (person)	8753	7119	7128	7452	6588	7737	7462
五、刑事立案监督、侦查活动监督（件）	**Supervision of Acceptance of Criminal** Cases and Investigation (case)	**89**	**263**	**368**	**284**	**162**	**118**	**79**
六、审查起诉案件受理件数（件）	**Examination and Prosecution (case)**	**6298**	**6747**	**6371**	**7278**	**6922**	**8090**	**8933**
七、起诉各类案件人数（人）	**Prosecution of Criminals of each kind(person)**	**8276**	**7307**	**7615**	**8399**	**8018**	**9445**	**10365**
起诉贪污贿赂犯罪被告人（人）	Prosecution of Criminals of Corruption and Bribery to be Defendants(person)	129	157	151	123	153	154	179
起诉渎职、侵权犯罪被告人（人）	Prosecution of Misprision and Tortious to be Defendants (person)	13	29	24	44	17	39	38
起诉刑事犯罪被告人（人）	Prosecution of Criminal to be Defendants (person)	8134	7121	7440	8232	7848	9252	10148

注：本表数据来源于市检察院。
本表数据为西安原口径数据。

21-32 西安市中级人民法院案件基本情况（2017年）

Law Cases Basic Data of Xi'an Intermediate People's Court（2017）

单位：件、万元 (case,10 000 yuan)

指 标	Item	全市结案（件） the whole City (case)	中级人民法院结案 the Intermediate People's Court	基层人民法院结案 the Basic People's Court
合 计	**Total**	**167808**	**24696**	**143112**
刑事	Criminal	11059	2983	8076
民事	Civil	108704	17028	91676
行政	Administration	1719	95	1624
执行	Execution	43652	3163	40489
其他类型	Other types	2674	1427	1247

注：本表数据来源于市中级人民法院。
本表数据为西安原口径数据。

主 要 统 计 指 标 解 释

艺术表演团体 指由文化部门主办或实行行业管理（经文化行政部门审批并领取营业性演出许可证），专门从事表演艺术等活动的各类专业艺术表演团体，含民间职业剧团。（不包括群众业余文艺表演团队）

艺术表演场馆 指由文化部门主办或实行行业管理（向文化行政部门备案或领取合资（合作）演出场所许可证），有观众席、舞台、灯光设备，公开售票、专供文艺团体演出的文化活动场所。附属于文化部门机构内非独立核算的剧场、排演场，公开营业的也应单独统计。

图书馆 指各类图书馆的管理与服务（对文献和信息的搜集、整理、存储、利用和管理，向社会公众开放并提供科学、文化等各种知识普及教育）。包括公共图书馆和各类机构内部举办的或单独举办的图书馆的管理与服务。不包括部队系统以及文化馆（文化中心、群众艺术馆）、文化站内设的图书室。

群众文化活动 指开展群众文化活动的场所的管理和组织活动。包括文化馆（含综合性文化中心、群众艺术馆）、文化站、文化宫、少年宫等群众文化活动。在本制度中，目前暂不统计文化部门以外的文化宫和少年宫。

文化馆 （含综合性文化中心、群众艺术馆）、文化站：指专门从事群众文化活动的群众文化场馆。不包括临时抽调人员组成、没有编制的农村和街道文化工作队、服务站等。

广播节目综合人口覆盖率 根据国家广电总局制定的《广播电视人口覆盖率统计技术标准和方法》进行统计调查的，分别反映中央、省级、地市级、县级广播节目在本行政区域的综合覆盖情况，反应以无线方式传输的广播节目综合覆盖情况，综合反映广播公共服务覆盖的规模、能力、水平。

电视节目综合人口覆盖率 根据国家广电总局制定的《广播电视人口覆盖率统计技术标准和方法》进行统计调查的，分别反映中央、省级、地市级、县级电视节目在本行政区域的综合覆盖情况，反应以无线方式传输的电视节目综合覆盖情况，综合反映广播公共服务覆盖的规模、能力、水平。

博物馆 指为了研究、教育、欣赏的目的，收藏、保护、展示人类活动和自然环境的见证物，向公众开放，非盈利性、永久性社会服务机构，包括以博物馆（院）、纪念馆（舍）科技馆、陈列馆等专有名称开展活动的单位。

等级运动员人数 指经考核正式批准授予等级运动员称号的人数。运动员等级分为国际级运动健将、运动健将、一级运动员、二级运动员、三级运动员、少年级运动员。

等级裁判员人数 指经考核正式批准授予等级裁判员称号的人数。裁判员等级分为国际裁判、国家级裁判、一级裁判、二级裁判、三级裁判。

医疗卫生机构 指从卫生（卫生计生）行政部门取得《医疗机构执业许可证》、《计划生育技术服务许可证》或从民政、工商行政、机构编制管理部门取得法人单位登记证书，为社会提供医疗服务、公共卫生服务或从事医学科研和学在职培训等工作的单位。包括医院、基层医疗卫生机构、专业公共卫生机构、其他医疗卫生机构。

医院 包括综合医院、中医医院、中西医结合医院、民族医院、各类专科医院和护理院，不包括专科疾病防治院、妇幼保健院和疗养院，包括医学院校附属医院。

基层医疗卫生机构 包括社区卫生服务中心（站）、乡镇(街道)卫生院、村卫生室、门诊部、诊所(医务室)。

专业公共卫生机构 包括疾病预防控制中心、专科疾病防治机构、妇幼保健机构（含妇幼保健计划生育服务中心）、健康教育机构、急救中心（站）、采供血机构、卫生监督机构、取得《医疗机构执业许可证》或《计划生育技术服务许可证》的计划生育技术服务机构。

其他医疗卫生机构 包括疗养院、临床检验中心、医学科研机构、医学在职教育机构、卫生监督（监测、检测）机构、医学考试中心、农村改水中心、人才交流中心、统计信息中心等卫生事业单位。

卫生技术人员 包括执业医师、执业助理医师、注册护士、药师(士)、检验及影像技师(士)、卫生监督员和见习医(药、护、技)师(士)等卫生专业人员。不包括从事管理工作的卫生技术人员(如院长、副院长、党委书记等)。

执业(助理)医师 指《医师执业证》“级别”为“执业（助理）医师”且实际从事医疗、预防保健工作的人员，不包括实际从事管理工作的执业（助理）医师。执业（助理）医师类别分为临床、中医、口腔和公共卫生四类。

提供住宿的社会服务机构 包括养老服务机构、精神疾病服务机构、儿童福利机构以及其他提供住宿机构。

烈士纪念建筑物管理机构 指民政部门管理的、独立核算的褒扬烈士的陵园、纪念馆等单位的总称。

殡葬服务机构 指为殡葬服务的单位总称。殡仪馆（含火葬场）、公墓、独立核算的骨灰堂、殡葬管理机构等。

公证人员 指在国家公证机关依法办理公证事务的司法人员，包括公证员、助理公证员和在公证处工作的其他人员。

办理公证文书 指公证处在一定时期内办结的公证文书件数。公证文书按司法部规定或批准的格式制作，包括国内公证和涉外公证两部分。国内公证分为经济合同公证和民事法律关系公证两大类。

调解人员 指在人民调解委员会担负调解民间一般民事纠纷和轻微违法行为引起纠纷的工作人员，包括调解委员会的委员和调解小组的调解员。

Explanatory Notes on Main Statistical Indicators

Arts Performance Troupes refer to the various professional performing arts groups, which sponsored by the cultural sectors or guided by the cultural society (Receive commercial performance license approved by the cultural administration authority),including non-governmental troupes. (The mass amateur arts performance troupes are not included.)

Arts Performance Places refer to the various sites for cultural activities, which sponsored by the cultural sectors or guided by the cultural society (approved by the cultural market administration, or receive joint/cooperative venues permit), with the facility of auditorium, stage and lighting, and selling tickets in public, including the opera halls and rehearse sites, etc. which are affiliated to the culture sectors without independent financial accounts and open to the public.

Library refers to all types of library management and services(collection, collation, storage, use and management of literature and information, open and provide scientific, cultural and other literacy education to the public). Including the management and services of public libraries and the libraries internally or separately organized by various sectors. Excluding the libraries in troops system and cultural palaces (cultural centers, mass art centers),cultural stations.

Mass Culture Center refers to the management and organization of the places where mass culture activities hold. Including cultural palace (cultural center ,mass art center), cultural stations, cultural palaces ,youth palaces and other mass cultural activities. In this system ,cultural palaces and youth palaces beyond cultural sectors are not counted at present.

Cultural Palaces (Cultural Centers, Mass Art Centers),Cultural Stations refers to the mass cultural venues specialized in mass cultural activities. Excluding rural and street cultural teams, service stations which made up by temporary without authorized strength.

Radio Coverage of Population refers to the comprehensive coverage which respectively reflected central, province, city, prefecture and county radio programs by wireless in the administrative region, and comprehensively reflect the size, capacity, level of the public broadcasting services, according to Statistical Standard and Method on Television and Radio Coverage of Population established by the State Administration of Broadcasting ,Film and Television

Television Coverage of Population refers to the comprehensive coverage which respectively reflected central, province, city, prefecture and county television programs by wireless in the administrative region, and comprehensively reflect the size, capacity, level of the public broadcasting services, according to Statistical Standard and Method on Television and Radio Coverage of Population established by the State Administration of Broadcasting , Film and Television

Museum refers to the non-profit, permanent society service sectors which collect ,protect ,show human activities and the witnesses of natural environment, including the units that organize activities with the proper name such as museum, memorial hall , science and technology museum, exhibition hall, etc.

Number of Athletes in Grades refers to the number of athletes who have been given titles through examination. The titles of athletes include international masters of sports, masters of sports, first-grade, second-grade and third-grade sportsmen and young athletes.

Number of Referees in Grades refers to the number of referees who have been given titles after examination. They are classified as international referees, national referees and referees of the first, second and third grades.

Medical and health institutions are the organizations that have got thepractice license of medical institutionandfamily planning technical services licensefrom health administrative departments or have obtained legal entity registration certificate from civil, industrial and commercial administration, organization management departments, to provide medical services, public health services or engaged in medical research and medical job training. Itincludes hospitals, primary medical and health institutions, professional public health institutions, and other medical and health institutions.

Hospitals include general hospital, hospital of traditional Chinese medicine, hospital of integrated traditional Chinese and Western Medicine, National Hospital, various specialist hospitals and nursing homes, excluding specialized disease prevention and treatment centers , Maternity and child care centers and sanatorium, including hospitals affiliated to medical colleges and universities.

Primary medical and health institutions include community health service centers (stations), township (street) health centers, village clinics, outpatient department, clinics.

Professional public health institutions include the center for disease control and prevention, specialized disease prevention and treatment centers, maternity and child care centers (including maternal and child health family planning service center), health education institutions, first aid agencies,collecting and supplying agencies, health supervision institutions, andfamily planning technical service institutions which have got the practice license of medical institution and family planning technical services license.

Other medical and health institutions include sanatorium, clinical inspection center, medical research institutions, medical in-service education institutions, health supervision institutions, medical examination center, Rural change water quality center, personnel exchange center, statistical information center and other health institutions.

Health technical personnel include practicing physician, practicing assistant doctors, registered nurses, pharmacists, inspection and imaging technicians, health supervisors and clerksand other health professionals. It does not include health technical personnel engaged in management work such as Dean, vice president, Secretary of the Party committee, etc.

Practicing physician(assistant) refers to the practitioner who is a practitioner (assistant) doctor and actually engaged in medical care and preventive health care, and does not include the practitioner (assistant) practitioner who is actually engaged in the management work. Practitioners (assistants) are classified into four categories: clinical, Chinesetraditional, oral and public health.

Social services providing accommodation include pension services, psychiatric care services, child welfare institutions, and other lodging establishments.

Martyr memorial buildings management organization refers to the floorboard of cemetery, memorial and other units which are independent accounting and managedby civil affairs department to praise the Martyrs

Funeral service agencies refer to the units that serve funeral services. It includesFuneral home (including crematorium), cemetery, independent accounting ashes hall, funeral and interment management organization, etc.

Notary Personnel refers to judicial workers of the state notary offices handling notarization work according to law. They include notaries, assistant notaries, and other people working for notary offices.

Notarized Documents refer to the documents settled by notary offices in a year. The notary documents are drawn up in accordance with the regulations of the Ministry of Justice, including domestic documents and foreign-related documents. Domestic documents are divided into two major categories, documents on economic contracts and documents on civil legal relations.

Mediators refer to workers on peoples mediation committees responsible for mediating in civil disputes and cases of slight infraction of the law. They include members of the mediation committees and mediators of mediation groups.

22 企业调查

ENTERPRISES INVESTIGATION

资料整理：薛　燕
Data management：Xue Yan
数据审核：黄雪冰
Data audit：Huang Xuebing

第二十二部分　企业调查

一、简要说明

本章资料主要包括各行业企业景气调查指数和企业家信心指数等，由西安市统计局社会经济调查中心提供。

二、主要指标

企业景气指数（第四季度）	125.0
企业家信心指数（第四季度）	126.0

22　ENTERPRISES INVESTIGATION

Ⅰ.Brief Introduction

Data in this chapter consists prosperity survey indices of various industries and Entrepreneur Expectation Indicator, provided by Xi'an Municipal Bureau of Statics .

Ⅱ.Major Indicators

Business Climate Index（Fourth Quarter）	125.0
Entrepreneur Expectation Indicator（Fourth Quarter）	126.0

22-1 企业景气指数（2017年）

Business Climate Index（2017）

指　标	Item	一季度 First Quarter	二季度 Second Quarter	三季度 Third Quarter	四季度 Fourth Quarter
企业景气指数	**Business Climate Index**	**117.3**	**119.8**	**123.1**	**125.0**
按行业门类分	**Grouped by Sector**				
工业	Industry	128.6	132.4	133.9	136.5
建筑业	Construction	101.7	103.8	105.0	109.5
批发和零售业	Wholesale and Retail Sales	111.7	116.0	119.1	123.1
住宿和餐饮业	Hotels and Catering Services	101.0	103.9	122.1	116.5
房地产业	Real Estate	117.2	120.5	122.5	126.0
社会服务业	Social Services	117.2	117.9	122.1	122.1

22-2 企业家信心指数（2017年）

Entrepreneur Expectation Indicator（2017）

指　标	Item	一季度 First Quarter	二季度 Second Quarter	三季度 Third Quarter	四季度 Fourth Quarter
企业家信心指数	**Entrepreneur Expectation Indicator**	**117.9**	**120.2**	**123.4**	**126.0**
按行业门类分	**Grouped by Sector**				
工业	Industry	127.8	130.4	131.4	137.8
建筑业	Construction	105.0	107.3	106.1	110.9
批发和零售业	Wholesale and Retail Sales	110.1	114.1	119.8	124.0
住宿和餐饮业	Hotels and Catering Services	98.6	105.6	120.3	117.5
房地产业	Real Estate	121.0	123.9	124.8	128.6
社会服务业	Social Services	118.7	119.4	124.8	122.6

主要统计指标解释

企业景气指数：是根据企业家对本企业综合生产经营情况所作的判断与预期（通常是对“良好”、“一般”、“不佳”的选择）而编制的指数，用以综合反映企业的生产经营状况。企业景气指数也称“企业综合生产经营景气指数”。

企业家信心指数：是根据企业家对企业外部市场经济环境与宏观政策的认识、看法判断和预期（通常是对“乐观”、“一般”、“不乐观”的选择）而编制的指数，用以综合反映企业家对宏观经济环境的感受与信心。企业家信心指数也称“宏观经济景气指数”。

景气指数的表示方式：景气指数的表示范围在0~200之间，其含义：100为景气指数的临界值，表明景气状况变化不大；100~200为景气区间，表明景气状况趋于上升或改善，越接近于200，状况越景气；0~100为不景气区间，表明经济状况趋于下降或恶化，越接近于0，状况越不景气。

Explanatory Notes on Main Statistical Indicators

Business Climate Index it is an index worked out according to the judgment and anticipation (normally a choice from good, ordinary, not good) of entrepreneurs made based on synthetic productive and operational situation of the enterprise. It is used to reflect synthetically the productive and operational situation of the enterprise. It is also referred to as synthetic and productiveoperational prosperity index of enterprise.

Confidence index of entrepreneur it is an index worked out according to the judgment and anticipation (normally a choice from optimistic , ordinary , not optimistic) of entrepreneurs made based on their understandings and views of the market and economic environment outside the enterprise and the macro policies. It is used to reflect synthetically the confidence and feelings of the entrepreneurs to the macro economic environment. It is also referred to as macro-economy prosperity index.

The way to express prosperity index the range of prosperity index is from 0 to 200; 100 is the critical value, and means economic situation didn't change largely; from 100 to 200 is the interval of prosperity; and from 0 to 100 is the interval of not prosperity, meaning economic situation is going down or worse, the closer to 0, the worse the economic situation.